Roe v. Dobbs

Roe v. Dobbs

*The Past, Present, and Future of a
Constitutional Right to Abortion*

Edited by

LEE C. BOLLINGER AND GEOFFREY R. STONE

OXFORD
UNIVERSITY PRESS

OXFORD
UNIVERSITY PRESS

Oxford University Press is a department of the University of Oxford. It furthers
the University's objective of excellence in research, scholarship, and education
by publishing worldwide. Oxford is a registered trade mark of Oxford University
Press in the UK and certain other countries.

Published in the United States of America by Oxford University Press
198 Madison Avenue, New York, NY 10016, United States of America.

© Oxford University Press 2024

Library of Congress Cataloging-in-Publication Data
Names: Bollinger, Lee C., 1946– editor. | Stone, Geoffrey R., editor.
Title: Roe v. Dobbs : the past, present, and future of a constitutional right to abortion /
[edited by] Lee C. Bollinger, Geoffrey R. Stone.
Other titles: Roe vs. Dobbs
Description: New York, NY : Oxford University Press, 2024. |
Includes bibliographical references and index.
Identifiers: LCCN 2023043399 (print) | LCCN 2023043400 (ebook) |
ISBN 9780197760369 (paperback) | ISBN 9780197760352 (hardback) |
ISBN 9780197760383 (epub)
Subjects: LCSH: Abortion—Law and legislation—United States. |
Pro-choice movement—United States. | Reproductive rights—United States. |
Constitutional law—Untied States.
Classification: LCC KF3771 .R64 2024 (print) | LCC KF3771 (ebook) |
DDC 342.7308/4—dc23/eng/20231003
LC record available at https://lccn.loc.gov/2023043399
LC ebook record available at https://lccn.loc.gov/2023043400

DOI: 10.1093/oso/9780197760352.001.0001

Paperback printed by Marquis Book Printing, Canada
Hardback printed by Bridgeport National Bindery, Inc., United States of America

To Jean and Jane
And to the next generation:
Colin, Katelyn, Cooper, Sawyer, and Emma
Julie, Mollie, Maddie, Jackson, Amaya, and Leni

Contents

Acknowledgments

We would like to acknowledge and extend our gratitude to the many people who contributed to the making of this volume: first and foremost are the experts and authors who provided their perspectives on the profound constitutional and other questions raised by "Roe v. Dobbs." Second, as has been true with almost all of our projects, our general editor Carey Bollinger Danielson brought her unflagging wisdom, precision, and care to the complex task of making a manuscript emerge out of these writings. We were all aided by the intelligence and organizational skills of Christina Shelby, who served as senior executive director in the Office of the President at Columbia. In addition, Noah Howard, Columbia Law School class of 2024, provided critical support in this process, as did Molly Hellauer from the Office of the President. Finally, Evelyn Schwalb, Executive Director of the Office of the President Emeritus, provided superb help to bring this project to completion.

We are grateful to Oxford University Press, and editor Dave McBride in particular, for staying with us on all of our efforts to illuminate critical constitutional questions of our time. We know that Columbia University and the University of Chicago make our work—and, specifically, this work—possible. And, most of all, as always, we express our most profound appreciation to our spouses, Jean Magnano Bollinger and Jane Dailey, whose links to the substance and process of undertaking this book are impossible to unravel.

And, perhaps it should not be regarded as too late to thank the justices for whom we clerked, Chief Justice Warren E. Burger and Associate Justice William J. Brennan, Jr., for having given us the extraordinary opportunity to be at the Court in the seminal 1972–73 term, when *Roe v. Wade* was decided.

Contributors

Jack M. Balkin, Knight Professor of Constitutional Law and the First Amendment, Yale Law School; founder and director, Yale's Information Society Project; director, Abrams Institute for Freedom of Expression and the Knight Law and Media Program, Yale University

Lee C. Bollinger, president emeritus and Seth Low Professor of the University, Columbia University

Khiara M. Bridges, professor of law, University of California, Berkeley School of Law

Erwin Chemerinsky, dean and Jesse H. Choper Distinguished Professor of Law, University of California, Berkeley School of Law

I. Glenn Cohen, deputy dean and James A. Attwood and Leslie Williams Professor of Law, and faculty director of the Petrie-Flom Center for Health Law Policy, Biotechnology & Bioethics, Harvard Law School

Nancy F. Cott, Jonathan Trumbull Research Professor of American History, Harvard University

Cary Franklin, McDonald/Wright Chair of Law, faculty director of the Center on Reproductive Health, Law, and Policy, and faculty director of the Williams Institute, UCLA School of Law

Tom Ginsburg, Leo Spitz Distinguished Service Professor of International Law, Ludwig and Hilde Wolf Research Scholar, professor of political science, The University of Chicago Law School

Michele Bratcher Goodwin, Chancellor's Professor, founding director of the Center for Biotechnology and Global Health Policy, University of California, Irvine, Law School; senior lecturer, Harvard Medical School

Linda Gordon, professor emerita of History, New York University

Aziz Z. Huq, Frank and Bernice J. Greenberg Professor of Law, The University of Chicago Law School

Michael W. McConnell, Richard and Frances Mallery Professor, Stanford Law School; director, Stanford Constitutional Law Center; senior fellow, Hoover Institution

Martha Minow, 300th Anniversary University Professor, Harvard Law School

Jonathan F. Mitchell, principal, Mitchell Law PLLC; former solicitor general of Texas

Melissa Murray, Frederick I. and Grace Stokes Professor of Law, faculty director of the Birnbaum Women's Leadership Center, NYU School of Law

Richard M. Re, Joel B. Piassick Research Professor of Law, University of Virginia School of Law

Dorothy Roberts, George A. Weiss University Professor of Law and Sociology and the Raymond Pace and Sadie Tanner Mossell Alexander Professor of Civil Rights, University of Pennsylvania Carey Law School

Katherine Shaw, professor of law, Cardozo School of Law

Reva Siegel, Nicholas deB. Katzenbach Professor of Law, Yale Law School

Geoffrey R. Stone, Edward H. Levi Distinguished Service Professor of Law, The University of Chicago Law School

David A. Strauss, Gerald Ratner Distinguished Service Professor of Law, faculty director of the Jenner & Block Supreme Court and Appellate Clinic, The University of Chicago Law School

Cass R. Sunstein, Robert Walmsley University Professor, founder and director of the Program on Behavioral Economics and Public Policy, Harvard Law School

Mark Tushnet, William Nelson Cromwell Professor of Law, Emeritus, Harvard Law School

Rebecca Wexler, assistant professor of law, faculty co-director, Berkeley Center for Law & Technology, University of California, Berkeley School of Law

Mary Ziegler, Stearns Weaver Miller Professor, Florida State University College of Law

Opening Dialogue

Lee C. Bollinger and Geoffrey R. Stone

Bollinger: This is our sixth project working together on major constitutional issues. Our driving philosophy has been, and remains, that a combination of voices from leading experts (including our own), along with focused recommendations on some of the nation's most significant contemporary issues, and typically at historic judicial anniversaries, will yield a useful overview for experts and nonexperts alike; and welcome insights and contributions toward answering or resolving the questions at hand. In 2002, *Eternally Vigilant: Free Speech in the Modern Era*[1] launched our ambitions for reflecting on the principles of freedom of speech and press at the turn of the new century. *The Free Speech Century*[2] in 2019 was a similar effort to mark the one-hundredth anniversary of the first Supreme Court cases interpreting the First Amendment's words: "Congress shall make no law . . . abridging the freedom of speech, or of the press . . . ."[3] This was followed on the fiftieth anniversary of the Pentagon Papers decision in 2021 by *National Security, Leaks and Freedom of the Press: The Pentagon Papers Fifty Years On.*[4] More recently, we took on the vexing issues of regulation (or not) of "bad speech" on the internet and social media platforms in *Social Media, Freedom of Speech and the Future of Our Democracy* (2022).[5] And earlier this year we published our own views on the constitutionality of affirmative action policies in higher education in *A Legacy of Discrimination: The Essential Constitutionality of Affirmative Action.*[6] Now, with this volume, *Roe v. Dobbs: The Past, Present, and Future of a Constitutional Right to Abortion*, we confront the remarkable beginning and end—once again, after a half-century—of the landmark Supreme Court decision in *Roe v. Wade*,[7] stunningly overruled by the Court in *Dobbs v. Jackson Women's Health Organization.*[8]

What makes this subject unique among our collaborations is how it intersects with our own lives, since both of us were law clerks in the year *Roe* was decided (1973)—you for Associate Justice William Brennan, and me for Chief Justice Warren Burger. So, let's start there. I would add that you have also written extensively, and deeply, about *Roe*, its context and the inner workings of the Court that produced this remarkable decision. Your book, *Sex and the Constitution: Sex, Religion, and Law from America's Origins to the Twenty-First Century*,[9] provides the best description and analysis of the pre-*Roe*, *Roe*, and post-*Roe* worlds that I know of. Can you lay out your observations, starting with *Roe* and how we got there?

Stone: As always, Lee, you're much too kind! But instead of dwelling on that, let me turn to the substance. During the Court's 1972–73 term, when *Roe* was decided, the Court was in a state of flux. President Nixon had just appointed four justices to the Court: Burger, Blackmun, Powell, and Rehnquist. The era of the Warren Court was clearly over. Yet although these justices were clearly thought to be "conservative" at the time, they were not nearly as conservative as, pardon the expression, the extremely right-wing Republican-appointed majority on the current Court. In those days, the justices were nonpartisan, often joined opinions across the political/ideological spectrum, and approached most cases with an open mind. That in large part explains why the Court could reach the decision it did in *Roe*, with five of the six Republican-appointed justices and two of the three Democratic-appointed justices in the majority, and one Republican-appointed justice (Rehnquist) and one Democratic-appointed justice (White) in dissent. It was a different Court and a different era.

But what led the justices to vote seven-to-two in *Roe* to recognize a constitutional right of women to terminate an unwanted pregnancy? In my recollection, at least two factors opened the justices' minds to such a decision. First, until the late 1960s, almost everyone assumed that abortion had been illegal from the beginning of Western history. But as the women's rights movement gained steam, and justices—especially Justice Harry Blackmun, who wrote the majority opinion in *Roe*—looked into the history, this turned out to be completely wrong. To the contrary, abortion had been legal (at least up to the midpoint of pregnancy) throughout Western history—from the ancient Greeks, to the Romans, to the Middle Ages, in England in the years leading up to the American Revolution, in the American colonies, and in all the states at the time the Constitution was adopted. Indeed, it was not until the mid-nineteenth century that abortion in America began to be criminalized. And what became clear was that the primary driving force for this movement was a combination of religion and disdain for the interests of women. Thus, by the end of the nineteenth century every state in the nation had made abortion a crime. Nonetheless, by the beginning of the twentieth century some two million women each year resorted to illegal abortions—which were often terrifying and dangerous. For most of the justices, knowledge of this history was both mind-opening and powerful.

Second, until the late 1960s almost all Americans assumed that illegal abortions were rare. The reason for this was that abortion was illegal and women who had abortions could not tell anyone (except perhaps close friends and some family members) what they had done. Not only was abortion illegal, but for the past century most Americans had been led to believe that it was profoundly immoral. Thus, it was seen as essential for women say anything. As a result, most people had no idea how many illegal abortions were being performed or how dangerous these illegal abortions were. Once again, as the women's movement gained steam in the late 1960s, these facts were increasingly made public. As we learned at the time, approximately one million women each year still had illegal abortions—many of them either self-induced with the use of coat hangers and similar objects, and many others through "back-alley abortions," which were often performed by people the woman didn't know, couldn't see, and who had little or no training. As these facts came to light, both the horrible consequences of making abortion illegal and the often desperate need for women not to have unwanted babies—as evidenced by their extraordinary willingness to resort to dangerous unlawful abortions—clearly affected both the nation and the justices.

With these two understandings in mind, the justices—or at least seven of them, both conservatives and liberals—came to understand that denial to women of the right to terminate unwanted pregnancies was a profound and fundamental violation of women's right to make these decisions for themselves and to be able to do so in much safer environments with the assistance of trained professionals.

Anyway, that's my sense of what motivated the justices to understand that the right recognized in *Roe* was both essential and warranted by our Constitution.

Bollinger: These points that the decision in *Roe* crossed judicial ideological lines at the time, and that the decision was the result of a growing realization about the relatively "recent" and extraordinarily injurious impact of bans on abortions and intimate decisions by women and their physicians, are well put. I would add two additional observations and then ask a question.

First, it seems important to understand that, while *Roe* unquestionably was an important decision of that Supreme Court term, it was not regarded either within the Court or by the general public as the most important, or controversial, decision of the period; nor was it regarded as a radical expansion of constitutional rights—certainly, nothing like how it came to be portrayed by the conservative establishment over succeeding decades. (How and why that happened is one of the most important questions for this book.) Indeed, the primary focus of that year was on the well-known intention of the newly appointed conservative justices to curtail First Amendment protections for speech deemed "obscene." The Nixon appointees, led by Chief Justice Burger, wanted to allow greater latitude by local communities to prohibit erotic speech, believing that this was needed and justified to preserve the "moral character" of society. They achieved this aim with narrow majorities in two very prominent cases, *Miller v. California* and *Paris Adult Theatre v. Slaton*,[10] which together provided a new and fundamental governing standard for how to treat obscenity under the First Amendment.

That raises the second point I would make about *Roe*, focusing now on its purported rationale. Here, too, the comparison with *Miller* and *Paris Adult Theatre* is interesting, but in another way. Both the obscenity decisions and *Roe* offered justifications that were challenged, expanded, and supplanted in the years to come by the women's rights movement in America. As you know so well, Blackmun's opinion in *Roe* emphasized a combination of interests supporting recognition of a right to an abortion—the woman's right, to be sure, but also that of her treating physician.[11] The latter seems to have arisen from Blackmun's prior long relationship with the medical community, most significantly by serving for many years as the general counsel of the Mayo Clinic. The woman's interest was also present, but not anywhere close to the degree that many came to understand as the reality of systemic discrimination. So Blackmun's comments about "distress" experienced by women in having to carry a pregnancy to birth and beyond was arguably weaker than the claim that women must have a right to control their reproductive lives in order to be fully equal citizens in society.

Similarly, but even more forcefully, this same transition in sensitivity to the interests of women transformed the debate about the regulation of obscenity. Within a few years of *Miller* and *Paris Adult Theatre*, the argument shifted from respecting the state's interest in preserving the "moral character" of the community to protecting women from discrimination in the production and distribution of pornography.

That leads, then, to my question: Do you think it would have made a difference over time if *Roe* had been grounded not simply or primarily in a "right of privacy" but in a more fully dimensional understanding of the often intentional and discriminatory consequences of laws banning abortions? (It is worth noting here that you and I have argued, in the context of the constitutionality of affirmative action, that it was highly unfortunate that the Court in 1978 abandoned the original rationale for affirmative action that was based on the value of achieving racial justice and instead embraced the much weaker rationale of the interests of higher education in achieving the benefits of "educational diversity.") Let me just quickly add that many others have made the point I'm making here, so I don't for a second present it as an original insight. Nevertheless, we experienced the origins of *Roe* and its thinking, and the changes in public values and debates that followed, and perhaps we can offer some perspective on how this area of constitutional law and political debate evolved or might have evolved. We also need to discuss the theories of constitutional interpretation that are implicated and came to be symbolized by the *Roe* decision.

Stone: You raise an interesting question: Why did Justice Blackmun rest the decision in *Roe* on the woman's "right of privacy" rather than on the reality that laws prohibiting abortion unconstitutionally "discriminated" against women?[12] I can offer three possible explanations.

First, in important cases, and for obvious reasons, the justice writing the majority opinion wants as many of the justices as possible to sign on to that opinion. Thus, in such cases the justice writing the majority opinion often must try to find common ground, even though some of the justices might prefer a different approach. Justice Blackmun was certainly faced with that challenge in *Roe*.

Second, Blackmun's invocation of a woman's "right of privacy" with respect to such fundamental decisions as whether to bear or beget a child was grounded in several important prior decisions of the Court.[13] At the outset, it should be noted that the Ninth Amendment clearly recognizes that there are constitutional rights beyond those expressly spelled out in other provisions of the Constitution, such as the freedom of speech, the freedom from unreasonable searches and seizures, and the freedom of religion. Indeed, the Ninth Amendment expressly provides that "the enumeration in the Constitution, of certain rights, shall not be construed to deny or disparage others retained by the people."[14] Thus, in a number of important decisions going all the way back to 1925, such as *Meyer v. Nebraska* and *Pierce v. Society of Sisters*, as well as *Griswold v. Connecticut* in 1965, the Court had recognized that an "unenumerated" but fundamental constitutional right to privacy protected such fundamental personal freedoms as the right to decide how to educate one's children and the right to decide whether to use contraceptives.[15]

I should note that "privacy" in this context does not mean "secrecy," but the right to make fundamental personal decisions for oneself.

Third, why didn't Blackmun focus expressly on the constitutional right of women not to be discriminated against or specifically disadvantaged? After all, it was a common phrase in the late nineteenth century that "if men could get pregnant, abortion would be legal." And that, no doubt, was true. But did the Fourteenth Amendment's Equal Protection Clause prohibit laws that discriminate against women? According to the Supreme Court until just a few years before *Roe*, the Court said no. Such laws, the Court held, were constitutional as long as they were "rational." Thus, for example, in *Bradwell v. Illinois*, the Court held in 1872 that state laws prohibiting women from being lawyers were constitutional.[16] As one justice explained, such laws did not violate the Equal Protection Clause because "the paramount destiny and mission of women are to fulfil the noble and benign offices of wife and mother."[17] Only two years later, in *Minor v. Happersett*, the Court unanimously held that although women are no less citizens than men, state laws that ban women from voting are constitutionally valid.[18] Moving closer to the present, in *Goesaert v. Cleary* in 1948, the Court upheld the constitutionality of a law prohibiting women from serving as bartenders because the state could rationally conclude that bartending could create moral and social problems for women.[19]

Indeed, the Court did not hold unconstitutional a law that expressly discriminated against women until 1971, in *Reed v. Reed*, in which the Court held that a state statute providing that males must be preferred to females in estate administration was irrational and therefore violated the Equal Protection Clause.[20] But the fundamental question remained whether laws that discriminate against women should be deemed unconstitutional under the Equal Protection Clause unless the laws survive "strict scrutiny" rather than "rational basis" review. Why didn't the Court embrace that theory in *Roe*? For those of us who were inside the Court at that time the answer was clear. In *Frontiero v. Richardson*, a case decided during the same term as *Roe*, the justices considered the constitutionality of a military policy that automatically gave benefits to the wives of male soldiers but gave them to the husbands of female soldiers only if the husband was dependent on his wife for more than half of his support.[21] Eight of the nine justices (all but Rehnquist) voted to hold the law unconstitutional, but only four of them, in an opinion by Justice Brennan, concluded that laws that discriminate against women are consistent with the Equal Protection Clause only if they satisfy the "strict scrutiny" test, which this law clearly did not.[22] The four other justices in the majority, however, refused to address the "strict scrutiny" issue, instead rather disingenuously arguing that the law was irrational, even though it wasn't.[23] They did this because the Equal Rights Amendment had been sent to the states for ratification in 1972 and they believed that it would be inappropriate for the Court to interpret the Equal Protection Clause in a way that would effectively render the Equal Rights Amendment redundant. It was for that reason that the justices in *Roe* could not muster the votes to strike down abortion laws on Equal Protection grounds, even though seven of the justices agreed that it was unconstitutional for states to deny women the right to terminate unwanted pregnancies on "right to privacy" grounds.

Bollinger: *Roe* may have crossed ideological lines when it was decided in 1973, and at the time it seemed to most legal experts as a natural step in the evolution of core fundamental rights, even among those that were "unenumerated" in the constitutional text. Moreover, as you noted earlier, it was received across the nation as a basically sound and reasonable result. But two things happened in the coming decades. One was an increased appreciation of the decision as our collective sensibilities about the rights of women developed. And the other was a demonization of the decision among the new and growing conservative segments of American legal and political life for the Court's purported abuse of judicial power with respect to the interpretation of the Constitution. The latter forces finally triumphed with the decision in *Dobbs*.

At the heart of the debate about abortion, then, is the fundamental question: How do we interpret the Constitution? At this point, everyone accepts that the Constitution protects certain rights of citizens against infringement by the state and that the role of the courts is to articulate those rights. We recognize, too, that the text itself is extremely brief and general ("Congress shall make no law . . . abridging the freedom of speech"),[24] barely providing a guide. (What constitutes "the freedom of speech"? Are all "actions" that "communicate" encompassed by "the freedom of speech"? What conditions necessary for "the freedom of speech" are protected? Expenditures of money? A decent education?). And (as you say) the Ninth Amendment specifically and explicitly charges us to protect rights that are not expressly enumerated in the text of the Constitution.[25] Thus, with respect to every single "right" recognized by the Court over the decades and centuries, there are extensive, sometimes labyrinthine, doctrines, analytical formulations, and decisions in concrete cases that altogether provide the foundation for those rights.

And there can be no doubt for any reasonable person that those collective decisions undergirding every single "right" go far beyond what the "Framers" thought about the Bill of Rights in 1789. Indeed, given the vagueness and brevity of the document they drafted and adopted, the only reasonable conclusion is that they intended it to evolve over time, which, of course, is exactly what has happened, in every Court in every period of American history.

That said, it is also vitally important that the Constitution not serve as a contentless charter for justices to implement their personal or political preferences under the guise of doing "law." That, too, would be as bad as setting constitutional rights in some sort of eighteenth-century amber, which would also essentially be an invented reality.

This is the dilemma of constitutionalism, and a profoundly serious one. *Roe v. Wade* came to symbolize this problem, and that is what we are struggling with throughout this volume. There is a natural wish in all of us to find simple answers for hard problems. You and I, and every author in this book, believe that there is something real in the process of constitutional interpretation that, while extremely difficult (perhaps even impossible) to articulate, nevertheless is different from making political judgments and is worthy of respect in a democracy. It is not a process captured by fictional notions of "original intent," and not one frozen in a distant past when our notions of right and wrong, fair and unfair, just and unjust, may well have been, from our current vantage point, embedded in error.

A good faith constitutional interpretation works like any good relationship, informed by knowledge of constitutional law and law more generally, sincere and genuine respect for the efforts of others to know and to discover the law, demonstrated actions of deciding against one's own likes and dislikes, and a sense of caring and patriotism for the nation.

Roe and *Dobbs* highlight these issues.

Stone: This leads me to a couple of final observations. First, in light of the complications of constitutional interpretation that you identify so well, one might sensibly ask why our Constitution even has a Bill of Rights and why we should trust the justices of the Supreme Court to give the Constitution's often vague and open-ended terms meaning. It's worth remembering that when the Constitution was first drafted, James Madison, perhaps the most important of the Framers, did not believe a Bill of Rights would serve any purpose. He believed that political majorities would interpret those rights in any way that suited their own self-interest, and that guaranteeing such rights in the Constitution would therefore lead only to cynicism and disillusion.

On December 20, 1787, though, Thomas Jefferson wrote to Madison from Paris that, after reviewing the proposed Constitution, he regretted "the omission of a bill of rights."[26] In response, Madison expressed his doubt that a bill of rights would "provide any meaningful check on the passions and interests of popular majorities." He maintained that, in practical effect, such constitutional guarantees would be mere "parchment barriers." "What use," he asked Jefferson, "can a bill of rights serve in popular Governments?"[27] Jefferson's answer was clear: the courts, he said, will make sure that the Bill of Rights is effective. "Your thoughts on the subject of the Declaration of Rights," he told Madison, failed to address one consideration "which has great weight with me, the legal check which it puts into the hands of the judiciary. This is a body, which if rendered independent . . . merits great confidence for their learning and integrity."[28] This exchange apparently helped persuade Madison. On June 8, 1789, Madison proposed a bill of rights to the House of Representatives. Echoing Jefferson's letter, Madison said that if these rights are "incorporated into the constitution, independent tribunals of justice will consider themselves . . . the guardians of those rights; they will be an impenetrable bulwark against every assumption of power in the legislative or executive; they will be naturally led to resist every encroachment upon rights guaranteed in the constitution."[29] It is this special responsibility for making our constitutional rights a reality—rather than, in Madison's words, a mere parchment barrier—that should animate the Court's approach to constitutional interpretation.

But what does that mean? In my view, and in the views of many, this means that we should distrust democracy in certain contexts and that we need to rely upon the courts to protect the relatively powerless against both hostile and indifferent majoritarian abuse. This suggests at least two contexts in which courts should be especially active in protecting our most fundamental values. The first of these involves the electoral process. If majorities have a free hand to structure that process in any way they see fit, they will inevitably do so in a way that guarantees their continued control of government. The second, and the context especially relevant to the abortion issue, concerns the tendency of those in control of the democratic process to disregard the fundamental rights—whether freedom of speech, freedom of religion, freedom from unreasonable searches and seizures, or the right to equal treatment—of those not in control of the government. It is in this sense that the gendered element of the abortion right comes into play—as I noted earlier, if men could get pregnant, abortion would be safe and legal.

And with that, I suggest we turn the "floor" over to our many distinguished authors who will provide a broad range of views on these and other issues.

PART I

THE SUPREME COURT

Roe v. Dobbs

1

Liberal Critics of *Roe*

David A. Strauss

In the decades before *Roe v. Wade*, the Supreme Court was the subject of intense partisan and ideological conflict. The Warren Court, beginning at least with *Brown v. Board of Education* in 1954, was bitterly attacked for "judicial activism"—exemplified, supposedly, by its decisions expanding the rights of criminal defendants, prohibiting state-sponsored prayer in public schools, and, in cases like *Brown*, trying to uproot Jim Crow segregation. Richard Nixon's successful presidential campaign in 1968 prominently featured attacks on the Warren Court. Against that background, it's natural to think that *Roe v. Wade*, decided in January 1973, less than four years after Chief Justice Warren's retirement, was simply a continuation of Warren-era conflicts between liberals who were identifying new constitutional rights and conservatives who were trying to preserve the status quo.

But that is not an accurate account either of the political reaction to *Roe* or of the relationship between *Roe* and the controversies that surrounded the Warren Court. *Roe* was a thoroughly bipartisan decision, and it scrambled Warren-era ideological lines. Of the seven members of the *Roe* majority, five had been appointed by Republican presidents. Three of the seven—enough to reverse the outcome—were appointed by Nixon, who had vowed that his appointments would change the direction of the Court from what it had been in the Warren era. Those three included Justice Harry Blackmun, the author of the opinion in *Roe* and its most passionate defender among the justices. One of the two dissenters in *Roe*, Justice Byron White, had been appointed by a Democratic president, John Kennedy, and was often aligned with the Warren Court majority.

Roe was decided less than two years after the deaths of two of the central figures of the Warren Court; had they still been on the Court, it would have been even more obvious how *Roe* crossed partisan and ideological lines. Justice John Marshall Harlan was the Warren Court's most prominent dissenter. But he can fairly be called the godfather of *Roe v. Wade*: he had

David A. Strauss, *Liberal Critics of* Roe In: *Roe v. Dobbs*. Edited by: Lee C. Bollinger and Geoffrey R. Stone, Oxford University Press. © Oxford University Press 2024. DOI: 10.1093/oso/9780197760352.003.0001 advocated a constitutional right to reproductive freedom since 1961.[1] Justice Hugo Black had been an intellectual leader on the Warren Court, noted for his commitment to freedom of speech and constitutional protections for criminal defendants, but he would certainly have dissented in *Roe*.[2]

So just as there were conservatives who supported *Roe*, there were liberal critics of *Roe*. Many of these critics believed that there should be a right to abortion, but they thought the Court made a mistake by establishing that right itself, at least in the way that *Roe* did, rather than leaving the issue to politics. Ruth Bader Ginsburg, then a judge on the District of Columbia Circuit, was one of the liberal critics of *Roe*, although her criticism was qualified.[3] Yale Law School professor John Hart Ely, a former law clerk for Chief Justice Warren, was an emphatic defender of the Warren Court, but he published one of the most strongly worded attacks on *Roe*.[4] The title of Ely's article, "The Wages of Crying Wolf," captured the reversal of liberal and conservative positions that *Roe* precipitated: Ely's argument was that the wrongheaded criticism of the Warren Court as impermissibly "activist" discredited the correct claim that the Court in *Roe* had badly overreached. There were several other critics of *Roe* who, like Ginsburg and Ely, held unmistakably liberal views.[5]

These liberal critics helped create the perception that there was something especially lawless about *Roe*: how could there not be, if *Roe* went too far even for pro-choice Warren Court enthusiasts? *Roe*'s opponents never tired of pointing out how many card-carrying liberals agreed with them that *Roe* was wrong. Unsurprisingly, the majority opinion in *Dobbs v. Jackson Women's Health Organization*[6]—the decision that overruled *Roe*—prominently featured Ely, Ginsburg, and other liberal critics.

But the liberal criticisms of *Roe* are important for reasons that go beyond the abortion controversy. For one thing, the trajectory of liberal commentators' opinions on *Roe* tells us something more general about how progressive views of the Constitution and the courts evolved between *Roe* and *Dobbs*. By the time *Dobbs* was decided, opinions about *Roe* had polarized. Hostility to *Roe* became a de facto litmus test for Republican judicial appointments—a sharp contrast with the Republican-dominated majority in *Roe* itself. On the other side, it is very difficult, today, to identify prominent figures who have liberal views on other issues but who applaud *Dobbs*. The way that anti-*Roe* opinion became a defining feature of legal and political views on the right, and what that reveals about how today's conservatives are different from their predecessors—has been discussed extensively and insightfully.[7] By the same token, the near-disappearance of liberal criticism of *Roe* tells us something about what happened to progressive constitutionalism in the half-century since *Roe*.

The evolution of liberal views about abortion rights has implications for the future, too. One of the bases of liberal criticisms of *Roe* was liberals' reservations about—sometimes overt hostility to—the idea that there are "unenumerated" rights in the Constitution, that is, rights other than those explicitly identified in the Bill of Rights or elsewhere in the text of the Constitution. Justice Black, in particular, made a point of insisting that the Court had no business enforcing unenumerated rights. Since *Roe*—and probably in part because of *Roe*—that strand of liberal constitutionalism has no champions. Instead, the majority opinion in *Dobbs* adopted a conservative version of that hostility to unenumerated rights, leaving behind earlier conservatives like Justice Harlan and those who joined the *Roe* majority. One of the most important questions *Dobbs* raises is how far this antipathy to unenumerated rights—once, but no longer, a core tenet for many liberals; now, but not previously, a conservative view—will extend in the future.

The Critics

Some liberal critics—Ginsburg was the most prominent—agreed that the Constitution protects abortion rights. Their objection was that *Roe* went too far, too fast, and that it did so unnecessarily because the normal political processes were working as they should. The Texas law that the Court invalidated in *Roe* forbade abortions unless the abortion was done to save the woman's life. Many other states had more liberal statutes that, for example, permitted abortions when necessary to protect the woman's health. The *Roe* Court itself noted that there was a trend, among state legislatures, toward liberalizing abortion laws. That led Ginsburg to say:

> *Roe,* I believe, would have been more acceptable as a judicial decision if it had not gone beyond a ruling on the extreme statute before the Court. The political process was moving in the early 1970s, not swiftly enough for advocates of quick, complete change, but majoritarian institutions were listening and acting. Heavy-handed judicial intervention was difficult to justify and appears to have provoked, not resolved, conflict.[8]

Whether *Roe* provoked conflict—or, as some liberal critics have suggested, a backlash—is far from clear; there is good reason to think that those claims are exaggerated, and that they oversimplify the complex political dynamics of the abortion issue at the time.[9] But Ginsburg's underlying point of principle—that when "majoritarian institutions [are] listening and acting .... judicial intervention [is] difficult to justify"—has been a central theme among liberals.

Other liberal critics, like Ely, asserted that the right to an abortion simply lacked any basis in the Constitution. The right to an abortion "is not inferable from the language of the Constitution, the framers' thinking respecting the specific problem in issue, any general value derivable from the provisions they included, or the nation's governmental structure."[10] *Roe* "is a very bad decision . . . because it is bad constitutional law, or rather because it is *not* constitutional law and gives no sense of an obligation to try to be."[11]

Criticisms like Ely's and Ginsburg's are important because they did not just attack the reasoning in the opinion in *Roe*; they asserted that the outcome was mistaken. The reasoning of the opinion was quite widely criticized, including by liberals. But today at least, the soundness of the reasoning in the *Roe* majority opinion is essentially beside the point. The Court's opinions in some of the most important and durable decisions in history provide weak justifications for the results they reached; at least that is a common view. *Marbury v. Madison* is often criticized for failing to make the best arguments in support of judicial review—it "begged the question in chief."[12] The unanimous opinion in *Brown v. Board of Education* was as much a diplomatic document as a justification for the outcome; it was designed to reduce the affront to segregationist states, and it did not provide anything like a full account of what the Court was doing and why. Especially after nearly fifty years, the question about *Roe* is not whether the majority opinion would get a good grade if it was an answer on a law school exam. The question is whether the result can be justified. The most significant liberal critics are those, like Ely and Ginsburg, who thought at the time that it could not be.

The Criticisms

Why were the liberal critics troubled by, or flatly opposed to, the outcome in *Roe*? There are, I think, three principal explanations. The first, illustrated by Ginsburg's criticism, was what many liberals took to be the central lesson of President Franklin Roosevelt's New Deal–era confrontation with the Court: in dealing with highly controversial issues, courts ought to proceed with the greatest caution, if they act at all. The second basis for liberal criticism, central to Ely's argument, was a variant of the first: while the Court should enforce rights enumerated in the Constitution, the Court in *Roe* invented a right that did not have an adequate (or, Ely argued, any) basis in the Constitution. The third is more speculative, but it seems to be a plausible explanation of why liberals were receptive to criticisms of *Roe*: there was an insufficient understanding, among the critics of *Roe*, of the extent to which abortion was an issue about women's equality.

In the decades since *Roe*, things have changed on all three of these fronts.

The New Deal Legacy and Judicial Restraint

When *Roe* was decided, a number of state legislatures had recently liberalized abortion laws, as Ginsburg and others emphasized. Some liberal critics of *Roe* drew a contrast with *Brown*. When *Brown* came before the Supreme Court, systematic disenfranchisement of Black people, and the filibuster and seniority system in the U.S. Senate, meant that the federal courts were arguably the only institution that could effectively deal with Jim Crow segregation. But nothing comparable was true of abortion. In fact, the wave of reform legislation showed that elected officials could be responsive. So, the critics said, it would have been better for the Court to minimize its role and to allow the political process to run its course.

This view of the Court's role—that, unless there is some defect in the normal political processes, controversial political issues are for elected representatives, not the courts—was central to progressive constitutionalism during much of the twentieth century. It is a position commonly associated with what is known as the *Carolene Products* footnote, a reference to a 1938 Supreme Court decision.[13] In the first third of the twentieth century, in several high-profile decisions—*Lochner v. New York*[14] was the most infamous—the Supreme Court invalidated social welfare and regulatory statutes enacted by Congress and state legislatures. Liberals of that period condemned those decisions as antidemocratic; they thought that courts were imposing their own small-government ideology on the nation. The New Deal–era clash between the Court and President Roosevelt—he attacked the Court, threatened to pack it, and the Court changed course—seemed to vindicate the liberals' view. The Court had to retreat, and the approach associated with *Lochner* was all but universally repudiated.

Carolene Products was decided right after that happened, at a time when Jim Crow segregation was, belatedly, becoming a focus of the Court's attention. The *Carolene Products* footnote provided a justification for treating discrimination against Black Americans as an exception to the general rule of judicial restraint, precisely because of the inability of the political process to address that issue. Even so, many liberals who supported *Brown*, including some of the justices, hesitated because they were acutely aware of the New Deal confrontation, and fear of a backlash shaped the way the Court approached segregation in the decade after *Brown*. The central theme of progressive constitutionalism remained: courts should intervene only when the normal political processes were in some way impaired. What Ely described as "crying wolf" was the failure of critics of the Warren Court to realize that what the Warren Court did was justified by the *Carolene Products* rationale in the way that *Roe* was not.

Lochner and Unenumerated Rights

The Constitution explicitly protects several rights, most of them in the Bill of Rights, and most of them familiar: freedom of speech and religion, freedom from unreasonable searches and seizures, rights that protect criminal defendants. Many of the Warren Court's most controversial decisions expanded those rights.

Probably the most common criticism of *Roe* from all sides was that the Court in *Roe* unjustifiably invented a new constitutional right that is not in the text. For many mid-twentieth-century liberals, this was another crucial lesson of the *Lochner* era and the New Deal confrontation: the Court should refuse to recognize extratextual rights. *Lochner* itself, and several other cases, had invalidated statutes on the ground that they infringed the "freedom of contract"; that right is not explicitly listed in the Bill of Rights or elsewhere in the Constitution, but the Court said it could be derived from the Due Process Clauses of the Fifth and Fourteenth Amendments (which apply to the federal government and the states, respectively). When the New Deal–era Court rejected that approach, Chief Justice Charles Evans Hughes tersely stated the new view about "freedom of contract": "What is this freedom? The Constitution does not speak of freedom of contract."[15] One of the common attacks on *Roe*—"the word 'abortion' is not in the Constitution"—is an unconscious echo of that line.

The idea that the Due Process Clause is the source of unenumerated rights—that it guarantees not just procedures but rights that cannot be abridged irrespective of process—became known as "substantive due process," an oxymoronic term (as its critics, of course, always point out). The post–New Deal era sensibility about unenumerated rights and substantive due process is captured in a passage of the Court's opinion in *Bowers v. Hardwick*,[16] a 1986 decision—overruled in 2003 by *Lawrence v. Texas*[17]—that held that there is no unenumerated right to same-sex sexual intimacy. Not coincidentally, the opinion in *Bowers* containing this passage was written by Justice White, one of the dissenters in *Roe*:

> The Court is most vulnerable and comes nearest to illegitimacy when it deals with judge-made constitutional law having little or no cognizable roots in the language or design of the Constitution. That this is so was painfully demonstrated by the face-off between the Executive and the Court in the 1930's, which resulted in the repudiation of much of the substantive gloss that the Court had placed on the Due Process Clauses of the Fifth and Fourteenth Amendments. There should be, therefore, great resistance to expand the substantive reach of those Clauses, particularly if it requires redefining the category of rights deemed to be fundamental. Otherwise, the Judiciary necessarily takes to itself further authority to govern the country without express constitutional authority.[18]

The Underdeveloped Protection of Women's Equality

Laws that forbid abortion force pregnant women, against their will, to bear children. That is a grievous affront to a woman's autonomy—her physical autonomy, of course, but well beyond that. To convey the message to women that they can be subject to that kind of imposition—when historically women's lives have been stunted by the norm that they should devote themselves to bearing and raising children—treats women unequally in a way that can be compared to the way that racial discrimination conveys messages about the inferiority of minority groups.

This kind of argument for abortion rights is fairly common today. But when *Roe* was decided fifty years ago, even its defenders seldom put the point in those terms. And the critics of *Roe*—including liberal critics, who should have been especially attuned to issues of autonomy and group subordination—did not engage that argument.

Part of the reason—maybe all of the reason—was that it was difficult to make this argument within the existing legal categories. Asserting that anti-abortion laws constitute sex discrimination is only the beginning, and even that argument was barely available when *Roe* was decided. Some of the liberal critics of *Roe* certainly did understand that abortion was an issue about sex discrimination and women's rights. Ginsburg, of course, was among them; she thought that *Roe* moved too quickly, but she defended abortion rights as necessary to secure women's equality.[19] Some contemporary defenders of *Roe*, notably Kenneth Karst, did the same.[20] Ely, the other liberal critic featured prominently in the *Dobbs* opinion, recognized that abortion could be treated as an issue of sex discrimination, although he thought the sex equality argument did not ultimately justify *Roe*.[21]

But several liberals who were skeptical about *Roe* did not mention women's equality at all, nor did some of *Roe*'s defenders. The principal progressive cause in the decades before *Roe* was the attack on Jim Crow segregation and other forms of discrimination against Black people. Constitutional law in the area of women's equality was in a primitive condition when *Roe* was decided; it reflected, and probably reinforced, the relative neglect of women's rights, even among liberals, especially compared to the progress on racial equality.

As the dissenting opinion in *Dobbs* pointed out, "Only a dozen years before *Roe*"—seven years after *Brown*—"the Court described women as 'the center of home and family life,' with 'special responsibilities' that precluded their full legal status under the Constitution." (The case in which the Court said that was *Hoyt v. Florida*,[22] which upheld a state law that exempted women from jury service unless they chose to opt in.) The first case in which the Supreme Court held a statute unconstitutional because it discriminated against women was *Reed v. Reed*,[23] which was decided just fourteen months before *Roe*, and the opinion in *Reed* treated the case as one about legislative irrationality rather than about women's equality per se. The Court did not explicitly say that laws discriminating on the basis of sex would be subject to a higher standard of review until 1976, three years after *Roe*.[24] And it did not emphasize the connection between abortion rights and women's equality until 1992, when it reaffirmed *Roe* in *Planned Parenthood v. Casey*.[25]

Unsurprisingly given the state of the law at the time, the plaintiffs' brief in *Roe* did not argue that the Texas law forbidding abortion violated the Equal

Protection Clause, the provision of the Constitution that prohibits invidious discrimination. The Court's opinion in *Roe* justified the result in the case entirely on the basis of an unenumerated right to privacy, not on the ground that a ban on abortion is impermissible discrimination against women. In fact, some passages in the *Roe* opinion notoriously pushed women into the background and suggested that the decision whether a woman would have an abortion was to be made primarily by the doctor. In summarizing its holdings, the *Roe* opinion said, "For the stage prior to approximately the end of the first trimester, the abortion decision and its effectuation must be left to the medical judgment of the pregnant woman's attending physician."[26]

In fact, in 1973—and today, too, apparently—a law forbidding abortion would not have been considered sex discrimination. In *Dobbs*, the majority summarily dismissed an Equal Protection Clause argument, relying entirely on a precedent from 1974: *Geduldig v. Aiello*, which upheld a state program that excluded pregnancy from the conditions covered by disability insurance.[27] Treating pregnancy differently from other medical conditions was not sex discrimination, the *Geduldig* Court said; it "merely remove[d] one physical condition—pregnancy—from the list of compensable disabilities."[28] It followed, the *Dobbs* majority thought, that anti-abortion laws also do not discriminate on the basis of sex.[29]

But even characterizing abortion as an issue of sex discrimination would not have been adequate. Forbidding a woman from getting an abortion—forcing a woman to bear a child—inflicts tangible and intangible harms that are in a different category from the kinds of sex discrimination that have been addressed in Supreme Court cases, such as excluding women from state-run institutions of higher education or structuring social insurance programs on the assumption that women are dependent on their male spouses' earnings.[30] The contemporary legal controversy about *Roe*—concerning issues of the role of courts, the existence of unenumerated rights, and whether anti-abortion laws even constituted sex discrimination—obscured the nature of those harms.

None of this addresses the concern that is advanced to justify laws forbidding abortion: the interest in protecting fetal life. The status of fetal life raises very difficult questions. But critics of *Roe*, including liberal critics, did not really grapple with those questions either, and, perhaps ironically, that is further evidence of the critics' relative insensitivity to the way in which anti-abortion laws affect women. Many of those critics, liberal and conservative, just assumed—as, for that matter, the Supreme Court did in *Dobbs*—that because questions about fetal life are so difficult and controversial, the regulation of abortion should be left to the political process.

But you cannot reach that conclusion so easily if you truly take into account the effects of anti-abortion laws on women. When rights to free speech or the freedom of religion are at stake, or when the government proposes, for example, to discriminate on the basis of race, we do not automatically say that the weight of any countervailing interest should be determined by the normal political processes. The opposite is true: those are the kinds of conflicts of values that are often removed from politics. Once you recognize that women's interest in having access to abortion—to not being forced to bear children—is at least comparable to those constitutionally protected interests, you cannot assume that the genuine difficulty of dealing with the interest in fetal life means that the issue should be left to the political process. The ease with which critics of *Roe* made that assumption suggested that they did not fully recognize what is at stake for women.

That is not to say that there is an obvious answer to the question of how to take fetal life into account in deciding about abortion rights. *Roe*, and the *Dobbs* dissent in defending *Roe*, implicitly took the position that, faced with such a conflict of values, a court should just strike the balance as best it can—somewhat like the way cases involving free speech or the exercise of religion might require that kind of balancing by a court. Alternatively, because women's autonomy and equality are at stake, the Constitution might require that the decision about fetal life be made by the woman herself, without intervention by the government; there is a rough analogy to saying that respect for the autonomy of local communities sometimes requires that they, not the larger nation of which they are a part, be allowed to decide even complex and crucially important issues.[31] Or perhaps an argument could in fact be made that this clash of values should be resolved by the normal political processes. But that conclusion would have to be justified, not assumed. The ease with which it was assumed by many liberal critics (among others)—understandable in light of the state of the law at the time—suggests an insufficient understanding of the effects on women of denying abortion rights.

What Changed?

Why were there several prominent liberal critics of *Roe* but few prominent liberal defenders of *Dobbs*? The polarization of opinion about abortion among legal commentators may have reflected the polarization in society. The fact that *Roe* had been in place for a half-century undoubtedly caused many of those who were originally skeptical to accept it for the same reasons that courts accept precedents.

But the change in views among liberals goes beyond *Roe* itself. Today a commitment to across-the-board judicial restraint, although recently embraced in some progressive circles, is not a mainstream liberal position and has not led to continued skepticism about *Roe*. Concerns about unenumerated rights seem to have faded among liberals—no doubt partly because the right to an abortion came to seem like a good idea, but not for that reason alone. Women's equality has become more of a priority and has become important in a different way from the way it was conceived in 1973.

Judicial Restraint and Unilateral Disarmament

Skepticism about judicial review was a central tenet of progressive thinking during the first half of the twentieth century. The view was that courts, in contrast to legislatures and executive branch agencies, were undemocratic institutions that lacked the capacity to resolve complex issues. Judges, who were generally relatively affluent and had often been corporate lawyers, were by nature biased against progressive initiatives. The *Lochner*-era courts' hostility to the emerging social welfare and regulatory state proved the point.

When the Supreme Court became willing to challenge racial discrimination, liberals opened the door to a more active role for the courts. But the belief in judicial restraint was still a central commitment among liberals. The Warren Court is not associated with judicial restraint, but in fact some of the most important Warren Court decisions—tellingly, decisions that were narrowed or effectively overturned by later conservative courts—were highly deferential to Congress.[32] That liberal commitment to judicial restraint led to the disquiet about *Roe*.

Very recently, some progressives have gone further, calling for a return to something closer to the across-the-board judicial restraint that characterized liberals' reaction to the *Lochner* era. That is, very likely, a reaction to the recent aggressive conservatism of the Supreme Court. But among liberals generally, across-the-board judicial restraint has not become the dominant creed that it was. One conspicuous example is the litigation that led to the Court's recognition of a constitutional right to same-sex marriage. In the case that recognized that right, *Obergefell v. Hodges*, it was a dissent—not by a liberal but by Chief Justice John Roberts—that emphasized that the political process was addressing the issue: "[O]ver the past six years, voters and legislators in eleven States and the District of Columbia have revised their laws to allow marriage between two people of the same sex."[33] The chief justice cited the law review article in which Ginsburg, before she joined the Court, had criticized the *Roe* Court for short-circuiting political progress.[34] But few liberals took that position about same-sex marriage; Justice Ginsburg herself joined the majority.

There are at least two plausible explanations for why a more across-the-board version of judicial restraint has not taken hold among liberals, so that the doubts about *Roe* that existed in 1973 have not returned with respect to *Roe* or *Obergefell*. One has to do with Congress. The idea that the courts should stay in the background because the political process would address problems was much more plausible in 1973 than it is today. *Roe* was decided not long after Congress enacted a series of civil rights laws: the Civil Rights Act of 1964, the Voting Rights Act of 1965, the Fair Housing Act of 1968, and Title IX of the Education Amendments of 1972. Since then, Congress has not enacted legislation of comparable importance protecting minorities and women.[35]

The second explanation is that in recent decades, conservatives have been anything but restrained. They have invalidated gun control laws, affirmative action measures, land use regulations, and campaign finance laws. The Court effectively nullified a central feature of the Voting Rights Act. No Court since the New Deal era had struck down a major piece of federal legislation comparable to the Affordable Care Act, but that statute barely and only partly survived in 2012.[36] With respect to issues that are politically or ideologically polarizing, judicial restraint is not going to be an appealing creed if only one side practices it.

Nor, arguably, should it be. Otherwise one side will be able to promote its agenda free from judicial review, while for the other side, it will not be enough to prevail in the legislative process: legislation will have to survive the judicial gauntlet, too, as was the case with the Affordable Care Act. So even if liberals believed that across-the-board judicial restraint is the right approach in an ideal world, they might be justified in insisting that it is not the best approach if they are the only ones who are practicing it. Given the path the Court has been on, to ask liberals to endorse *Dobbs* or reject *Obergefell* seems like demanding unilateral disarmament.

The Present and Future of Unenumerated Rights

The sound-bite criticism of *Roe*—"the word 'abortion' is not in the Constitution"—was easily conjoined with an accusation that liberal supporters of *Roe* were hypocritical. They rejected unenumerated rights they did not like, as in *Lochner*, but supported unenumerated rights they liked, as in *Roe*. Those criticisms were made by both conservative and liberal critics of *Roe*. But today the wholesale rejection of unenumerated rights is not a widely held position—most people are willing to accept some unenumerated rights—which makes that criticism less telling. The significant question about the trajectory of progressive constitutionalism is why the post-*Lochner* hostility to unenumerated rights, one of the bases for liberal criticisms of *Roe*, has dissipated. And the significant question about the future is whether *Dobbs*, by rejecting an unenumerated right to abortion, will lead to the rejection of other currently established unenumerated rights—in particular, the right to obtain contraceptives and the right to same-sex marriage.

The Persistence of Unenumerated Rights

The argument that support for *Roe* cannot be squared with the rejection of *Lochner* was one of Ely's main criticisms of *Roe*, but the ur-text is a dissenting opinion Justice Black wrote in *Griswold v. Connecticut*.[37] *Griswold* held unconstitutional a Connecticut statute that made it unlawful for anyone, even married couples, to use contraceptives. *Griswold*, of course, was one of the principal precedents the Court relied on in *Roe*.[38]

The majority in *Griswold* held that several provisions of the Bill of Rights taken together—the First, Third, Fourth, Fifth, and Ninth Amendments—created a "right of privacy" that the Connecticut law violated, even though none of those amendments explicitly states that there is such a right. Justice Harlan, in a concurring opinion, said instead that the Connecticut statute violated the Due Process Clause of the Fourteenth Amendment because it was inconsistent with "basic values 'implicit in the concept of ordered liberty.'"[39] Later decisions have followed Justice Harlan and treated *Griswold* as having been based on the Due Process Clause.[40] Justice Black's dissent attacked both the majority and Justice Harlan; there is no enumerated right of "privacy," he said, and to rely on the Due Process Clause as a source of unenumerated rights was to commit the error of the *Lochner* Court: inventing rights that are not in the Constitution.

In *Dobbs*, Justice Clarence Thomas, in a concurring opinion, took a position like Justice Black's, disparaging the idea that the Due Process Clause could be a source of substantive rights.[41] But no one else on the *Dobbs* Court agreed. The majority acknowledged that the Due Process Clause "has been held to guarantee some rights that are not mentioned in the Constitution." The majority insisted that "any such right must be 'deeply rooted in this Nation's history and tradition'"—which, according to the majority, the right to an abortion was not.[42] But the majority in *Dobbs* made a point of distancing itself—at least for now—from Justice Thomas's view, and the majority's discussion showed, perhaps unwittingly, how deeply entrenched unenumerated rights have become.

Justice Thomas called for the Court to "reconsider all of this Court's substantive due process precedents, including *Griswold*, *Lawrence*, and *Obergefell*."[43] But the majority listed a dozen cases, including those three, that recognized various unenumerated rights and made a point of not calling those decisions into question. Those substantive due process cases, the majority said, "do not support the right to obtain an abortion" because they did not involve the interest in protecting fetal life, but "by the same token, our conclusion that the Constitution does not confer such a right does not undermine them in any way."[44] The majority repeated this point several times.[45] So the position taken by Justices Black and Thomas—that there are no unenumerated rights—has been, at least for now, marginalized.

That position, which was central to liberals' (and others') criticism of *Roe*, is at least superficially appealing: the Constitution protects only the rights that are listed in the Constitution; if judges can recognize other rights, they can usurp the legislature's role. So why has that position, which was close to a mainstream view in the New Deal era, lost ground? One answer, which may reveal something basic about U.S. constitutional law, begins with the currently recognized unenumerated rights that the *Dobbs* majority said it was not questioning: "the right to marry while in prison, the right to obtain contraceptives, the right to reside with relatives, the right to make decisions about the education of one's children, the right not to be sterilized without consent, and the right in certain circumstances not to undergo involuntary surgery, forced administration of drugs, or other substantially similar procedures."[46]

These are all very appealing rights, the kind of rights, one might think, that a decent society will protect. Of course it does not follow that courts should protect them; elected officials can. But if a case does arise in which a government seeks to deny an individual a right like these, it is easy to see why a court will want to find some way it can use the Constitution to rule in favor of the individual, even if that means establishing an unenumerated right as a matter of substantive due process. That is, in fact, what the Supreme Court did in the cases that *Dobbs* listed.

So the persistence of unenumerated rights may be a result of the way U.S. constitutional law often develops: case by case, like the common law, with courts responding to particular facts and shaping the law accordingly, rather than working deductively from the text. There remains the concern that courts that aren't limited by the text will effectively usurp the role of elected officials, but there are, possibly, two complementary reasons that this concern did not deter the Court from continuing to recognize unenumerated rights. One was given by Justice Harlan in *Griswold*, in response to Justice Black: " 'Specific' provisions of the Constitution, no less than 'due process,' lend themselves as readily to 'personal' interpretations by judges.' "[47] Freedom of speech, freedom of religion, and freedom from unreasonable searches and seizures are quintessential examples of "enumerated" rights, but of course it is not clear what, specifically, those rights guarantee, and "interpreting" those provisions leaves judges plenty of room to impose their own views.

The second possible reason that the concern about giving judges too much leeway did not deter the Court from recognizing unenumerated rights is also related to the case-by-case way in which constitutional law develops. The real limits on judicial discretion are provided not so much by the text—much of which is open-ended—as by precedents. This should have been obvious all along, but the Warren Court may have been a turning point. The Warren Court expanded the protections of the Equal Protection Clause and the First, Fourth, Fifth, and Sixth Amendments. In addition, one of the central projects of the Warren Court was to extend many of the provisions of the Bill of Rights to the states; some had applied only to the federal government. The result was a profusion of cases deciding difficult issues presented by those provisions. The text did not begin to resolve those issues. Instead, the arguments in those cases, on both sides, predominantly concerned the precedents the Court had established.

With that experience, it is especially clear that, in general, limits on what the courts can plausibly say are determined by precedents, not by the text. A court committed to following precedent cannot simply make up an unenumerated right to suit its own policy preferences, just as it cannot make up any interpretation of "freedom of speech" that it prefers. By the same token, a court that is willing to play fast and loose with precedent is not going to be very limited by open-ended language in the Constitution. In the decades after *Roe*, it should have become more and more clear that, for these reasons, the concerns about unenumerated rights were at least overstated and perhaps just unwarranted. By 1986, in *Bowers v. Hardwick*, when the Court refused to recognize a right to same-sex intimacy, four justices, in dissent, were already willing to reject Justice White's caution—which echoed the common New Deal–era view—about unenumerated rights. For similar reasons, the parallel liberal criticism of *Roe* was becoming more and more untenable.

Unenumerated Rights after *Dobbs*

The current conservative majority's apparent willingness to tolerate some unenumerated rights does not mean that it will continue the status quo; one important question is whether, in the wake of *Dobbs*, the Court will begin to reject other unenumerated rights. The *Dobbs* dissent accused the majority of being disingenuous in claiming that its reasoning extended only to abortion and not to, among other things, contraception and same-sex marriage. The majority's test for whether an unenumerated right should be recognized—whether it was "deeply rooted" in "history and tradition"—is potentially indeterminate and manipulable; in any event it would not be difficult to argue that a constitutional right to obtain contraceptives, and certainly a right to same-sex marriage or intimacy, is not "deeply rooted" in history.

If history is in fact the test, then, as the dissent also pointed out, the assertion that abortion is different because it concerns fetal life is just a red herring. Cases protecting other rights, having nothing to do with fetal life, could be overruled if they do not have what a majority of the Court considers sufficiently deep roots in history. As the dissent said, the majority's willingness to overrule *Roe* and *Casey* suggests that no precedent is safe, and *Lawrence* and *Obergefell* are not as long-standing as *Roe* was.

Probably the best way to understand the implications of *Dobbs* for the future is that the Court is leaving its options open. The Court could uphold the rights to contraception and to same-sex marriage by pointing to the language in *Dobbs* that said abortion is different, and to the repeated statements in the *Dobbs* majority opinion that the Court was not casting doubt on other unenumerated rights. Or the Court could go in the other direction: it could conclude that the unenumerated rights established by *Griswold*, *Lawrence*, and *Obergefell* are not sufficiently rooted in history—that was the test that *Dobbs* endorsed, so presumably that test must be satisfied, irrespective of the assurances in the *Dobbs* opinion—and overrule those cases.

The *Dobbs* dissent identified a recent analogue to this kind of (possibly deliberate) ambiguity. *Lawrence*, the case that established a right to same-sex intimacy, was decided at a time when same-sex marriage was a highly controversial issue. The Court wrote its opinion in *Lawrence* in a way that did not commit it to holding that there was a right to same-sex marriage but did not close the door on that possibility, either. For example, *Lawrence*, which was a criminal prosecution, held that individuals could not be convicted of a crime for engaging in a same-sex sexual act, but the opinion explicitly noted that the case did "not involve whether the government must give formal recognition to any relationship that homosexual persons seek to enter."[48] That gave the Court a chance to wait and see before it decided about same-sex marriage. *Dobbs* gives the Court a chance to wait and see before it decides whether it will continue to accept *Griswold, Lawrence,* and *Obergefell.*

Realistically speaking, the Court is unlikely to overrule any of those three cases outright. The more likely scenario is that the Court will allow them to be eroded. States might insist, for example, that some contraceptives are in fact abortifacients and therefore can be banned; the Court would then have to decide how much deference it should give to the state's determination. Courts might be more receptive to religion-based claims by government employees who do not want to provide contraceptives or facilitate same-sex marriages. And *Dobbs* will complicate efforts to recognize constitutional rights for transgender individuals.

The opposite scenario, in which *Dobbs* does not lead to any further undermining of unenumerated rights, is also possible. Same-sex marriage has not aroused nearly as much opposition as abortion, and substantial restrictions on the availability of contraceptives would be very unpopular. The *Dobbs* opinion does repeatedly say that abortion is different. So the Court may stop at overruling *Roe*. But *Dobbs* certainly does not leave other unenumerated rights secure.

Abortion as an Issue of Women's Equality

One way to describe the change since *Roe* is that liberals have increasingly come to see abortion in terms of all its effects on women, without trying to fit the right to abortion into preexisting categories. Here, for example, is the opening passage of the dissenting opinion in *Dobbs*:

> For half a century, [*Roe* and *Casey*] have protected the liberty and equality of women. *Roe* held, and *Casey* reaffirmed, that the Constitution safeguards a woman's right to decide for herself whether to bear a child. *Roe* held, and *Casey* reaffirmed, that in the first stages of pregnancy, the government could not make that choice for women. The government could not control a woman's body or the course of a woman's life: It could not determine what the woman's future would be. Respecting a woman as an autonomous being, and granting her full equality, meant giving her substantial choice over this most personal and most consequential of all life decisions.[49]

This passage focuses strictly on women. It tries to paint a picture of both the tangible effects on women and the effects on women's status in society. It does not seem concerned with such questions as exactly what rights are at stake, where they come from in the Constitution, and what their limits are, or whether anti-abortion laws discriminate "on the basis of sex" within the meaning of the Court's decisions. Those questions in isolation failed to identify, and probably obscured, the constitutionally significant ways that anti-abortion laws harmed women. Abortion is an issue that has elements of sex discrimination, of reinforcing traditional gender roles, of invading physical autonomy, of preventing women from shaping their lives, and of interfering with the most intimate decisions about one's family, all reinforcing each other. This perspective became more apparent when abortion was considered from women's point of view; it was lacking in the contemporaneous liberal criticisms of *Roe*.

Explaining the change between then and now is obviously a matter of speculation, but it is clear enough that in the last third of the twentieth century, there were many advances in the status of women in U.S. society. Women entered the workforce in greater numbers, and more women began to occupy elite ranks in, among other places, the legal profession, including the Supreme Court. These developments very likely contributed to a change in the way people thought about the constitutional issues surrounding abortion. At the very least, the effect that the availability or unavailability of abortion would have on women's lives became a bigger part of the legal controversy.

It also mattered that *Roe* was a fifty-year-old precedent, and, paradoxically, it mattered that *Roe* was so controversial that it became a central focus of debates about constitutional interpretation. Depriving people of what they have come to believe are their rights generally has a greater effect than refusing to grant them a right in the first place, so once women came to think of reproductive freedom as a part of their lives—both concretely and symbolically—it became more difficult to address the issue without seeing it from the point of view of women.

Beyond that, the long controversy over *Roe* affected the legal landscape. The central issues about abortion stopped being whether the Supreme Court had learned the lesson of *Lochner*, whether the Court had gone too far, too fast, or whether laws forbidding abortion were technically "sex discrimination." The issue became the right to an abortion itself and the effect that denying that right would have on women. That issue cannot be confined within the categories that *Roe* used or that critics used when they attacked *Roe*. It became increasingly clear that the legal controversy over the right to an abortion required more of a focus on women and the effects that denying that right would have on women. The understanding that abortion is primarily an issue about women's equality, understood in complex ways, took some time to develop. But in retrospect, *Roe*—the outcome, if not the reasoning—was ahead of its time.

2

Equality Emerges as a Ground for Abortion Rights in and after *Dobbs*

Cary Franklin and Reva Siegel

Is *Dobbs*[1] the end of the abortion right? Or is *Dobbs* a stage in the struggle over abortion rights? If the U.S. Supreme Court had invented the abortion right, the Court might have the power to kill it. But if in deciding *Roe v. Wade*[2] the Court interpreted the Constitution's liberty guarantee in light of public belief that people ought to have control over certain life decisions, in particular the belief that it is wrong for government to coerce a woman to continue a pregnancy, then the Court cannot unilaterally eradicate that belief.

In 1973, a time when women barely had any role in state or federal government, in the courts, or in the legal academy, converging movements for the decriminalization of abortion and for recognition of women's equal citizenship helped move a nearly all-male judiciary to extend the right to privacy to protect decisions about whether to carry a pregnancy to term.[3] At the time *Roe* was decided, Justice Harry Blackmun had a Gallup poll showing supermajority support for leaving the abortion decision to a woman and her doctor, support that consolidated after the Court's ruling and has remained remarkably steady.[4]

In the intervening half-century, the constitutional framework the Court forged in 1973 has been the locus of conflict.[5] For a half-century the Court vindicated that right, reaffirming it countless times, famously in 1992 in *Planned Parenthood v. Casey*,[6] and as recently as 2016 and 2020. But three justices appointed, in procedurally contested circumstances, by President Donald Trump have formed a Court to declare *Roe* and *Casey* egregiously wrong and reverse those decisions.[7]

In this chapter we consider the Supreme Court's repudiation of *Roe* and *Casey* as a time of transition in the form of abortion rights rather than as a time of their abolition. The Court's decision to repudiate *Roe* and *Casey* destroys protections that federal courts afforded the right for fifty years.

Cary Franklin and Reva Siegel, *Equality Emerges as a Ground for Abortion Rights in and after* Dobbs In: *Roe v. Dobbs.* Edited by: Lee C. Bollinger and Geoffrey R. Stone, Oxford University Press. © Oxford University Press 2024. DOI: 10.1093/oso/9780197760352.003.0002

At the same time, it opens the door for advocates of reproductive justice to defend the abortion right in terms consistent with twenty-first-century understandings of women's equal citizenship.

The focal point of our attention is equal protection as a ground for abortion rights claims. In *Dobbs*, before reversing *Roe*, Justice Samuel Alito reached out in dicta to assert that equality supplied no basis for abortion rights—betraying his anxiety that the Equal Protection Clause in fact supplied abortion rights claims a natural constitutional home. As there was no equal protection claim asserted in *Dobbs*, Justice Alito could not rule on the claim in the *Dobbs* case.[8] The question of how equal protection speaks to the regulation of abortion is open now in a way it has not been open in half a century. Contestation over this question will unfold in federal court, in Congress and the executive branch, in state courts and legislatures, and in the court of public opinion—in every arena in which conflicts over abortion rights continue.

For fifty years, the framework the Court adopted in *Roe* has structured legal and popular contestation over abortion. That framework analyzed the abortion right as grounded in the Fourteenth Amendment's due process liberty guarantee, even as the Court increasingly came to reason about that liberty right as infused with equality values that advocates have asserted since the 1960s.[9] Now that the Court has overruled *Roe* and *Casey* and demolished the due process framework it created in 1973 for reasoning about the constitutional values at stake when government controls pregnancy and childbirth, it is time to ask in what ways the Equal Protection Clause might speak directly to the question.[10]

What is at stake in examining equal protection as an alternative constitutional ground for challenging laws criminalizing abortion if a conservative majority of the Court is now implacably hostile to abortion rights? First, even with this majority, there may be opportunities for advocates to challenge the vague and draconian abortion bans now causing doctors and hospitals to refuse or delay care until death is proximate in cases involving cancer treatment, ectopic pregnancies, miscarriages, and hemorrhaging.[11] A pregnant person who is deprived of needed medical care because providers fear prosecution under an abortion ban with a narrow or ill-defined life exception could assert liberty and equality claims that might split the coalition that overturned *Roe* and *Casey*.

The equal protection analytic can also guide actors in the executive branch and Congress, as well as actors in state courts and legislatures. The equal protection questions we raise are relevant in crafting new legislation and new constitutional provisions, in interpreting existing constitutional texts, and in everyday debates over the justice of abortion bans. This chapter is a call not for abandoning liberty-based arguments for reproductive justice but for expanding the repertoire.

Because liberty-based arguments have taken center stage for so long in contestations over abortion, the implications of modern equal protection law for the regulation of abortion are not well understood. Women's rights advocates have long offered equality-based arguments against stringent abortion regulation. The Court itself emphasized the conflict between such regulation and equal protection law as a key reason for reaffirming *Roe* in *Casey* and for applying *Casey*'s undue burden standard to strike down an abortion statute.[12] But the full implications of modern equal protection law for the regulation of abortion have not been explored and developed.

This chapter begins by showing how sex discrimination law has evolved since *Roe*, which was handed down at a time when only one sex-based equal protection case had been decided. Sex discrimination law today is a much more powerful body of law than it was fifty years ago. It declares sex-based state action presumptively unconstitutional, and especially suspect when it enforces traditional family roles. Before regulating by sex-based means that force people into such roles, government must show why it cannot achieve its ends by more inclusive, less restrictive means. This equal protection sex discrimination framework extends to laws regulating pregnancy and, thus, to abortion restrictions.

As the next section shows, the equal protection analytic provides powerful tools for probing the ways that anti-abortion jurisdictions protect life. Asking equal protection questions of abortion bans raises disturbing questions about their sex-, class-, and race-based animus and impact. The *Dobbs* Court was itself sufficiently disturbed by the power of this alternative constitutional framework that it reached out in dicta to insist that laws governing pregnancy are not subject to heightened equal protection scrutiny, and to assert in its merits decision that nineteenth-century abortion bans protected unborn life and did not express constitutionally suspect judgments about women.

In the third section we show how *Dobbs* misrepresents the past and present logic of abortion bans. Bans on abortion were adopted at a time when the law enforced gender hierarchy in the public and private spheres. Advocates argued that abortion bans were needed to protect unborn life *and* to enforce women's roles and the procreative ends of marital sex. Over time, abortion was codified as a morals crime, a sex crime, and a crime against the family. As we show, this understanding of abortion restrictions persists to the present day. Judgments about women's roles and about sex continue as a part of the abortion argument, sometimes in the register of paternalism, sometimes in the register of punishment. Even when it is not openly expressed, sex-role-based reasoning continues to shape the structure of abortion regulation and its justifications, demonstrating why equal protection scrutiny is warranted.

Equal protection permits abortion regulation of some kinds, but the regulation of women in our constitutional order can no longer be premised on the view that "[t]he paramount destiny and mission of woman are to fulfil the noble and benign offices of wife and mother," as Justice William J. Brennan observed in *Frontiero v. Richardson*[13] a half-century ago, just after the Court decided *Roe*. This chapter's fundamental claim, delineated in the fourth section, is that the regulation of abortion must take account of that fundamental shift in the law and social understanding of women's civic membership. In the era in which abortion bans were first adopted, lawmakers understood women as caregiving dependents of male heads of household; today women are recognized as equal and independent members of the polity. Evolving understandings of women's citizenship have implications for *how* the state protects new life. The state must protect new life in ways that respect women as equals in the constitutional order, not simply in the formal sense—can we find a male comparator?—but with historical memory of the ways that the state for too long restricted women's civic status and instrumentalized women's lives in the service of family care.

Put differently, we argue that women's status as equal citizens—recognized in Supreme Court equal protection case law—gives rise to an *anticarceral presumption*. A state seeking to protect life must do so in ways that are consistent with women's equal citizenship; to demonstrate that a state regulating abortion is acting on a bona fide interest in protecting new life—rather than controlling and punishing those who resist maternity—the state must first endeavor to protect new life by supporting those who nourish new life. The labor of lifegiving is no longer to be coerced or extracted by law—as states enforcing the law of gender status historically assumed it could be, and abortion abolitionists still insist it can be.

In what ways must the forms of law employed to protect and respect new life evolve with evolving understandings of women's citizenship? This is a debate we need to be having in courts and legislatures and in the court of public opinion. Some decision-makers might say that in 2023 the *only* way that public authorities can protect life consistent with equal protection is to employ noncoercive means. Others might question this exclusively noncoercive view and conclude that women's equal citizenship imposes a condition: that a jurisdiction must at least provide its citizens resources to avoid becoming pregnant and to navigate pregnancy in health and dignity *before* the state can adopt an abortion ban consistent with equal protection. The authors of this chapter are committed to the exclusively noncoercive view. But what we think most critical in the wake of *Dobbs* is that legislatures and courts conduct this debate on terms that make clear that women have rights as equal citizens that they did not when abortion bans were first enacted and that these rights need to be taken into account whenever Americans deliberate about the protection of potential life and the regulation of abortion.

The Evolution of Equal Protection Law and Its Implications for Abortion Regulation

A half-century ago, law protecting sex equality and sexual freedom was born under two different clauses of the Fourteenth Amendment. The Court's 1965 decision in *Griswold v. Connecticut*[14] was decided so early that the Court did not even see it as constitutionally relevant that Connecticut enforced its criminal ban against contraceptives used by women but allowed drugstores to sell condoms over the counter to men.[15] In *Roe*, the Court famously had difficulty remembering whether doctors or women were the rights' holders.[16]

Litigants were remarkably creative in devising ways to make women's voices heard in a system where women were still radically underrepresented[17] and where abortion was so stigmatized from a century of criminalization that it was difficult to conduct ordinary democratic debate about the question. They used speak-outs and other storytelling techniques to point out the systemic inequalities that laws criminalizing abortion intensified. They emphasized that because a gender-hierarchical society organized sex roles around reproduction, taking control over pregnancy from women not only took control over women's bodies but also took control over women's lives in matters of sex, health, family relations, education, work, and politics. They invoked most every constitutional clause to say so. And they emphasized that these harms were intersectional, enforcing inequality along lines of race and class as well as sex.[18]

An all-male Court responded, slowly. As Justice Blackmun revised the *Roe* opinion in colloquy with his colleagues, the Court expanded *Roe* from a case about injuries to doctors to include the injuries to pregnant women[19] and expanded the time women's decisions were protected to two trimesters to ensure that poor and young women could access the right.[20]

But *Roe* was still a transitional decision, unfolding in the footprint of the criminalization regime. *Roe* simply took for granted that the state has a benign interest in protecting potential life that becomes compelling over the course of pregnancy. The Court did not recognize that what *Roe* terms "the state interest in potential life" was at one and the same time a state interest in *regulating women's decisions about motherhood, the role determining women's civic status*—or recognize that this was state action that might warrant heightened scrutiny given what the Court would call, only a few months later, the nation's "long and unfortunate history of sex discrimination."[21] Reasoning in a world before its equal protection sex discrimination opinions, *Roe* did not express concern about stereotyping or the coercive imposition of maternity. The Court built *Roe*'s trimester framework on a premise of "physiological naturalism."[22] Abortion laws regulate women because women are where the fetus happens to be. Any imposition on women is reasonable, explained by features of women's bodies.[23] The Court reasoned as if objective facts about the body—rather than assumptions about social structure or social roles—explained the architecture of its decision. It meted out privacy rights to women and their doctors in accordance with different stages of fetal development, never asking how laws that regulate abortion— past or present—expressed, enforced, or structured women's membership in the community: "When the fetus is considered as an object of regulatory concern distinct and apart from the woman bearing it, it becomes possible to reason about regulating women's conduct without seeming to reason about women at all."[24]

It is not surprising that the Court adopted this approach at the time of *Roe*. In 1973, the Court had not yet held that sex-based state action is subject to heightened scrutiny, and it was not ready to integrate pregnancy, a so-called real difference, into the logic of its nascent sex discrimination jurisprudence. Feminists in this period argued that laws regulating pregnancy were a core site of sex stereotyping. But in 1974, the Court held in *Geduldig v. Aiello* that a pregnancy classification was not a sex classification for the purposes of equal protection, based on the same physiological naturalism evident in *Roe*. The Court in this early period viewed pregnancy as a distinct physical condition,

affecting some subset of women, and not as part of the sex role of motherhood. It could not yet recognize the ways in which regulation of pregnant
women might enforce sex-role stereotypes, nor could it conceive of applying
constitutional equality protections across biological difference.[25]

In dicta in *Dobbs* dismissing equal protection as an alternative ground for
the abortion right, the Court invoked *Geduldig* as if equal protection law was
fully formed in the early 1970s, before the Court had even adopted a framework for analyzing sex-based state action. But the law has evolved substantially since *Geduldig* and the very first sex discrimination cases. Over the past
fifty years, there has been intense debate about the Equal Rights Amendment,
a veritable stream of cases litigated under the Constitution, and the development of a rich body of case law under the nation's civil rights statutes, including debate over civil rights law addressing pregnancy. (In 1978, Congress
repudiated the Court's efforts to import *Geduldig*'s reasoning into federal employment discrimination law and enacted the Pregnancy Discrimination Act
[PDA], which defines discrimination on the basis of pregnancy as discrimination on the basis of sex for purposes of Title VII of the 1964 Civil Rights Act.)[26]

The all-male bench that decided *Geduldig* imagined women as equal to
men only to the extent they were like men. Two decades later, in *United States
v. Virginia*,[27] the Court summarized its equal protection sex discrimination cases emphasizing that women are entitled to be treated as men's equals
notwithstanding " '[i]nherent differences' between men and women."[28] The
Court affirmed that law classifying on the basis of sex "may be used to com-
pensate women 'for particular economic disabilities [they have] suffered,' to
'promot[e] equal employment opportunity,' and 'to advance full development of the talent and capacities of our Nation's people.' "[29] But, the Court
explained, "such classifications may not be used, as they once were, to create
or perpetuate the legal, social, and economic inferiority of women."[30]

To make clear that pregnancy is the primary object of this analysis—the
main "inherent difference" to which this passage refers—the Court points
to a state law governing pregnancy (a maternity leave benefit, upheld under
the PDA in *California Federal Savings and Loan Association v. Guerra*)[31] as a
paradigmatic example of a law classifying on the basis of sex that is constitutional because it advances women's equality.[32] The Court explains in this
passage that equal protection does not require the state to ignore the physical
reality of pregnancy, but that regulation of pregnancy must be designed to
promote equal opportunity and may not perpetuate women's subordination.
Rather than "reasoning from the body"[33]—as the Court did when it declined

to apply heightened scrutiny in *Geduldig* on the ground that "pregnancy is an objectively identifiable physical condition with unique characteristics"[34]— the Court in *Virginia* reasons about laws regulating pregnancy in an institutional context, asking whether the law regulating pregnancy is promoting equal opportunity or perpetuating the inferiority of women. To determine whether a law regulating pregnancy is consistent with equal protection, the Court does not consult a medical dictionary; it asks how the law regulating pregnancy structures social relationships.

By 2003, when Chief Justice William Rehnquist wrote for the Court in *Nevada Department of Human Resources v. Hibbs*,[35] he emphasized not only that laws regulating pregnant women may constitute sex discrimination but that redress of such discrimination is a core concern of sex-based equal protection law. In *Hibbs* the Court held that Congress could enforce the Equal Protection Clause by enacting the family leave provisions of the Family and Medical Leave Act in order to redress the stereotyping and exclusion of pregnant workers. Chief Justice Rehnquist held that Congress's provision of family leave was an appropriate means of enforcing equal protection because many states' maternity leave policies were "not attributable to any differential physical needs of men and women, but rather to the pervasive sex-role stereotype that caring for family members is women's work."[36] The Court echoed Congress's observation that, "[h]istorically, denial or curtailment of women's employment opportunities has been traceable directly to the pervasive presumption that women are mothers first, and workers second," and that "[t]his prevailing ideology about women's roles has in turn justified discrimination against women when they are mothers or mothers-to-be."[37]

The Court's equal protection decision in *Hibbs* reflects growing awareness of the central role that regulation of pregnancy has played in women's marginalization. Five of the six justices in the majority in *Geduldig* were born before women obtained the right to vote. (The sixth, Justice Rehnquist, was born just after, in 1924.) All of those justices came of age in an era in which the exclusion of pregnant women and mothers from the public sphere was viewed as entirely natural, an outgrowth of biological difference and a benign reflection of the fact that women's primary calling is to have children and care for their families. Justice Blackmun's views evolved over time as he lived through the firestorm directed at the *Roe* opinion he authored; Justice Rehnquist's shift in understanding may well be attributable to his role in helping his daughter, a lawyer who was a single mother, navigate work and child care.[38]

Another major factor driving this evolution was the Court's involvement in enforcing the PDA. After the PDA's enactment, the Court was enlisted in enforcing the prohibition on pregnancy discrimination in the workplace and began to issue major opinions combating such discrimination.[39] Once it started this work, the Court stopped invoking *Geduldig* in equal protection cases. We have not found a majority opinion (prior to *Dobbs*) invoking *Geduldig* to interpret the Equal Protection Clause since Congress repudiated its reasoning in the late 1970s. *Virginia* and *Hibbs* supersede *Geduldig's* reasoning. In these cases, the Court reasoned from the experience it acquired enforcing the PDA and explained that laws regulating pregnancy must be closely scrutinized to ensure they do not stereotype, reinforce traditional assumptions about women's roles, or perpetuate women's second-class standing.

Yet Justice Alito invoked *Geduldig* in *Dobbs*. Before overturning *Roe* and *Casey*, Justice Alito reached out to assert that there are no equal protection grounds for challenging abortion bans under the federal Constitution. To tie his dicta to the litigation—the parties were not raising equal protection claims—he cited two amicus briefs, including one that relied on *Virginia* and *Hibbs*, to show that *Geduldig* has been superseded and that the Court had identified the regulation of pregnancy as a key concern of sex-based equal protection law.[40] In keeping with the majority's nostalgia for the world before recognition of women's equal citizenship, Justice Alito cited *Geduldig* and a decision about abortion protests that had nothing to do with state action or sex-based classifications[41] and, without addressing the arguments or the major equal protection cases on which the amicus brief relied, asserted that equality arguments were "squarely foreclosed by our precedents."[42] Justice Alito's fidelity to pregnancy discrimination precedent from a half-century ago, before the rise of sex discrimination law, was a fitting prelude to a decision that overturned a half-century of substantive due process law—by tying the meaning of the due process liberty guarantee to laws enacted in 1868.

Applying Equal Protection to Criminal Abortion Bans Post-*Dobbs*

Dobbs unleashed—and sanctioned—a wave of anti-abortion regulation unlike any in living memory.[43] As of this writing there are now twelve states where abortion is banned entirely[44] and several others where bans are in the litigation pipeline.[45]

These new (and revived) abortion bans are breathtakingly extreme, surprising even many opponents of abortion with their rigidity and punitiveness.[46] On the one hand there is the shock of states enforcing abortion bans enacted before women were granted the right to vote.[47] On the other hand there are new laws that surpass the old laws in the severity of their penalties. A new Texas law threatens abortion providers with life or twenty years in prison.[48] A new Tennessee law makes it a felony to perform any abortion, providing doctors who acted to save the life of a woman an affirmative defense to this criminal charge if they carry that burden at trial.[49]

Many of these new laws ban abortion with no exceptions for rape or incest or the health of the pregnant person. The bans generally except abortions needed to protect maternal life. But as *Dobbs* allowed criminal bans to go into effect immediately with no transition period, it is unclear which medically necessary abortions the exceptions authorize.[50] With exceptions vaguely drafted, and prosecutors ready to enforce exorbitant criminal penalties, healthcare administrators and providers have proceeded cautiously, afraid to intervene to save their patients' lives. In most cases it is unclear how near death's door a pregnant person needs to be before a life-saving abortion is legal.[51]

These draconian new (and old) bans have been in effect for only months, but they have already begun to present serious threats to the well-being of women and others capable of pregnancy. Pregnant women who are miscarrying or suffering ectopic pregnancies have been denied abortions because doctors have determined they are not yet close enough to death to qualify for care under the law.[52] Growing numbers of pregnant women experiencing various life-threatening complications have been turned away and told to return to hospitals only when they can prove their deaths are imminent.[53]

Some of these bans are so extreme it is not clear that equal protection heightened scrutiny would be required to establish their unconstitutionality. There is no rational basis for a law (let alone a law that purports to preserve life) that deters doctors from providing life-saving medical care. Even Justice Rehnquist, dissenting in *Roe*, declared that "the Fourteenth Amendment undoubtedly does place a limit . . . on legislative power to enact laws [that] . . . prohibit an abortion even where the mother's life is in jeopardy."[54] Doctors and hospital administrators are interpreting many of the laws enacted after *Dobbs* as doing just that. The scope and contours of the life exceptions are so vague that doctors are deterred from providing care even in life-threatening circumstances.[55] Even under rational basis, that is constitutionally illicit. It is irrational to enact regulations designed to preserve and express respect for life that endanger people's lives in the way these regulations do. Indeed, even committed anti-abortion advocates are trying to disavow these consequences and the extreme disregard these laws show toward women and others capable of pregnancy—suggesting such people merit little concern and have no value apart from their baby-making capacity.[56]

Under heightened scrutiny, these laws fare even worse. Heightened scrutiny requires the state to justify its decision to regulate by discriminatory means and to show why the state could not have adopted less restrictive means to accomplish its aims.[57] States enacting criminal bans classify by sex,[58] singling out pregnant women, without endeavoring to achieve the compelling end of protecting life and health by more inclusive, less coercive means.

States claim that their aim is to nurture and protect potential life. But there are many ways for states to nurture potential life and reduce the incidence of abortion that are not punitive and do not strip women and other pregnant people of agency. Evidence-based sex education programs can help to reduce unplanned pregnancies, which are far more likely than planned pregnancies to result in abortion. Making contraception widely available and mandating its coverage in health insurance plans can also reduce the incidence of unplanned pregnancies.[59] States can expand Medicaid to ensure people receive essential pre- and postnatal care; they can provide pregnant people with nutrition and housing support and access to drug and alcohol treatment programs; they can guarantee high-quality child care and paid parental leave; and they can pass laws protecting pregnant workers, to help people—women in particular—surmount the many obstacles to combining work and parenting in an at-will employment context with few social supports for poor and low-income parents.[60]

These are just a few of the less restrictive alternatives to criminalization that states purporting to prioritize protecting unborn life could adopt. In fact, many of the states enacting criminal abortion bans are openly hostile to offering social supports for pregnant people that other states routinely provide.

Take Mississippi, the state whose fifteen-week abortion ban was at issue in *Dobbs*. The anti-abortion legislators who control the Mississippi legislature frequently proclaim their commitment to protecting potential life. But their policy choices help place Mississippi last, or near the bottom, on nearly every measure related to fetal and maternal health. Infants in Mississippi are likelier to die before their first birthday than infants in any other state, and Black babies are twice as likely to die as their white counterparts.[61] In part, this is because Mississippi has the country's highest rate of premature birth—a leading cause of infant death that is linked to chronic conditions such as high blood pressure and diabetes among mothers.[62] Increasing access to pre- and postnatal care could address many of these problems, but Mississippi is one of twelve states that have not expanded Medicaid coverage under the Affordable Care Act—leaving approximately 25% of Black women in Mississippi without health insurance.[63] The state has repeatedly refused to provide a full year of Medicaid coverage to people who have given birth, despite evidence showing that extending this postpartum benefit to the Medicaid eligible would make a critical difference in protecting maternal life and health.[64] (Even though the decision to extend postpartum benefits from two months to a year would not increase the number of people eligible for Medicaid, the Mississippi Speaker of the House explained the state's refusal by asserting, "We need to look for ways to keep people off [Medicaid], not put them on." He also claimed he had seen no evidence proving the benefit would save the state money, and when asked whether it could save lives, responded, "That has not been a part of the discussions that I've heard.")[65] Nor is the state taking steps proven to reduce the number of unplanned pregnancies: the widespread lack of health insurance reduces access to contraception and the state refuses to provide comprehensive evidence-based sex education. Unsurprisingly, the 2019 *Health of Women and Children Report* ranked Mississippi fiftieth among the states on a range of metrics related to the health of women, infants, and children.[66]

Just about the only thing Mississippi does to vindicate its purported interest in protecting potential life is criminalize abortion.[67] In this, it is not an outlier. States enacting criminal abortion bans after *Dobbs* generally share Mississippi's antipathy to expanding health insurance, to enacting any kind of social support for poor and low-income people, and to educating students about safe sex and contraception.[68] As a result, Mississippi is joined at the bottom of the charts regarding fetal, infant, and maternal health and morbidity by all of the most zealous anti-abortion states.[69] Their policy is not only to employ criminal law means to protect unborn life but to do so while denying the people coerced into giving birth forms of social provision commonly offered in other jurisdictions. The states that have rushed to criminalize' abortion in the wake of *Dobbs* are the states *least likely* to have pursued any of these other means of protecting potential life.[70]

Assuming Mississippi sought only to protect potential life, then, the state is wildly underinclusive in the means it employs, to the point of irrationality. It has targeted women who seek to end pregnancies and has elevated control of women's decision-making over most every other policy measure it might employ to reduce abortion or to protect life in utero, even policies known to protect maternal health and potential life.

Banning abortion and coercing resistant women to serve as mothers over their objections might sound rational to some, on the assumption that women are simply instruments the state can employ for gestating and nurturing potential life. But simply criminalizing abortion does not stop the practice.[71] As the image of the coat hanger recalls, women, even poor and young women, resist abortion bans: "Nearly six months since the Supreme Court overturned *Roe v. Wade*, triggering abortion bans in more than a dozen states, many antiabortion advocates fear that the growing availability of illegal abortion pills has undercut their landmark victory."[72] Meanwhile, lack of prenatal care can be deadly for newborns; the U.S. Department of Health and Human Services found that newborns whose mothers had no early prenatal care are almost five times more likely to die.[73] Mississippi's hostility to Medicaid and social provision must be one of the reasons the state has the highest infant mortality rate in the nation. And lack of a safety net plainly contributes to abortion. Seventy-five percent of women who seek abortions are poor or low-income.[74] At the same time it is clear that coercing birth without adequate social supports poses a threat to maternal health and human dignity.[75] There is no self-evident rationale for choosing most-restrictive over least-restrictive means for supporting healthy pregnancies and nurturing fetal life.

Under *Virginia*, equal protection law requires the government to justify its use of sex-based coercive means over less restrictive means and to provide reasons for its policy choices that do not rely on sex-role stereotyping or perpetuate traditional inequalities between the sexes.[76] Mississippi and like-minded states think it is reasonable to protect life by pushing pregnant women into motherhood against their will, without providing healthcare, providing social support or child care for them and their children, or protecting them against job loss. To put the point modestly, Mississippi's method of protecting life rests on certain presuppositions about women. As Justice Blackmun observed thirty years ago in *Casey*, the "assumption—that women can simply be forced to accept the 'natural' status and incidents of motherhood—appears to rest upon a conception of women's role that has triggered the protection of the Equal Protection Clause."[77] For these and other reasons, under *Virginia* and *Hibbs* and the body of sex discrimination case law the Supreme Court has decided in the past half-century, Mississippi's exclusively carceral approach to protecting life violates equal protection.[78]

Dobbs rejected the claim that laws criminalizing abortion trigger equal protection scrutiny, and not only in opening dicta where Justice Alito asserted that equal protection imposes no limits on laws regulating pregnancy. The Court's due process decision depicted *Roe* and *Casey* as illegitimate usurpations of state authority to ban abortion and represented the Court as returning the authority to ban abortion to the states: "The Constitution does not prohibit the citizens of each State from regulating or prohibiting abortion. *Roe* and *Casey* arrogated that authority. We now overrule those decisions and return that authority to the people and their elected representatives."[79] *Dobbs*'s story of "return" is not only jurisdictional, but substantive, of handing power back to *Roe*'s critics.[80] It is about going back in *time* to a democratic tradition of banning abortion.

Conceding intermittently that the common law prohibited abortion at quickening—that is, midway through pregnancy only—the Court's due process opinion depicts America as a nation with a deep-rooted tradition of banning abortion. To construct this tradition, *Dobbs* expressly rejected the argument of amici who claimed that nineteenth-century abortion bans were enacted for sexist and nativist reasons and so are unfit to guide constitutional interpretation today. Acknowledging the historians' objection that nineteenth-century abortion bans were enacted not simply because of a constitutionally legitimate interest in protecting unborn life but also because of a constitutionally illegitimate interest in enforcing women's marital roles and in preserving the religious and ethnic character of the nation,[81] Justice Alito responded that he simply didn't believe it: "Are we to believe that the hundreds of lawmakers whose votes were needed to enact these laws were motivated by hostility to Catholics and women? There is ample evidence that the passage of these laws was instead spurred by a sincere belief that abortion kills a human being."[82] By setting up a dichotomy—either nineteenth-century abortion laws were motivated by "hostility to Catholics and women" *or* by "a sincere belief that abortion kills a human being"—Justice Alito excused himself from considering how prevailing beliefs about gender shaped the campaign to ban abortion at a time when sex-role divisions were so systematically enforced by law that the Supreme Court itself authorized states to bar women from voting[83] and to deny women the right to practice law.[84]

In adopting this dichotomy—that abortion bans reflect constitutionally illicit status-based judgments *or* abortion bans reflect constitutionally licit beliefs about the importance of protecting unborn life—the majority reasoned about the regulation of pregnancy within the logic of physiological naturalism, as *Roe* and *Geduldig* once did.[85] *Dobbs* perpetuates the naturalist claim that abortion bans may stop women from ending pregnancies, but laws compelling women to continue a pregnancy reflect no judgments about women; women are simply where the embryo/fetus happens to be.

In deciding that the United States had a constitutionally cognizable tradition of banning abortion, the Court rejected the view that abortion bans, past or present, express any particular judgments or send any particular messages about women's roles and social status. As the next section shows, however, abortion regulation has never been focused exclusively on protecting fetal life. In the nineteenth century, advocates for banning abortion emphasized the laws' dual purpose of protecting the unborn and enforcing traditional norms governing sex and women's family roles.

The Long History of Dualism in Abortion Regulation

In Justice Alito's telling, advocates of banning abortion had one aim in mind: protecting fetuses. But this account of our history is simply wrong. Abortion regulation has long had a dual focus. It has never been concerned exclusively with protecting fetuses. It has always also been about the regulation of sexuality and motherhood.

In the 1850s, Boston obstetrician Horatio Storer launched a "physicians' crusade" to criminalize abortion before quickening.[86] The physicians sought to consolidate and professionalize the practice of medicine, excluding the "irregulars," including midwives, who often provided abortions in this era, and granting male physicians monopoly control over reproductive healthcare.[87]

Many doctors came to believe that life began at conception and that abortion was wrongful life-taking—murder, they called it. Their campaign prominently featured a fetal-protective argument.[88] But to persuade Americans to abandon customary and common law views of pregnancy that permitted abortion before quickening, that is, sixteen to twenty weeks into a pregnancy, it was not enough to advise the public that life began at conception. Opponents of abortion added to their ethical arguments for protecting life ethical arguments for protecting the social order. Many emphasized the prevalence of abortion among married, native-born, white, Protestant women, and advocated abortion restrictions as a means of preserving the country's religious and ethnic makeup.[89] Even more pervasively, doctors argued that banning abortion was necessary to preserve the family.

A core theme of anti-abortion crusaders was that women were abandoning their wifely and maternal roles for improper pursuits and distractions. Abortion enabled women to betray their family responsibilities for pleasure and for politics. Advocates of criminalizing abortion returned to this theme constantly, arguing that childbearing was "the end for which [married women] are physiologically constituted and for which they are destined by nature."[90] If women—married women in particular—sought to evade their true destiny by ending their pregnancies, Storer and others argued, they would face devastating consequences: such infringement of nature's laws "must necessarily cause derangement, disaster, or ruin."[91]

The debate over abortion featured open debate about sex. Many advocates of criminalization argued that allowing married women to access abortion turned marriage into "legalized prostitution,"[92] in which women could trade sex—freed of reproductive consequences—for spousal support and engage in all manner of activities without the obligations of motherhood.

When Storer and others argued that laws banning abortion were needed to prevent marriage from becoming "legalized prostitution," they were attacking claims for voluntary motherhood advanced by the women's movement of the era. Before and after the Civil War, women seeking the vote—and power to reform marriage law that gave a husband rights in his wife's person, labor, and property—supported "voluntary motherhood": the right to say no to sex in marriage. Suffragists argued that without voluntary motherhood, marriage was little better than "legalized prostitution."[93] Given the conditions of conception and childrearing, they condoned—without endorsing—women who ended a pregnancy.[94] But Storer and others who sought to ban abortion argued that it was *freeing wives from compulsory childbearing* that would turn marriage into "legalized prostitution."

In 1871, the newly formed American Medical Association denounced women who obtained abortions, claiming that when a woman ends her pregnancy, "[s]he becomes unmindful of the course marked out for her by Providence . . . [and] overlooks the duties imposed by the marriage contract."[95] Some doctors explicitly blamed the emergence of new notions of women's roles for the uptick in abortion rates, arguing that "the tendency to force women into men's places" was creating insidious "new ideas of women's duties."[96]

The physicians' arguments against abortion were pronatalist. The campaign against abortion promoted birth, to protect unborn life, to enforce wives' marital roles, and to preserve the religious and ethnic character of the nation. In the 1870s, states and the federal government criminalized contraception for the first time, often enacting statutes that simultaneously banned contraceptives and abortifacients together; both interfered with the procreative ends of sex.[97]

For Storer and his allies, criminalizing abortion was the answer, and it seemed obvious that criminal penalties ought to be imposed on *everyone* involved in abortion-related crimes, including women who procured abortions. Storer argued it would make no sense to exempt pregnant women from punishment, for "[i]f the mother does not herself induce the abortion, she seeks it, or aids it, or consents to it, and is, therefore, whether ever seeming justified or not, fully accountable as a principal."[98] In the 1850s, he developed model legislation that reflected this understanding. The legislation imposed criminal penalties not only on providers but also on women who obtained abortions.[99] The legislation allowed for increased punishment of married women,[100] as their sex-role violations were even more heinous than those of unmarried women.

The physicians' campaign was stunningly successful. Between 1860 and 1880, it "produced the most important burst of anti-abortion legislation in the nation's history."[101] States and territories enacted at least forty anti-abortion statutes, and many of those statutes reflected the physicians' argument that abortion ought to be criminalized from the moment of conception.[102]

But the body of law that grew in the campaign's wake did not exert control over women through the imposition of criminal sanctions on them. Some of the criminal abortion statutes enacted in the wake of the physicians' campaign exempted from liability women who obtained abortions; other statutes imposed liability on women who obtained abortions, but prosecutors and judges refused to enforce the law against them.[103] In jurisdictions where the law explicitly criminalized obtaining an abortion, judges read in exemptions, insisting that women who did so were victims and could not be held responsible for their actions. Judges reasoned that, regardless of what statutory texts said, "[t]he public policy which underlies this legislation is based largely on protection due to the woman—protection against her own weakness as well as the criminal lust and greed of others."[104] Judges insisted that a woman who obtained an abortion was "[m]isguided by her own desires, and mistaken in her belief,"[105] not thinking straight and therefore not culpable of any crime. Over time judges enforcing the bans reasoned that women who sought abortions should be considered "the object of protection rather than of punishment" and should "be regarded as the victim of the crime rather than as a participant in it."[106]

This very prominent feature of abortion law—the general exemption from punishment of pregnant women who choose abortion—persists to this day, and it coheres with all the other natalist features of the campaign we have described—prominently including the first laws criminalizing contraception. Nineteenth-century changes in abortion law were not simply about protecting fetuses. Along with innumerable other features of social structure, abortion bans coerced and channeled women into dependent caregiving roles.[107]

Abortion bans were dualist in structure; they enforced judgments about protecting the unborn *and* sex-role judgments about women.[108] In the nineteenth century, a time when women were beginning to protest the many forms of public and private law that pushed them into dependent family roles, it "made sense" to protect unborn life by coercing motherhood.

Abortion bans offered a new and a newly legitimate form of coverture, adopted at a time when suffragists were challenging old common law doctrines of marital status. With the modernization of marital status law, "a wife was gradually transformed from a juridical appendage of her husband into one who performed the physical and social work of reproducing family life."[109] Criminalization of abortion offered a new way of regulating and a "new way of reasoning about wives' obligations . . . physiologically, deriving women's duties from facts about the female body."[110] Even as legislators began to recognize wives as juridically independent of their husbands, facts about their bodies supplied reasons for laws that continued to enforce their family roles.[111] Reasoning from the body naturalized assumptions about gender, autonomy, and dependence long rooted in coverture.

It is because abortion law regulated family roles that abortion was commonly codified in the nineteenth century as a crime against the family or a sex crime—*not* as homicide.[112] For instance, David Dudley Field classified abortion law along with "Crimes against the Person and against Public Decency and Good Morals" in his New York Penal Code.[113] As historian

David Sklansky has observed, the crimes that accompanied abortion in this category were "rapes[,] . . . child abandonment, bigamy, indecent exposure, and lotteries."[114] In the twentieth century, the Model Penal Code classified abortion under "Offenses against the Family."[115]

In a 1959 commentary accompanying the draft Model Penal Code's section on abortion, the American Law Institute referenced the dual aims of abortion laws quite explicitly. The ALI acknowledged that as "the fetus develops to the point where it is recognizably human in form" or "manifests life," as in quickening or at viability, "destruction [of the fetus] comes to be regarded by many as morally equivalent to murder."[116] But in the next sentence the ALI observed that "abortion is opposed by many on moral grounds not directly related to the homicidal aspects," and immediately began discussing condemnation of abortion as rooted in beliefs about religion and the proper ends of sex. The 1959 commentary expressed in twentieth-century idiom the heteronormative, pronatalist objections to abortion expressed in the nineteenth-century campaign: "For some it is a violation of the divine command to be fruitful from which has been inferred also the sinfulness of homosexuality, contraception, masturbation, and in general all sexuality which is 'unnatural' in the sense of not being procreative. Furthermore, legalizing abortion would be regarded by some as encouraging or condoning illicit intercourse."[117] The fact that criminal law codes grouped abortion alongside rape, bigamy, homosexuality, neglect/abandonment of wife and children, contraception, and masturbation as crimes against public decency and good morals, or offenses against the family,[118] instead of treating abortion as contract killing or some other form of first-degree murder, underscores the degree to which abortion restrictions have been understood as regulating women's sexuality and family roles rather than simply protecting fetuses.

Today the dual concerns of abortion law may not be as prominent as in the past. Yet abortion law is unmistakably shaped by judgments about women as well as the unborn. When abortion is banned, pregnant women who obtain abortions are still exempt from any sort of criminal punishment. And abortion bans typically have exceptions reflecting judgments about pregnant women: "Nearly three-quarters of adults (73%) say abortion should be legal if the woman's life or health is endangered by the pregnancy, while just 11% say it should be illegal. And about seven-in-ten say abortion should be legal if the pregnancy is a result of rape, with just 15% saying it should be illegal in this case."[119] Broad-based support for health, life, and rape exemptions demonstrates that beliefs about abortion depend on judgments about

women's sexuality and whether it is fair to coerce women into motherhood—
not only judgments about when life begins.[120]

The application of abortion law to fertility practices demonstrates again
that abortion law cannot be explained simply by beliefs about when life
begins. A number of states now banning abortion expressly *permit disposal
of embryos created through in vitro fertilization*, only characterizing acts that
prevent the embryo's development *as abortion if the embryo is in a woman's
uterus*.[121] These states seem to reason that it is permissible to destroy embryonic life in the quest to conceive but not in the effort to avoid parenthood.
This policy is as natalist as the bans on contraception that began during the
nineteenth-century anti-abortion campaign. In the wake of *Dobbs*, we can
also see dualist judgments fueling efforts by anti-abortion advocates to redefine the term "abortion" to exclude pregnancy terminations that take place
during the treatment of miscarriages, in cases involving pregnant ten-year-
olds, and in other contexts in which advocates are uncomfortable forcing
people to continue pregnancies.[122]

The simple desire to protect life from the moment of conception cannot
explain these various exemptions and exceptions. We see instead that the
regulation of abortion, in the nineteenth century and today, has consistently
had a dual focus concerned with protecting fetuses *and* regulating women's
sexuality and family roles.

In fact, for decades now the modern anti-abortion movement has insisted
that the case for prohibiting abortion depends on protecting *women* as well
as the unborn, as advocates argue that abortion harms women or that women
have been coerced into abortions.[123] *Dobbs* and the two Supreme Court cases
before it involved challenges to laws that restricted abortion purportedly
to protect *women's* health. Of course, sex-role reasoning undergirds these
woman-protectionist claims. The architect of the Louisiana law at issue in
June Medical Services L.L.C. v. Russo explained her thinking thus: "What's
good for the child is good for the mother."[124]

One of the most striking features of Justice Alito's opinion in *Dobbs* is its
denial of the dual focus of abortion law and its insistence that restrictions
on abortion are, and always have been, exclusively about protecting fetuses.
The opinion frames its question about the nineteenth-century record in binary terms: are abortion bans focused on protecting fetuses *or* on regulating
women? But Justice Alito never explained why the desire to protect fetuses
and the desire to regulate women are mutually exclusive—why evidence that
regulators cared about fetuses means they can't have had any particular views

about women. (Just where are fetuses?) This fetal-focused account of abortion bans is all the more striking given that the Mississippi ban at issue in *Dobbs* asserted the legislators' claims that coerced motherhood is good for women's health in the text of the statute itself.[125]

In his concurring opinion Justice Brett Kavanaugh also insistently denied the dual focus of abortion bans. The central theme of his opinion is that the Constitution is neutral with respect to abortion bans: it neither requires nor prohibits them. This almost shrill insistence on the Constitution's "neutrality"[126] with respect to abortion bans erases the dual focus of abortion regulation—the historical and ongoing ways in which carceral approaches to abortion implicate women's liberty and equality.

The *Dobbs* Court has authorized lawmakers opposed to abortion to revive the carceral regime their predecessors developed over a century and a half ago. In some cases, contemporary lawmakers are simply reinstating bans from the nineteenth and early twentieth century, while in others, they are dramatically increasing criminal penalties.[127]

Just as *Dobbs* has nostalgia for a national past that the Court itself is in part reviving and in part inventing, so too anti-abortion advocates and lawmakers are returning to a past that they are playing a role in creating. When lawmakers today argue for protecting women, as Louisiana did in *June Medical* and Mississippi did in *Dobbs*, they revive protectionist traditions in contemporary feminist and public health idioms.[128] And when lawmakers argue for *punishing* abortion, they resume carceral conversations that reach back to the nineteenth century, often supercharged with a quite contemporary appetite for use of the criminal law—as in a Louisiana bill that would have granted constitutional rights to "all unborn children from the moment of fertilization" while classifying abortion as a homicide. The bill was withdrawn amid public uproar at the plan to charge women and their doctors with murder for obtaining or providing abortion services.[129]

This escalation to classifying abortion as homicide suggests that interest in punishing abortion may rise with women's civic status. Nineteenth-century doctors may have talked about abortion as murder, but nineteenth-century legislators did not generally ban abortion as homicide. (Infanticide was distinct from abortion, and to prosecute infanticide at common law, courts reasoned, "a child must be born alive. It cannot be the subject of a homicide until it has an existence independent of its mother.")[130] It wasn't until the 1980s that states began passing fetal homicide statutes (with abortion-rights carveouts) that broke with this common law tradition.[131] Today there are natural lawyers and originalists who urge *judges* to impose draconian penalties for abortion. They talk about giving unborn persons equal treatment under homicide laws,[132] asserting that "unborn children are *persons* within the original public meaning of the Fourteenth Amendment's Due Process and Equal Protection Clauses,"[133] and urging courts to apply homicide laws to abortion. ("Most States have laws tailormade for 'feticide'; any carve-outs for elective abortion would be disregarded by courts as invalid.")[134] This is living constitutionalism,[135] advancing a carceral claim rooted in the 1980s, not in the 1860s, that would enforce modern forms of coverture. Observe that as the embryo and fetus appear, women disappear. And because women disappear the question never comes into view: What forms of law for protecting unborn life are appropriate today, given women's equal civic status?

The anti-abortion movement is now advancing equal protection claims for fetuses, even as the Court is denying equal protection rights for women. It is precisely because abortion bans raise questions under contemporary sex discrimination law that the justices in *Dobbs*—and those defending their decision—are so intent on reasoning from the body and so insistent that abortion laws are exclusively motivated by concern for protecting fetal life. Denying the dual focus of abortion bans, in doctrine and in history, is part of a concerted effort to shield abortion laws from the scrutiny that contemporary sex discrimination doctrine demands.

Anticarceral Presumption

This chapter opened by showing how the Court integrated pregnancy into the framework it developed for adjudicating sex-based equal protection cases. Well into the 1970s, the Court continued to view pregnancy through the lens of physiological naturalism. But after years of enforcing the PDA, the Court began to appreciate the centrality of laws regulating pregnancy in constructing and maintaining gender-based hierarchies and cementing women's secondary status. Justice Ruth Bader Ginsburg's opinion in *Virginia* and Chief Justice Rehnquist's opinion in *Hibbs* superseded the Court's reasoning in *Geduldig*. Rather than assert that women are equal to the extent they are like men, the Court announced that women are men's equals, notwithstanding their differences. Once *Virginia* and *Hibbs* applied antisubordination and antistereotyping principles to pregnancy, the government cannot appeal to pregnancy as a physical difference between men and women to justify laws that perpetuate women's second-class standing or enforce traditional family roles.

In a Court that was willing to apply equal protection doctrine faithfully, this body of law would give rise, in the context of abortion, to an anticarceral presumption. When the government engages in sex-based state action—including when it regulates pregnancy—the government must show why less restrictive means will not serve its ends, especially here, where government is enforcing a role historically associated with restrictions on women's civic status. There are many ways the state can protect life that *support rather than coerce* those who gestate, nurture, and provide for developing dependent humans that do not "perpetuate the legal, social, and economic inferiority of women."[136]

In a gender-egalitarian society, government efforts to protect potential life should look different than in a world in which the work is performed by a disfranchised caste. Centrally, a government committed to women's equal citizenship would recognize that commitment as changing its relationship to the family and to those who do the work of raising the next generation. As we have shown, there are a multitude of ways states can protect new life that are compatible with women's equal citizenship. To reduce abortion, the state can assist those who are sexually active and wish to avoid becoming parents; to protect potential life, the state can assist those who are expecting children and would become parents if they could afford to do so.

When a state rejects this array of nondiscriminatory means of nurturing potential and born life, and protects life by means that instrumentalize women and inflict on them bodily, economic, and dignitary harms, this violates modern equal protection law. It may have been acceptable, in the view of the law and of many Americans, in the nineteenth century to threaten and coerce women, to compel them to become mothers by criminalizing abortion. But that anti-abortion regime did not treat women as equal members of the polity. It exacerbated inequality, endangered pregnant women's lives and well-being, stripped women of agency, and subjected them to forms of coercion and control incompatible with twenty-first-century understandings of liberty and equality. When a state today eschews other means of protecting fetuses—when it refuses to employ the many egalitarian, less violent means of supporting the health and well-being of fetuses and pregnant people—and seeks to discipline and punish, it violates this anticarceral presumption.

While there are members of the *Dobbs* majority who might yet rule that the Constitution imposes some limits on abortion bans—for example, to protect a pregnant woman's right to life,[137] it is of course exceedingly unlikely that the Court responsible for *Dobbs* will actually enforce an anticarceral presumption. But this presumption does not reside only in federal judicial doctrine. It also resides in other governmental actors' and the public's understanding of the limits on state power to coerce motherhood. Even without a Supreme Court to give it uniform articulation, we can expect to see federal and state actors—many legislative—giving this presumption varying expression in the coming years. Indeed, some states took action immediately after *Dobbs* to incorporate aspects of this presumption into their state constitutions. A few months after the Court's decision, Michigan and Vermont amended their constitutions to include explicit protections for reproductive freedom that subject abortion regulations to strict scrutiny, requiring the state to show that it has a compelling interest and is employing "the least restrictive means" to effectuate that interest.[138] California also amended its constitution to protect reproductive rights; like Vermont, its amendment explicitly references equal protection, making clear that abortion rights vindicate both liberty and equality values.[139]

Public opposition to the recent carceral turn in abortion regulation was also evident in the aftermath of *Dobbs* in red states such as Kansas and Kentucky, where voters rejected proposed constitutional amendments that would have outlawed abortion.[140] Like the Louisiana law referenced above, which would have treated abortion as homicide and had to be withdrawn after public outcry,[141] these extreme carceral measures induce discomfort even among many conservatives. They are too harshly punitive and too obviously disrespectful of women's well-being and social standing to move through legislatures and succeed at the ballot box even in some very conservative, anti-abortion states.

Indeed, we can read electoral backlash to the Court's decision in *Dobbs* as expressing skepticism of its account of public values. In the 2022 midterm elections, voters—especially young voters and women—turned out in great numbers to repudiate the Court's decision in *Dobbs*.[142] The public does not appear to credit the claim made by *Dobbs* and its advocates that abortion bans contain no judgments about women, that bans are simply the most effective way of communicating the state's profound concern for fetal life.[143]

Does declaring that abortion bans communicate only fetal-focused messages make it so? Did declaring that separate was equal make it so? As Elizabeth Anderson and Richard Pildes have observed, "[e]xpressive meanings are socially constructed"; they are "a result of the ways in which actions fit with (or fail to fit with) other meaningful norms and practices in the community."[144] For this reason, "a proposed interpretation must make sense in light of the community's other practices, its history, and shared meanings."[145] The expressive meaning of an act of government emerges only when analyzed "in the full context in which it is adopted and implemented."[146]

If we situate abortion bans in the historical and social contexts in which they arose and continue to operate, the depiction of these bans as gender-neutral, incorporating no suspect judgments about women and simply expressing concern for fetal life, is not plausible. Abortion bans were enacted in the nineteenth century—by an electorate from which women were excluded—for purposes including enforcing women's marital and maternal roles, at a time when law was first enlisted to criminalize the means of contraception and to direct sex to natalist ends.[147]

To suggest that reviving this regime—a hybrid of ancient and modern status laws—reflects only judgments about embryos and fetuses and has nothing to do with women's equality is ridiculous. We have examined the gender stereotypes and judgments that fueled abortion bans historically and the way the revival—and the shocking intensification—of these bans perpetuates women's secondary status. But history is only one lens for looking at these bans; there are all sorts of indicia of sexism surrounding the new wave of anti-abortion lawmaking after *Dobbs*. Polling in the aftermath of *Dobbs* shows that "[s]exist beliefs are highly correlated with and predictive of views toward abortion" and that false stereotypes about women and women who have had abortions are very strong predictors of opposition to abortion—stronger than party identification, gender, or religiosity.[148] For example, a majority of anti-abortion adults in a recent poll agreed with the statement that "feminism has done more harm than good." Just 20% of anti-abortion adults agreed "the country would be better off with more women in political office," compared to 64% of adults who support legal abortion.[149] There is no independent, or fetal-focused, reason why support for abortion bans would be so strongly correlated with a dislike of women holding political office: traditional gender ideology is clearly the driver of and the link between these views.

Or we could shift from polling to consider the people most affected by the new abortion bans. As we have noted, the vast majority of women who obtain abortions are poor, and they are disproportionately Black and brown. The overrepresentation of Black women among those who seek abortions is particularly pronounced in Mississippi, where *Dobbs* arose. Anti-abortion advocates in Mississippi have long insisted that their primary motivation in pursuing abortion bans is to protect new life. But Black women in Mississippi have been lobbying state legislators to protect new life and those who nurture it for years, to no avail.

Shortly after *Dobbs* came down, organizations devoted to Black women's health in Mississippi held a press conference called "We Are the Data" to dramatize the crisis in Black maternal and infant mortality[150] and to persuade the state legislature to implement measures proven to improve health outcomes, such as extending Medicaid coverage for postnatal care by a few months.[151] One of the organizers emphasized, "What we're asking for here is just a right to life"—some basic measures to curb the unnecessary suffering and death experienced by so many Black mothers and babies. The majority-white legislature rebuffed their demands. The only thing the Mississippi legislature appears willing to do to address this crisis is to pass abortion bans that close clinics that predominantly served Black and poor women. This regulatory approach imposes on these women conditions that the majority of state legislators in Mississippi would not impose on their own families. It treats vulnerable women with contempt, it disregards their health and well-being, and it subjects them to forms of coercion and control all too familiar to Black women living in the former Confederacy.

As Professor Charles Black once said of *Plessy v. Ferguson*'s claim that separate was equal:

> [I]f a whole race of people finds itself confined within a system which is set up and continued for the very purpose of keeping it in an inferior station, and if the question is then solemnly propounded whether such a race is being treated "equally," I think we ought to exercise one of the sovereign prerogatives of philosophers—that of laughter.[152]

The Court has the power to control the narrative it constructs about abortion, within the four corners of its opinions. It can assert that punitive abortion laws convey no judgments about women's social status—just as the Court in 1896 asserted that the segregation of railroad cars conveyed nothing about Black people's social status. But there are limits to the Court's power, even in the context of imperious landmark decisions such as *Plessy* and *Dobbs*. Simply announcing that nineteenth-century status regimes are compatible with egalitarian ideals and constitutional protections does not make it so. And defending and maintaining such a regime today ought to be even more of a challenge than it was at the time of *Plessy*, because despite what the Court suggests, we now have a robust body of equal protection law that requires the state to respect women as equal citizens. We are beyond the day when the state can simply dominate and control women, using punitive measures to coerce them to continue pregnancies and become mothers against their will. The majority in *Dobbs* seems determined to kill this body of law, and although it didn't succeed this time, it is likely to keep trying.

But equal protection doctrine and equality principles have taken root in too many places, have been embraced by too many actors across too many levels of government and by too high a percentage of the American people, for the Court to eradicate them everywhere. The goal now is to figure out how best to nurture and protect these commitments, not by debating women's rights versus fetal rights but by talking about the kind of support families need to meet the real challenges families face and to enable new understandings of women's citizenship to flourish.

PART II
CLOSE READINGS OF *ROE*

3

Why Was *Roe v. Wade* Wrong?

Jonathan F. Mitchell

Being asked to write an essay on why *Roe v. Wade* was wrongly decided is a daunting request—and accepting the invitation can seem like an act of hubris. The opinion in *Roe* has already been dissected, critiqued, scrutinized, and pored over by some of the most brilliant jurists and constitutional scholars who have ever lived. So how can one hope to add something new to a debate that has been raging for over fifty years and over which the battle lines have been clearly defined for decades?

As audacious as this claim may seem, I believe there is still room for commentators to weigh in on *Roe*—and especially for commentators who oppose *Roe* to explain why the case was wrongly decided. And that is because the conventional critique of *Roe* is (in my view) undertheorized and unsatisfying. The critique, in a nutshell, claims that *Roe* was wrong because there is nothing in the text of the Constitution suggesting that abortion is a constitutional right. This argument proceeds from textualist interpretive premises, which not everyone shares, yet it undergirds most of the scholarly and judicial criticism of *Roe*. John Hart Ely's magisterial essay, published shortly after *Roe*, hammered the *Roe* opinion for its insouciance toward constitutional text,[1] and echoes of Ely's critique can be heard in Justice Antonin Scalia's *Casey* dissent[2] and Justice Samuel Alito's opinion in *Dobbs*.[3]

Yet *Roe* was hardly the first time that the Supreme Court imposed a constitutional right that lacks textual support. Defenders of *Roe* have observed that there are many other Supreme Court rulings whose textual foundation is nonexistent or shaky at best, which include not only the usual suspects, like *Griswold v. Connecticut*[4] and *Loving v. Virginia*,[5] but also the Warren Court's voting rights cases, the so-called dormant commerce clause, the right to interstate travel, modern sex-equality jurisprudence, and perhaps even *Brown v. Board of Education*.[6] Ely was sensitive to this problem, as he went out of his way to defend *Griswold*[7] and the right to travel[8] and wrote an entire book defending the Warren Court's jurisprudence on the ground that

Jonathan F. Mitchell, *Why Was* Roe v. Wade *Wrong?* In: *Roe v. Dobbs*. Edited by: Lee C. Bollinger and Geoffrey R. Stone, Oxford University Press. © Oxford University Press 2024. DOI: 10.1093/oso/9780197760352.003.0003 it ensured the integrity of representative government and protected discrete and insular minorities, while distinguishing those projects from decisions like *Roe*, which involved (in his view) nothing more than the naked imposition of "fundamental values" favored by judges at the expense of the political branches.[9] Yet the gnawing fact remains that so many of the Supreme Court's canonical pronouncements have little or no grounding in constitutional text—and it is not immediately apparent what makes *Roe* more egregious than other Court-created rights that have won broad acceptance across the political and jurisprudential spectrum. There's always been a sense that the conventional critique of *Roe* proves too much, which may explain why many have been reluctant to embrace it.

The typical response to this challenge has been to narrow the attack on *Roe* in an attempt to explain how *this* particular act of atextual judicial adventurism is uniquely worse than the others. Justice Scalia's dissent in *Casey*, for example, argued that abortion could not be a constitutional right for *two* reasons: "(1) the Constitution says absolutely nothing about it, and (2) the longstanding traditions of American society have permitted it to be legally proscribed."[10] That eventually became the rationale of *Dobbs*, which rejected *Roe* both because "[t]he Constitution makes no reference to abortion" *and* because the right to abortion is not "deeply rooted in this Nation's history and tradition."[11] On this view, the problem with *Roe* is not that it imposed a right without textual support in the Constitution, but that it imposed an atextual right that lacked a "deeply rooted" historical pedigree. This idea that courts may enforce unenumerated constitutional rights—so long as those textually unenumerated rights are "deeply rooted" in history and tradition—finds support in judicial precedent.[12] And by invoking a history-and-tradition test, the *Dobbs* majority opinion appeared to find a way to salvage other nontextual rights (such as the right to interstate travel), while simultaneously announcing a test for unenumerated rights that can appeal to constitutional originalists, Burkean traditionalists, and even some common-law constitutionalists who look to precedent as a means to discipline judicial decision-making.[13]

Yet there are many problems with using history and tradition as the touchstone for unenumerated constitutional rights. The first problem is that the history-and-tradition test does nothing to salvage the constitutional holdings of *Griswold* or *Loving*. The right to contraception is not deeply rooted in this nation's history and tradition—one needs only to look at the federal Comstock laws, which until 1971 criminalized the mailing, transporting, or

importation of contraception and contraceptive advertising.[14] And neither is
the right to interracial marriage, as antimiscegenation laws were widespread
at the nation's founding and at the time of the Fourteenth Amendment's ratification.[15] The *Dobbs* opinion refuses to say whether *Griswold* and *Loving*
were correctly decided or whether they should be overruled, perhaps because
the five justices who joined the majority opinion could not agree on how to
explain or distinguish the holdings of those cases.[16] But those questions must
be confronted and answered if tradition is to be the test for determining
whether an unenumerated right can be recognized or enforced as a constitutional entitlement.

The second problem is that there are many unenumerated rights that are
"deeply rooted in this Nation's history and tradition" yet are not recognized
as constitutional entitlements by the Supreme Court. The common-law right
of employers to hire and fire employees at will was deeply rooted in history
and tradition,[17] but it has been superseded by federal labor statutes and
antidiscrimination laws that the Supreme Court has upheld and enforced.
The marital rape exemption was deeply rooted at common law and remained
in existence until the 1970s; it has now been repealed in all fifty states. Many
other traditional common-law entitlements have been jettisoned by the political branches without encountering resistance from the Supreme Court.[18]
So the history-and-tradition test appears not only underinclusive—by failing
to account for *Griswold* and *Loving*, which continue to exist as precedents
of the Supreme Court—but overinclusive as well, and it has no standard for
determining which of the time-honored rights that go unmentioned in the
Constitution should nonetheless be enshrined as constitutional entitlements.

The third and most serious problem is that the history-and-tradition test
has no account for *why* traditional rights and practices should be entrenched
as constitutional mandates when they were never formally incorporated into
constitutional text. Burkean theories that glorify tradition as the embodiment
of accumulated wisdom must account for the fact that many of the rights and
practices that are "deeply rooted in this Nation's history and tradition" are
today looked upon with horror and revulsion. They must also account for the
possibility that past adherence to tradition can be the product of instinctive
and uncritical groupthink rather than a vast sum of thoughtful, independent
contributions to the collective wisdom.[19] And even if there were a reliable
theory to explain how the constitutional entrenchment of traditionally
recognized yet textually unenumerated rights is normatively desirable, that
still would not justify the judicial imposition of those rights in the absence of

legal authority to do so. The text of the Due Process Clause offers no support for the idea that courts may recognize and enforce unenumerated rights if (but only if) those rights are "deeply rooted in this Nation's history and tradition."[20] And neither the *Dobbs* opinion nor any other ruling of the Supreme Court has persuasively explained why a right that was omitted from textual protection in the Constitution should be accorded the same status as a textually guaranteed right, or why a traditionally recognized (yet unenumerated) right should have any more claim to this status than an unenumerated right of more recent vintage. So efforts to use history and tradition as a way of distinguishing the "legitimate" substantive due process rulings from *Roe* are unconvincing—and a better theory is needed to explain not only why *Roe* is wrong but also why *Roe* can be overruled while other nontextual precedents (such as *Griswold* and *Loving*) are left undisturbed.

The principal goal of this essay is to defend the conventional critique of *Roe*—as well as Ely's claim that courts lack authority to identify and impose "fundamental values"[21] that cannot be found in the constitutional text—against objections that this stance would imperil the continued existence of precedents such as *Griswold*, *Loving*, and *Brown v. Board of Education*. But it does not take the approach of the *Dobbs* majority, which sought to narrow Ely's critique by allowing courts to impose unenumerated rights that are "deeply rooted in this Nation's history and tradition."[22] Instead, it acknowledges and confronts head-on the fact that the rights to contraception, interracial marriage, and school desegregation are *not* deeply rooted in tradition and cannot be salvaged by invoking a history-and-tradition test for unenumerated constitutional rights. And it defends the legitimacy of those cases by looking outside the Constitution to other sources of federal law, such as federal statutes and agency rules, and by invoking those extraconstitutional legal authorities to support the correctness of those rulings or (at the very least) to rebuff efforts to overrule them. Many (though not all) of the rights that the Supreme Court has imposed under the rubric of substantive due process or equal protection are independently protected by nonconstitutional sources of federal law. And that is all that is needed to distinguish those cases from *Roe*, which has never been codified as a federally protected right—and it explains why the *Roe* regime can and should be regarded as uniquely indefensible and an improper imposition of judge-held preferences.

A secondary goal is to respond to those who reject the premise of Ely's critique by embracing consequentialist theories of judging over textualism.

Too often in debates about *Roe* the participants are talking past each other, and an argument that denounces *Roe* for its lack of textual foundation gets nowhere with those who accept the legitimacy of textual departures from the document, or who interpret the text in a manner that vests the judiciary with a limited or wide-ranging authority to impose unenumerated rights. My claim here is that there are reasons to doubt the wisdom of *Roe* even from the standpoint of those who embrace consequentialism over textualism and support legal abortion as a matter of policy, as *Roe* triggered a backlash that eventually undid the decision and has undercut progressives' credibility in attacking the atextual (or textually dubious) constitutional pronouncements of the Roberts Court.

My tertiary goal is to rehabilitate the jurisdictional holding of *Roe v. Wade*, while critiquing the reasons the Court gave for allowing Norma McCorvey's claims to escape dismissal for mootness. The Court was right to allow McCorvey's challenge to the Texas abortion ban to proceed despite the fact that she was no longer pregnant, but not because McCorvey's claims were "capable of repetition yet evading review."[23] Instead, the Court should have allowed McCorvey's claims to proceed on the theory that abortion bans inflict injury in fact on women regardless of whether they are currently pregnant, as abortion bans can injure even nonpregnant women by causing them to alter their sexual behavior or spend more money on other means of birth control.

Finally, in criticizing *Roe* I do not mean to suggest that everything in the *Roe* opinion is wrong. Justice Harry Blackmun's explanation for why an embryo or fetus should not be regarded as a "person" under the Fourteenth Amendment was well reasoned and carefully presented.[24] His reliance on the use of the word "person" throughout the Constitution—and especially in section 2 of the Fourteenth Amendment, which requires members of the House to be apportioned in accordance with "the whole number of *persons* in each State," and which has never been interpreted to include the unborn—presents a textual argument capable of convincing even the most ardent opponent of abortion that the word "person," as used in the Constitution, does not encompass those who have yet to be born.[25] It is unfortunate that this nugget of textual analysis in *Roe* has been overshadowed by the remainder of the opinion, which has been deservedly excoriated for its indifference to constitutional text. The irony of the *Roe* opinion is that it simultaneously serves as an exemplar of constitutional textualism while demonstrating the pathologies that arise when judges invent rights without regard to the text of legal enactments. Few decisions of the Court can claim this unique distinction.

Roe's Jurisdictional Analysis

Before discussing the merits of *Roe*'s constitutional holding, one must begin (as always) with jurisdiction. The relentless attacks on *Roe*'s decision to announce a constitutional right to abortion have obscured the equally deserved criticisms of its jurisdictional analysis,[26] and too many of *Roe*'s defenders have skated past the jurisdictional obstacles in their zeal to defend its imposition of a nationwide right to abortion.

The jurisdictional problem in *Roe* was evident: McCorvey, aka "Jane Roe," had given birth long before the Supreme Court announced its judgment in *Roe v. Wade*, and there was no certified class of pregnant women that Roe was purporting to represent.[27] Roe stood before the Supreme Court as a solitary litigant who was no longer pregnant, and she had no more interest in challenging the continued enforcement of the Texas abortion law than a woman who had never been pregnant in the first place.

The Court's opinion, however, claimed that it could disregard this justiciability problem because (according to the Court) the appellate courts otherwise would never be able to rule on whether abortion is a constitutional right: "[T]he normal 266-day human gestation period is so short that the pregnancy will come to term before the usual appellate process is complete. If that termination makes a case moot, pregnancy litigation seldom will survive much beyond the trial stage, and appellate review will be effectively denied. Our law should not be that rigid."[28] This passage is transparently false. There are many ways to obtain an appellate court ruling on whether pregnant women have a constitutional right to abort consistent with the case-or-controversy requirement of Article III. The most obvious path is to bring a class-action lawsuit on behalf of all pregnant women affected by an abortion restriction, and then ask a district court to certify that class before the representative plaintiff (or plaintiffs) give birth or obtain an abortion. Once a class is certified, there is no risk that the case will become moot after the pregnancies of the representative plaintiffs come to an end.[29] This is what Roe's lawyers should have done to avoid the mootness issue that they encountered on appeal—and their failure to take this step did not warrant the Supreme Court bailing them out with a false assertion that "pregnancy litigation" cannot otherwise survive past the trial court stage.

There is a second problem with *Roe*'s claim that the plaintiffs' constitutional arguments would have "evaded" appellate review absent an exception to mootness. The constitutional claims asserted by Roe could have been litigated by an abortion provider—either as a defense to criminal prosecution[30] or in a pre-enforcement lawsuit seeking to enjoin the enforcement of the state's abortion laws.[31] Claims asserted by the abortion provider would not become moot before the case reaches an appellate court, so creating an ad hoc exception to mootness in Roe's lawsuit was unnecessary to ensure that the appellate courts could resolve the merits of the abortion controversy.

There was also a better argument for jurisdiction in *Roe*—though not one that the Court made. The Court could have held that even nonpregnant women like Roe have standing to challenge the enforcement of criminal abortion laws because it removes the availability of abortion as a fallback method of birth control, thereby inflicting injury in fact by making sexual intercourse more risky (and more costly). Even a nonpregnant woman should be able to establish Article III standing in those circumstances, especially if an abortion ban would cause her to change her sexual behavior or spend more money on other means of birth control. *That* is the rationale that the Court should have used if it wanted to assert jurisdiction in *Roe v. Wade*.

Instead, the Court's opinion seems to concede that a nonpregnant woman would lack standing to challenge the enforcement of a criminal abortion ban, yet insists that it should nonetheless assert jurisdiction in *Roe v. Wade* because otherwise the appellate courts would be powerless to rule on whether abortion is a constitutional right.[32] This reflects a belief that appellate courts *must* be given some way of resolving the constitutionality of abortion bans, even when Article III justiciability doctrines would otherwise stand in the way, and that courts may (or perhaps must?) create or recognize exceptions to mootness to preserve their ability to reach an issue that would otherwise "evade" appellate review. That understanding of the judicial role is hard to reconcile with Article III, which empowers the federal courts to resolve "cases" or "controversies" and confers no freestanding power to rule on the constitutionality of legislation. But it wasn't even necessary for the Court to open this can of worms. It should have simply held that McCorvey, as a woman who remained capable of becoming pregnant, continued to suffer injury in fact from a law that eliminated an after-the-fact method of birth control— and that sufficed to give McCorvey a stake in the outcome of the litigation even though she was no longer pregnant by the time her case reached the Supreme Court.

Roe's Constitutional Holding

On the merits, *Roe* held that the Constitution protects the right to abortion before viability, while allowing a very limited role for state regulation.[33] This became one of the most controversial and fiercely disputed pronouncements in the history of constitutional law. Critics of *Roe*, led by Ely, pounced on the absence of any language in the Constitution to support the idea that abortion is a constitutional right, and declared that the *Roe* majority had simply imposed its preferred abortion policy from the bench under the guise of constitutional interpretation.[34]

Yet it is not immediately apparent what makes *Roe* all that different from other rights recognized by the Supreme Court that lack a clear foundation in constitutional text. And supporters of *Roe* have been quick to point out that declaring *Roe* wrong for its lack of textual support in the Constitution would call into question some of the Supreme Court's most canonical constitutional rulings. Chief among them is *Loving v. Virginia*,[35] which recognized a substantive constitutional right to marry a person of another race. Defenders of *Roe* often seek to tie *Roe* and *Loving* together and challenge the critics of *Roe* to explain how *Loving* can be right if *Roe* is wrong. The *Casey* plurality opinion, for example, correctly observed that "[m]arriage is mentioned nowhere in the Bill of Rights and interracial marriage was illegal in most States in the 19th century,"[36] and it invoked *Loving* (and other cases) to justify *Roe* and reject the history-and-tradition test for unenumerated constitutional rights proposed by Justice Scalia in dissent.[37] The *Dobbs* dissent also relied on *Loving* to defend *Roe*, noting that the right to abortion has no more pedigree in constitutional text or historical practice than the right to interracial marriage.[38]

None of *Roe*'s critics have (to my knowledge) offered a satisfactory explanation for how *Loving* can be correct if *Roe* is wrong. Justice Scalia's dissent in *Casey* addressed *Loving* only in a footnote,[39] and he tried to distinguish *Loving* from *Roe* by insisting that the right to interracial marriage was compelled by the text of the Equal Protection Clause, which (according to Justice Scalia) "explicitly establishes racial equality as a constitutional value."[40] But the Equal Protection Clause says nothing of the sort. The

Fourteenth Amendment does not even mention race, let alone enshrine a textual prohibition on government-sponsored racial classifications.[41] And a command to provide the "equal protection of the laws" does not require equal *treatment*[42]—and it certainly does not allow "persons" to marry whomever they wish. Laws prohibiting first-cousin marriage do not withhold the "equal protection of the laws"; they simply define the scope of permissible marriage partners. Laws prohibiting interracial marriage (or same-sex marriage) are no different as far as the language of the Equal Protection Clause is concerned. The text merely requires "equal protection of the laws"—and it is unconcerned with whether a statutory restriction on the right to marry is based on race, sex, or consanguinity.

The *Dobbs* majority tried to distinguish *Loving* from *Roe* by observing that abortion terminates the life of a human embryo or fetus, while the court-created right to interracial marriage does not inflict (or arguably inflict) harm on third parties.[43] But none of that explains how *Loving* can survive when the *Dobbs* majority insists throughout its opinion that unenumerated constitutional rights must be "deeply rooted in this Nation's history and tradition."[44] The right to interracial marriage is no more "deeply rooted in this Nation's history and tradition" than the right to abortion, so *Loving* and *Roe* should be equally doomed if history and tradition determine the legitimacy of an unenumerated yet court-imposed right.

Then there is *Griswold v. Connecticut*,[45] which established a constitutional right to contraception that was initially limited to married couples but later extended to all individuals in the successor case of *Eisenstadt v. Baird*.[46] The right to contraception has no more textual grounding in the Constitution than the right to abortion,[47] and it is not "deeply rooted in this Nation's history and tradition."[48] The *Dobbs* opinion did not deny any of this, but it distinguished *Griswold* and *Eisenstadt* on the same ground as *Loving*: by declaring that contraception (unlike abortion) does not involve the purposeful destruction of a human embryo or fetus, and therefore does not implicate harm to third parties.[49] Yet that does not explain how the Supreme Court could have recognized (or could continue recognizing) a constitutional right to contraception after announcing that unenumerated constitutional rights must be "deeply rooted in this Nation's history and tradition."

History and tradition should not be the test for determining the legitimacy of a court-imposed substantive due process right. Too many of the atextual constitutional rights that the justices have recognized yet are unwilling to overrule have no grounding in the nation's history or tradition. And at the same time, many rights that *were* deeply rooted in the common law—such as employment at will and the marital rape exemption—have been curtailed by modern legislation despite their long-standing pedigree,[50] and no one thinks that the "deeply rooted" nature of these common-law rights should shield them from legislative modification when the Constitution has nothing to say about them. More important, the Court has never attempted to explain *why* unenumerated yet "deeply rooted" common-law rights should be elevated to the status of constitutional rights that are immune from legislative revision. Its only justification has been to cite statements from its precedents, but none of those precedents provides a reason for this idea.[51]

The better approach is to ask whether an unenumerated right can be found in other sources of positive law, such as federal statutes or agency regulations, and use those nonconstitutional sources of law to defend (or rehabilitate) the court rulings that imposed the disputed right. All too often litigants and judges look to the Constitution for answers that are found in other sources of law, and these extraconstitutional legal authorities obviate the need to render a constitutional pronouncement. *Loving* is a prime example. The Court had no need to invoke the Fourteenth Amendment or a supposed constitutional right to marry a person of another race, because the Civil Rights Act of 1866 provided all the authority needed to set aside Virginia's antimiscegenation law. The Civil Rights Act provides, in relevant part, that "citizens, of every race and color, . . . shall have the same right, in every State and Territory in the United States, to make and enforce contracts . . . as is enjoyed by white citizens . . . any law, statute, ordinance, regulation, or custom, to the contrary notwithstanding."[52] There is abundant authority establishing that marriage is a contract,[53] and the Civil Rights Act gives every citizen the "*same right . . . to make and enforce contracts . . . as is enjoyed by white citizens.*"[54] That language indicates that minority citizens must be treated *as if they were white citizens* for each of the rights listed in the statute—and that the precise scope and content of the rights held by white citizens must be extended to minority citizens on equal terms. If a white citizen has the right to marry a white spouse, then one cannot escape the conclusion that an antimiscegenation law withholds that "same right" from a minority citizen. Perhaps one could say an antimiscegenation regime offers a *similar* right to minorities by allowing them to marry within their race—but that is not the "same right" to marry that is "enjoyed by white citizens," especially when antimiscegenation laws leave minorities with a smaller pool of permissible spouses. So *Loving* remains good law despite the absence of textual support for a constitutional "right to marry" and despite the lack of historical pedigree for a right to marry a person of another race.

Griswold and *Eisenstadt* are harder to defend because there was no federal statutory right to use contraception at the time of those decisions, and the Comstock laws continued to criminalize the mailing or shipment of contraceptive drugs and devices.[55] But Congress has since repealed those provisions of the Comstock laws,[56] and the Affordable Care Act and the Contraceptive Mandate now secure a federal right to contraception by compelling private insurers to cover FDA-approved contraceptive methods as preventive care.[57] That does nothing to defend the correctness of *Griswold* or *Eisenstadt* at the time they were decided. But it does allow the present-day Court to continue holding that contraception is a federally protected right and that states cannot outlaw contraception, while simultaneously denouncing and overruling *Roe* for its decision to impose a right to abortion that lacks any textual basis in the Constitution or in any other source of federal law.

Many other nontextual rights that the Supreme Court has imposed can be defended by looking outside the Constitution to other sources of supreme federal law. The Civil Rights Act of 1964, for example, outlaws racial discrimination in every school that receives federal funds.[58] This provides an independent source of authority for the holding of *Brown v. Board of Education*,[59] and it puts to rests the lingering doubts that many have expressed about whether adherence to *Brown* can be supported by the text or original meaning of the Fourteenth Amendment.[60] Congress's civil rights statutes also protect women from sex discrimination at the hands of state and local governments,[61] which allows the courts to enforce these antidiscrimination rules without relying on a supposed equal protection right to be free from government-sponsored sex discrimination. The problem with the right to abortion is that it cannot be found in the text of any federal law that existed at the time of *Roe* or at any time since. And rejecting *Roe* for this reason does not entail or imply the rejection of other court-created rights that are now secured by other sources of supreme federal law.

So there is no reason to fear that a repudiation of *Roe*—or that a full-throated rejection of court-created substantive due process rights—will somehow undermine the continued existence of *Loving*, *Griswold*, *Eisenstadt*, or *Brown*. The rights established in those cases are enshrined in federal statutes and agency regulations, and that is all that is needed to support the continued judicial enforcement of those rights, even for those who harbor doubts about the constitutional foundations of those rulings. And no one should hesitate to proclaim *Roe* wrong for the simple reason that federal judges have no authority to enforce rights that cannot be found in the text of the Constitution or other sources of federal law. Justice Blackmun and his colleagues may have believed very strongly that women should be allowed to abort their pregnancies for any reason prior to viability, and doubtless there are many others who hold that belief with sincerity and conviction. But that is not a basis on which a Court can declare a statute unconstitutional or enjoin its enforcement. A statute cannot be *un*constitutional unless it contradicts something in the Constitution; it is not enough that a statute offends a judge's sense of morality or justice. The Fourteenth Amendment does not enact the ideology of the sexual revolution, and supporters of *Roe* need to amend the Constitution or enact a federal statute before demanding that the federal judiciary impose their preferred abortion policy on all fifty states.

Roe and Consequentialist Theories of Judging

The critique of *Roe* that I have outlined and defended is rooted in a textualist judicial philosophy that not everyone shares. Textualism is primarily concerned with ensuring that the judiciary derives its authority from sources exogenous to its own pronouncements and beliefs. And it assesses the correctness of court rulings not by the consequences that follow from those decisions but by their fidelity to the authorities that establish the courts and endow them with power to act. Ely's critique of *Roe* is unabashedly textualist, and so are nearly all of the subsequent criticisms of the *Roe* opinion.

But not everyone accepts the premise of textualist interpretive methodologies, and there are other approaches to judging that proceed from a more consequentialist orientation. Consequentialist theories of judging seek to ensure that judicial decisions produce normatively desirable results and may be willing to tolerate at least some judicial improvisation to effectuate that end. Consequentialists can defend the Warren Court by pointing to the undeniable fact that many of its constitutional pronouncements led to lasting improvements in American society, even when those decisions have been hard to defend as a matter of constitutional text or original understandings.[62] And consequentialists may be at least open to the idea of allowing the judiciary to recognize and enforce rights that cannot be found in the constitutional text if the right is sufficiently important (in their view) to warrant protection despite its lack of textual pedigree.

My own sympathies are with the textualist camp, because I have never thought that consequentialist arguments or reasoning present a satisfying way for judges to resolve disputes between litigants. People fiercely disagree over what counts as a normatively desirable outcome (especially on an issue such as abortion),[63] and there are no reasons to think that life-tenured judges have any comparative advantage in deciding whether or when it is "better" to protect the life of a human embryo or fetus or a pregnant woman's freedom to terminate an unwanted pregnancy—or in presenting arguments capable of persuading others to abandon or reconsider their beliefs on this issue.[64] I've never met anyone who felt persuaded to jettison their anti-abortion beliefs after reading Justice Blackmun's opinion in *Roe* or the joint opinion in *Casey*, and it is hard to imagine that such a person could exist. It is also unclear whether and to what extent concerns for rule consequentialism (such as the systemic benefits that come from adhering closely to legal texts or following rule-bound interpretive methodologies, even when they produce injustices in particular cases)[65] should trump act consequentialism (the desire to en- sure a normatively desirable outcome in the particular case before the court), and there is no obviously right answer to this question.

By contrast, arguments rooted in the language of authorities that everyone accepts as law (such as the Constitution and federal statutes) can at least have the *potential* to persuade people who dislike a court's decision to nonetheless accept it as rooted in law. Consider Justice Blackmun's textual argument in *Roe* regarding how the word "person" throughout the Constitution is used only to refer to those who have already been born, and how embryos and fetuses have never been considered "persons" when allocating House seats under section 2 of the Fourteenth Amendment. It is hard to deny Justice Blackmun's conclusion that the word "person" excludes embryos and fetuses without rejecting the authority of the written Constitution, or without presenting an argument for why the word "person" should have different meanings in the same constitutional amendment (no small task).[66] So *Roe*'s textual argument on the meaning of "person" has (unsurprisingly) had more staying power than its consequentialist argument for why abortion should be a constitutional right.

But it is a mistake (in my view) to offer a textualist critique of *Roe* while pretending that consequentialists do not exist. Textualists who denounce *Roe* should either admit that their critique proceeds from premises that not everyone shares, or they should meet the consequentialists on their terms and explain why *Roe* should be rejected even by those who embrace a living constitution and regard access to abortion as normatively desirable. As it happens, there are reasons to be skeptical of *Roe* even for those who reject the textualist premises of Ely's critique.

A consequentialist who supports access to abortion could defend the Court's actions in *Roe* with an argument along these lines: It is undeniable that the Supreme Court has recognized nontextual rights under the Constitution that have won widespread acceptance and produced normatively desirable consequences, such as the rights to interracial marriage and contraception. Therefore, those who support access to abortion should also support *Roe* because the judicial imposition of a constitutional right to abortion will accelerate societal acceptance of abortion and increase access to the procedure in locations where it would otherwise remain banned.

The problem with this argument is that it underestimates the resolve and perseverance of the anti-abortion movement and ignores the reality of checks and balances on the Supreme Court. The justices who joined the *Roe* majority and authored the joint opinion in *Casey* may have believed (or hoped) that opposition to abortion would eventually die out, in the same way that opposition to contraception and interracial marriage have largely disappeared.[67] But that did not happen, and it was naïve for anyone to think that it would. The erstwhile resistance to interracial marriage and legal contraception rested on squeamishness or social taboos that were easily overcome by movements to legalize and destigmatize these practices. Opposition to abortion, by contrast, is rooted in a belief that the intentional termination of a human embryo or fetus is a murderous and unjustifiable act of violence against the most vulnerable members of the human family. Opponents of abortion may or may not be right to hold that belief, but they will not be persuaded to abandon their convictions by a court ruling that insists that a right that is nowhere to be found in the text of the Constitution is actually a constitutional right.

So a backlash to *Roe* predictably ensued, which triggered a realignment in American politics and contributed to the election of Republican presidents and senators who were determined to appoint justices who would overrule *Roe v. Wade. Roe* managed to survive its initial brush with death in 1992, when a Court stacked with Republican appointees surprised by voting to reaffirm rather than overrule *Roe* in a 5–4 vote.[68] But *Roe* could not survive the change of membership brought about by President Donald Trump, who had promised to appoint anti-*Roe* justices to the Supreme Court and delivered on each of his three nominees.

The life and death of *Roe* show the limits of a living-constitution philosophy. One can choose to embrace the idea of a living constitution in the hope that the Supreme Court will use its powers to impose normatively desirable policies from the bench. But there is no mechanism to ensure that the members of the Supreme Court will share your values, and past performance is not indicative of future results.[69] Rights created by judges will last only for as long as a majority of the Supreme Court is willing to adhere to those court-created rights, and the members of the *Roe* Court had no way to ensure that their pro-abortion majority would last in perpetuity. It is the national political branches that control the gateways of membership to the Supreme Court, and they will use their appointment powers to bend the Court toward their views on *Roe*. One can always hope that Supreme Court vacancies will be filled at a time when the presidency and the Senate are controlled by *Roe*-supportive politicians, but there is no way to guarantee that will happen.

Some may still think that it was better to have had forty-nine years of judicially enforced abortion rights—even knowing with the benefit of hindsight that *Roe* would eventually be overruled—than to have abortion policy left to the states during that forty-nine-year window of time. Many states would never have legalized abortion in the absence of *Roe*. And it is plausible to think that the half-century of nationwide abortion on demand brought about by *Roe* shifted behavior, expectations, and public opinion in favor of continued abortion legalization, which gives supporters of abortion access the upper hand in a post-*Dobbs* world where abortion policy has been returned to the political process.

But even here, one has to consider the systemic consequences of embracing a decision like *Roe*, especially at a time when conservative Republicans hold a supermajority on the Supreme Court and are using their powers to impose or expand constitutional doctrines whose textual foundations are questionable or nonexistent. There have been many textually dubious constitutional pronouncements emanating from the Roberts Court, despite the Court's professed fealty to constitutional textualism.[70] These include but are not limited to (1) the use of Court-created Article III standing doctrines to limit congressionally created causes of action;[71] (2) the use of Court-created state sovereign-immunity doctrines to limit congressionally authorized lawsuits against states;[72] (3) the decisions to override congressionally imposed restrictions on the president's authority to remove subordinate officers;[73] and (4) the invocation of an "equal sovereignty" doctrine—a phrase that is nowhere to be found in the Constitution—to override Congress's decision to reauthorize section 5 of the Voting Rights Act.[74] Progressives have been critical of those decisions, but the criticisms fall flat when the left simultaneously embraces and defends *Roe* and the forty-nine-year regime of judicially imposed abortion rights. It isn't easy to defend the idea that left-of-center judges get to recognize nontextual rights and doctrines while simultaneously insisting that conservative judges play by a different set of rules. Of course, there may be single-issue voters who think the cause of abortion access is of such overriding importance that they will gladly embrace the *Roe/Casey* regime even if it undermines the progressive critique of atextual Roberts Court decisions or emboldens conservative jurists to impose textually questionable constitutional doctrines from the bench. But now those individuals are facing what may be (from their perspective) the worst of both worlds: *Roe* has been overruled, while a conservative-dominated Supreme Court is perpetuating and reinforcing atextual constitutional doctrines without compunction.

It is always difficult (if not impossible) to prove a consequentialist legal argument, and that is especially true when assessing the consequences of *Roe*. But there are reasons to question whether the *Roe* decision and its forty-nine-year reign brought about normatively desirable consequences—even from the standpoint of those who support legal abortion as a matter of policy.[75] For all that *Roe* did to expand access to abortion, it also galvanized an anti-abortion movement that eventually led to the decision's undoing, and it has undercut the credibility of progressives when they critique the atextual constitutional pronouncements of the Roberts Court. This should give even supporters of abortion access pause before embracing *Roe*'s decision to impose that policy through judicial decree.

4

Justice Blackmun Got It Right
in *Roe v. Wade*

Erwin Chemerinsky

In *Dobbs v. Jackson Women's Health Organization*, the Supreme Court explicitly overruled *Roe v. Wade*[1] and held that the issue of abortion is left to the political process.[2] The Court said that *Roe* was "egregiously wrong and deeply
damaging."[3] It said that "*Roe* was incorrectly decided, but that decision was
more than just wrong. It stood on exceptionally weak grounds."[4] Justice
Samuel Alito's majority opinion—which was joined by Justices Clarence
Thomas, Neil Gorsuch, Brett Kavanaugh, and Amy Coney Barrett—
declared, "All in all, *Roe*'s reasoning was exceedingly weak, and academic
commentators, including those who agreed with the decision as a matter of
policy, were unsparing in their criticism."[5] Justice Alito quoted a number of
law professors, including liberals, criticizing the reasoning in Justice Harry
Blackmun's majority opinion in *Roe v. Wade*.

I doubt I would speak of a colleague's or former colleague's work as "egre-
giously wrong" or "exceedingly weak." It is notable that both Republican and
Democratic appointees to the Court were part of the majority in *Roe* and its
many reaffirmations. *Roe* was a 7–2 decision, the majority opinion written by
Justice Blackmun, who had been appointed by Republican president Richard
Nixon and was joined by Nixon appointees Chief Justice Warren Burger and
Justice Lewis Powell.

Even more dramatic, in 1992, in *Planned Parenthood v. Casey*, the Supreme
Court reaffirmed *Roe v. Wade* and again held that states cannot prohibit
abortions before viability.[6] It was a 5–4 decision, with all five justices in the
majority having been appointed by Republican presidents: Justice Blackmun
by President Nixon, Justice John Paul Stevens by President Gerald Ford,
Justices Sandra Day O'Connor and Anthony Kennedy by President Ronald
Reagan, and Justice David Souter by President George H. W. Bush.

Erwin Chemerinsky, *Justice Blackmun Got It Right in* Roe v. Wade In: *Roe v. Dobbs*. Edited by: Lee C. Bollinger and
Geoffrey R. Stone, Oxford University Press. © Oxford University Press 2024.
DOI: 10.1093/oso/9780197760352.003.0004

Was *Roe v. Wade* "egregiously wrong" and "exceedingly weak" in its reasoning? It is true that many academics have criticized Justice Blackmun's opinion in *Roe*. But I would strongly disagree and contend that he and the majority in *Roe* got it exactly right in their reasoning.

The Court in *Roe* faced three questions, as, for that matter, did the Court in *Dobbs*. First, are there rights to privacy and autonomy protected by the Constitution even though they are not mentioned in the document's text? Second, if so, are the rights infringed by a prohibition of abortion? Third, if so, does the state have a sufficient justification for upholding laws prohibiting abortion?[7]

Are Rights to Privacy and Autonomy Protected by the Constitution?

The first question—Is there a right to privacy protected by the Constitution?—was presented as the central focus of the Court in *Dobbs*. The Court declared, "We hold that *Roe* and *Casey* must be overruled. The Constitution makes no reference to abortion, and no such right is implicitly protected by any constitutional provision, including the one on which the defenders of *Roe* and *Casey* now chiefly rely—the Due Process Clause of the Fourteenth Amendment."[8]

This has been the focus of opponents of *Roe* from the beginning, contending there is no such right because it is not mentioned in the Constitution and was not part of its original intent. The most famous critique of the decision—quoted by Justice Alito in *Dobbs*—was written by Professor John Hart Ely, where he declared, "It is, nevertheless, a very bad decision. . . . It is bad because it is bad constitutional law, or rather because it is not constitutional law and gives almost no sense of an obligation to try to be."[9] Ely's objection was that abortion and privacy are not mentioned in the Constitution, and therefore no such rights exist. This, of course, is the criticism that conservatives have launched at *Roe* since it was decided.[10]

The problem with this argument is that it is wrong as a matter of constitutional law and it would be a radical change in constitutional law to reject the idea of rights of privacy and autonomy. Before *Roe*, the Court had expressly recognized a right to privacy, including over matters of reproduction, even though there is no mention of this in the text of the Constitution. In *Griswold v. Connecticut* in 1965, the Court declared unconstitutional as violating the right to privacy a state law prohibiting the sale, distribution, or use of contraceptives.[11] In *Eisenstadt v. Baird* in 1972, the Court invalidated a state law keeping unmarried individuals from having access to contraceptives and declared, "If the right of privacy means anything, it is the right of the individual, married or single, to be free from unwarranted governmental intrusion into matters so fundamentally affecting a person as the decision whether to bear or beget a child."[12]

Indeed, long before these decisions, the Court safeguarded many aspects of autonomy as fundamental rights even though they are not mentioned in the text of the Constitution and were never contemplated by its drafters. For example, for almost a century, the Court has expressly held that certain aspects of family autonomy are fundamental rights and that government interference will be allowed only if the government can prove that its action is necessary to achieve a compelling purpose. In the 1920s, the Supreme Court held that parents have a fundamental right to control the upbringing of their children and used this to strike down laws prohibiting the teaching of the German language and forbidding parochial school education.[13] In the 1940s, the Court ruled that the right to procreate is a fundamental right and declared unconstitutional an Oklahoma law that required the sterilization of those convicted three times of crimes involving moral turpitude.[14]

In the 1960s, the Court proclaimed that there is a fundamental right to marry and invalidated a Virginia law prohibiting interracial marriage.[15] This, of course, was the foundation for the Court declaring that laws prohibiting same-sex marriage are unconstitutional as infringing upon the fundamental right to marry.[16] Thus, under the rubric of "privacy," the Court has safeguarded the right to marry, the right to custody of one's children,[17] the right to keep the family together,[18] the right of parents to control the upbringing of children, the right to procreate, the right to purchase and use contraceptives, the right to refuse medical treatment,[19] and the right to engage in private, consensual same-sex sexual activity.[20]

Unless the Court intends to overrule all of these decisions, it is clear—and it was clear at the time of *Roe*—that the Constitution is interpreted as protecting basic aspects of personal autonomy as fundamental rights even though they are not mentioned in the text of the document or protected under its original meaning or safeguarded by a long unbroken tradition. Put another way, the Court never has adopted the position of originalists, such as Justices Antonin Scalia and Thomas (and others) who insist that the

Constitution is limited to those rights explicitly stated or originally intended at the time of its ratification.

Of course, opponents of *Roe* could argue that all of these decisions were wrong and that there should be no protection of privacy or other nontextual rights.[21] This would be a dramatic change in the law. Professor Cass Sunstein has explained, "[The rejection of privacy rights] is a fully plausible reading of the Constitution. But it would wreak havoc with established law. It would eliminate constitutional protections where the nation has come to rely on them—by, for example, allowing states to ban use of contraceptives by married couples."[22]

Strikingly, the majority opinion in *Dobbs* expressly rejected this position and was clear that it does regard the Constitution as protecting privacy and autonomy. Justice Thomas was explicit that there are no such rights protected by the liberty of the Due Process Clause, and he argued that the implication of *Dobbs* should be the overruling of the prior decisions safeguarding privacy and autonomy. He wrote, "For that reason, in future cases, we should reconsider all of this Court's substantive due process precedents, including *Griswold*, *Lawrence*, and *Obergefell*. Because any substantive due process decision is 'demonstrably erroneous,' we have a duty to 'correct the error' established in those precedents [and] overrul[e] these demonstrably erroneous decisions."[23] The dissent, too, saw this as the potential implications of the holding in *Dobbs*.[24] But Justice Alito's majority opinion expressly responded to this and said that none of these other precedents are in jeopardy because they do not involve "potential life." The Court stated, "What sharply distinguishes the abortion right from the rights recognized in the cases on which *Roe* and *Casey* rely is something that both those decisions acknowledged: Abortion destroys what those decisions call 'potential life' and what the law at issue in this case regards as the life of an 'unborn human being.' "[25] Later in the opinion, the Court stated, "And to ensure that our decision is not misunderstood or mischaracterized, we emphasize that our decision concerns the constitutional right to abortion and no other right. Nothing in this opinion should be understood to cast doubt on precedents that do not concern abortion."[26] And near the end of the opinion, the Court stated once more:

> But we have stated unequivocally that "[n]othing in this opinion should be understood to cast doubt on precedents that do not concern abortion." We have also explained why that is so: rights regarding contraception and same-sex relationships are inherently different from the right to abortion

because the latter (as we have stressed) uniquely involves what *Roe* and *Casey* termed "potential life." . . . It is hard to see how we could be clearer.[27]

Justice Kavanaugh, in a concurring opinion, also stated, "I emphasize what the Court today states: Overruling *Roe* does *not* mean the overruling of those precedents, and does *not* threaten or cast doubt on those precedents."[28]

It is difficult to know what weight to give to these reassurances. The Court, at the outset of its opinion in *Dobbs*, says that rights should be protected only if they are in the text of the Constitution, part of its original meaning, or there is a long unbroken historical tradition. None of these other rights of privacy are justified under this approach to constitutional interpretation. And *Dobbs* shows a Court that gives little weight to precedent.

But more important, the reassurances of the Court demonstrate something profoundly correct about Justice Blackmun's opinion in *Roe*: the Constitution protects rights of privacy and autonomy that are not stated in the Constitution. Justice Alito's opinion in *Dobbs* does not question these rights and stresses that they will remain protected. For that reason, on close examination, *Dobbs* cannot be seen as about rejecting rights of privacy and autonomy and is not really about abortion not being protected by the text or original meaning or long historical tradition. It is all about the Court's judgment that states can protect potential life.

Put another way, by saying that no other rights are in jeopardy, the Court is conceding that fundamental rights of privacy and autonomy are safeguarded under the liberty of the Due Process Clause even though they are not in the text, part of the original meaning, or safeguarded by a long unbroken tradition. That, then, is not really why the Court overruled *Roe* and disagreed with Justice Blackmun. It was all because of the Court's judgment about the state's interest in protecting "potential life."

Do Laws Prohibiting Abortion Infringe Privacy and Autonomy?

The second question before the Court in *Roe* was whether laws that prohibit abortion impinge on a woman's right to privacy. Interestingly, no one, not even the staunchest opponents of abortion rights, disputes that they do. Opponents of *Roe* argue against there being a right to privacy or claim that the state has a sufficiently important interest in prohibiting abortion. There is little disagreement that a prohibition of abortion interferes with a woman's autonomy.

Obviously, forbidding abortions interferes with a woman's ability to control her reproductive autonomy and to decide for herself, in the words of *Eisenstadt v. Baird*, whether to "bear or beget a child."[29] Also, no one can deny that forcing a woman to continue a pregnancy against her will is an enormous medical, financial, psychological, and social intrusion on her control over her body. Justice Blackmun forcefully expressed this view in his majority opinion in *Roe*, where he stated that the "detriment" imposed by the state against a pregnant woman when denying her the choice of terminating her pregnancy "is apparent."[30]

Justice Blackmun and his fellow justices recognized that "[s]pecific and direct harm medically diagnosable even in early pregnancy may be involved" when denying a pregnant woman the right to an abortion.[31] In addition, the Court underscored how "[m]aternity, or additional offspring, may force upon the woman a distressful life and future."[32] The justices stressed that not only might "[p]sychological harm . . . be imminent," but that "[m]ental and physical health may be taxed by child care."[33] These were concerns not only for the pregnant woman, as the Court noted, because "for all concerned [or] associated with the unwanted child . . . there is the problem of bringing a child into a family already unable, psychologically and otherwise, to care for it."[34]

The Court in *Dobbs* does not directly dispute that laws prohibiting abortion infringe upon a woman's rights to privacy and autonomy. But at one point, the Court seems to question this when it states:

> [A]ttitudes about the pregnancy of unmarried women have changed drastically; that federal and state laws ban discrimination on the basis of pregnancy; that leave for pregnancy and childbirth are now guaranteed by law in many cases; that the costs of medical care associated with pregnancy are covered by insurance or government assistance; that States have increasingly adopted "safe haven" laws, which generally allow women to drop off babies anonymously; and that a woman who puts her newborn up for adoption today has little reason to fear that the baby will not find a suitable home.[35]

Twice at the oral argument, Justice Barrett suggested that laws prohibiting abortion are not a burden because women could put the children up for adoption.

At the very least, this suggests that the Court recognizes that Justice Blackmun was right at the time of *Roe* in seeing laws prohibiting abortion as infringing on privacy and autonomy; it just is saying that things have changed. More important, this aspect of the majority's opinion in *Dobbs* is fundamentally misguided. Forcing a woman to continue her pregnancy against her wishes and to put the baby up for adoption makes her exactly what she does not want to be: a mother. Laws forbidding abortion directly impinge on a woman's bodily autonomy and her right to decide whether "to bear or beget a child." This aspect of Justice Blackmun's opinion in *Roe* is unassailable.

Do States Have a Compelling Interest in Protecting Fetal Life?

The third question before the Supreme Court in *Roe v. Wade* was whether states have a compelling interest in protecting fetal life. Once it was decided that there is a fundamental right to privacy and that laws prohibiting abortion infringe upon it, then the question became whether laws prohibiting abortions are needed to achieve a compelling government interest. This is the test the government must meet whenever it burdens or infringes upon a fundamental right.

In *Planned Parenthood v. Casey* in 1992, the plurality opinion shifted to using "the undue burden" test rather than strict scrutiny.[36] This later came to be adopted by a majority of the Court.[37] But in *Roe*, the Court saw the appropriate test as strict scrutiny. This was the right approach. Strict scrutiny is used for other fundamental rights, and as explained above, the law was clear before *Roe* that privacy and autonomy are fundamental rights under the Due Process Clause. The "undue burden test," which the Court invented later, is used for no other rights under the Constitution. The only justification for its application in the abortion context is that abortions involve "potential life." But that begs the question of whether the state should be deemed to have an interest in prohibiting or limiting abortions based on the presence of potential life.

As explained above, this was the real basis for the Court's decision in *Dobbs*. By my count, the majority opinion in *Dobbs* refers to "potential life" twelve times.

In *Roe,* the Court rejected a state interest in outlawing abortions from the moment of conception and concluded that the state has a compelling interest in prohibiting abortion only at the point of viability, the time at which the fetus can survive outside the womb. Justice Blackmun, writing for the majority, stated, "With respect to the State's important and legitimate interest in potential life, the 'compelling' point is at viability. This is so because the fetus then presumably has the capability of meaningful life outside the mother's womb."[38]

In *Planned Parenthood v. Casey,* the Court reaffirmed this, and the plurality explained:

> [T]he concept of viability, as we noted in *Roe,* is the time at which there is a realistic possibility of maintaining and nourishing a life outside the womb, so that the independent existence of the second life can in reason and all fairness be the object of state protection that now overrides the rights of the woman. Consistent with other constitutional norms, legislatures may draw lines which appear arbitrary without the necessity of offering a justification. But courts may not. We must justify the lines we draw. *And there is no line other than viability which is more workable. . . .* The viability line also has, as a practical matter, an element of fairness. In some broad sense it might be said that a woman who fails to act before viability has consented to the State's intervention on behalf of the developing child. The woman's right to terminate her pregnancy before viability is the most central principle of *Roe v. Wade.* It is a rule of law and a component of liberty we cannot renounce.[39]

Ultimately, the question is who should decide whether the fetus before viability is a human person: each woman for herself or the state legislature? Harvard law professor Laurence Tribe, in an article written soon after *Roe,* put this well: "The Court was not, after all, choosing simply between the alternatives of abortion and continued pregnancy."[40] Instead, as he explains, "[i]t was . . . choosing among alternative allocations of decisionmaking authority, for the issue it faced was whether the woman and her doctor, rather than an agency of government, should have the authority to make the abortion decision at various stages of pregnancy."[41]

Why leave the choice as to abortion to the woman rather than to the state? There was then, and is now, no consensus as to when human life begins.[42] In other words, "[s]ome regard the fetus as merely another part of the woman's body until quite late in pregnancy or even until birth; others believe the fetus must be regarded as a helpless human child from the time of its conception."[43] Moreover, according to Tribe, "[t]hese differences of view are endemic to the historical situation in which the abortion controversy arose."[44] The choice of conception as the point at which human life begins, which underlies state laws prohibiting abortion, thus was based not on consensus or science but on religious views.

In fact, as the dissent in *Dobbs* points out, historically abortions were not illegal in the United States.[45] Rather, due to political, medical, and religious movements—particularly the agitation of Anthony Comstock—abortion, contraceptive access, and contraceptive use became crimes.[46] Indeed, states jailed women for violating Comstock's "chastity laws" because they disseminated information about human anatomy, family planning, and birth control. Comstock claimed that the women and the materials they distributed promoted vice and thereby implicitly and explicitly associated birth control advocates with men who sex-trafficked and bootlegged liquor. In part, one could argue that Comstock's campaign against contraception and abortion reflected "a statement of religious faith upon which people will invariably differ widely."[47]

Legislatures could cloak religious objections to abortion in secular arguments (and often they do this) by claiming that potential human life exists at the point of conception and therefore the state may restrict abortion after that point, because a compelling interest exists in preserving that potential life. This was the core of the Court's approach in *Dobbs*. The problem with this approach is that it is factually absurd and medically inaccurate. According to this line of argument, absent an abortion, all or the overwhelming majority of pregnancies develop fetuses to term and produce babies. This is wrong.

Rather, pregnancy is more precisely described as bounded in uncertainty. For example, statistically, roughly 10% to 20% of known pregnancies will spontaneously terminate, resulting in miscarriages. Moreover, 33% "of all human embryos fail to develop successfully" and terminate before women even know they are pregnant.[48] Even in the most controlled, hormone-rich circumstances, such as in vitro fertilization, over 65% of the embryos end in miscarriage.[49] In other words, there is not a probable chance that but for an abortion there will be a baby resulting from conception. Instead, there may be a reasonable chance—but clearly no more than that—that there will be a baby but for an abortion.

Equally, the same logic applies to contraception. Obviously a potential life can result from sex without the use of contraception (or even with it if there is. contraceptive failure). That is, but for the use of contraception, there is a reasonable possibility that a baby may result. For example, data on fertility and infertility indicates that "[w]hen trying to conceive, a couple with no fertility problem has about a 30 percent chance of getting pregnant each month."[50]

Arguments framed in protecting "potential life" justify a ban on contraceptives as much as they do when applied to abortion. The Catholic Church takes exactly this position.[51]

When examined closely, as we have here, Tribe's argument that there is no secular basis for a prohibition on abortion and contraception makes enormous sense. Put in this way, it becomes clearer why the choice whether to continue a pregnancy or terminate should reside with the pregnant woman and is not for the state to make.

The Court's repeated declaration in *Dobbs* that the state has an interest in protecting the "potential life" of the fetus begs the crucial question of who should decide the status of the fetus: the woman or the government. Justice Blackmun was right in saying that this should be left to each woman to resolve for herself until the point of viability, for that is when the fetus can survive outside the womb. Any other judgment requires that the Court allow the government to make a determination that is unquestionably based on a religious judgment that should not be for the government to make.

Conclusion

The central difference between *Roe* and *Dobbs* was about whether the issue of abortion should be left to the political process. Justice Blackmun was right in saying that the issue should not be left to the political process because privacy and autonomy are safeguarded as fundamental rights under the liberty of the Due Process Clause. It is a central tenet of constitutional law—accepted by both liberals and conservatives—that fundamental rights are not left to the political process. Once this is accepted, it must be for the Court and not the political process to decide whether the state has a compelling interest in protecting the "potential life" of the fetus. Justice Blackmun was correct in saying that given the enormous disagreement over this in society, and in light of the burden on a woman in being forced to carry a pregnancy to term against her will, this is a choice that should be left to each woman.

Justice Blackmun's opinion in *Roe* was neither "egregiously wrong" nor "exceedingly weak." Quite the contrary, he and the Court were following well-established constitutional principles and precedents. It is Justice Alito's opinion in *Dobbs* that abandons these out of a conservative desire to end abortion rights. I hope someday there will be a different Court that will embrace and praise Justice Blackmun's reasoning in *Roe* and explain that it was the Court's opinion in *Dobbs* that was egregiously wrong and exceedingly poorly reasoned.

PART III
THE PATH FROM *ROE* TO *DOBBS*

5

Abortion, Partisan Entrenchment, and the Republican Party

*Jack M. Balkin**

The Supreme Court's 2022 decision in *Dobbs v. Jackson Women's Health Organization*[1] achieved a long-sought victory of the conservative legal movement that began following Ronald Reagan's election in 1980. And it is a key moment in an ongoing conservative constitutional revolution. In this essay, I will explain why *Roe v. Wade*[2] lasted as long as it did, many decades after the Republican Party became a pro-life party. I will also describe the processes of partisan entrenchment that led to *Dobbs* and the central role of the conservative legal movement in *Roe*'s overruling and suggest what the future holds, both for the conservative legal movement and for the Republican Party.

Although the Republicans dominated appointments to the Supreme Court from 1969 until 2020, it was not until 2018 that the members of the conservative legal movement, as opposed simply to Republican appointees, gained a majority on the Court. At that point *Roe*'s days were numbered, because eliminating a constitutional right to abortion had long been one of the central goals of the movement. But for a series of contingencies, *Roe* might have been overruled much earlier. But once movement-affiliated justices gained a majority, *Roe*'s demise was all but certain.

But that demise, in turn, has created new problems for the Republican coalition. Like *Roe* itself half a century ago, *Dobbs* creates opportunities for politicians to break apart existing coalitions of voters and create new ones.

Dobbs and the Conservative Constitutional Revolution

What do I mean by "a constitutional revolution in doctrine"? Constitutional law is always changing. There are new decisions every Supreme Court

Jack M. Balkin, *Abortion, Partisan Entrenchment, and the Republican Party* In: *Roe v. Dobbs*. Edited by: Lee C. Bollinger and Geoffrey R. Stone, Oxford University Press. © Oxford University Press 2024.
DOI: 10.1093/oso/9780197760352.003.0005

term. Constitutional understandings about which arguments are plausible and implausible, "on-the-wall" and "off-the-wall," are also constantly changing because of social movement contestation, political entrepreneurship, and ever-changing circumstances.[3] Whenever a significant change in the law occurs, people are tempted to call it revolutionary. But by "a constitutional revolution," I mean a significant change in doctrines, conventions, assumptions, and understandings in multiple areas of the law in a relatively short period time, perhaps a decade or so.[4]

Here are a few examples: Following the constitutional struggle over the New Deal in the mid-1930s—the turning point was the spring of 1937—constitutional law began to change rapidly in several areas, including the commerce power, spending power, taxing power, war power, due process, equal protection, and the dormant commerce clause. By 1942, when the Court decided *Wickard v. Filburn*,[5] which dramatically expanded the regulatory authority of the federal government, constitutional law had become very different from what it was only seven years before.

So too, during the final years of the Warren Court, between about 1962 and 1969, there was a constitutional revolution in the law of civil rights and civil liberties. These seven years produced significant changes in the protection of voting rights; in the law of freedom of speech, press, and religion; in the Establishment Clause; in equal protection law; in criminal procedure; in the application of the Bill of Rights to the states; and in Congress's power to enforce the Reconstruction amendments. And on top of all this, the Court began a second era of substantive due process law in *Griswold v. Connecticut*,[6] protecting the right of married couples to use contraceptives.

Something similar is happening once again, but in a different ideological direction. U.S. constitutional law has been moving to the right in several areas for a very long time, and especially in the decade following 2006 after Justice Samuel Alito replaced Justice Sandra Day O'Connor. But the conservative trend appears to have been turbocharged since 2017, when the first of three new conservative justices joined the Court, and the doctrinal changes are far from over. We are in the middle of significant changes in many different areas of the law, including free speech law, establishment clause law, free exercise law, voting rights law, the law of substantive due process, and the Second Amendment, not to mention changes in the law of separation of powers and the presidency.

Partisan Entrenchment

Constitutional revolutions in doctrine usually occur because of a phe-nomenon that Sanford Levinson and I call *partisan entrenchment*.[7] In the U.S. constitutional system, presidents nominate judges to the lower federal courts and the Supreme Court, subject to the Senate's advice and consent. The political parties, and the presidents who lead them, tend to appoint ide-ologically allied judges and justices—who tend to agree with the appointing president on basic commitments of ideology and interest—at least from the standpoint of the time the appointment is made. I emphasize this last point because new issues may arise that cause life-tenured judges to become out of step with the views of the party or the president who appointed them.

Partisan entrenchment of ideological allies is the general tendency rather than a hard and fast rule. Presidents take many political considerations into account in appointing justices. They may need to pay off political favors, please demographic or regional constituencies, respect the wishes of senators of the same party (especially for the lower federal courts), or fulfill campaign promises. They may have to hedge their bets if they face a Senate controlled by their political opponents. But all other things being equal, presidents try to stock the courts and appoint Supreme Court justices who are ideologically similar to them and who agree with their basic commitments of ideology and interest with respect to the issues of the day.

There are always exceptions, of course. Dwight Eisenhower, for example, wanted to show that he was moderate and above party politics, and his Supreme Court appointments reflected this.[8] His appointment of California governor Earl Warren, for example, paid off a political favor; without Warren's help, Eisenhower might not have gotten the Republican presidential nom-ination in 1952. Another Eisenhower appointment—of the liberal justice William Brennan of the New Jersey State Supreme Court—was an attempt to win the Catholic vote in the 1956 election.[9] In our far more polarized times, it is difficult to imagine a contemporary president behaving in the same way.

Even if a president's appointments reflect the party's values at the time of appointment, partisan entrenchment doesn't guarantee that judges and justices will move in lockstep with the party's positions later on. The center of gravity of the party's views may change over time, while the judge or justice doesn't go along. Or new issues may arise for which a judge or justice wasn't appointed.[10] Richard Nixon appointed justices to get tough with criminals and limit court-ordered busing, but he wasn't thinking about abortion or gay rights.[11] Franklin Roosevelt appointed justices primarily to uphold his New Deal programs. But after the New Deal's legitimacy was settled, the Court moved on to new issues in the 1940s and 1950s involving civil rights and civil liberties, and the justices began to disagree among themselves. The further we move out from the time of appointment, the greater the chances that these disagreements and divergences will occur.

Suppose, however, that a president is able to appoint many new justices in a relatively short space of time. Suppose further that the new judges are able to ally themselves with ideologically friendly jurists already on the bench. (These ideological allies may have been appointed by a president of the same party or of a different party.) Then we are likely to see significant changes in constitutional law over a brief period of time. We will see, in other words, a constitutional revolution.

That's exactly what happened during the New Deal period, when the Roosevelt-appointed justices allied with the liberal/progressive holdovers already on the Court. That's also what happened during the Warren Court. A bipartisan collection of liberal justices—some appointed by President Eisenhower, a Republican, others appointed by Presidents Roosevelt and Kennedy—formed a liberal coalition that decided the key cases in the Warren Court's constitutional revolution.

And that is also what appears to be happening today. In the present case, all of the justices engaged in the conservative constitutional revolution were appointed by Republican presidents. Perhaps more important, all of them are *movement-identified* conservatives.[12] That is, all of them are either part of or were significantly shaped by the conservative legal movement that began during the Reagan administration. The three newest Trump appointees—Neil Gorsuch, Brett Kavanaugh, and Amy Coney Barrett—have joined forces with the Court's other three movement conservatives: Clarence Thomas, Samuel Alito, and, to a lesser extent, Chief Justice John Roberts. Although Roberts is very conservative and cut his teeth in the conservative legal movement, he has been partly constrained by his institutional role as chief justice. The decision in *Dobbs* is an example. While Alito and four other movement-identified justices sought to rid themselves of *Roe* immediately, Roberts counseled greater restraint, seeking to overturn elements of the right to abortion gradually through a series of steps.[13]

Partisan Entrenchment and Democracy

In Bruce Ackerman's famous theory of constitutional moments, constitutional revolutions are inherently democratic. They reflect the judgment of We the People who deliberate about fundamental questions of constitutional law over the course of a decade.[14] Once the people have spoken through a series of key elections, politicians consolidate the meaning of the revolution through a series of framework statutes and transformative appointments to the Supreme Court.[15]

Levinson and I disagree with Ackerman's account in several respects. First, we do not think that constitutional revolutions necessarily reflect the considered judgments of the American people.

Second, although we agree that presidents can effect changes in doctrine through transformative appointments, presidents may achieve this without the support of a broad or sustained majority of Americans. Instead, changes in doctrine may reflect the entrenchment of the values of party elites or activists.

Third, Ackerman recognizes only three constitutional moments, of the Founding, Reconstruction, and the New Deal, and one smaller "constitutional solution," involving the civil rights revolution. We think that constitutional revolutions in doctrine occur far more frequently, and they don't always correspond to relatively rare periods of heightened and serious deliberation about constitutional questions by We the American People. The present conservative constitutional revolution exemplifies all three of these differences from Ackerman's model.

Our view is that partisan entrenchment can be roughly but imperfectly democratic.[16] But it guarantees neither correct judicial decisions nor democratically responsive decisions. Again, the current constitutional revolution is an example.

Because of life tenure, partisan entrenchment tends to entrench the political views of past political coalitions on the Supreme Court, and this, in theory, can act as a moderating influence on current politics. The ideological center of the Supreme Court is composed of the justice or justices in the middle who cast the deciding votes in the most controversial cases. This ideological center is a lagging indicator of national politics. It reflects the vector sum of the forces of national politics considered over long periods of time.[17]

When the ideological center of the Supreme Court gets too far out of line with the political center of the country, new presidential elections may produce new appointments that move the median justice or justices back into better alignment with national popular opinion. Under these circumstances, partisan entrenchment can be roughly if imperfectly democratic. Note that this process connects the Court only to national public opinion. In different parts of the country the views of local majorities may vary widely. But the Supreme Court is a national institution whose members are appointed by national politicians, and so at best it tends over time to fall in line with national public opinion.

But because Supreme Court justices serve for life, this process of adjustment between the ideological center of the Court and the ideological center of the country may take many years. And it is hardly foolproof. Suppose that one of the parties is unlucky and its presidents get relatively few Supreme Court appointments despite often enjoying majority support. Suppose that the other party is able to make many appointments and control the Court despite representing only a minority of the national electorate. Then the ideological center of the Supreme Court won't be well aligned with the ideological center of the country.

And there are further complications. The Supreme Court is composed of legal elites. It is far more likely to represent elite opinion than national popular opinion whenever the two diverge.[18] We must also factor in political polarization, both among elites and among the country as a whole. During the middle of the twentieth century the parties were not as polarized as they are now and there was far greater consensus among well-educated legal and political elites in the two parties.[19] But if the country is highly polarized, as it is now, there is less reason to think that the ideological center of the Supreme Court will have much relationship to the center of public opinion. It is far more likely to reflect the center of elite opinion in whichever major party currently controls the Court.[20]

In our current political climate, elites and party activists are probably even more polarized than the public as a whole. The distribution of their views is essentially bimodal. So if the Supreme Court tends to reflect the views of national elites, and if there is a wide gap in the views of political and legal elites of different parties, then the ideological center of the Supreme Court may be quite distant from the center of national public opinion.[21]

Partisan entrenchment tended to align the Supreme Court with public opinion far better in the middle of the twentieth century than it does today. In the New Deal and Warren Court revolutions, the Supreme Court was buoyed by majority support for liberal policies. These Supreme Courts generally worked with Congress and the president rather than in opposition to them. The Warren Court upheld the Civil Rights Act of 1964 and the Voting Rights Act of 1965; Roosevelt's Supreme Court appointments were designed to uphold New Deal programs, like the Wagner Act, the Fair Labor Standards Act, and the Social Security Act. To be sure, the Warren Court did strike down many state laws and police practices, but in doing so it reflected national rather than local values.

The current conservative revolution is a bit different, and it shows why partisan entrenchment may not be all that democratically responsive in our current era. First, the country is strongly polarized, and elites and party activists are even more polarized. So whichever party manages to get firm control of the Court, the median justice on the Court is likely to be far from the center of public opinion, and the Court's work may change rapidly as a result of a few appointments.[22]

Second, the Republican Party has managed to maintain and even increase a conservative Supreme Court majority while losing its status as the majority party in the United States. The Republican Party has benefited from the Senate's malapportionment, which allows less populated states that tend to vote Republican to have disproportionate influence in the Senate, and hence disproportionate influence over judicial appointments. In addition, since 2000 the Republican Party has won the presidency twice without winning the national popular vote. In fact, from 1992 onward, the Republican Party has won the popular vote in a presidential election only once, in 2004.

Finally, the Republican Party has adeptly used constitutional hardball to keep the Court under conservative control. After Justice Antonin Scalia died in February 2016, Senate Republicans refused to consider any Supreme Court appointments by President Barack Obama because it was an election year. After Donald Trump won an Electoral College victory and became president, Senate Republicans eliminated the filibuster on Supreme Court appointments to push through Neil Gorsuch. After Ruth Bader Ginsburg's death in September 2020, Republicans abruptly abandoned the principle against considering Supreme Court appointments during an election year. They pushed through the appointment of Barrett on October 26, 2020, a little more than a week before the 2020 election.

Because Republicans have been laser-focused on controlling the federal courts, they have managed to create a strong conservative majority without the support of a national popular majority. The current ideological center of the court is Brett Kavanaugh, a movement-identified conservative. Kavanaugh is hardly a moderate; he is fairly far to the right of the ideological center of the country. Immediately to his left is Roberts, who is also very conservative and far from the country's ideological center. Moreover, because Republicans have sought to appoint relatively young judges who will stay on the Court for many years, the Court's ideological center will probably stay far to the right for many years to come.[23]

The Republican Party's Appointments Advantage

One might well ask why overturning *Roe* took so long when the Republican Party has dominated Supreme Court appointments for more than half a century. From 1969, when Warren retired and was replaced by Warren Burger, to September 2020, when Ginsburg died and was replaced by Barrett, the Republican Party made fifteen appointments to the Supreme Court, and the Democratic Party made only four. In fact, there was a stretch between 1969 and 1992 in which the Republicans made ten straight appointments and the Democrats made none at all.

That is an overwhelming advantage for the Republican Party. If partisan entrenchment is the best explanation for constitutional revolutions, you would think that *Roe v. Wade* would have been overturned a long time ago.

That would be the case if the Republican Party in 1969 was the same as the Republican Party now. But it is not. The Republican Party has changed considerably over the course of half a century. The 1969 version was a far more heterogeneous party than the party we see today, with many liberal and moderate elements. Supreme Court justices, who stay on the Court for long periods of time, tend to be a lagging indicator of party politics. A judge appointed in 1969 when Harry Blackmun joined the Court, or 1976, when John Paul Stevens joined, will reflect a different balance of political forces and a different set of constituencies within the party of appointment than a judge like Alito, appointed four decades later. These earlier Republican appointees were not placed on the Court to overturn *Roe*. In fact, several of them were part of the original *Roe* majority.

The Rise of the Conservative Legal Movement

There are two important events in the transformation of the Republican Party. The first is the rise of the New Right in the 1970s and the election of Reagan, who welcomed conservative Catholics and Evangelical Protestants into the party. Both of these religious groups had been suspicious of each other, and many had voted Democratic. But they found a way to make common cause in the emerging culture wars. Conservative social movements helped secure Reagan's election in 1980, and in the succeeding years the Republican Party increasingly became a movement-driven party. One of the key targets of the conservative movement, of course, was overturning *Roe v. Wade* and outlawing abortion.

The transformation of the Republican Party into a movement party did not happen all at once; it took many years to accomplish. This slow transformation is quite important in understanding the effects of partisan entrenchment. With the exception of William Rehnquist, who was a Barry Goldwater conservative, the justices appointed before Reagan became president were not movement conservatives. Many of them turned out to be moderate, like Lewis Powell, or even liberal, like Blackmun and Stevens. Even Burger, who was regarded as staunchly conservative in his own time, was, by today's standards, moderate and even liberal on many issues. For example, Burger denied that the Second Amendment protected an individual right to self-defense: he considered the claim "one of the greatest pieces of fraud, I repeat the word fraud, on the American public by special interest groups that I have ever seen in my lifetime."[24]

The second important event in shaping Republican judicial politics was the creation of the conservative legal movement, a network of conservative legal organizations, think tanks, public interest law firms, lawyers, judges, and law students, funded and supported by wealthy conservative donors, sometimes anonymously or through various intermediaries.[25] The conservative legal movement has sought to transform American law through litigation and judicial appointments.

Overturning *Roe v. Wade* has long been a central goal of the conservative legal movement. Abortion was the most prominent of many culture war issues that motivated conservatives, and it crystallized in a single issue the decline of traditional morality, increasing secularism, women's liberation, and threats to the "traditional" family. In addition the attack on *Roe* brought together many conservative beliefs about the Constitution. In *Roe* the Supreme Court had struck down dozens of state statutes on the basis of a fundamental right to abortion, which, conservatives claimed, had no basis in the text or history of the Constitution. *Roe* simultaneously symbolized the lawlessness of liberal decision-making, liberal judges' lack of judicial restraint, their opposition to democratic majorities, and their hostility to federalism. The attack on *Roe* allowed legal conservatives to promote their political goals through making claims about law, about the Constitution, and about the separation of law from politics.

The conservative legal movement employed originalism as a common language for articulating conservative claims. Conservative originalism offered a language for movement conservatives to express their political aims in the language of fidelity to the Constitution and the rule of law.[26] But judges allied with the conservative legal movement have generally invoked originalism only selectively, and mostly when it furthers the political and policy goals of the movement. When originalism does not further conservative policy goals, movement-identified justices have largely ignored originalism—for example, in many First Amendment cases.[27] As it happened, Justice Alito's decision in *Dobbs* was not originalist. It relied on doctrines about substantive due process, which most conservative originalists think is inconsistent with the Constitution's original meaning and understanding.[28]

The most famous and prominent organization in the conservative legal movement is the Federalist Society, which began as a debating society for law schools but soon morphed into a central organization for the conservative legal movement.[29] The Federalist Society offered a way for young legal conservatives to find each other and to connect with powerful and influential conservatives in law firms, government, and the judiciary. It provided a way to identify and promote rising talent, as well as a salient path for young conservatives to move up the ranks and obtain jobs and influence. Finally, the many connections the Federalist Society fostered among conservative lawyers made it easier for them to organize to influence judges and justices who were also part of the movement through litigation and amicus briefs.[30]

The Federalist Society famously does not take official positions on any question of law or policy. But it does not have to, because that is not its central goal. Its real purpose is to create a platform for conservative ideas and a network for nurturing, credentialing, and promoting conservative legal talent.

When Reagan took office in 1980, there was not a conservative legal movement in today's sense. The Federalist Society did not yet exist. Therefore, the Reagan administration and the Reagan Justice Department took on the task of creating a cadre of bright young conservative lawyers who would promote the conservative movement's causes.[31] Many prominent legal conservatives began their careers in the Reagan administration and especially in the Reagan Justice Department. For example, both Roberts and Alito were in the Reagan Justice Department, with Roberts moving to the White House Counsel's office in the Reagan administration.

Reagan was able to appoint three justices to the Supreme Court and elevate Rehnquist to chief justice. But in the early 1980s, he did not have much of a farm team of reliable movement conservatives ready to appoint. Two of his three Supreme Court appointments—O'Connor and Anthony Kennedy—were not part of the conservative legal movement.

Reagan was further hemmed in by his campaign promise to appoint the first woman justice. This limited his choices because he had to find a suitably conservative woman judge to appoint. There weren't all that many in the early 1980s, and so Reagan finally settled on an intermediate appellate court judge in Arizona, O'Connor, a westerner who cared deeply about federalism. Reagan's next appointment, Scalia, was a movement conservative and known to be staunchly pro-life. The next year, when the Court's median justice, Powell, retired, Reagan sought to appoint another movement conservative, Judge Robert Bork, to fill Powell's seat. But by that point Republicans had lost control of the Senate and the Bork nomination was defeated. Reagan had to find a replacement quickly, and after the libertarian Douglas Ginsburg withdrew, Reagan selected Kennedy, another westerner who, like O'Connor, was not a movement conservative.

Luck often plays a role in the effects of partisan entrenchment. For example, if Reagan had nominated Bork in 1986—when Republicans still controlled the Senate—and Scalia in 1987, *Roe* might have been overturned much earlier. Replacing Burger's vote with Bork's in 1986 would not have seemed to change the Court's balance of power very much. So Bork might have been appointed without difficulty. Then, in 1987, when Powell retired, Reagan could have nominated Scalia, who lacked Bork's paper record and would have been far easier to confirm. In this scenario, *Roe* would very likely have been overturned when the Court decided *Planned Parenthood of Southeastern Pennsylvania v. Casey* in 1992.[32] Unlike Kennedy, Bork would probably not have provided a fifth vote to retain *Roe*.

Another contingency of partisan entrenchment concerns who led the Republican Party after Reagan's second term as president. Reagan chose George H. W. Bush as his running mate in 1980 because he sought to balance the national ticket. Bush was not originally part of the conservative movement. Although he lived in Texas, he came from a moderate New England brand of Republican politics that gradually declined in importance as the conservative movement came to dominate the party, and the party's balance of power shifted to the South and Mountain West.

Because Bush was from a different wing of the party, installing movement conservatives on the Supreme Court was not a high priority for him. Instead, he mostly wanted to avoid political setbacks like the Bork nomination.[33] His first Supreme Court appointment, David Souter, like Bush himself, came from the moderate New England branch of the party and was increasingly seen as liberal as the Republican Party moved further to the right. Bush picked Souter mostly because he thought that, in contrast to Bork, Souter would be easily confirmable; Souter's appointment is an example of how the contingencies of politics at the moment of nomination affect partisan entrenchment. The need for confirmability also affected Bush's second Supreme Court nomination of Thomas, a D.C. Circuit judge. Thomas, unlike Souter, was a movement conservative—and eventually became a central figure in the movement. But that was not why Bush appointed him. Bush faced the problem of how to replace retiring Justice Thurgood Marshall, the Court's first African American justice and a hero of the Civil Rights Era. Bush's aides believed that the only way they could confirm a conservative justice was to nominate a Black conservative.[34]

The Triumph of the Conservative Legal Movement

Between 1980 and 1992, Presidents Reagan and Bush made five appointments to the Supreme Court. (Once again, I do not count making Rehnquist chief justice since his vote remained the same.) But of the five, only two—Scalia and Thomas—were movement-identified conservatives.

Why do I emphasize this fact? Conservative legal elites who are members of the conservative legal movement care much more about what other members of the conservative movement think than they care about what liberal legal elites think.[35] Or, to use Lawrence Baum's expression, movement conservatives are movement-identified judges' most important audience.[36] Movement-identified conservatives are much more likely to see themselves as isolated and put upon by liberal institutions that do not understand their views and do not take them seriously. Members of the conservative legal movement are also more likely to pay attention to and credit arguments and research produced by other members of the movement. Because lawyers' arguments often offer competing accounts of history, movement-identified judges and justices may be more likely to gravitate to the accounts of history offered by voices they trust.[37]

Moreover, because the conservative legal movement identifies and promotes conservative legal talent, connects like-minded individuals, and provides an important source of professional and personal validation, members of the movement have strong incentives to stay connected with and loyal to the movement's basic concerns and ideas over time, even if they disagree among themselves about particular questions.[38] Indeed, disagreements on specific issues are much less important than membership in the conservative legal movement itself and identification with its basic values and goals. Therefore, in contrast to nonmovement judges, movement-identified jurists are much less likely to become moderate or liberal over time.[39] If the views of movement conservatives evolve over time, it is likely that this is because the views of the movement as a whole are evolving, and they are influenced by these changes.

Justices Blackmun, Stevens, O'Connor, Souter, and Kennedy were all appointed by Republican presidents. But their professional identities and reputations were not formed within or connected to the conservative legal movement. So they did not have strong incentives to hew to the goals of the movement. Their views diverged from the conservative movement in many respects—and especially on abortion, an issue that was very important to the movement. In fact, by the end of their tenure on the Court, Blackmun, Souter, and Stevens were considered judicial liberals.

By contrast, Scalia and Thomas were part of the conservative legal movement from its earliest days. Their views remained tied to the goals and values of the movement as it evolved. Indeed, Thomas is now the most prominent symbol and intellectual leader of the conservative legal movement.

In 1992, the Supreme Court considered whether to overturn *Roe v. Wade* in *Planned Parenthood of Southeastern Pennsylvania v. Casey*. Of the five justices in the majority in *Casey* who voted to protect the right to abortion— Blackmun, Stevens, O'Connor, Kennedy, and Souter—all five were appointed by Republican presidents. But none were movement conservatives. The two movement conservatives—Scalia and Thomas—were in dissent. They were joined by the two original dissenters in *Roe*, Rehnquist, a Goldwater conservative, and Byron White, the Court's only remaining justice appointed by a Democratic president.

Republican dominance in Supreme Court appointments, therefore, was not enough to overturn *Roe*. What mattered was appointing members of the conservative legal movement. And this would take considerable time.

By the time Republicans won the White House in 2000, the conservative legal movement had matured. The Federalist Society had grown rapidly from a few law school chapters into a powerful professional network with multiple connections to law firms, think tanks, federal judges, and conservative donors. Equally important, there was now a much larger farm team of smart young conservatives to draw on for judicial appointments. Bush's two Supreme Court appointments—Roberts and Alito—worked as young lawyers in the Reagan administration in the early days of the conservative legal movement.

After George W. Bush's election, all Republican Supreme Court nominees would be members of the conservative legal movement. In fact, when Bush considered appointing someone who was not part of the conservative legal movement—his personal counsel, Harriet Miers—he faced enormous pushback from members of the movement, who did not regard Miers as one of their own.[40] Bush soon withdrew Miers's nomination and substituted Alito, a conservative judge who had served in the Reagan Justice Department and had strong movement credentials. This marked an important moment in the history of the conservative legal movement. Years later, when Trump ran for president in 2016, he felt that he had to assure Republican activists that his Supreme Court appointments would be reliable members of the conservative legal movement. So he took the unusual step of releasing a series of lists of potential Supreme Court candidates, vetted by the Heritage Foundation and members of the Federalist Society.[41]

Successful partisan entrenchment of movement-identified conservatives turned out to be the key ingredient in the conservative constitutional revolution that finally overturned *Roe v. Wade*. And the Supreme Court did not have a majority of movement-identified conservatives until 2018, when Justice Kennedy retired and Justice Kavanaugh joined the Court, soon to be joined by a sixth movement-identified justice, Barrett. Fifty years after Republicans began to dominate Supreme Court appointments, the Court had a majority of members of the conservative legal movement. At that point, *Roe*'s demise was more or less in the cards. The only question was whether it would be overturned slowly, as Chief Justice Roberts wanted to do, or very quickly, as Justice Alito wanted to do. As it turned out, five movement-identified conservatives wanted to move quickly. *Dobbs* was the result.

The Future of the Conservative Legal Movement

With *Dobbs*, the conservative legal movement has achieved one of its long-cherished goals, and the Court's conservative revolution is only just beginning. The next several years will probably produce multiple changes in constitutional doctrine, from affirmative action to the First Amendment.

Once the conservative legal movement has achieved many of its central goals, however, it may lose cohesion, as the country faces new issues and the Republican Party continues to evolve into a Trumpist party. Different parts of the conservative legal movement may find themselves increasingly at odds—for example, religious conservatives and secular libertarians, or conservatives who support Trump's MAGA movement and conservatives who are less enthusiastic or even opposed.

Tensions will also form within the Supreme Court's conservative majority. Movement-identified justices may begin to differ among themselves about how far to take the conservative constitutional revolution, and how far and how fast to extend the revolution's decisions. And although *Dobbs* purported to return the issue of abortion to the states, the courts will likely continue to decide multiple federal constitutional issues related to abortion. These include the right of women to travel out of state for abortions, regulation of abortion by medication, the status of in vitro fertilization, and the regulation and surveillance of pregnant women. The nation's two political parties are likely to struggle over federal laws that attempt to secure the right to abortion or that prohibit abortion nationwide. If passed, these laws will likely be challenged in the federal courts.

Equally important, once the conservative legal movement achieves its most sought-after victories, new issues will emerge for which the conservative legal movement was not organized. These new issues may create fractures among the Court's conservative majority. The best analogy is the justices appointed by Franklin Roosevelt and Harry Truman between 1937 and 1950. All of them were appointed by Democrats and all of them supported Roosevelt's New Deal. But once the New Deal's legitimacy was settled, the Court's agenda turned to new questions: criminal procedure, the incorporation of the Bill of Rights, the rights of Black people, the rights of Communists, political dissenters, and religious minorities. These became important constitutional issues in the 1940s and 1950s. The justices appointed by Roosevelt and Truman disagreed with each other on these questions—often quite bitterly—in part because they had not been put on the Court to answer them.

In the same way, justices who were placed on the Court primarily to resolve the culture war issues of the late twentieth century may disagree about the constitutional questions of the 2030s and 2040s.

Not only are the issues before the Court changing rapidly, but so is the Republican Party itself. The post-Trump version will be quite different from the party of Reagan that gave birth to the conservative legal movement. Much of the party is in thrall to Trump's false claim that the 2020 presidential election was stolen. The party emerging from the Trump presidency is an anticosmopolitan party, driven by cultural grievances and conspiracy theories, with elements of nativism, authoritarianism, and Christian Nationalism.

The Court's conservative justices, who have been drawn from the ranks of highly educated legal elites, may not embrace all of the new party's values in equal measure. Some of the conservative justices may align themselves with the new Trumpist dispensation, while others, whose careers were formed in elite legal networks, may distance themselves from it on certain questions.

For some time now, Republican Party activists have sought to limit voting rights, gerrymander districts, and challenge nonpartisan voting administration to keep Republicans from losing political power. In general, the Court's movement-identified justices have been eager to adopt narrow readings of voting rights, hamstring the federal Voting Rights Act, and defer to restrictions on the right to vote and the manipulation of the political process.[42] But at some point a few of them may begin to push back at the most egregious techniques for holding on to power.[43]

The Supreme Court and Party Coalitions

The theory of partisan entrenchment argues that large-scale changes in constitutional doctrine are shaped by the appointments process, which, in turn, is shaped by presidential elections and party coalitions. But the converse phenomenon is just as important. The doctrines that courts create can help shape—and fracture—party coalitions.

Two familiar arguments about the Court's use of judicial review contend that it is countermajoritarian, a view most famously associated with Alexander Bickel, or that it tends to reflect the dominant political forces in American politics, a view often associated with Robert Dahl and Robert McCloskey.[44]

But there is a third view, developed by Mark Graber, which seems most relevant in the case of *Roe* and *Dobbs*.[45] Graber argues that political actors have reasons to leave certain issues to courts to decide, even when politicians disagree with the decisions.

In particular, judicial decisions can make some kinds of party coalitions easier to keep together, and other kinds of coalitions more difficult to manage. That is, instead of party coalitions affecting the exercise of judicial review, the exercise of judicial review affects party coalitions. Judicial review can make it easier for a political party to maintain its base of voters; conversely, judicial review can create openings for a party's opponents to pick off its voters and split its coalition.

Party leaders hope to make certain issues—those which unite their coalition, fracture their opponents' coalition, and attract new voters—especially salient. Conversely, they want to make other issues—those which divide their coalition, unite their opponents, and cause the party to lose voters—less salient. In other words, party leaders usually want politics to be about the issues that strengthen their coalition and keep it together, and not about the issues that divide and weaken it.[46] Sometimes this puts them at odds with party activists and donors, who want to win on certain issues regardless of the effects on the party's coalition of voters.

Courts play an important role in this process. They do more than simply uphold laws or strike them down, forbid things or permit them. Courts structure the set of available choices that politicians have in making laws that courts will uphold and enforce.

Court decisions place some policies on the table as constitutional and others off the table. For example, before *Brown v. Board of Education*,[47] both racial segregation and racial integration were available policy choices. Both were on the table. After *Brown*, racial segregation became (officially at least) off the table. Before the Court's New Deal revolution, certain kinds of labor and economic regulations were off the table. After the New Deal revolution, they were on the table.

In addition to changing the *scope* of what politicians may do, courts also change the *salience* of certain issues. Court decisions can raise or lower the salience of particular political issues that affect party coalitions. A controversial decision can raise the salience of an issue regardless of how it is decided, either because it opens up new opportunities for legislation or because it gives politicians a convenient reason to attack the courts. Conversely, once courts settle an issue in one way or another, it can lower the salience of the issue, because politicians decide to move on to other subjects. The important point is that courts do not make issues salient simply by their own actions. Rather, politicians use the opportunities created by judicial decisions to make certain issues salient or to switch to other topics and controversies.

Abortion is a good example. Abortion did not become the flashpoint it is today immediately after *Roe* was decided. Rather, the New Right later seized on abortion as a central issue and figured out how to use it to attract both Catholics and Evangelical Protestants to the Republican Party.[48] *Roe* created an opportunity to make the issue of abortion central to American politics, but it was political actors who decided to make it central, thereby causing the two political parties to divide over abortion beginning in the late 1970s.

Judicial review affects both the scope of permissible legislative action and the salience of particular issues. How are these two dimensions related? You might think that if an issue is off the table, politicians might not want to make it salient because there is nothing they can do about it. But often politicians may want to run on an issue that the courts have taken off the table because it allows them to blame the courts for the state of the country. Moreover, politicians may actually *prefer* that courts have taken a certain issue off the table. If the issue were on the table, having to decide what to do about it might split their coalition.

Consider this last point in the context of *Roe v. Wade*.[49] The Republican Party is a collection of people with different ideologies and interests. It includes people who are very strongly pro-life and want to prohibit all abortions with no exceptions for health, rape, or incest. There are other members of the party who are pro-life but who want these kinds of exemptions. There are still others who want some degree of access to abortion, say, in the first twelve weeks or so, and there are some who are essentially pro-choice.

Even though the Republican Party is officially a pro-life party, all of these people have been able to vote Republican because *Roe v. Wade* took abortion prohibition off the table. No matter how much politicians catered to the most strongly pro-life parts of their base, people understood that courts would strike down laws eliminating the right to abortion. Republican politicians could chip away at the abortion right, but they couldn't actually outlaw abortion completely. This meant that voters who supported other parts of the Republican agenda—lower taxes, less regulation, strong national defense, restrictions on immigration, opposition to affirmative action, opposition to social programs for the poor, and so on—could still vote Republican secure in the knowledge that the party's politicians would not destroy a right they wanted protected.

In this way, *Roe v. Wade* helped form the modern Republican coalition.[50] It was the Supreme Court opinion the G.O.P. loved to hate. It allowed strongly pro-life voters to be in the same party as people who voted Republican for other reasons.[51] In fact, Republican politicians could have the best of both worlds. They could chip away at abortion rights or make symbolic gestures and gain plaudits from their most strongly pro-life constituents. But chipping away at the right to abortion was not as salient as getting rid of the right entirely, so it did not endanger their coalition.

Dobbs changed this calculus. Now that *Roe v. Wade* is gone, complete prohibitions of abortion are on the table. Politicians can vote for any regulations they like. What *Dobbs* did not do is lower the salience of abortion as a political issue. Quite the contrary, abortion is as salient an issue as ever, especially for more moderate Republicans and for independents.

The fact that abortion prohibition is now on the table and remains highly salient will place different parts of the Republican coalition in tension with each other. The staunchest pro-life advocates will demand complete prohibition with no exceptions (other than perhaps a clear and immediate threat to the mother's life). Previously, Republican politicians could cater to this part of the party without much consequence. But following *Dobbs*, pro-life forces may demand that politicians put up or shut up and enact complete or near-complete bans.

Other parts of the party may regard these laws as harsh or extreme. Moreover, new pro-life abortion restrictions may be badly drafted or unclear, leading to horror stories about women whose lives and health are ruined because hospitals are uncertain about their potential liability for terminating pregnancies under new abortion restrictions.

These new laws and their consequences in human suffering may alienate some independents and Republican voters. Yet if Republican politicians announce that they will take a more moderate position on abortion, they risk being attacked by the most fervent elements of the party, who are among the most vocal and active, and—perhaps more to the point—who play an outsized role in the primary voting that selects Republican candidates for office.

Republican politicians are now caught between a rock and a hard place, trying to find language and positions that will keep as many people as possible in their electoral coalition while continuing to placate the hardline constituents who control the primary process.

For this reason, Republican politicians may seek to downplay abortion as an issue, trying to make it less salient to voters, even though previously they had strong incentives to trumpet their pro-life bona fides. Republican politicians may eliminate mention of abortion from their campaign literature and advertisements, or adopt increasingly ambiguous language making it unclear what kinds of abortion regulations they actually support. Democratic politicians, by contrast, may now find it useful to make abortion a highly salient issue in politics. They will try to portray Republican politicians as staunchly pro-life and extreme because they think it may split apart the Republican coalition and allow Democrats to pick off enough voters to win close elections.

Meanwhile, Republicans who are moderate on abortion issues and Republican-leaning independents must decide whether they will continue to support a party that now is able to push for extreme measures on abortion. In response, these voters may leave the party, vote for non-Republican candidates, or not vote at all.

What was true of *Roe* in 1973 is also true of *Dobbs* in 2023. The Court's decisions do not create or destroy coalitions all by themselves. They merely create opportunities for politicians of different parties to attack existing coalitions or create new ones. They do not foreordain the electoral results. Much will depend on the voting population in particular states, the agility of politicians and party donors, and whether other issues displace abortion from the public's attention. But the general tendency of *Dobbs*, at least at the outset, will be to pressure and shrink the Republican coalition.

Political decisions are always made in the shadow of other institutional features of the American constitutional system, including judicial review. Politicians respond to the political environment they find and attempt to use and alter that environment to gain office and stay in power. The Court's decisions affect political coalitions, but that is because of decisions made by political actors over whom they have no control. Supreme Court decisions may make or break political coalitions, but not as the justices either understand or intend.

6

Some Realism about Precedent in the Wake of *Dobbs*

Michael W. McConnell

Dobbs v. Jackson Women's Health Organization[1] involved the most divisive issue in American public life: abortion. Roughly a third of the population regard abortion as the taking of innocent human life, to be permitted only under the gravest of circumstances; roughly a third of the population regard the right to abortion as essential to the autonomy and equality of women; and roughly a third are somewhere in between, favoring some restrictions and recoiling from the extremes. Ordinarily, such a question would be resolved through legislative debate, compromise, and vote, as in other democratic nations, but in the United States it has been governed for the past fifty years by *Roe v. Wade*.[2] *Roe* is without doubt the most enduringly controversial decision in the history of the Court—controversial not only because of divisions over the underlying moral question but also because the legal reasoning of the *Roe* opinion was exceptionally weak. Even supporters of an abortion right as a matter of policy have found the *Roe* opinion difficult to defend,[3] and most have retreated to a smorgasbord of alternative constitutional theories never tested, let alone adopted, by the Court.[4]

The political explosion that followed the *Dobbs* decision was mostly about the pros and cons of an abortion right, a genuinely wrenching issue with powerful moral claims on both sides. But it also presented itself as a debate about the usually obscure legal doctrine of stare decisis, a shortened form of the Latin legal maxim *stare decisis et quieta non movere* (to stand by the decisions and not to disturb what is settled).[5] The respondents' brief began with, and spent most of its pages on, precedent, with little attempt to show that *Roe* was correct as an original matter.[6] Editorial writers, politicians, activists, and many others professed to be shocked—*shocked!*—that the Court finally did what dissenting justices and outside critics have been demanding for years: overrule *Roe v. Wade* and return the issue of abortion to

Michael W. McConnell, *Some Realism about Precedent in the Wake of* Dobbs In: *Roe v. Dobbs*. Edited by: Lee C. Bollinger and Geoffrey R. Stone, Oxford University Press. © Oxford University Press 2024.
DOI: 10.1093/oso/9780197760352.003.0006

the democratic processes of the states. The dissenting justices in *Dobbs* told the public that the Court had "discarded" the principle of stare decisis.[7] The very legitimacy of the Court is said to be in question.

The actual doctrine of stare decisis is far less rigid than the dissenters and their supporters let on. Scarcely a year goes by when the Court does not overrule one or more cases, usually without much commotion. The Supreme Court has never treated precedent as anything close to untouchable. Twenty-two times in recent years the Court has commented that stare decisis is not an "inexorable command."[8] The Court has stated that stare decisis, though "tending to consistency and uniformity of decisions," is "entirely within the discretion of the court."[9] *Planned Parenthood v. Casey* is lauded (in some quarters) for its reaffirmation of *Roe*, but in fact it overruled much of the earlier decision's specific holdings. Moreover, the Court has repeatedly said that stare decisis is "at its weakest" in cases of constitutional interpretation,[10] a view that goes back at least to Justice Louis Brandeis if not earlier.[11] Justice Lewis Powell—no radical, he—wrote that it was the Court's "*duty* to reexamine a precedent where its reasoning or understanding of the Constitution is fairly called into question."[12] The strong view, espoused by the *Dobbs* dissenters, is almost always found in dissents. Much of the rhetoric about stare decisis in *Dobbs*, on and off the Court, was overblown.

We are in serious need of realism about precedent.

How Strong Is Precedent, Really?

There are at least three forms in which the "doctrine" of stare decisis occurs, and they must not be confused. One involves the obligation of inferior courts to follow precedents set by courts above them in the hierarchy. This, which may be called "vertical stare decisis," is the strictest form. It is essential to the achievement of uniformity in the interpretation of national law, which is the foremost purpose of the federal judiciary. It is enforced through appeals and reversals. A second form, which may be called "cross-jurisdictional stare decisis," involves consideration by courts of precedents set by parallel courts in other jurisdictions. This is the weakest form. Cross-jurisdictional precedent is not binding and carries force only by power of persuasion. The third form is stare decisis within a court, over time, the practice of continuing to adhere to past decisions even when the current court may not be persuaded that that past decision was correct when made. This is the most contested version of stare decisis and is the version at issue in *Dobbs*.

Even within this category, there are variations. In the federal courts, the decision of a district court does not bind other district judges even in the same district, though as a matter of practice such precedents are usually followed. At the appellate level, courts of appeals are free to overrule circuit precedent by vote of the full en banc court. Because en banc proceedings are inconvenient and time-consuming, this is a natural check in favor of precedent unless the reasons for overruling are genuinely powerful. There is no need for a "doctrine" of stare decisis under those circumstances. Only in the Supreme Court, which always sits en banc, is the "doctrine" of stare decisis a matter of contention. In the Supreme Court, there is no enforcement mechanism for stare decisis (or indeed for adherence to any other legal principle)—no requirement of going en banc and no prospect of reversal. Stare decisis is purely a matter of comity within the Court.

On the surface, precedent is by far the dominant mode of interpretation in Supreme Court opinions and briefs. Virtually every Supreme Court decision cites precedent, often dozens of them. Whether precedent is genuinely constraining is harder to know. A lot of citations to precedent are window dressing. Moreover, precedents are most often followed because the Court regards them as correct, or at least as not wrong, or as producing acceptable results even if not analytically sound. Professor Michael Gerhardt, author of *The Power of Precedent*, writes that there is no "clear evidence" that precedents "*ever* have forced the Court into making a decision contrary to what it would rather have decided."[13] It is easy to find cases where individual justices agree to follow a precedent they think was wrongly decided—when the effects are nonharmful or unimportant, or when they do not have the votes to overrule. I am not sure there are any cases where justices have adhered to a precedent (1) that they regard as wrongly decided, (2) that they regard as having significant harmful consequences, and (3) where a majority shares their view. Very often, even if the justices do not expressly overrule a precedent with which they disagree, they fail to follow it, offering unpersuasive grounds for distinction or even simply ignoring it.

To be sure, there is a "doctrine" of stare decisis, which consists of a nonexclusive list of "factors" that are typically taken into consideration when a justice decides whether to vote to overturn a precedent. These are surprisingly cross-ideological. There is no apparent difference between the factors stressed by conservative justices and those stressed by progressive justices.

It is widely agreed that, other things being equal, a decision should be left in place unless it is not merely wrong but egregiously wrong; if it has engendered reasonable reliance, which is especially powerful in cases involving property law and contract law; if it has been repeatedly reaffirmed by a variety of judges over time; and if it has been embraced by the political branches and been treated as the predicate for legislation and executive action. Similarly, it is widely agreed that precedents have less force if they involve constitutional rather than statutory or common law interpretation; if they have proven unworkable in application or have been eroded by subsequent decisions; if the factual circumstances bearing on the decision are perceived to have changed; or if there have been strong dissents, and especially if those dissents persist over time. Perhaps most powerful, though not usually listed, is the justices' perception of real-world consequences. Justices are usually willing to leave even a demonstrably erroneous precedent in place if it does not matter, or if the effects are benign—and not otherwise.

Unfortunately, although these factors are transideological in the abstract, they are highly malleable and can be deployed in different ways in any particular case. Their application is heavily influenced by the same sorts of jurisprudential and ideological currents that lead to disagreement about other legal materials. It is almost never possible to say, in a contested case, that the factors objectively point in one direction or the other. One scholar writes, "[T]he modern doctrine of *stare decisis* is essentially indeterminate. The various factors that drive the doctrine are largely devoid of independent meaning or predictive force."[14] Arguments about stare decisis thus almost always map onto arguments about the merits.

If the "doctrine" of stare decisis provides scant constraint, the principal force behind stare decisis is some combination of the Court's reputational interest in not appearing to change its mind too often and any influence that may come from comity/mutuality. As discussed below, the comity/mutuality point has worn thin in these hyperpartisan days. The reputational interest point, though, appears strong, even if not strong enough to prevail in cases of particular importance to one side or the other (or both), like *Dobbs*. Observationally, it seems evident that the Court as an institution perceives a cost to overruling and therefore overrules relatively rarely. It may sound flip, but I think the Court has an unconscious—maybe even a conscious—"budget" for overruling: one or two cases a year. To avoid exceeding that budget, the Court reserves its overruling for what the majority regards as the most important matters in that year. In the past term, the Court overruled

Roe v. Wade but refrained from overruling *Employment Division v. Smith* or the *Chevron* doctrine, to mention two examples of doctrines that very likely no longer command the assent of a majority of the Court. Interestingly, although the Court in substance overruled *Lemon v. Kurtzman*,[15] and the dissenters asserted it did so,[16] the opinion for the Court conspicuously refrained from uttering the word "overruled," and the Library of Congress did not include it on the list it keeps of cases overruling precedents.[17]

However skeptical one might be about the "doctrine" of stare decisis, the *practice* of stare decisis thus turns out to be surprisingly stable across time. In the past ten years, according to the tally kept by the Library of Congress, the Court explicitly overruled fourteen cases. That is not a large number, especially compared to the number of mistaken past decisions that would be overruled if all that mattered was whether they were wrong. In the ten years before that, the Court overruled . . . fourteen cases. (Are we getting a sense of the overruling "budget"?) In the ten years before that, the Court overruled a somewhat larger number: nineteen—still fewer than two a year. The practice of stare decisis is alive and well. It is just not a doctrine. It does not tell the justices which precedents should be overruled. It is an inclination or disposition—a presumption, or a thumb on the scales—rather than a rule of law. The only truly common, predictable, and reliable "factors" are that justices vote to overrule when they think the prior decision was both clearly wrong and harmful.

Arguments for a Presumption, but Only a Presumption, of Following Precedent

The plain fact is that the Supreme Court makes mistakes, though it may take decades to recognize them. Some of these wreak grievous harm on the nation and its constitutional ideals. They scream out for correction. Others, while less consequential, do damage to the economy, the administration of justice, the protection of civil liberties, or other important national values. In every other field of human endeavor—*ex cathedra* pronouncements of the pope excepted—the correction of error is seen as natural, necessary, and unavoidable. It would be strange indeed for the Court to adopt a strong principle against correcting mistakes.

On the other hand, error correction has its costs. When precedents are overruled, this generates uncertainty and instability in the law. The possibility that legal interpretations will change reduces the predictability and consistency that are hallmarks of the rule of law. The idea of stare decisis thus serves, properly, as a powerful *presumption*. Just how powerful cannot be expressed in words or "doctrine." It will depend on the norms of the particular nine human beings who make up the Court. The single most important determinant, as discussed below, is mutuality: justices are most likely to abide by precedents they think wrongly decided if other justices do the same. Aside from rejection of the extremes—no overrulings and no respect for precedent—there is no right or wrong about the balance.

In the heat of the *Dobbs* reaction, it may seem heretical to say so, but no one—left, right, or center—should wish for a strong rule of stare decisis. Justice Brandeis famously commented, "Stare decisis is usually the wise policy, because in most matters it is more important that the applicable rule of law be settled than that it be settled right."[18] It is not often noted that he quoted this aphorism in an opinion in which he advocated *overruling* the applicable precedent. It surely is true that in many matters it is more important that the issue be settled. But the opposite is also true: in many matters it is more important that the issue be settled right. Ask yourself, on the assumption that you do not know which way precedent points: Is it better that the abortion question be settled correctly (meaning the way you think it should be decided), or that we stick with a decision made fifty years ago by justices who had never previously given the issue much thought? If *Roe* had come out the other way, how many of the Court's critics would now be demanding that the Court follow stare decisis? *Lawrence v. Texas* and *Obergefell v. Hodges* both overruled precedent that was squarely on point, without worrying about the stare decisis "factors," simply because majorities came to believe that the precedents were grievously wrong.

There are four principal arguments in favor of adhering to precedent. First and most important, following precedent is necessary for the rule-of-law values of consistency, stability, and predictability. If every judge felt free to adopt the interpretation he or she regarded as best, without regard for what other judges are doing (and indeed, without regard to what the judge's own court had done in the past), litigants would face a mass of inconsistent, changing, and unpredictable decisions.

Second, stare decisis is a defining feature of our legal system. It is the way we do things. As Professor Henry Monaghan, a wise man, put it, "Precedent is, of course, part of our understanding of what law is."[19] In this sense, stare decisis in some form is supported by originalist evidence that when the

people established a judicial branch, they understood that following precedent is one of the practices that is constitutive of being a "court." Alexander
Hamilton famously wrote in *The Federalist*, No. 78, "To avoid an arbitrary
discretion in the courts, it is indispensable that they should be bound down
by strict rules and precedents, which serve to define and point out their duty
in every particular case that comes before them."

Third, stare decisis might tend toward better substantive results. Judges,
being human, are fallible, but an interpretation reached by many judges over
a long period of time is more likely to be correct than the best effort of any
particular judge or of one court at any particular point in time. Professor
David Strauss, the leading academic theorist of what he calls "common
law constitutionalism," argues that precedent-based constitutional interpretation develops "over time, not at a single moment; it can be the evolutionary product of many people, in many generations." Its legitimacy stems
from its "evolutionary origins and its general acceptability to successive
generations."[20]

Finally, sometimes precedents become embedded in the way our society conducts itself; they gain a democratic (or republican) warrant when
legislatures and executives embrace them and act on the supposition that
they are true.

These are good reasons, but they support only a moderate view of precedent. It is true that the rule of law requires that courts enforce the same interpretation of the Constitution in like cases. Those rule-of-law concerns
strongly support vertical stare decisis—the requirement that lower courts
follow the precedents set by higher courts—but they provide little support
for the idea that the Supreme Court should have a heavy presumption against
overruling its own past decisions. An explicit overruling provides as clear
and uniform a rule as a reaffirmation.

Indeed, the Court's reluctance to overrule cases is one of the principal
causes of doctrinal inconsistency. When faced with precedent they do not
wish to follow, but when unwilling (or unable to get the votes) to overrule,
the justices typically distinguish the precedent, often on lame or spurious
grounds. This leaves in place two essentially inconsistent lines of precedent,
leaving lower court judges free to choose the line they prefer. For example, in
Washington v. Glucksberg, the Court held that substantive due process claims
of unenumerated rights must be "objectively, deeply rooted in this Nation's
history and tradition."[21] But in *Lawrence v. Texas*, the Court ignored that
holding (without overruling, indeed without even mentioning *Glucksberg*),[22]

which meant that lower courts could decide substantive due process claims on the basis of history and tradition, or not, as they wished. *Bivens*[23] is repeatedly distinguished rather than followed, leaving lower courts in a quandary.[24] The same treatment has been given to *J. I. Case v. Borak*.[25] In the Establishment Clause area, the Court played this game for almost forty years, drawing so many incomprehensible lines and distinctions that a lower court called the Court's cases "a vast, perplexing desert."[26] It took several square overrulings to bring consistency to the field.[27] Abortion jurisprudence is rife with these inconsistencies. I defy anyone to reconcile the two partial-birth abortion decisions, *Gonzalez* and *Stenberg*.[28]

This suggests, paradoxically, that open overrulings are sometimes more faithful to the values and purposes of stare decisis than strained distinctions and sub silentio disregard of applicable precedent. A serious doctrine of stare decisis would hold that if a legal interpretation adopted in a prior case would apply in the case now before the Court, the Court is obliged either to follow it, to overrule it and state the reasons why, or to candidly limit it in some intelligible fashion. If the Court is not willing actually to follow an applicable precedent, it would be better to overrule it than to pretend to comply with stare decisis and merely distinguish it. That way, lower courts, legislatures, executive officials, and citizens would know what the law is. The Court's reluctance to bite the stare decisis bullet is, paradoxically, one of the most significant causes of doctrinal uncertainty.

Similarly, it is true that following precedent is a constitutive feature of our system of adjudication, one that is blessed by the authority of *The Federalist*. But this can carry us only as far as past practice establishes that precedent is followed. If, through our history, precedent has often been ignored or overruled, then "our practice" is one of only presumptive stare decisis. From a very early time, error correction has been seen as a legitimate basis for overruling erroneous precedents. In his influential *Commentaries on American Law*, first published in 1826, Chancellor James Kent wrote that "the judges are bound to follow that decision so long as it stands unreversed, unless it can be shown that the law was misunderstood or misapplied in that particular case."[29] He described stare decisis as a "presumption in favor of [the prior decision's] correctness." Justice Brandeis took a similar view. Indeed, until abortion rights became the dominant issue, it was hard to find justices who espoused the more rigid view. Viewed realistically, "our practice" cannot support a strict version of the doctrine.

The theory that stare decisis helps to weed out incorrect from correct interpretations by the process of evolutionary development by many judges over time makes a great deal of sense, but Supreme Court adjudication is not evolutionary. Unlike common law development, which occurs across many courts and jurisdictions, the modern doctrine of stare decisis makes a single decision of the Supreme Court—even if reached by a 5–4 majority and even if contrary to past interpretations—binding the day it is handed down. This modern doctrine is not Darwinian or Burkean but positivist. It assumes that the Constitution is what a current majority of the Supreme Court says it is. There is no test of time. Strauss's theory of common law constitutionalism, based on the ideal of incremental change over long periods of time, bears no resemblance to this positivist reality. If we wanted a genuinely evolutionary system of constitutional adjudication, we would allow judges to make up their own minds about the wisdom of decisions, until enough time had passed and enough judges had concurred to establish a consensus. This evolutionary process would include overruling mistaken decisions, since there can be no evolution and no self-correction without it. Extinction is an essential part of evolution.

Finally, it is also true that some precedents have gained democratic warrant by virtue of becoming embedded in legislation and executive action. A familiar example is the Court's expansive interpretation of the Commerce Power. Even if one were to conclude those interpretations were incorrect as an original matter, it is too late in the day to correct the mistake. Too much of modern statutory law rests on them. If precedents gain democratic warrant by legislative acceptance, however, it would seem equally true that precedents lose democratic warrant by legislative resistance. But the Court in *Planned Parenthood v. Casey* attempted to tell us that when its decisions encounter resistance, that is all the more reason for the Court to dig in its heels.[30] That makes little sense.

The Lesser Role for Stare Decisis in Constitutional Cases

Since at least the time of the New Deal, the Court has held that stare decisis has lesser force in the context of constitutional law, if it applies there at all.[31] This is not a change wrought by the modern Court or by the conservative justices. In *Smith v. Allwright*, a key voting-rights case from the New Deal era, the Court held that "[i]n constitutional questions, where correction depends upon amendment and not upon legislative action this Court throughout its history has freely exercised its power to reexamine the basis of its constitutional decisions."[32] Justice Brandeis, the progressive lion, wrote that "in cases involving the Federal Constitution, where correction through legislative action is practically impossible, this Court has often overruled its earlier decisions."[33] The decade between 1935 and 1945 probably saw more overrulings of more significant lines of precedent in more different areas of constitutional law than any other time in our history. For a more recent example, Justice Ruth Bader Ginsburg wrote or joined twenty-four majority opinions overruling past decisions and thirteen dissents calling for the overruling of decisions relied on by the majority.[34]

The usual reason given why constitutional precedents have lesser force than cases of statutory interpretation is that it is very difficult to amend the Constitution, while Congress can correct decisions involving statutory interpretation by amending the statute. There is force to this argument, though perhaps it is overstated. Statutory correction is far from easy. More important, the status of the Constitution as our highest law suggests that a judge's conscientious interpretation of the document must take precedence over past interpretations if they are seriously wrong. As Justice William O. Douglas observed, "it is the Constitution which [a justice] swore to support and defend, not the gloss which his predecessors may have put on it."[35] The Constitution was deliberately made difficult to change; it would be odd if the justices could effectively make an amendment by five votes and their successors would be unable to return to the original.

The strong view of stare decisis is not consistent with any major school of thought regarding constitutional interpretation. Originalism is based on the idea that the Constitution should be interpreted, as nearly as possible, to mean what it meant to those who had authority to adopt or amend it. Prudence may incline even an originalist justice not to disturb a long-standing precedent abruptly (as in *Dobbs*), but over the long haul precedent must necessarily take a back seat to the original meaning of the constitutional text.

It is sometimes said that originalist judges have a particular obligation to follow precedent because precedent was part of judicial practice at the time of the Founding. One variety of originalism, called "original methods originalism," holds that the Constitution should be interpreted today in the manner in which it would have been interpreted at the Founding (as opposed to being interpreted according to the meaning it would have been understood to have at that time).[36] And indeed, the Court very rarely overruled past decisions in the early years of the Republic. This is not a convincing argument. For the most part, the early Court was writing on a clean slate; only occasionally did precedent loom large in constitutional interpretation. Chief Justice John Marshall sometimes did not bother to cite precedents even when they would be supportive. For a conspicuous example, in *Marbury v. Madison*, he did not cite *Hylton v. United States*, a clear example of constitutional judicial review some seven years before *Marbury*.[37] Moreover, it took decades before the Court first had to deal with the prospect that its precedents may have been wrong. When that happened, possibly for the first time, Chief Justice Roger B. Taney wrote (in dissent) that the Court's "opinion upon the construction of the Constitution is always open to discussion when it is supposed to have been founded in error, and that its judicial authority should hereafter depend altogether on the force of the reasoning by which it is supported."[38] There is no particular reason for originalists—more than anyone else—to take a strong view of stare decisis.

The so-called Living Constitution approach to interpretation is equally inconsistent with a strong view of stare decisis. Living Constitutionalism interprets the words and concepts of the Constitution in accordance with present-day needs and understandings, as perceived by the judge. It seems obvious that if a past decision conflicts with the judge's perception of present-day needs and understandings, the precedent should be discarded. There is no more logical reason to adhere to the decisions of past courts than there would be to adhere to the understandings of long-dead framers and ratifiers. Indeed, to the extent that Living Constitutionalism is associated with the progressive left, which advocates sweeping changes in our social and political arrangements, one would expect to see more departures from precedent than from conservatives, with their ostensible attachment to the status quo and to slowing the pace of change.

Common law constitutionalism, as explicated by Strauss, at first blush appears more in line with stare decisis, because it is based on incremental change over long periods of time. But a strong view of stare decisis would prevent change, incremental or otherwise, and the evolutionary approach requires change. Thus, even a common law constitutionalist justice (if there were one) would treat precedent as only presumptively authoritative, much like the other two methodologies. To be sure, common law constitutionalism, if practiced faithfully, would be minimalist, but that is not the same as stare decisis. A minimalist judge decides a case on the narrowest convincing ground and seeks to avoid rapid and large changes in doctrine.

Thayerian deference to political institutions, like the other approaches, is orthogonal to stare decisis. Some precedents defer to the decisions of executives and legislatures, and some do not. A Thayerian would be disposed to follow the former and correct the latter. *Roe v. Wade* is an especially conspicuous example of the latter.

Each of the methodologies must come to grips with the pragmatic and prudential value of adhering, most of the time, to precedent—but for each, following precedent sacrifices the purity of the jurisprudential approach. Perhaps we should think of stare decisis as a foot on the brake, keeping originalist and living constitutionalist judges alike from moving too fast, too soon. The point is that for none of them is precedent a natural constitutive element; all rely on a vision of constitutional interpretation that is at odds with following old cases because they are on the books.

Stare Decisis and the Pace of Change

Even if the Court is not strictly bound to manifestly erroneous interpretations a majority no longer shares, it does not follow that they will necessarily overrule the old cases abruptly. The nation may need time to adjust. Thurgood Marshall and the NAACP Legal Defense Fund did not try to convince the Court to uproot *Plessy v. Ferguson* root and branch at the first opportunity, but instead undermined the decision bit by bit over a long period of time.[39] The first signs that the Court was dissatisfied with *Lemon v. Kurtzman* appeared as early as 1980, but it took another forty years of fits and starts for the doctrine finally to be interred. The most disquieting feature of the *Dobbs* decision was not its abandonment of *Roe*, but the decision of the Court to do it in one leap. The "undue burden" test of *Casey* had appeared to offer a gradual off-ramp from the extremes of *Roe*, but it never developed into a coherent middle-ground position, and indeed in *June Medical*, the Court appeared to be moving back in a more absolutist direction. Then came *Dobbs*.

Dobbs may give the appearance of returning the nation to where we would have been if *Roe* had not been decided, with state legislatures able to enact laws in accordance with the various shades of opinion around the country. But a U-turn is rarely the same as never taking the problematic route to begin with. As Justice Ginsburg famously commented, *Roe* interrupted a process of reconsideration of abortion law that was then underway,[40] which might well (we can only speculate) have produced laws somewhere between the poles of prohibition and abortion on demand. *Roe* profoundly affected American politics, as it did the process of judicial nomination and selection. By promising judicial invalidation of any state enactment impinging on the abortion right, *Roe* liberated politicians on the pro-life side of the spectrum to advocate prohibitory laws with the knowledge that those laws would not be enforced, and thus without facing serious political repercussions. There was no political incentive for moderation. On the other side, *Roe* accustomed supporters of abortion to think of it as a fundamental right and not as a matter of difficult moral trade-offs. This made any middle-ground policy seem to be an offense against principle. (Much the same seems to be occurring with respect to guns.) *Roe* also nationalized the abortion issue in an unhelpful way, rendering it possible to have national pro-choice or anti-abortion laws passed by Congress if and when one party or the other gains control of the House, Senate, and presidency.

It is a sign of the polarization of American politics—and increasingly, American jurisprudence—that Chief Justice John Roberts's concurring position attracted not a single other vote, and indeed that not a single one of the 130-plus amicus briefs in the case had a good word to say for it. It is particularly noteworthy that justices like Elena Kagan and Stephen Breyer, who are often amenable to middle-ground positions that might ward off a more decisive change in constitutional doctrine, did not move in that direction. The tenor of the pro-*Roe* amici and the dissenting opinions seemed to discourage rather than encourage moderation on the part of the majority.

Roberts's approach—to uphold Mississippi's fifteen-week limit on late abortions but leave the broader question to a later day—would have given state legislators some breathing room to explore approaches to abortion law that might command a broader base of assent. True, it likely would have been a waystation toward eventual overruling of *Roe*, but in other areas of constitutional law the Court has seen the virtue of proceeding by smaller steps.

The Most Important Determinant of the Strength of Stare Decisis Is Mutuality

As already noted, in the lower courts stare decisis is enforced through procedural mechanisms such as requiring an en banc proceeding to overrule circuit court precedent or nearly guaranteed review and reversal for refusing to follow Supreme Court precedent.[41] At the Supreme Court level, there are no external enforcement mechanisms. The force of precedent comes only from each justice's perception that overruling too many decisions too fast will undermine their collective institutional credibility, along with the constraints of comity and mutuality. When one side believes that the other side will not hesitate to overrule decisions they do not approve of, the constraint of mutuality will be at their weakest. At this particular juncture in the Supreme Court's history, there is very little mutuality. After *Dobbs*, the constraint will be weaker still.

Looking at precedent through the lens of game theory, stare decisis is a game of *tit-for-tat*.[42] When both sides accommodate the other, tit-for-tat can produce periods of stability, which in this context would mean periods with high regard for precedent on both sides. But when one side offends, the other side cannot be expected to continue to cooperate; indeed, it would be foolish to do so. When a prior system of mutual cooperation breaks down, both sides tend to blame the other. It is always possible to point to more or less convincing reasons why one's own transgression was justifiable, but the effect is predictable: tits follow tats, and vice versa, with each response requiring less in the way of special justification, until some exogeneous force inspires a new negotiation of terms.

No doubt there are other candidates for when the current round of mutual distrust began, but I nominate 1985, when Justice Harry Blackmun, the author of *Roe*, provided the fifth vote to overrule *National League of Cities v. Usery*,[43] a federalism decision that Justice William Rehnquist regarded as one of his most important achievements. Blackmun had voted with Rehnquist in *Usery*, and nothing had changed except that Blackmun shifted allegiance from one wing of the Court to the other. (This is not to say there weren't good reasons to overrule *Usery*, but there always are.) The tone of Rehnquist's dissent made it clear that any hesitation he might have had to overrule Blackmun's favorite decision had been erased. Prior to 1985, Rehnquist and most of the Court had generally been precedent followers. Thereafter, Rehnquist and his allies on the Court voted repeatedly to overrule *Roe*.

In the past few decades, the abortion issue has been the most salient battleground over stare decisis, with the result that the progressive wing has been more rhetorically supportive of stare decisis. During confirmation hearings, Democratic senators grill Republican nominees about their commitment to stare decisis, hoping to get them to commit to not overrule *Roe*. In terms of actual results, however, overrulings in the past century have come from both left and right. Whenever the current composition of the Supreme Court is more conservative than the Court in the past, liberals are advocates of precedent, and whenever the composition is more liberal than in the past, conservatives take that role. Justices on both the right and the left offend against the principle of stare decisis when they have the opportunity, which does not stop some of those same justices from waxing indignant when the other side so offends. Arguments about stare decisis are thus fraught with hypocrisy and should be received with a degree of cynicism.

The professions of shock over the overruling of *Roe* were heavily inflected with this sort of selective indignation. Just about everyone who bemoaned the overruling of *Roe* would be happy to overrule decisions they feel were wrongly decided. How long would *Heller, Citizens United, Shelby County, Parents Involved*, capital punishment, *Rucho*, or *Hobby Lobby* survive a 5–4 progressive majority?

Consider the issue of capital punishment. The Court has held in dozens of cases that capital punishment is not categorically unconstitutional under the Eighth Amendment. Yet over the years, some of our most esteemed justices have persisted in voting to overrule these precedents. Among them was Justice Breyer, who was a dissenter in *Dobbs*. It is easy to understand why Breyer and others (including my former employer, Justice William J. Brennan) took this position: capital punishment is a question of life and death, the enormity of which outweighs the pragmatic benefits of adhering to precedent. The *Dobbs* dissenters think the same of abortion.

Capital punishment is not the only issue where progressives openly espouse the overruling of precedents they disagree with. Just this term, Justice Sonia Sotomayor declared that recent Establishment Clause decisions were, in her opinion, wrongly decided, and voted not to follow those precedents.[44] The liberal/progressive icon Justice Ginsburg voted to overturn precedent with some frequency, commenting simply that "stare decisis is not an inexorable command."[45] Hillary Clinton, running for president, made the overruling of *Citizens United* a plank of her platform.[46] Liberal/progressive legal academics do not hide their intention to promote the overruling of the many conservative decisions they dislike, as soon as they have the power to do so. Professor Mark Tushnet, whose credentials as a leader of the liberal/progressive movement in legal academia cannot be disputed, let the cat out of the bag when Justice Antonin Scalia died and he believed President Barack Obama would name a replacement. Here is what he wrote:

Liberals should be compiling lists of cases to be overruled at the first opportunity on the ground that they were wrong the day they were decided. My own list is *Bakke* (for rejecting all the rationales for affirmative action that really matter), *Buckley v. Valeo* (for ruling out the possibility that legislatures could develop reasonable campaign finance rules promoting small-r republicanism), *Casey* (for the "undue burden" test), and *Shelby County.* . . . Others will have their own candidates. What matters is that overruling key cases also means that a rather large body of doctrine will have to be built from the ground up.[47]

Tushnet may have been more candid than is typical, but when conservatives hear this kind of talk from the left, they are entitled to suspect that stare decisis will not be a two-way street. It is no wonder that the conservative justices in the *Dobbs* majority decided the abortion question as they thought it should be decided, without worrying overmuch about what their decision would do to stare decisis.

The only reliable generalization is that when the majority on the Court shifts from one side to the other, as it has very recently, the new majority will engage in more overrulings and their counterparts will resist them. Because of the liberal/progressive slant of academia and the news media, we do not hear much anguish about stare decisis when there is a liberal/progressive majority, but that does not mean that stare decisis is honored more often when they are in control. In the end, the *Dobbs* decision should be regarded as persuasive or unpersuasive on the merits of its constitutional arguments.

PART IV
CLOSE READINGS OF *DOBBS*

7

The *Dobbs* Gambit

Gaslighting at the Highest Level

Khiara M. Bridges

In *Dobbs v. Jackson Women's Health Organization*, the Court upheld
Mississippi's fifteen-week abortion ban and, in the process, overturned *Roe
v. Wade*.[1] One of the most striking features of the majority opinion in *Dobbs*
is its commitment to the pretense that it is a "neutral" decision, taking no
particular side in the contentious debate over the propriety and legality of
abortion.

The majority's most explicit articulation of its faithfulness to the idea of
its own neutrality occurs when it chides the dissent for observing that the
majority's reasoning in the case imperils other fundamental rights. The
dissenting opinion, authored by Justice Stephen Breyer, argues that the
majority's method of constitutional interpretation—by which the Due
Process Clause of the Fourteenth Amendment is construed to protect only
those rights that were recognized or enjoyed at the time that the amendment was ratified in 1868—calls into question many of the cases upon
which *Roe* relied, as well as several cases that were decided subsequent
to *Roe*. Specifically, the dissent contends that *Dobbs* imperils *Griswold
v. Connecticut*[2] and *Eisenstadt v. Baird*,[3] which recognized a right to access
and use contraception, as well as *Lawrence v. Texas*[4] and *Obergefell v. Hodges*,[5]
which recognized the right to consensual same-sex sexual contact and the
right to marry someone of the same sex, respectively. The dissent is right,
of course. In 1868, governments did not protect a right to access contraception. As the dissent convincingly observes, "The majority could write just
as long an opinion showing, for example, that until the mid-20th century,
'there was no support in American law for a constitutional right to obtain
[contraceptives].'"[6] Neither did governments in 1868 recognize a right to engage in consensual same-sex intimacy or the right to marry a person of the
same sex. Indeed, LGBTQ people were subjected to punishment, censure,

Khiara M. Bridges, *The* Dobbs *Gambit* In: *Roe v. Dobbs.* Edited by: Lee C. Bollinger and Geoffrey R. Stone,
Oxford University Press. © Oxford University Press 2024. DOI: 10.1093/oso/9780197760352.003.0007

and erasure until very recently in our nation's history. As such, the dissent is correct that divining the scope of the Constitution's protections by looking to the nation's practices in the mid-nineteenth century jeopardizes the Court's decisions in *Lawrence* and *Obergefell* as well.[7]

The *Dobbs* majority argues that the dissent errs by suggesting that *Griswold, Eisenstadt, Lawrence,* and *Obergefell* are appropriately analogized to *Roe,* proposing that the dissent raises the question of the continued legitimacy of those cases because it may disingenuously seek to "stoke unfounded fear that our decision will imperil those other rights."[8] The majority contends that *Griswold, Eisenstadt, Lawrence,* and *Obergefell* are not analogous to *Roe* insofar as the right to access contraception, the right to engage in same-sex intimacy, and the right to marry a person of the same sex do not implicate the destruction of fetal life, which is part and parcel of the right to terminate a pregnancy. The majority argues that the dissent's claim that the right to an abortion is in any way *like* the rights recognized in *Griswold, Eisenstadt, Lawrence,* and *Obergefell* reveals that the dissent believes that fetal life has no significance; according to the majority, it reveals that the dissent's interpretation of the Constitution would embrace and embody this conviction about the (non)value of fetal life.

The majority contends that interpreting the Constitution to reflect any idea about the value of fetal life is incorrect. It claims that it will not commit this error—an error that the seven justices who signed the majority opinion in *Roe* also committed. It proclaims that "[n]othing in the Constitution or in our Nation's legal traditions authorizes the Court to adopt that 'theory of life.'"[9] It announces that, unlike the *Roe* majority opinion and the *Dobbs* dissenting opinion, the majority's own "opinion is not based on any view about if and when prenatal life is entitled to any of the rights enjoyed after birth."[10] In essence, the majority proposes that it will be atheoretical, embracing no "theory of life." It will be neutral.

This idea runs beneath Justice Brett Kavanaugh's concurring opinion—which repeats "neutral" or a variation of the word thirteen times over the course of twelve pages.[11] Kavanagh argues that on the question of the moral significance of the fetus and the consequences that the fetus's moral status should have on the ability of the person gestating the fetus to decide whether or not to carry the pregnancy to term,

[t]he Constitution is neutral and leaves the issue for the people and their elected representatives to resolve through the democratic process in the

States or Congress. . . . Instead of adhering to the Constitution's neutrality, the Court in *Roe* took sides on the issue and unilaterally decreed that abortion was legal throughout the United States up to the point of viability (about 24 weeks of pregnancy). The Court's decision today properly returns the Court to a position of neutrality and restores the people's authority to address the issue of abortion through the processes of democratic self-government established by the Constitution.[12]

However, the *Dobbs* majority certainly embraces a "theory of life," its protestations to the contrary notwithstanding. Littered throughout the majority opinion is the language of those who consider themselves champions of fetal life—those who believe that life begins at, or shortly after, conception. Indeed, even *before* the majority opinion begins, the reader confronts this language. The syllabus, which is longer than most, contains a reference to an "abortionist"[13]—a term that abortion opponents have deployed to deny that those who provide abortion care are highly trained, credentialed medical providers.[14] The majority opinion goes on to reference "abortionist" three additional times.[15] The usage of a term that tends to be used only by those who oppose abortion is not a demonstration of the absence of a theory respecting life. It is not a demonstration of "neutrality." Instead, it reveals the political and ethical commitments that motivate the majority.

Another revelation of the *Dobbs* majority's stance on the question of when life begins occurs when the opinion describes a dilation and evacuation abortion procedure, albeit briefly.[16] This tactic, designed to illicit disgust for abortion care, is one that Justice Anthony Kennedy once employed, first in a dissent in *Stenberg v. Carhart*,[17] and then as the author of the majority opinion in *Gonzales v. Carhart*.[18] As others have noted, many medical procedures—from rhinoplasty to open-heart surgery—can seem "barbaric"[19] when described in graphic detail.[20] It seems apparent that the *Dobbs* majority insists upon describing the dilation and evacuation procedure, which it renders as involving the "crush[ing] and tear[ing of] the unborn child,"[21] because it endeavors to depict abortion as gruesome or brutal. This is not a rhetorical move that someone who is "neutral" on the moral status of the fetus and the propriety of abortion would embrace. Instead, it is a rhetorical move that those who oppose abortion and abortion rights have long deployed.

The majority opinion also references "wombs" a dozen times.[22] In telling contrast, there is not one mention of a "uterus." Thus, the majority intentionally eschews the more dispassionate language of medicine and science, instead embracing terminology that is designed to invoke a particular emotional reaction to reproductive organs and the fact of pregnancy. Further, while there are many mentions of the "fetus" and "fetal" life, there are also numerous references to "unborn human being[s]" and "unborn child[ren]," terms that are far from neutral.[23] Further still, the majority opinion includes a long description of the fetus's biological development that is contained in the challenged Mississippi act[24]—a strategy that opponents of abortion and abortion rights have long used to make the argument that the fetus is the moral equivalent of a baby, and that, consequently, abortion is the moral equivalent of murder.

In this way, it seems plain that the *Dobbs* majority embraces a particular "theory of life." Thus, its disagreement with the justices who joined the *Roe* majority and *Dobbs* dissent is not that they embraced a "theory of life" when they ought to have eschewed one, but rather that they embraced a different "theory of life" than the one that the justices in the *Dobbs* majority preferred. Had the *Dobbs* majority been truthful, it would have admitted this. Instead, it chose dishonesty.

If the majority believed it appropriate, or even necessary, to use the language of those who believe themselves to be champions of fetal life, it might have attempted to achieve some semblance of neutrality in its opinion by *also* identifying the myriad harms that occur when governments seek to protect fetal life by forcing birth. That is, a Court committed to being as neutral as possible in the abortion debate might have articulated the position that abortion is a morally objectionable act—an articulation that the *Dobbs* majority achieves through the rhetorical moves that it undertakes—alongside an acknowledgment of the harms that are inflicted when safe and legal abortion is made unavailable. Quite tellingly, the majority opinion makes no mention of these harms—quite likely because it believes that they are insignificant or nonexistent.

Although the *Dobbs* majority thought them unworthy of mention, the harms attendant on the forced continuation of an unwanted pregnancy and forced birth are immense. To begin, the experience of an unwanted pregnancy is deeply painful—sometimes physically, but invariably mentally and emotionally.[25] In an amicus brief submitted in *Thornburgh v. American College of Obstetricians and Gynecologists*, the National Abortion Rights Action League centered the experiences of those who carry unwanted pregnancies in their argument that the Court ought to reaffirm *Roe*.[26]

The brief quoted women who described themselves as "terrified" by the fact of their unwanted pregnancies.[27] Another woman stated, "It is difficult to adequately describe the difference between a wanted and an unwanted pregnancy. It is sometimes like the difference between darkness and despair, and light and joy."[28] One woman explained:

> Today I am a little more than two months pregnant. My husband and I are thrilled about it. Almost exactly a decade ago, however, I learned I was pregnant, and my response was diametrically opposite. I was sick in my heart and I thought I would kill myself. It was as if I had been told my body had been invaded with cancer. It seemed that very wrong.[29]

Beyond the emotionally excruciating experience of an unwanted pregnancy and the physical trauma of being compelled to give birth, researchers have documented that the people who are denied abortions have poorer social outcomes than those who are able to terminate an unwanted pregnancy. People who carry pregnancies to term unwillingly are more likely to remain in poverty than those who access abortion care.[30] Years after being denied an abortion, they are more likely to lack money for essentials like food and shelter.[31] They are also more likely to remain in violent relationships.[32]

Further, criminalizing abortion exacerbates existing inequality. That is, people with privilege will always be able to access safe abortion. This was true before the Court decided *Roe* in 1973.[33] It remains true after *Dobbs*. However, those who are able to access abortion in a country that permits states to criminalize the procedure tend to be people who have some degree of privilege.[34] In a nation where *Dobbs* is the law of the land, those who can legally terminate unwanted pregnancies are those who either live in a jurisdiction where abortion is permitted or those who can travel to such a place. The individuals in the latter group are not the most marginalized among us. They can afford the costs of travel. They can afford to take time off from work or to forgo the wages that they might have earned. They can afford childcare. Moreover, they do not have to hide their whereabouts from an abusive partner or parent. They do not have a physical or mental disability that makes travel difficult or impossible. They are not undocumented, and they can freely move past immigration checkpoints without fear of detention and deportation.

Thus, the criminalization of abortion produces a distinct sociological injury. It is one in which those with privilege have the ability to access the healthcare that they need and, in so doing, control the content and trajectory of their lives; meanwhile, those without privilege are forced to attempt to terminate their pregnancies without the assistance of trained and licensed healthcare providers[35]—a strategy that was nothing short of horrific for many of the millions of people who undertook it annually in the pre-*Roe* era[36]—or to give birth against their will.

The *Dobbs* majority opinion mentions none of the harms, only sketched above, that are inflicted when governments are permitted to make abortion care illegal. In this way, the majority's decision to use the language of those who position themselves as defenders of fetal life, while at the same time taking absolutely no notice of the concerns that motivate those who insist that abortion services be safe and legal, gives the lie to its declaration of its own neutrality.

However, if we are completely honest, we will admit that no majority or plurality opinion—even those that ultimately protected abortion rights—has ever provided an adequate accounting of the harms that governments exact when they force pregnant people to give birth. In *Roe* itself, the majority opinion contained an exceedingly limited discussion of the harms of forced birth, observing:

> The detriment that the State would impose upon the pregnant woman by denying this choice altogether is apparent. Specific and direct harm medically diagnosable even in early pregnancy may be involved. Maternity, or additional offspring, may force upon the woman a distressful life and future. Psychological harm may be imminent. Mental and physical health may be taxed by child care. There is also the distress, for all concerned, associated with the unwanted child, and there is the problem of bringing a child into a family already unable, psychologically and otherwise, to care for it. In other cases, as in this one, the additional difficulties and continuing stigma of unwed motherhood may be involved.[37]

The discussion of the injury inflicted when individuals are forced to give birth was even more constrained in the plurality opinion in *Planned Parenthood v. Casey*, which affirmed what it called the "central holding" of *Roe*.[38] There, the plurality observed:

> The mother who carries a child to full term is subject to anxieties, to physical constraints, to pain that only she must bear. . . . Her suffering is too intimate and personal for the State to insist, without more, upon its own vision

of the woman's role, however dominant that vision has been in the course of our history and our culture.[39]

Indeed, it appears that the *Casey* plurality attempted to achieve the appearance of neutrality through relating the positions of both sides of the abortion debate. It describes the perception that abortion is an "act of violence against innocent human life"[40] while at the same time defending the ability of people to terminate a pregnancy if they believe it is in their best interest to do so. It describes the view that pregnancy is a "wonder of creation" that "ought to be welcomed and carried to full term no matter how difficult it will be to provide for the child and ensure its well-being."[41] And then it describes the view that "the inability to provide for the nurture and care of the infant is a cruelty to the child and an anguish to the parent."[42]

But it is important to observe that even if the *Dobbs* majority opinion had taken pains to describe the positions of those on both sides of the abortion debate—an approach that the *Casey* plurality opinion takes—*Dobbs* still would not have been a neutral, atheoretical decision. *Dobbs* embraces the theory that a pregnant individual's desire to control what happens to their body and their life is not more significant than their fetus. The theory is that a pregnant person can be subordinated to the fetus that they gestate. This is not the absence of a theory. This is not an example of a Court that is being "scrupulously neutral" in a national controversy.[43] In the context of abortion, there is no neutral position. The *Dobbs* Court has taken the position that the fetus can be prioritized over the person who gestates it.

Importantly, it is not a demonstration of neutrality to interpret the Constitution in this way.[44] When the Constitution contains a guarantee of "liberty"—and when there is a hundred years of precedent interpreting this term to protect the individual from state intervention in matters involving the family, as well as close to fifty years of precedent interpreting this term to protect the individual right to terminate a pregnancy—it is not neutral to interpret that term as silent on the question of abortion rights. Instead, it is an interpretive act that permits the Court to take a side in the abortion debate. The Court has sided with those who believe that it is acceptable to force birth.

We then might ask why. Why did the five justices who signed the majority opinion feel the need to announce that they are being neutral when they reverse half a century of precedent regarding a contentious social issue—even when only the most naïve and/or gullible will believe their protestations about their neutrality? It seems reasonable to conclude that the answer likely involves a concern about the Court's continued legitimacy.

We have been asked to pretend that the judiciary is the apolitical branch of our government—even while we observe that the composition of the Court is subject to the most political of contests. We observed Senator Mitch McConnell's refusal to hold Senate hearings on Merrick Garland's nomination to the Supreme Court in order to prevent the appointment of a liberal justice who, among other things, would be likely to vote to affirm *Roe*.[45] We observed that one of Donald Trump's many campaign promises during his bid for the presidency was that if elected, he would appoint justices to the Court who were willing to overturn *Roe*,[46] and we knew that Justice Neil Gorsuch was confirmed by only fifty-four votes—after McConnell abolished the filibuster for Supreme Court nominees—because Democratic senators recognized that Gorsuch was a fulfillment of that campaign promise.[47] We observed the bitter fight over Justice Kavanaugh's confirmation to the Court, knowing that he secured only one Democratic senator's vote in his favor, not solely because credible allegations of sexual assault had been made against him[48] but also because Democratic senators knew it was likely that he would vote to overturn *Roe* if given the opportunity. We observed the hasty nomination and confirmation of Justice Amy Coney Barrett after Justice Ruth Bader Ginsburg's death some six weeks before the 2020 presidential election, knowing that Republicans sought to install a conservative supermajority on the Court that would be willing to shape the country in line with its vision, including on the issue of abortion.

And so we know that the Court's decision in *Dobbs* is a political strategy coming to fruition. It is made possible by politics.[49] It is the materialization of political commitments. That *Dobbs* is an act of political will, of course, calls the legitimacy of the Court—squarely affixed in the purportedly apolitical branch of government—into question.

Justice Sonia Sotomayor raised this issue during oral arguments in *Dobbs*. She observed that the sponsors of the Mississippi bill said quite openly that they sought to raise the immediate challenge to *Roe* "because we have new justices on the Supreme Court."[50] If the Court accepts the invitation to overturn *Roe*, she asked, "[w]ill this institution survive the stench that this creates in the public perception that the Constitution and its reading are just political acts? I don't see how it is possible. . . . If people actually believe that it's all political, how will we survive? How will the Court survive?"[51]

The *Dobbs* majority's declaration of its neutrality suggests that this is how it thinks the Court will survive. It will survive by declaring that it is atheoretical when a theory clearly informs it. It will survive by asserting that political commitments do not motivate it when they obviously do. It will survive by proclaiming things to be true that evidence unambiguously disputes.

In this way, the Court demonstrates that it shares a key feature with the shape that the Republican Party has taken in the past five years: mendacity. This is more than the observation that one of the most obviously dishonest presidents in the history of the country appointed three of the nine justices on the Court at the time that *Dobbs* was decided.[52] Instead, it is an observation that one of the most striking features of the Republican Party of the past half-decade is its method of incessantly repeating falsehoods until millions of people believe them to be true.

We observed this in the manufactured culture war over what the Republican Party called "Critical Race Theory." Although Critical Race Theory had existed for forty years as an advanced legal theory that interrogates the relationship between law and racial inequality, the Republican Party used the term to refer to a "Marxist" philosophy, capable of being taught to kindergartners, that proposed that white people were inherently and inevitably racist.[53] The Republican Party repeated this lie about what "Critical Race Theory" is and proposes so many times that significant numbers of those who belong to the Republican Party—representing tens of millions of people—are convinced that this falsehood is true.

Perhaps even more devastating, significant factions of the Republican Party have repeated the treacherous, democracy-destabilizing lie that the 2020 presidential election was stolen from Trump. The lie has been retold so many times that despite the fact that all the evidence suggests the 2020 election was overwhelmingly secure and there was no significant voter fraud, millions of people currently believe that Trump actually defeated Joe Biden in the election.

Numerous other examples might be recounted. They all show that it has been an effective strategy for the Republican Party to continuously repeat a statement that is demonstrably untrue; over time, significant numbers of people will believe in the truth of the thing. This strategy appears to be on display in the *Dobbs* majority opinion. Now, this should not be read to argue that the *Dobbs* majority consciously adopted the strategy. Instead, it is simply an observation that analogous rhetorical formations have developed within the Court and the larger, obviously political sphere in which the Court is embedded.

Some will find convincing the *Dobbs* majority's declaration of the atheoretical nature of its analysis and its practiced neutrality in the abortion debate. Undoubtedly, scores of observers, from lay persons to serious scholars—quite likely including some of those who consider themselves supporters of abortion rights[54]—will assess the opinion as a neutral interpretation of the Constitution. They will point to it as an exemplar of dispassionate legal reasoning, appropriately contrasted to the motivated reasoning on display in *Roe*. In essence, the *Dobbs* majority's gambit will work—a demonstration of gaslighting at the highest level.

8

Dobbs and the Travails of Due Process Traditionalism

Cass R. Sunstein *

Due Process Traditionalism

The Court's opinion in *Dobbs v. Jackson Women's Health Organization*[1] offers a distinctive understanding of the meaning of the Due Process Clause of the Fourteenth Amendment. In short, the *Dobbs* majority is committed to *due process traditionalism*. That commitment is the engine for the Court's ruling, which overrules *Roe v. Wade*.[2] For the future of constitutional law, it is also the most important feature of the *Dobbs* opinion.

The Court urges that while the Due Process Clause "has been held to guarantee some rights that are not mentioned in the Constitution," its reach is limited to rights that are (1) "deeply rooted in this Nation's history and tradition" *and* (2) "implicit in the concept of ordered liberty."[3] The Court emphasizes that the very idea of "substantive due process," by which the Due Process Clause extends beyond procedural guarantees, "has long been controversial."[4] (By itself, the text of the clause might be taken to suggest a purely procedural interpretation.)[5] At the same time, the Court acknowledges that its decisions have protected two categories of substantive rights. Both categories are, in the Court's view, to be understood directly by reference to tradition.

The first category consists of rights guaranteed by the first eight amendments. The Due Process Clause has long been understood to "incorporate" most of those rights; the Court takes the relevant cases as given. The second category consists of "a select list of fundamental rights that are not mentioned anywhere in the Constitution."[6] According to the Court, this list is limited to those that are deeply rooted in tradition and essential to our nation's "scheme of ordered liberty."[7] Noting that "the Constitution makes no mention of abortion,"[8] the Court emphasizes that for purposes of evaluating *Roe*, the second category—the "select list"—is the relevant one.

Cass R. Sunstein, Dobbs *and the Travails of Due Process Traditionalism* In: *Roe v. Dobbs.* Edited by: Lee C. Bollinger and Geoffrey R. Stone, Oxford University Press. © Oxford University Press 2024.
DOI: 10.1093/oso/9780197760352.003.0008

But crucially, the Court urges that the analysis of the two categories is *essentially the same*. In the context of incorporation, the Court's decisions involving excessive fines and the right to keep and bear arms paid exceedingly close attention to practices at the time of ratification, and thus the Court rooted its incorporation holdings in "relevant historical evidence."[9] With respect to incorporation itself, this is a form of due process traditionalism.[10] In the Court's view, "it would be anomalous if similar historical support were not required when a putative right is not mentioned anywhere in the Constitution."[11]

This is a key claim, and the *Dobbs* Court is not the first to offer it. Similar ideas have occasionally played a role in several of the Court's rulings.[12] In the *Michael H.* case, Justice Antonin Scalia, for a plurality, argued that consultation of specific traditions—that is, traditions understood at a low level of generality—ensures that judges will remain faithful to "the society's views."[13] Justice Scalia urged that the problem with general readings of traditions is that they provide "such imprecise guidance, they permit judges to dictate rather than discern the society's views."[14] And if judges are not bound "by any particular, identifiable tradition," they are not bound by the "rule of law at all."[15] The Court notes that in refusing to recognize a right to assisted suicide in the *Glucksberg* case, the Court had emphasized that such a right was not "objectively, deeply rooted in this Nation's history and tradition."[16] There is a direct line from the plurality opinion in *Michael M.* to *Glucksberg* to *Dobbs*, and at least some of the incorporation cases support the central idea. (Notably, *Glucksberg* seemed, until *Dobbs*, to be a failed effort to entrench due process traditionalism, an outlier superseded by *Lawrence* and *Obergefell*; *Glucksberg* is back.)

According to the *Dobbs* Court, one reason for limiting the term "liberty" in these ways is that the term is "capacious," and there is a "natural human tendency to confuse" what the Fourteenth Amendment "protects with our own ardent views about the liberty that Americans should enjoy."[17] With that point in mind, "the Court has long been 'reluctant' to recognize rights that are not mentioned in the Constitution."[18] Unless it respects "the teachings of history," the majority notes, the Court could well fall "into the freewheeling judicial policymaking that characterized discredited decisions such as *Lochner v. New York*."[19] Due process traditionalism is an alternative to a freewheeling Supreme Court.

Does the abortion right find support in "relevant historical evidence"? According to the *Dobbs* Court, it does not. Until late in the twentieth century, "there was no support in American law for a constitutional right to obtain an abortion."[20] In every state, "abortion had long been a crime."[21] The common law made abortion "criminal in at least some stages of pregnancy," and in the 1800s, American law "expanded criminal liability for abortions."[22] When the Fourteenth Amendment was adopted, "three-quarters of the States had made abortion a crime at any stage of pregnancy, and the remaining states would soon follow."[23] The *Dobbs* Court offers a great deal of detail in an effort to support these historical claims.

Consequences and Implications

Thus far, then, the *Dobbs* Court's approach to the Due Process Clause seems reasonably straightforward (and theoretically ambitious). The Due Process Clause does not protect a substantive right unless the purported right can claim support from deeply rooted traditions *and* is essential to ordered liberty as the United States has long understood it. Some rights might claim support from tradition but might not be essential to ordered liberty; consider, as possible examples, the right to eat catfish, the right to box, and the right to cut down trees. If, by contrast, a state prohibited heterosexual marriage or imposed on married (heterosexual) couples a limit of one child per family, we might be able to say that it was violating the Due Process Clause as the Court understands it.

For the Court's argument, the largest challenge comes from an assortment of cases purporting to protect "intimate and personal choices" that are "central to personal dignity and autonomy."[24] These are hard to square with due process traditionalism.[25] Consider the following:

1. the right to marry a person of a different race
2. the right to live with one's grandchildren
3. the right to use contraceptives within marriage
4. the right to obtain contraceptives within or without marriage
5. the right to allow one's young children to be educated in a language of one's choice
6. the right to send one's children to private schools
7. the right not to be sterilized without one's consent
8. the right to engage in private, consensual sexual acts
9. the right to marry a person of the same sex.

Are these rights protected by the Due Process Clause? To put it gently: under the method suggested in *Dobbs*, the answer is not clearly yes. In each case, it would be necessary to ask about the teachings of history *and* about ordered liberty as this Nation has understood it.

For consensual sexual acts and same-sex marriage, at least, history's teachings do not seem to support a substantive right under the Due Process Clause. With respect to racial intermarriage and living with one's grandchildren, it cannot be said that American history speaks plainly in favor of a constitutional right under the Court's approach. Due process traditionalism fits uneasily with a large number of rulings.

Perhaps with these challenges in mind, the Court does not attempt to show that prior holdings are, in fact, supportable by reference to an inquiry into traditions and ordered liberty.

Instead, the Court urges, the relevant cases did not involve "the critical moral question posed by abortion."[26] The reason is that they did not involve "potential life" or an "unborn human being."[27]

This is a gesture in the direction of a minimalist opinion, and of course the claim is *true*. But why, exactly, is it *relevant*? The central thrust of the Court's opinion is theoretically ambitious. It is *not* that the interest in protecting unborn human beings, or the rights of unborn human beings, outweighs, or might reasonably be taken to outweigh, the right to choose; it is that under the framework of due process traditionalism, the right to choose does not fall in the category of presumptively protected interests.[28] I will return to this issue.

In a gesture toward a degree of modesty, the Court accepts, (only) for purposes of argument, the proposition that the scope of the Due Process Clause, in its substantive form, might not be defined by reference to the specific practices of the states at the time that the Fourteenth Amendment was ratified. (Again: But why?) Accepting that assumption for purposes of argument, the *Dobbs* Court emphasizes that abortion is nothing new, that "the fundamental moral question that it poses is ageless," and that no "new scientific learning calls for a different answer to the underlying moral question."[29] In this light, the Court concludes, *the only question is whether restrictions on the right to choose abortion are rational.* This is of course a critical conclusion; under "rational basis" review, legislation is nearly always upheld. The doctrinal consequence, maximalist in nature, is that if a purported right does not qualify as presumptively protected under the tradition/ordered liberty test, a state is nearly always entitled to act as it chooses.

To be sure, the state must have legitimate reasons for imposing restrictions. In the context of abortion, those legitimate reasons include "respect for and preservation of prenatal life at all stages of development," as well as "the preservation of the integrity of the medical profession" and "the protection of maternal health and safety."[30] In that light, the Court finds it straightforward to uphold the Mississippi law at issue in the case.

The Court's opinion thus (1) offers due process traditionalism as the framework for understanding the protection of substantive rights under the Due Process Clause, (2) seeks to preserve existing substantive due process holdings except those involving abortion, and (3) subjects abortion restrictions to rational basis review. The Court aims to accomplish (2) by emphasizing that abortion involves a unique moral question. That is fair enough. But when we focus on (1), we immediately see that some or many of the existing substantive due process holdings are exceedingly vulnerable. And if we focus on (3), we immediately see that if a purported right is not supported by the tradition/ordered liberty framework of (1), then it is subject only to rational basis review (and as just noted, it will almost certainly be upheld).

For example, it would not be easy to argue that bans on same-sex marriage are irrational as that term is standardly understood in constitutional law. Return to the list above.

Would *anything* on that list constitute a right, under due process traditionalism, whose infringement would be struck down under rational basis review as it is now understood? (Short answer: Probably not.)

It follows that the *Dobbs* Court's efforts to preserve existing substantive due process holdings are unsuccessful. If those holdings survive, it is because they are "grandfathered," for one or another reason.[31]

Common Law Constitutionalism?

The Court is intensely concerned with the problem of judicial discretion. The Court does not want courts to seize on the capacious word "liberty" to entrench their own preferred understandings of the concept. For those who share that concern, "originalism" might seem to be the right solution. But the Court's opinion is emphatically not originalist. To be sure, the draft does make a strong gesture toward *textualism*: "Constitutional analysis must begin with 'the language of the instrument,' which offers a 'fixed standard' for ascertaining what our founding document means. The Constitution makes no express reference to a right to obtain an abortion, and therefore those who claim that it protects such a right must show that the right is somehow implicit in the constitutional text."[32] Still, the Court devotes essentially no attention to the original public meaning of the Due Process Clause, or to the original understanding of its framers and ratifiers. It is possible that due process traditionalism would emerge from the relevant history, or perhaps that privileges or immunities traditionalism would so emerge, but the Court does not defend that conclusion. In this light, the endorsement of due process traditionalism is best seen as a form of common law constitutionalism, with a large dose of Burkeanism and Thayerism. That is a compressed claim that requires some explanation.

First: The *Dobbs* opinion can be seen as a form of common law constitutionalism in a broad sense, at least if we understand that idea capaciously, and to authorize a measure of pluralism. It is a form of common law constitutionalism insofar as it works hard with, and attempts to preserve, existing precedents (with the exception, of course, of those relating to abortion). The Court devotes much more space to prior Supreme Court cases than to the understanding of the Due Process Clause at the time of ratification. (In fact the Court spends no time on the understanding of the Due Process Clause at the time of ratification.) At the same time, the common law constitutionalism of *Dobbs* is pluralistic insofar as it includes references to the text, historical practice, precedent, broader constitutional values, and institutional capacities. (If we see common law constitutionalism as an alternative to pluralism, *Dobbs* is best seen as pluralistic.)[33] *Second*: The *Dobbs* opinion is Burkean insofar as it emphasizes national traditions and deplores moral theorizing.[34] It is proudly and self-consciously backward-looking with respect to the definition of liberty. This is of course due process traditionalism.[35] *Third*: The opinion is Thayerian insofar as it emphasizes the need to give a wide berth to the judgments of the political process. A constant preoccupation of the opinion is the risk that, unmoored from traditions, judges will be giving liberty the content they like, and so depriving the political process of the authority to make moral judgments.

Regrettably, we need one more -ism: Dworkinism. Ronald Dworkin famously argued that in law, interpretation involves "fit" and "justification." Judges need to fit the existing legal materials, and within the constraints of fit, they need to put those materials in the best constructive light. The Court aims to do that, which means that it might be approved or criticized on the ground of either fit or justification. (As we have seen, it is not perfect on grounds of fit.) Notably, however, Dworkin also believed that the Supreme Court should be a "forum of principle" in American government. He was no Burkean. Can a Dworkinian be a Burkean? Absolutely.[36] The *Dobbs* Court demonstrates the point.

Options

Consider the following understandings of the Due Process Clause (the list is not exhaustive):

1. The Clause is purely procedural; it protects no substantive rights at all.
2. The Clause is largely procedural, but it has a substantive dimension insofar as it includes substantive protection of the first eight amendments. Otherwise it is not substantive.
3. The Clause is largely procedural, but it includes substantive protection of the first eight amendments and also includes substantive protection of unenumerated rights that were widely understood as fundamental at the time of ratification, and that were taken to be fundamental in the particular sense that they were essential to ordered liberty. This is, of course, the understanding in the Court.
4. The Clause is substantive as well as procedural, and for purposes of both substance and procedure, the concept of "liberty" is not frozen in time. It develops in common law fashion. The development is principled, but it is not backward-looking, or at least, it is not *exclusively* backward-looking.

With respect to the Court in *Dobbs* and *Roe* and *Casey*, the contest is between (3) and (4). To be sure, one could embrace (4) while also thinking that *Roe* and *Casey* are wrong.

How shall we choose among the four alternatives? To answer that question, we need a theory of interpretation. If we are originalists, the choice among competing views is largely historical. What was the original public meaning of the Due Process Clause? To say the least, the answer to that question is disputed. The topic is complicated by the Privileges or Immunities Clause. We might be keenly interested in a purely procedural reading of the Due Process Clause and insist that the Fourteenth Amendment's substantive clause is the Privileges or Immunities Clause. But what are the privileges or immunities? On that question, we might again have a contest between a view that would be close to (3) and one that would be close to (4).[37] This point was recognized in the Court by way of footnote, where it is urged that even if the Privileges or Immunities Clause is the proper source of substantive rights, those rights "would need to be rooted in the Nation's history and tradition."[38] Hence (3).

How should the contest between (3) and (4) be resolved? Originalists might be able to give an answer. But imagine that we are not originalists and that we think the choice must be defended not by reference to history but as a matter of principle.[39] Suppose that we believed, with reason, that long-standing traditions are excellent, or excellent enough, and that judicial judgments, with respect to the content of "liberty," are highly unreliable; suppose too that we believed that democratic thinking about that concept will broaden it over time, when it deserves to be broadened. If so, we should endorse (3) and reject (4). Or suppose we believed, with reason, that long-standing traditions are not excellent, or excellent enough, in the sense that they will not include certain practices within the domain of "liberty" that deserve to be so included; that judicial judgments, with respect to the content of liberty, are likely to be reliable; and that democratic thinking will sometimes fail to protect liberty when it ought to be protected. If so, we would favor (4) and reject (3). In insisting on "the forum of principle," Dworkin himself favored (4) on roughly that ground.[40]

In my view, he was correct, and the arc of American history supports his view. To see why, note that the choice between (3) and (4) depends on a long-standing contest between Burkeans, who emphasize the importance of respecting long-standing traditions, and non-Burkeans, who turn longevity against them. Those who reject Burke urge in response that *we are the ancients*. They believe in progress on multiple fronts. Hence Pascal:

> Those whom we call ancient were really new in all things, and properly constituted the infancy of mankind; and as we have joined to their knowledge the experience of the centuries which have followed them, it is in ourselves that we should find this antiquity that we revere in others. They should be admired for the results which they derived from the very few principles they possessed, and they should be excused for those in which they failed rather from the lack of the advantage of experience than the strength of reasoning.[41]

Bentham spoke in similar terms, urging that "the wisdom of times called old" is in reality "the wisdom of the cradle."[42] One version of this idea is that we know much more about facts. We create vaccines. We produce cell phones and electric cars. We build airplanes and laptops.

Another version of this idea is that there is moral progress. We have learned a few things about liberty and equality. It is true that even if we believe that (and we should), we need not think that Supreme Court justices (consisting of a small group of not-young lawyers) should be authorized to understand the Constitution to incorporate their own assessment of what they think we have learned, or of what they have learned. But Supreme Court justices live in society, and perhaps we might agree that some forms of moral progress are legitimately introduced, by them, into judgments about basic rights. (I believe that.) At the very least, a commitment to (4), and a rejection of (3), must depend on a belief of that general sort.

Consider, then, an alternative to due process traditionalism, also with foundations in existing law: the Due Process Clause gives substantive protection to a certain category of interests, which qualify as presumptive rights because they are so fundamental to self-determination. The right not to buckle one's seatbelt does not fall within that category. The right to use contraceptives and the right to live with one's grandchildren do. The list of rights that fall within the protected category is to be developed cautiously, but it is not frozen and closed. It depends on the relevant arguments, and on questions of principle.[43] (On this view, *Roe* might be right, though one can embrace this view without *necessarily* thinking that *Roe* was right; that question turns on the legitimacy and importance of protecting prenatal life.)

What the Constitution Mentions

This statement in *Dobbs* is true: "[T]he Constitution makes no mention of abortion."[44] It is also true that the Constitution makes no mention of the following:

1. blasphemy
2. libel
3. false statements of fact
4. incitement
5. sedition

6. obscenity
7. commercial advertising
8. expenditures on political campaigns
9. the nondelegation doctrine
10. school prayer
11. one person, one vote
12. the right to vote[45]
13. segregation
14. education
15. sex discrimination[46]
16. affirmative action
17. injury in fact
18. regulations that diminish the value of property.

This is a list of just a few of the things that the Constitution does not mention that have been taken to give rise to serious constitutional challenges, and in many cases to invalidation of state or federal legislation. The *Dobbs* opinion raises a fundamental question: How are we to think about such cases,[47] which are emphatically non-Burkean and non-Thayerian? Should we be constitutional traditionalists in general? Free speech traditionalists in particular? Property rights traditionalists? Equal protection traditionalists?

It is natural to answer that *Dobbs* was about the Due Process Clause of the Fourteenth Amendment, which means that it has nothing at all to say about Article I, Article III, the First Amendment, the Fifth Amendment, or the Equal Protection Clause.[48] Perhaps that is correct. But as we have seen, the Burkean and Thayerian strands in the draft cannot be simply "read off" the Due Process Clause. They are meant as a way of making best sense of the Clause, and of the Court's own precedents. (Recall that they seem to be incorporated by reference into the Court's understanding of the Privileges or Immunities Clause.) Would it make sense to incorporate Burkean and Thayerian strands into the Supreme Court's thinking about freedom of speech? We might note that while "the freedom of speech" is a narrower concept than "liberty," it is not exactly narrow, and it can be specified in many different ways. We might notice that, just as with the Fourteenth Amendment, there is a "natural human tendency to confuse" what the First Amendment "protects with our own ardent views about the [freedom of speech] that Americans should enjoy."[49] Ought judges to be keenly interested in the reach of the concept of the freedom of speech before ratification of the First

Amendment, or before ratification of the Fourteenth Amendment, perhaps for originalist reasons, or perhaps for Burkean reasons?

Or consider the reach of the Equal Protection Clause (or perhaps the Privileges or Immunities Clause, if we think that the Equal Protection Clause has a narrow scope because of the word "protection"). The words "affirmative action" do not appear in the Fourteenth Amendment; the words "preferential treatment" do not appear there, either. For Thayerian reasons, ought we to be cautious about judicial deployment about a broad concept like equality, for fear that there is a "natural human tendency to confuse" what the Fourteenth Amendment "protects with our own ardent views about the [equality] that Americans should enjoy"?

These questions could easily be proliferated. It is a fun game, and anyone can play. Let us suppose that the theoretical foundations of the *Dobbs* opinion should not be applied to constitutional questions not involving the Due Process Clause. If so, it must be because (controversially, of course) that particular clause is best understood to protect (only) those substantive rights that are vindicated by tradition, whereas (for example) the First Amendment is best understood to establish broad principles whose reach encompasses rights that extend well beyond those vindicated by tradition, and (for example) the Equal Protection Clause is best understood to establish broad principles of nondiscrimination that extend well beyond what tradition establishes.[50] If we think that the First Amendment and the Equal Protection Clause are best understood in this way, it must be because we are comfortable, or comfortable enough, with the normative judgments, informed but not defined by tradition, that judges are inevitably required to make.

If we are comfortable, or comfortable enough, with those judgments, it must be because we are not, and should not be, across-the-board traditionalists.[51] It must be because we are at best ambivalent Burkeans (on principle; recall Pascal and Bentham) and are not thoroughgoing Thayerians (again on principle). It must be because we believe in some forms of moral progress and have at least some faith in the judicial capacity to incorporate one or more of those forms of progress in constitutional law.

9

Should Gradualism Have Prevailed in *Dobbs*?

Richard M. Re[*]

Gradualism should have won out in *Dobbs v. Jackson Women's Health Organization*,[1] exerting gravitational influence on the majority and dissenters alike. Disruptive doctrinal changes necessarily implicate judicial discretion and statecraft, and so cannot be reduced to any simple rule. Yet at least one principle is generally worth adhering to: the Supreme Court should not impose massive disruption without first providing notice of its contemplated course of action. That precept, which I have called the doctrine of one last chance,[2] has been a hallmark of decision-making during the Roberts Court but failed to carry the day in *Dobbs*. Only the chief justice followed the doctrine, and as a result his opinion is the most compelling of the bunch.

The other *Dobbs* opinions are far less persuasive. Justice Samuel Alito's majority sometimes claimed to be strictly formalist, particularly when doing so helped it dismiss prudential objections. Yet the majority's most plausible rationale was, inevitably, steeped in judicial statecraft. In essence, the majority claimed that only grand, decisive action could meet the challenge at hand. But that approach blinked the case for gradualism. By acting in haste, the Court compromised its own deliberative process and prevented the public from adequately preparing for an avulsive shift in the law. On balance, the majority's approach was incautious, self-contradictory, and harmful. *Dobbs*'s maximalism should accordingly be remembered, not as a new way forward but as a worrisome exception that proves the need for a more circumspect rule.

The joint dissent's treatment of precedent was, if anything, even less persuasive. Apart from the merits, two ideas underlie the dissent. First, the Court is subject to a strong duty to follow precedent. Second, changes in the Court's composition cannot justify overruling. Neither of these claims is correct, and the first is hardly plausible. The dissent's own uses of precedent demonstrate

Richard M. Re, *Should Gradualism Have Prevailed in* Dobbs? In: *Roe v. Dobbs.* Edited by: Lee C. Bollinger and Geoffrey R. Stone, Oxford University Press. © Oxford University Press 2024.
DOI: 10.1093/oso/9780197760352.003.0009

how readily case law is thrown overboard—not just in the past few years, but throughout many decades. And because changes in the Court's composition stem from democratic politics, new personnel can offer a uniquely compelling basis for revisiting case law. So if the majority had reason to moderate, the dissenters did, too—by joining a gradualist opinion like the chief's.

The stakes in this debate aren't limited to *Dobbs* or abortion rights. Every theory of law has to be mindful of the *when* and *how* of change, not just the *if* or *whether*. Substance and procedure are entangled, and the questions teed up by *Dobbs* therefore arise in every area of litigation. Anyone who cares about the law's future should be interested in whether gradualism should have prevailed in *Dobbs*.

The Case for Gradualism

The Court has ample reason to deploy its "judicial Power" only gradually.[3] In particular, gradualism can improve deliberation, mitigate harms, and defuse backlash.[4] At least the first two of these reasons strongly counseled against the result in *Dobbs*.

Improving Deliberation

Gradualism fosters better results through improved deliberation.[5] Because high-stakes questions are often charged with political and emotional significance, jurists can arrive at the bench with strong preconceptions about what to do, even when those views are based on incomplete understandings or partial experiences. The result is a worrisome tendency toward bias and overconfidence. The judicial process accordingly fosters various forms of gradualism, allowing the Court to learn, experiment, reflect, and garner feedback before making a precipitous decision.

In extraordinary cases, special caution is warranted. But even the Court's normal decisional process exhibits gradualism. First, issues usually "percolate" in lower courts until a division of authority develops, so as to allow the development of competing views. Second, the Court grants reviews of discrete issues, thereby giving public notice and an opportunity for amicus curiae filings as well as public debate. Finally, the Court considers and decides only the issues vetted in the foregoing ways.

In *Dobbs*, however, the Court displayed no special caution and, in fact, barreled through each of its normal procedural guardrails. First, the Court granted review of a petition concerning the viability rule—one of the most well-settled issues in the law.[6] The case thus posed no traditional basis for Court review. Second, the Court allowed Mississippi to change its position midstream. The question presented concerned the viability line, and Mississippi's request for review disavowed any need to overrule case law.[7] But after Justice Ruth Bader Ginsburg was replaced by Justice Amy Coney Barrett, Mississippi filed a merits brief that primarily argued for overruling all abortion precedents.[8] The case's evolving character misled the public, with many commentators initially expecting only an incremental change.[9] Finally, the justices discussed and ultimately reached conclusions about matters not presented by the case at hand. For example, justices asked both parties questions about important abortion-related issues that were not at stake in that case, prompting demurrals.[10] The Court's opinion nonetheless addressed those unpresented matters on the way to a sweeping outcome.[11]

And *Dobbs* wasn't a normal case. Many millions of people had a stake in how *Dobbs* came out—not just in the bottom line but also in the details of the Court's reasoning. Hearing from the full range of relevant views could have benefited the Court. Yet that diversity found almost no voice. As the Court was keen to observe, the abortion providers in the case insisted that there was no middle way.[12] The providers went so far as to say that "*any* abandonment of viability would be no different than overruling *Casey* and *Roe* entirely."[13] Yet that hardline position was false, as well as adverse to the interests of their patients and many other people. The *Dobbs* dissent pointed out the obvious: "[N]o one should think that there is not a large difference between upholding a 15-week ban on the grounds [the chief] does and allowing States to prohibit abortion from the time of conception."[14]

What could explain the almost total absence of that viewpoint from the litigation? The abortion providers' brinksmanship could represent a canny strategy—indeed, it echoed a similarly absolutist and false position advanced in *Planned Parenthood v. Casey*.[15] There, the abortion providers argued, "To adopt a lesser standard, to abandon strict scrutiny for a less protective standard such as the undue burden test . . . would be the same as overruling *Roe*."[16] That claim, however, was obviously incorrect, as Justices Sandra Day O'Connor and Anthony Kennedy immediately pointed out.[17] And when *Casey* did abandon "strict scrutiny" in favor of the "undue burden" test, nobody seriously thought that the result was "the same as overruling *Roe*."

There is some irony that, about thirty years later, the abortion providers in *Dobbs* were again taking a hardline position—except, this time, it was *Casey* that supposedly had to be honored in every particular, or else it might as well be entirely overruled. Perhaps this irony is unembarrassing. The providers' hardline position in *Casey* worked, after all, in the sense that robust abortion rights survived. So experience arguably counseled in favor of a similar strategy in *Dobbs*. Other explanations sound in politics. A party or lawyer who offered a middle way could be viewed as weak or a sellout. And some left-wing politicos preferred a big loss on abortion before the 2022 midterm elections rather than just after.

The cause of the parties' extremism is ultimately less important than its existence. From the Court's standpoint, the providers' absolutist position in particular should have been a red flag. So instead of prominently relying on the abortion providers' implausible absolutism, the Court should have treated it as a reason to slow down and consider a wider range of views.

The chief was therefore right to complain that the other justices exhibited "a relentless freedom from doubt."[18] *Dobbs* involved a high-stakes, politically charged issue that had long divided the Court, the bar, and the public. The justices were bound to approach such a matter with deeply held, even axiomatic views already in mind. But, for the same reasons, those views should have been suspect: they posed a heightened risk of having been the products of partial consideration and political circumstances. What felt like certitude could actually have been prejudice. Yet the justices failed even to abide by their normal decisional process, instead leaping to transform an important area of law in a single, procedurally flawed case.

Mitigating Harms

Another reason for gradualism has to do with mitigating harms. When the Court issues a disruptive ruling, many people are aggrieved. Advance notice can then help those individuals protect themselves and their interests. The point is not that reliance on preexisting law should forever prevent legal change, as a stringent stare decisis analysis might demand. Rather, the point is that harmful disruptions should be reduced where feasible. And that principle applied with extraordinary force in *Dobbs*.

While the fate of abortion rights has long been a topic of political and legal controversy, relevant case law had long been fundamentally stable. In fact, the Court's most recent abortion case was an abortion rights victory.[19] In that context, only an especially strong signal could credibly indicate that radical change was afoot. Moreover, a specific foreboding of impending change is generally necessary either to motivate actual changes in behavior or to give fair notice. In *Dobbs*, the notice associated with gradualism would have allowed for at least three forms of self-help.

First, many people made reproductive choices before *Dobbs* on the assumption that relevant law was stable. Even if the *Dobbs* oral argument supplied adequate notice of the Court's plan, that event occurred just seven months before the Court's final decision—substantially less than a typical gestational period. And assisted reproduction can take still longer. This point sounds in the kind of immediate, "concrete" reliance interests that even the majority recognized as important under stare decisis.[20]

Second, many people decided where to live and work based in part on their access to abortion-related medical care. Those choices take far more time to unwind or correct than the Court allowed. This concern bears not just on individuals but also on families and businesses. In the wake of *Dobbs*, for instance, some firms announced that they will shift the location of their operations or make other arrangements in order to retain and support their employees.[21]

Third, people lacked political notice of the need to update or clarify old abortion regulations. Instead of providing that notice, the Court allowed very old or extreme abortion restrictions to go into immediate effect. Voters had not selected their representatives with these defunct laws in mind, and even some pro-life legislators were surprised by the consequences.[22] Meanwhile, medical providers were unsure about the state of the law. The result was gratuitous confusion and harm, such as delays in treating ectopic pregnancies that are life-threatening and cannot result in a viable fetus.[23] Gradualism, by contrast, would have allowed individuals, the public, and legislators to become more informed and then to update or refine the law.[24]

For all these reasons, gradualism would have advanced interests consistent with the Court's avowed posture of neutrality with respect to abortion.[25] Large, abrupt rule changes are almost always costly, and the political process needs time to catch up to a new constitutional landscape. These claims pertain to transition effects, particularly the widespread appeal of notice and planning, and so stand even if the Court cannot competently engage in a broader assessment of "the effect of the abortion right on society and in particular on the lives of women."[26]

* * *

Perhaps the Court actually *did* honor gradualism, albeit indirectly. Consider *Dobbs*'s context. In the months before oral argument, Texas implemented a statute known as SB8, which cleverly manipulated procedural law to effectively ban abortion after six weeks.[27] On September 1, 2021, the Court declined to enjoin SB8.[28] As a result, a major state transitioned to a post-*Roe* world well before *Dobbs* was decided. Later, the Court's antipathy to *Roe* became explicit during the *Dobbs* oral argument.[29] And, still later, the draft majority opinion in *Dobbs* leaked to the public, creating even crisper notice as well as an unprecedented chance for public criticism to influence the precise content of a Court decision.[30] While these events did not slow things down, they did afford increasingly powerful forms of notice.

But even these extraordinary events could not substitute for actual gradualism.[31] For one thing, the relevant events occurred too late. The briefing in *Dobbs* was already well underway when SB8 went into effect, and the justices cast their initial votes on *Roe*'s fate before much could be learned from Texas's example. At most, the Court had enough time to gain insight into the degree of public hostility that would result from abandoning *Roe*; much greater clarity would have followed from additional public deliberation and feedback, including the possible appointment of new justices. The SB8 litigation also focused on complicated procedural issues adjacent to abortion rights, and so did not add to the range of perspectives bearing on *Dobbs* itself. Finally, affected parties gained little or no time to adjust their behavior in anticipation of what the Court would do. So while the windup to *Dobbs* did mitigate some gradualist objections, the core reasons to reject the Court's precipitous course of action remained.

Implementing Gradualism

The *Dobbs* opinions feature an unusually rich and instructive judicial debate on how gradualism might work in practice.

Finding a Narrow Ground

The doctrine of one last chance strives to strike a delicate balance: credibly signaling an inclination to take disruptive action, without committing to doing so. That approach is compatible with leaving case law intact in the short term. For example, the Court could have dismissed *Dobbs* as improvidently granted due to Mississippi's abrupt change in position, perhaps with a separate writing that revealed the majority's tentative views.[32] The resulting notice would have improved the Court's deliberation while enabling self-help. And it would also have shown that the justices cared more about getting things right than hurrying toward a predetermined destination.

The chief instead proposed that the Court simply answer the question it had selected: "Whether all pre-viability prohibitions on elective abortions are unconstitutional."[33] This relatively muscular form of gradualism may have been the only approach that could hope to peel off a necessary vote. And it also had the advantage of affording strong notice by substantially changing and unsettling case law.

Perplexingly, the Court read the chief as saying that "the viability line . . . can . . . be 'discarded' without disturbing any past precedent."[34] The Court accordingly devoted considerable effort to showing that case law had embraced the viability line—something that the chief readily conceded.[35] Perhaps the Court wanted to head off any possible argument that *Roe* could be narrowed rather than overruled. That is, the chief could have tried to shrink precedent by creatively interpreting it not to apply to certain facts, rather than by replacing it with a new view of the law.[36] But the chief did not narrowly read the case law. Instead, the crux of the chief's position was that the viability rule was wrong from the beginning.

There are at least two ways of understanding the chief's proposal, and each is not only legally plausible but also attractive.[37]

First, the Court's abortion case law could have been viewed as a collection of distinct precedential rules. One of these assorted rules had to do with viability, and the chief proposed rejecting that precept while leaving the rest where they lay. As he put it, "*Roe* adopted two distinct rules of constitutional law: one, that a woman has the right to choose to terminate a pregnancy; two, that such right may be overridden by the State's legitimate interests when the fetus is viable outside the womb."[38] On this view, the "right to choose" rule would essentially step up to resolve cases that the more sharp-edged viability rule used to resolve. And because Mississippi's law preserved a considerable right to choose (namely, a right to choose up to fifteen weeks), it was facially constitutional. One could object that there actually was no precedential rule regarding a right to choose as such. For practical purposes, after all, a robust "right to choose" operated only before viability, and the Court had often said as much. Yet the chief adduced a number of decisions, including *Roe* itself, where the Court discussed a right to choose without tying it to the viability line.[39]

Second, abortion case law could be viewed as a set of operational rules that are derived from a deeper balance of competing interests. In *Roe*, the Court evidently balanced certain interests in a way that produced the viability rule, and *Casey* reinforced that result by noting the rule's workability.[40] Yet *Roe*'s balancing act was unreasoned, and later cases had cast the viability line into doubt by both clarifying and expanding the interests at stake.[41] *Dobbs* therefore offered an opportunity to revisit the relevant interests and rebalance them in light of deeper reflection and more recent case law. Doing so, the chief rejected the viability rule. At most, he concluded, the relevant interests supported a different operational rule, namely, a right to abortion up to fifteen weeks.[42] So the Court could sustain Mississippi's law without addressing any broader questions. This framing assumes that the viability rule was clearly wrong in a way that other aspects of abortion case law weren't. And that premise was plausible, especially given the cross-ideological criticisms that have always been leveled against *Roe*'s circular adoption of the viability rule.[43]

Under either reading, the chief's middle way depended on a number of more abstract points about legitimate adjudication. Most explicitly, the chief invoked a specific kind of gradualism—namely, minimalism, or the idea that rulings unnecessary to decide a case are generally impermissible.[44] To wit, the chief ended his opinion by quoting Justice Felix Frankfurter for the idea that the justices must "confine ourselves to deciding only what is necessary to the disposition of the immediate case."[45] Thus, a broad ruling cannot be justified by its mere possibility or even desirability. Just what qualifies as "necessary" then becomes critical, as explored below.

Reinforcing the chief's familiar minimalism was a related if implicit idea: the Court must give adequate notice before causing a large disruption. I have called this precept "the doctrine of one last chance," and it has been a staple of the Roberts Court.[46] The point of this maxim is to insist, in a rule-like fashion, that exceptional change should not occur until a period of noticed deliberation and harm mitigation can take place—typically, about two years. The distinctive effect of this asserted doctrine is to require at least one postponement, without requiring a series of incremental steps or persistent caution over a longer period of time. This idea is visible in the chief's insistence that the "decision to overrule *Roe* and *Casey* is a serious jolt to the legal system," suggesting the need for special hesitancy.[47] It is also discernible in the chief's celebration of the idea that, after deferring *Roe*'s fate just a single time in *Dobbs*, the Court "would then be free to exercise our discretion in deciding whether and when to take up the issue, from a more informed perspective."[48]

Finally, the chief's middle way assumed a lack of mandatory rules that could curtail judicial discretion and thereby compel a broader decision. To wit, the chief's first principle of stare decisis was that "[w]hether a precedent should be overruled is a question 'entirely within the discretion of the court.'"[49] This statement suggests that precedents are not mandates but permissions.[50] They allow the Court to do what it has done before, without requiring anything. That permissive view allowed the chief to rely on case-specific, prudential considerations when selecting which precedents to overrule. For example, the chief was sensitive to the case's high stakes as well as its procedural defects. In stark contrast, Justice Clarence Thomas's concurrence reiterated his claim that the Court has a "duty" to overrule "demonstrably erroneous" decisions.[51] Thomas's rule-like, mandatory understanding of stare decisis curtailed the range of considerations that could be marshaled in support of precedent or gradualism.

When a Narrow Ground Is "Right"

When rebutting the chief, the majority invoked his past writings on minimalism. This exchange provides an opportunity to deepen and improve the chief's account.

The *Dobbs* majority drew from the chief's separate opinion in *Citizens United v. FEC*, which had overruled precedent and upheld corporations' and unions' First Amendment rights to political speech.[52] In particular, the *Dobbs* majority noted the chief's assertion that stare decisis is "a doctrine of preservation, not transformation."[53] "Therefore," the majority continued, "a new rule that discards the viability rule cannot be defended on stare decisis grounds."[54] But stare decisis plainly *is* a "doctrine of . . . transformation," at least in the sense that it applies when doctrinal change is at issue. And what looks like a "new rule" can result from preserving some rules while jettisoning others.

The majority also invoked the chief's rejection of half-measures in *Citizens United*. In among the chief's most memorable turns of phrase, he asserted,

"[W]e cannot embrace a narrow ground of decision simply because it is narrow; it must also be right."[55] But what does it mean for the narrow ground to be "right"? The Court appears to have thought that the ground must represent the view that should be adopted in the absence of relevant precedent. We might imagine that abortion case law is a complex structure and that the removal of the viability rule causes the whole edifice to collapse, leaving the Court with nothing but its own first-principles view of the law.

But why? Precedential interests can be honored or diminished to varying extents and degrees. And when courts chip away at precedent, they do not assume that the slightest revision to any part requires an immediate reconsideration of all the rest. *Casey* supplied an example, as the Court overruled some abortion holdings while relying on stare decisis to preserve others.[56] Likewise, the chief could conclude that considerations of reliance and prudence supported overruling the viability rule alone, at least for the time being. Alito himself had arguably acted similarly, such as by cabining *Abood v. Detroit Board of Education* years before overruling it.[57]

There is a better way to understand when a "narrow" ground is "right": the ground cannot be wrong. That is, it must be consistent with other legal principles. On this view, a narrow ground might fail because it is at odds with the reason for altering case law in the first place. In *Citizens United*, for instance, the Court rejected narrower grounds that would themselves have transgressed the First Amendment by chilling protected speech.[58] A narrow ground could also fail because it runs afoul of a separate precept, such as a principle of nondiscrimination. That is why the Court could not declare capital punishment unconstitutional *only with respect to Christians*, even if the claimant at hand happened to be Christian. The chief's *Dobbs* opinion posed neither of these problems. How could it? The chief essentially proposed switching from one timing rule (viability, or roughly twenty-three weeks) to another (at most fifteen weeks).

For its part, the majority suggested that the chief's middle ground was untenable (that is, not "right") for prudential reasons. While a final reckoning with the abortion question "would not be long in coming," the intervening period "would be fraught with turmoil until the Court answered the question that the concurrence seeks to defer."[59] Therefore, it would be "far better— for this Court and the country—to face up to the real issue without further delay."[60]

But what, exactly, is the "turmoil" that the majority feared? Lower courts would surely have disagreed on how to draw the boundaries of the "right to choose," but that kind of temporary dissensus is normally viewed as valuable percolation. Moreover, the chief's rebalancing of interests could have generated an interim rule. Having overruled precedent to the extent it protected abortion rights after fifteen weeks, for instance, the Court might have concluded that precedent securing abortion rights up to fifteen weeks continued to bind lower courts. In all events, litigants, the public, and the courts would have been invited to debate the desirability or shape of abortion rights. And that, of course, is the point. By postponing its final decision, the Court could arrive at a "more informed perspective"[61] while allowing affected parties to mitigate harms.

Dobbs hinted at a subtler answer. Perhaps the Court did not want to insinuate itself in a public debate with such extraordinary political valence. Inviting a national colloquy on abortion rights could have brought special risks "for this Court" as well as for individual justices. While *Dobbs* was pending, one justice became the object of an attempted murder plot at his home.[62] And in an apparent act of internal sabotage, a draft of the *Dobbs* opinion itself was leaked to the press.[63] The prospect of being under that kind of pressure for even longer could not have been enticing. That self-interested point tees up an institutionalist case for maximalism. Quickly overturning *Roe* might have promised to remove the Court from the political stage. The one-person, one-vote cases offer a template: those rulings generated intense short-term disruption, but the political system quickly adjusted to the new rules, quelling any abiding discontent.[64] Likewise, the majority might have felt that the Court would be less politicized if the transition to a post-*Roe* world occurred as quickly as possible.

That the Court only hinted at these points is no coincidence. The justices do not want to seem either bullied into their ruling or to be lashing out in the face of pressure. And understandably so. No legitimate decision could rest on such grounds. By contrast, the institutionalist case for a rapid overruling is plausibly viewed as legitimate on its own terms. But institutionalist arguments were questionable at best. Unlike the one-person, one-vote rule, abortion rights are a substantive issue of ongoing importance. And in deciding *Dobbs*, the Court hurriedly took a huge institutional risk. In particular, it may have placed itself permanently at odds with a major political party that had already begun to flirt with Court-packing and other modes of judicial discipline.

There is one wrinkle. The chief cited evidence that "almost all" pregnancies are discovered in the first trimester and, therefore, that fifteen weeks is generally adequate time to exercise the "right to choose." However, the chief also noted that more time might be needed "in rare circumstances."[65] This elliptical comment went unexplored, and the majority quite fairly underlined it.[66] The chief might have expected as-applied challenges to be available in cases where a woman needed more than fifteen weeks to learn key information about her pregnancy and then obtain an abortion. Regardless, this caveat would have created some confusion and litigation if the chief had prevailed. Yet even the majority did not claim that this limited problem in itself would have amounted to "turmoil." And perhaps the chief failed to clarify this issue for the simple reason that he had no need to do so, since he ultimately failed to command the Court.

The *Dobbs* majority raised one additional if indirect objection. During its tussle with the dissent, the majority argued that the separate but equal doctrine associated with *Plessy v. Ferguson*[67] was so wrong and harmful that there was no need to wait for any changed facts or law before overruling it. Instead, the majority declared, *Plessy* should have been overruled "at the earliest opportunity."[68] Though directed at the dissent, this reasoning posed an implicit challenge to the chief and other gradualists. While the "earliest opportunity" would presumably follow some delay—enough time for *Plessy*'s defenders to file a brief, for instance—should the Court have insisted on more?

The *Dobbs* majority thought that the answer was no, but that view traded on anachronism. It implicitly assumed both that there was nothing more for the Court to learn and that any delay would be counterproductive. But while those premises may appear self-evident today, they did not obtain for much of the time before *Brown v. Board of Education*.[69] For many justices, constitutional history and case law seemed to support the lawfulness of segregation, and the threat of public backlash and widespread noncompliance was quite real.[70] The Court accordingly engaged in extensive gradualism during the period before *Brown* as well as during *Brown* itself, which was argued at the Court three separate times.[71] And that gradualist strategy was effective: it helped both to convince the justices of what they had to do and to legitimate *Plessy*'s demise in the eyes of lawyers and the public at large. The *Brown* Court may ultimately have engaged in *too much* gradualism.[72] But gradualism still played an indispensable role in making *Brown* a reality. As this history illustrates, gradualism can be desirable not for honoring the status quo but rather for helping to change it.

Dobbs's Inconsistent Formalism

Most fundamentally, the Court rejected the chief's gradualism for the same reason it rejected *Casey*'s deployment of stare decisis: for blurring hard-edged legal reasoning with irrelevant political considerations. As the Court put it, "[W]e cannot allow our decisions to be affected by any extraneous influences such as concern about the public's reaction to our work."[73] The Court accordingly professed no interest in "how our political system or society will respond to today's decision."[74] In a similar vein, the Court disqualified almost all reliance interests from its stare decisis analysis, including "the effect of the abortion right on society and in particular on the lives of women."[75] These passages are of a piece. They attempt to narrow the range of considerations to relatively formal matters, at the expense of prudence. The apparent goal was to rule out of bounds the entire category of reasons that underlay the chief's gradualism and, before that, the doctrinal recalibration arrived at in *Casey*.

Yet the Court's focus on formal law was conveniently inconsistent. When making the case to overrule, the Court explicitly indulged in political and sociological analysis. Why was the "nature of the error" in *Roe* so "damaging"?[76] Because *Roe* did "not concern some arcane corner of the law of little importance to the American people" but instead "usurped the power to address a question of profound moral and social importance."[77] Quoting Justice Antonin Scalia's *Casey* dissent, the *Dobbs* majority elaborated that "*Roe* fanned into life an issue that has inflamed our national politics in general, and has obscured with its smoke the selection of Justices to this Court in particular, ever since."[78] All these arguments were explicitly concerned with "social importance" and "our national politics." It was for *these* reasons— avowedly functional, prudential reasons outside of formal law—that the Court concluded, "Together, *Roe* and *Casey* represent an error that cannot be allowed to stand."[79] Judicial statecraft was thus deemed in-bounds, but only to show that overruling was mandatory.

The Court's opportunistic rejection of prudence rendered its entire opinion self-refuting. Take the Court's repeated insistence that "[n]othing in this opinion should be understood to cast doubt on precedents that do not concern abortion," such as cases on rights to contraception or same-sex marriage.[80] Those assurances represented a form of judicial statecraft or gradualism akin to the chief's, except at a higher level of abstraction. Instead of picking out the viability rule while passing over surrounding abortion case law, the Court picked out abortion case law while passing over related case law on substantive due process and unenumerated rights. And much as the majority suggested that the chief's half-step would cause doctrine to topple, the dissent conjured images of a "Jenga tower" that is bound to "collapse" after the majority finished its work.[81] The live question, then, was not whether to engage in prudential or gradualist reasoning, but how to do so. Unfortunately, that was not a question that the majority was prepared to contemplate, much less answer.

Gradualism versus Inaction

The *Dobbs* dissent poses a different kind of challenge to gradualism: In light of stare decisis, how could *any* legal change have been appropriate?

Overplaying Stare Decisis

The *Dobbs* dissent argued that stare decisis generally imposes a strong, mandatory rule: absent certain conditions, precedent must stand. That position served rhetorical aims, allowing the dissenters to claim the legalistic high ground even for readers who had their doubts on the merits. But the dissenters' rigid view of stare decisis was implausible, both as a description of actual practice and as a normative prescription. While procedural rules like the doctrine of one last chance are defensible, a strong rule in favor of indefinitely preserving precedent is not.

The dissent's problems with precedent began, ironically enough, with its creative use of case law. In an opinion that harps on the importance of stare decisis, you might expect to see a canonical statement of that doctrine. But none appears in the dissent. Instead, the dissent follows the majority (and, for that matter, most Court opinions on this topic) by assembling its own bespoke stare decisis analysis, cobbling together phrases from past rulings without being faithful to any one of them. The only discernible explanation for the gerrymandered test that resulted is that it tended to preclude overruling on the facts of *Dobbs*. Consider the dissent's initial summary of relevant case law:

> [In past cases that overruled precedent, t]he Court relied on one or more of the traditional stare decisis factors in reaching its conclusion. The Court

found, for example, (1) a change in legal doctrine that undermined or made obsolete the earlier decision; (2) a factual change that had the same effect; or (3) an absence of reliance because the earlier decision was less than a decade old.[82]

No prior case had endorsed just these three illustrative factors, and it does not appear that any case had ever quite articulated the third one at all. The most conspicuous omitted factor is the quality of the precedent's reasoning.[83] And if that factor were added, the majority would seem to have abided by the dissent's demand to find a "special justification," apart from the merits, warranting an overruling.[84]

When it came time to distinguish the specific past overrulings that the Court relied on, the dissent grew increasingly strained. For example, the dissent (like the chief) thought it important that *Brown* was decided by an opinion "in which the entire Court could speak with one voice."[85] The apparent idea is that *Brown*'s decision to overrule somehow depended on its being unanimous. But that argument gets things backward. *Brown* was unanimous only because the majority planned to reject the separate-but-equal doctrine whether or not holdout justices got onboard.[86] If overruling had actually required unanimity, then *Brown* wouldn't have overturned *Plessy* at all.

In one sense, the dissent's creativity with precedent was consistent with the history of modern stare decisis. But, in this instance, that creativity was at odds with itself. Stare decisis has never been the rigid doctrine that the dissent imagines.

Dobbs as Democratic Constitutionalism

At any rate, why hadn't there been a "factual change" sufficient to undermine *Roe*, even under the dissent's view of stare decisis? After *Casey*, political contestation around abortion had continued for another thirty years—a point well made by the majority.[87] Moreover, that contestation played a significant role in supporting the selection of five new Republican-appointed justices, all of whom voted in *Dobbs* to overrule *Roe* at least in part. Consistent with its avowed formalism, the majority mostly ignored the link between politics and judicial appointments, and even the dissent only vaguely gestured toward it. The dissent instead framed the case as being a clash between precedent and "the proclivities of individuals," without inquiring into how those specific "individuals" happened to get on the Court.[88] And, most important, the dissent claimed that neither ongoing political contestation nor recent changes in the Court's membership could justify revisiting precedent.[89]

But precedent has frequently given way after relevant changes in the Court's personnel. The dissent's lament is thus like accusing the ocean of suddenly being wet. In fact, the dissent's own citations prove this point. When the dissent opened its peroration by declaring that "[p]ower, not reason, is the new currency of this Court's decisionmaking," it was quoting a dissent from 1991.[90] And when the dissent concluded by declaring that "[i]t is not often in the law that so few have so quickly changed so much," it was reciting a dissenting bench statement from 2007.[91] In the past, justices have sometimes been candid enough to recognize the link between personnel and outcomes. As Justice Scalia frankly observed in a 1989 dissent, "Overrulings of precedent rarely occur without a change in the Court's personnel."[92]

The dissent also overlooked many good reasons to think that doctrine *should* change based on changes in personnel. Like all people, justices who have botched a decision may have trouble recognizing or owning up to their error, especially when it has come to be associated with their personal legacies. Moreover, new justices are more closely tied to recent political events and so arguably have superior democratic legitimacy. Finally, new justices are likely to be younger and more in tune with ascendant social facts and trends. Given all this, the legal updating that results from new appointments often has a progressive effect. Left-leaning scholars have accordingly advocated for different versions of "democratic constitutionalism," whereby political movements do or should shape the Court and constitutional law.[93] To take account of these points would not be "retreating under fire," as *Casey* suggested, but responding to democratic feedback.[94]

And *Dobbs* finds an especially strong foundation in democratic constitutionalism. Curtailing or overruling *Roe*, after all, has long been an explicit goal of Republican politicians.[95] In a 2016 presidential campaign debate with Hillary Clinton, for example, Donald Trump famously, or infamously, declared, "If we put another two or perhaps three Justices on, [overruling *Roe*] will happen. And that will happen automatically, in my opinion, because I am putting pro-life Justices on the court."[96] Clinton agreed that *Roe*'s fate was hanging in the balance—as indeed it was. Justice Scalia had recently passed away, Senate Republicans were preventing President Barack Obama from filling the resulting vacancy, and Trump therefore had the opportunity, if elected, to "flip" the Court. Moreover, there was reason to expect additional vacancies among the aging justices. With the benefit of hindsight, we now know that, on this occasion, Trump accomplished exactly what he promised the electorate.

Broader consideration of democratic constitutionalism could point in a different or more ambiguous direction. Trump lost the popular vote, after all, as President George W. Bush once did. And the 2016 presidential election was of course about much more than just abortion rights. Yet democratic politics is premised on the actual rules in place, including the electoral college. And campaigning against *Roe* had repeatedly succeeded. When Trump became president, five of the previous nine presidential terms were occupied by anti-*Roe* Republicans. Perhaps arguments from democratic constitutionalism were in equipoise, especially given President Joe Biden's recent election. But a tie would likely go to *Roe*'s critics. When it comes to showing democratic support, the burden of proof should be on the side that wants to impose a constitutional limit on politics.

To be clear, democratic constitutionalism alone cannot—and does not—demonstrate that *Dobbs* was rightly decided. Judges have several obligations that check or even preclude consideration of democratic constitutionalism. They take an oath of fidelity to the law, not political mandates. They also have life tenure precisely to be insulated from political bias and democratic tides. And, as we have seen, they have reason to engage in gradualism—not to rush toward major issues as soon as a personnel change makes it possible to do so, or while they still have the votes. At most, then, political movements and resulting changes in the Court's personnel provide reasons for revisiting precedent, not a decisive case or specific plan for doing so.

Conclusion: The Rule of Restlessness

If the *Dobbs* dissenters were wrong to cast political opposition to *Roe* and the Court's changed membership as impermissible grounds for reconsidering precedent, how *should* the dissenters have regarded those considerations? One attractive answer would shift focus from deciding issues to exploring them. Even if the dissenters were mostly secure in their fundamental views, the tides of judicial politics might supply a reason to reassess or moderate, perhaps along the lines that the chief proposed. Similar logic might have supported past instances of consensus gradualism. Take *NAMUDNO v. Holder*, where the Court faced a constitutional challenge to an important part of the Voting Rights Act.[97] The Court deferred that issue based on its preference to avoid difficult constitutional questions. And the liberal justices, who presumably had little doubt of the Act's constitutionality, all joined the Court's opinion.

That line of thought supports a "rule of restlessness": when in doubt, the justices should err in favor of taking a gradualist step toward an overruling or some other disruptive action. Again, many people, and perhaps lawyers especially, are biased toward the status quo. And judges who have supported old rulings may be particularly stubborn about admitting error. So when the justices see reason to doubt the past, they probably also have reason to investigate it. Gradualism, broadly understood, affords a means of conducting that investigation without generating excessive costs or instability. Modest examples include dissents from denials of certiorari in which pivotal justices announce their interest in revisiting a settled area of law. Recalibrating the law, as the chief proposed, offers another, more robust approach.

Gradualism thus both pulls and pushes. It pulls rash justices back from the brink. And it pushes complacent justices to experiment. But these two effects are asymmetrically strong. For instance, the doctrine of one last chance is rule-like in generally demanding notice before a major disruption. The *Dobbs* majority accordingly erred. By comparison, the rule of restlessness creates only a factor to consider or a weak presumption. So if the *Dobbs* dissenters were certain that existing doctrine was correct, then the push of gradualism should not have altered their positions. If, however, the dissenters saw even a little merit in the many criticisms leveled against abortion doctrine, then the rule of restlessness would have counseled in favor of experimenting with the case law and, perhaps, supporting the chief's middle way.

10

Dobbs's Democratic Deficits

Melissa Murray and Katherine Shaw[*]

Introduction

The politics of abortion played an important role in the 2022 midterm elections. Ballot initiatives expanding abortion rights succeeded in a number of states,[1] while initiatives that would have restricted abortion rights failed in others.[2] In some states, abortion-protective ballot measures buoyed statewide candidates, who far exceeded expectations.[3] At the same time, a number of states were moving to implement, or had already implemented, total or near-total bans on abortion for the first time in nearly half a century.[4]

All of this unfolded less than six months after the Supreme Court's decision in *Dobbs v. Jackson Women's Health Organization*,[5] which overturned *Roe v. Wade*[6] and *Planned Parenthood v. Casey*,[7] once the twin pillars of the Court's abortion jurisprudence. To some commentators, these events, along with other post-*Dobbs* developments, vindicated the *Dobbs* majority's insistence that "[i]t is time to heed the Constitution and return the issue of abortion to the people's elected representatives."[8]

This response was perhaps unsurprising. After all, Justice Samuel Alito's majority opinion in *Dobbs* repeatedly invoked democratic deliberation as the proper mechanism for resolving the competing interests at stake in abortion.[9] On Justice Alito's telling, the Court in *Roe* and *Casey* had "usurped the power to address a question of profound moral and social importance"[10] and had "short-circuited the democratic process by closing it to the large number of Americans who dissented"[11] from these two decisions. According to Justice Alito, the *Dobbs* decision laying waste to nearly fifty years' worth of precedent was best understood as the proper correction of an egregious act of judicial overreach.

Yet despite this talk of returning the question of abortion "to the people,"[12] there are a number of reasons to be skeptical of the *Dobbs* Court's claim that its decision rests on or furthers principles of democracy. This chapter

Melissa Murray and Katherine Shaw, *Dobbs's Democratic Deficits* In: *Roe v. Dobbs*. Edited by: Lee C. Bollinger and Geoffrey R. Stone, Oxford University Press. © Oxford University Press 2024.
DOI: 10.1093/oso/9780197760352.003.0010

examines the *Dobbs* majority's invocation of democratic deliberation, highlighting its profoundly limited conception of democracy. These limitations include a cramped conception of the processes and institutions the Court seems to view as constitutive of democracy; a limited acknowledgment of the direction of change the opinion expects the mechanisms of democracy to produce; a limited conception of how to understand and gauge political power; and a complete failure to grasp the profoundly antidemocratic quality of its method for identifying the rights worthy of constitutional protection. After identifying and describing these limitations, we turn our attention to cases outside of the abortion context, canvassing a series of Roberts Court decisions that have systematically undermined and distorted the promise of inclusive democratic deliberation. In the aggregate, these decisions ensure that the very sites to which the Court purports to "return" the abortion question are unlikely to produce policies that genuinely reflect majority will.

Taken together, the Court's myopic vision of democracy in *Dobbs*, and its distortions of the democratic landscape across a number of other cases, make plain that *Dobbs* cannot be genuinely understood to rest on, or further, principles of democracy.

Dobbs's Democratic Limitations

The *Dobbs* Court insists that its opinion rests on and implements principles of democracy. But *Dobbs* purports to "return" the issue of abortion to the democratic process while revealing an extraordinarily limited, even myopic conception of democracy. This includes a limited understanding of the processes and institutions the Court understands as constitutive of democracy, with state legislatures playing a central role to the exclusion of other democratic institutions; a narrow, even unidirectional vision of the type of change that the mechanisms of democracy are expected to produce; a profoundly limited conception of political power and the composition of the political community; and a failure or refusal to acknowledge the antidemocratic quality of its method for identifying the rights worthy of protection.

In detailing these limitations in the *Dobbs* Court's discussion of democracy, we do not mean to suggest that they are the *only* such limitations. The Court's apparent equation of democracy with majoritarian politics belies the fact that genuine democracy arguably demands much more than bare expressions of majority will. True democracy requires procedures that are "conducted under certain background conditions,"[13] participants who enjoy genuine political equality,[14] and circumstances that provide opportunities for meaningful deliberation.[15] But even on its own narrow and limited vision of democracy as majoritarian politics, as we discuss below, *Dobbs's* appeal to democracy is shallow, underdeveloped, and profoundly cynical.

Democratic Institutions

First, when the Court discusses democracy, it focuses almost exclusively on state legislatures, repeatedly treating those bodies as proxies for democracy. Consider the Court's claim that its decision to overrule *Roe* "allows women on both sides of the abortion issue to seek to affect the *legislative* process."[16] It similarly explains that "the *Casey* plurality's speculations and weighing of the relative importance of the fetus and mother represent a departure from the 'original constitutional proposition' that 'courts do not substitute their social and economic beliefs for the judgment of *legislative* bodies.'"[17] Elsewhere, the Court insists that "the States may regulate abortion for legitimate reasons, and when such regulations are challenged under the Constitution, courts cannot 'substitute their social and economic beliefs for the judgment of *legislative* bodies.'"[18]

As scholars have shown, however, state legislatures are often the least representative institutions in state government,[19] largely as a result of the extreme partisan gerrymandering that the Supreme Court has approved. Further, the emphasis on state legislatures as pillars of democracy belies the role that state *judiciaries* have played in interpreting and enforcing state constitutional provisions, including in contexts involving abortion and reproductive freedom. Surely Justice Alito knew that in places like Iowa and Kansas, state courts have identified protections for abortion in state constitutions.[20] Notably, in those states, like many others in which judicial candidates run for office, jurists on state high courts are selected by many more voters than the average member of a state legislature, or even than the voters who select a majority of the members of the state legislature.[21] Taking a statewide view, then, state courts may be more democratically accountable than state legislatures.

To be clear, our point is not that elected judges "represent" voters in precisely the same way legislative representatives do,[22] or are imagined to do.[23] Rather, our point is more straightforward and modest: that state *democracy* is in no way synonymous with "state *legislative* activity," as Justice Alito suggests in *Dobbs*.

Beyond the role of state courts in state democracy, state executive-branch officials, and those who serve in state agencies, play important roles in forging state law.[24] Many state executive-branch officials, for example, again in contrast to state legislative officials, are elected statewide. Governors, elected statewide in every state, are of course participants in state legislative processes and may veto restrictive abortion laws, including on the basis of state constitutional principles.[25] Attorneys general, who in most states are elected, may utilize enforcement discretion, and even control over litigation,[26] to implement abortion policy. Other state officials, whether appointed or independently elected,[27] may issue rules and take other regulatory action that facilitates or impedes access to abortion.[28] They, too, are strikingly absent from the Court's conception of state-level democracy.

Perhaps even more conspicuous is the Court's omission of any mention of *direct* democracy in its discussion of democratic deliberation on the abortion question. Today nearly half of the states have at least some mechanisms by which the people can make policy directly, without the participation of legislative intermediaries.[29] The post-*Dobbs* era has already seen significant direct democracy initiatives on questions surrounding abortion, with a number of states relying on ballot initiatives and voter referenda to protect reproductive rights under state law, as well as attempts—so far unsuccessful—to use direct democracy to curtail those rights.[30]

Beyond overlooking the array of opportunities for state-level democratic deliberation, Justice Alito's *Dobbs* opinion is also conspicuously silent on the prospect of the *federal* legislature as a site of future democratic deliberation on abortion rights. Congress could of course seek to regulate abortion under federal law; indeed, in 2003, Congress prohibited an abortion procedure it termed "partial-birth abortion,"[31] and the Supreme Court, in an opinion by Justice Anthony Kennedy, upheld that law in the 2007 case *Gonzales v. Carhart*.[32] Despite this recent history, there is no mention of the possibility of federal legislation in Justice Alito's majority opinion—a fact made all the more notable by Justice Brett Kavanaugh's explicit acknowledgment of this possibility in his concurrence.[33] There is similarly no acknowledgment in the majority opinion of the role of the federal executive branch in policymaking around abortion and reproductive healthcare—an area in which the Biden administration has sought to play a role in the wake of *Dobbs*.[34]

In short, democracy is not coextensive with state legislatures. And it is striking, and likely no accident, that the opinion chooses to single out state legislatures in the way that it does. Today state legislatures are likely to be less responsive to and reflective of majority will than other democratic institutions.[35] And the disconnect between the output of state legislatures and the policy preferences of voters is particularly striking when it comes to abortion. Consider a state like Oklahoma, where polling reveals that 51% of the population supports access to legal abortion in most or all circumstances, but in which the state legislature has enacted one of the most sweeping abortion bans in the country.[36] Other states in the post-*Dobbs* era are already displaying a similar disconnect between the preferences revealed by polling and the enactments of state legislatures.[37]

Unidirectional Democracy

In addition to focusing narrowly on state legislatures, when the *Dobbs* majority invokes democracy, it appears fixated on deploying democracy in one direction—limiting, rather than expanding, access to abortion. Tellingly, the Court's repeated references to democratic deliberation imagine democratic interventions that curtail, rather than expand, reproductive rights. For example, the opinion explains that "the Constitution does not prohibit the citizens of each State from regulating or prohibiting abortion. *Roe* and *Casey* arrogated that authority. We now overrule those decisions and return that authority to the people and their elected representatives."[38] Similarly, the opinion reasons that "the Court short-circuited the democratic process by closing it to the large number of Americans who dissented in any respect from *Roe*. Together, *Roe* and *Casey* represent an error that cannot be allowed to stand."[39]

Indeed, whenever the opinion details the prospect of state abortion regulation, it credits potential state efforts to make abortion *less accessible* rather than more available. There is one passing mention of a state that might wish to protect abortion, but it is paired with a much more detailed discussion of Mississippi's fifteen-week abortion ban, the law challenged in *Dobbs*, whose proponents the Court describes with evident sympathy as animated by their belief that "abortion destroys an 'unborn human being.' "[40]

It is true, of course, that it was only state efforts to restrict or prohibit abortion that *Roe* and *Casey* prevented. But given the majority's insistence that, before *Roe*, democratic debate and deliberation were ongoing and active, with proponents of liberal abortion rights occasionally succeeding in persuading their fellow citizens of the rightness of their cause, it is curious that the *Dobbs* opinion does not admit the possibility that democratic deliberation might yield outcomes that are *favorable* to abortion rights.

This neglect is especially striking when compared to Justice Kavanaugh's separate concurrence. Though he joined the majority opinion in full, Justice Kavanaugh wrote separately to stake out a more moderate position, reiterating that the Constitution is "neutral" on abortion and suggesting that states could not seek to prohibit interstate travel for abortion care.[41] As Kavanaugh maintained:

> To be clear . . . the Court's decision today *does not outlaw* abortion throughout the United States. On the contrary, the Court's decision properly leaves the question of abortion for the people and their elected representatives in the democratic process. Through that democratic process, the people and their representatives may decide to allow or limit abortion. As Justice Scalia stated, the "States may, if they wish, permit abortion on demand, but the Constitution does not *require* them to do so."
>
> Today's decision therefore does not prevent the numerous States that readily allow abortion from continuing to readily allow abortion.[42]

Kavanaugh's language here is striking. Rather than speaking in general terms about a state-by-state settlement of the abortion question, but adverting in concrete terms only to abortion *restrictions*, as the majority does, Justice Kavanaugh actually credits the possibility that states might move to protect abortion. Strikingly, Kavanaugh even allows the possibility that states, in Justice Antonin Scalia's terms, might permit "abortion on demand."[43] In openly acknowledging the prospect of state-level democratic deliberation that might curtail *or protect* abortion rights, Kavanaugh's concurrence is therefore a startling contrast to the majority opinion's insistence on unidirectional deliberation.

Democracy and Political Power

The *Dobbs* majority opinion also demonstrates an exceedingly narrow vision of political power, suggesting that political power is reducible to voting and *perhaps* running for office.[44] To be sure, as Justice Alito notes,[45] women today are registered to vote, and also turn out to vote, at higher rates than men.[46] But even setting aside the significant obstacles that women, who are often the primary caregivers in their families, may need to surmount to actually exercise the franchise—particularly in states that erect hurdles to voting— if we use metrics beyond voter registration and turnout to measure democratic participation and political power, the picture looks decidedly different. When it comes to seats in state and federal legislatures, for example, women are grossly underrepresented. Women today occupy a mere 31% of the 7,383 seats in state legislatures.[47] In some states, the number of women serving in the state legislature is far lower. As Justice Alito noted, with obvious relish, in Mississippi, the state in which *Dobbs* arose, women are registered to vote and vote in higher numbers than men. Yet despite their presence at the ballot box, women comprise just 14.9% of Mississippi's state legislature. In Tennessee the number is 14.4%, and in West Virginia it is 13.4%.[48] This state legislative underrepresentation is particularly striking in view of Justice Alito's suggestion, discussed above, that the abortion question should properly be reserved for democratic deliberation in state legislatures.

The composition of the federal legislature is also woefully uneven in terms of gender representation. Today just twenty-four women serve in the hundred-member U.S. Senate. The picture is slightly rosier in the U.S. House of Representatives, where 123 women serve today, out of a total of 435 representatives.[49] Still, these figures represent only about a quarter of each chamber.

Women are also strikingly underrepresented in the ecosystem that surrounds Congress. Women, for example, account for only 37% of the lobbyists working in Washington, D.C.[50] Women are also much less likely than men to donate to political campaigns. Indeed, a 2020 study showed that men out-donated women in state legislative elections by a 2:1 ratio.[51] These disparities are also present in federal elections, both congressional and presidential; a recent paper analyzing contributions from 1980 to 2008 found that in 1980, women made only 20% of federal campaign contributions, and that by 2008 the number was still only 37%.[52] Another recent study found an even starker divide in the context of women of color, who accounted for merely 2% of contributions to House races in 2010, despite constituting approximately 18% of the population.[53]

These metrics reveal the enduring disparity in women's political power at both the state and federal levels. And important recent work reveals the impact of women's underrepresentation on abortion policy: there is "a very significant relationship between women's presence in the legislature and the degree of permissiveness of abortion policy."[54] In short, legislatures with higher percentages of women consistently enact policies that are more protective of abortion access than legislatures with lower levels of women's representation.[55]

In addition, the Court's uncritical account of women's political power is intimately connected to its limited understanding of *who* comprises the polity. On one level, the Court's vision of the polity is limited to those who have managed to overcome state-imposed obstacles to voting—obstacles that the Court, through many of its voting rights decisions, has credited and blessed.[56] On another level, however, the Court's vision of democratic deliberation prioritizes and privileges moments of democratic debate that included only some members of the political community. For example, when the *Dobbs* majority insists that *Roe* interrupted state-level deliberation around abortion, it is often referring to midcentury debates over whether to repeal or liberalize then-extant abortion restrictions. What is missing from the Court's account of these debates is the fact that the laws and policies being debated had been enacted through democratic processes that were categorically closed to all but white men. That is, they were democratic processes in which "the polity" affirmatively did not include women and people of color. On this account, the "debates" that *Roe* preempted—and that the *Dobbs* majority prioritizes and seeks to vindicate in returning the abortion issue to the states—were debates over whether to retain or liberalize laws enacted under conditions of extreme democratic deficit.

Meaningfully, the impulse to invoke such laws as reflecting democratic deliberation endures in the aftermath of *Dobbs*. Consider the recent debate over Wisconsin's 1849 abortion prohibition. This prohibition, which predates the Nineteenth Amendment by seventy years and the amendment granting women's suffrage in the Wisconsin Constitution by eighty-five years,[57] was enacted at a time when women were without formal political power. Despite this demonstrably undemocratic provenance, Republican politicians now argue that, after *Dobbs*, Wisconsin should be permitted to enforce the 1849 law, which remained on the books after *Roe* in a state of desuetude. And critically, even though women and people of color *are* eligible to participate today, the current "debate" over whether the law should be retained will not occur in conditions of genuine democratic deliberation. Wisconsin is subject to one of the worst gerrymanders in the country, meaning that there is virtually no prospect of repealing the 1849 law through ordinary legislative processes.

Methodology and Democracy

Finally, and related to the above, the *method* the Court uses in overruling *Roe* and *Casey* and holding that the Constitution does not protect the right to terminate a pregnancy reveals the hollowness of the Court's professed commitment to principles of democracy. The Court explains that when determining whether a right that is not explicitly enumerated in the Constitution is nevertheless a protected liberty, courts must rely exclusively upon "history and tradition." The opinion announces that "guided by the history and tradition that map the essential components of our Nation's concept of ordered liberty, we must ask what the *Fourteenth Amendment* means by the term 'liberty.' "[58] The opinion then deploys this "history and tradition" method to conclude that "[w]hen we engage in that inquiry in the present case, the clear answer is that the Fourteenth Amendment does not protect the right to an abortion."[59]

But on what, specifically, does the Court's "history and tradition" analysis rely? *Dobbs* places primary reliance on the existence, both before and following the enactment of the Fourteenth Amendment, of an ongoing nationwide effort to ban abortion. This effort resulted in a slew of mid-nineteenth-century statutes, which Justice Alito cites and reproduces in a lengthy appendix. But in recounting this legislative activity, Justice Alito does not acknowledge that this effort to restrict abortion was linked to a wave of nativist furor explicitly aimed at increasing the birth rate among native-born (white) women.[60] As Reva Siegel has demonstrated, "the campaign to ban abortion unfolded at a time when America was rife with religious, ethnic, and racial reasoning, and doctors advocating for abortion restrictions coupled arguments for protecting unborn life with arguments for protecting the ethno-religious character of the nation."[61] Justice Alito offers these laws as evidence of a historical tradition that would not have admitted the prospect of a constitutional right to abortion. But at no point does he genuinely engage with "the Fourteenth Amendment's larger historical context or animating aims or purposes,"[62] nor does he consider the additional historical evidence that points to the problematic social and cultural contexts in which these laws were enacted.

This context matters in terms of the Fourteenth Amendment's substantive goal of advancing equality. But perhaps more important, this context matters because it makes clear that all of the laws on which the majority stakes its conclusion that the Fourteenth Amendment does not protect abortion rights were enacted in an era in which women could not vote, run for political office, or participate in any way as full and equal members of the polity.[63] Put differently, the *Dobbs* majority's method of analysis and interpretation binds the contemporary meaning of the Constitution to a body of law and authority in whose enactment and creation neither women nor people of color played any part. This is a methodological approach that reifies conditions of democratic deficit—it is the antithesis of a methodology that values democracy and seeks true democratic engagement.[64]

Beyond this, the *Dobbs* decision entirely fails to grapple with the ways in which withdrawing the abortion right would restrict the full citizenship participation and equality of women. There is a powerful argument that women's full citizenship under both the Equal Protection Clause of the Fourteenth Amendment and the Nineteenth Amendment entails control over their reproductive lives.[65] These arguments were presented to the Court in the briefing and arguments in *Dobbs*, yet there is only glancing engagement with them in the opinion.[66] The majority's conspicuous refusal even to fully acknowledge, let alone to take seriously, those arguments is further evidence of the opinion's crabbed and thin commitment to democracy.

The Roberts Court's Democratic Distortions

Considering the *Dobbs* opinion from these perspectives reveals the hollowness—indeed, the cynicism—of the Court's paeans to democracy. But the disingenuousness of *Dobbs*'s commitment to democracy is even more apparent when viewed alongside the Court's many other interventions to distort and disrupt the landscape of democracy. Indeed, *Dobbs* follows on the heels of a series of high court decisions that together have made our democracy decidedly less representative and less democratic.[67] The topic of the Court's undermining of democracy is vast and well canvassed,[68] so we offer here just a few representative examples.

First is the Court's approach to partisan gerrymandering, a process that permits self-interested politicians to draw legislative district lines in ways that consolidate partisan power. Wisconsin supplies a particularly egregious recent example of this practice and its impact. The 2022 election in that state produced a victory for the Democratic governor, who was reelected statewide by a margin of 51.2% to 47.8%.[69] Despite this statewide Democratic majority in the governor's race, Republicans won approximately 64% of seats in the state assembly and 67% of seats in the state senate.[70]

For many years and across a number of cases, the Court wrestled with how to define, and then how to remedy, the constitutional problem of excessive partisan gerrymanders. But in the 2019 decision *Rucho v. Common Cause*, a 5–4 majority of the Court concluded that while excessive partisan gerrymanders are "incompatible with democratic principles"[71]—and lead to "results that reasonably seem unjust"[72]—federal courts are powerless to stop them. According to the *Rucho* Court, challenges to partisan gerrymanders present nonjusticiable "political questions," so that challenges to such efforts to distort the democratic process are properly left to state politicians and legislatures—the very actors who stand to benefit from the practice.

In the wake of *Rucho*, a number of states have tried to address partisan gerrymandering, either by creating independent commissions to draw legislative maps, or through litigation in state courts under state constitutional provisions. These outcomes proceed directly from *Rucho*, which emphasized that the federal courts' inability to address partisan gerrymandering did not in any way foreclose anti-gerrymandering efforts undertaken by other actors and institutions, like state redistricting commissions and state courts.[73]

And yet, notwithstanding *Rucho*'s assurances, there is every reason to worry about how these interventions might fare before this Court. In 2015, Chief Justice John Roberts insisted in a dissent that independent redistricting commissions were unconstitutional,[74] and in light of intervening personnel changes that have occurred at the Court since 2015, there may be sufficient votes to enshrine that view into law. And although the Court's 2023 decision in *Moore v. Harper* did not embrace the broadest possible version of the so-called independent state legislature theory, the Court *did* preserve the possibility of federal court supervision of state court enforcement of state constitutions, at least when it comes to federal elections.[75] This could empower federal courts to further undermine state-level efforts to combat partisan gerrymandering.

The Court has also hobbled the federal Voting Rights Act (VRA), a statute enacted in 1965 with the explicit purpose of ending racial discrimination in voting. The VRA, in the words of Justice Elena Kagan, "marries two great ideals: democracy and racial equality. And it dedicates our country to carrying them out."[76] Despite these lofty aspirations, the Roberts Court has repeatedly undermined these ideals and the landmark legislation intended to enshrine them into law. In 2013, the Court in *Shelby County v. Holder* (once again a 5–4 decision) struck down a provision of the VRA that required states and localities with especially egregious histories of racial discrimination in voting to obtain preclearance from a federal court or the Department of Justice before implementing any changes to their voting policies or procedures.[77] Two terms ago, in *Brnovich v. DNC*, the Court narrowly interpreted Section 2 of the VRA, rendering meaningful enforcement of the VRA's key remaining prohibition on discriminatory voting laws exceedingly difficult.[78] And the Court's 2023 decision in *Allen v. Milligan*, while affirming a lower court's conclusion that Alabama's legislative map discriminated on the basis of race in violation of Section 2,[79] turned on the vote of Justice Kavanaugh, who indicated in a concurring opinion that he would be receptive to future existential challenges to what remains of the VRA.[80]

Beyond the VRA, the Court has hollowed out other federal laws that aim to protect political participation. In 2018's *Husted v. Phillip Randolph Institute*,[81] the Court in a 5–4 decision allowed states to aggressively purge voter rolls, notwithstanding a provision of federal law that appears to limit states' authority to do just that.[82] The *Husted* Court concluded that Ohio could remove eligible voters from voting rolls for no other reason than neglecting to vote for several election cycles.[83] The Court's decision in *Husted* put a significant percentage of voters at serious risk of being purged from voter rolls and thereby being made ineligible to vote without undertaking a new registration.

The Court has also blessed the voter identification requirements that have gone into effect in many states, and whose ostensible predicate—preventing fraud in voting—has been squarely repudiated in the years since the Court allowed states to enforce such requirements in the 2008 case *Crawford v. Marion County*.[84] And yet in the fifteen years since *Crawford* was decided, many states have implemented and enforced such requirements.[85] Some lower courts have invalidated such laws,[86] but they remain in force in many jurisdictions.[87] And it is clear that their impact is felt disproportionately by low-income voters, voters of color, and the youngest and oldest voters.[88]

In addition, just one year after *Crawford*, the Court in *Citizens United v. FEC*[89] opened the floodgates to corporate spending in federal elections, allowing moneyed interests to dominate political campaigns.[90] The *Citizens United* decision not only invalidated long-standing limits on corporate spending in federal elections; it fundamentally transformed the campaign finance landscape,[91] dramatically limiting lawmakers' ability to enact reforms designed to combat both corruption and the appearance of corruption in campaigns for office.[92]

There are many other examples of this Court's efforts to limit democratic participation. In fact, the Roberts Court has *never* invalidated a state or federal law on the grounds that it impermissibly undermined or interfered with the right to vote.[93] Where it has invalidated election-related laws, it has done so on the grounds that they violate the speech rights of campaign donors[94] or the right of states to regulate elections.[95] It is impossible to miss how aggressively the Court has moved across a number of areas of law—a series of decisions that, in tandem, make democracy less representative and less democratic.

Conclusion

The rhetoric of democratic deliberation in *Dobbs* is both hollow and revealing. It displays an incomplete and distorted conception of democracy, and its appeal to democratic deliberation cannot be reconciled with the Court's recent dismantling of core structures that would enable such deliberation. It also offers an incredibly narrow vision of who is genuinely in the polity, a view that is reflected in the majority's adherence to a "history and tradition" analysis. That analysis not only ties us to a past in which very few Americans were meaningful participants in the production of law and legal meaning; it also fails to take seriously the impact of the *Dobbs* decision on women's equal citizenship, or the ways in which the decision opens the door to the enforcement of laws that in no way reflect contemporary popular will.

Focusing on the deficiencies of the *Dobbs* majority's discussion of democracy may also reveal a more profound truth about the opinion: that the Court's "democratic deliberation" settlement is merely a waystation en route to a final destination: the abolition of legal abortion in the United States. Here, past may be prologue. In the aftermath of *Roe*, abortion opponents' principal complaint was not that *Roe* improperly deprived the people of their say in the fraught and divisive debate over abortion rights. Rather, the initial resistance to *Roe* focused on the *wrongness* of the right the decision identified. And, as important, the initial mobilization against *Roe* sought to correct the Court's error by pressing for a constitutional amendment that would make clear that there was no constitutional right to terminate a pregnancy. It was only when this effort failed that abortion opponents began to issue a *cri de cœur* to return abortion to the states—and the people—for democratic debate. Put differently, post-*Roe* abortion opponents initially did not seek to restore the abortion issue to the democratic process, but rather to end it entirely.

With this history in mind, one might speculate that the *Dobbs* settlement may be not an endpoint but rather an intermediate step—one whose aim is to shift political dynamics while at the same time anesthetizing the population to the deprivation of access to legal abortion in significant swaths of the country. For now, fights around access to abortion, both legal and political, will be waged in state legislatures, state courts, state and federal agencies, the commercial marketplace, and through the mechanisms of popular democracy. But it seems all but certain that, despite the claim that it is returning abortion to the realm of democratic deliberation, the Supreme Court has not spoken its final word on this question.

PART V
HISTORICAL PERSPECTIVES

11

The Failure of *Dobbs*

The Entanglement of Abortion Bans, Criminalized Pregnancies, and Forced Family Separation

Dorothy Roberts

Introduction

For most of its history, the mainstream reproductive rights movement centered its advocacy on safeguarding the constitutional right to abortion. This focus prioritized the interests of the most privileged women in the nation and obscured the experiences of Black, Latina, Indigenous, and other marginalized women whose childbearing was socially devalued.[1] Women of color were disproportionately subjected to white supremacist and eugenicist policies that punished them for having children, including mass sterilization abuse, pregnancy-related prosecutions, harsh welfare regulation, and state child removal. *Roe v. Wade* was a victory for the narrow protection against state laws criminalizing abortion, but it failed to recognize the full scope of reproductive freedom, leaving in place these forms of reproductive violence that targeted women of color.

The Supreme Court's decision in *Dobbs v. Jackson Women's Health Organization* spotlights the entanglement of abortion bans, criminalization of pregnancy, and family separation, which *Roe* failed to address. After *Dobbs*, we can see more clearly a right-wing strategy of reproductive control that includes not only abortion laws that compel pregnant people to give birth, but also a broader criminalization of people who give birth to and raise children. Especially telling is how the Court's attention to adoption ties together these forms of reproductive violence. Justice Samuel Alito's majority opinion refers favorably to relinquishing babies for adoption as an answer to denying access to abortion. Its rosy recommendation of adoption paints a false picture of both reproductive servitude's history and the child welfare system's current operation. The Court ignores how forced reproductive labor

Dorothy Roberts, *The Failure of* Dobbs In: *Roe v. Dobbs.* Edited by: Lee C. Bollinger and Geoffrey R. Stone, Oxford University Press. © Oxford University Press 2024. DOI: 10.1093/oso/9780197760352.003.0011 and forced family separation were entwined during the slavery era, as well as opposed by the abolitionists who crafted the Fourteenth Amendment. Moreover, compelling pregnant people to give birth will increase state removals of children from parents charged with neglecting them in the womb or after they are born.

Black feminists have long argued that reproductive freedom includes both bodily and family autonomy. The human right not to have a child, to have a child, and to raise children in safe and supportive communities are all essential to the reproductive justice framework they developed—a framework made more urgent than ever by *Dobbs*.

The Mythical Adoption Remedy

Dobbs and Adoption

Anti-abortion advocates have long held out adoption as a remedy for the harms of compelling pregnant people to give birth. They argue that the availability of adoption eliminates the obligation to raise unwanted children and therefore serves as a substitute for having an abortion. The anti-abortion movement has installed deceptive crisis pregnancy centers throughout the nation that pressure pregnant people to carry their pregnancies to term and surrender their babies for adoption.[2] By linking abortion to adoption, conservatives hope to make abortion restrictions seem less onerous, thereby gaining popular support for them.[3] Liberals, too, have embraced adoption as a seemingly noncontroversial child welfare policy that can build common ground with conservatives on the hot-button issue of abortion.[4]

The adoption remedy became a significant aspect of the *Dobbs* decision. Some anti-abortion activists who gathered outside the Supreme Court during the *Dobbs* oral arguments carried signs with the message "I will adopt your baby." During Julie Rickelman's argument on behalf of abortion clinics, Justice Amy Coney Barrett suggested that the burdens experienced by pregnant people who are denied abortions could be easily relieved by placing the resulting babies in state custody:

> So petitioner points out that in all 50 states, you can terminate parental rights by relinquishing a child after [birth]. . . . It seems to me, seen in that light—both *Roe* and *Casey* emphasize the burdens of parenting. And insofar as you and many of your amici focus on the ways in which forced

parenting, forced motherhood, would hinder women's access to the workplace, and to equal opportunities, it's also focused on the consequences of parenting and the obligations of motherhood that flow from pregnancy—why don't the safe haven laws take care of that problem?[5]

Justice Alito picked up this idea in his majority opinion. He recited without criticism anti-abortion advocates' argument "that States have increasingly adopted 'safe haven' laws, which generally allow women to drop off babies anonymously; and that a woman who puts her newborn up for adoption today has little reason to fear that the baby will not find a suitable home."[6] He then backed up this claim with a footnote that quoted a 2008 Centers for Disease Control and Prevention report: "[N]early 1 million women were seeking to adopt in 2002 (i.e., they were in demand for a child), whereas the domestic supply of infants relinquished at birth or within the first month of life and available to be adopted had become virtually nonexistent."[7] The Court suggested that forcing pregnant people to give birth created a win-win situation: by surrendering their babies for adoption, pregnant people would escape the burdens of parenting while meeting the unfilled demand for adoptable babies. This vision of a well-functioning market for babies conveniently omitted the physical and mental costs of gestating a fetus and the ethical problem of overriding pregnant people's autonomy over their bodies. The Court considered only the burdens that arise after the compelled birth and not those that occur during the pregnancy. Moreover, the adoption market imagery falsely treats the decision to surrender the baby as if it were a freely made reproductive choice when, in reality, it was coerced by the inability to obtain an abortion.[8]

Dobbs and Family Separation

The Court's baby market imagery also grossly mischaracterizes how the adoption system operates. Justice Alito's portrayal of the transfer of babies from birth mothers to adoptive couples as equitable transactions masks the coercive power arrangements that underlie the transfers. To begin with, pressuring people to relinquish their babies for adoption typically takes a profound emotional toll. More than one million U.S. unwed women bowed to enormous family and social pressure to give away their babies in the decades between World War II and *Roe*.[9] Many of them reported enduring lifelong emotional trauma from the experience. One woman described herself to author Ann Fessler as an "illegal mother" who was "robbed" of her child. "It's as if I was an unwilling accomplice to the kidnapping of my own child," the birth mother stated.

Indeed, the pain of losing a newborn is so severe that people who are denied an abortion rarely surrender their babies for adoption.[10] Instead, compelling people to give birth to a child whom they are economically, socially, or psychologically unprepared to raise often intensifies the hardships faced by them and their families. The Turnaway Study, which tracked one thousand women who sought abortions over ten years, found that the women who were denied abortion care suffered serious physical, emotional, and economic harm. Those forced to carry unwanted pregnancies to term were far more likely to be living in poverty, undergo evictions and bankruptcies, and experience mental health problems than their counterparts who had abortions.[11]

The hardships that abortion bans impose on people who keep their babies create another avenue for family separation and coercive adoptions. Impoverished families, especially those that are Black or Indigenous, are at high risk of investigation by government child protective services (CPS). Many Americans view the child welfare system as a benign social service provider that safeguards children from abuse and neglect in their homes. This government regime is better described, however, as a family policing system: it is a powerful state apparatus that intensively regulates marginalized communities by accusing family caregivers of child maltreatment, investigating and monitoring them, taking away their children, and permanently severing their familial bonds.[12] Child protection agents gain their power to regulate families by wielding the threat of removing children from their homes and permanently severing their relationships with their parents.

In 2020 alone, child protection agencies investigated accusations of maltreatment involving three million children.[13] In cities across the nation, CPS surveillance is concentrated in impoverished Black neighborhoods, where all parents are ruled by the agencies' threatening presence.[14] Most Black children in America (53%) will experience a CPS investigation at some point before their eighteenth birthday, and the rate is even higher in many large counties.[15] During CPS investigations, caseworkers may inspect every corner of the home, interrogate family members about intimate details of their lives, strip-search children to look for evidence, and collect confidential information from schools, healthcare providers, and social service programs.[16] If caseworkers detect a problem, like drug use, inadequate medical care, or insecure housing, they will coerce families into an onerous regimen of supervision that rarely addresses their needs.

More disruptive still is the forcible family separation that often follows CPS investigations. Most of the more than $30 billion spent on child welfare services goes to keeping children away from their families—using foster care and adoption assistance—rather than prevention and family services.[17] Every year child welfare agencies take more than 200,000 children from their homes and put them in the formal foster care system. At the same time, these agencies informally separate about the same number of children from their parents each year based on so-called safety plans—arrangements parents are pressured to agree to in lieu of a formal court proceeding.[18] At the end of 2021, the national foster care population stood at nearly 400,000, with untold numbers in the "shadow" foster system.

As a 2021 study concluded, Black children experience "exceptionally high rates" of traumatic child welfare interventions. Black children have long been grossly overrepresented in the national foster care population: although they were only 14% of children in the United States in 2019, they made up 23% of children in foster care. More than one in ten Black children will be taken from their families before they reach age eighteen. While President Donald Trump's cruel policy of separating migrant children from their parents at the U.S.-Mexico border drew national condemnation, few experts connected it to the far more widespread family separation that takes place every day in Black neighborhoods. Empirical studies have documented rampant anti-Black racial bias in the decision to remove children from their homes, and the U.S. and state governments have wielded child removal as a measure to quell Black people's rebellion against racial injustice.[19]

Most children in foster care were removed from their homes based on accusations of parental neglect. Only 17.5% of children enter foster care because they are found to be physically or sexually abused.[20] The conflation of poverty and neglect is written directly into state statutes that define child maltreatment. Many states broadly permit intervention into families whenever parents fall short of supplying "the proper or necessary support for a child's well-being." A 2020 fifty-state survey of neglect statutes found that most "are very open-ended, allowing child protective investigators and their supervisors to declare a child neglected based on their own unbounded opinions as to what is 'proper' or 'necessary care.' "[21] Based on state child neglect laws, child protection investigators interpret conditions of poverty, such as lack of food, insecure housing, and inadequate medical care, as evidence

of parental unfitness. Forcing people to give birth to children they are unprepared to care for will increase their odds of being deemed neglectful and
becoming entangled in the family policing system.

The fate of many families separated by family policing is their legal destruction. Parents who are unable to complete agency requirements to
recover their children from foster care within an imposed timeframe face termination of their rights: a judge permanently severs their legal relationship
with their children. The dissolution of the legal relationship between foster
children and their parents is known as the "civil death penalty" because it is
the ultimate punishment family courts can impose.[22] A 2019 study estimated
that one in one hundred U.S. children will experience this permanent loss
of family ties before they reach age eighteen, with the risk highest for Native
American and African American children. Parental rights termination "is far
more common than often thought," the authors concluded.[23]

Adoption of children from foster care requires the termination of their
parents' rights. Far from being a free market transaction, as the *Dobbs*
Court implied, the availability of foster children for adoption results from a
system that relies on coercion, threats, and terror. The justices' promotion of
adoption also elides the untold numbers of "legal orphans" in foster care—
children who were legally severed from their families but never adopted.[24]
Many of these children "age out" of the foster system, abandoned by the state
and vulnerable to homelessness, poverty, and incarceration.[25] Denying access to abortion will likely increase the numbers of children consigned to and
spat out of the foster system without any family ties at all.

Slavery's Entanglement of Reproductive Servitude and Family Separation

The connection between abortion bans and family separation, which *Dobbs*
intensified, has deep roots in U.S. history. Exploitation of enslaved women's
reproductive labor entailed enslavers' domination of both childbearing and
childrearing. Considering the violence inflicted on Black women by compelling their pregnancies under bondage helps to elucidate the violence inflicted
on pregnant people today by compelling them to give birth under abortion
bans. Because enslavers had a vital economic stake in Black women's childbearing, they made control of reproduction a central aspect of the slavery
regime.[26] Enslavers claimed a property right in enslaved women's bodies

and enslaved women's children from the moment of conception. A 1662 law passed by the Virginia Assembly giving the children born to Black women and fathered by white men the status of their mothers permitted white men to enslave the children and to profit from raping enslaved women.[27]

Enslavers' legal control over Black women's reproductive capacity and the law's failure to afford enslaved women any legal right to bodily autonomy cast an archetype for laws that compel pregnant people to give birth. "Where is the precedent for the appropriation of a person's body by the state? Where did we learn in this country that the state could define a fetus as a distinct matter of law and property and state intervention?" asks historian Jennifer Morgan.[28] "We learned that from the long and violent history of hereditary racial slavery." Although there are obvious distinctions between exploiting the reproductive labor of enslaved women and prohibiting abortion, there is also a profound resemblance in the denial of autonomy caused by compelled pregnancy.

Family separation was inextricably tied to reproductive servitude. One of the most awful atrocities inflicted by the slavery regime was the physical separation of enslaved parents from their children.[29] Enslavers had absolute discretion to buy and sell family members separately from each other. They could dismember Black families at will whenever doing so became economically expedient. A nineteenth-century South Carolina court noted, for example, that planters could sell children away from their mothers no matter how young, because "the young of slaves . . . stand on the same footing as other animals." Only Louisiana and, in 1852, Alabama enacted laws that placed any restrictions at all on the ages at which children could be sold separately from their mothers. According to historian Heather Andrea Williams, "Approximately one third of enslaved children in the Upper South experienced family separation in one of three possible scenarios: sale away from parents, sale with mother away from father, or sale of mother or father away from child."[30] A slaveholder might decide to sell a mother, a father, or their children to pay off a debt or to punish perceived disobedience. Black people were devised in wills, wagered at horse races, and awarded in lawsuits. Bonded families were disbanded when the heirs of an estate decided not to continue the patriarch's business or when young children were hired or apprenticed out to work on another plantation. Enslaved women's loved ones routinely "got rented out, loaned out, bought up, brought back, stored up, mortgaged, won, stolen or seized," Toni Morrison wrote in *Beloved*. "Nobody stops playing checkers just because the pieces included [their] children."[31]

Even when enslaved families remained physically intact, Black parents were denied authority over their children. Slavery law installed the white patriarch as the head of an extended plantation family that included the Black people he enslaved. White people considered the plantation family, ruled by white men, to be the best institution to teach moral values to Africans, whom they deemed to be uncivilized. "Abrogation of the parental bond was a hallmark of the civil death that United States slavery imposed," writes law professor Peggy Cooper Davis in *Neglected Stories: The Constitution and Family Values*.[32] Slaveholders proclaimed their moral authority by reinforcing the message of parental helplessness, frequently whipping enslaved parents in front of their children. Likewise, enslavers had unbridled authority to force Black children to labor, to punish them, and to sexually assault them, while denying enslaved parents any power to protect their children. "These messages of parental vulnerability and subordination were repeatedly burned into the consciousness of slave parents and children," Davis explains, "undermining their sense of worth, diminishing the sense of family security and authority, eroding the parents' function as a model of adult agency and independence, and, most importantly for our purposes, kindling a determination that freedom would entail parental prerogatives."[33]

Black mothers resisted reproductive servitude by self-inducing abortions, fending off enslavers' sexual violence, and caring for their children.[34] Enslavers, however, used children as hostages to prevent bonded women from running away or to lure escaped women back to plantations.[35] Slaveholders could threaten enslaved women who were rebellious with the sale of their children to make them more compliant. This strategy is one of the reasons far fewer women than men fled from bondage. Most enslaved women were unwilling to abandon their children in order to increase their chances of escape; most fugitive women took their children with them. Thus, there is a long history of the white male elite, on one hand, devaluing Black mothers' relationships with their children while, on the other hand, using the threat of child removal to control and punish Black mothers.

The rights of family were central to the antislavery movement. In petitions to the government, enslaved people often based their claims for freedom on the natural right to family integrity. Abolitionists also focused their condemnation of slavery on its immoral destruction of families—"the greatest perceived sin of American slavery."[36] Images of crying mothers and children clinging to each other as merciless slave traders wrenched them apart were widely circulated in antislavery pamphlets, slave narratives, and newspapers.

The Reconstruction Congress was moved to draft the Thirteenth and Fourteenth Amendments both by formerly enslaved people's heart-wrenching accounts of family separation and by the argument that the right to family integrity is inalienable.[37] For example, Republican senator James Harlan of Iowa advocated for the Thirteenth Amendment by accusing slavery of causing "the abolition practically of the parental relationship, robbing the offspring of the care and attention of his parents, severing a relation which is universally cited as the emblem of the relation sustained by the Creator to the human family." His colleague Senator Henry Wilson of Massachusetts promised accordingly, "When this amendment to the Constitution shall be consummated . . . the sharp cry of the agonizing hearts of severed families will cease to vex the weary ear of the nation."[38]

Just as the child welfare system can trace its disruption of Black families to slavery, contemporary notions of family liberty can trace their roots to Black people's resistance against this form of state violence. Thus, the *Dobbs* Court grossly misread the Fourteenth Amendment and ignored its history by holding it provided no support for reproductive freedom. Indeed, the *Dobbs* decision will intensify the kind of destruction of family bonds that the Reconstruction amendments were meant to eradicate.[39]

Criminalizing Pregnancy

Criminalizing Abortion and Fetal Abuse

We can fill out the trajectory of the foundational exploitation of enslaved women's reproductive labor with the history of policies punishing Black women's childbearing throughout the twentieth century. Black women's historical experiences of reproductive violation help to illuminate the intersection of laws that compel pregnancy and laws that criminalize pregnancy loss. The first laws enacted in the colonies treated Black women as innately unrapeable and their children as innately enslaveable, laying the foundation for long-lasting notions of Black women's hypersexuality and hyperfertility. The belief that Black women pass down a depraved lifestyle to their children persisted after the passage of the civil rights laws through the circulation of popular icons of Black maternal unfitness, such as the "welfare queen,"[40] and social scientific research, such as Daniel Patrick Moynihan's 1965 report "The Negro Family: The Case for National Action,"[41] fueling harsh welfare and law enforcement policies that continue to target Black communities.[42]

Of particular significance is the prosecution of Black women for being pregnant and using drugs, launched during the so-called war on crack in the late 1980s. Stoked by false depictions of "crack babies" as irredeemable monsters, the devaluation of Black women's procreation turned the public health issue of drug use during pregnancy into a crime.[43] Over the ensuing decades, the fetal-personhood movement developed a unified legal strategy of criminalizing pregnancy outcomes while shutting down access to abortion services. Legal theories crafted to prosecute Black women set the stage for more widespread criminalization for fetal harm: by 2020, more than seventeen hundred women were arrested, detained, or subjected to forced medical interventions because of pregnancy-related accusations.[44]

Over the same period, state legislatures enacted fetal-protection laws that criminalize pregnancy by giving fetuses the status of already-born children.[45] As states mounted legislative assaults on access to abortion, they constructed a legal apparatus to charge pregnant people criminally for putting their fetuses at risk, including for pregnancy losses. Women have been arrested both for stillbirths and for attempted abortions under the same fetal-protection laws.[46] By eliminating *Roe*'s protection of abortion before viability, which some courts considered a limitation on fetal-abuse prosecutions, *Dobbs* unleashed state power to criminalize pregnant people who fail to deliver a healthy baby.[47]

Policing Fetal and Child Neglect

Just as criminalizing abortion will increase the number of children forcibly removed from their homes, so criminalizing fetal abuse will expand the grounds for family separation. Fetal neglect has become evidence of parental unfitness. Hospital staff routinely screen certain newborns for evidence of their mother's drug use during pregnancy and report positive results to child protection authorities. Over the past thirty years, states have increasingly included prenatal drug use in their definitions of child maltreatment. Despite the lack of scientific support, states began to define exposing a fetus to drugs as a form of child maltreatment or as evidence of unfitness as a parent. In 2003, Congress amended the Child Abuse Prevention and Treatment Act of 1974 to require states to put in place policies and procedures "to address the needs of infants born with and identified as being affected by illegal substance abuse or withdrawal symptoms resulting from prenatal drug exposure."[48] These measures must include a "requirement that health care providers involved in the delivery or care of such infants notify the child protective services system of the occurrence of such condition in such infants." Congress left it to the states to establish their own definitions of what constitutes child abuse and neglect.

The number of states with prenatal drug use policies increased from one in 1974 to forty-two states and the District of Columbia in 2016. Whether considered a crime, infliction of civil child maltreatment, or reason to question the ability to parent in the future, using drugs during pregnancy is often seen as warranting a call to child protection authorities.[49] Most states don't have either universal drug testing or clear testing rules.[50] Nor do they have any checks on when to report positive toxicologies to CPS. As a result, healthcare providers have wide latitude in determining which newborns exposed to drugs or alcohol get investigated. Their decisions whether to test and report rely on their subjective suspicions about the likelihood a mother used drugs—or, perhaps more telling, her fitness to care for her baby. This free-for-all invites rampant discrimination against Black mothers by hospital staff. Since the 1990s, numerous studies have shown that healthcare professionals report Black women who use drugs during pregnancy far more readily than they report their white patients.[51] Parents who are found to have maltreated a fetus, bringing them under CPS surveillance, automatically may be put at risk of losing any children they have in the future.

Racial Capitalism, Punitive Logic, and the Mirage of Benevolence

I have shown that the *Dobbs* decision's denial of constitutional protection for abortion is intimately connected to state punishment of pregnancy and parenting, creating a broader incursion on reproductive freedom. Throughout U.S. history, Black women have experienced the brunt of these entangled punitive policies. Their experiences of reproductive servitude and family separation illuminate the fallacy of the *Dobbs* Court's appeal to adoption as a benevolent alternative to abortion. The rhetoric of saving babies is a guise to justify expanding the government's power to regulate individuals, families, and communities even beyond what is currently permitted by the criminal legal system. The veneer of benevolence obscures how these integrated reproductive violations support racial capitalism—the U.S. system of wealth accumulation grounded in racist hierarchy and ideology—and impose a punitive approach to meeting families' material needs.

Adoption serves as a market-based solution for meeting the needs of children in struggling families. As I discussed above, parental failure to provide material support for children is the main reason the state places children in foster care and makes them available for adoption. The family policing system revolves around an ideology that confuses poverty with child neglect and attributes the suffering caused by structural racism, poverty, and other inequities to parental pathologies. The government then prescribes useless therapeutic remedies in place of the social change needed to eliminate those inequities. Not only does the state separate families for failing to provide for their children, but it is structured to deprive these families of the income, housing, medical care, and other resources required to meet their children's needs. Moreover, the family policing system is structured to offer state resources for children only when parents have lost custody of those children. Whether resulting from forced births or forced family separation, adoption inflicts an unjust bargain: the price of receiving care for children is giving up custody of them.

The relationship between adoption and lack of state support for families is illuminated by comparing abortion laws and welfare policies among states. The states that enacted the most severe restrictions on abortion are the ones with the highest child poverty rates, worst healthcare systems, and fewest supports for struggling families.[52] Moreover, these same states have the highest maternal and infant mortality rates in the nation—rates that are far worse for Black people.[53] States in the South, which have the largest share of the Black population, have especially abysmal birth outcomes. It is safer for Black women to be pregnant in Kenya or Rwanda than in the Mississippi Delta.[54] In short, the states that compel pregnant people to give birth—and rely on adoption as a remedy—are the ones that are the riskiest for Black people to be pregnant.

The relationship between adoption and lack of state support for families is also exemplified by the Clinton-era federal consolidation of welfare retrenchment and carceral expansion. In the late 1990s, Congress passed back-to-back major legislation that simultaneously intensified law enforcement surveillance of Black communities, stripped away support for struggling parents, and sped their children into adoptive homes. First came the controversial Violent Crime Control and Law Enforcement Act of 1994, which imposed harsher prison sentences for federal offenses and showered states with funds to expand their police forces and build more prisons.[55] In 1996, Congress passed the Personal Responsibility and Work Opportunity

Reconciliation Act, ending the federal guarantee of cash assistance to families living in poverty and giving states wide latitude to decide how to implement extensive welfare reform policies.[56] Welfare's purpose was no longer to provide aid to families with children but instead to coerce mothers who receive welfare to change their behaviors by getting married, taking low-wage jobs, and having fewer children.[57]

A year later, President Bill Clinton signed the Adoption and Safe Families Act of 1997,[58] after directing the federal government to take steps to double the number of foster children adopted annually by 2002.[59] ASFA prioritized getting foster children adopted over reuniting them with their families through a set of mandates and incentives to state child welfare departments. Falsely equating permanency with adoption, the law loosened the requirement that agencies make "reasonable efforts" to keep families together and established swifter timetables for terminating parents' rights, shifting the presumption in favor of termination when children have spent more than fifteen of the previous twenty-two months in state custody.[60] Some states have established even shorter timelines for termination. ASFA also offers financial incentives to states to increase the number of children adopted out of the foster system, with no comparable incentives to increased family preservation. By 2014, the federal government had handed states $424 million in adoption-incentive bonuses, exceeding the amount saved in foster care costs.[61] The coinciding passage of the welfare and adoption laws marked the first time in modern U.S. history that the federal government mandated that states protect children from parental neglect—centered on taking them from their families—but failed to guarantee a minimum economic safety net for impoverished families.

Racist mythology about Black families, such as the "welfare queen" and "crack baby," helped to fuel these punitive bipartisan measures. When ASFA's backers argued for increasing adoptions to reduce the mushrooming foster population, Black children were four times as likely as white children to be removed from their homes and made up the largest group in the foster system.[62] Advocates portrayed Black families' ties as the chief impediment to permanency for children in foster care. The solution, they argued, was to "free" Black children from their mothers by permanently extinguishing their legal bonds to make them available for adoption.[63] Some transracial adoption advocates portrayed expedited terminations of Black mothers' rights as a means for facilitating adoptions of Black children by white couples.[64]

ASFA dealt a devastating blow to families. Chicago, where virtually all the children in foster care were Black, felt its immediate impact; according to the *Chicago Reporter*, by 1999, just two short years after ASFA's enactment, "[t]erminations grew from 958 to 3,743 in that period, meaning that three out of every five cases ended with parents losing custody."[65] High incarceration rates intersect with ASFA to put Black families at risk of legal demolition.[66] Imprisonment itself constitutes statutory grounds for termination of parental rights in some states, and some judges consider the law's swift timetable for termination proceedings as sufficient grounds for ending incarcerated parents' ties to their children forever.[67] A 2003 study discovered that the number of cases terminating incarcerated parents' rights more than doubled in a few years after ASFA became law.[68]

First Lady Hillary Clinton, one of ASFA's leading champions, plainly stated the adoption remedy for abortion: "[I]nstead of yelling at one another about abortion, we should spend our energy making adoptions easier."[69] Yet she expressed a baffling ignorance of the adoption system's toll on families when she tweeted in response to the Trump administration's family separation policy, "There's nothing American about tearing families apart."[70]

Conclusion: The Urgency of Reproductive Justice

The *Dobbs* decision not only permits making abortion a crime but also intensifies state punishment of pregnancy and parenting that was already expanding under *Roe*'s regime. The Court's reasoning envisions a society where adoption is forced upon politically marginalized people as a response to crises caused by racial capitalism and structural inequities. Black feminists developed a reproductive justice analysis that accounts for the entanglement of abortion bans, criminalization of pregnancy, and forcible child removal. The reproductive justice framework includes the freedom not to have children or to have children and to raise children in safe and sustainable communities.[71]

Rather than center on defending legal protections for the most privileged people, the reproductive justice movement should center on creating a society that meets human needs without policing pregnancy and families. We should connect activism to guarantee the legal right to abortion to the growing movement to dismantle the family policing system led by parents and youth who have been ensnared in it. These activists promote legislation to curtail mandated reporting, guarantee legal representation for parents, and require informed consent for drug testing of pregnant people and their newborns. They advocate for policies that shift government funds away from coercive interventions in families toward putting resources directly in parents' hands. And they are creating community-based approaches to support families and keep children safe. With a common radical vision for meeting human needs, we can build a society where all aspects of reproductive violence—compelling people to give birth, punishing people for pregnancy outcomes, and forcing people to surrender their children—would be unimaginable.

12

A Requiem for *Roe*

When Property Has No Privacy

Michele Bratcher Goodwin

Introduction

What is the requiem for *Roe v. Wade?*[1] In 1973, in a 7–2 opinion, exactly one hundred years after the Supreme Court upheld states' laws barring women from suffrage in *Minor v. Happersett*[2] and from practicing law in *Bradwell v. State*,[3] the Court acknowledged the disturbing social conditions associated with centuries of shaming, stereotyping, and stigmatizing women when it struck down laws that criminalized abortion. In doing so, the Court finally recognized the "detriment" that states had long inflicted on women when legislatures denied them choices about their reproductive destinies and aspirations beyond motherhood or being bound to their husbands.[4]

Although unstated in *Roe*, the Court also initiated the work of dismantling its ugly record of complicity in affirming harmful laws that tethered women to motherhood. Laws banning women from full participation in society and suffrage arguably rooted in coverture—the troubling legal theory advanced by Sir Matthew Hale and Sir William Blackstone that women's identities and legal rights are subsumed within the bundle of rights possessed by their husbands.[5] Such laws were never meant to enrich women or to recognize their constitutional personhood, but rather to secure familial harmony for men even to the detriment and abuse of their wives and daughters. According to Blackstone, "[b]y marriage, the husband and wife are one person in law: that is, the very being or legal existence of the woman is suspended during the marriage, or at least is incorporated and consolidated into that of the husband."[6] Supposedly, a woman gained protection by being "under [her husband's] wing, protection and *cover.*"[7] Blackstone declared that a wife was to "perform[] every thing; and is therefore called in our law . . . a *feme-covert.*"[8]

Michele Bratcher Goodwin, *A Requiem for* Roe*: When Property Has No Privacy* In: *Roe v. Dobbs.* Edited by: Lee C. Bollinger and Geoffrey R. Stone, Oxford University Press. © Oxford University Press 2024. DOI: 10.1093/oso/9780197760352.003.0012

In 1736, Sir Matthew Hale's highly acclaimed treatise, *Historia Placitorum Coronae, History of the Pleas of the Crown*, declared that it was inconceivable for a woman to be raped by her husband. Hale argued that a "husband cannot be guilty of rape" because marriage conveys unconditional consent, whereby a wife has entered a binding contract and "hath given up herself in this kind unto her husband, which she cannot retract."[9] Importantly, no prior English common law articulated this standard, but this rule found broad support among parliamentarians and subsequently influenced legal developments in the British colonies and in the United States. Nearly every state legislature enacted laws that safeguarded husbands from criminal punishment for raping their wives (and sometimes even girlfriends). The harmful vestiges of such principles instantiate deeply in law and remain difficult to uproot. It wasn't until 1993 that North Carolina rescinded its marital rape exemption.

Egregiously, in *Dobbs v. Jackson Women's Health Organization*[10] the decision authored by Justice Samuel Alito that struck down *Roe,* the Court invoked Blackstone and Hale. In doing so, the Court embraced legal theorists who rejected the idea that women possessed any identity apart from their husbands. Blackstone too rejected the concept of marital rape, and thus denied the principle that married women could defend themselves against sexual violations committed by their husbands. Seemingly, because Hale and Blackstone espoused the view that marital rape was nonexistent, so too did states' legislatures.

Undoubtedly, Blackstone and Hale provided convenient cover for male legislators already inclined toward patriarchal interpretations of law. In a society that also embraced and greatly profited from slavery, race and sex hierarchies served as the architecture and organization of American life, not only in southern states but in northern states as well. As such, invidious norms became justified and maintained by laws. Problematically, American courts became complicit in upholding dangerous, patriarchal ideals and citing Blackstone and Hale in justification of invidious norms, violating what can be described as "minimal standards of the rule of law."[11] Applying Gerald Postema's theory of the rule of law, American courts became complicit in laws that "embed, authorize, or encourage patterns of invidious discrimination, because they violate the core rule-of-law principle that all who are subject to law's requirements are entitled to law's protection (equality in the eyes of the law)."[12]

In other words, in their advancement of the view that domestic "corrections" were unpunishable and sexual assaults nonexistent in marital relationships, such ideologies became incorporated in American jurisprudence. Lower courts came to interpret domestic violence as inoffensive to law. In North Carolina, for example, while the state supreme court eventually rejected the idea that wives could be subjected to whipping, in 1874 it maintained that, "if no permanent injury has been inflicted, nor malice, cruelty nor dangerous violence shown by the husband, it is better to draw the curtain, shut out the public gaze, and leave the parties to forget and forgive."[13] Similarly, in *Abbott v. Abbott*,[14] the Supreme Court of Maine in 1877 denied relief to a married woman whose injuries were so severe as to require hospitalization. According to the court, the "husband and wife are one person," and as such the wife was denied recovery.[15]

This sophistry extended to daughters as well. In *Roller v. Roller*, for example, the Washington Supreme Court held that it would undermine public policy if a victimized teen could recover after being serially raped by her father.[16] Evidence of the repeated sexual molestations was not at issue in the case, as sufficient proof was provided at the lower court adjudication. Rather, the justices explained that preserving domestic "harmony" took priority over the interests of the daughter and that this principle was manifested from the "earliest organization of civilized government ... [and] inspired by the universally recognized fact that the maintenance of harmonious and proper family relations is conducive to good citizenship, and therefore the welfare of the state."[17] American courts twisted and distorted basic rule-of-law values in order to embed and maintain patriarchal conceptions in law even in the most grievous cases. Obviously, the harmony and safety of girls and women mattered very little in cases of rape and incest, and courts could not be trusted to correct invidious discrimination in the most odious instances involving harms against girls and women.

Judges insisted that spousal and familial immunity furthered important policy goals, including discouraging intrafamilial litigation.[18] As Reva Siegel has explained, courts claimed that "[i]nterspousal litigation violated fundamental precepts of the doctrine of marital unity."[19] Judges ignored that minimizing marital tensions and discord for men did not alleviate tensions for women. Moreover, enshrining marital harmony as a priority in American jurisprudence did not serve women or remedy physical, emotional, and sexual abuse they experienced in marital homes.[20] This judicial philosophy did not consider, let alone ensure, the safety, care, and betterment of women and girls.

Dorothea Dix, a prominent nineteenth-century activist, put it this way:

It is impossible to enter upon individual histories here, and I think that the plain facts, stating recent outward conditions, are sufficient to show that society at large is unfaithful to its moral and social obligations. . . . I know of sisters and daughters subject to abusive language, to close confinement, and to "floggings with the horse-whip." . . . I know of many cast out from dwellings, to wander forth, and live or die, as the elements, less merciless than man, permit.[21]

Obviously, *Roe* did not directly address the devastating multitude of patriarchal harms, even related to sex or concerns raised in this essay. It even reeked of paternalism, tying women's reproductive decision-making to consultations with their physicians. Nevertheless, the decision was a powerful departure from prior court rulings on matters of women's personhood and bodily autonomy. It was a corrective to the notion that women's destinies necessarily and fundamentally attached to sexual subordination, mothering, and providing care to men—even their husbands. *Roe* was a salve to and acknowledgment of the invidious social, economic, educational, physical, and psychological injuries women experienced in unwanted pregnancy, childbearing, and mothering.

The *Dobbs* Court's turn to the past—framed as originalism—in dismantling *Roe* was selective, if not opportunistic. The Court's radical conservatives pointed to specific moments in history that shaped a narrative fitting an outcome that appeared predetermined from the outset. Justice Alito highlighted states' laws criminalizing abortion before ratification of the Fourteenth Amendment, though he neglected to provide a descriptive or analytical account as to why. The majority in *Dobbs* avoided glaring, inconvenient truths, including that the Framers were not opposed to abortion. Indeed, Benjamin Franklin wrote about how to procure a safe abortion,[22] and Thomas Jefferson, Patrick Henry, and John Marshall were all of the view that abortion was a private, family matter.[23] Neither was abortion illegal in any state at the nation's founding.

Notably, some legislatures criminalized abortion in the years leading up to the Civil War, as concerns about enslaved Black women and men becoming freed from the grips of slavery loomed. Relevantly, the Court in *Dobbs* ignored that the lobbyists who demanded criminal abortion laws in those years—disgruntled, newly minted male obstetricians—sought to push women out of the practice of reproductive healthcare and thus monopolize the profession for themselves. Dr. Horatio Robinson Storer—a leader among them—comes to mind. After the war, he bemoaned that too few white people inhabited "the great territories of the far West, just opening to expansion, and the fertile savannas of the South, now dis[e]nthralled" due to the abolition of slavery. He queried whether those regions of the country would come to be "filled by our own children or by those of aliens? This is a question our own women must answer; upon their loins depends the future destiny of the nation."[24]

Rather than stamping out the vestiges of coverture, Justice Alito tellingly resurrected them, justifying the Court's overturning of *Roe* by citing Blackstone, Hale, and other legal theorists who advanced coverture principles—or women as property. The Court in *Dobbs* showed extreme solicitude and deference to Mississippi, a state whose notorious patterns of invidious sex and race discrimination throughout slavery and Jim Crow sadly continue to manifest in disparate rates of maternal mortality, maternal morbidity, and poverty. When the Court declared, "*Roe* and *Casey* must be overruled," it stripped away a fundamental right on which millions of women had come to rely, including low-income Black women.[25] *Dobbs* will likely be remembered as one of the most haunting Supreme Court decisions ever issued, in company with *Dred Scott*,[26] *Plessy v. Ferguson*,[27] and *Buck v. Bell*.[28]

In overturning *Roe,* the Court rejected decades of precedent affirming abortion rights. Only six years before *Dobbs*, in 2016, in *Whole Woman's Health v. Hellersted,* the Court struck down two Texas laws that unconstitutionally infringed on abortion rights. The Court debunked Texas's erroneous claims that laws imposing surgical center requirements and mandating hospital admitting privileges for providers that perform abortions advance the health interests of women seeking abortions. Instead, the Court held that laws that provide few, "if any, health benefits for women seeking abortions," and that create substantial obstacles "to women seeking abortions," will not stand.[29] In her concurring opinion, Justice Ruth Bader Ginsburg noted that so long as the Court adheres to *Roe* and *Casey,* laws that "strew" obstacles to abortion will not "survive judicial inspection."[30] Like *Roe,* those days are gone.

This eulogy for *Roe* now proceeds in two brief parts. First I address forced reproduction and pregnancies—the conditions normalized before *Roe,* during coverture and slavery. The discussion centers on the concerns of Black women by reflecting on Margaret Garner, her escape from slavery and subsequent trial for murder. I then turn to post-*Dobbs* risks and harms—the new coverture and New Jane Crow.

Pre-*Roe* Coverture, Slavery, and Jane Crow

In 1861, Harriet Jacobs penned the illuminating and enduring memoir, *Incidents in the Life of a Slave Girl*,[31] adding an important narrative and witness account to the canon of American history. If Tocqueville's *Democracy in America* compellingly captured the new nation's dream, Jacobs revealed the nightmare. She presented a chilling examination of antebellum America, captured through the lens of a child—an enslaved girl—trapped in the hungry and predatory grasps of American slavery. The despair that dripped from her pen landed in terrifying prose about sexual violence, forced pregnancies, and efforts to escape those terrifying realities. Her autobiography exposed a system of laws, practices, and behaviors far less gentle and kind and far more sinister than the labor-focused accounts of slavery that largely center on men: forced, uncompensated production and harvesting of cotton, rice, tobacco, and sugar cane.

Rather, the horrors Jacobs recounts—kidnapping, sexual coercion, confinement for the purpose of sexual abuse, rape, and torture—the far too common terrors of chattel slavery, demand a more nuanced view of the period. Jacobs provided a view into a largely neglected archive of American legal and social history now made increasingly relevant by the Supreme Court and contemporary debates involving forced pregnancy, reproductive freedom, and abortion.

Jacobs was by no means alone. In 1851, in a powerful oration recorded as *Ain't I a Woman*, Sojourner Truth implored the crowd of men and women gathered at the Women's Rights Convention in Akron, Ohio, to consider the gravity and utter depravity of American slavery in the lives of Black women. It was an appeal not only to abolish slavery but to understand its unique toll on the reproductive lives of Black women. Reported by newspapers and recorded through history, Truth stated that she had borne thirteen children and seen nearly each one ripped from her arms, with no appeal to law or courts.[32] As she explained the devastating psychological and physical toll of American slavery, she left the audience with a penetrating question: Wasn't she a woman too?

By no means rhetorical, Truth's question touched on a profound matter of human rights, hotly debated in American law: *Was she (and for that matter all other non-manumitted Black women) property—and therefore with no rights a court was bound to respect? Or was she a woman, and therefore entitled to the legal protections accorded white women? Was she mere property and therefore*

not worthy of privacy? The answers to such questions mattered not only politically but economically.

In a letter to John Wayles Eppes on June 30, 1820, Thomas Jefferson wrote,
"I know no error more consuming to an estate than that of stocking farms
with men almost exclusively. I consider a woman who brings a child every
two years as more profitable than the best man of the farm. [W]hat she
produces is an addition to the capital, while his labors disappear in mere consumption."[33] Notably, Eppes was a politician as well as a relative of the former
president. At the time of Jefferson's epistle lauding the economic gains to be
wrought from exploiting Black women's forced reproductive labor and servitude, Eppes had already served in the Virginia House of Delegates as well
as in the U.S. House of Representatives and the Senate. He was Jefferson's
nephew and an owner of enslaved people. Thus, while this was an exchange
among businessmen with family ties, it was also a communication among
politicians who shaped state and federal law.

Across a series of events in the 1850s and 1860s, these matters would
be contested and sorted at trials and even before the U.S. Supreme Court.
Whether Black women were property, entitled to privacy, shared the legal
status of white women—at least regarding rape—were questions that
dominated the concerns of abolitionists, including those in Congress. By
the late 1850s, the tragic narratives of women like Sojourner Truth, Harriet
Jacobs, Margaret Garner, and Celia, a slave, among others, were central to the
concerns of abolitionists. They are once more relevant in light of the Supreme
Court's ruling in *Dobbs*.

In the wake of a ten-year-old rape survivor fleeing Ohio to obtain an
abortion in Indiana, mere days after *Dobbs*,[34] like a page ripped from history, Margaret Garner comes to mind.[35] Margaret, memorialized in Toni
Morrison's Pulitzer Prize–winning book, *Beloved*, fled a Boone County,
Kentucky, plantation and the Gaines family, which claimed ownership of
her. In the frigid depths of winter, on January 27, 1856, at twenty-two years
old and pregnant, safeguarding her meager belongings, Margaret escaped on
foot with her children, a mule, and companions.

Margaret's goal was to reach Cincinnati, a key stop on the underground
railroad, a place of at least temporary respite and safety for escapees brave
enough to risk physical punishments, including whippings, the chopping
off of limbs, and even death. Such cruelties were strong disincentives against
attempting freedom, and without federal protections Black women and girls
were incredibly vulnerable. State and federal laws even punished individuals

who aided and abetted so-called runaways or fugitives from slavery.[36] In *Ableman v. Booth,* the U.S. Supreme Court in 1856 queried whether the Wisconsin Supreme Court had the authority to issue writs of habeas corpus for the release of Sherman Booth, an abolitionist who aided in the escape of Joshua Glover, a "runaway slave," held in federal custody in Wisconsin.[37]

Jurisdictional struggles ensued between courts regarding whose authority defined the law related to a formerly enslaved Black person in a city or town, leading famously to the Supreme Court's decisions in *Ableman*[38] and three years later in *United States v. Booth.*[39] Was an enslaved person still so after escape; were they property or person? Specific to the *Booth* cases, did the supreme court in Wisconsin, then a "free state," have authority to issue writs of habeas corpus for the release of Booth? The Supreme Court ruled that it did not. In this light, *once a slave, always a slave, regardless of the laws in other states.*

To become free or legally recognized as free to govern her own body, to travel, and to control possessions was by no means simple. It was not enough for a woman to flee a plantation, endure an arduous journey, and reach a free state. Notably, Ohio was a "free state" on paper, but a complicated one at best. Lawmakers had abolished slavery years before, and in 1841 even allowed Black people who made their way to the state to claim freedom. However, according to Julius Yanuck's illuminating work on the Garner case, "in southern Ohio there was a marked antipathy toward abolition" and lawmakers were hostile to Black refugees escaping the torments of slavery.[40]

A border state, Ohio was situated directly across the river from Kentucky, and business leaders and lawmakers tolerated slaveholders who traveled interstate with their cargo of kidnapped and trafficked Black children, women, and men on their journeys north and south. As noted in my prior work, "the Fugitive Slave Laws of 1793 and 1850 were accelerants on an already raging fire, they legalized an enterprise whereby nonelite, white bounty hunters and 'slave catchers' traveled to northern states and territories to hunt Black people who, by skill and wit, escaped."[41] It was not uncommon or extraordinary that bounty hunters kidnapped Black children, women, and men who had never been enslaved.[42]

Often, they made mistakes or purposely flouted the law, disrupting families, capturing and selling Black people never previously enslaved as far north as Boston and New York. Judges were complicit in this. Judge Richard Riker "was infamous in the 1800s for abusing the Fugitive Slave Act to send (or sell) African Americans in New York to slaveowners in the

South."[43] Solomon Northup's chilling memoir, *Twelve Years a Slave*, offers a detailed and distressing account of this general practice, while Richard Bell's powerful book, *Stolen: Five Free Boys Kidnapped into Slavery and Their Astonishing Odyssey Home*, exposes the broader depths of the reverse underground railroad, where thousands of legally "free" Black people in the North were kidnapped and trafficked to the American South.

By January 1856, Margaret was desperate to be liberated from the sexual abuse of Archibald Gaines and the intergenerational physical abuse and psychological torment she and other women in her family endured. She was the daughter of an enslaved Black woman who is believed to have been raped by John Pollard Gaines, a prominent politician and her mother's owner. Being the daughter of a slaveholder did not spare Black girls and women, as they took on the status of their mothers, not their fathers, which shielded white men from economic and moral responsibility for their Black offspring and allowed them to hold their children in bondage to mortgage, rent, and sell for profit.

Among the earliest legal questions to be settled in the colonies was *whether the offspring of white men and enslaved Black women were free or enslaved.* Early legislation answered that the children would take the status of their enslaved mothers. This troublingly tied slavery to forced pregnancy, tethering Black women to involuntary reproduction. It fastened capitalism to rape, embedding a horrific practice into the culture of southern economics.[44]

By age twenty-two, Margaret had become the victim of serial rapes and birthed at least four children. Some accounts suggest she had six births and married at sixteen. It is unclear how many of her children were the product of sexual abuse by Archibald, the younger brother of John Pollard. During her trial, however, the coroner's jury reported that the dead child "was almost white, and was a little girl of rare beauty," killed by Margaret, her mother. The abolitionist Lucy Stone Blackwell, who traveled south to meet Margaret and attend her trial, told members of the court, "The faded faces of the Negro children tell too plainly to what degradation female slaves submit. Rather than give her little daughter to that life, she killed it."

On that frigid January evening, when the air was so cold that the Cincinnati River, usually a barrier to freedom, froze, Margaret made her escape. The river served as a literal pathway to freedom. Margaret's freedom would not last long, however. Archibald Gaines and his party were in hot pursuit, arriving in Cincinnati early the next morning, where they obtained a warrant for Margaret's arrest under the Fugitive Slave Act. Along with his group of friends and a deputy U.S. marshal, Gaines successfully tracked Margaret down.

With Gaines and his mob approaching, Margaret grabbed a knife and slit the throat of her daughter, then grabbed her son, "sobb[ing] that she would rather kill every one of her children than have them taken back across the river." It is said that Margaret fought wildly, resisting capture until she was overpowered and brought down.

In an internationally covered trial, several critical legal issues arose: If an enslaved woman spent previous time in a "free state," did this confer automatic freedom for the future? If a Black woman's offspring were conceived after travel to a free state, did that confer freedom on the child? If an enslaved woman returned to a slave state after being in a free state, was her freedom revoked?

The case was of national concern. Francis T. Chambers, who represented the slave owners, argued, "We have the Union yet, and let those who would dissolve it for the sake of the slave remember that in achieving the liberty of three millions of blacks they are periling those of twenty-four millions of the white race."[45] In response, Margaret's lawyers urged that she be charged with murder in Ohio's state court; even if convicted, this would keep her safer than returning to Kentucky as a slave, where she might be put to death, sold, or subjected to her pre-escape conditions: enslavement, confinement.

Margaret's case ultimately centered on a question far beyond Gaines's Boone County plantation and his enslaved property. If Margaret was mere property, she could not be guilty of killing the child. If she was a person and not mere property, this would suggest that she and other Black women like her were human—possessing personhood, deserving freedom, autonomy, and liberty—something that the South was unwilling to concede. If Margaret possessed personhood this would upset the troubling, unstable legal foundations on which slavery was justified—even articulated in the near-future Supreme Court decision in *Dred Scott v. Sandford* that Black people were reduced to property for their own well-being.[46] Simply put, it was illegal for enslaved Black women to claim freedom and control of their bodies, including in matters involving sex and reproduction. They were mere property. And property has no privacy rights or interests to defend. After the trial, Gaines sold Margaret and her baby, shipping her south to Mississippi, where she died before her twenty-fifth birthday.

Rather than isolated or rare, key aspects of Margaret's tragedy played out for Black women throughout the South, written by abolitionists. In 1951, Horace

Mann delivered a speech on the Fugitive Slave Law, remarking, "[T]here was one girl, who after her recapture . . . was sold six times in seven weeks, in Maryland and Virginia for her beauty's sake. . . . Like Rebecca, the jewess, she would have flung herself from the loftiest battlement, rather than yield her person to a villain."[47] Representative Mann further reported, "[H]er body was found scarred and waled with whip marks, which the villains inflicted upon her because she would not come to their bed."[48] Equally, Representative Joshua R. Giddings brought attention to the degradations experienced by a Black woman "as she flees from the inhumanity of a worse than savage oppressor."[49]

Post-*Dobbs*: The New Jane Crow

Today tensions between free reproductive states and nonfree reproductive states have reemerged now that *Roe v. Wade* has been overturned. In the aftermath of *Dobbs,* there is no federal protection for abortion. And though a strong case can be made that the Thirteenth Amendment, which abolished slavery and involuntary servitude, legally protects a ten-year-old girl from forced pregnancy, the Supreme Court has craftily handed these issues back to the states—just as the Court did during slavery.

Now legal controversies over extradition, extraterritoriality, whether doctors in reproductive sanctuary states can be charged with murder after performing abortions for patients residing in nonfree states, the right to travel, and lack of federal protections for girls, women, and people capable of pregnancy expose the instability of law in the wake of *Dobbs.*

Although over 160 years apart, the reproductive liberty interests at stake with Margaret Garner resonate today as a ten-year-old girl became a modern-day fugitive from Ohio's abortion law, which bans abortion after six weeks of pregnancy, with no exceptions for rape or incest.

For all the deserved criticisms of *Roe,* from its trimester framework to important critiques that it centered on the concerns of doctors, *Roe* acknowledged that unwanted motherhood could be oppressive and dangerous. The ruling directly challenged the premise that a woman's destiny was confined to motherhood and heterosexual spousal care. The enduring profundity of *Roe* is that a century after *Minor, Bradwell, Goodell,* and the many tragic stories of forced and involuntary motherhood during slavery and beyond, *Roe* articulated that motherhood and childbearing could be injurious to women.[50] According to Justice Harry Blackmun, the author of *Roe,* to force or coerce women into those destinies violated their constitutional right to make such fundamental decisions for themselves. Justice Blackmun wrote:

> Maternity, or additional offspring, may force upon the woman a distressful life and future. Psychological harm may be imminent. Mental and physical health may be taxed by child care. There is also the distress, for all concerned, associated with the unwanted child, and there is the problem of bringing a child into a family already unable, psychologically and otherwise, to care for it. In other cases, as in this one, the additional difficulties and continuing stigma of unwed motherhood may be involved.[51]

Apparently dissatisfied with the prevailing assumption that existing criminal bans on abortion could inform the Court on the history of abortion, Blackmun undertook a rigorous empirical review. A century after *Minor* and *Bradwell,* and for the first time, the Court acknowledged that "[s]pecific and direct" injuries "medically diagnosable even in early pregnancy" may result when women are forced by the state to bear children.[52] To have decided any differently would have been to ignore the grave medical consequences mounting at the time.

According to the Guttmacher Institute, "[t]he toll the nation's abortion laws took on women's lives and health in the years immediately before *Roe* was substantial."[53] Data from the era suggest that roughly one million illegal abortions took place each year, with hundreds resulting in death and numerous others requiring emergency hospital interventions.[54] Sometimes women were left infertile as a result of illegal procedures. Indeed, by the "early 1960s, [illegal] abortion-related deaths accounted for nearly half, or 42.1 percent, of the total maternal mortality in New York City."[55] These deaths were not inevitable but the result of harmful legal policies.

As Leslie Reagan, author of *When Abortion Was a Crime: Women, Medicine, and Law in the United States,* describes that period, "[p]hysicians and nurses at Cook County Hospital saw nearly one hundred women come in every week for emergency treatment following their abortions."[56] She observed how women needlessly suffered hemorrhaging, burns, and infections. They were the lucky ones; others died. Cook County Hospital and other medical facilities organized entire wards to address "abortion-related complications," which impacted "[t]ens of thousands of women every year" who needed emergency care following self-induced or back-alley abortions.[57] Deaths were particularly acute among women of color.

Similar concerns surface today, almost immediately after *Dobbs*. For example, the United States is now the deadliest country in the industrialized world in which to be pregnant. It ranks fifty-fifth in the world. Nationally, Black women are 3.5 times more likely to die due to maternal mortality than their white counterparts. In Mississippi a Black woman is 118 times more likely to die by carrying a pregnancy to term than by having an abortion. As well, in Mississippi, Black women comprise 80% of the cardiac deaths during pregnancy.

The tragic consequences of overturning *Roe* were both predictable and immediate. Mere weeks after the decision, a patient in Wisconsin bled excessively, the hemorrhaging lasting more than ten days, during an incomplete miscarriage. In her case, doctors refused to intervene, fearing potential criminal and civil punishment.[58] Prior to *Dobbs*, physicians would have relieved the pregnant woman's suffering and terminated the pregnancy. After *Dobbs*, fear interferes with the practice of medicine. In Louisiana, a woman was refused an abortion in a pregnancy where the fetus had no skull.[59] In Florida, a teenager was denied a judicial bypass to terminate a pregnancy where the judge ruled the girl too immature to terminate a pregnancy, but strangely the result either assumes or ignores whether the girl possesses the capacity for motherhood at sixteen years old.

As Judge Carlton Reeves explained in a 2018 order enjoining the Mississippi law at issue in *Dobbs*, "legislation like H.B. 1510 is closer to the old Mississippi—the Mississippi bent on controlling women and minorities. The Mississippi that, just a few decades ago, barred women from serving on juries 'so they may continue their service as mothers, wives, and homemakers.'"[60]

Conclusion

The scale of the harms brought about after *Dobbs* cannot be described as anything less than significant and tragic. Nor would it be appropriate to describe the cases of near-death and desperation as isolated or episodic. Sadly, threats of criminal and civil punishment for aiding or abetting in the termination of a pregnancy now shape whether and how medical providers will care for their patients.[61] With the Court's decision in *Dobbs*, many states will once again cast into the wind the fundamental right of women to control their own lives, dignity, and destiny.

13

Where History Fails

Nancy F. Cott [*]

Supreme Court opinions can make history in more than one way. First, obviously, the Court's power to declare what the law is and how it should be applied can make dramatic changes in national policies and in everyday life. Second, and less noticed, the Court's opinions can include assertions about history. Judge-made law is a historical practice. Relying on previous cases and precedents as evidence for legal reasoning, it looks to the past, as history does. Historical claims made in Supreme Court cases are taken as accurate, enshrined and quoted in subsequent cases—even if the Court's claims rest on faulty grounds. When the Court uses historical narrative to advance its reasoning, its account becomes, for later cases and for matters of state, "true"—unless and until dislodged by a subsequent overruling opinion. Yet of course this historical "truth," like any other, rests on interpretation. As much as justices may assert that legislative text and previous holdings require what they assert, their opinions are always interpretive.

Dobbs v. Jackson Women's Health Organization[1] offers extravagant evidence of this double effect. It immediately "made history" by ending fifty years of abortion rights. The majority opinion also devoted 40% of its length (counting its appendices) to historical inquiry. Surveying Anglo-American law from the thirteenth century to the year of the Fourteenth Amendment's ratification, Justice Samuel Alito found no positive "right" of abortion.[2] It meant little to his survey or his reasoning that at the time of the founding of the United States and the writing of the Constitution and the Bill of Rights, no law prohibited or punished abortion before "quickening" (a pregnant woman's sensing of fetal movement at around four and a half months). Though Alito conceded that the common law and early American state laws allowed abortion before quickening, he passed over this lightly, giving it no significance because "the quickening rule" was later "abandoned."[3] He gave

Nancy F. Cott, *Where History Fails* In: *Roe v. Dobbs*. Edited by: Lee C. Bollinger and Geoffrey R. Stone,
Oxford University Press. © Oxford University Press 2024. DOI: 10.1093/oso/9780197760352.003.0013

even shorter shrift to the fifty years of history since *Roe v. Wade*'s[4] recognition of a constitutional right to abortion, not even treating those decades as history and dismissing the reliance interest then incurred (meaning people's expectation that abortion would be available if necessary).[5]

The history that mattered to Alito was not those earlier and more recent eras, but only the mid-nineteenth-century decades when numerous American states made performing an abortion a crime. He saw those criminal laws, which lasted well into the twentieth century, as decisive evidence for his view that American history and tradition lacked any "constitutional right to an abortion."[6] How did it happen, we might well ask, that only that slice of history mattered to the majority?

Privacy as a Dimension of Liberty before *Roe v. Wade*

Some attention to history was not surprising, given Alito's aim to deny any legitimacy to *Roe v. Wade*. *Roe* incorporated a historical view of abortion regulation, as a supportive rather than a dispositive element. The Court in *Roe* found the right of a pregnant person to choose to terminate a pregnancy in the personal liberty underwritten by the Fourteenth Amendment, and in so doing consulted the past history of abortion regulation and of rights to make choices around intimate relationships, marriage, and parentage previously affirmed by the Court. Alito responded not only by controverting *Roe*'s historical account but also by stressing the constitutional necessity of consulting history. "Historical inquiries of this nature are essential whenever we are asked to recognize a new component of the 'liberty' protected by the Due Process Clause," Alito wrote, "because the term 'liberty' alone provides little guidance."[7]

Alito's reference to a "new" component might be called disingenuous, since privacy in intimate conduct dealing with childbearing and childrearing had been recognized by the Court as an aspect of liberty for almost a century. Substantive due process—reading the Fourteenth Amendment's promise that no state shall deprive any person of "life, liberty, or property, without due process of law," as a substantive, not simply a procedural, guarantee—was born under a cloud in *Lochner v. New York* in 1905.[8] It was revived in the mid-1960s not in regard to the employer-employee relation, as in *Lochner* and other labor or business cases, but rather in regard to family and sexual issues.

Interpreting the Fourteenth Amendment's "liberty" became newly central in 1965, in decriminalizing contraception for married couples. In *Griswold v. Connecticut*,[9] the majority opinion written by Justice William O. Douglas relied on it, as did two additional justices' concurrences. Justice Douglas had worked up his reasoning about marital privacy and contraception four years before, in *Poe v. Ullman*,[10] which had previously challenged Connecticut's ban on contraception but was dismissed on procedural grounds. (It and *Griswold* were both brought as test cases.) Douglas would have struck down the law then, and in his *Poe* dissent, he explained, "Though I believe that 'due process' as used in the Fourteenth Amendment includes all of the first eight Amendments, I do not think it is restricted and confined to them.... 'Liberty' is a conception that sometimes gains content from the emanations of other specific guarantees or from experience with the requirements of a free society."[11] He cited previous Supreme Court holdings that had expanded the meanings of "liberty" in the Fourteenth Amendment's Due Process Clause in relevant ways, perhaps most importantly *Meyer v. Nebraska*.[12]

In *Meyer*, decided in 1923, the Court struck down as an unreasonable infringement of Fourteenth Amendment liberty a state statute that forbade teaching of any modern language to a pupil who had not yet passed the eighth grade. Addressing the expansive though inexact meaning of this liberty, the Court cited thirteen previous cases and wrote:

> Without doubt, it denotes not merely freedom from bodily restraint, but also the right of the individual to contract, to engage in any of the common occupations of life, to acquire useful knowledge, to marry, establish a home and bring up children, to worship God according to the dictates of his own conscience, and generally to enjoy those privileges long recognized at common law as essential to the orderly pursuit of happiness by free men.[13]

The early date of *Meyer* and the Court's mention of marital and childrearing freedoms as if there were no questions about their inclusion made the decision a rock to stand on.

In *Griswold*, Douglas set aside *Lochner*'s approach and looked to the Bill of Rights to fill out the meaning of due process, asserting that "specific guarantees in the Bill of Rights have penumbras, formed by emanations from those guarantees that help give them life and substance." He found guarantees that created "zones of privacy" in the First Amendment's right of association broadly understood, and also in the Third, Fourth, Fifth, and Ninth Amendments' protections against state actions. While Douglas conceded that "penumbral rights of 'privacy and repose'" had more than once been controversial for the Court, his task in *Griswold* was made easy by the Connecticut law, which banned not only the sale and advertising of contraception (as had many other states) but also its use. "Would we allow the police to search the sacred precincts of marital bedrooms for telltale signs of the use of contraceptives?" Douglas wrote. "The very idea is repulsive to the notions of privacy surrounding the marriage relationship." In Douglas's words, marital privacy was "a right of privacy older than the Bill of Rights," sacralized by its "noble" purpose.[14]

Not every one of the six other justices who joined Douglas's majority agreed with his precise reasoning, but in differing they emphasized the scope of due process liberty. Justice John Harlan declined to endorse Douglas's resort to the Bill of Rights, confident that "the Due Process Clause of the Fourteenth Amendment stands . . . on its own bottom."[15] Though the Bill of Rights or "radiations" from it might be relevant to the inquiry, Harlan saw no need to rely on them. Justice Byron White also concurred, simply because "this Connecticut law, as applied to married couples, deprives them of 'liberty' without due process of law, as that concept is used in the Fourteenth Amendment."[16]

Griswold was crucial for *Roe v. Wade* eight years later. The reasoning in *Griswold* paved a path of constitutional interpretation in which the "liberty" assured in the Due Process Clause of the Fourteenth Amendment protected freedom of choice in regard to family, marriage, procreation, and intimate behavior. Indefinite as the words "penumbras" and "emanations" might be, the majority opinion in *Griswold* secured a line of twentieth-century holdings after *Meyer*, protecting freedom within this "zone of privacy," including *Pierce v. Society of Sisters*[17] (childrearing), *Prince v. Massachusetts*[18] (family privacy), *Loving v. Virginia*[19] (marriage); and *Skinner v. Oklahoma ex rel. Williamson* (procreation).[20] Notably, the *Griswold* opinion did not search within American history and traditions for the marital privacy right, beyond Douglas's eloquence about its ancient origins and indubitable rightness.

Soon the Court (down to seven members because of sudden retirements) faced the question whether unmarried persons shared the same intimate freedoms. In 1972 in *Eisenstadt v. Baird*,[21] the answer was yes, with only one dissent: depriving single persons of the personal liberties attached to married persons (to use contraception) violated the Fourteenth Amendment's promise of "equal protection of the laws." Justice William Brennan, who wrote the opinion, took the opportunity to include this significant point:

> It is true that, in *Griswold,* the right of privacy in question inhered in the marital relationship. Yet the marital couple is not an independent entity, with a mind and heart of its own, but an association of two individuals, each with a separate intellectual and emotional makeup. If the right of privacy means anything, it is the right of the individual, married or single, to be free from unwarranted governmental intrusion into matters so fundamentally affecting a person as the decision whether to bear or beget a child.[22]

This comment implicitly acknowledged unmarried sexual freedom and also significantly reversed the traditional legal premise that the married couple was a single entity represented by the husband.

Thus, when *Roe v. Wade* followed soon after *Eisenstadt,* the Court had already made a remarkable pronouncement on intimate and familial privacy as a dimension of liberty. In deciding *Eisenstadt,* the justices knew that they would soon face the issue of abortion.[23] It was a time of intense and multifaceted abortion activism, as well. A movement for abortion law reform had been under way since the mid-1960s, sparked initially by conscience-driven doctors and lawyers opposing the damages wrought by the criminality of abortion, soon joined by a more insistent and more public women's movement. As a result, a dozen or more states had passed reform statutes widening the ambit of legal abortion performed by medical professionals, and four states (New York, Washington, Hawaii, and Alaska) had fully decriminalized abortion by licensed doctors during a specified number of weeks or months of pregnancy.[24] The Republican Party, moving in the opposite direction, had newly seized on opposition to abortion as a way to rally Catholic and Evangelical Protestant voters to its side. President Richard Nixon made this clear in anticipation of the 1972 elections, announcing his personal belief in the "sanctity of life."[25] Abortion was still criminal in the great majority of states, except (typically) if the pregnant woman's life was endangered.

Adding History into *Roe*

The Court accepted review of *Roe*'s challenge to Texas's abortion law, which allowed abortion only "for the purpose of saving the life of the mother," alongside a related case, *Doe v. Bolton*,[26] which challenged Georgia's new abortion reform law for its over-restrictiveness and/or vagueness in setting boundaries for responsible medical professionals to follow. The latter case seemed more difficult to Justice Harry Blackmun, who was assigned the task of drafting opinions in both cases. Initially, he thought it credible to strike down the Texas law simply for vagueness, without engaging larger questions, such as liberty or privacy, because the Texas law did not clearly specify the determinants for "saving" a life. *Doe* seemed to him to require more intensive reasoning. Blackmun and other members of the Court were very concerned about the legal risks faced by abortion providers, as medical professionals who saw the reasonableness of abortion for individuals and for public health yet faced criminal prosecution for performing their professions as they saw fit.[27]

In the spring of 1972, Blackmun sensed that several of his liberal colleagues were leaning, as he was, toward striking down the Texas law and much of the Georgia law as well. Nonetheless, his initial drafts of opinions for both cases met with little enthusiasm. He then moved successfully to postpone the cases until the fall, with reargument before a full Court of nine members, even though the two new justices recently appointed by President Nixon, William Rehnquist and Lewis Powell Jr., were expected to be conservative.

The Court's opinion in *Roe*—especially the inclusion of its historical section—would not have taken the shape it did without that postponement, which enabled Blackmun to do further research and thinking over the summer of 1972. He spent a week in July at the Mayo Clinic library, reading medical and other sources and surveys about the history and practice of abortion, set out for him by the library staff. This was familiar territory for him. He had been in-house counsel for the Mayo Clinic for nine years prior to his career as a judge, and he respected medical expertise.

Roe v. Wade was reargued with new briefs in the fall, as was *Doe v. Bolton*. At the justices' fall conference, Blackmun solidified his view that the pregnant woman had a "fundamental personal liberty"—lodged in the Fourteenth and Ninth Amendments—to seek and receive medical care, including abortion services, to secure her life and her physical and mental health. Sufficient precedents (*Griswold* most prominently) had established a right of privacy "broad enough to encompass the decision whether to terminate a pregnancy."[28] Blackmun framed the pregnant person's right to choose abortion as a decision to be made in concert with a physician. He developed this reasoning to address *Doe v. Bolton*. The more liberal justices embraced

Blackmun's approach, and so did the new justice Powell, surprising his colleagues. It was Powell who made the crucial suggestion that Blackmun apply his reasoning to *Roe*, and make *Roe*, not *Doe*, the leading case of the two.[29] Blackmun's new draft for *Roe* relied on this privacy argument, derived from the Fourteenth Amendment's Due Process Clause. He cited numerous precedents, including *Griswold* and *Eisenstadt*.[30]

The opinion focused noticeably on the medical practitioner. American criminal laws restricting abortion historically targeted the abortion provider rather than the woman who sought an abortion. The opinion's framing of the issues this way reflected the concerns raised in *Doe* and elsewhere about physicians' risk of prosecution in performing abortions under unclear criminal laws. Feminist activists who championed the pregnant individual's decisional freedom rued that emphasis then, and for years afterward. The Court elevated professional integrity over women's rights claims when the majority affirmed "the right of the physician to administer medical treatment according to his professional judgment up to the points where important state interests provide compelling justifications for intervention. Up to those points, the abortion decision in all its aspects is inherently, and primarily, a medical decision, and basic responsibility for it must rest with the physician."[31]

Blackmun also clearly recognized the state's stake in defending the fetus's "life or the potential of life." Neither the woman's nor the state's claim was absolute; a balancing of interests was required, he concluded. The opinion was equally clear that "the right of personal privacy includes the abortion decision" and "that this right is not unqualified and must be considered against important state interests."[32] But when should state interests enter? Blackmun, wanting to locate the point when the state's interests became "compelling" and thus could limit the privacy right, chose the end of the first trimester, though he admitted to his colleagues that this choice was "arbitrary."[33] Powell suggested the much later point of fetal viability instead. Other justices, especially Thurgood Marshall, while not endorsing Powell's view, worried that enabling state regulation at the end of the first trimester might enable prohibition at that early point. They urged a more gradual design. As a result of the justices exchanging their views in the fall of 1972, Blackmun's opinion in *Roe* embraced a three-part approach.[34] During the first trimester of pregnancy, "the attending physician, in consultation with his patient, is free to determine, without regulation by the State, that, in his medical judgment, the patient's pregnancy should be terminated." State regulation "reasonably related to maternal health" could enter thereafter, but only when the fetus reached viability could the state regulate to the extent of prohibiting abortion. The opinion took as a premise that a fetus was not a "person" within the meaning of the Constitution and declined to address "when life begins."[35]

The Court's opinion also included a long discussion of the historical legal treatment of abortion.[36] Blackmun's historical reading over the summer had persuaded him that the state could not undergird its interest by asserting a long-standing tradition of prohibiting abortion. American criminal laws, such as the one in Texas, were relatively recent and their reign brief, in his view, compared to centuries of greater openness to legal abortion before the mid-nineteenth century. The historical account in *Roe* began with the ancients and continued through the Anglo-American common law, English law from its first criminalization of abortion in 1803 to liberal revisions in 1967, and American states' laws from the first criminalization in 1821 to the 1950s.

Blackmun found a varied history of partial allowance of abortion and was impressed that criminalizing abortion except to save the mother's life, so common in American state laws like that of Texas, "was not of ancient or even of common-law origin" but stemmed "from statutory changes effected, for the most part, in the latter half of the 19th century."[37] His historical survey emphasized the leniency of the common law toward abortion before "quickening" (which he put at typically sixteen to eighteen weeks) and the practice of many states, when they instituted criminal laws, of exempting or only lightly punishing abortion before that point, as well as enabling therapeutic exceptions. In considering the motives for the mid-nineteenth-century criminalization of abortion, the sources Blackmun read led him to give equal or arguably greater credence to claims for the laws being passed to protect maternal health rather than to protect potential life.[38]

Blackmun's historical narrative, like any other, was inevitably an interpretation of the sources he found. It led him to the conclusion that from the time of the common law through much of the nineteenth century, abortion in the United States "was viewed with less disfavor than under most American statutes currently in effect," so that "a woman enjoyed a substantially broader right to terminate a pregnancy than she does in most States today." He saw "the opportunity to make this choice" as available as before the second half of the nineteenth century "at least with respect to the early stage of pregnancy" and "very possibly" afterward.[39]

A responsible historian today would shy away only from the last of these points. Blackmun was mistaken to give credence to the idea that the common law did not criminalize post-quickening abortion. His timing was also slightly off when he asserted that replacement of the common law by state codes "generally" did not begin until after the Civil War, since it was well under way by 1860. As an admittedly broad-brush history, however, his overall portrait was sound, highlighting the importance of distinctions in punishment based on quickening, and acknowledging that these distinctions gradually disappeared in the middle to late nineteenth century, when "the degree of the offense and the penalties were increased."[40]

Was Blackmun's history dispositive in the case? No. The decision rode on privacy. What the Court would hold was evident before Blackmun's summer of reading. The history served as merely a narrative backup.

Dobbs: A Counterhistory

After *Roe*, a veritable industry arose among abortion foes to counter Blackmun's historical narrative. From the 1970s to the present day the resulting stream has flowed, arguing that there was a centuries-long Anglo-American legal tradition of criminalizing abortion, contrary to Blackmun's understanding.[41] This avalanche of anti-*Roe* historical research included recondite common law references going back to the thirteenth century (evidence unknown to American lawyers and judges in the eighteenth and nineteenth century) and fussy disputation over the meaning of "quick" and "quickening" in medieval treatises (despite overwhelming consensus in American trials and opinions that "quickening" meant the pregnant woman's sensation of fetal movement).[42] This work always blasted Cyril Means, a New York law professor whose two arcane articles about the early common law were cited in *Roe* and gave rise to Blackmun's surmise that the common law may not have criminalized abortion at all. Because Means consulted with abortion rights activists, reference to his articles fatally tainted *Roe* in the minds of opponents, despite the opinion's use of numerous other sources besides Means.[43]

At the core of almost all this criticism was furor that Blackmun had not sufficiently emphasized that criminalization was meant to protect the life of the fetus—an interpretation strongly maintained by opponents of abortion rights. In their view, the common law had always recognized abortion as a punishable wrong at any point in pregnancy, because the life of the fetus was primary. (This claim rests on very doubtful evidence, and even if true, knowledge of it was not available to lawyers, judges, and juries in nineteenth-century America, who adhered to the quickening rule.)[44] They called the quickening threshold merely "evidentiary"—that is, evidence of a live pregnancy—at a time when the progression of gestation was little understood; in their view, the appearance of punitive criminal abortion laws in the nineteenth century responded to scientific clarification of the course of fetal life. They were offended that the *Roe* opinion took seriously the point that criminal abortion laws in the nineteenth century arose in response to dangers to women's lives and health in septic abortions, though this is historically accurate.[45]

Justice Alito sprinkled the results of this counterhistory sparingly throughout his opinion in *Dobbs* but adopted its main points and the same perspective, in which disapprobation and criminalization of abortion dominated a long history and stemmed from concern for fetal life, not for a pregnant woman's life or health. Passing lightly over centuries of common law, he acknowledged the "quickening rule" but countered its significance by stressing that abortion was a common-law crime "at least" by the sixteenth to eighteenth week of pregnancy.[46] He also regarded as nugatory the numerous American cases and commentaries that declared abortion before quickening unindictable, citing a distinct outlier to indicate that consensus was not universal.[47] Most definitively, he dismissed the quickening rule because it was eventually "abandoned."[48] Alito cherry-picked textual scraps calling abortion "unlawful" even when it was not prohibited or punished, whereas Blackmun had highlighted historical points of variability and permissibility of abortion.[49]

Blackmun's historical narrative had been an add-on or backup to his constitutional reasoning. Alito, following a route marked out over twenty years, made "American history and traditions" far more central. As substantive due process justifications for expanding intimate liberties had become more frequent in cases after *Griswold*, members of the Court called control mechanisms into play, ostensibly to assure that their reasoning was constitutionally sound.[50] These standards were backward-looking (although theoretically they could produce progressive results).[51] A newly articulated liberty had to be "so rooted in the traditions and conscience of our people as to be ranked as fundamental"[52] or "implicit in the concept of ordered liberty"[53] or "deeply rooted in this Nation's history and tradition."[54] By 1997, conservative justices on the Court had made de rigueur the approach modeled by Chief Justice Rehnquist in 1997 in *Washington v. Glucksberg*: "We begin, as we do in all due process cases, by examining our Nation's history, legal traditions, and practices."[55] The history and traditions approach in *Glucksberg* became a touchstone for constitutional credibility going forward, a purposeful drag on the expansion of liberty rights.[56]

Alito made the "history and traditions" requirement in *Dobbs* even less likely to be met by defining what he was looking for not as a practice of abortion or a freedom of choice or a permissible possibility unnoticed by the law, but as a stated "right" in a statute or constitution. Of course, he did not find it. Indeed, in all the centuries he examined, women had no stipulated rights except the general rights of inhabitants and citizens under the U.S. Constitution. Those were few. The Supreme Court in 1875 affirmed, against the claim of a woman citizen, that the "privileges and immunities" of citizens did not include a woman's right to vote.[57]

Alito's main historical claim was simple—so simple that it sidestepped public meaning, social practices, enforcement, or American case law in the nineteenth century. By his count, more than half the states had laws criminalizing abortion when the Fourteenth Amendment became part of the Constitution in 1868.[58] Because the Fourteenth Amendment at the time of its enactment was not understood to expressly invalidate those criminal statutes, he inferred that the Amendment's potential to protect reproductive freedom today was nil. His reasoning was not new. Justice Rehnquist argued this line in 1973, in his dissent in *Roe,* also including an appendix listing criminal statutes, as Alito did. But Rehnquist's view failed to change the minds of seven of his colleagues, who interpreted the Fourteenth Amendment as having more far-reaching meaning in 1973 than in 1868. That was then. Now, in 2022, Alito had no difficulty getting four other justices to agree with him that *Roe* was "egregiously" wrong.[59]

Mississippi's brief in *Dobbs* gave Alito a template for the Court, calling both *Roe* and *Planned Parenthood v. Casey*[60] (the 1992 decision that reaffirmed the core holding of *Roe,* although on altered terms) "egregiously" wrong. Mississippi also posited, as did the *Dobbs* majority, that the right to abortion was fundamentally different from other expanded due process liberties because it involved "purposeful termination of a potential life."[61] Sharply distinguishing *Roe* from *Griswold,* Mississippi flatly denied that abortion could be seen as a liberty or justified by a broad right to privacy. Citing *Glucksberg* language and bringing to bear the contemporaneity of the

Fourteenth Amendment's ratification and the presence of state criminal statutes, Mississippi took the cue of the anti-abortion history chorus to claim
that the state legislators who ratified the Fourteenth Amendment saw no
conflict between it and the criminalization of abortion.[62]

Comparing the historical account in *Dobbs* to that in *Roe* forces recognition that what we know as "history" is not immovable "fact" (out there, back
there) but intentional selection of evidence and interpretation. This painful
truth nonetheless should not be taken to mean that history is all "relative" or
that one historical interpretation is as good as another.

Dobbs was met with public outrage from many quarters, not least for its
historical distortions and its carelessness about women's lives and rights.[63]
That outrage will have to be translated into forceful real-world effects that
are electoral and more, if the history that the Supreme Court has made is to
be resisted. To swallow the majority's claims in *Dobbs* (and its disclaimers,
including its refusal to respect any reliance interest) in full view of the
conclusions embraced by Supreme Court majorities from *Griswold* to *Roe*
and beyond, is to enter a time warp. Recall Justice Brennan in 1972: "[I]f the
right of privacy means anything, it is the right of the individual, married or
single, to be free from unwarranted governmental intrusion into matters so
fundamentally affecting a person as the decision whether to bear or beget a
child."[64]

Justice Harlan explained in 1961:

> Due process has not been reduced to any formula; its content cannot be de-
> termined by reference to any code. The best that can be said is that, through
> the course of this Court's decisions, it has represented the balance which
> our Nation, built upon postulates of respect for the liberty of the individual,
> has struck between that liberty and the demands of organized society.[65]

The *Roe* majority explicitly aimed at such a balance. The *Dobbs* opinion
"discards that balance" (in the words of the dissent)[66] and supplies no other.
Regarding our nation's tradition as "a living thing," Justice Harlan opined that
"a decision of this Court which radically departs from it could not long survive."[67] All that can be hoped is that Harlan's prediction applies to *Dobbs*.

14

How Contraception and Abortion Got Divorced

Linda Gordon

The phrase "birth control" was coined by Margaret Sanger early in the twentieth century in a campaign to distinguish contraception from abortion and thereby decriminalize the former. That campaign succeeded, but at a cost, since it is partly responsible for the anti-abortion movement that has been so destructive for over half a century.

Since the 1920s in the United States, birth control has come to mean contraception, but this definition masks its larger meaning and its role in human history. Both contraception and abortion are included in the phrase "reproduction control," but that phrase is not colloquial; it is found more often in technical and scholarly speech and writings. In common use today, most people understand birth control and abortion as distinct practices and methods, and that distinction shapes policies and debates about reproduction control. The process by which that distinction developed, the history of that "divorce," illuminates much about the often intense emotional and political weight the terms carry today. Yet the "divorcees" may be reuniting today, as recent medical developments have all but erased the distinction.

Because "reproduction control" is a cumbersome and somewhat official term, I prefer to use "birth control," with the same, generic, meaning. I invite readers to understand birth control not as a device or a method but as a universal human aspiration. And not only universal but also ancient. Birth control was widely practiced for many centuries, albeit with mixed success. There are no societies, however ancient or "primitive," in which people did *not* try to control conception and birth. The modern medicalization of birth control has of course vastly improved the ease and effectiveness of how people do this, but it has also blurred, even mystified our sense of what the

Linda Gordon, *How Contraception and Abortion Got Divorced* In: *Roe v. Dobbs*. Edited by: Lee C. Bollinger and Geoffrey R. Stone, Oxford University Press. © Oxford University Press 2024.
DOI: 10.1093/oso/9780197760352.003.0014

practice is and has been about. I want to try to undo this mystification a bit, to restore what one scholar has called "mindfulness" to the practice of birth control. Doing this may also clarify why aspects of the practice remain so controversial.

Three important generalizations about human reproduction: One, it is a mysterious experience, a common subject of myths in all religions. Even in a world in which there is no longer magic, in which we are accustomed to invisible chemical and physical changes, women often report feeling amazed when they see a baby emerge from their body. Second, reproduction has, until recently, always involved men and women, so regulating it involves regulating gender and family relations—not just sexual relations but overall power relations. Third, like sexual activity, reproduction has always been socially regulated. Birth control practices and rules are so ancient that they have had to be excavated not only by historians but also by anthropologists and archaeologists. There is simply no such thing as "natural" sexual and reproductive practices; creating rules about reproduction seems to be part of the definition of being human.

For eons, the need to control reproduction was primarily economic. Especially in nomadic and hunting-and-gathering societies, children were an economic burden, often literally because they had to be carried. Controlling reproduction was vital to whole communities as well as families.[1] Settled agricultural societies shifted the calculus somewhat, as children provided crucial labor power—becoming less a burden and more a source of labor power.

A variety of birth control practices already thrived in ancient societies. They included, in fact, all the basic forms of birth control known today except one, hormonal preparations. Women used natural spermicidal douches; even a slightly acidic juice, such as lemon juice, will kill sperm. Women manufactured rudimentary diaphragms, using sea sponges or matted grass to block sperm from getting through the cervix. People manufactured male or female condoms made of animal skins. These so-called barrier methods of contraception remained fundamentally the same until the twentieth century; if you prevent sperm from entering the uterus, or kill it as it travels there, you stop reproduction.

But the most reliable method of birth control was abortion, which was practiced universally. Ancient abortion techniques ranged from the relatively safe and effective to the dangerous and ineffective. Potions taken by mouth were usually in the latter category; those that worked usually did so by causing an abortion only as a side effect of systemic poisoning, as in the case of strong cathartics. Better methods included inserting a foreign object into the uterus, causing the uterus to expel its contents. For this purpose women used smooth stones or carefully smoothed sticks, for example; more recently these became knitting-needle abortions. There is a recipe for herbal abortion in the Ebers Scroll, an Egyptian papyrus dated between 1550 and 1500 BCE. Soranos, an ancient Greek medical writer of the early first century CE, offered recipes for vaginal suppositories for abortion. Recent abortion-rights arguments often refer to the dangers of premodern, premedicalized abortion, but without historical context they often exaggerate the dangers. Long into the modern era, traditional midwives—who often provided both abortion and birthing help—had good safety records, while many women died from medicalized procedures that were not sterile.[2] Even in the United States in much of the twentieth century abortion was far and away the safest birth control method. It was also much safer than childbirth—five times as many women died in childbirth as from abortion.[3] High infant mortality rates meant that women underwent twice as many pregnancies and childbirths as the number of children they wanted, and these repeated pregnancies and deliveries increased women's mortality and morbidity.

Until about two hundred years ago, and throughout the world, some forms of birth control were legal and uncontroversial in most societies so long as it was practiced in conformity with dominant rules and values. It was also often perceived as a women's matter, even as a woman's natural right, part of the biological processes of reproduction. In the United States and much of the world, an informal compromise made abortion before "quickening" legitimate. "Quickening" was the term for the moment when a woman could feel a fetus kicking, usually in the middle of the second trimester of pregnancy, and was imagined as the moment the fetus took on life. (Here we meet an ancestor of today's arguments about what constitutes human life.) The quickening standard was flexible, because no one but the pregnant woman could know when it occurred, so the quickening rule gave women a degree of control. Some fetuses might become "quick" in the fourth month, some in the sixth. For most of the nineteenth century abortion remained common, especially among married women who already had children and could not afford to support more.

Despite the relatively inefficient means of reproduction control in use, in the mid-nineteenth century an anti-birth-control campaign arose, propelled by anxieties about gender, class, and racial change—often combined. A growing women's rights movement sought to overthrow the legal, economic, and social restrictions under which American women suffered. Women could not vote, serve on juries, or participate in any part of the formal political process; if they married, all their property, including their own wages, belonged to their husbands; should they wish to leave an abusive husband, for example, they would automatically lose their children to him; a husband who beat or raped his wife did not commit a crime. Conservative rhetoric in this period revealed a central contradiction: on the one hand, women were destined, by God and/or nature, to be wives and mothers, submissive to their husbands, and that they could achieve true fulfillment only from these roles; on the other hand, coercion by laws and by husbands' authority was needed to make women fit into those roles.

In the late nineteenth century falling birth rates intensified these concerns. Not everywhere: only among women of "superior stock." Elites built a mini-panic around the fact that allegedly "superior" women were rejecting motherhood, seeking education or careers. Reflecting awareness that reproduction could be controlled, the discourse charged that women were becoming selfish, trying to escape domestic obligations in order to venture outside their proper sphere. Their behavior threatened to let people of "inferior stock" overwhelm the nation and sap its strength. Meanwhile, the growing immigrant population would drown out the "true" Americans (an early version of today's "replacement" theory).

Although the concern about birth rates extended only to privileged women, in the United States the problem was called "race suicide" in the then-vague understanding of "race." At the time the term had ethnic and religious as well as racial meanings: Irish Catholics, Italian Catholics, and Eastern European Jews, for example, were not then "white." Promoters of race suicide fears soon promoted a solution: eugenics, the "science" of human breeding. It had a positive side, encouraging reproduction by "superior" whites, and a negative, trying to stop reproduction among "inferiors." Negative eugenics would later justify large campaigns of forced sterilization of women of color and poor white women. Indeed, the whole race suicide hysteria reflected the increasing view that controlling reproduction was vital to the nation's health.

Meanwhile a women's movement for full citizenship was developing. Its best-known demands were for suffrage, property rights, child custody, and educational rights, while a smaller left wing within the movement began promoting birth control as a woman's right. Pioneered by utopian socialists and anarchists, better-known women's rights advocates such as Elizabeth Cady Stanton later joined the campaign. Their first proposals may sound shocking today and were unlikely to be well-received even then: that wives should allow sexual intercourse only when they wanted to conceive a child. They condemned contraception and abortion for allowing men to exploit and "ruin" women without accepting responsibility for marriage and fatherhood. The radicalism of this proposal appears if you consider the context: the idea of rape in marriage was alien, because wives' sexual submission to their husbands upon demand was part of the understanding of what marriage *was*. Challenging this standard, feminists spoke of "voluntary motherhood"; they even used rhetoric that would be repeated a century later, that women "own" their bodies. Thus birth control also meant a campaign to criminalize marital rape. In other words, they believed that before women could get *reproductive* self-determination they had to have *sexual* self-determination.

Voluntary motherhood advocates' comfort with restricting even marital sex to such infrequency also tells us something important about their understanding of what sex was. Official morality of the age defined "sex" as intercourse. Official physiology of the age also assumed that women had little or no sex drive, and that they married and submitted to intercourse as a result of their maternal drive, their innate desire to bear children. Put these two beliefs together and it seems likely that many twentieth-century wives rarely experienced orgasm and may not have found sex enjoyable at all. For such women abstinence may not have seemed much of a sacrifice.

We have no way of measuring the influence of voluntary-motherhood talk, but the backlash was visible and punitive. Women who sought to control births were labeled self-indulgent, frivolous, selfish, in love with fashion and "fast living." If women could escape motherhood at will, there would be no holding them back. In other words, the risk of pregnancy was a means of disciplining women. Those who feared "voluntary motherhood," including abortion, explained their goals less as protection of health, economic well-being, or even "race suicide," instead focusing on the imperative to control women's behavior. In the United States, major cultural and political campaigns charged that birth control (referring to all forms of birth control, not just abortion) would allow women to engage in activities inappropriate to their gender, including sexual immorality but also ambitions in the public sphere, such as higher education. These campaigners rarely if ever spoke of birth control, including abortion, as taking "life," of murdering fetuses or the "unborn." This argument could be found occasionally, as for example in the use of the term "feticide," which included what we today call contraception. But even "feticide" was a sin of transgressive women.

In the Western world it was Protestant, not Catholic, countries, and in the United States Protestant ministers, not priests, that led in criminalizing all forms of reproduction control. Because of the federal structure of the United States, outlawing birth control was the prerogative of the states, and by about 1880 almost all the states had done so. Birth control opponents, however, soon found a way to prohibit birth control federally, by calling on the federal government's constitutional power to regulate interstate commerce. The 1873 Comstock Act, an amendment to a postal law, prohibited sending any obscene material through the post office—and specifically defined any material related to birth control as obscene. The prohibition extended not only to shipping birth control devices but even to academic discussion of the value of smaller families. Birth control was then illegal in the United States for almost a century.

Its practice did not appear to decline, however. A small population of prosperous, cosmopolitan people were getting contraceptives—notably pessaries—smuggled in from Europe, always less prudish than the United States. Soon, thinner, flexible sheets of rubber made diaphragms possible, and they were far easier to use. Spermicidal douches were advertised openly, however, in American newspapers, such as this ad: "The most philosophic of all instruments . . . cheapest, most effect [sic] to hygienic practice. A thousand times more effect [sic] than pills or powders, and without the slightest danger." Yet abortion remained the main form of birth control practiced. Most women probably found abortionists through word of mouth, but practitioners also advertised their services through widely understood euphemisms: "Madame Grindle, Female Physician, guaranteeing relief to all female complaints" or "guarantees certain relief to ladies in trouble . . . sure relief to the most anxious patient at one interview; elegant rooms for ladies requiring nursing."[4]

Enforcement of Comstock and state laws varied greatly, not only from state to state but even from neighborhood to neighborhood.[5] As waves of public concern rose and fell, as particular district attorneys built campaigns around suppressing these immoralities, police enforcement and conviction rates swung between laxity and strictness. Enforcing the prohibition against contraception was of course difficult because it was used in private. But lenience dominated even abortion because it continued to be so widespread, and so few juries were willing to convict for this traditional practice. Indeed, at the turn of the twentieth century, as many as two million illegal abortions were being performed in the United States annually, and almost a third of all pregnancies ended in abortion.[6]

But the nineteenth-century anti-birth-control law forced abortion underground, which no doubt made it less safe than when it was legal. Illegal abortions were usually discovered only when women were so injured that they turned to hospitals or other doctors for help—a tiny fraction of abortions. The resultant prosecutions were gruesome when they occurred. Anyone tending an injured woman was asked to get a "dying declaration"—questioning a woman on her death bed. (This practice resulted from the legal precedent that dying declarations were exempt from the rule against hearsay—which excludes secondhand testimony—because a dying person was believed not to lie as she was "about to meet her maker.") District attorneys gave doctors lists of the proper questions to ask: "Do you believe that you are about to die? [Correct answer: yes.] Have you any hope of recovery? [Correct answer: no.]" When a woman was reluctant to name her abortionist, doctors were urged to threaten to refuse to treat her unless she did so. One DA marveled at the loyalty of so many women who refused to reveal their abortionists' names; dying declarations were successfully obtained in only four of ten such cases.

Small networks of countercultural women then transformed birth control ideas in what has been called an early twentieth-century "sexual revolution." An influential, upscale population of urban, educated women brought the ideas of the marginal nineteenth-century radicals to a new public. Women who prided themselves on being "modern" began articulating, and acting on, a more positive view of women's sexuality—as a right, even a value, as opposed to an activity aimed at reproducing. In doing so they were creating a new feminism, breaking with a nineteenth-century women's rights orientation that had considered sexual activity a component of male domination, even exploitation of women.

Greenwich Village was for a time the epicenter of this new, unprecedented social movement for birth control. Two radical women—Jewish immigrant anarchist Emma Goldman and Irish Catholic socialist Margaret Sanger—embarked on civil disobedience. Goldman began distributing leaflets explaining how women could practice birth control. Then Sanger opened a clinic on Amboy Street in Brownsville, Brooklyn, which fit women with vaginal diaphragms imported from Europe, where they were plentiful. The day it opened there was a line of women around the block waiting to get in.

The next day the police closed it. But to little long-term avail: Sanger's clinic sparked a nationwide movement for legalizing birth control.

The new contraceptives represented an explicit break from the Victorian acceptance of sexual abstinence as a healthful discipline. Contraception was not only for birth control but also for sexual pleasure. Furthermore, the new contraception—mainly diaphragms—required women to become comfortable handling their "private parts" and to express or at least acknowledge sexual intent. Vaginal diaphragms were not only easier (and safer) to use than pessaries but had to be used at the time of sexual intercourse. Meanwhile condoms became widely available after World War I, but they, of course, gave women little control.[7]

Birth control as a social movement thus arose from a major break with Victorian prudery but built on a new strategy inaugurated by Sanger: pushing for legalizing contraception without challenging the prohibition on abortion. That distinction would shape reproductive politics and science for almost a century.

The distinction also helped the social movement secure support from eugenists, a move that ultimately resulted in justified suspicions of racism, including vilification of Sanger herself.[8] Eugenics "experts" were certain that "white" and middle-class people were superior in almost every way and supported legalizing contraception aimed at other populations in order to retain the quality of the population. Their greatest impact, however, resulted not from encouraging contraception among "inferiors"—which typically failed due to lack of access—but from promoting forced sterilizations. At this they were considerably successful. In the 1920s, Henry Goddard's famed Kallikak study of "defectives" convinced some thirty states to impose coercive sterilization on at least sixty-four thousand allegedly "genetically defective," "feeble-minded" women, Native Americans and African Americans particularly. The eugenists were by no means right-wing outliers; in the 1920s eugenics was taught widely in college biology and sociology textbooks. Eugenics also exerted a major influence on the passage of the first omnibus federal immigration restriction law of 1924, which set quotas according to ethnic, national, and religious groups adjudged inferior or superior. Testing arrivals at Ellis Island, Goddard "found" that 83% of Jews, 80% of Hungarians, and 79% of Italians were either morons or imbeciles.[9] This was respectable science at the time. These quotas remained in place for forty years.

In the bargain between advocates of contraception and eugenists, Sanger's birth control movement gained little and lost much. The birth control clinics mainly served middle-class and some working-class whites and did little for the poor or people of color. Many American Blacks in particular concluded, somewhat understandably, that birth control was a plot to shrink their numbers and thereby diminish their political and economic power. (This suspicion was reinforced after exposure of the 1930s Tuskegee study, in which unknowing African American men were medically infected with syphilis and other diseases in order to provide a population on whom researchers could then chart the progress of the diseases.) This opinion long damaged not only the white-dominated birth control movement but Black women's health concerns in general. Sanger surely harbored the personal bigotry that saturated the American white mainstream, but there is no evidence that her views were more racist than that of other white progressives. By contrast, some outspoken Black feminists and leftists such as W. E. B. Du Bois staunchly supported the birth control movement.

The birth control movement gained more through alliances with physicians, but at a cost. A small but growing number of liberal doctors were persuaded to work at the clinics or otherwise support the effort. Sanger and others believed they needed this legitimacy and expertise. (We now know that they may have needed the legitimation but not the expertise, as it seems clear that nonprofessionals could have learned to fit diaphragms with virtually no risk, as there is not much injury that a diaphragm can cause.)[10] But the movement's decision to depend on doctors made them the gatekeepers of access to contraception. This subjected women for many decades to medical moralizing about the prescribing of diaphragms. Worse, it radically raised the cost of access to female contraception for decades. By contrast, male condoms were cheap and widely available at drug stores.

By 1920 nearly every big city in the country had a birth control league that not only advocated for contraception but established and operated clinics. The leagues became active in state politics and gradually succeeded: state legislatures began legalizing contraception. The process was slow. In 1936 the U.S. Court of Appeals for the Second Circuit in *U.S. v. One Package* (of pessaries) ruled that government erred in seizing a package of pessaries sent by a Japanese physician to an American physician.[11] Still it took another thirty years until contraception became legal in the last state, when the U.S. Supreme Court in 1965 ruled in *Griswold v. Connecticut*[12] that the Constitution protects the liberty of married couples to buy and use contraceptives without government restriction, thereby overturning the last remaining state law prohibiting contraception.

Legalizing contraception by no means ended women's reliance on abortion. This was partly because *Griswold* applied only to married women[13] and partly because of the limited availability of contraceptives. Clinics were not widespread and served only married women. Many women still relied on abortion as birth control, especially working-class women. This pattern endangered many: a 1960s study showed that one in ten low-income women in New York City had had abortions, and of those, eight in ten tried to do it themselves, with only 2% saying that a physician had been involved in any way.[14] The escalating abortion rate in this era also tells us something about popular attitudes, men's as well as women's: the development of what has been called a birth control *mentality*—an expectation that sex could be enjoyed without fear of conception. Few women *choose between* contraception and abortion, and no one would prefer abortion to contraception. In fact, making contraception easily accessible and affordable tends to lower the abortion rate.

At the same time, contraception became more reliable. In 1950, Sanger persuaded wealthy supporter Katherine McCormick to donate $2 million (about $25 million in 2023 dollars) to fund research on hormonal contraceptives.[15] "The pills," as they became known, were marketed in 1960, and within a year one million women had used them. By the 1970s, the vast majority of American women used contraception. In the 1980s the proportion of sexually active fertile women *not* using some form of contraception (including surgical sterilization) was down to 6%. Contrary to common expectations, religion made little difference in patterns of contraceptive use. Only a small minority of Catholics relied on the Church-approved method of periodic abstinence ("rhythm"), and 78% of Catholic physicians prescribed contraception. Physicians hesitated to refuse because they knew women would only go elsewhere if they did.[16] Contraception spread through an informal, irresistible social movement.

Meanwhile, media coverage of unsafe abortions slowly led organizations and people of influence to reconsider the ban on abortion. In 1955 Planned Parenthood held the first conference on the issue of abortion. Physicians increasingly wanted immunity from prosecution for abortions they deemed necessary. Moreover, technology, primarily ultrasound scans, allowed physicians to see inside the uterus, and the resultant detection of fetal abnormalities contributed to demand for therapeutic abortions. Rubella among pregnant women often created fetal deformities. Class inequality contributed both to the detection of fetal abnormality and awareness of it. In

1962 the case of Sherri Finkbine, a children's TV host, spread this awareness and displeasure with bans on abortion. Having taken the drug thalidomide, and then learning that her fetus was defective, Finkbine was nevertheless denied an abortion in Arizona; she went public and secured an abortion in Sweden. (Her refusal to hide ultimately led to a TV film about her case, *A Private Matter*, starring Sissy Spacek.)

Roe was thus a response to several related—and mutually reinforcing— social changes: a break with Victorian sexual morality, women's demands for access to education and jobs, families' increasing dependence on women's wages, the economic costs of multiple children, the impact of contraception on making childbirth and children a choice, and pregnant women's desire to make sure their children would not have serious disabilities.

So when *Roe* was decided, few thought it controversial. Before the decision, eighteen states had already partly decriminalized abortion. Some progressive Catholic leaders criticized the Church's hypocrisy in denouncing abortion while supporting capital punishment and opposing "welfare."[17] Even some of the most influential conservative Protestant Evangelicals saw no problem with the decision. W. A. Criswell, the president of the Southern Baptist Convention, wrote, "I have always felt that it was only after a child was born and had a life separate from its mother that it became an individual person and it has always, therefore, seemed to me that what is best for the mother and for the future should be allowed."[18]

The anti-abortion movement arose through an alliance inaugurated by a secular New Right developing within the Republican Party with conservative Protestant Evangelicals. Before 1976, New Right publications rarely mentioned abortion.[19] New Right leaders soon recognized, however, the mobilizing potential of a "pro-family" agenda that included opposition to gay rights and sex education as well as abortion. Previously many if not most Evangelical leaders had avoided entanglement with secular politics. Nor did they imagine themselves falling in line with Catholics. Their change of heart came largely as a result of a New Right campaign to break apart the then-dominant Democratic voting majorities and move voters to the right. Paul Weyrich, founder of the Heritage Foundation, was particularly influential in convincing his antiestablishment Republican allies that these "family issues" could win support from nonelite people who were not attracted by traditionally conservative economic policies.[20] "Abortion Knits Religious Right into G.O.P. Fabric," the *New York Times* headlined in 1986.[21]

Discursively, calling this campaign "Right to Life" rather than anti-abortion was crucial. Earlier anti-abortion arguments and rhetoric focused on gender issues, specifically women's changing roles and aspirations. The massive 1970s feminist movement became a particular target, accused of undermining family values that were allegedly threatened by abortion. The turn to focus anti-abortion propaganda on the fetus, and thereby "life," was supported by the same fetal-imaging technology that had been used to discover fetal defects. Now it allowed widespread images of fetuses in utero. Tiny plastic fetuses became symbols of the life that abortions were murdering.[22]

But technology and science have more recently blurred the very distinction between contraception and abortion. IUDs and new hormonal medications, including notably RU-486 and "Plan B," can be described as preventing or interrupting pregnancy. Some can be purchased and received by mail. In response to these developments some anti-abortion organizations and spokespeople began to denounce contraception. A majority of anti-abortion campaigns quickly extended to attempts to exclude medical insurance from covering contraception of any kind.

Thus reproduction control politics has to some extent moved in circular fashion, annulling the divorce of contraception from abortion. Both supporters and opponents of reproductive rights may be returning to the dominant late nineteenth-century view of contraception and abortion as a seamless set of options to control reproduction.

Postscript

It is important to bear in mind that building an anti-abortion movement was part of a wholesale transformation of the Republican Party, the effects of which are felt so strongly in recent politics. Moving away from its traditional corporate agenda toward right-wing populism, the party's most important mobilizing issue may no longer be abortion. But the exploitation and politicizing of abortion played a key role in these new developments.

15

The Anti-Abortion Movement and the Punishment Prerogative

Mary Ziegler

The criminalization of abortion figured centrally in the Court's decision to dismantle abortion rights in *Dobbs v. Jackson Women's Health Organization*. The *Dobbs* Court honored only unenumerated rights that the majority deemed to be deeply rooted in history and tradition. Writing for the majority, Justice Samuel Alito told a story about how American law had long disapproved of abortion, if not prohibited it altogether. "Not only was there no support for such a constitutional right until shortly before *Roe*," Alito wrote, "but abortion had long been a *crime* in every single State."[1]

Alito's fixation on crime is revealing. Regardless of what one believes about the history of criminalization before *Roe*, criminal penalties *have* become central, both to the fate of abortion rights and to the regulation of reproductive rights after *Dobbs*. But why have criminal sanctions become so prominent? In the months since *Dobbs*, abortion opponents have revived discussion about who should be punished, with a group of self-proclaimed abortion abolitionists demanding criminal penalties for at least some who have abortions. The desirability of punishment, and the priority put on incarceration or equally harsh alternatives, have received almost no discussion at all.[2]

This chapter traces the history of how and why the anti-abortion movement came to embrace punishment as a defining priority, and it argues that this punitive focus has been profoundly destructive. While harming pregnant people and their families, carceral policies have done comparably little to prevent abortions. To begin with, a focus on punishment resulted from a series of historical coincidences rather than growing inevitably out of the principles of anti-abortion constitutionalism. The threat of incarceration

Mary Ziegler, *The Anti-Abortion Movement and the Punishment Prerogative* In: *Roe v. Dobbs*. Edited by: Lee C. Bollinger and Geoffrey R. Stone, Oxford University Press. © Oxford University Press 2024.
DOI: 10.1093/oso/9780197760352.003.0015

has not effectively or consistently discouraged those seeking abortion, but increasingly harsh penalties—together with shifting definitions of "abortion"—have stopped doctors, universities, and others from providing crucial emergency medical treatment and even contraceptive access.

Harsh punishments are discriminatory and unlikely to consistently discourage abortion, all while dramatizing the suffering of those forced to continue a pregnancy. These are the very stories that make real the constitutional arguments about the equality and liberty at issue in forced childbearing.

The Origins and Efficacy of Criminalization

Historians contest the degree to which the law has always treated abortion as a crime, especially early in pregnancy, and most reject the narrative that Alito adopts. But the treatment of pre-quickening abortion aside, the first anti-abortion movement, led by the American Medical Association (AMA), clearly championed criminal laws. This focus on penalties was not novel—the AMA simply sought to expand criminal laws that were already in place. In the nineteenth century, states began expanding their criminal laws on abortion to address harms to pregnant women; at first, in the 1820s, a handful of states began expanding laws criminalizing the use of poisons to include drugs marketed as abortifacients, many of which were dangerous to women. By 1840, however, only eight states had passed statutes that authorized criminal punishment for abortion.[3]

But abortion soon became fodder for newspaper readers, especially consumers of the sporting press, contemporary publications for men eager for salacious stories. Reporters routinely carried stories of women seduced by dishonest men and then negligently killed by profiteering entrepreneurs. These stories motivated legislators committed to protecting women from unscrupulous seducers, and some states began introducing harsher criminal penalties when abortions resulted in the death of patients.[4]

In the 1850s and 1860s, the AMA, led by Dr. Horatio Storer of Boston, expanded on these modest laws by leading a campaign to criminalize abortion throughout pregnancy. Storer argued that abortion was wrong because it involved the taking of fetal life—an argument that would resonate with an entirely different anti-abortion movement a century later. Storer also focused on what he saw as the evil done by married Anglo-Saxon women who chose abortion. He worried that Catholic immigrants, who more often had large families, would swamp the nation with "inferior" children, while the "better sort" of woman shrugged off her responsibilities to her husband.[5]

What Storer did not offer was an explanation of why criminal punishment was the best solution for those opposed to abortion. Instead, criminal punishment was the default for an organization that argued against the quickening distinction. Earlier in the nineteenth century, states had expanded abortion regulation mostly to address harm to women, and Storer and his colleagues, who derided the quickening line, simply expanded on that criminal model, proposing penalties for women who sought out procedures and managed their own terminations and authorizing especially strict penalties for married women.[6]

By the end of the nineteenth century, states across the country had passed laws that criminalized abortion throughout pregnancy and authorized relatively minor punishments; five years in prison was a common penalty. But if the AMA had success in passing criminal abortion laws, the statutes themselves failed to significantly lower abortion rates. Abortion remained common throughout the United States—most estimates suggested that the numbers remained steady or even increased—and prosecutions remained uncommon. One judge suggested that in the 1890s, hundreds of thousands of abortions took place in New York City alone.[7]

Defending the Status Quo

In the 1960s, when states began reforming abortion laws, anti-abortion activists again defaulted into a defense of criminal penalties. The early anti-abortion movement, which at first was heavily white, Catholic, and middle class, mobilized to defend the status quo: rather than offering an argument *for* criminal penalties per se, anti-abortion activists criticized the legalization of the procedure. As important, describing abortion as a crime highlighted the violence that abortion foes identified with the termination of pregnancy. This strategy was clear in 1962 when some Catholics responded to the story of Sherri Finkbine, a married mother and former television presenter who took thalidomide for morning sickness during her pregnancy. She later learned that the drug caused serious birth defects. Denied an abortion in the United States, she traveled to Sweden to seek out the procedure, detailing her journey to the press.[8]

Finkbine and her husband framed the abortion decision as deeply personal, while Pope John XIII argued instead that abortion was a crime, "morally, [and] legally wrong."[9] In the years after Finkbine's abortion, states began seriously considering a model law patterned on a 1962 proposal offered by the American Law Institute (ALI), which legalized abortion in cases of rape, incest, fetal abnormality, and certain maternal health threats. In responding to the ALI bill, abortion foes again stressed that abortion was a crime, but they did not simply point to existing criminal statutes; they argued that abortion was an act of homicide, if not premeditated murder.[10]

Framing abortion as murder advanced a constitutional agenda emerging in the anti-abortion movement of the mid-1960s. Anti-abortion leaders insisted that a fetus qualified as a "person" under the Fourteenth Amendment and therefore enjoyed constitutional protection. To make this point, anti-abortion leaders championing personhood routinely argued that if any killing was murder, so must be abortion. "Abortion and infanticide are unspeakable crimes," explained a statement against the legalization of abortion issued by Catholic bishops in New York State.[11] "[T]he unjustified taking of a human life is murder," reasoned a group of bishops opposed to California's abortion reform.[12]

This argument was complicated by the fact that state laws had not treated abortion as murder. Indeed, by the 1960s, police forces sometimes delegated enforcement of abortion laws to the vice patrol, which, as Connecticut's *Hartford Courant* explained in 1960, dealt with "bookies, prostitutes, illegal liquor sales, abortions, fortune tellers and dope peddlers."[13] Even when physicians did kill pregnant patients, juries did not always opt for a serious sentence. For example, when a New York doctor killed a nineteen-year-old patient during an illegal abortion in 1960, a jury sentenced him to only two years in prison when he could have faced up to ninety-nine. Law enforcement leaders likewise signaled at times that abortion was not a serious crime: Captain Hugh Brown of the Los Angeles Police Department explained that his colleagues rarely made abortion-related arrests unless a provider was making large amounts of money. "Our efforts," he explained, "are directed to people who are doing abortions for profit."[14] In 1967, the President's Commission on Crime similarly questioned the legitimacy of abortion laws, noting that only about 1% of all procedures were subject to prosecution.[15]

The argument that abortion was murder, then, was not a defense of existing law but a move made in the argument for constitutional personhood. "Every living fetus is truly a person, just as you and I," wrote one anti-abortion advocate in a 1967 letter to the editor of the *New York Times*. "Consequently, every direct abortion, no matter the motive, is as much a crime as the assassination of President Kennedy."[16] For others, calling for the criminal punishment of murder solidified the secular bona fides of a growing anti-abortion movement. "Abortion is a moral problem that transcends any particular sectarian approach," stressed Cardinal Krol of Philadelphia. "The Biblical prohibition 'thou shalt not kill' is not the invention of any particular sect."[17]

Enforcing Fetal Personhood: Criminalization and Its Alternatives

In 1973, when the Supreme Court decided *Roe*, emphasis on criminal punishment faded for a time. Indeed, for the first time in years, anti-abortion activists discussed what the law should look like rather than defending criminal laws that were already in place. While the anti-abortion movement rallied around a constitutional personhood amendment, members of the movement did not agree on or sometimes even discuss the need for criminal punishment. There were twenty-seven personhood amendment proposals circulating in Congress by August 1973. Many followed a model set by Senator James Buckley in his draft: changing the word "person" in the Fourteenth Amendment to include "unborn offspring" at "every stage of development." In the early 1970s, the anti-abortion movement was fractious but unified almost completely around the idea of an amendment.[18]

Lawyers charged with drafting a "human life amendment" often discussed the importance of banning abortions performed by private citizens as well as state actors. As Joseph Witherspoon, a law professor and anti-abortion activist, explained, a human life amendment not regulating private actors would mean that "court action [would] have to be instituted to compel a State Legislature or Congress to enact anti-abortion law to protect unborn children." The point, as Witherspoon saw it, was "to provide immediate legal protection for the unborn child."[19]

Many anti-abortion activists agreed with Witherspoon but divided when it came to the role that criminal punishment should play in enforcing a constitutional ban. Charles Rice, another anti-abortion professor, argued that a constitutional personhood amendment would not only render permissive abortion laws unconstitutional but also revive nineteenth-century criminal laws. Nellie Gray, the founder of March for Life, proposed "an amendment which places the death of the unborn child within the homicide laws enacted to deal with the death of any human being." Her argument was based on equal protection: if the law recognized personhood at fertilization, she claimed, then equal protection required identical treatment of fetal killing and homicide.[20]

But other anti-abortion attorneys paid little attention to criminal penalties. Robert Byrn, a leading anti-abortion attorney, worried that it would be politically costly to prohibit abortions except in cases of state action, since anything else would involve "more in the way of constitutional protection for the lives of unborn children" than everyone else. To the extent that a Thirteenth Amendment–style solution was feasible, Byrn favored an enforcement mechanism like the one he had championed before *Roe:* the appointment of a guardian ad litem for unborn children to bring a class action against hospitals and doctors and enjoin further procedures.[21] Anti-abortion scholar John T. Noonan went further, explaining, "A Constitution is not a criminal statute. If an amendment is to act at a criminal level, it is not the appropriate place to incorporate the details and qualifications of a criminal law."[22]

While the fight for an amendment continued, some in the anti-abortion movement even argued that their movement had put too much emphasis on criminal penalties. Led by activists like Marjory Mecklenburg, a Minnesota advocate who championed anti-abortion crisis pregnancy centers and better access to birth control, these groups promoted what they described as alternatives to abortion: modest funding for birth control, changes to the law of adoption, support for anti-abortion crisis pregnancy centers, and new laws against discrimination on the basis of pregnancy or illegitimacy. Mecklenburg and her colleagues believed that their movement should do more to address the reasons that some who might want to carry a pregnancy to term nevertheless sought a termination. Such activists at times held prominent positions in the movement; Mecklenburg was for a time the chairman of the National Right to Life Committee (NRLC).[23]

The Advantages of Decriminalization

In the 1970s, there was reason to believe that de-emphasizing criminal penalties benefited pregnant people—and hardly harmed the anti-abortion movement. True, the abortion rate increased each year between 1970 and 1980, but the largest increases took place before *Roe,* between 1970 and 1972.

After *Roe*, the most visible changes involved when and where abortions took place; after 1973, many more procedures took place early in pregnancy and in the home state of a pregnant person, and abortion became far safer as a result—the case fatality rate decreased 90% between 1972 and 1987. To the extent that abortion numbers were really increasing, the rate often reflected contraceptive failure: the authoritative 1970 National Fertility Study found that one-third of women trying to prevent birth suffered contraceptive failure. (Two decades later, a panel convened by the National Academy of Sciences found that the United States remained decades behind many European countries in contraceptive effectiveness.) If a lack of criminal laws did not explain high abortion rates, de-emphasizing criminal penalties seemed to have a broad political appeal, especially for an anti-abortion movement that struggled to find political allies. In 1976, Gerald Ford hired Mecklenberg to lead pro-life outreach for his reelection campaign. Jimmy Carter, Ford's rival, took a more pro-choice position under pressure from feminists in the Democratic National Committee, but in office he continued to stress the importance of Mecklenberg's policy priority, alternatives to abortion, juxtaposing his opposition to abortion funding with his support for better access to contraception and subsidies to facilitate the adoption of hard-to-place foster children.[24]

Fetal Victims and the War on Crime

By the 1980s, however, a rapidly changing political landscape began pushing many in the anti-abortion movement toward a greater focus on criminal punishment. Ronald Reagan, who had proudly proclaimed his support for an anti-abortion amendment, easily won the 1980 presidential race, and anti-abortion Republicans took control of Congress. Nevertheless, there were not enough votes for a personhood amendment, and anti-abortion groups could not agree on an alternative. With a constitutional amendment off the table, anti-abortion groups invested more in incremental restrictions. Reagan capitalized on panic about crime by demanding funding for private prisons, limits on pretrial release, federal sentencing guidelines, and more mandatory minimum sentences. While Reagan presented himself as a defender of victims' rights—and argued that the best way to defend victims was to impose harsh penalties on those who wronged them—Americans United for Life and other anti-abortion groups suggested that a victims' rights approach should protect fetuses too. Anti-abortion groups championed laws that fit well in the Reagan administration's new approach to criminal law and racial justice: fetal homicide laws and statutes criminalizing drug or alcohol abuse during pregnancy. As Michele Goodwin has shown, these prosecutions disproportionately targeted people of color.[25]

Demonizing "the Abortion Industry"

By the 1990s, the anti-abortion movement increasingly stressed the criminalization of doctors. By 1982, over 80% of abortions took place in freestanding clinics. Their rise improved access to abortion but also isolated providers and made clinics more vulnerable to attack. It was no surprise that the early 1980s witnessed a wave of vandalism and fire bombings at clinics across the country.[26]

The more separated clinics became from other medical facilities, the more anti-abortion leaders defined providers as greedy and amoral. These claims captured greater attention after 1978, when reporters Pamela Warrick and Pamela Zekman published an exposé in the *Chicago Sun-Times* titled "The Abortionists." Warrick and Zekman had worked undercover for five months in six of the thirteen clinics then operating in the Chicagoland area. Their conclusions were nuanced: "The Abortionists" detailed everything from substandard care and fraudulent billing practices to abortion procedures performed on people who were not pregnant. But Zekman and Warrick also told the stories of clinics that provided safe and compassionate services. The *National Right to Life News*, which reran much of the *Sun-Times* series, stripped out this nuance. The term "abortionist" became part of the anti-abortion movement's lingua franca, as shorthand for profiteers who had no ethical commitment to their patients or their professions. Women, wrote the chairperson of Westchester Right to Life in 1981, had "a right to be protected from the exploitation of the $500 million-a-year abortion industry."[27]

These arguments caught on even more because of a 1979 book, *Aborting America*, by Bernard Nathanson, a former abortion provider, founding member of the National Abortion Rights Action League, and a pro-life convert. *Aborting America*, like "The Abortionists," held itself out as an exposé of the inner workings of a profit-driven abortion industry. Nathanson's insider status—he claimed to have performed sixty thousand abortions over the course of his career—helped to popularize his arguments. "The pricing structure of abortions suggests that, with 1.5 million performed annually, what's good for the 'well-being of the patient' can be even better for the financial well-being of doctors toiling in the abortion industry," argued anti-abortion columnist Colman McCarthy in 1983, citing Nathanson's work.[28] When the Supreme Court struck down a 1983 model anti-abortion law, Doug Johnson of NRLC made a similar argument, arguing that the Court had "defended the interests not of women, but of the assembly-line abortion industry."[29]

Demonizing abortion providers made sense as leading anti-abortion groups took aim at Planned Parenthood. As early as 1982, *National Right to Life News* argued that Planned Parenthood ran "the nation's largest abortion clinic chain."[30] Planned Parenthood also had begun a successful public-interest litigation campaign. "Litigation initiated and funded by Planned Parenthood," noted Ed Grant of Americans United for Life, "has made it virtually impossible for state legislators to act against abortion."[31]

Throughout the 1980s, as Reagan gradually changed the composition of the Supreme Court, anti-abortion leaders began imagining the best laws for a post-*Roe* United States, most of them centered on different criminal punishments for abortion providers. NRLC, for example, privileged a law in politically contested states that would allow abortion only in cases of rape, incest, certain fetal conditions, and extreme threats to the health of a pregnant person. These laws almost all targeted what anti-abortion leaders described as a criminal and "unregulated abortion industry."[32]

But a focus on criminalizing abortion came at a steep cost. The new focus on policing the conduct of pregnant patients resulted in the prosecution of at least fifty low-income women of color between 1987 and 1990 alone. These prosecutions—and the punitive ideas about pregnancy and the "abortion industry"—did not lower the abortion rate, which actually increased more than 2% between 1989 and 1990. Subsequent research suggested that higher rates of maternal incarceration led to spikes in infant mortality, particularly in communities of color.[33]

By 1992, the Supreme Court's conservative majority had signaled interest in reversing *Roe*, but the majority in *Planned Parenthood of Southeastern Pennsylvania v. Casey* turned away requests to undo abortion rights, preserving what the joint opinion called the essential holding of *Roe*: that there was a right to choose abortion until viability, the point at which fetal survival outside the womb became more realistic.[34] *Casey* increased interest in a punitive strategy targeting providers. In its aftermath, larger anti-abortion groups like Americans United for Life and NRLC concluded that the way to undo both *Roe* and *Casey* was to convince the Court (and the public) that women could not and should not rely on abortion access to lead more equal lives because the abortion industry was willing to hurt them for a price. Americans United for Life legislative director Judith Koehler argued that the "abortion industry" had conspired to "deny women this important preventive health information [which] is both sexist and cruel."[35] Some of these groups began championing targeted regulations of abortion providers, onerous clinic regulations that often forced some clinics to close.[36]

Regional Realignment, a Changing Supreme Court, and Punishment

By 2007, when the Supreme Court upheld a law criminalizing dilation and extraction, the procedure that anti-abortion leaders called "partial-birth abortion," the anti-abortion movement had fully embraced criminal punishment. The regional realignment of the anti-abortion movement—which became increasingly evident after 2010—further strengthened the movement's commitment to carceral solutions. In earlier decades, a predominantly Catholic anti-abortion movement had not been especially influential in the American South, and white Evangelical Protestants were not particularly active in the anti-abortion movement. Because of the legacy of the Democratic Party's effort to write white supremacy into law during and after Reconstruction, the so-called Solid South voted for Democrats for president in every election but one between 1876 and 1948 (rejecting Catholic Democrat Al Smith); Democrats won congressional and state elections for far longer. At the national level, Republicans like Reagan easily won election across the South starting in the 1980s, and following the so-called Republican Revolution of 1994, led by Georgia representative Newt Gingrich, seats in the House of Representatives long held by Democrats were in Republican hands. But at the state level—where most abortion restrictions arose—Democrats retained majorities until 2010.[37]

That year, the so-called Tea Party wave delivered a swath of state legislatures to Republicans. The gains were particularly notable in the South, which became a new laboratory for abortion restrictions. The South had a long history of punitive laws: southern states had long incarcerated more of their citizens—and a far higher percentage of their citizens of color—even after the region's "tough on crime" approach later spread elsewhere in the United States. (Between 1965 and 2000, the number of prisoners in the United States increased by 600%.) Even as the rest of the nation embraced mass incarceration, the South was unique. Southern states used the death penalty more since the 1970s than all other regions combined and incarcerated the most people before the trial. Eight of the ten states with the highest rates of incarceration of any kind were in the South.[38]

As the anti-abortion movement found its most promising partners in southern state legislatures, criminal enforcement of abortion laws—including personhood proposals—seemed far more natural. At first, this shift was less visible because the anti-abortion establishment, embodied by groups like Americans United for Life and the NRLC, privileged strategies designed to chip away at *Roe* in the U.S. Supreme Court. Overly punitive policies, many of which polled badly, also seemed likely to alienate swing justices or leaders of the national Republican Party. Nevertheless, from time to time, the movement's new focus on punishment was obvious. In March 2016, at a townhall on MSNBC, primary candidate Donald Trump answered a question about whether people who had abortions should be punished. Trump insisted that there should be "some kind of punishment" for people who terminated pregnancies. The answer produced a backlash from supporters of the anti-abortion movement, who described pregnant people as the second victims of abortion. "Being pro-life," wrote Jeanne Mancini of March for Life, "means wanting what is best for the mother and the baby."[39]

But the reaction to Trump's comment made clear that criminal punishment *was* central to the anti-abortion movement. Most groups responding to Trump's misstep stressed their support for fining and imprisoning doctors and those who aided them. "Punishment," explained the anti-abortion Susan B. Anthony List in a spring 2016 press release, "is solely for the abortionist who profits off of the destruction of one life and the grave wounding of another."[40]

Punitive laws spread in the wake of changes to the Supreme Court. The anti-abortion movement's incremental approach—centered on laws that the movement argued could be reconciled with *Roe* and *Casey*—had gained influence in state legislatures because lawmakers did not want to sabotage the campaign to undo federal constitutional abortion rights. After Senator Mitch McConnell refused to hold a hearing on President Barack Obama's last Supreme Court nominee, Merrick Garland, Trump pushed through the nomination of Neil Gorsuch, and after Anthony Kennedy announced his retirement in 2018, Brett Kavanaugh survived credible accusations of sexual assault to become the Court's new median justice.[41]

With Kavanaugh on the Court, state lawmakers bet that the Court already had a majority prepared to reverse *Roe* and saw no reason to be as careful about the laws they passed. First came a wave of so-called heartbeat laws that banned abortion at six weeks, or roughly two weeks after a missed period. These and similar laws prescribed harsh penalties for doctors who performed abortions after this time; in Alabama, a new law prescribed up to ninety-nine years in prison. Some were unclear about exactly who would be punished—in Georgia, for example, lawmakers did not include statutory language they had previously used to exempt people from punishment for ending their own pregnancies, a step some commentators interpreted as proof that pregnant people as well as doctors could face punishment for abortion. Even after the Court struck down a Louisiana targeted regulation of abortion providers, with Chief Justice John Roberts casting the deciding vote, state lawmakers continued to pass sweeping criminal laws. In part, this switch reflected changes to the Republican Party, especially in certain states that were politically uncompetitive. In states like Alabama, legislators had little to fear from passing laws that criminalized all abortions, even when taking steps that might play poorly for the national Republican Party. But even more cautious lawmakers were reassured by the Fall 2020 confirmation of Amy Coney Barrett. With Barrett on the Court, Roberts's potential defection no longer mattered as much; there were still five conservatives who might vote to reverse *Roe*.[42]

Even when some anti-abortion strategists moved away from purely criminal strategies, their focus remained on punishing those who performed abortion. Texas's SB8, the best-known abortion bill of the year, began with efforts to ban abortion in a small Texas town with no abortion clinics. Mark Lee Dickson, a pastor and anti-abortion activist in East Texas, had already drafted a bill prohibiting the procedure in Waskom, Texas, and he worked with legislator Bryan Hughes and former Texas solicitor general Jonathan Mitchell in refining a model ordinance for other towns. Hughes and Mitchell set out to ensure that no one challenging the law would have standing to sue by allowing only private citizens to enforce the law—and would be unable to overcome the state's arguments about sovereign immunity under Ex parte *Young*. But even the champions of SB8 clearly endorsed the idea of punishment. The bill used the language of criminal laws, describing those who assisted in abortions as aiders and abettors, for example, and adopted as a minimum amount of damages the fine that would accompany the most serious felonies under Texas law.[43]

The Wages of Criminalization

In 2022, after the Supreme Court reversed *Roe v. Wade* in *Dobbs v. Jackson Women's Health Organization*, nearly half of the states stood ready to reinstate old criminal punishments for abortion or to introduce new ones. States with trigger laws, statutes that would criminalize abortion were *Roe* to be overturned, authorized punishments ranging from one year to life in prison, while pre-*Roe* bans set out comparably modest penalties. Following the leak of Justice Alito's draft majority in *Dobbs*, more states passed punitive laws. The most intense debates were not about whether anyone should be punished but about how and how much. For example, those who favored criminal punishment for women and pregnant people were more organized and influential, introducing model bills in a handful of states and backing a Louisiana bill that received serious consideration.[44]

At a time when state and federal governments may seriously consider writing fetal personhood into American law, it is worth remembering that protecting personhood does not lead inexorably to incarceration in other countries (Germany being a key example). The equation of fetal rights and mass incarceration is no more natural or unavoidable in the United States.[45]

And history also gives us reason to think that criminalization will continue to harm vulnerable communities while doing little to make abortion less common. After the 1990s, abortion rates began a steady decline, partly reflecting improved access to contraception in the decade. Opposition to criminalization, by contrast, remained steady: only between 10% and 20% of Americans polled by Gallup between 1976 and the present have said that abortion should be illegal under all or most circumstances. And to the extent criminal punishment ever affected abortion rates, states may have already reached a point of diminishing returns when it comes to imposing new restrictions. A 2022 study by the Guttmacher Institute found that for the first time in thirty years, the abortion rate had increased, between 2017 and 2020. Conservative states in this period had continued to pass restrictions on abortion, but at the same time any marginal effect from those laws was overshadowed by the effects of progressive states' increases in Medicaid funding for abortion. At the same time, cuts to Title X funding and other changes to federal family planning policy appear to have increased demand for abortion. Criminal laws will primarily (though not exclusively) apply in states that already limit access to abortion; progressive states seem likely to step up support for low-income people seeking abortion, even if they travel from another state.[46]

Even the most effective criminal laws seem unlikely to significantly reduce abortion rates. Before 1973, abortion was as common as it was rarely prosecuted; in other countries with unusually punitive abortion laws, such as Ecuador and Kenya, abortion rates remain high. And criminal abortion laws will be extraordinarily difficult to enforce, especially given the availability of medication-based abortions. Criminal abortion laws will likely face a fate similar to the drug laws that formed the "war on drugs" waged between the 1960s and the present, or even the Prohibition battle that briefly banned the transportation, sale, and manufacture of alcohol in the United States—they will be ineffective in preventing people from ending their pregnancies but likely to increase rates of incarceration, especially for those in communities of color that are the most heavily policed. Rates of incarceration, in turn, will contribute to higher rates of infant mortality and poorer outcomes for families of color.[47]

The years between *Roe* and *Dobbs* suggest that any constitutional argument for reproductive rights and justice, no matter how good, would have de-escalated a profound national conflict around abortion. In the aftermath of *Dobbs*, this constitutional impasse has become only more pronounced: while supporters of reproductive rights and reproductive justice have pressed new claims about constitutional equality, anti-abortion activists have revived the movement for fetal personhood and insisted that abortion is unconstitutional. Interstate conflicts are also brewing, as conservative lawmakers contemplate the extraterritorial application of their criminal abortion laws, and progressive states introduce shield laws to protect physicians and others from subpoena, extradition, and other legal consequences.

These interstate struggles all assume that criminalization will preoccupy the anti-abortion movement, but history shows that it does not have to be this way. An emphasis on incarceration has not done much to lower abortion rates, all while alienating ambivalent voters. More important, de-emphasizing punishment would certainly lead to better outcomes for pregnant people and their families. The post-*Dobbs* era will almost certainly be one of profound inequalities and constitutional chaos, but it need not be the start of a new chapter in the nation's troubled story of mass incarceration.

PART VI
INTERNATIONAL PERSPECTIVES

16

Abortion Policy Aimed at Promoting Life As Much As Possible

Mark Tushnet

This chapter argues that people whose sole concern in devising abortion policies is protecting human life and who regard the fetus/unborn child as a human life should seriously consider a set of abortion-related policies that would resemble those adopted in most Western European nations with strong traditions of social democracy and Christian democracy. The centerpiece of such policies are strong systems of social support for childbearing, childbirth, and childrearing. Such systems reduce the costs associated with those activities and thereby reduce the demand for abortions. Important collateral features of these systems include some degree of regulation of abortion procedures and some complex rules about when abortions are lawful (in some sense) and when unlawful. These regulations are designed to reduce the size of the underground or "gray" market for abortions because abortions performed in that market pose risks not only to the fetus/child (of course) but to the woman as well. These policies operate as a package: take away one or another significant element, and the case for the others weakens dramatically.

These Western European policies stand in sharp contrast to the policies typically advocated in the United States by those who purport to seek a reduction in the number of abortions. The typical U.S. policy focuses solely on abortion and seeks to raise its cost by imposing substantial restrictions upon its availability, including criminal penalties for those who perform abortions inconsistent with the restrictions, and sometimes for those who assist women seeking such abortions (and sometimes, though rarely, for the women themselves). Among the things these policies ignore is the inevitable existence of the underground or gray market. And, though the evidence is inevitably contestable, there's some reason to think that Western

Mark Tushnet, *Abortion Policy Aimed at Promoting Life As Much As Possible* In: *Roe v. Dobbs.* Edited by: Lee C. Bollinger and Geoffrey R. Stone, Oxford University Press. © Oxford University Press 2024.
DOI: 10.1093/oso/9780197760352.003.0016

European–style abortion policies actually reduce the incidence of abortion more than strict restrictions on availability do.[1]

I observe at the outset that one need not take promoting life (including that of the fetus/child) as much as possible as the sole goal of abortion-related policy. One might well be concerned in addition with quality of life. As the German Constitutional Court observed, the history of concern for the quality of the lives of newborns is troubling, focusing on what that court described as the view that some newborns were "unworthy of life" and similar discriminatory attitudes. On the other hand, concern for the quality of the woman's life—comparing her life after obtaining an abortion with the way her life might have gone had she carried the pregnancy to term—has no similar history. Many women considering obtaining an abortion apparently are concerned about the quality of their lives. Abortion-related policies might respond to their belief that the quality of their lives would be adversely affected were they to carry the pregnancy to term. That would qualify the policy focus on promoting life as much as possible in ways that make the Western European approach unattractive.[2]

After laying out the argument for the Western European policies, which are rooted in Social and Christian Democratic policies, this chapter offers a political analysis that seeks to explain why they have not been and are unlikely to be available in practice in the United States. Neither of the major party coalitions has strong incentives to pursue such policies independently. That would make the set of policies, were they somehow to be adopted, quite unstable, weakening the political incentives to pursue them. I conclude with the suggestion that an entrepreneurial politician, probably a Democrat but perhaps a Republican, might someday find it advantageous to develop a comprehensive political platform one part of which, but only a part, would be the Social and Christian Democratic package of abortion-related policies.

An Outline of Western European Policies

The injunction that abortion-related policies should be designed solely to protect human life as much as possible is of course a normative and contestable one, which this chapter does not defend. I take the injunction to refer to human life as such, meaning that in any case in which abortion becomes an issue, the life of the woman and the life of the fetus/child count just the same. In the political analysis I note some reasons offered for treating the life of the fetus/child as more valuable than that of the woman, but those reasons aren't a feature of the argument for the Western European policies. Another feature of the injunction is that policies are to be insensitive to their distributional effects: the policymaker doesn't care that abortions might be available without legal sanction more readily to one group of women than another. Here too the political analysis will point out that distributional concerns do matter in U.S. politics today.

The case for Western European–style abortion policies also rests on the empirical assumption, which I think well-founded, that there is an ordinary market for abortion services—"ordinary" here meaning that the market involves willing buyers (the people seeking abortion) and willing sellers. What counts as being a "willing" buyer, though, can itself be contested, and the policies to be described make the assumption, again empirical, that in at least some cases the seemingly willing buyer is ambivalent about whether she should purchase the service (or, more pointedly, is ambivalent about actually following up on an initial decision to explore the possibility of having an abortion).

Experience with policies purportedly prohibiting ordinary market transactions in alcohol (Prohibition) and recreational drugs shows that such policies can reduce the size of the market for the banned goods but will not eliminate it. An underground economy will inevitably emerge. The underground market for abortions is different at least in degree from the underground markets for alcohol and recreational drugs, though. Abortion is a medical procedure. Except in highly unusual circumstances, it leads to the death of the fetus/child, but as a medical procedure it entails risks to the woman's life as well. And when those risks eventuate, you end up with two dead people rather than just one. Policies aimed at bringing the underground market into the open can reduce that risk.

It's not just abortion that's risky in that sense. So is pregnancy itself. Women who attempt to carry their pregnancy to term sometimes suffer severe medical setbacks, to the point of death itself. The stresses of pregnancy, both physical and mental, can also be life-threatening, with cases of attempted and completed suicide known to happen. Here too policies regulating but not prohibiting abortion might be life-preserving, with the loss of the fetus/child's life offset by the preservation of the woman's.

I turn to the case for Western European–style abortion policies with these normative and empirical assumptions in hand. Western European abortion policies are founded on two tightly connected bases. First, abortion is available essentially on request during the early stages of pregnancy—from ten weeks to fourteen weeks or so. Second, strong systems of social support are in place for medical care generally, including contraception (important because the primary driver of a decision to obtain abortion is that the pregnancy is unintended), prenatal care and postbirth care, and for providing relief from the financial stresses associated with pregnancy, childbirth, and childrearing, including paid leave from work for a substantial period postdelivery and readily accessible infant- and child-care facilities for working parents. Notably, most features of these systems are not abortion- or pregnancy-specific; they are applications of more general social support programs such as the program for providing medical care of all sorts to all persons. Their universal character reduces concerns about whether abortions are available only to a privileged segment of society.

Why are these features important as part of a policy aimed at preserving life as much as possible? One might think that the availability of abortion on request would have to be non-life-preserving. The systems of social support, though, reduce the financial pressures on women who might consider having an abortion, and the availability of medical care reduces the risks associated with pregnancy. They also reduce what we might call the moral pressures on women who think it irresponsible to bring children into the world before they are financially stable.

The effect of the systems, then, is to reduce the demand for abortion during pregnancy's early stages. The German Constitutional Court, which offers the most extended judicial discussion of the rationale for the Western European approach, contends that—when coupled with other features of the regulatory system, to be discussed in a moment—the reduction in demand can reasonably be thought to drive demand below the number of abortions that would otherwise take place in an unregulated underground market. On that view the two features (and supplemental measures) do indeed preserve life as much as possible.

The Western European approach allows for abortions even after the period when abortion on request is available. Women seeking later abortions typically must show to a doctor or a panel of doctors what the German court calls "indications" for termination. These ordinarily include serious medical risks to the woman, whether directly life-threatening or seriously impairing her psychological or physical well-being, and the possibility that the fetus/child will be born with serious and life-threatening medical conditions. If we assume that the lives of the woman and the fetus/child are of equal value, much of this system can also be seen as preserving life as much as possible.

One might have reservations about the indication invoking physical or psychological well-being because on its face an abortion under those conditions takes the life of the fetus/child when the woman's life is not at risk. Here too we have to consider the role of the underground—and life-risking—market for abortions: women who believe that carrying the pregnancy through to birth would cause them substantial physical or psychological harm might seek abortions in the underground market. So, again, an indication that on its face seems incompatible with the policy of preserving life as much as possible might be understood as compatible with that policy. Or at least we can assume that the Western European approach believes that it is.

The concern for directing abortions away from the underground market interacts with the Western European systems of social support to reduce the distributional effects of that market's existence in a way that differs from the U.S. gray market. The systems of social support mean that a woman's wealth has a smaller impact on her access to abortion than would occur without such systems. That is, in the absence of systems of social support, relatively better-off women would have easier access to the underground market than their less well-off counterparts. Distributional effects don't disappear, of course, because better-off women who can't satisfy the regulatory requirements of an "indications" model will be able to access the gray market more easily. But, one might reasonably think, the distributional effects are weaker.

So far I have described three aspects of the Western European approach. The "indications" model for abortions after the early stages of pregnancy shows that there is a fourth aspect to consider. As Mary Ann Glendon put it, the Western European approach names the problem as seen by those who seek abortion policies that promote life as much as possible. The approach makes it clear that abortion is different from other medical procedures because it inevitably involves the taking of a human life (again, from the specified perspective).

The German Constitutional Court makes the naming explicit. It rejected a legislative provision that described some abortions as justified, that is, as not wrongful under the circumstances identified by the "indications." Instead it said that continuing some pregnancies was "non-exactable." This concept appears to operate in a space similar to that of excuse in the criminal law: a woman's decision to have an abortion under the circumstances is wrongful but understandable, and it would be unfair to her or disrespectful of her personal autonomy to block her from having an abortion. The German Constitutional Court's naming of abortion as involving the taking of a life is explicit. A similar naming is implicit in any system of regulation that treats abortion as a medical procedure requiring regulations not imposed when patients seek other forms of medical care, including risky operations to correct chronic illnesses. This differential treatment of abortions can be understood—and, the Western European approach assumes, will be understood by the people—as explained by the fact, as the approach has it, that abortion involves the taking of a human life.

Stating or clearly implying that abortion is wrongful is an exercise of law's expressive function. Such an expression can be reinforced or undermined by other features of a nation's laws. In particular, naming abortion as wrongful is compatible with a general "culture of life" that finds expression in the universal European prohibition of capital punishment. Western Europeans assume that women who participate in a general "culture of life" will think more seriously about obtaining a legally available abortion than they would were they located in a culture more ambivalent about the general value of life as such.[3]

Taken in all its parts the Western European approach can be defended as protecting life as much as possible by (1) reducing the financial and other stresses associated with pregnancy, childbirth, and childrearing; (2) bringing out of the shadows gray market abortions that threaten the lives of both the woman and the fetus/child; and (3) encouraging women to see themselves as full members of a society generally committed to a culture of life.

The Political Background of the Western European Approach

How did Western Europe reach this point? The story is complex and varies from one nation to another. Concerns about gray market abortions appear to have played a larger role in Ireland than elsewhere, for example. The general contours, though, can be discerned in the politics of abortion and in particular in the stances taken by Social Democratic and Christian Democratic parties (which have different formal names in different countries).

Two aspects of the history matter. The first is institutional, the second substantive. The institutional aspect is that social policy in Western Europe has not traditionally been highly "juridified," that is, subject to close judicial examination. Traditions of parliamentary supremacy, political constitution-alism in which constitutional concerns are the subject of legislative but not judicial attention, and opposition to government by judges—all contributed to a political culture in which political compromises didn't have to sat-isfy lawyers' demands for doctrinal consistency. Messy and unprincipled compromises could survive in such a culture.

The central substantive theme in the story is the development of the sys-tems of universal social support. These originated in the late nineteenth cen-tury and were grounded in both political and moral considerations. Socialist parties of that period pushed for the development of systems of social sup-port because, they argued, the capitalist-dominated market could not assure workers a living wage, understood to include the ability to pay for adequate levels of food, shelter, education, healthcare, and the like. Socialists argued as well that systems of social support were ways in which everyone in the so-ciety demonstrated their solidarity with everyone else.

At the outset some programs were initially contributory, such as old-age pension schemes and workers' compensation programs, and others implic-itly or explicitly were reserved for the "deserving" poor, such as unemploy-ment compensation programs available only to those who lost their jobs (and so had them in the first place). The socialist arguments about capitalism and solidarity led to the transformation, typically gradual but sometimes sudden, of these programs into more general systems of social support available to everyone without condition.

Conservatives understood that the socialist programs were politically at-tractive, and as democracy deepened conservatives responded to electoral threats by creating their own versions of social support. As a result such sys-tems became parts of the programs of socialist and conservative parties by the mid-twentieth century. Though of course the contours of the systems conservatives supported were different from the socialist versions, the idea that the nation as a whole should provide wide social supports settled into the conventional understanding of good social policy.

Paralleling the socialist arguments based on solidarity, Catholics, often as-sociated with conservative parties, developed—or retrieved—a tradition of social solidarity among all the children of Christ. In 1891 Pope Leo XIII is-sued the encyclical *Rerum Novarum*, described as setting out the "rights and duties of capital and labor." It supplemented the political defense of systems of social support with a Christian normative defense. Subsequent encyclicals in 1931 (*Quadregesimo Anno*), 1981 (*Laborem Exercens*), and 1991 (*Centesimus*

Annus, on the centennial of *Rerum Novarum*) further elaborated the Catholic Church's scriptural commitment to relatively thick systems of social support.

The systems of social support became entrenched social policies throughout Europe by the middle of the twentieth century. European nations were then ethnically homogeneous. The social support systems' distributional effects were almost entirely class-based and not, as they would be in the United States, compounded with race-based effects.

When abortion policy became the focus of political contention in the second half of the twentieth century, leftist and conservative parties had a long heritage of endorsing stable and substantial systems of social support. With such systems in place the religious, and at the time mostly Catholic, opposition to abortion because it involved the taking of a human life, became easier for secularists associated with leftist parties to accept. And as the Catholic Church moved incrementally against capital punishment—including the encyclical *Evangelium Vitae* in 1995, which said that in modern reasonably well-ordered societies cases in which capital punishment could be justified were "very rare, if not practically non-existent"—the idea that Western European societies aspired to have a culture of life became increasingly credible.

The overall result was that leftist and conservative parties were able to converge on a somewhat messy and somewhat unprincipled consensus on abortion-related policies that satisfied them and their constituents. The lack of principle can be seen in the difficulty of explaining how some of the "indications" for abortions after the early stages of pregnancy can be justified, a point to which I'll return.

The Western European consensus can reasonably be seen as promoting life as much as possible. Indeed, the German Constitutional Court requires that abortion-related policy take as fundamental the goal of promoting life as much as possible and has concluded that the policies I've described are constitutionally required. Elsewhere in Western Europe, in nations whose constitutional traditions don't require that courts give their stamp of approval to legislative compromises by finding them consistent with a highly rationalized set of constitutional doctrines, the messy consensus seems reasonably stable as well.

But, it seems, the Western European approach is in practical terms unavailable in the United States. The reasons include some features of the U.S. constitutional tradition and, more important, some aspects of U.S. politics. Here too the institutional setting matters. In the United States courts are regularly called upon to determine whether a policy is consistent with the Constitution. As they do so they develop legal doctrine that, they say, enforces a requirement of rational consistency. The European political culture tolerates messy compromises, but the U.S. political culture is uncomfortable with them.

Doctrinal Difficulties in Developing Legally Coherent Abortion Policies in the United States

Judicial action defining the constitutional contours of abortion-related policies along Western European lines would require a high degree of doctrinal creativity in the United States, which, though not impossible to imagine, is unlikely to occur. National legislation could unproblematically adopt the social-support aspects of Western European policies. Other features of those policies—specifically, the use of the criminal law to express a culture of life while simultaneously limiting the actual impact of criminal sanctions—might face doctrinal obstacles. More important, the structure of U.S. political parties as it has developed doesn't have the characteristics that made it politically possible for Western European parties to converge on the policies they've adopted: the U.S. Democratic and Republican parties are organized around traditions quite different from those animating Western European Social Democratic and Christian Democratic parties.

Begin with a judicial effort to build the Western European approach into the constitutional law of abortion. The form would be something like this: Here are a number of conditions that are constitutionally required if you seek to regulate the availability of abortions. You have to create a system of social supports for childbearing, childbirth, and childrearing. You can use your criminal law to express the judgment that abortion is morally wrongful, but you have to build in "defenses" for situations in which requiring the woman to carry the pregnancy to term would be unfair, analogous to the German notion of "non-exactability," such as extreme stress and risks to the woman's health. And you have to ensure that your regulations actually promote life as much as possible, which requires that you take into account the possibility that your regulations will drive too many abortions into the underground economy. There's nothing inherently "unjudicial" about a constitutional regime with such conditions built in, but it is quite a ways outside the U.S. tradition, which has been notably reluctant, for example, to impose substantial responsibility on governments to maintain a social safety net.[4]

What about legislation? Western European nations deploy their approach in what are, with respect to abortion, centralized rather than federal systems. In the United States the approach would, I think, have to come through national-level legislation. No single state nor even a group of states has the resources to provide the social supports to every woman who might otherwise obtain an abortion—nor could we assume that such women would relocate to states that did provide such supports.

The social-support requirement is straightforward under accepted notions of congressional power to tax and spend to advance the general welfare. The expressive dimension is more problematic. Perhaps the Fourteenth Amendment might be the source of congressional power to enact a nationwide criminal ban on abortion coupled with the kinds of exceptions built into the Western European approach. Whether such a statute could preempt state-level regulations, especially criminal laws with different contours, is unclear. It's not unthinkable that the U.S. Supreme Court could find such a statute "inappropriate" because of its intrusion on domains traditionally left to the states.

A final difficulty arises from the drive for rational consistency in doctrine—or, put another way, from the difficulty in the U.S. system of robust constitutional review of coming up with defenses of compromises on fundamental rights. Consider the apparently widespread intuition that regulatory exceptions should be available in cases of rape and incest. The intuition rests on the idea that pregnancies resulting from nonconsensual sex are relevantly different from those resulting from consensual sex. The relevant difference, though, can't be about the preservation of life. Abortions in such cases terminate one life without unusual risks to another, at least if we assume that pregnancies resulting from rape and incest are no more risky for the woman than pregnancies resulting from consensual intercourse. These exceptions thus show that something other than an injunction to promote life as much as possible is at work.

One red herring can be associated with the culture of life discussed earlier. Some who defend restrictive abortion laws but support capital punishment argue that abortion involves the taking of an innocent life, whereas capital punishment involves the taking of a guilty one. A woman who becomes pregnant after being raped might easily be described as innocent *and* unusually burdened by pregnancy, the latter fact perhaps justifying the taking of the innocent life of the fetus/child. But to complete the argument one would have to say that women who become pregnant after consensual intercourse are in some sense guilty. What that sense might be, though, is unclear unless one holds the view that consensual intercourse is wrongful.[5] So it can't be that the exceptions for rape and incest are defensible on the ground that they are available to innocent women whereas broader exceptions would be available to "guilty" ones.[6]

With ideas about innocence and guilt put to one side, we can see that the difference lies in the idea of consent to sexual intercourse. As the German account of "non-exactability" shows, though, the idea that lack of consent can offset the wrongfulness of abortion opens up a can of worms. Even with substantial social support, pregnant women can experience psychological stresses that make carrying the pregnancy to term unfair. And if somehow we're able to limit the relevance of consent to the moment of sexual intercourse, many women experience pressures in that moment that can reasonably be said to impugn the apparent consent they give.[7]

The push for rational consistency creates another difficulty. Centuries ago religious and legal doctrine identified "quickening" as a key moment in pregnancy. Quickening indicated that the entity within the womb had become "ensouled" and was therefore a person entitled to moral respect. And quickening was detected when the pregnant woman could feel that entity moving within the womb. The idea of ensoulment faded, but the thought that there was a line between non-personhood and personhood persisted. As science replaced religion the line came to be drawn at the moment of conception, when the entity—now the fetus—had the capacity to become an unquestioned person (a day before emerging from the womb, for example) in the ordinary course. Religious sensibilities shifted as well, perhaps under the indirect influence of science, to push to an earlier time the moment when abortion was understood to be the taking of a human life. As a matter of fundamental principle, then, those committed to promoting the lives of all persons were pushed by the demands of consistency to oppose abortions from the moment of conception—making problematic the Western European compromise allowing early-term abortions on request.

All well and good, but that opposition ran into an obstacle and generated an important counterreaction. The obstacle was a widespread sense in ordinary people not deeply committed to one or the other side of the abortion debate that there was a real moral difference between early- and late-term abortions, the latter involving the termination of a life, the former perhaps not. The counterreaction was to offer a competing principle, colloquially captured in the phrase "An acorn is not an oak tree." That is, what's morally significant is not the capacity to become an unquestioned person in the ordinary course but actually being such a person. (The counterreaction also ran into an obstacle, the flip side of the anti-abortion principle: it couldn't distinguish between early- and very late-term abortions even though ordinary people thought that such a distinction made a great deal of sense.)

The demand for rational consistency, that is, pushed the activists on abortion policy into irreconcilable claims of principle. Messy compromises when successful obscure that irreconcilability. But in a juridified culture demanding rational consistency (and enforcing that demand in the courts), such compromises are extremely difficult to arrive at.

Another obstacle to compromise arose in connection with contraception. Analytically the issue of contraception should be mostly independent of issues associated with abortion because contraception, when successful, operates to prevent a life from coming into existence. Some abortion opponents, though, believe that some modern methods of contraception actually operate after life has come into being (by blocking the implantation and therefore the growth of a fertilized egg, for example), and those beliefs have slopped over into a generalized objection to making contraception more readily available. In addition, objections of that sort sometimes originate in a vague sense that ready availability of contraceptives makes nonmarital intercourse more likely, which is for some morally objectionable independent of any relation to abortion or preserving life.

Political Difficulties in Developing Legally Coherent Abortion Policies in the United States

This doctrinal analysis might well be beside the point because neither of the major U.S. political parties now is structured to support a Western European approach to abortion policy. Notably, U.S. policy analysis uses the language of compromise rather than consensus to describe the political process. Not only is it essentially impossible to imagine a consensus emerging between the major parties on abortion-related policy; it's almost equally difficult to imagine the parties embracing, grudgingly or enthusiastically, compromises on such policies.

As in Western Europe, the story for the United States combines history, ideology, and party structures. The Democratic and Republican parties aren't equivalent to Western European Social Democratic and Christian Democratic parties. The latter were parties historically organized on a national basis around ideological platforms. Parties in the United States were historically organized on a state basis, responding to local concerns, including patronage. At the national level, U.S. parties were coalitions of state-level parties, coming together around a handful of policies that united each party and distinguished it from the other. This party structure encouraged relegating social welfare policies to the state level, where—among other things—social provision could be administered by patronage-dominated bureaucracies, and wide variations in social provision could and did arise. Importantly, some of those variations were driven by white racism: states with substantial Black populations were particularly reluctant to develop social supports that would be available disproportionately to Blacks.

During the twentieth century U.S. political parties became coalitions of often disparate interest groups united not by coherent ideologies but by vaguer notions of conservatism and liberalism. One notable feature is especially significant for abortion-related policies: fiscal conservatives and relatively rich people combine in the contemporary Republican Party with conservative Catholics and Protestant Evangelicals. The former groups are committed to low-tax policies, which means that they oppose developing thick general programs of social support. And that slops over into opposition, perhaps less strong, to systems of social support specific to pregnancy, childbirth, and childrearing. Conservative Catholics who might favor social provision in line with the Church's social teachings have accepted a deal with fiscal conservatives in which the latter support restrictive abortion laws in exchange for the religious groups' acceptance of low-tax policies (which might well not be in the material interests of members of the religious groups). The result is that the Republican Party has no real constituency for offering a Western European–style compromise on abortion-related policy. So, for example, though Senator Lindsey Graham defended as similar to policies existing in Western Europe his proposal for national regulation of abortion, a ban after fifteen weeks with limited exceptions, his proposal says nothing whatever about expanding social support.

And there's no real constituency in today's Democratic Party for either offering or accepting such a compromise. For a relatively short period some prominent Democratic politicians said that they favored policies that would make abortion "safe, legal, and rare." By the second decade of this century that position had disappeared from Democratic politicians' discourse. Some center-left pundits occasionally revive the idea in various forms, including some that advert to Western Europe. The suggestions are met with scorn by political activists and (as yet) have had no purchase among leading Democratic politicians. The reason for that, to the extent we can discern it, is that the term "rare" connoted that abortions were wrongful.[8] And important components of the Democratic Party coalition didn't regard it as wrongful.

The moment for policies that would make abortion safe, legal, and rare passed because of changes in the Democratic Party coalition. For much of the twentieth century labor unions representing members of the traditional working class were important components of that coalition. In part paralleling the structure of European politics, traditional labor unions supported strong systems of social support for a blend of socialist-like reasons and religion-based reasons, in light of the fact that many union members were Catholics. National labor policy and changes in the national economy led to a gradual, then rapid decline in traditional industrial labor unions. Today's major unions represent teachers and low-wage service workers. Working-class voters, no longer organized into strong unions, migrated to the Republican Party, in part because they saw the rise of a different type of interest group within the Democratic Party.

That new-ish type of interest group was identity-based. Black Americans had shifted from the Republican Party of Abraham Lincoln to Franklin Roosevelt's Democratic Party because the latter supported, and the former came to oppose, systems of social support that benefited Black Americans— and because Black Americans migrated from the segregationist (and Democrat-dominated) South to urban centers in the North and West, where local Democratic parties were strong and could provide patronage jobs and help in navigating welfare bureaucracies. The increasing role of Black Americans in the Democratic Party led many members of the working class to shift their party affiliations, for what we can now see were fundamentally racist reasons. The effect within the Democratic Party was to reduce support for thickening the U.S. system of social provision, which had collateral effects on abortion-related policy.

More directly, the organized feminist movement became an important identity-based interest group within the Democratic Party. That movement's class base was in relatively well-to-do social sectors, which have been relatively more secularist and less committed to religion than has been the U.S. working class. Some social supports—family and medical leave, for example—were important for that interest group. More important, though, was opposition to restrictive abortion laws and, in particular, to the idea embodied in such laws that abortion was wrongful. As secularists or only moderately religious people, members of the organized women's movement tended to see abortion as simply another medical procedure.

Thin systems of social support interact with the interest-group character of the Democratic Party coalition to bring distributional issues to the fore in developing abortion-related policies. Democratic politicians simply can't afford to ignore the fact that, absent a thick and universal system of social supports, any moderately restrictive abortion law will make the lives of Black (and other minority) women, and the lives of poor women, worse than they would be with unrestrictive abortion laws. As noted earlier, relatively restrictive abortion laws won't eliminate the gray market for abortions, but in the United States that market would probably have a significant distributional character, substantially more available to relatively well-off women than to others. As we've seen, there's basically no one on the Republican side who is willing to couple restrictive regulations with thicker systems of social support. Concerned about distributional effects, Democrats correctly treat unrestrictive laws as the only available policy.

The political conditions for compromise over systems of social support and over restrictive abortion regulations don't exist in the United States. What of the culture of life? At one point prominent Catholic leaders described social policy as a "seamless garment," coupling their opposition to abortion with opposition to capital punishment. At least by the second decade of the current century, Catholic leaders clearly elevated opposition to abortion over opposition to capital punishment.[9] On the Supreme Court, Justice Clarence Thomas's practice of reciting in detail the awful facts of cases where the death penalty was imposed conveys rhetorically the sense that he believes that the death penalty is not merely constitutionally permissible but morally appropriate in the cases before him. Other components of the Republican coalition are traditional law-and-order conservatives. Opposition to the death penalty is greater among Democrats but not enough to make credible the claim that the United States has a culture of life, much less that abortion opponents hope that such a culture might be created.

Possibilities for the Future?

This analysis of U.S. politics suggests that politicians have few incentives to promote Western European–style abortion-related policies. One can imagine the United States stumbling along a path toward the Western European–style policies. In the absence of national legislation or with vague national laws in place, some states will adopt restrictive abortion policies, others dramatically less restrictive ones. That regime might prove unsatisfactory largely for distributional reasons. Social supports might expand for reasons unrelated to their effects on abortion.

Perhaps a handful of entrepreneurial and ambitious politicians outside each party's core might see an opportunity to make names for themselves by advocating for Western European policies. Whether Republican or Democrat, they would initially focus on expanding social supports. A Republican might propose such expansions as anti-abortion measures explicitly aimed at reducing the costs of pregnancy, childbearing, and childrearing. Perhaps the expansion could be designed to make the new social supports available almost exclusively to women who might otherwise obtain abortions. A Democrat might propose wider expansions of social supports and defend them as good in general but also specifically because of their effects on reducing the demand for abortions. Support for enhanced social supports might be accompanied, again in the ambitious politician's program, by explicitly defending generous versions of the Western European "indications" model as life-preserving because they shift abortions from the risky gray market and hold out the prospect of saving one life when two would otherwise be lost.

At the moment the pool of such politicians seems dry. Someday, perhaps, a politician who takes seriously all of the Catholic Church's teachings—those on abortion, social supports, and capital punishment—might come forward. Until then the United States seems unlikely to pursue abortion-related policies that hold out the possibility, as Western European ones do, of promoting life as much as possible.

17

American Exceptionalism and the Comparative Constitutional Law of Abortion

*Tom Ginsburg**

Although the phrase "American exceptionalism" dates only to the 1930s, it has become a common placeholder for a much older idea: the received wisdom that the United States is a special nation, immune from the forces that beset other nations. For the most part, of course, these claims are overstated. Our country, it turns out, is deeply polarized and vulnerable to many of the same forces of democratic backsliding found in other countries. It remains marred by a legacy of slavery and racial inequality, like many other countries in the New World. It suffers many of the other afflictions of early twenty-first-century political life, including disinformation and media capture.

One area in which our country *is* exceptional is the particular role of abortion politics in our current ailment. While many countries struggle with the question of how abortion should be treated within the constitutional order, the United States is distinct in the degree to which the abortion question has warped our politics more generally. The constitutionalization of the abortion issue in the 1973 decision of *Roe v. Wade* set in motion five decades of increasingly intense conflict, most recently manifested in the 2022 decision in *Dobbs v. Jackson Women's Health Org.*, which overruled *Roe*.[1]

This chapter considers how a range of other countries have dealt with the constitutional questions surrounding abortion. The survey suggests that, for the United States, there have been jurisprudential roads not traveled that might have generated greater compromise, or at least would not have created a scorched-earth conflict with massive implications for politics more generally. Of course, abortion is a deeply contested moral issue in many countries because it involves a trade-off between the interests of an unborn fetus and those of a prospective mother confronted with an unwanted pregnancy.

Tom Ginsburg, *American Exceptionalism and the Comparative Constitutional Law of Abortion* In: *Roe v. Dobbs*. Edited by: Lee C. Bollinger and Geoffrey R. Stone, Oxford University Press. © Oxford University Press 2024. DOI: 10.1093/oso/9780197760352.003.0017

But at least some other countries have adopted compromise solutions that recognize the various interests at stake without experiencing decades of extreme partisan warfare. Understanding that possibility is itself illuminating for observers of the American scene.

One consequence of the U.S. approach is that, in some instances, American partisan warfare has spilled over into the politics of other countries, raising the salience of abortion in potentially destabilizing ways. American activists on the right have mobilized to lobby decision-makers in other countries to become more strict with regard to abortion. Indeed, the Constitution of Kenya almost failed to pass at referendum in 2010 because of lobbying by American churches, as will be described below. This illustrates that we are in an era in which abortion politics have become partly globalized. American exceptionalism, then, can generate the conditions for its own demise by virtue of its impact on other countries. The constitutional politics of abortion are increasingly transnational. Law, too, is, increasingly transnational, as regional human rights systems have had to grapple with the issue along with national supreme and constitutional courts.

The chapter is organized as follows. First, I make some introductory remarks about the United States. Next, I examine the jurisprudence of abortion in several other countries in different parts of the world. The goal is not to be comprehensive so much as to provide illustrative examples of different jurisprudential approaches and their relationship with constitutional politics. I then turn to international law, in particular the regional human rights courts found in some parts of the world, to explicate how they have approached the issue. The final section concludes.

Abortion and the Zero-Sum Poisoning of American Politics

In the United States, political entrepreneurs have framed abortion as an either/or choice: either we must insist on absolute protection of unborn life, or alternatively we must have absolute freedom from state interference on decisions to terminate a pregnancy. This framing means that one must be either an advocate of the murder of innocent babies or an advocate of women dying unnecessarily because of lack of access to healthcare. These absolutist views are out of step with those of most Americans, who for fifty years have held relatively stable public opinions on the issue, supporting the availability of abortion in many but not all circumstances.[2]

How did we get here? The world before *Roe* was worse for women, but also one in which abortion was not a central issue in American politics. Before that 1973 decision, more Republicans than Democrats favored leaving the abortion decision to a woman and her doctor. There were passionate opponents of abortion, but it was not a defining issue of partisan identity. No longer. The issue has now poisoned our politics, with U.S. Supreme Court appointments as a central battleground. Presidential elections are now won and lost on the power to appoint pro- or antichoice justices, notably in 2016, when Senator Mitch McConnell blocked the nomination of Merrick Garland so as to make the fall election a referendum on the Court. It is not much of a stretch to say that abortion politics gave us Donald Trump, along with the three new anti-abortion justices he was able to appoint. These justices then gave us the decision in *Dobbs v. Jackson Women's Health Org.* in 2022, overturning *Roe* and returning the issue to the states.[3] Many of the states promptly enacted a wide range of new restrictions, building on over a thousand statutes already in place.[4] The consequence was a dramatic decline in the number of legal abortions in the United States.

Processes of politicization, once set in motion, are very hard to reverse. Both American political parties have mobilized around the *Roe* decision for decades. GOP state legislators have passed numerous statutes trying to whittle it away, and many restrictions automatically came into force with *Dobbs*. But *Dobbs* has not settled the issue, as new restrictions continue to be adopted. Meanwhile, some Democrat-dominated states have codified the right to abortion in state constitutions in the aftermath of *Dobbs*. Litigation involving these new measures will likely continue. For example, restrictive states are likely to try to prevent their residents from traveling to other states to undertake abortions, and this will lead to new litigation in which the Supreme Court weighs the fundamental right to travel against "states' rights" to criminalize abortion. Laws singling out abortion providers for special scrutiny by medical regulators or that impose mandatory counseling and consent requirements may be challenged as well.

Roads Not Taken

Some other countries have taken a different, less absolutist path that starts with recognizing that there are indeed multiple interests at stake. Germany provides the best example in this regard, and a counterpoint to the United States. For obvious reasons, postwar Germany had strong reasons to embrace a culture of life. During World War II, Nazi eugenics laws facilitated selective abortion of "undesirable" populations, while enforcing an absolute prohibition on abortion for "Aryans." In reaction to this experience, the German Constitution of 1949 declared human dignity to be a core value, and abortion remained prohibited. Human life was to be protected as a way of marking a break with the past.

As in other parts of the Western world, however, the 1960s led to massive social change, and women began demanding greater control over reproductive issues. In 1975, Germany's Constitutional Court held that protection of human dignity required that the right to life attach to an unborn fetus.[5] The Court specifically rejected the framework of *Roe* that an unborn fetus had no constitutional interests in the first trimester. At the same time, the Court argued that prevention of abortion was to be preferred over punishment, and so gave room to the legislature to craft a compromise. In 1976, Germany legislated a new framework, in which abortion was decriminalized in the first twelve weeks of pregnancy if accompanied by counseling and a waiting period. Later abortions were to be allowed in cases of serious risk to the physical or mental health of the woman. This remains the basic framework in Germany today, and it is not particularly controversial.

The German solution recognizes that there is common ground between those who oppose abortion and those who want to ensure that women remain in charge of their own decisions regarding reproduction. Unsafe abortion is a major cause of maternal deaths, and both sides can agree that no woman should die from avoidable complications in her pregnancy. Both sides can agree that minimizing the number of abortions is a desirable goal; after all, for legalization advocates, safe and effective contraception is always preferable to terminating a pregnancy, with its attendant emotional harms. The advantage of the German system is also that it recognizes that both sides have legitimate arguments. As a result, abortion has not become a central issue in their electoral politics.

The technique used by the German Constitutional Court was proportionality doctrine, which has been become a favorite tool of constitutional adjudicators around the world.[6] Proportionality recognizes that any particular dispute may have multiple interests at stake, and so valid rights can clash. The role of the court is not to find that any one interest (say, that of the fetus in being born, or that of a woman to control reproductive decisions) trumps all others. Instead, adjudication involves an effort to *optimize* among constitutional rights in situations when they clash.[7] Proportionality involves a weighing of interests and a search for solutions that recognize competing rights, while minimizing infringement on both. This is not a technique explicitly deployed by the U.S. Supreme Court, although scholars have called on it to do so.[8] As a political matter, proportionality communicates the legitimacy of both positions in a bilateral dispute; while one or the other may come out ahead, the decision does not deny the legitimacy of either. This contrasts with the scorched-earth quality of American abortion politics.

There are a number of other countries that have dealt with abortion in a less conflictual way, generally through legislative solutions and sometimes through court decisions. For example, Canada, perhaps the closest comparator to the United States, has some of the most liberal abortion laws in the world. Abortion is not criminalized in any circumstances, and the procedure is funded by the country's medical system. Prior to 1988, Canada had some laws in place restricting abortion access, and an 1869 law formally banned abortion. The 1969 Criminal Law Amendment Act legalized abortions when a committee of doctors certified that the pregnancy would endanger the life or health of the pregnant person. In 1988, the Canadian Supreme Court struck down that law in the landmark case *R. v. Morgentaler*. The Court found that restrictions on abortion violated Section 7 of the Canadian Charter of Rights and Freedoms, which stipulates that everyone has the right to life, liberty, and security of the person.[9] In 1989, the Canadian Supreme Court issued another decision, in *Tremblay v. Daigle*, holding that a fetus has no legal status in Canada as a person under Canadian Civil Law.[10] Although these decisions were essentially a triumph for the forces in favor of abortion access, it is important to note that they seem to have settled the issue politically for the most part.

Nepal provides an example of an affirmative duty on the part of the government to provide access to safe abortions. Nepal originally legalized abortion in 2002 with an amendment to the civil code following the deaths of many women who had procured unsafe abortions. The law allowed abortion of pregnancies up to twelve weeks' gestation on request, up to eighteen weeks' gestation in cases of rape or incest, and at any time if the pregnancy threatened the life or physical or mental health of the pregnant person or if there is a fetal abnormality.[11] In 2009, the Supreme Court of Nepal found that the government had a duty to guarantee access to safe and affordable abortion services in light of deep inequities in socioeconomic status, which hindered availability. The court ordered the government to adopt a comprehensive abortion law that established a national fund for abortion costs, ensured greater protection of women's privacy, and established means for disseminating information about safe abortion services to the public and healthcare providers.[12] In 2018, the government passed the Safe Motherhood and Reproductive Health Rights Act, which, among other things, requires healthcare services to provide safe abortions to pregnant women.[13]

Jurisdictions in East Asia influenced by Confucianism, such as Japan, South Korea, and Greater China, also tend to be tolerant of abortion, even where it remains formally illegal.[14] For example, in Taiwan, abortion is technically illegal except in specified circumstances, including rape, incest, and genetic defects.[15] Nevertheless, it is widely available, and not a major political issue.

Episodic Conflict

In a number of other countries, abortion politics have been intense but episodic, and once liberalization has occurred, the issue has been settled. For example, in South Korea, abortion was illegal for many decades, though the criminal penalties were rarely enforced. A 2012 decision in the Constitutional Court upheld the ban in a divided decision.[16] But some years later, in April 2019, the Court reversed course, announcing that the criminal ban violated women's freedoms, and gave the legislature a set period in which to reform the law or else it would lose its constitutional status.[17] When the National Assembly failed to act, abortion become legal in 2021. The change was brought about by a broad coalition of activists and healthcare providers and has not led to much backlash.

Ireland stands out for the manner in which legal change occurred. While Ireland's abortion law now aligns with most other European countries, its route to liberalization was unique. Although abortion has long been illegal in the largely Catholic country, it was not until 1983 that the Constitution was amended by referendum to provide for the right to life of the unborn on the same level as that of the mother.[18] This was a result of work by anti-abortion advocates, who were concerned that judges would rule in favor of abortion access. The relevant section provided:

> The State acknowledges the right to life of the unborn and, with due regard to the equal right to life of the mother, guarantees in its laws to respect, and, as far as practicable, by its laws to defend and vindicate that right. This

subsection shall not limit freedom to travel between the State and another State. This subsection shall not limit freedom to obtain or make available, in the State, subject to such conditions as may be laid down by law, information relating to services lawfully available in another State.[19]

As the language suggests, women were allowed to travel abroad (mainly to the United Kingdom) to obtain the service, but this restriction increased the number of maternal deaths.

In the 2000s, women's groups in Ireland increased lobbying to repeal the amendment. In a remarkable process, the country convened a "Citizen's Assembly" in 2016, in which randomly selected citizens and political appointees deliberated for a year on several divisive issues, including the status of abortion. The Assembly recommended repeal of the prior amendment so that Parliament could legislate on the topic, and this was achieved by a two-thirds majority at a referendum in 2018.[20] Following the referendum, lawmakers passed a law which allowed abortion for any reason up to the end of the first trimester, and later in cases of fetal abnormalities considered fatal after birth or a potential risk to the woman's health. The process has been held up as an example of how democracies can deal with issues of deep moral disagreement. Bringing together ordinary citizens who profoundly disagree with each other to deliberate can change minds and lead to compromise.[21]

Several Latin American countries have also recently liberalized abortion rights through intense episodes of political mobilization. Latin America is a largely Catholic region, and so many countries have long had outright bans on abortion. The 1969 American Convention on Human Rights provides in Article 4 that the right to life is to be protected from conception.[22] But recent years have seen a trend toward expanding access in some countries. And as we shall see, the interpretation of the international convention has changed over time, being deployed for liberalization in some countries.

In Argentina, abortion was legal only if the mother's life was in jeopardy or if the pregnancy was the result of rape; anyone who obtained an abortion outside these parameters could face criminal charges.[23] But in 2020, abortion law was liberalized through legislation with the adoption of the Voluntary Interruption of Pregnancy Bill. This development surprised observers, since the debate "emerged overnight in remarkable scope and intensity."[24] The bill, passed in the Senate by a thirty-eight to twenty-nine vote with one abstention, legalized elective abortions throughout the first fourteen weeks of pregnancy. The professed goal of the bill was "to regulate the access to voluntary termination of pregnancy and post-abortion care . . . in order to help reduce preventable morbidity and mortality."[25] The bill outlines a set of rights for those who are able to become pregnant: to decide to terminate the pregnancy, to have access to termination of pregnancy at centers of the healthcare system, to request and receive postabortion care at healthcare centers even if the abortion was illegal, and to have access to information and means to prevent unwanted pregnancy.[26] The bill allows healthcare workers to conscientiously object to performing abortions except in cases where the life or health of the pregnant person is at risk.[27] Notably, the bill also mentions Article 75(22) of the Argentinian Constitution, which recognizes a range of international treaties as providing complementary sets of rights to those already provided in the Constitution. The bill repeatedly refers to international treaties such as the Universal Declaration of Human Rights, the Convention on the Elimination of All Forms of Discrimination Against Women and its Optional Protocol, and the Convention on the Rights of the Child, among others.

Similarly, the legislature decriminalized abortion access in Uruguay in 2011. The law, passed with a seventeen to fourteen majority in the Senate, allows women to have an abortion in the first twelve weeks of pregnancy on request, during the first fourteen weeks in the case of rape, and without a time limit when the woman's health is at risk or in the case of fetal anomalies. Again, this was the result of a brief period of political salience.

While Argentina and Uruguay liberalized abortion law through legislation, Colombia did so through a ruling of the Constitutional Court. Before 2006, Colombia had a total ban on abortion with no exceptions. In that year, the Constitutional Court ruled that the total ban was unconstitutional and that there needed to be certain exceptions to the rule, including instances when there is a risk to the person's physical or mental health, when the fetus is inviable, and when the pregnancy is the result of rape or incest. On February 21, 2022, in response to a lawsuit brought by women's groups, the Constitutional Court decriminalized abortion up to twenty-four weeks of gestation. After the twenty-fourth week, pregnant people may seek abortions with no gestational limit in cases of risks to health (including mental health), rape, and nonviability of the fetus.[28] In the majority opinion, the Constitutional Court addressed Article 11 of the Constitution, which states that "the right to life is inviolable."[29] While this right implied a duty of the state to protect life, including that of a fetus, the right is not absolute and must be weighed against other constitutional principles, including women's rights to privacy and dignity.[30] In this sense, it followed the German approach of treating the interests of mother and fetus within a single framework. As in Argentina, the Court also considered international treaties, since the Constitution stipulates that international treaties ratified by Congress have domestic priority.[31]

Mexico has also partially decriminalized abortion access through the judiciary. On September 7, 2021, the Mexican Supreme Court ruled that it was unconstitutional to punish abortion as a crime. The Court struck down the existing law, which punished people who had procured abortions, with up to three years in prison, even if they had become pregnant because of rape. In 2008, the Supreme Court found that there was no absolute constitutional protection of life in gestation that could be construed to violate the fundamental rights of women. However, the 2008 ruling was limited to the federal district of Mexico City, whose government had sought to legalize abortion. It did not have the broad implications of the 2021 ruling, which asserted federal decision-making power rather than the supremacy of the states to determine abortion laws. Since the 2021 ruling, eight Mexican states and Mexico City have created pathways to abortion.[32]

This means that, as of this writing, five countries in Latin America have legalized abortion on request: Cuba (1965), Guyana (1995), Uruguay (2012), Argentina (2020), and Colombia (2022), as well as some states in Mexico. Looking outside Latin America, many countries in Sub-Saharan Africa, such as Niger, Chad, Cameroon, and the Central African Republic, allow abortions to preserve the health of the mother. South Africa, Mozambique, Benin, and Guinea Bissau have the most liberal abortion laws in the region, allowing abortions on request with various gestational limits. Zambia, Ethiopia, and Rwanda allow abortions on social or economic grounds.

This survey has demonstrated that there have been instances of liberalization of access to abortion as a result of episodic politics, whether through a judicial or a legislative mechanism. In most of these countries, abortion is an issue of deeply held views, but it has not assumed a central, defining role in political identity as it has in the United States.

The one recent case in which conflict over abortion has spilled over into broader constitutional politics, other than the United States, is the recent failed constitution-making episode in Chile. Chile has long had an absolute ban on abortions, and the 1980 Chilean Constitution states that "the law protects the life of the one about to be born."[33] The Pinochet regime instituted a total ban in 1989, although this did not prevent high rates of illegal abortion and little enforcement.[34] In 2017, the Senate voted to loosen the existing ban on abortions by legalizing abortions in cases where the mother's life is at risk, when the fetus would not survive the pregnancy, during the first twelve weeks of pregnancy in the case of rape, and during the first fourteen weeks of pregnancy for a minor under the age of fourteen.

In 2019, restrictive access to abortion was one of the major issues that motivated widespread social protests in Chile, which triggered a new process of drafting a Constitution. Women's groups staged major public demonstrations. While the draft produced thereafter was ultimately rejected at referendum in September 2022, it was stark in its reversal of the prior policy. Article 61(2) of the draft read, "The State guarantees . . . all women and people with the capacity to gestate the conditions for a pregnancy, a voluntary interruption of pregnancy." This proposal would have been the broadest in the world in guaranteeing the right to terminate a pregnancy. Other countries' constitutions sometimes *allow* legislatures to take the step of legalizing; Chile's draft would have directly required it.[35] Even though the draft failed, it is highly likely that there will be a renewed discussion on the rights of fetuses and abortion law more broadly in Chile in years ahead.

Backlash

While in all these cases changes over time have generally moved in a more liberal direction, a countertrend is also apparent. Abortion is completely prohibited in four Latin American countries: El Salvador, the Dominican Republic, Nicaragua, and Honduras. Other countries in South and Central America allow abortion in certain circumstances, such as in the case of rape, to save the mother's life or health, or if the fetus is impaired. These countries include Guatemala, Paraguay, Venezuela, Brazil, Costa Rica, Peru, Ecuador, Chile, Panama, and Bolivia.

El Salvador illustrates how the political dynamics have changed in a more restrictive direction, perhaps in response to transnational politics that followed *Roe*. Under the country's 1973 Penal Code, a pregnant person could access an abortion if their life was endangered, if the pregnancy was the result of rape or incest, or if there was a serious defect in the fetus. However, the government enacted a new Penal Code in 1998 that removed all exceptions in the 1973 law. Under the 1998 law, any person who performs or receives an abortion can be imprisoned for two to eight years. Observers note, though, that illegal abortion remains common.[36] Still, enforcement impacts the

ability of doctors to provide maternal care, and there are cases in which innocent women have been convicted for abortions they did not receive.

The Dominican Republic provides an interesting case of competing abortion agendas between the legislature and the courts. The country's 1884
Penal Code prohibited abortion in all circumstances, and Article 37 of the
Dominican Republic's current Constitution provides a right to life: "[T]he
right to life is inviolable from conception until death."[37] This provision effectively prohibited abortion in all cases. In 2012, the abortion law came under
fire when a pregnant teenage girl could not receive treatment for leukemia
because the chemotherapy would threaten the life of the fetus. In the time
it took for doctors to decide whether they could provide the treatments or
risk criminal prosecution, her cancer progressed. By the time they decided to
provide chemotherapy, her body did not respond, she suffered a miscarriage,
and shortly afterward died from cardiac arrest.[38] The case sparked widespread outrage in the country. In 2014, the legislature amended the penal
code to decriminalize abortion in cases of rape, incest, fetal impairment,
and when the pregnant woman's life is at risk. However, the Constitutional
Tribunal of the Supreme Court declared the amendment unconstitutional.[39]

European countries generally have liberal abortion laws, allowing
abortions in cases of socioeconomic distress with varying gestational limits.
However, several predominantly Catholic countries have been notable
exceptions, and as a result, there is no uniform approach within the regime
of the European Convention of Human Rights. Some countries seem to have
moved toward an intense, zero-sum approach to the issue.

One such country is Poland. During the Soviet era, Poland had some of
the most liberal abortion laws in Europe, but in 1993, following the collapse
of the Soviet Union, Parliament passed a law banning abortion except in
cases of danger to the mother's health or life, rape or incest, or severe fetal
abnormalities. In October 2020, the Constitutional Tribunal struck down
this law, ruling that abortion even in cases of severe and irreversible fetal
defects was unconstitutional.[40] Parliament had previously tried and failed
to pass a law on the same issue. In 2021, the legislature passed the Act on
Pregnancy Planning of Poland which made abortion illegal except in cases of
pregnancies resulting from rape or incest or pregnancies posing a risk to the
mother's life. These actions generated widespread protest against the ruling
Law and Justice Party, posing the biggest challenge to its rule.

Going one step further, Malta prohibits abortion in all cases. Even ectopic
pregnancies are terminated only on case-by-case decisions. Malta's criminal

code states that anyone causing the miscarriage of a woman by food, drink, medicine, violence, or any other means, whether or not the woman consents, shall be liable to imprisonment between eighteen months and three years.[41] The law stipulates the same punishment for a woman who procures her own miscarriage. It places a harsher punishment of eighteen months to four years imprisonment and removal from the profession of any physician or apothecary who knowingly prescribes or administers the means for a miscarriage. This law has recently faced intense criticism due to the case of an American woman who was visiting Malta with her husband while sixteen weeks pregnant. She suffered an incomplete miscarriage, but because the fetus's heart was still beating, the doctors could not perform an operation to complete the miscarriage even though they found that the fetus would not survive outside the womb. The woman faced risks of potentially fatal hemorrhaging and infection and had to be medically evacuated to Mallorca for the procedure.[42] Such evacuations are not an option for Maltese women. The publicity associated with this incident generated some debate in Malta, but it remains an outlier.

Abortion is also completely prohibited in Madagascar, Mauritania, Sierra Leone, and Congo.[43] The abortion ban in Madagascar is particularly stringent. Article 317 of Madagascar's Penal Code inherited from the French colonial period criminalizes abortion in all circumstances. While there have been efforts to reform the law to make abortion a minor offense, they have not been successful.[44] To make matters worse, there are no laws prohibiting domestic sexual abuse. This leaves women who become pregnant after being raped by their husbands with no options to terminate the pregnancy or seek legal recourse against their spouses.[45]

Transnational Mobilization

As the above discussion has suggested, transnational forces play a role in abortion politics. The Catholic Church is obviously one such force, but American evangelical groups have recently entered the fray.

In 2009, Kenya was drafting a new constitution, and the drafters were being pressured to include a provision on abortion. Christian groups wanted an absolute ban on abortion in the new constitution, but the prior constitution had been silent on it, and the initial draft remained so.[46] Members of Parliament, in reviewing the draft, inserted quite strict language prohibiting abortion.[47] The Committee of Experts charged with drafting the document, however, amended this to allow significantly broader access to abortion on therapeutic grounds. Kenya's final text of its Constitution, put up for referendum in 2010, restricts abortion "unless, in the opinion of a trained health professional, there is a need for emergency treatment, or the life or health of the mother is in danger, or if permitted by any other written law."[48] This was viewed as overly liberal, as it allowed the legislature to further liberalize conditions for abortion.

This in turn led to mobilization of church groups to urge a "no" vote in the referendum. The opposition was coming from Kenyan churches—Anglican, Catholic, Evangelical, and others. But it was also coming from abroad. A group called the American Association of Pro-Life Obstetricians and Gynecologists lobbied the U.S. Congress and the Obama administration to oppose the draft. The Vatican also criticized the proposed constitution and mobilized Catholics to oppose it.[49] The American Center for Law and Justice (ACLJ), a U.S.-based Christian lobbying group founded by Pat Robertson, opened up a branch in Kenya (the East African Center for Law and Justice) and lobbied against the draft.[50] And an anti-abortion U.S. congressman from New Jersey, Chris Smith, assailed the draft and the Obama administration's support for the process. He argued that it constituted illegal lobbying for abortion rights.[51]

The new Kenyan Constitution was 191 pages long, containing 261 articles and six additional "schedules" providing additional detail. A wide variety of provisions decentralized power, cleaned up the judiciary, and guaranteed basic rights. It even contained a novel section titled "Leadership and Integrity" to set new standards for Kenya's traditionally venal politicians. Abortion was mentioned in a single article. But that threatened to derail the entire constitution-making process. Abortion was the single biggest topic of public debate, and many observers in the spring of 2010 feared that the Constitution would not pass. While the government and the Committee of Experts were coordinating a vast civic education campaign to inform the public of the contents of the proposed draft, the churches organized a campaign of their own. They brought graphic videos showing aborted fetuses to poor, rural areas. Misinformation was common, with many rural women told that they would be *forced* to have abortions under the new Constitution. In the end, the draft was approved by 67% of voters.[52] But the vote was arguably much closer than it would have been had the Constitution remained silent on abortion.

The transnational anti-abortion alliance kept up the pressure after the adoption of the Kenyan Constitution. Locally, the director of Human Life International, a branch of a U.S.-based Roman Catholic organization, blamed the Obama administration for the passage of the Kenyan Constitution as he appealed to U.S donors for more funds.[53] And the U.S. allies were just as active. Even before the constitution-making process had been completed, Representative Smith along with his Republican colleagues Darrell Issa and Ileana Ros-Lehtinen wrote to USAID and the General Accounting Office (GAO) complaining that the Obama administration had violated a little-known provision of the Foreign Aid Act. That provision, called the Siljander Amendment after its congressional sponsor, prohibits the use of foreign aid funds to lobby "for or against abortion." The legislators asserted that Obama administration funding of civic education and technical support to the Kenyan drafters constituted "lobbying" for abortion. (I should disclose that I myself was implicated in this accusation on the basis of a technical report that I organized on the draft Constitution for the International Development Law Organization, an international organization based in Rome.) The GAO duly conducted an investigation and ultimately exonerated the Obama administration but urged USAID to come up with a definition of "lobbying" to guide future efforts. Nevertheless, administration opponents and anti-abortion activists seized on the GAO report to argue that Obama had violated the law.[54]

The Kenyan story illustrates the transnational quality of constitutional politics in many countries. Learning from the Kenya process, the ACLJ opened an office in Zimbabwe to lobby against abortion and homosexual rights in the new constitutional drafting process.[55] Foreign groups also worked with local churches and organizations, including the Evangelical Fellowship of Zimbabwe, to influence the abortion debate there. The groups sought to "affirm that Zimbabwe is a predominantly Christian nation founded on biblical principles," define life as "beginning at conception," define marriage "as being between a man and a woman," prohibit same-sex marriage or civil unions, and criminalize same-sex intercourse.[56] The Zimbabwe branch of the U.S.-based Women Weapons of Warfare was also involved; the Zimbabwe branch is led by the African Center for Law and Justice's executive director, Vicky Mpofu.[57] (These efforts paid off: the new Zimbabwe Constitution, adopted in a 2013 referendum with limited turnout, included a prohibition on homosexual marriage.)

Transnational mobilization is also found on the side of those supporting access to abortion. One notable effort is that of the group Women on Waves, a European nongovernmental organization which has sought to provide off-shore access to abortion and contraception in countries in which they have been limited, beginning with Ireland in the early 2000s.[58] The organization operates outside a country's territorial sea and facilitates women's transit to its boats to receive services.

Regional Norms

Because abortion implicates rights discourse, it has occasionally become the subject of transnational adjudication by regional human rights courts. These operate in Africa, Europe, and Latin America.

Africa

The African Union features a human rights system, centered on the African Charter on Human and People's Rights. It includes the 2003 Maputo Protocol on the Rights of Women, which requires that states authorize medical abor-tion in cases of rape or incest and where the mental or physical health of the mother is in jeopardy.[59] This is the very first international treaty to provide for an explicit articulation of a right to abortion. Although widely ratified, access to abortion remains severely limited on the continent. But it has informed legislative changes in Rwanda, the Democratic Republic of the Congo, and other countries.

While there are no cases interpreting the Protocol at the regional level, it has been consequential in national courts. For example, in a 2014 case, *Mildred Mapingure v. Minister of Home Affairs and 2 Others*, the Supreme Court of Zimbabwe relied on the Protocol in a case brought by a rape victim for damages against the state.[60] Her claim was that bureaucratic ineptitude prevented her from obtaining pregnancy-preventing drugs within the legal timeframe for an abortion. Because of this, she was forced to carry her preg-nancy to full term. The Court gave her a partial award and found an obliga-tion on the part of the state to clarify its laws around abortion access and to increase public awareness of abortion procedures. In doing so, it relied on

Article 14 of the Maputo Protocol, which mandates that states must ensure that women have access to sexual and reproductive healthcare and that states must authorize medical abortion in cases of rape.

Europe

The presence of a regional convention, the European Convention on Human Rights (ECHR), means that citizens in countries with restrictive policies can challenge them outside the borders of the state. The most common bases for such complaints concern the European Convention's right to privacy, the notion of discrimination against pregnant women, and inhuman/degrading treatment suffered by women looking to receive abortions.[61] In addition, in a case involving the Women on Waves, the European Court of Human Rights ruled that norms of free expression found in the ECHR required member states to restrict this group only in ways that were proportional.[62]

In *A, B, and C v. Ireland*, three applicants had to travel to England from Ireland to receive abortions.[63] Each applicant suffered complications postprocedure. They challenged the Irish laws under Articles 3, 8, 13, and 14 of the Convention. Third parties also submitted complaints regarding the availability of postabortion care, the denial of abortion for women with a diagnosis of fetal abnormality, and the fact that traveling for the purpose of abortion would require admitting an abortion, which would in turn undermine the right to privacy. The government responded, claiming a failure on the part of the applicants to exhaust domestic remedies. The court dismissed this objection and held that the complaints concerning Articles 8, 13, and 14 were admissible, and that there was a violation of Article 8, which protects the right to privacy and family life.

In *R.R. v. Poland*, the applicant, having reason to believe the fetus was suffering genetic abnormalities, sought the requisite referrals to obtain an abortion. Section 4(a) of the 1993 Family Planning Act specified that an abortion could be carried out if, among other situations, there was a high risk the fetus would suffer from an incurable life-threatening condition. Such cases were limited by time and procedural constraints and must be carried out by a physician working in a hospital and certified by a separate physician. Yet increasing delays meant that the timeframe within which the applicant was able to seek an abortion totally elapsed. The applicant in *R.R.* gave birth to a child with Turner syndrome and instituted criminal proceedings against the doctors (as public servants) involved in her case, arguing that they failed to safeguard her interests due to a lack of timeliness in performing examinations. The government denied that the case involved the mother's private life, as covered by Article 8 of the ECHR, or torture as protected by Article 3. Further, the government declared that Turner syndrome is not itself a condition that fits the criteria for legal abortion because it is not life threatening. The government further claimed that the applicant contributed to the delays in testing due to her specifying that the testing take place at a specific location, and that the government had no positive obligation to provide an abortion for eugenic reasons. In *R.R.*, the court held that the ECHR was violated under Articles 3 and 8.[64]

In other cases, the European Court has insisted on a right to information regarding abortion. In the case of *Open Door and Dublin Well Woman v. Ireland*, the applicants were nonprofit organizations that provided counseling and women's health services. The activities of these organizations involved counseling and educating pregnant women with regard to their options (including, but not limited to, arranging travel to the United Kingdom to seek abortion). Such actions were found to be unlawful by the Irish High Court in light of Article 40.3.3 of the Irish Constitution criminalizing abortion. Further, section 16 of the Censorship of Publications Act (1929) provided that the printing, publication, and distribution of information advocating or reasonably supposed to advocate for abortion or miscarriage or delineate methodology was unlawful. The Irish courts thus imposed an injunction against the organizations. The decision of the high court was appealed to the ECHR on the grounds that it violated Article 10 of the Convention, protecting freedom of expression. The ECHR agreed and compensated the applicants.

In short, the ECHR has been held to provide an arena in which abortion politics are extended outside the national constitutional sphere. Transnational dialogues occur among courts, governments, and civil society groups. In some ways the presence of a supranational level to which national policies can be appealed reduces the stakes of national constitutional conflict; the fact that a decision is an expression of a continent-wide consensus on the range of acceptable policies is a limiting factor preventing scorched-earth warfare.

Latin America

The role of the Inter-American Court of Human Rights, a principal enforcer of the American Convention and the American Declaration of Human Rights, is important in the region. The Inter-American Court has held that its interpretation of Convention rights is directly applicable throughout the region, and while this position has been resisted by some of the member countries, it provides an avenue for distinct regional dynamics. Relatively few cases, though, have come before the Court to date.

A case involving El Salvador provides an interesting example of the potential relevance of international human rights law. As noted, El Salvador has some of the most restrictive abortion laws in South and Central America. In 2008, a thirty-three-year-old woman had an obstetric emergency and had a miscarriage. She was accused of having an abortion and was convicted of aggravated homicide and sentenced to thirty years in prison. She died of cancer during her imprisonment. On November 30, 2021, the Inter-American Court of Human Rights found El Salvador responsible for her death. The ruling, which applies to all countries throughout Latin America and the Caribbean under the Court's jurisdiction, stipulates that healthcare staff cannot refer women who come to their hospitals for abortion care to law enforcement. The Court ordered El Salvador to make reparations to the woman's family and reform its legal and healthcare policies.[65]

Beyond the role of the Inter-American Court of Human Rights in protecting rights, the Inter-American system features a commission which plays a role in interpreting and promoting rights. In a 2017 report, the Inter-American Commission called on all states to respect women's reproductive autonomy. These kinds of pronouncements provide resources for domestic mobilization, even if they are not legally binding.

Conclusion

As the chapter's survey demonstrates, countries around the world have a diverse array of approaches to abortion. Religion seems to be a critical factor in determining access. Countries in the Confucian tradition tend to have more moderate, less politicized approaches, while those influenced by monotheistic traditions, such as Poland, the Philippines, and Indonesia, tend to be more restrictive.[66] Like those of some Latin American countries, the constitution of the largely Catholic Philippines protects "the life of the un-born from conception."[67]

Another factor that has led to a more intense constitutional politics of abortion has been the rise of transnational movements seeking to promote or restrict access. U.S.-based Christian movements have for many years tried to achieve in foreign countries what could only be dreamed of in the United States: a total ban on abortion. But cutting against this development have been transnational rights regimes in Latin America, Europe, and Africa that have tolerated diverse approaches among member states. The transnational language of rights has led to the framing of abortion as a women's rights issue, giving ideational support to domestic movements.[68]

Michele Oberman writes that the war over abortion is ultimately a war over abortion *law*.[69] This suggests that legal and jurisprudential techniques might help to frame compromise solutions. Proportionality analysis, in which both interests are identified and a mechanism optimizes the competing interests without overriding any of them, is central here.

Some legal frameworks, such as that of the United States, do not critically engage with the legal value of a fetus compared to the rights of the mother. An explicit recognition that there are multiple rights-holders and interests at stake is a good step toward crafting compromise and lowering the political temperature.

The Irish Citizens' Assembly is a legislative technique that accomplishes much the same goal. Instead of aggregating a fixed set of preferences among voters, with the majority decision becoming law, it created a process for a genuine public discussion about a contentious issue, leading to a major legislative change. The deliberative public became a kind of tiebreaker in an environment of contentious politics.

As in so many other areas, the American political system is failing to deliver on policies supported by a majority of citizens. Five decades of polarized politics of the fetus are unlikely to go away soon: politicians have become addicted to the issue. But perhaps if we recognize that the complex moral questions around abortion are too important to leave to the politicians, we might begin to do better. We could start by finding ways to bring ordinary Americans together to understand that their views are not as divided as their politics.

PART VII

IMPLICATIONS FOR THE FUTURE

18

Reproductive Technologies and Embryo Destruction after *Dobbs*

*I. Glenn Cohen**

Introduction

Upon the release of the *Dobbs* decision, indeed upon the leak of Justice Samuel Alito's draft opinion, the public and legal academic conversation about the decision very quickly shifted to its implications for other rights closely connected to substantive due process.

Justice Clarence Thomas, concurring, wrote that "[b]ecause any substantive due process decision is 'demonstrably erroneous,'" future cases "should reconsider all of this Court's substantive due process precedents, including *Griswold*, *Lawrence*, and *Obergefell*," the cases protecting contraception, same-sex sexual intimacy, and same-sex marriage, because the Court had "a duty to 'correct the error' established in those precedents."[1]

Justice Alito's opinion for the Court nevertheless tries to suggest that the *Dobbs* decision does not necessarily spell the end of those cases, arguing that "[w]hat sharply distinguishes the abortion right from the rights recognized in the cases on which *Roe* and *Casey* rely is something that both those decisions acknowledged: Abortion destroys what those decisions call 'potential life' and what the law at issue in this case regards as the life of an 'unborn human being'" and emphasizing that "[n]one of the other decisions cited by *Roe* and *Casey* involved the critical moral question posed by abortion."[2]

The dissenting justices would have none of it, arguing, "[I]t is impossible to understand (as a matter of logic and principle) how the majority can say that its opinion today does not threaten—does not even 'undermine'—any number of other constitutional rights," and that even taking the "majority at its word . . . Scout's honor," that "law often has a way of evolving without regard to original intentions—a way of actually following where logic leads, rather than tolerating hard-to-explain lines."[3]

I. Glenn Cohen, *Reproductive Technologies and Embryo Destruction after* Dobbs In: *Roe v. Dobbs*. Edited by: Lee C. Bollinger and Geoffrey R. Stone, Oxford University Press. © Oxford University Press 2024. DOI: 10.1093/oso/9780197760352.003.0018

Only time will tell who correctly foresaw the shape of what is to come as to these constitutional rights. But as to reproductive technologies, specifically those that involve the destruction of embryos, I argue in this chapter that the situation is more clear-cut. If a state were to prohibit entirely the destruction of embryos, the exact language Justice Alito uses to distinguish abortion from other constitutional rights directly applies—embryo destruction just as much as abortion "destroys . . . 'potential life' and what" such a potential state law "regards as the life of an 'unborn human being.' "[4] For reproductive technologies, the caller is already in the house.

When it comes to in vitro fertilization (IVF), embryo destruction is very common.[5] "Data collected by the US Centers for Disease Control and Prevention reveal that virtually every IVF clinic in the nation provides embryo cryopreservation services, an essential adjunct to treatment when more than 1 or 2 embryos are produced in a single cycle."[6] While most IVF cycles do produce more than two eggs for fertilization, the current standard of care is to implant no more than two embryos to avoid the risk of multiple pregnancies.[7] Those embryos are often destroyed when the parties die or divorce; or when they decide they will have no more children and want to stop paying cryopreservation fees.[8] Moreover, "nearly half of all IVF cycles in the US involve preimplantation genetic testing, in which cells are biopsied from a developing embryo to determine the health of any resulting child," and those for which "test results reveal genetic abnormalities potentially associated with negative health outcomes" are often destroyed (or "discarded," to use the term preferred within the reproductive technology community).[9]

Nor are restrictions on embryo destruction in the United States merely hypothetical. Louisiana has a statute, dating all the way back to 1986, reading:

> A viable in vitro fertilized human ovum is a juridical person which shall not be intentionally destroyed by any natural or other juridical person or through the actions of any other such person. An in vitro fertilized human ovum that fails to develop further over a thirty-six hour period except when the embryo is in a state of cryopreservation, is considered non-viable and is not considered a juridical person.[10]

Clinics in Louisiana do not destroy embryos, but they do sometimes arrange transfer to more permissive states, I am told off the record; it is possible that in a post-*Dobbs* world this option may at some point cease to be available.[11] Kentucky has a similar prohibition—"Public medical facilities may be used for the purpose of conducting research into or the performance of in-vitro fertilization as long as such procedures do not result in the intentional destruction of a human embryo"—but by its terms limits itself to public (i.e., state) medical facilities.[12]

Outside the United States we see other possible models for restrictions. In Italy, a 2004 law prohibited creating more than three embryos in an IVF cycle and prohibited cryopreservation, the idea being that all would be implanted, though the law was struck down in 2009.[13] Germany also prohibits the creation of more than three embryos per IVF cycle.[14] One could imagine a similar law passed by a U.S. state or, much less likely, one that requires that any unused embryos be made available for "embryo adoption" by other individuals.[15]

The rest of this chapter focuses on the normative question, what should one's views about restricting abortion tell us about one's views on restricting embryo destruction in one of these ways? Should those who seek to prohibit abortion also prohibit embryo destruction as part of IVF or other reproductive technology use? By contrast, should those who oppose restrictions on abortion also oppose restrictions on destroying embryos as part of IVF or other reproductive technology use? I think many people assume one's views on abortion should carry over to one's views about embryo destruction, but a main contribution of this chapter is to question that assumption and to show for both sides of the abortion debate that the question of embryo destruction is more complicated and a lot will depend on one's theory of embryonic/fetal personhood and when it obtains.

Before doing so, though, I want to very briefly address two other questions.

The Constitutional and Political Questions

The first question is about U.S. constitutional law: Can states lawfully prohibit embryo destruction in this way as a matter of the U.S. Constitution? After *Dobbs*, the language I quoted above from Justice Alito's opinion suggests to me that they plausibly can.

Indeed, even in the pre-*Dobbs* period I think advocates would have faced considerable difficulties in arguing that the Constitution protects a right to destroy embryos as part of IVF. In earlier work I have labored to show why foundational substantive due process cases pertaining to contraception, sterilization, and abortion (before *Dobbs*) are most fairly read as not establishing a constitutional right to use IVF or other reproductive technologies.[16] What is more, there is very little case law of courts below the U.S. Supreme Court suggesting there is any such right—and what case law exists seems adjacent, not central, to the claim.[17] What would have been a hard row to hoe constitutionally before *Dobbs* seems to me essentially foreclosed by the opinion.

Second is a political question: Are the states that prohibit abortion, in particular those that prohibit abortion from the very start of pregnancy, likely to adopt measures that restrict embryo destruction as part of IVF? Here the available polling and other data on public attitudes suggest that at least currently such measures are unlikely to be a priority or perhaps even supported in most states.

As Heather Silber Mohamed writes in her 2018 analysis (looking at data from a 2013 nationally representative survey by the Pew Research Center), "questions of embryo disposal and destruction in IVF have not been subject to the same fierce political debates surrounding abortion and, to a lesser extent, ESC [embryonic stem cell] research," with reproductive technologies occupying "an intermediate policy space, 'stretch[ing] the boundaries of current conceptualizations of morality policy,' while also incorporating business and scientific interests."[18] Her pertinent findings include the fact that

> a majority of respondents describe IVF as "not a moral issue," while only about a quarter of respondents categorize abortion in this way. Nearly 57% of respondents view abortion as morally wrong, compared with just 13% for IVF. These results support the first hypothesis and suggest that there is unlikely to be broad support for expansive fetal personhood laws that would also impact access to IVF. . . .
>
> [Do] respondents who describe abortion as morally wrong feel similarly about ESC research and IVF[?] . . . [W]hile nearly 41% of respondents who describe abortion as morally wrong oppose ESC research, nearly *half* of those who say abortion is morally wrong describe IVF as not a moral issue.[19]

Much has changed in America since 2013, and there are limits on using these data to predict the current state of play. I am not a pollster or a political operative, but my own view is that it is much more likely a state will inadvertently restrict embryo destruction related to IVF in the course of introducing more general personhood language (or perhaps more accurately, I should say "without that being its specific goal") than that states will target embryo destruction related to IVF as Italy and Germany have done (and Louisiana at the dawn of this technology in the United States).[20]

If I am right in that prediction, it provides another way of understanding the next section: Should we be puzzled that those who are pushing strict limits on abortion *are not* pursuing these policies? Is this merely politics, or are they acting in a way that is normatively consistent with their established views?[21]

The Normative Question

Should those who seek to restrict abortion also seek to restrict embryo destruction? On the other side, should those who oppose restricting abortion also oppose restricting embryo destruction? In this section my goal is to unsettle some likely intuitions on this question. One might have thought that in both directions one's answer to the question of abortion will track one's answer to the question of embryo destruction. In fact, I want to show that divergent views about abortion and embryo destruction are not only possible but plausible; on some views one can plausibly believe that abortion should be restricted and embryo destruction as part of IVF be permitted, and on other views one can plausibly believe that the opposite configuration should obtain. While I think the divergence is possible for both "pro-life" and "pro-choice" views,[22] I will start my discussion by focusing on the pro-life side for two reasons. First, because they are the ones currently in the pole position in the United States in terms of introducing post-*Dobbs* legislative changes and most likely to change a status quo that largely permits embryo destruction. Second, because one of the most provocative ideas I want readers to consider is that the current status quo in several pro-life states where abortion is heavily prohibited but embryo destruction is permitted in some ways has things upside down. It is *easier* to justify prohibiting embryo destruction than it is to justify prohibiting abortion, and yet we see the opposite configuration enacted into law.

At the start it is useful to distinguish opposition to some reproductive technologies on the ground that in their regular course they involve embryo destruction, versus other reasons to oppose such technologies. My focus is on the former, but it is worth noting that some conservatives who oppose abortion also have certain foundational commitments to the purpose of reproduction, sexual morality, and conceptions of parenthood that make them wary about some forms of reproductive technology apart from concerns about embryo destruction per se. Leon Kass's famous essay "The Wisdom of Repugnance" comes to mind.[23] A different strand opposes reproductive technology for its reconfiguring of gender roles and for moving away from traditional notions of what reproduction is and is for.[24]

While there may be some commonalities between these reasons to oppose reproductive technologies and the reasons some oppose abortion, even from the early days of IVF[25] the clearer link to abortion for those opposing reproductive technologies has been the risk of embryo destruction. Why? As I have put it elsewhere, if we pressed them to state their views in philosophical terms most individuals who want to prohibit abortion subscribe to something like the following two premises:

1. Fetuses are persons and/or get some of the rights of persons from early on in their development, particularly the right of inviolability.
2. Whatever interest the mother has in protecting her bodily integrity, protecting her reproductive autonomy, and so on does not outweigh her fetus's right of inviolability.[26]

If one replaces the word "fetuses" in first premise with the term "early embryos,"[27] the exact same argument entails opposing embryo destruction just as it does abortion.

For this reason, to understand what those opposed to abortion and those who defend an abortion right should think about embryo destruction, we should look closely at each premise and whether it fully applies to embryo destruction. I will take them in reverse order.

The Second Premise

Many people are surprised when I tell them that the argument for prohibiting embryo destruction is *stronger* (or, if you prefer, "easier") than the argument for prohibiting abortion. Why? Because the second premise is less relevant (or, on some accounts, irrelevant) in the case of early embryos that have not yet been implanted. While prohibiting abortion requires favoring the right of a fetus to inviolability over the right not to gestate of the woman seeking an abortion, a bodily autonomy right, there is no countervailing right to control one's body at issue in a prohibition on embryo destruction. That is, prohibiting abortion directly restricts a right not to be a gestational parent, whereas prohibiting embryo destruction does not.[28] In other words, the second premise is a strong reason to support abortion rights, but it is weaker when it comes to opposing embryo destruction because prohibitions on embryo destruction do not involve forced gestation. For that reason one can plausibly be in favor of permitting abortion but also in favor of prohibiting embryo destruction as part of IVF.

This is not to say the aggrieved party has no potential rights claim to make against a policy that restricts embryo destruction, but such a rights claim is harder to characterize, may depend on exactly the state policy in question, and may be less persuasive. If individuals were required to make their excess embryos available for adoption, aggrieved individuals would argue for a violation of a right not to be a genetic parent—the state is forcing them to allow other people to rear their genetic children.[29] Here, the state could respond that the individuals could have avoided the dilemma by only fertilizing embryos one or two at a time. If the individuals respond that this would be economically infeasible, then one might wonder if the argument is more in the style of a *positive* liberty right to be a genetic parent that is stymied by the background rule on the fate of cryopreserved embryos.[30]

The rights claim is weaker still on what I consider a more plausible policy intervention: if a state prohibited the creation of more than three embryos per cycle and forbade cryopreservation, similar to the German or prior Italian approach, in that case too it seems as though the aggrieved party is really arguing for a right *to* be genetic parent. A person burdened by such a policy might argue that the prohibition imposes expenses upon them that will stop them from succeeding at IVF before they run out of money, that it will prevent them from achieving the number of children they want to have via IVF before they run out of money. One might push back that in an extreme case, as time passes through the repeated cycles of harvesting eggs and fertilizing them, their chance of success dwindles because of advancing maternal age.[31] As I discuss later, if the success rates of using frozen eggs that are later thawed approaches that of fresh eggs, the pushback loses more of its force: the state's policy will permit egg retrieval as it currently does and "merely" requires that one freezes rather than inseminates any eggs one does not currently intend to fertilize and implant with the knowledge that those frozen eggs can later be thawed as needed for insemination and implantation.

To be sure, the state has imposed on the aggrieved person's preferred reproductive process. It is not that these potential rights claims by the aggrieved individuals are worth nothing. It is just that they are a much less "clean" and, in my view, forceful, countervailing rights claim than the classic one regarding forced gestation that women make in the abortion context. The most famous argument as to why forced gestation is particularly morally noxious is associated with Judith Jarvis Thomson's famous article "A Defense of Abortion."[32] I have tried elsewhere to briefly summarize her key thought experiment:

> She asks us to imagine that one morning one wakes up having been kidnapped and hooked up to an unconscious famous violinist dying from a rare kidney disease, but who will survive if one allows him to use you as a human dialysis machine for nine months. The violinist is not at fault for your predicament, instead the kidnapping and attachment was the work of the Society of Music Lovers who are devoted to his music and saving his life. Should you unhook yourself, the violinist will die. Thomson argues that one has a right to disconnect oneself from the violinist in this situation, that his mere need does not create an obligation upon you to sustain him, though it would not be immoral if you did—superogatory to sustain him, but not immoral to disconnect. She then argues that this is what abortion is like. In doing so she argues that even if the fetus is a person, that does not change the prerogative to disconnect—after all there is no dispute that the violinist is a full person as well.[33]

As Thomson puts it, "[A] right to life does not guarantee having either a right to be given the use of or a right to be allowed continued use of another person's body—even if one needs it for life itself."[34] The argument also allows us to draw analogies to related court decisions—for example, the holding in *Mcfall v. Shimp* that an individual has no duty to donate life-saving bone marrow to a cousin.[35] Indeed, some have drawn explicit U.S. constitutional comparisons to a Thirteenth Amendment right against slavery.[36]

To be sure, Thomson's argument and variations on it have been attacked by other philosophers either on the argument's own terms, as the wrong analogy for abortion, or as applying to only some kinds of abortion (such as pregnancy stemming from rape) and not others.[37] But for those who are convinced by it, and I count myself among them, it provides a normative reason to favor permitting abortion *even if one believes fetuses have the moral status of persons* (the first premise). It is precisely because the strongest version of this premise is not available in the case of restricting embryo destruction that even some individuals who support a right to abortion might oppose a right to destroy embryos—or at least find the argument more difficult.

The First Premise

The first premise, again, is "Fetuses are persons and/or get some of the rights of persons from early on in their development, particularly the right of inviolability." Earlier I noted that the argument for prohibiting embryo destruction equates "early embryos" with "fetuses" in the premise. One could thus argue for prohibiting abortion but *not* for prohibiting embryo destruction if one believes there are morally relevant differences as to personhood claims for early embryos as opposed to fetuses.

Are there? The answer is very law-professorial: it depends, and it depends on a very deep question: When does personhood begin? There are several leading views pertinent to our inquiry.

The Time of Fertilization
One view is that personhood begins—and indeed, more importantly, is fully "there"—at the point of fertilization. This has been the position of the Catholic Church:

> Thus the fruit of human generation, from the first moment of its existence, that is to say from the moment the zygote has formed, demands the unconditional respect that is morally due to the human being in his bodily and spiritual totality. The human being is to be respected and treated as a person from the moment of conception; and therefore from that same moment his rights as a person must be recognized, among which in the first place is the inviolable right of every innocent human being to life.[38]

Why start at fertilization? As the conservative philosophical bioethicists Robert George and Patrick Lee put it in 2009 in defending this view:

> [T]he argument is that the adult is identical to the embryo he or she once was because there are no essential differences in the kind of being one is between any two stages—whether the two stages are adjacent to each other or not—in the development of a human individual from embryo to fetus, infant, child, adolescent and adult. There are of course several significant

differences between an embryo, an infant and an adult—such as size and degree of development. But there is no difference in the kind—that is, there is no difference in the fundamental nature of the entity—between any two stages of the developing living being—whether those stages are adjacent to each other or are several months apart in his or her life cycle.

Whether a new human organism exists is a question to which the answer must be either yes or no—there is no in between.

Again, the human embryo, from fertilization forward, develops in a single direction by an internally directed process: the developmental trajectory of this entity is determined from within, not by extrinsic factors, and always toward the same mature state, from the earliest stage of embryonic development onward. This means that the embryo has the same nature—it is the same kind of entity, a whole human organism—from fertilization forward; there is only a difference in degree of maturation between any of the stages in the development of the living being.[39]

The time-of-fertilization view has been criticized on a number of grounds. A common *reductio* style argument in circulation suggests those who hold this view should favor saving a large number of fertilized but not yet implanted embryos from a burning building instead of saving a smaller number of children from the same building.[40] Another line of argument against this view suggests that "the possibility that identical twins can develop from a single fertilized egg" may problematize the position because "if the fertilized egg is already an individual human being that directs its own development, it is difficult to explain how one human being can divide into two or more."[41] The argument is that the possibility of twinning before the fourteen-day mark "leaves us with no rational basis on which to describe the fertilized egg as an earlier stage of either one of the twins," which in turn "means that we cannot say that the fertilized egg is identical with a specific individual."[42] Defenders of the time-of-fertilization view have their rejoinders—including attempts to show that the possibility of twinning does not negate the moral status of the entity before twinning.[43]

My charge here is not to offer a full analysis of the merits of the time-of-fertilization view, but instead to show that unlike some other views on the first premise it leaves no space to distinguish abortion from embryo destruction. This is not true of its main rival views—I will focus on two prominent ones, fourteen days and Capacity X views.

Fourteen Days or Later

One rival view to time-of-fertilization would treat embryonic personhood as starting at or after fourteen days of development. Why that marker?

> Several developments at this point are especially significant. The first is that the cells of the early embryo begin to function either as part of the embryo proper or as extraembryonic supporting materials that will be discarded later. The second is that it is irrevocably settled by this time that an embryo proper that is distinct from the membranes that nourish it is present. A third is that twinning can no longer occur.[44]

Since embryos used for IVF are never allowed to develop anywhere near the fourteen-day point, if this is the marker for the first premise to activate then embryo destruction is morally distinct from abortion; one can justifiably oppose abortion but not embryo destruction as part of IVF or other reproductive technologies.

To be sure, those in favor of the fourteen-day rule do not say anything goes before the fourteen-day point; instead they have argued that the early embryo deserves "special respect" before that point.[45] This concept is quite fuzzy, but it is usually thought to rule out their destruction as part of research that did not have significant value, or that researchers should destroy embryos only as a last resort when other ways of answering a scientific question are not available.[46] The primary discussion of the fourteen-day limit has occurred in the debate over *research* on embryos that will destroy them or otherwise rule them out for implantation; indeed until fairly recently scientists had adopted a self-imposed fourteen-day rule as a hard limit on embryo research, albeit one with a complicated history and some incompletely theorized agreements.[47]

In the reproductive technology context, "special respect" has primarily been discussed in cases of embryo disposition disputes (e.g., when couples with frozen embryos divorce). In particular, in one of the earliest such cases, the Tennessee Supreme Court (itself relying on language from the Ethics Committee of the American Fertility Society) "conclude[d] that preembryos are not, strictly speaking, either 'persons' or 'property,' but occupy an interim category that entitles them to special respect because of their potential for human life."[48] This language has been frequently quoted by later courts, but largely as a background statement of principle. While there have been occasional suggestions that *particular* reproductive technology practices, like sex selection, *may* fail to show "special respect" to the embryo,[49] the discard of embryos as part of IVF by and large has not been viewed as a failure to show "special respect."

Of course, one can press deeper and ask why. It would certainly be *more* respectful to the early embryo to create only as many as we intend to implant in a cycle to avoid embryo discard. Why is a rule to that effect, the German or previous Italian approach, for instance, not justified on "special respect" grounds? Even if costlier for financial or health or stress reasons, doesn't showing "special respect" sometimes require such costs? The deeper we dive, in my opinion, the more the nebulous nature of the "special respect" constraint becomes apparent. It seems more as though the "real" rule has been the fourteen-day one, and the constraint of "special respect" is invoked only to avoid biting the bullet of permissibility in extreme cases.[50] That may be rhetorically and politically very useful, but not particularly intellectually satisfying. In any event, if one believes the first premise is "fully" activated only at the fourteen-day mark, with a weaker constraint of showing special respect before that, one can justifiably seek to prohibit abortion but not the destruction of embryos associated with IVF and other reproductive technologies.

Capacity X Views (Including Potentiality Views)

A second rival theory, or really set of theories, I will loosely call "Capacity X" theories. Such theories specify a capacity that a person must have to be a person. Such views begin by filling in "X" with different candidate capacities: to feel pain, for embodied consciousness, to have awareness of self over time, to communicate, to experience emotion, to solve new and complex problems, and so forth.[51] They then specify whether a particular capacity or joint or alternating set of capacities is necessary and/or sufficient to confer personhood on the entity. They then branch out, again loosely speaking, as to what the entity's relationship to the Capacity X (or Capaci*ties* X, but I will henceforth just use the singular for ease of exposition) must be.

One branch treats an entity as a person only if/when the entity *actually attains* Capacity X; for example, only those entities that actually have awareness of themselves over time are persons. The theories in this family further branch out as to whether that means the entity *currently* has it versus a more capacious view that it is enough that the entity *once had* it even if it does no longer have it. (Humans in irreversible comas are a test case par excellence.)

This branch often faces objections aimed at showing that adopting them requires revising very closely held moral beliefs. If actual attainment is required and the Capacity X selected is too demanding, it is argued that the view implies that infants or individuals with significant intellectual disabilities are not persons and that this is a *reductio* of the view.[52] If the Capacity X selected is not demanding enough, then it leads to a view that we ought to treat animals as persons, which for some (but not others) is a *reductio*. That said, there certainly can exist a Capacity X or a set of jointly sufficient or necessary Capacities X that identify the early embryo as a nonperson and the fetus as a person. Whether they are plausible or not is another question.

A second main branch, sometimes called "potentiality theories," determines that an entity is a person if it has the potential to *actually attain* Capacity X in the ordinary course of its development. As Cynthia Cohen puts the view as relevant to our context, an early embryo is

a potential human being and will, in the normal course of events, grow into an actual one. It develops gradually from conception through the various stages of prenatal development until it emerges completely actualized. Consequently, those presenting this potentiality view argue that the fertilized egg and the embryo and fetus that develop from it are owed protection from destruction from the time of conception onward.[53]

As recognized by Cohen—I think fairly, even if she is clearly not a fan of potentiality arguments—a lot will depend on the concept of "the normal course of events." She quite correctly rejects an interpretation that what matters is "what happens to [the entity] statistically" that would "count up how many zygotes develop in a certain way and then draw conclusions about their potential in the normal course of events from this," and instead argues that the concept depends on the idea that "the relevant processes will unfold in virtue of the child's biological constitution, not by virtue of certain exigencies in that child's environment."[54] The statistical interpretation might lead one to adopt a very easy way of distinguishing abortion from embryo destruction as to personhood that would trade on an act-omission type distinction— that the embryo must be transferred to the woman's body in IVF to develop, whereas in abortion it is stopping a process that has already begun by destruction. Though attractive on its surface, such an argument seems problematic (or even circular) in suggesting that what we may permissibly do with an embryo (i.e., its moral status) depends on what we choose to do to it to enable its development or not.[55]

Instead, the relevant concepts of "potential" and "normal course of events" should be connected to something about the biology of the fetus or early embryo. That is, "the fertilized egg is morally significant because it is potentially the very same being as the later human being that emerges from the process of prenatal development—and that human being is morally significant." Otherwise put, what is important about the early embryo is that "it has the power, within the normal course of events, to become one and the same being as the later morally significant individual human being."[56] If *this* is what matters, it puts a lot of pressure on the continuity between the early embryo and the person that will come—whose rights are the ones that "loop back."

One line of attack on such views is whether rights do "loop back" because of potentiality; acorns are potential trees and eggs are potential chickens, but that does not mean we automatically confer on either eggs or acorns the kind of regard we do for trees or chickens.[57] From a legal perspective, consider the legal processes surrounding the cutting down of trees in a neighborhood or the animal protection laws for poultry; they do not attach to acorns or eggs at those stages of development simply because acorns and eggs have the potential to become those other things. But defenders of potentiality personhood arguments can reply that they are not making a *general* argument about potentialities' relation to rights conferral, but one that is specific to human persons. Your mileage may vary as to whether you find this persuasive.

A different attack on potentiality arguments centers on the premise of continuity between embryo and potential adult. Cohen, for example, distinguishes two different kinds of potential: the "potential to *become* a distinct being in the future" versus the "potential to *produce*" an entity or state of affairs.[58] To use her example, hydrogen and oxygen *produce* water but do not *become* it, and she argues the important moral relation is the latter, not the former. Similarly, sperm and egg *produce* an embryo but do not *become* the embryo, hence why it is not plausible to suggest that sperm or egg alone has the moral status of an adult person. This leads her to argue that the fertilized egg does not *become* the eventual adult person but merely *produces* it. As she puts it:

> The fertilized egg will not eventually become a human subject because it is not the same entity as the embryo proper or the human individual at the other end of the developmental process. . . .

The embryo proper that forms around the primitive streak . . . is not the entire collection of cells that develop from the fertilized egg but a small subset of them. It is this set of cells that is the embryo proper from which the individual human being develops. The other cells form extraembryonic material that supports it. Consequently, the fertilized egg does not stand at the beginning of the process of development of the embryo proper, for it does not become the embryo proper. Instead, it produces or causes the embryo proper. It is not itself numerically identical with the embryo proper.[59]

One possible response is to accept this claim and have potentiality begin later in the process of development, when there is a numerical identity between the embryo and the person it becomes. Such a view, once again, might distinguish destruction of the early embryo (for which the right kind of potentiality has not yet "activated") from abortion of a fetus (for which the potentiality has activated).

* * *

Where does all this leave us as to the first premise? I have suggested that the time-of-fertilization view cannot distinguish the personhood of the early embryo and the fetus, and thus at least on this premise should treat abortion and embryo destruction similarly. By contrast, the fourteen-day or later view would easily distinguish the two, finding personhood only in the fetus and at best give "special respect" to the early embryo which is conventionally viewed as compatible with IVF. Of the Capacity X views, for the actual attainment branch some can draw a distinction between the fetus and the early embryo as to their personhood, but it will depend on exactly how the X is filled in. The potentiality branch as conventionally articulated would seem to have a harder time drawing such a distinction, but there may exist views focused on continuity and numerical identity that would "start" the potentiality "clock" after the point of development in which embryos are typically discarded as part of IVF.

Should pro-life activism, as it succeeds more and more in prohibiting abortion in the United States, now turn its sights on restricting embryo destruction? One answer is that they view such a policy as outside the current Overton window, as some of the polling above suggests, but are waiting, as it may not always be so.[60] But a different take is that unlike abortion, attempts to restrict embryo destruction require resolution of deep and difficult questions of when personhood begins and why. Except for perhaps abortions very early in pregnancy, the movement to restrict abortion could take advantage of incompletely theorized agreements on when personhood begins since fetal personhood was present on many of the rival theories. Debates about embryo destruction require making much finer distinctions. On the flipside, pro-choice activism on abortion also took advantage of the incompletely theorized agreements on when personhood begins. In the mold of Thompson, one could accept or deny the personhood of fetuses and still maintain that an abortion right should be available solely based on the second premise. The question of embryo destruction, by contrast, requires engagement with the question of when personhood begins and potential divisions within those who opposed restrictions on abortion.

Conclusion

My conclusions are that some but not all of those who believe abortion should be restricted, as a normative matter, should also oppose embryo destruction and push for laws restricting it. Perhaps more surprising, some but not all who oppose abortion restrictions should *not* oppose restrictions on embryo destruction, because they do not involve trumping women's rights as to bodily autonomy. Interestingly, there is a kind of push and pull between the two premises and abortion versus embryo destruction. For the second premise it is harder to defend embryo destruction than it is to defend abortion. For the first premise the opposite is true.

As a political matter, I do not believe that even in states that are maximally restricting abortion rights there will be political momentum to restrict IVF or embryo destruction connected to reproductive technology usage. Finally, as a constitutional matter after *Dobbs* it seems very clear that any such attempt at restriction would not violate the federal Constitution, such that state constitutional law would be the main challenge if such statutes were enacted.

Nevertheless, we have seen that some states have already restricted embryo destruction—Louisiana most forcefully, though its prohibition far predates the current debates. In response to a law like Louisiana's, what would citizens of that state be able to do? One possibility is to travel to another state for the entirety of their treatment. Another might be to transfer embryos from the restrictive state to one that permits embryo destruction either at the time of cryopreservation or at a future moment when they want the embryos destroyed.

This raises the question about whether a state could prohibit the transfer of embryos out of state for the purpose of destruction. There is a similar question regarding whether one state can restrict its citizens' travel to a sister state for abortion.[61] Justice Brett Kavanaugh's *Dobbs* concurrence explicitly weighs in—though somewhat blithely and without much clarification as to its application to extraterritorial criminalization as opposed to restricting travel: "[M]ay a State bar a resident of that State from traveling to another state to obtain an abortion? In my view, the answer is no based on the constitutional right to interstate travel."[62] Even if this turns out to be the correct reading of the constitutional law for the purpose of abortion, it is far less clear to me whether the same could be said about transferring an embryo from one state to another. That is, the potential right to travel in the abortion case belongs to the mother who is herself undertaking the travel. In the case of the embryo the state is not restricting the *mother's* right to travel; instead, it is restricting her right to transport the embryo (which might be viewed by that state as either property or another person with its own right) for the purpose of the embryo's destruction. While it is possible that other portions of the federal Constitution, such as the dormant Commerce Clause, would create obstacles for a state prohibition on out-of-state embryo transport for destruction, I am less confident about a right to interstate travel being the obstacle for such a prohibition.

A different possibility for individuals in restrictive states would be to shift to egg freezing—that is, harvesting and freezing eggs that will not be used for immediate implantation, such that what would be retained is frozen eggs, not embryos, that could be thawed and fertilized should a future need arrive.[63] Even if this was cost-effective for the individual and even if rates of success after thawing were comparable to that using frozen embryos, this would only be a solution for embryo destruction connected to excess embryos as opposed to discard related to preimplantation genetic testing that finds a problem with an embryo. It is possible that states prohibiting destruction may include carve-outs for such instances.

A different option might be to prohibit embryo destruction but permit indefinite freezing. I think it is difficult to argue that such a fate is "better" for "the embryo" than destruction. Perhaps some might believe this to be a kind of liminal state between existence and destruction. One might wonder whether banks would agree to do such freezing knowing that after the genetic parents die they themselves may face liability if they destroy the embryo. Moreover, one might rightly wonder whether freezing is just a delay in destruction since it is plausible that at some point a freezer will fail, freezing will have gone on so long that thawing is not possible, or, to invoke Robert Frost, the world will end in fire (or ice). Nonetheless, the firing (or misfiring?) of act-omission distinctions as to, or the diffusion of responsibility for, the end of such embryos might give some comfort or political cover.

Finally, it is possible some such states may permit so-called compassionate transfer of the embryo to a woman's uterus during a nonfertile time in her cycle such that the embryo fails to implant rather than is destroyed.[64] Whether that should be viewed as normatively different from embryo discard, and whether a restrictive state would treat it as legally different if it prohibits embryo destruction, are open questions. Perhaps this approach, like indefinite freezing, is really about the expressive effect, a sort of solemnization, of our treatment of embryos—a cousin to the "special respect" perspective discussed above.

At the end of this journey you, dear reader, may find yourself more confused as to what you think about embryo destruction than when you started reading. That, I will humbly suggest, might be a good thing. The U.S. debate about restricting abortion was ossified and largely binary. It was tempting to think one's position in the "last war" would determine one's position on embryo destruction, but I hope to show you that these questions are more open—not just in the possible positions one takes but in the terms of the debate itself.

19

Dobbs and Our Privacies

Aziz Z. Huq and Rebecca Wexler[*]

This right of privacy, whether it be founded in the Fourteenth Amendment's concept of personal liberty and restrictions upon state action, as we feel it is, or, as the District Court determined, in the Ninth Amendment's reservation of rights to the people, is broad enough to encompass a woman's decision whether or not to terminate her pregnancy.[1]

In the beginning, of course, was privacy. Justice Harry Blackmun's argument in *Roe v. Wade* turned upon the idea of a zone of privacy that shielded an individual's "decision" respecting whether to carry a child to term. But what counts as "privacy" in the first place? Famously, the word does not appear in the text of the Constitution. The general concept, also famously, abides in disarray. In the abstract, privacy is valued by almost all of us. But even as we all value it, we also all profoundly disagree about what the concept means. Both celebrated and misunderstood, privacy has come to take on a plethora of meanings. These range from the zone of autonomy to make decisions about our bodies, which was described by Justice Blackmun, to a freedom from physical intrusions into physical spaces such as homes, vehicles, and similar spaces. They range from the right not to have certain embarrassing or intimate facts or activities revealed to the right to keep chosen communications, facts, or actions secret from all or most of the world.[2] The term "privacy" is so attractive, so positively charged, that it runs the risk of simply being used to describe "things you and I should like." At the same time, there seems to be little or no link between the various ideas that come under the resulting rubric of privacy.[3] Even as they're discussed in the same treatises and casebooks, the diverse values flagged as "privacy" seem to lack any real

Aziz Z. Huq and Rebecca Wexler, Dobbs *and Our Privacies* In: *Roe v. Dobbs*. Edited by: Lee C. Bollinger and Geoffrey R. Stone, Oxford University Press. © Oxford University Press 2024.
DOI: 10.1093/oso/9780197760352.003.0019

connective tissue. They are a jumble. Their association seems an accident of history.

The Supreme Court's decision to overrule *Roe*, however, creates an urgent need to reconsider the apparently discontinuous character of "our privacies." The end of *Roe*, we argue in this chapter, created powerful incentives for state and private actors who are opposed to abortion to act in ways that intrude on both bodily autonomy and other zones of privacy—in particular, data privacy.[4] Meanwhile, in a post-*Roe* world, the long-critiqued underprotection of data privacy in the United States creates new and distinct risks to reproductive autonomy. Data privacy and sexual privacy, that is, turn out to be profoundly entangled.

What do we mean by data privacy, and how does it relate to *Roe*? Our increasingly frequent interactions with digital devices and platforms create a universe of personal data that can illuminate our behavior and intentions. Personal data is now extensively used by private firms such as Google, Amazon, and Meta to power behavioral advertising and recommendation engines. Moreover, there is a lively secondary market in which personal data is bought and sold by those firms and by a rather murky group of commercial "data brokers." Much of that personal data can be exploited by anti-abortion officials and activists to target those who are pregnant, who search for information about reproductive choice, or who seek clinical or medication abortion. Indeed, the state already uses personal data in law enforcement and other domains.[5] *Dobbs* creates a new and powerful spur for the anti-choice state and its allies to acquire and exploit personal data.

At the same time, this will not be all that hard to do, at least as of 2022. The United States is notorious for the minimalism of its data privacy protections. State and federal law, alas, offers few limitations on private firms' collection and analysis of vast swaths of personal data. By and large, there is also either weak or no legal protection for this data against the state. When a police officer or a prosecutor can point to a plausible prosecution under a state's abortion proscriptions, information will usually be vulnerable to disclosure. As a result, the stakes of digital privacy after *Dobbs*—at least for those contemplating or risking pregnancy—are quite different from the pre-*Dobbs* era.

Note also that this new pressure on privacy is distributed in unexpected ways. On the one hand, it will not be confined to those states where abortion is restricted for the simple reason that abortion regulators have powerful motives to investigate and move against providers and patients outside their home state. *Dobbs*'s effect on digital privacy, in short, will be national. On the other hand, regulators have an obvious reason to focus on those who become pregnant. In practice, this is likely to translate into a focus on those identifying as, or who are identified as, women. New burdens on digital privacy will not evenly spread across the population. They will instead track familiar, gendered lines.

By eliminating one sort of privacy (reproductive autonomy), then, the Supreme Court in *Dobbs* generated great pressure on another species of privacy (data privacy). In so doing, it has cast light on the ways in which various meanings of privacy entwine—facets that seem disconnected initially, but that turn out on closer inspection to be more entangled than first impressions suggest. Specifically, post-*Dobbs* efforts to restrict abortion access nationwide will incentivize anti-abortion prosecutors and vigilante civil plaintiffs to exploit digital personal data, creating new invasions of data privacy and spillover data privacy harms. At the same time, inadequate existing protections for data privacy will extend the reach of these anti-abortion actions, further threatening reproductive autonomy.

We devote the bulk of this chapter to fleshing out the dialectical relationship between our reproductive autonomy and data privacies. First we introduce the scope of anti-abortion criminal and civil investigations after *Dobbs* and explain why these investigations will seek to exploit digital personal information, creating new risks to the pregnant and their care providers as well as broad spillover harms to data privacy more generally. We describe the expansive production of digital personal data in the information economy and explain how the data can expose efforts to seek, obtain, and provide reproductive care, putting reproductive autonomy at risk. We argue that the role of, and risks from, digital data in the coming abortion wars will ultimately be determined by two groups of actors: private tech firms and state actors who will set the rules for anti-abortion investigators' access to the data. We then provide a detailed prescriptive account of what tech firms and state actors should do to protect digital privacy after *Dobbs*. In the conclusion, we loop back to the question of how our privacies are hitched together.

Dobbs's Consequences

For all its talk of federalism, democratic self-determination, and tradition, the Supreme Court's decision in *Dobbs v. Jackson Women's Health Organization*[6] had its most direct and immediate effect on bodies. It eviscerated the individual right to decisional privacy recognized by Justice Blackmun's 1973 opinion and opened the gate to new state coercion of bodies. Thirty-eight clinics in seven states that had been providing reproductive care closed in the month after *Dobbs*.[7] There is simply no good reason to think that this didn't immediately foreclose opportunities for care—especially on the part of those too poor or too constrained otherwise to travel. Indeed, empirical studies of pre-*Dobbs* laws that targeted specific kinds of abortion suggest that any legal ban—let alone the sweeping, draconian ones enacted after *Dobbs*—can lead to hundreds of thousands of pregnant people seeking out the procedure and then not being able to obtain it.[8] Many of the people who are unable to get medical care will carry their pregnancy to term. And in the course of that, many will experience adverse physical and psychological consequences, quite apart from additional financial strains.[9] These—we should be clear up front—are the principal reasons to criticize *Roe*'s end. Our focus on digital privacy should not be taken to suggest otherwise.

But *Dobbs* also created another dynamic. Pregnant people and providers will inevitably continue efforts to access and facilitate reproductive care despite closures of registered clinical facilities. They may do so within restrictionist states by engaging prohibited services through underground markets. They may also try to cross state lines to obtain or provide services in pro-choice jurisdictions. Anti-abortion officials and activists, of course, are not going to sit on their hands and allow their restrictionist efforts to be undermined. They will mobilize two resources to prevent what, even considering conduct that is lawful out of state, they likely perceive as circumvention: criminal prosecutions and civil damages lawsuits. And—key for our purposes—both criminal and civil efforts will require information. Digital personal information is one of the most potent sources of inference about reproductive choice in the contemporary world. So it will quickly be targeted as fuel for the fight to restrict reproductive choice.

Let's take a closer look at these enforcement mechanisms. Many states have made the provision of abortion a felony. Louisiana's criminal prohibition, for example, imposes sentences up to ten years, or fines between $10,000 and $100,000. Idaho's allows sentences between two and five years, as well as the suspension or termination of medical licenses.[10] Criminalizing abortion isn't new. One study found 1,331 instances between 2006 and 2020 in which pregnancy was a predicate for criminal prosecution.[11] With *Roe* discarded, there's every reason to expect that this number will rise sharply and rapidly.

Meanwhile, prosecutors are not the only people enforcing new anti-abortion prohibitions. Texas, Idaho, and Oklahoma have all enacted statutes permitting private citizens to seek civil penalties against abortion providers and others. Texas's law, for example, allows *any* private party to bring a suit for damages of no less than $10,000 or injunctive relief against a person who "performs or induces" a covered abortion or "aids or abets the performance or inducement of an abortion," whether knowingly or not.[12] The law allows anyone—including someone who doesn't live in Texas—to sue. And it seems to allow a damages action against a defendant who also doesn't live in Texas.

Now consider how these criminal and civil anti-abortion laws will play out for the provision of abortion services across state lines. It is easy for states to stop registered clinical facilities from offering abortion services. It is less easy for them to stop their residents taking advantage of out-of-state opportunities for reproductive care. These come in two forms. If you live in a state where abortion is outlawed, you can cross state lines to find care elsewhere. This was happening even before *Dobbs*. In 2020, only 167 abortions were performed in Missouri, which had onerous regulation of reproductive care. But 3,201 Missouri residents received such care in Kansas in the same year.[13] In the immediate weeks after *Dobbs*, there was a storm of national news stories about a ten-year-old girl who had been raped and then crossed state lines from Ohio to Indiana to abort her pregnancy.[14] A second way of reaching across state lines is digital access to medicated abortion, using mifepristone and misoprostol. Telemedicine providers in *Dobbs*'s wake have been "pushing the envelope" to meet a surging demand for medicated abortion. And overseas nonprofits such as Aid Access offer abortion to patients remotely within the first ten weeks of a pregnancy at a cost of $150.[15] Both of these routes for the cross-state provision of abortion services will be targets for restrictionist prosecutions and vigilante civil lawsuits.

But in order to bring any prosecution or civil action for damages, information is needed: the instigator of such an action needs to know whom to target, and then needs to secure evidence that they were pregnant, that they terminated the pregnancy, and that there are people who can be targeted for penalties because they were involved. In the contemporary context, their investigative search will focus increasingly on digital personal information. This is arguably especially so for those prosecutions and civil lawsuits that concern conduct occurring across state lines, in which other sources of evidence, such as physical traces or eyewitness testimony, may be harder for investigators to obtain. This is a new development. Fifty years ago, before

Roe was initially handed down, there was very little such data. A technological leap since then changed this. That revolution is familiar to most of
us through our daily experience with the internet, social media and search,
smartphones, and other digital devices. Behind those devices and their con-
venience is a large, ever-growing commercial economy of "personal data"
that can be used to observe directly a person's behavior and beliefs, or indirectly to infer them. And that universe of digital data might end up being a
rich stream for prosecutors and anti-abortion activists to exploit.

Personal Data and Reproductive Choice

Just as prosecutors and anti-abortion activists will increasingly target digital
personal data in their quest to curtail reproductive autonomy, creating new
threats to data privacy in the process, so too the seemingly ever-expanding
collection, analysis, and sale of digital personal data will render abortion
seekers and their care providers more vulnerable to investigation and prosecution, further undermining reproductive choice.

Personal data is usually created as an unintended byproduct of access to
internet search tools, social media platforms and other communication apps,
and web-based services to make purchases or access services via a smart-
phone or another digital device. There are approximately 313 million internet
users in the United States, of which 276.8 million access the internet via mobile devices.[16] Each produces a steady stream of data as a byproduct of their
daily activities. Personal data is also generated by one's physical movement
through the world. It is produced, for example, because of location-tracking
tools in cell phones, Fitbits, and other devices carried or worn on the body. It
is an output of the digital movement and location sensors built into many private vehicles. There is also the kudzu-like "internet of things," a rather vague
term that's used to describe the way in which ordinary devices are armed
with sensors and capable of transmitting data to a central server without
any human intervention. The result of these cumulative developments—
all facilitated by advances in computing science—is a quite new "exaflood"
of data concerning individuals' physical states, movements, interests, and
moods updated on a minute-by-minute, if not second-by-second, basis. To
the extent this data either concerns or can be used to draw inferences about
specific individuals, we can usefully call it "personal data."

Personal data is increasingly commercially valuable because it can be
analyzed to "infer and deduce the feelings, thoughts, intentions, and interests

of individuals."[17] These insights are monetized mainly through the sale of digital advertising. The resulting market is staggeringly big. A handful of dominant social media platforms in the United States currently have a market capitalization of more than $4 trillion.[18] Like other firms that capture data, these feed into a multimillion-dollar secondary market of "brokers." These buy and sell that personal data.[19] This downstream market takes on a new, more sinister significance after *Dobbs*.

Personal data will become important in the abortion wars for several reasons. To begin with, ours is an era when most people use search engines or social media to access information and services. Search and social media data alike can be used to infer the fact of a pregnancy or its termination. When patients transact with providers or secure prescriptions online, this also generates a range of data trails: search histories associated with a person's internet protocol address, details of any financial dealings, and details of any medication and procedures researched or obtained.

Second, many people engage in "self-tracking," which is the collection and analysis of biometric data about "health and wellness" through wearable devices.[20] About one in five Americans uses a smart watch or wearable fitness tracker.[21] By gathering data on exercise, diet, and more, self-tracking apps enable individuals (or third parties such as spouses, employers, or physicians) to take preemptive action in respect to their health. Most relevant here are period-tracking apps. These gather information on menstrual cycles, moods, fetal movements, and more. Some can predict a pregnancy less than a week after conception. Almost one-third of women in the United States have used or now use period-tracking apps.[22] Another part of the multibillion-dollar workplace wellness industry allows employers to purchase self-tracking tools for their workers, retaining access to, and even sharing with insurers, the data thereby generated. For example, Progyny is a highly profitable company that manages fertility benefits for employees at large companies. Other apps marketed directly to employers "focus on the aspects of women's health linked to reproduction, including menstruation, fertility, pregnancy, and menopause."[23] All of these devices and apps generate information that directly pinpoints pregnancies and their termination.

Third, as we have explained, state prohibitions on abortion create an incentive for those seeking reproductive care to cross state borders and seek services in another jurisdiction. But individuals' movements generate digital traces because of the presence of location-tracking capabilities in phones, wearable devices, and vehicles. Unless a patient makes a conscious decision to avoid generating such digital data trails (which is tough), it is very likely that they will inadvertently create a record of their activities. For example, the use of an Alphabet app generates locational data because the company logs GPS data "about every two minutes" so long as one of its apps is in use.[24] A person who uses Google Maps or communicates via Google Chat while physically accessing an abortion-related service generates a corresponding data trail. And a person who does not realize that their apps are generating and sharing this data will unwittingly create a record of their search for abortion-related information and services.

Private firms are not the only entities in possession of relevant information. States also maintain large stocks of locational data because they manage highway toll systems and surveillance cameras. Under current law, that data can also be secured through legal process and used in coercive actions. In Illinois, for example, EZ Pass data has been disclosed through civil process in divorce proceedings.[25] The regulation of such state-held data will be a matter of state law, and we will concentrate hereinafter on privately held data—where the legal regime will be more uniform.

How Firms shape Reproductive Choice

In August 2022, Nebraska police reportedly used a warrant to acquire digital data from Facebook in order to indict a forty-one-year-old woman on a felony charge related to her decision to seek an abortion.[26] This will not be the last time digital data is used to advance an anti-choice end after *Dobbs*. The importance of such data in determining the availability of abortion—and the legal risks of seeking one out—will turn on decisions by two sets of actors: on the one hand, the firms that create, collect, and circulate personal data, and on the other hand, the state actors (including courts and legislatures) that determine when and how prosecutors and vigilante plaintiffs can access such data.

Users' Digital Access

Start with the way that private firms' decisions will influence the risk that digital privacy will be compromised in order to stifle reproductive privacy. The digital architecture and data-retention policies of those platforms determine first whether the pregnant person can access medically accurate advice and information about needful services, and then whether the mere act of doing so places them in peril by leaving a discoverable digital trace. After *Dobbs*, for example, Facebook and Instagram both promptly removed posts offering abortion medication.[27] Online access to information and services depends on internet service providers (ISPs). But ISPs have in the past "throttle[d]" access to certain sites.[28] Alternatively, a host might decide to withdraw protection from disabling attacks by hackers aimed at preventing a site from operating or being reached by internet users.[29] Or it can limit access to sites at the domain-name-system level such that the sites become inaccessible from other parts of the internet.[30]

Second, platforms, search engines, and other firms in the personal-data economy can decide whether to retain data; to remove identifying details from data; to shift it from the jurisdiction in which it was created; and to either sell or retain it. Because personal data is the basis for a lucrative trade in personalized advertisements, there is tremendous fiscal pressure to retain, use, and trade such data. But that pressure doesn't mean firms aren't making a choice when they continue retaining and selling such data after *Dobbs*.

There is a third way in which the decisions of private firms shape digital privacy in relation to reproductive choice: firms must decide whether and how to respond to law enforcement demands for information. We return to this question below—since it makes more sense to explain first *how* officials can get information from firms, and then examine whether or how firms might resist such efforts.

Digital Access by the State

Now consider the ways in which personal data can be accessed by police, prosecutors, or vigilante plaintiffs. The law offers them a range of tools to get information. These include search warrants, grand jury subpoenas, and "administrative" subpoenas. But we also should recall that officials and anti-abortion activists can ask firms to voluntarily disclose information, or else they can buy information on the secondary market.

It is already common practice for prosecutors to secure data directly from tech firms such as ISPs and search providers. Google alone receives tens of thousands of requests annually from law enforcement.[31] To make such a request, police and prosecutors can use a search warrant. These must be solicited from an independent magistrate judge. They are issued on a showing of probable cause that the search will produce evidence of a crime. Under the same standard, an official can obtain wiretap orders to require real-time disclosures of such data as it is being created.[32] Warrants and wiretaps can thus be used when an official already has some evidence of reproductive care being provided. They cannot be used for open-ended "fishing expeditions," by which officials trawl large pools of data in order to winnow out suspects for further investigation. So a warrant wouldn't allow a Texas prosecutor to demand that Facebook hand over (say) all posts related to abortion that originated within fifty miles of the Texas border. But it would allow the official to demand the social media records of a specific person or provider, on the ground that there was "probable cause" to believe they were involved in prohibited reproductive care.

Until recently, officials could obtain locational information—say, from a cell phone provider, without a warrant. In 2018, however, the Supreme Court ruled that "an individual maintains a legitimate expectation of privacy in the record of his physical movements as captured through [cell-site locational data]."[33] If this holding is applied to other forms of locational data, it means that a warrant regime will apply there. Another related but controversial tool is the geofence warrant. These can be used to compel a telecommunications company or an ISP to disclose information about everyone who passed through a particular location at a particular time or searched the web for a particular keyword. For instance, a geofence warrant can identify a specific location and time-slice, and then mandate that a cell phone company conduct sweeping searches of their location databases and provide a list of cell phones and affiliated users found at or near a specific area during that timeframe.[34] These warrants remain controversial and subject still to ongoing Fourth Amendment challenges.[35]

Warrants, however, will offer only very limited protection against police and prosecutors' demands for data in abortion-related prosecutions. Where a warrant is used, the Fourth Amendment hitches the scope of police search authority to the scope of substantive criminal law. A probable cause determination requires a magistrate to consider whether there is evidence pertaining to the elements of a cited criminal law. Of course, anti-choice prosecutors will be able to point to criminal statutes in seeking evidence about abortion. And the broader those laws are, the easier it will be to show probable cause. As a result, there will be many instances in which a warrant will not be difficult to obtain because there is a readily pertinent and applicable statutory hook for probable cause—that is, a legal prohibition on abortion backed by criminal sanctions. The fact that the Supreme Court has, rather remarkably, said "almost nothing" about the way in which a judge goes about making a probable cause determination or what substantively that standard means compounds the discretion afforded to anti-abortion actors.[36] This uncertainty might well give pregnant persons and providers even more reason for concern.

But while warrants will offer minimal protection, other forms of process will offer even less. Warrants are not the only or the easiest search tool for the government to acquire digital personal data. There are several other options for officials (and, in some instances, civil plaintiffs) that do not require the government to have as much preexisting knowledge about the existence of a possible crime.[37]

A grand jury subpoena also allows a federal investigator to extract documentary or digital evidence with almost no constitutional limitation other than a rather weak demand that a request be "reasonable"[38] and "relevant to the general subject of the grand jury's investigation."[39] Similarly, federal and state legislatures have granted executive branch officials power to compel document production or testimony during an administrative or civil investigation. These so-called administrative subpoenas can also be obtained without a showing of probable cause.[40] There are several specialized statutes that allow officials to demand personal data under threat of legal penalties in the absence of probable cause.

The most important here is a 1982 statute called the Stored Communications Act, or SCA.[41] This law applies to most electronic communication service providers, including ISPs, email providers, and hosting services. It rests on a set of complex distinctions between content and noncontent elements of covered communications. The SCA is now four decades old, and its taxonomies have not fared well in the face of technological change. Some of its provisions, moreover, have been invalidated in an influential federal appellate court decision.[42] Its application to new configurations of data, therefore, often raises complex questions of statutory interpretation. But some generalizations can be ventured. The SCA restricts electronic communications service providers' voluntary disclosure of the contents of stored communications, such as emails and chat messages.[43] But it contains exceptions for disclosures to law enforcement on a mere showing "that there are reasonable grounds to believe that the [data] . . . are relevant and material."[44] It also imposes no restrictions whatsoever on the ability of private entities to compel the disclosures of noncontent data. In short, anti-abortion prosecutors will be able to satisfy these minimal process requirements even more easily than they can obtain a warrant.

In contrast to the SCA, other federal statutes create heightened protections for some elements of the data trails left by pregnant persons. Yet even these statutes tend to have law-enforcement exceptions that authorize disclosure pursuant to legal process to police and prosecutors. In other words, these statutes add *zero* privacy protections from criminal investigation beyond what is already built into the baseline warrant and subpoena procedures. Under a Privacy Rule issued pursuant to the Health Information Portability and Accountability Act (HIPAA), disclosures by covered providers are prohibited absent a court order, subpoena, or warrant.[45] The Privacy Rule also has an exception for law enforcement, which allows disclosures that are otherwise required by legal process.[46] Health data can also be reidentified without violating the HIPAA privacy rule. Moreover, what limited protections HIPAA affords cover only traditional healthcare providers, health plans, and healthcare clearinghouses—and not most digital apps.[47] Similarly, the Gramm-Leach-Bliley Act prohibits disclosures of personal financial information but carves out the release of information upon legal process by law enforcement.[48] Entities covered by HIPAA, Gramm-Leach-Bliley, and the SCA in short, may be barred from some voluntary disclosures but must respond to criminal investigations and, in many instances, to civil subpoenas as well. State privacy law in the five states with comprehensive schemes tends to follow the same basic pattern.

Where the prosecutor cannot or does not wish to seek a warrant to obtain information from an ISP or the like, grand jury subpoena, or administrative subpoena, other options are open. One possibility is to simply purchase the data outright—say, from data brokers—on the open market.[49] In May 2022, *Vice News* bought a week's worth of location data for people visiting Planned Parenthood for slightly over $160 from a data broker called SafeGraph.[50] Data brokers like SafeGraph obtain and aggregate location data from a variety of sources, including cell phone apps that have location services enabled.[51] After *Dobbs*, more than two dozen data brokers have continued to market information about expecting parents in the United States, ignoring calls from Democratic lawmakers to limit the circulation of such data given its effect on reproductive choice.[52] Law enforcement and vigilantes can also purchase services from data brokers such as Beware, which "analyzes consumer information compiled by data brokers to provide officers real-time red, yellow, and green threat scores for addresses and individuals."[53] Often data is nominally anonymized. But de-anonymization is technologically feasible, even if beyond the reach of the ordinary state prosecutor.

In addition to these legal means of extracting information, technically so-
phisticated vigilante hackers may be tempted to employ creative and novel
methods to circumvent or "work around" data protections, like exploiting
encryption vulnerabilities or back doors in order to access data.[54] One such
tactic may be to use "malware," or "software designed to conduct surrepti-
tious surveillance on a target's computer or network" to access information.
Even when such tactics are illegal, vigilante groups could use them and pass
the resulting data to law enforcement.

The risk here is not limited to data that directly indexes pregnancy. The fact
of an individual's pregnancy can also be inferred from data that had no prima
facie connection to that condition using machine learning tools. Almost a
decade ago, the retailer Target made the news for its "pregnancy predictor,"
which applied data analytics to shoppers' consumption behavior to predict
the fact of a pregnancy. In the subsequent decade, the technique of "machine learning," which is used to mine large pools of data for unanticipated
correlations and inferences, has improved dramatically. Using machine-
learning tools, otherwise "private" information can be acquired without an
intrusive search or seizure. Machine learning can implicate privacy through
category-jumping inferences. For example, health conditions can be inferred
from spending-related information, and behaviors or dispositions can be
gleaned from health-related data.[55] Just as Target mined its transactional
data, so too an anti-abortion actor might try to leverage another large pool of
data for predictive ends.

This may sound implausible now. But several federal agencies, including
the Internal Revenue Service and the Securities and Exchange Commission,
have developed bespoke predictive tools to mine governmental and private
data in order to identify regulatory violations.[56] Is it so far-fetched to suggest
that the state of Texas will not be lagging far behind in the creative exploitation of retail or social media data?

The world after *Dobbs*, in short, looks very different from that before *Roe*.
Anti-abortion officials and activists have an array of new investigative tools
within reach. These allow them to examine in microscopic detail the activity and decisions of pregnant persons and providers. *Dobbs* dramatically
increases prosecutors' incentives to exploit digital data as a way of rooting
out reproductive choice. This places a new kind of pressure on digital privacy. The disclosure-forcing tools that we have described—from administrative subpoenas to geofence warrants and data-mining—were lawful prior to
Dobbs. They were certainly used by law enforcement agencies. But their use

was constrained by the fact that most of the serious felony investigations upon which police and prosecutors focus did not turn on personal data. In more run-of-the-mill cases, there is commonly another available source of evidence. Abortion-related offenses, however, are different. In many instances, there will not be an alternative source of evidence, such as eyewitness testimony or biological traces from which fingerprints or DNA can be extracted. Further, prosecutors in restrictive states have political incentives to pursue high-profile abortion indictments in ways that make the exploitation of personal data particularly tempting. Hence, the tempo at which prosecutors use personal data will likely increase, perhaps dramatically. Indeed, it is quite possible that abortion prosecutions operate as a "gateway." That is, they may alert prosecutors to the piecemeal and haphazard legal protections for personal data. This might in turn elicit greater exploitation of such data across the board.

How to Protect Choice Through Digital Privacy

Tech companies that wish to shield reproductive choice in states where it is legal, and the pro-choice states themselves, have a few options for responding to these pressures. We focus here on a couple of ideas that have not received as much attention as they should. We don't want to suggest that what follows is exhaustive; it is only suggestive. And we also don't mean to assume that all tech companies, any more than all states, will be open to these suggestions. The behavior of data brokers—exploiting *Dobbs* for a fleeting profit—is evidence enough of that. We consider first private firms, then states, and finally Congress (recognizing that the chances of federal legislative action are slim).

Private firms

Let's start with what private firms can do. Technology firms should obviously reduce patients' exposure to harmful disclosures in the first instance by limiting the kinds of information collected and retained, curbing their economic reliance on resale, and minimizing the possibility of inference of individual attributes relevant to pregnancy and abortion using machine-learning tools. In the wake of *Dobbs*, for example, Google announced that it would start proactively deleting users' location information tracking them to abortion clinics and other sensitive healthcare providers.[57] Taking a further step, it (and other firms) should also commit to noncollection and nonretention of any identifying information associated with abortion-relevant web searches. They should disable their own internal, automated scanning of message and email contents for abortion-relevant text. Information that could be targeted for anti-abortion ends would thus not be collected in the first place. And firms should decouple the data from personally identifying information to the greatest extent possible.

Is this incentive enough given the profits to be made by selling personal data? We think so—but that doesn't mean that all companies will follow through. For companies where abortion-relevant data remains a small percentage of the overall business model, such as Google and Meta, the costs involved should be relatively limited. These expenditures will also likely be offset by gains among users who value privacy related to reproductive choice. And for companies where abortion-relevant data is a substantial part of the business model—such as period-tracking or other reproductive health apps that may specialize in predicting pregnancies or identifying new parents for advertisers—limiting unnecessary risk to their users should be viewed as a necessary cost of doing business without compromising important privacy interests—much as pollution control may be an appropriate cost incurred by manufacturers. Indeed, the period-tracking app Flo has already announced that it would offer a "privacy" mode for users (an improvement that nonetheless puts the onus of responsibility on the user).[58] In contrast, many other pregnancy-related apps still make it difficult, perhaps even impossible, to opt out of sharing personal data. But there are plenty of data sources from which to profit. Seeking gain by trafficking in data that puts users' intimate privacy at risk without installing appropriate safeguards should not be one of them.

We mentioned earlier that firms could also change their responses to compulsory legal demands for disclosure. Indeed, firms can go a long way toward protecting pregnant people's choices simply by reducing the alacrity and ease with which anti-abortion actors access data. Many major technology companies have a two-tier system for responding to legal process demands for user data. Companies such as Alphabet and Meta have built special online "portals" that maximize efficiency and waive requirements for in-person service of process. Law enforcement requesters certify their identity via these portals and upload digital copies of their warrants or subpoenas. The requests then go directly to human reviewers inside the companies, who sometimes reach out to a law enforcement requester for clarifying information before providing responsive data in an easily downloadable format. This "portal system" reduces transaction costs for companies and law enforcement alike. But not all legal process requests receive this special treatment. Many companies do not currently permit nongovernmental litigants to use the online portals, so these litigants must follow standard service of process rules for their subpoenas. For instance, when criminal defense counsel seek data from technology companies, their requests are shunted to a second-tier process seemingly designed to maximize *in*efficiency. Not only are defense counsel barred from using the online portals, but some major technology companies will not even accept in-person service of process on their company representatives located in the counsel's state. Meta, for instance, requires that criminal defense subpoenas from counsel located anywhere in the country must be domesticated into California law through the California courts and served in-person on Meta's agent in Menlo Park.[59]

This two-tier filtering structure is an opportunity in the post-*Dobbs* context. Firms should modify their systems for responding to legal process to vary transaction costs depending on whether the entity demanding the data can certify that the information is not for an abortion-relevant legal suit. They could operationalize this policy easily by conditioning law enforcement's access to the hyperefficient online portals on submission of an affidavit that the alleged crime under investigation concerns a specific list of topics, and not abortion. Absent such an affidavit, firms should treat law enforcement service of process the same way they treat criminal defense subpoenas. If the second-tier system has been lawful and adequate for criminal defense counsel (and civil litigants) across the country, then that same second-tier system should be lawful and adequate for law enforcement requests as well.

We should emphasize that technology companies need not even implement any novel infrastructure or procedures to slow legal process for interstate collection of data by anti-abortion regulators. It is enough that they allocate restrictionist warrants and subpoenas to the same processing track that they currently employ for criminal defense counsel and subpoenas in civil cases.

Even when regulators demanding data have what appears to be a valid warrant or subpoena, there may be opportunities for companies to move to quash the legal process in court. Technology firms should commit publicly to challenging the scope and validity of all abortion-related legal process they receive.[60] Successful challenges will end a disclosure demand. Meanwhile, even challenges that ultimately do not receive a favorable ruling in court will nonetheless raise the costs (and slow the pace) of restrictionist search activity in a fashion that accords with users' privacy expectations and firms' *ex ante* commitments to privacy.

Pro-Choice States

What, then, should pro-choice states (or a pro-choice Congress) do to advance digital privacy? The pro-choice state response to *Dobbs* has been halting and incomplete when it comes to digital privacy. Quickest off the mark, both California and Connecticut enacted laws limiting law enforcement cooperation with abortion prosecutions. They shored up data-privacy rules for providers. And they permitted countersuits against out-of-state vigilante plaintiffs. In September 2022, California's legislature also voted to enact a measure that protects medical records (but not the full exaflood of personal digital data) from out-of-state anti-abortion subpoenas.

But these laws are still hazardously incomplete. Courts may still facilitate cross-jurisdictional evidence collection even without assistance from local law enforcement, and privacy statutes generally offer no protection from compulsory legal process. For instance, the "My Body, My Data Act of 2022" would restrict technology companies' *voluntary* collection, retention, use, and disclosure of "personal reproductive or sexual health information," but the Act does not block, or indeed even mention, warrants, subpoenas, or other court orders.[61] Apart from the limited scope of California's law (covering only medical records), their privacy measures are toothless in the face of warrants and court orders from anti-abortion states. Nothing prevents law enforcement from using subpoenas for locational information or commercial transactional records to identify abortion providers and patients, say, in Connecticut, as a means to shame and threaten them into inaction.

Pro-choice states, however, have options to do better. In other work, we have suggested both proactive tools to enable self-defense by the pregnant and a shield for digital privacy.[62] We focus on the latter here. Pro-choice states (or, indeed, Congress) could create what is called an "evidentiary privilege," like the lawyer-client privilege, to shield abortion-related data. This is, to be sure, not the only step that a pro-choice state could take, but it is one that squarely responds to the distinct perils to digital privacy. (In other academic writing, we've suggested other measures that these states should take, and we urge readers interested in learning more to turn there.)[63]

Evidentiary privileges are powerful shields for privacy because they shield the communication of information from most forms of legally compelled disclosure and use in litigation.[64] Many people are already familiar with the lawyer-client privilege. When you confide with a lawyer for purposes of seeking their legal advice, no one—not even law enforcement—can then force them to share your secrets. Not only do privileges bar protected information from being admitted into evidence at trial, but—unlike any other evidence rule—they also preclude the use of protected information at all other stages of a judicial proceeding. That means privileges do not just bar juries from considering protected information; they also bar judges from doing so. Privileges apply to bail hearings, settlement agreements, plea negotiations, sentencing proceedings, and more. They also prevent litigants, including criminal prosecutors and vigilante civil plaintiffs, from ever learning the information in the first place. And privileges have the power to block subpoenas,[65] discovery orders,[66] searches and seizures,[67] and even wiretaps.[68] This is so regardless of probable cause and *ex ante* judicial review.

A state statute could create a privilege covering any and all information that reveals a person's reproductive health choices. This would reach internet searches, locational data, social media communications, medical data, biometric data, related financial records, and more. Next, make the privilege applicable to all anti-abortion subpoenas, warrants, court orders, and judicial proceedings. It would set up a zone of privacy around reproductive choice, like the one we already have when we deal with lawyers. Importantly, this zone would cover many of the sources and the species of digital data that we've discussed above, including data brokers.

Such an abortion data privilege should include no statutory exceptions. It should also expressly preclude court-created or common law exceptions. This absolutism diverges from standard privilege practice. Even those privileges that are facially absolute generally have particularized exceptions for circumstances such as self-defense, child abuse prosecutions, and disclosures of an ongoing or future crime or fraud.[69] But the problem with including such exceptions in an abortion data privilege is that it would work as a loophole for anti-abortion judges to reject the privilege's effect. At the same time, we are sensitive to the risk that a truly absolute privilege might cause unintended, harmful consequences. To account for these countervailing concerns, we propose an extraordinarily narrow application for the privilege: it should apply solely to proceedings to hold a person criminally or civilly liable for seeking, obtaining, providing, or assisting in seeking, obtaining, or providing abortion services that would have been lawful before *Dobbs*. In other words, for medical liability disputes, domestic violence cases, child abuse prosecutions, or any other form of litigation, this privilege would not exist at all.

Ideally, the U.S. Congress would enact such a privilege to apply in courts nationwide. In that case, if a Texas prosecutor or vigilante plaintiff somehow got their hands on the data despite state-level protections, the federal privilege would stop them from lawfully using it in any anti-abortion court proceeding—including trials, sentencing, or even pretrial proceedings to keep someone in jail. But of course, federal action faces hurdles, and states shouldn't wait for gridlock on Capitol Hill to abate.

Conclusion

Our privacies are entangled with each other. Tear one down, and another comes under undue pressure. *Dobbs*'s defenestration of the right of privacy over the body leads inexorably to new pressure on a different sort of privacy: the interest embedded in personal data that is created and trafficked as part of the present data economy. This interest, to be sure, is not always protected by law—or at least not well protected by law. And that underprotection, in turn, loops back to impose new vulnerabilities on pregnant people and new risks to reproductive autonomy.

In short, then, *Dobbs* creates a new, hydraulic pressure on such privacy. At least for those who might become pregnant, certain state actors now have a far sharper interest in their personal data, and hence are much more likely to try to obtain and exploit it. And those who have an interest in protecting reproductive choice now have all the more reason to concern themselves with safeguarding data privacy as well.

So perhaps Justice Blackmun, in the beginning, was right to talk in *Roe* of the right to privacy. Perhaps both the right to reproductive choice and the right over digital personal data comprehend a similar ambition to invest a person with control over an autonomous sector of decision-making over their lives and bodies. If so, *Dobbs* has compromised something quite fundamental to being human—and in more ways than one.

20

The Unraveling

What *Dobbs* May Mean for Contraception, Liberty, and Constitutionalism

Martha Minow[*]

A hand-knitted American flag hangs in front of a copy of the U.S. Constitution, printed on fabric.[1] Bit by bit, day by day, the knitting is unraveled, its yarn hanging from the diminishing stripes on the flag. Adrienne Sloane, a fiber artist, created this artwork, *The Unraveling*, after the 2016 election, as a response to actions of the Trump administration.[2] She later explained, "Set against the backdrop of the constitution, I will continue to unravel this piece as long as I continue to see our civil and political rights eroding under the current administration."[3]

By 2021, the administration of President Donald Trump had ended, but the unraveling continues. It continues in the repeated claims that the 2020 election was "stolen" by President Joe Biden, claims that continued to dominate the 2022 midterm elections, despite sixty lawsuits in which judges rejected challenges to the 2020 election returns.[4] The unraveling continued with the violent insurrection on January 6, 2020, that interfered with the certification of the 2020 election and with the disrespect for the rule of law it signaled and amplified.[5] What remains to be seen is how much unraveling will occur through the courts with the influence of the judges appointed by Trump. During his one term in office, he appointed 33% of the Supreme Court justices and 30% of the federal judiciary, and their lifetime appointments will last for decades.[6] Trump's three justices made possible the five-person 2022 majority opinion in *Dobbs v. Jackson*, overturning a pregnant person's right to terminate a pregnancy.

In overturning the right to control one's body and reproduction as recognized fifty years previously in *Roe v. Wade*, the Court shaped by Trump has already had an immediate and stark impact on access to abortion.[7] More constitutional decisions are at genuine risk of reversal.[8] The issue takes no

Martha Minow, *The Unraveling* In: *Roe v. Dobbs*. Edited by: Lee C. Bollinger and Geoffrey R. Stone,
Oxford University Press. © Oxford University Press 2024. DOI: 10.1093/oso/9780197760352.003.0020

detective work. In his concurring opinion in *Dobbs*, Justice Clarence Thomas expressly called for reconsideration and overturning of precedents governing contraception, same-sex intimacy, and same-sex marriage.[9] Not unrelated, respect for the courts and the Constitution is itself unraveling.[10]

This chapter explores the implications of the Supreme Court's revocation of a pregnant person's right to choose to terminate a pregnancy; specifically, it explores implications for individuals' right to choose to prevent a pregnancy through the purchase and use of contraceptives.[11] In the language of case names, this chapter explores what *Dobbs v. Jackson* means for *Griswold v. Connecticut*,[12] *Eisenstadt v. Baird*,[13] and *Carey v. Population Services International*.[14] Millions of people, and notably millions of women, immediately face grave uncertainty and heightened risks not only of unwanted pregnancies but also of job and wage insecurity.[15] Also in jeopardy is public confidence in the courts and law. Of relevance, as explored here, is what the justices themselves said and what they did not say. What will matter from now on are consequences already unfolding and what may well ensue.

What the Justices Themselves Said

Justice Samuel Alito's opinion for the *Dobbs* majority states and restates that abortion differs from contraception, and hence the *Dobbs* decision does not itself in any way erode the cases recognizing the right to access contraception. The opinion for the Court states, "None of the other decisions cited by *Roe* and *Casey* involved the critical moral question posed by abortion. They are therefore inapposite. They do not support the right to an abortion, and by the same token, our conclusion that the Constitution does not confer such a right does not undermine them in any way."[16] Because abortion involves a " 'potential life,' " it differs from contraception, maintains the majority.[17] And quoting itself by way of responding to the dissent, the majority states, "[W]e have stated unequivocally that '[n]othing in this opinion should be understood to cast doubt on precedents that do not concern abortion' because 'rights regarding contraception and same-sex relationships are inherently different from the right to abortion because the latter (as we have stressed) uniquely involves what *Roe* and *Casey* termed 'potential life.' "[18] Moreover, prior decisions about contraception are each subject to their own analysis about the weight of precedent.[19]

Justice Brett Kavanaugh, while fully joining the majority, wrote separately to emphasize the point. After asking how the *Dobbs* decision will affect other precedents "involving issues such as contraception and marriage," he asserts that "[o]verruling *Roe* does *not* mean the overruling of those precedents, and does *not* threaten or cast doubt on those precedents."[20] (He also stressed that the Court was not outlawing abortion but simply allowing the states to do so.)[21]

Justice Thomas reads the majority rather differently, as he joins it fully even as he explicitly calls for overturning the entire line of fundamental personal privacy cases under the Fourteenth Amendment.[22] His analysis does not merely state that he would go further than the majority and wipe out rights of access to contraception and same-sex relationships. His opinion announces that "[c]ases like *Griswold v. Connecticut*, 381 U.S. 479 (1975) (right of married persons to obtain contraceptives); *Lawrence v. Texas*, 539 U.S. 558 (2003) (right to engage in private, consensual sexual acts); and *Obergefell v. Hodges*, 576 U.S. 644 (2015) (right to same-sex marriage), are not at issue."[23] The majority opinion thus does not disturb those precedents *because their validity was not presented in the case.* Justice Thomas could sign on fully to the majority without any commitment to—without even a hint of protection for—those other precedents.

Modest incremental judgments are not likely in the offing with a Court majority rapidly casting aside precedents and inventing doctrines garnering more power to itself. Receiving no support from the majority, Chief Justice John Roberts called for minimal steps in his separate concurrence; he hoped the Court would decide only the lawfulness of Mississippi's ban on abortions after fifteen weeks of pregnancy.[24] Even though this was in fact the issue initially presented in *Dobbs*, no one else on the Court endorsed his approach.

Justice Thomas's eagerness to overturn precedents involving contraception and same-sex intimacy is explicit in his repeated call to eliminate the entire doctrine of substantive due process.[25] Indeed, specifically on contraception, his opinion criticizes as distortion of equal protection the application of contraception access rights to unmarried individuals.[26] Justice Thomas does acknowledge that some other constitutional provisions, such as the Privileges and Immunities Clause of the Fourteenth Amendment, might come into play for some areas that have fallen within the substantive due process personal privacy doctrine, although further hurdles then would include whether any rights not unenumerated in the Constitution gain such protections.[27] He additionally disparages as evidence of incoherence and inconsistency the efforts by amici to describe the protected personal liberties as " 'bodily integrity' " and " 'personal autonomy in matters of family, medical care, and faith' " and " 'women's equal citizenship.' "[28]

Perhaps the only Fourteenth Amendment personal family decision that is safe from his call for excision is the one not mentioned anywhere in his concurrence. That is the unanimous decision overturning a ban on interracial marriage, *Loving v. Virginia*.[29] There, the Court relied on the Fourteenth Amendment's due process protection of what it described as the "freedom to marry," a basic civil right that is "fundamental to our very existence and survival." We cannot know, because he does not discuss the case, whether Justice Thomas would knock out this Fourteenth Amendment fundamental liberty reasoning and preserve *Loving* on its alternate grounding in the guarantee of equal protection of the laws, guarding against invidious racial discrimination.[30]

Hence, Justice Thomas agrees with the dissenters that the Court's precedents about contraception (and same-sex relationships) cannot stand after *Dobbs*. Of course, for the dissenters, this is further reason to disagree with the majority, while for Justice Thomas this is grounds to emphasize the issues that remain for future cases. The dissent, unusually presented by all three dissenting justices without a named author, acknowledges that the scope of the decision's effects will unfold but certainly already include "the curtailment of women's rights, and of their status as free and equal citizens . . . [who] will incur the cost of losing control of their lives."[31] Underscoring the centrality of women's bodies and lives at issue in the case, the dissent rapidly turns to the repercussions for "other settled freedoms involving bodily integrity, familial relationships, and procreation."[32]

Here the dissent underscores the long-standing link, historically and conceptually tying the Court's abortion precedents with precedents concerning the right to purchase and use contraception.[33] Warning that the majority may not be "done with its work," the dissent stresses that those precedents and the subsequent cases recognizing rights to engage in same-sex intimacy and marriage "are all part of the same constitutional fabric, protecting autonomous decisionmaking over the most personal of life decisions."[34]

Most tellingly, the dissent shows how the rationale and method of analysis used by the majority directly apply to the rest of the cases addressing bodily integrity, familial relationships, and procreation:[35] "The lone rationale for what the majority does today is that the right to elect an abortion is not 'deeply rooted in history.' "[36] The dissent observes that the same analysis—tracking state bans against abortion from the mid-nineteenth century until the mid-twentieth century—would find no support in American law for a constitutional right to obtain contraceptives because these too were banned in many states through the same period of time.[37] Supreme Court precedents about contraceptive access have no further foundation, so what could explain the majority's assertion that its decision has no effect on their durability? The dissent speculates that "[e]ither the majority does not really believe in its own reasoning," leaving other methods and approaches alive for future challenges to contraceptive restrictions, or "all rights that have no history stretching back to the mid-nineteenth century are insecure."[38] Given the absence of legal protection for contraceptives during the late nineteenth century, or protections against sterilization without consent, or interracial marriage, or same-sex marriage, "it is impossible to understand (as a matter of logic and principle) how the majority can say that its opinion today does not threaten—does not even 'undermine'—any number of other constitutional rights."[39]

The dissent builds on the large number of prior decisions that treat the substantive due process cases as a line of cases—tied together as a woven fabric or a physical structure.[40] In this light, the dissent questions how the majority can "neatly extract the right to choose from the constitutional edifice without affecting any associated rights. (Think of someone telling you that the Jenga tower simply will not collapse.)"[41] The dissent emphasizes how Justice Thomas could both join the majority and write separately to call for eliminating the entire line of substantive due process cases.[42]

Tethering rights protected by the Fourteenth Amendment only to those well-known and well-regarded in the mid-nineteenth century gives no room for a right to purchase and use contraception. Justice Thomas makes the point and invites challenges to allow the Court to reach this conclusion. Despite its assertions that the *Dobbs* decision leaves contraceptive rights intact, the majority's own reasoning leads to Justice Thomas's conclusion. The dissent hammers the point home: "The Constitution, of course, does not mention [contraception]. And there is no historical right to contraception, of the kind the majority insists on. To the contrary, the American legal landscape in the decades after the Civil War was littered with bans on the sale of contraceptive devices."[43]

The dissent speculates that the Court's majority may shy away from overturning its precedents protecting the liberty to choose contraception, while predicting (and at the same time acknowledging proposals already pending) that the decision in *Dobbs* will "fuel the fight to get contraception, and any other issues with a moral dimension, out of the Fourteenth Amendment and into state legislatures."[44] The dissent notes, "Because laws in 1868 deprived women of any control over their bodies, the majority approves States doing so today."[45] Thus, the *Dobbs* decision not only "eliminates a 50-year-old constitutional right that safeguards women's freedom and equal station"; it "also places in jeopardy other rights, from contraception to same-sex intimacy."[46] The only people skeptical about this conclusion seem to be the justices—well, some of those justices—who joined the majority opinion.

What None of the Justices Discuss

Using "potential life" as the distinguishing characteristic between abortion and contraception does not work, as some people—and some religious groups in particular—treat both activities as unacceptable interference with potential life. The current Supreme Court knows this well, as it decided *Little Sisters of the Poor Saints Peter & Paul Home v. Pennsylvania*.[47] In that case, seven members of the Court divided across four opinions in the case's treatment of a religious employer's objection to coverage of contraception mandated under federal health insurance, even when that governing rule provided an opt-out mechanism for those with religious or conscience objections.[48] That division presaged the decision in *Dobbs* by a Court with two new members, Justice Amy Coney Barret and Justice Ketanji Brown Jackson.

The *Dobbs* dissent observed that the majority's decision created new questions "about the application of abortion regulations to medical care most people view as quite different from abortion. What about the morning-after pill? IUDs? In vitro fertilization? And how about the use of dilation and evacuation or medication for miscarriage management?"[49] The line between abortion and these activities is not answered by reference to "potential life" as all pertain to it. Basic reproductive and medical facts should shield from regulation the removal of a dead fetus and treatment for an ectopic pregnancy, in which a fertilized egg implants outside the main cavity of the uterus but cannot survive and may cause complications threatening the life of the pregnant person.[50] Yet confusion and questions arise as medical personnel and individuals seeking medical care delay or avoid necessary actions in the wake of new abortion bans.[51] Besides reluctance to get close to the line of illegality with criminal as well as civil sanctions, such problems reflect politicized fights and potential ignorance about reproductive facts. The contrasting views in the *Dobbs* opinions proceed without discussion of the stages of human reproduction and laws affecting each stage.

The anti-abortion movement has targeted contraception as well as abortion and has done so in part by confusing the distinction between the two.[52] Contraception is meant to prevent pregnancy, while abortion terminates a pregnancy. But "pregnancy" includes multiple stages and steps, ranging from the activity producing a fertilized human egg to the journey of that egg from the ovary to the fallopian tube, division into multiple cells, and implantation in the uterus.[53] During the first day or so after fertilization of an egg, the cell divides rapidly and becomes a blastocyte.[54] The blastocyte stays in the fallopian tube for several more days; in the next stage, the blastocyte moves into the uterus. Once there, it needs to attach to the endometrium to grow, and that stage is called implantation.[55] Hence, after fertilization, cell division becoming a blastocyte, and further growth as an "embryo" (from around the second to the eighth week of development), the next stage after implantation in the womb is growth for about eight to ten weeks, after which it becomes known as a "fetus."[56]

For some people, any interference with sexual activity that is designed to prevent pregnancy involves obstruction of the "potential life" of a new being. Indeed, the human egg and the human sperm are themselves living cells and already alive.[57] Immature eggs—oocytes—are present in a newborn female; indeed, all the eggs that individual will ever have are present at birth.[58] These female germ cells await puberty for the processes that enable both ovulation—maturation of the immature egg and development of the uterus, onset of menarche (first menstrual period)—and then monthly release of a mature egg from the ovary into the fallopian tube, where the egg, still alive, can be available for fertilization by sperm.[59] Sperm development similarly moves from a stem cell to a mature cell.[60] Fertilization of the egg by the sperm is a further point in the journey of these living cells toward the development of a born and living human child, but there are several stages before that happens, including stages known as "contraception" rather than "abortion." For example, emergency contraception (known as "Plan B") can work to prevent fertilization and can also prevent a fertilized egg from attaching to the uterus (also known as a womb).[61] This medication is different from abortion medication which terminates a pregnancy.[62] Nonetheless, people seeking emergency contraception face objections by some pharmacists and others who view it as an agent of abortion.[63]

The *Dobbs* majority repeatedly used the term "potential life" without defining it.[64] They also refer to "'fetal life'" and "'unborn human being,'" references to nomenclature used in *Roe* and *Casey*.[65] "Prenatal life" is another phrase adopted by the *Dobbs* majority.[66] Some of these references, to some readers, encompass all of these stages of development starting with egg fertilization; "potential life" for some includes the egg and the sperm, while still separate and not united. Some states authorize religious exemptions for pharmacists with such beliefs.[67] Several states have already enacted legislation treating fertilization as the critical stage after which medical termination is illegal.[68] Still, by using the phrase "potential life," the majority asserts why contraception is "inherently different from the right to abortion."[69]

None of the other opinions discusses these multiple stages of prenatal development; Justice Thomas calls for reconsideration of the personal liberty substantive due process cases, including those involving contraception.[70] The dissent seems on strong grounds in predicting fights to come over contraception.[71] Even before the *Dobbs* decision, state abortion restrictions reduced contraceptive use.[72] Some groups and some public officials contemplate restricting contraceptives by law.[73]

Common understandings and practices, however, treat abortion and contraception quite differently. Opinion polls ask about abortion separately from questions about contraception.[74] Opinion polls show that even people who identify as pro-life predominantly do not oppose contraception, and significant majorities across the country support insurance coverage for contraception.[75] Very little difference in views appears for people with different political party affiliations.[76] In recent polls, some 90% of Americans support birth control as a lawful practice.[77] Despite highly visible opposition to covering contraception within the federal Affordable Care Act, an estimated 99% of American women used birth control at some time during their lives.[78] The vast majority of American women (regardless of religious or political affiliation) have used highly effective forms of birth control.[79] Birth control medication is also the treatment for other conditions, such as endometriosis, severe pain from menstrual cramping, and polycystic ovarian syndrome.[80] This level of belief and practices around contraception may indicate why the *Dobbs* majority and dissent both suggest (but cannot guarantee) different treatments of the matter by the Court.

After *Dobbs*, How Might the Justices Overturn
the Contraception Right Precedents?

As the dissent in *Dobbs* notes, it is hard to figure out how the test announced by the majority's analysis leads anywhere except allowing restrictions on contraception.[81] The majority announced it would confine recognition of unenumerated rights made under the Fifth and Fourteenth Amendments' Due Process Clauses to those "deeply rooted in this Nation's history and tradition" and "implicit in the concept of ordered liberty."[82] The Court traced this test to *Washington v. Glucksberg* and sidestepped the rejection of the test in *Obergefell v. Hodges* and its inconsistency with *Loving v. Virginia* and *Lawrence v. Texas*.[83] It expressly rejected general assertions of "broadly framed rights" such as "privacy" or "personal dignity and autonomy."[84] Defining the right at issue in *Dobbs* solely as "the right to obtain an abortion,"[85] the Court asserted that such a right could be recognized appropriately only if such a right existed at the time of the enaction of the Fourteenth Amendment. With that limited focus on the state of laws and practices in 1868, the majority concluded that no such support existed and hence there was no "right to an abortion" at the time the Fourteenth Amendment was adopted.[86] The Court gave no acknowledgment to the exclusion of women from voting and other legal rights at that time, despite the dissent's reference to this basic fact.[87] Nor did the majority suggest any significance to decades of evolving social norms and practices or doctrinal development as articulated by the Court itself, nor of subsequent constitutional amendments, such as the Nineteenth Amendment's extension of the right to vote to women, ratified in 1920.[88]

If applied in the same way to contraception restrictions, the Court's "history and tradition" test would again look to the late nineteenth century and ignore earlier legal and social practices. The *Dobbs* dissent aptly notes that laws against contraception were common in the United States by the late nineteenth century, and pegging the analysis to, say, 1873, when the Comstock Act was enacted, could be the beginning and the end of its analysis if and when the Court takes up new restrictions on contraception. Anthony Comstock and his supporters feared especially wanton sexuality and moral corruption of unmarried youth.[89] As the dissent in *Dobbs* noted, "the majority could write just as long an opinion showing, for example, that until the mid-20th century, 'there was no support in American law for a constitutional right to obtain [contraceptives].'"[90]

Yet a wooden application of the method used in *Dobbs* exposes its strange, selective idea of "history" and "tradition" perhaps even more so than what troubles critics of *Dobbs* (and indeed, critics of other recent decisions).[91] As two leading organizations of historians have noted, by narrowing the relevant time period to right around the Fourteenth Amendment's origin, the *Dobbs* majority downplayed strong evidence that from the American Revolutionary period to the Civil War, the states did not interfere with terminations of pregnancy before the third to fourth month.[92] Criminalization spread in the later decades of the nineteenth century and coincided with efforts by the emerging male obstetrical physicians to displace female relatives, neighbors, and midwives in birth-related care.[93] But abortion had been practiced without sanction in most of the United States in the first half of the nineteenth century, though often hidden due to concerns about illegitimacy.[94]

The Court may well be similarly selective about contraception history and ignore its long legal and social histories. Ancient teachings and techniques of contraception as well as centuries of practices in Europe made their way to the colonies and the early United States.[95] Alongside expectations about childbearing and mothering for white women in particular, many married women worked on controlling their fertility.[96]

Physicians may have declined to assist such efforts, but individuals could purchase "feminine hygiene" products for birth control as well as condoms and popular medical books that were available to the public.[97] One author who advocated family planning explained how he and his wife decided to practice birth control in the 1840s following painful and sad experiences of many pregnancies and births.[98] While dominant religious authorities and physicians stressed that sexual intercourse should be aimed at procreation, no government policies or practices forbade sharing information or contraceptive materials in the United States until the 1870s.[99] Many point to 1873 as the moment when Congress enacted the federal law punishing dissemination of advertising and sales of "obscene, lewd or lascivious," "immoral," or "indecent" publications through the mail. The law also made it a misdemeanor for anyone to sell, give away, or possess an "obscene book, pamphlet, picture, drawing, or advertisement" across state borders.[100] If the critical time relevant to a constitutional challenge to potential restrictions on abortion is 1868, when the Fourteenth Amendment was enacted, the turning point in legal treatment of contraception required several more years to take place.[101]

The federal law was named for Anthony Comstock, head of the New York Society for the Suppression of Vice, who waged a campaign against distribution and sale through the mail of "obscene, lewd or lascivious," "immoral," or "indecent" publications.[102] The Comstock Law of 1873 included no definition of obscenity. Congress authorized Comstock to serve as a special agent for the U.S. Postal Service, and in that role, he treated the law as covering writings and materials related to contraception and abortion and medical information, including information about how to prevent pregnancy.[103] As part of a "social purity" campaign, Comstock pressed for suppression of information and materials related to contraception as obscenity and inducements to immorality.[104] In response, the subject of contraception disappeared from medical books, but low birth rates persisted among white families.[105] Some states became even more restrictive than the federal government in this field.[106]

Yet before such enforcement of the Comstock Law, the distribution of and public education about birth control was common in the United States.[107] Actually, before such laws were enacted starting in 1873, distributing information about contraception was not unlawful.[108] In the late nineteenth century, a movement for "voluntary motherhood" represented convergence across women's groups seeking the vote for women, moral reform movements for temperance and social purity, and "free love" anarchists.[109] Notable individuals in the early twentieth century engaged in active advocacy and spurred a social movement that ultimately led to the repeal of restrictions on contraceptive information and material in most states and then to *Griswold v. Connecticut*.[110] Starting in 1911, Margaret Sanger drew on her training as a nurse as she wrote articles and gave speeches about health and sex, and soon focused on birth control.[111] Prosecuted and convicted on two counts of obscenity for sharing birth control information in a pamphlet, she continued to challenge legal restrictions, coined the term "birth control," created what became the Planned Parenthood organization, and succeeded in judicial interpretation permitting physicians to prescribe birth control despite prior interpretations of the Comstock Act.[112] Contemporary critics correctly identify and criticize Sanger's association with eugenics and racist ideas, but alongside these disturbing features of her work, she sought to empower women of every race and background to take control over reproduction and use contraception to manage their families and to avoid the risks of dying during childbirth or an abortion.[113]

Information about contraception circulated in the nineteenth and twentieth centuries as it had even before the founding of the nation. Besides oral traditions, a book published in 1684 in England and in 1685 in Boston—with twenty-seven editions over the next 150 years—provided a guide to human reproduction, assisting couples, midwives, and others.[114] It was precisely during those pre–Civil War decades that the size of American families declined, so historians suggest that birth control knowledge and usage spread.[115] Pamphlets and books spread across the country with information about reproduction and avoiding pregnancies.[116] American couples and individuals in the Civil War era used the same methods known for centuries throughout the early modern world to prevent pregnancy: abstinence, *coitus interruptus* (withdrawal), the rhythm method (timing intercourse to avoid peaks in the woman's ovulation cycle), and devices, including vaginal suppositories or pessaries (to physically block the cervix), syringes combined with acidic solutions for douching, antiseptic spermicides, and condoms made of animal intestines or, by the mid-nineteenth century, rubber.[117] Governmental respect for people's private homes and practical limitations on surveillance made contraceptive use an unlikely target of regulation.[118] A 1919 journal article reported only one state (Connecticut) then banned contraception, though others may have sought to deter it.[119]

None of this actual history, however, is likely to matter in litigation challenging future contraception restrictions, given how the *Dobbs* majority selected particular historical moments of the late nineteenth century and ignored both prior and subsequent practice. Following this same selective use of historical moments in the late nineteenth century, the Court could reverse the contraception precedents and explain away the majority's effort to distinguish contraception by noting that the issue simply had not been posed in *Dobbs* precisely as Justice Thomas suggested.[120]

After *Dobbs,* How Could the Court Reaffirm the Contraception Precedents?

To reaffirm *Griswold* and its progeny, it is always possible for the Court to change course again. But if the Court's majority cares about the appearance of consistency, that could be difficult. Assuming that a majority maintains the "history" and "traditions" test as used in *Dobbs*, it could once again be selective about what history to use and look only at the period after 1873.

In order to uphold the contraception precedents, the Court would need to apply the test by focusing on the pervasive legality of contraception in 1868, when the Fourteenth Amendment was ratified, and accordingly find "history" and "tradition" sufficient to find access to contraception "deeply rooted" and a basis for an unenumerated right. Doing so would expose, however, the oddity of relying on "history" and "tradition" that was altered shortly thereafter with the Comstock Act.

Alternatively, the Court could double-down on the asserted differences between abortion and contraception and uphold the contraception precedents essentially because they do not involve abortion. But then the Court would have to address the meaning of "potential life," the very phrase it used to distinguish abortion and contraception and acknowledge the details of the stages of reproduction continuously involving "potential life." And to uphold contraception as a right the Court would have to pick a point in the reproductive process when potential life begins, even though that choice will inevitably trigger debates in terms of science, religious beliefs, and community practices. If the chosen point is implantation of a fertilized egg in the uterus, some will object and stress that the prior moment of fertilization is the critical moment; after all, that is when the unique genetic structure of a "potential life" takes hold. If the moment selected is fertilization, how would the Court deal with the fact that widely used contraceptive techniques, such as Plan B and intrauterine devices, operate both shortly after fertilization and to prevent fertilization?[121]

Leaving the states to decide to permit such techniques would offend those who view any postfertilization method as interfering unlawfully with "potential life," while letting states forbid such contraceptive measures would mean bringing government in before pregnancy begins. And the selection of a point when contraception is permitted would elicit objections from those who oppose any prevention of conception by stressing that "potential life" is already present in the egg and sperm.[122] Many anti-abortion activists claim that methods of contraception like birth control pills and the IUD are "abortifacient" because they destroy potential life.[123]

Or, as a third avenue for affirming *Griswold*, *Eisenstadt*, and *Carey*, the Court might try to uphold the contraception precedents by finding that the weight of those precedents operates differently than the abortion precedents. (Doing so would put the Court in the position of turning its newly announced "history" and "tradition" test as a binding precedent, unlike the Court's own treatment of precedent in the plurality opinion in *Planned Parenthood v. Casey*.)[124] Justices might apply the five factors examined by the *Dobbs* majority in weighing deference to stare decisis and decide to affirm the precedents recognizing the right to contraceptive choice. Coming out differently would be challenging, though, due to the first factor, "the nature of the Court's error" in the precedents. The *Dobbs* majority focused on the "pro- found moral and social importance" of abortion;[125] coming out differently in the case of contraception simply replays the debates over what is "potential life." The *Dobbs* majority also treated *Roe* as erroneous because it "usurp[ed] the people's authority" by "find[ing] in the Constitution principles or values that cannot fairly be read into that document."[126] This objection applies with equal force to the unenumerated right to contraception that is used to reject measures enacted by legislatures elected and reelected by the people.

On the second *Dobbs* factor for stare decisis—the quality of the precedent's reasoning—the Court could point to lack of support in text, history, and precedent in assessing the "quality of the reasoning" in the contraception precedents, just as the majority found these elements wanting in *Roe*. The case of contraception would not give rise to an elaborate critique of the "vi- ability" line used in *Roe*, though the Court could well challenge the slide from "marital couple" to "individual." Justice William J. Brennan reasoned in *Eisenstadt*, "If the right of privacy means anything, it is the right of the individual, married or single, to be free from unwarranted governmental intrusion into matters so fundamentally affecting a person as the decision whether to bear or beget a child."[127] The phrase "if the right of privacy means anything" does not exactly demonstrate a reason to depart from the regard for "the right to marital privacy" deployed in *Griswold*. And if the implicit ra- tionale is one of equal protection—that single individuals should be accorded the same protections of the law as married individuals—that would cast doubt on all the other laws that treat married and single people differently. A further defect in reasoning arises in extending the contraception right to single individuals if the contraception right lacks a basis for married couples, as opponents of the entire substantive due process doctrine maintain.

Perhaps, though, the Court could find a meaningful difference between the deference due to the contraception and abortion precedents on the third factor, workability. There is, at least to date, no "long list of Circuit conflicts," as in the lower courts' debates over the meaning of *Casey*'s "undue burden test."[128] And although an academic can debate the precise line between per- missible and unconstitutional restrictions on contraception, so far that has not generated litigation, as the distinctions among abortion restrictions had.

With the fourth factor, the Court traced to the abortion cases undesirable "effect[s] on other areas of law." What would be such undesirable effects in the case of the contraception precedents? The chief effect that could generate concern for the Court would be extension to abortion and same-sex intimacy and marriage. Having overturned *Roe*, the Court might say it has cabined features of *Griswold* that it finds undesirable, although that would leave *Lawrence v. Texas* and *Obergefell v. Hodges* vulnerable to reversal. Those who support and those who oppose legal protections for same-sex intimacy would face uncertainty and incentives to pursue law reforms and litigation. It remains difficult and unknown how the Court would conclude the impact on other doctrines due to recognition of rights to intimacy and marriage regardless of sexual orientation.

The final consideration about deference to precedent by the *Dobbs* majority directly bears on the situation of contraception in a way that could strengthen deference to *Griswold* but would probably involve modifying the treatment of reliance by *Dobbs*. There, the Court set aside traditional reliance interests in the context of abortion because "getting an abortion is generally an unplanned activity" while "reproductive planning could take virtually immediate account of any sudden restoration of state authority to ban abortions."[129] Because contraception is available, people are not unduly disadvantaged by restrictions on abortion and not affected in ways that alter how people plan and organize their lives, reasoned the *Dobbs* Court. Or perhaps, for the Court's majority, contraception requires sufficient advance planning—though some contraception steps can take place moments before sexual activity, and some a day later. This notion of unplanned versus planned activity as key to a reliance interest was new in *Dobbs*. The Court treated counting on the possibility of an abortion as not the kind of thinking in advance that should qualify as a reliance interest deserving respect. The Court would have some complex steps to explain why it would respect, for reliance purposes, people using a condom minutes before intercourse or turning to Plan B during the following day. (If the Court were in future years to overturn the contraception precedents, it would make this reasoning in *Dobbs* operate like a "bait and switch.")

Distinguishing the contraception and abortion precedents in terms of reliance interest might not work if reason and logic matter. The *Dobbs* majority noted and rejected as not the kind of reliance interest deserving respect an interest recognized in *Casey*: "the ability of women to participate equally in the economic and social life of the Nation."[130] That interest, dubbed "intangible" by the Court, is precisely how individuals rely on the right to contraception.[131] Taking the five factors together, it would not be impossible, yet also not easy, for a Court following *Dobbs* to assess stare decisis differently for the contraception precedents compared with the abortion precedents. Of course, even that would assume that the Court would defer to the test articulated for respecting precedent by the *Dobbs* majority, a test that the dissent emphasizes departs from prior treatment of stare decisis in both statement and practice.[132] Indeed, because the Court's new "history and tradition" test rejects both methods and results of the Court's prior substantive due process decisions, affirming *Griswold* would undermine the reasoning in *Dobbs*.

What of the Quality of "Legal Reasoning"?

The *Dobbs* majority seems to have crafted a test for determining when the Constitution protects an unenumerated right that lacks both an honest treatment of prior cases and logical reasoning. It embraces an originalist approach to constitutional interpretation contrary to the framers' own insistence on evolving interpretations.[133] It enshrines for legal protection "potential life" despite no text in the Constitution supporting that idea. The majority relies on the Court's 1997 decision in *Washington v. Glucksberg* and acknowledges that not all rights protected by the Constitution are explicitly stated in it.[134] The Court in *Glucksberg* rejected a challenge to a statutory prohibition on assisted suicide.[135] While it acknowledged a long line of judicial decisions recognizing fundamental constitutional rights, the Court reasoned that no constitutionally based right to die nor to determine the circumstances of one's death exists in the traditions of the nation and instead considerations of such a right belong in the democratic process.[136] In his opinion concurring in the judgment in *Glucksberg*, Justice David Souter reviewed a list of Supreme Court decisions spanning the entire history of the nation, in which the Supreme Court relied on the Constitution in rejecting legal restrictions while working to balance the liberty of individuals and demands of organized society.[137]

The *Dobbs* majority pegs judicial interpretation to specific moments in time rather than full views of either legal traditions or American history.[138] Picking historical moments and selecting dicta from prior opinions, the Court does not acknowledge, much less discuss the traditions that informed two centuries of American jurists and the European and English lawyers and judges whose work informed them.[139] In its selectivity and assertions of historical roots, this methodology ironically resembles the misleading claims that the "substantive due process" doctrine itself continuously protected decisions about family formation, dissolution, and reproduction.[140] The *Griswold* Court may have exaggerated continuous protection for such intimate decisions—drawing as it did on two cases from the 1920s—but it nonetheless connected its analyses to undisputed regard for marriage and family among the Constitution's framers.

Moreover, as emphasized by the dissent, the Court's time-machine approach to legal analysis puts aside how the legal rights of women have changed from the time of the enactment of both the Constitution and the Fourteenth Amendment: "Those responsible for the original Constitution, including the Fourteenth Amendment, did not perceive women as equals, and did not recognize women's rights. When the majority says that we must read our foundational charter as viewed at the time of ratification (except that we may also check it against the Dark Ages), it consigns women to second-class citizenship."[141] The *Dobbs* majority has a problem of inconsistency if it acknowledges women's equality in future Fourteenth Amendment treatment of contraception and a problem of current public acceptance if it does not support women's equal citizenship.

What Happens to the Perceived Legitimacy of the Court?

Although some rejoice over the *Dobbs* decision, its reversal of *Roe* has brought anger, sadness, and worry for others, and even concern about division among those ostensibly agreeing with the result.[142] For many, the Court's reversal of *Roe* has occasioned a surge of questions about the legitimacy of the Supreme Court's reasoning and decisions.[143] These questions concern not only the result in *Dobbs* but also the majority's apparent appetite for reversing other precedents, its use of a procedure to reach decisions without briefing or published opinions, and the growing assertions of power over legislative, administrative, and social matters at both state and federal levels.[144] Such concerns may be overblown or misplaced, assert some commentators and justices.[145] In contrast, the dissent in *Dobbs* bluntly stated the concern that the Court's decision reflects simply a change in membership, not the predicates for decisions that have mattered in the past.[146] If legal decisions reflect the identities of the judges in a newly created majority more than the methods of legal reasoning, legitimacy concerns follow.[147]

Respect and trust for any social institution can be strained amid political and religious divisions. Another division particularly affecting the

Supreme Court contrasts public opinion and views among legal experts.[148] Judicial legitimacy, as Richard Fallon has explicated, could refer to the respect and deference of the public regarding court decisions or to moral soundness or to justification in terms of established legal methodologies and commitments.[149] Clashes with public opinion are salient especially after the abortion decision, although before the Court's decision in *Dobbs* public opinion about the Court mirrored the nearly equal division in the country of views about gun control, immigration restrictions, and public funding of religious schools.[150] This division may also be based on moral views, especially around abortion.[151] Notable as well is the dismay expressed by legal experts about the disregard for logic, transparency, doctrine, and precedent by the Court in *Dobbs*.

Legitimacy of the Supreme Court's decisions has occupied scholars of constitutional democracies for decades.[152] Especially during periods when the Court's decisions repeatedly diverge from public opinion, the Court's processes and very legitimacy become topics for political debate and protest. At the turn of the twentieth century, when the Court rejected legislation protecting conditions, wages, and hours for workers and other Progressive-era legislation, its decision in *Lochner v. New York* triggered long-lasting debates over not only those policies but also the role of courts compared with legislatures in the regulation of the economy and the status of economic and moral theories in judicial thinking.[153] When the Supreme Court struck down key elements of the New Deal legislation adopted in the wake of the Great Depression, the clash between the Court and public desires for action produced a crisis that led to rumored "Court-packing"—enlargement of the Court's membership to enable new appointments by President Franklin Delano Roosevelt as well as the leak of a speech suggesting he would defy an adverse decision by the Court.[154] Scholars continue to debate whether that crisis resolved because members of the Court changed their views in response to the public debate.[155] Researchers report that the Court generally is in line with public opinion, and when it is not, public backlash can fuel changes in both political and legal domains.[156]

What if the clash between public opinion and Supreme Court trends persists? It is in the design of the Constitution that voters' views about the Court can influence presidential and Senate elections, and over time, new administrations nominate different justices.[157] This design builds in a lag, awaiting new elections, and public opinion can change. Dysfunction in the political process, itself a product in no small part of Supreme Court decisions, can allow small groups to attain great influence in no small part as parties search for large financial sources to use in campaigns.[158] The result may oust established positions and leadership of a political party, as Mary Ziegler indicates in her study of abortion and the Republican Party.[159] The reversal of *Roe* also exposes the outsized influence of an advocacy group, the Federalist Society, and individuals, such as its leader, Leonard Leo.[160] A related feature is "dark money" from anonymous donors influencing judicial selection to achieve results serving the donors' interests.[161] Such influences may increase questions about the legitimacy of not only the Supreme Court but also of the American political process.

Perhaps some combination of judicial attentiveness to public opinion and appointments to the Court over time will prevent judicial rejection of the contraception precedents. Public opinion favors legality of contraception even more than abortion.[162] This will not escape the awareness of the justices and political candidates.

And for Those Who Can Become Pregnant and Those Who Care about Them

Current research shows that women's access to birth control is a top driver of women's increased economic success and also one of the largest influences in transforming businesses.[163] Being able to plan childbearing allows women to pursue education, jobs, and economic security.[164] It also protects women from the risks of pregnancy and childbearing, some of which are life-threatening.[165]

Birth control techniques can actually address women's health issues far beyond preventing conception. Barrier methods, such as a condom, protect against sexually transmitted diseases.[166] The birth control pill, with regular use, assists with the timing and scale of menstrual bleeding; reduces cramps, mood swings, weight gain, and anemia associated with periods; relieves painful symptoms of endometriosis (a condition in which the lining grows outside rather than inside of the uterus); and can prevent ovarian cysts, fibroids, and polycystic ovarian syndrome.[167] Its use also can reduce the risk of some cancers and have other health benefits.[168]

The doubt cast on the durability of the contraceptive precedents will spur more legislative and other governmental action to restrict access. Such efforts have already started.[169] Emergency contraception—which can involve an

IUD or medication (such as Plan B and ella)—can be effective and, according to medical professionals, does not involve aborting a pregnancy because it is effective only before a pregnancy is started.[170] These medications delay ovulation (the process in which mature eggs leave the fallopian tube).[171] Emergency contraception thickens cervical mucus in ways that interfere with the mobility of sperm and hence make the sperm less likely to fertilize the egg.[172] Emergency contraception may prevent implantation of a fertilized egg.[173] Such methods are commonly used; research indicates that three in ten women of reproductive age have used emergency contraception, and the number of women who have used it has been steadily increasing.[174]

Nonetheless, reflecting factual confusion and misinformation as well as contrasting religious beliefs and misleading labeling as "abortifacients" or abortive contraception, some states have prohibited the purchase of emergency contraception.[175] The effects of this confusion are already being felt. Universities in Idaho are warning their employees that providing emergency contraception in most situations (excluding rape) puts them at risk of imprisonment.[176] Other states may put legal restrictions on prescriptions of emergency contraception, such as requiring in-person meetings and requiring prescription by physicians.[177]

The bans on emergency contraceptives are particularly concerning in today's age of digital data collection. Information about sales and purchases of contraception can be used by prosecutors in those states to assist with criminal prosecutions. Relevant data collected can include location information pinpointing where purchasers and providers of emergency contraception are located, electronic search history detailing who investigated ways to acquire emergency contraception, period-tracking devices, purchase histories of those who acquired emergency contraception, and pharmacy rewards program data that tracks purchases along with personally identifying information.[178]

None of this material is governed by the privacy requirements attached to medical records, and the data are in the hands of private actors, including pharmacies and digital platform companies, which can decide how to shield from or share with law enforcement bodies the geolocation and other data. For example, Google indicated it would automatically delete the location data of individuals visiting abortion clinics, but according to some reports the data are still being collected, perhaps in response to government pressure.[179] How will tech companies respond to requests from law enforcement? How will they moderate information and disinformation related to

contraception? The Biden administration has responded with efforts to ensure access to contraception and reproductive healthcare, but a different federal administration could take a different stance.[180] For people who could
become pregnant and who might want or need access to contraception in
many parts of the United States, the world has already changed.

What Will Unravel Next?

When Adrienne Sloane created *The Unraveling*, juxtaposing a copy of the
U.S. Constitution and textile U.S. flag, unwound day-by-day, President
Trump was in office violating separation of powers to bypass Congress
in paying for a wall on the U.S.-Mexico border and in bombing Syria,
blocking social media platform users from his announcements after they
criticized him, undermining federal inspectors general, and calling his political opponents "human scum" and journalists "enem[ies] of the people."[181]
Created before Trump's involvement in the January 6 insurrection, efforts to
intimidate election officials and block certification of the election, and the
"big lie" denying the results of the 2020 election, the artwork also predated
Trump's appointees to the Supreme Court overturning *Roe v. Wade*. Sloane
explained to an interviewer, "I'm seeing the flag as a symbol of what's happening governmentally. . . . What I'm doing here is really a representation of
how the underpinnings of our democracy are being ripped out from under
us."[182] Sadly, the artwork has become only more relevant and haunting, as
not only reproductive rights but also respect for precedent and reason unravel through the actions of the Supreme Court. With more unraveling still
to come, it is not clear how to begin reweaving rights, law, and respect for
others. The work must start with honest witnessing of what is happening.

Closing Dialogue

Lee C. Bollinger and Geoffrey R. Stone

Bollinger: Let's pick up where we left off with the opening dialogue, namely with the large and difficult question about the framework for, or the theory of, constitutional interpretation. I think it's fair to say that *Dobbs*[1] puts us in a new constitutional world that is the antithesis of the era of the Warren Court. *Roe v. Wade*,[2] in many respects, was the end (one might say the culmination) of that era, and *Dobbs* is the beginning of the new one. We do not yet know what the *Dobbs* universe will look like, but some of the elements are already clear and the sensibilities manifest. State efforts to remediate the ongoing legacy of racial discrimination (whether in affirmative action policies in higher education, or with respect to voting, or elsewhere) are in jeopardy, as are attempts to control and reduce the distorting and dangerous effects of money in the political system. Freedom of religion will have a higher value than separation of church and state. And the powers of the federal government will be narrowed in favor of states' rights. One never knows where the currents of constitutional debate will flow over the course of a generation, but, given the majority opinion in *Dobbs* seemingly relishing the opportunity to declare *Roe* an illegitimate constitutional decision,[3] it would seem naïve to think that the spirit of the Warren Court, which more or less carried constitutional jurisprudence forward into this new century, will continue to do so in the next few decades.

And the shock of that reality seems to me to pervade nearly all of the essays in this volume. In other words, it is not just the brazen overturning of a constitutional right to an abortion after a half-century that is disturbing, but also, and even more so, the evident attitude of hostility, even mockery, toward the *Roe* Court. It is not too much to say of the *Dobbs* opinion that it reflects a breach of judicial norms of respect, which is what foreshadows a much more contrarian Court still to come (despite the oft-noted efforts of the majority to say its *Dobbs* rationale doesn't mean what it logically requires).

Stone: Following up on your point, it's worth noting that, from 1973 to the present, among the eleven Republican-appointed justices not on the Court when *Dobbs* was decided, nine supported the fundamental decision in *Roe* (Harry Blackmun, Warren Burger, Lewis Powell, Potter Stewart, William Brennan, John Paul Stevens, Anthony Kennedy, Sandra Day O'Connor, and David Souter), and only two Republican-appointed justices (William Rehnquist and Antonin Scalia) opposed that decision. On the current Court, though, in *Dobbs*, Clarence Thomas, Samuel Alito, Neil Gorsuch, Brett Kavanaugh, and Amy Coney Barrett all voted to overrule *Roe* outright.[4] That is the product not of a principled approach to law but of aggressive and illegitimate politics intentionally determining the makeup of the Supreme Court with a specific goal in mind. That isn't to say that reasonable people can't disagree with *Roe*, but it is to say that in a system based on stare decisis, it is clear that *Dobbs* was the product not of judicial integrity but of the aggressively partisan distortion of our judicial process.

What, though, of the future? Well, barring a wholly unlikely shift in the makeup of the Court, hundreds of thousands of women—mostly poor and minority—will once again be subjected each year to the nightmare world of illegal abortions. That is not a step forward in our nation's history.

Bollinger: With that said, I have nothing more to add.

Notes

Opening Dialogue

1. ETERNALLY VIGILANT: FREE SPEECH IN THE MODERN ERA (Lee C. Bollinger & Geoffrey R. Stone eds., Chicago: University of Chicago Press, 2002).
2. THE FREE SPEECH CENTURY (Lee C. Bollinger & Geoffrey R. Stone eds., New York: Oxford University Press, 2019).
3. U.S. CONST. amend. I.
4. NATIONAL SECURITY, LEAKS & FREEDOM OF THE PRESS: THE PENTAGON PAPERS FIFTY YEARS ON (Lee C. Bollinger & Geoffrey R. Stone eds., New York: Oxford University Press, 2021).
5. SOCIAL MEDIA, FREEDOM OF SPEECH AND THE FUTURE OF OUR DEMOCRACY (Lee C. Bollinger & Geoffrey R. Stone eds., New York: Oxford University Press, 2022).
6. A LEGACY OF DISCRIMINATION: THE ESSENTIAL CONSTITUTIONALITY OF AFFIRMATIVE ACTION (Lee C. Bollinger & Geoffrey R. Stone eds., New York: Oxford University Press, 2023).
7. Roe v. Wade, 410 U.S. 113 (1973).
8. Dobbs v. Jackson Women's Health Org., 142 S. Ct. 2228 (2022).
9. GEOFFREY R. STONE, SEX AND THE CONSTITUTION: SEX, RELIGION, AND LAW FROM AMERICA'S ORIGINS TO THE TWENTY-FIRST CENTURY (New York: Liveright Publishing Co., 2017).
10. Miller v. California, 413 U.S. 15 (1973); Paris Adult Theatre I v. Slaton, 413 U.S. 49 (1973).
11. *Roe*, 410 U.S. at 116–67.
12. *Id.*
13. *Id.* at 152–55.
14. U.S. CONST. amend. IX.
15. Meyer v. Nebraska, 262 U.S. 390, 399–401 (1923); Pierce v. Soc'y of the Sisters of the Holy Names of Jesus & Mary, 268 U.S. 510, 534–35 (1925); Griswold v. Connecticut, 381 U.S. 479, 483–86 (1965).
16. Bradwell v. Illinois, 83 U.S. 130, 139 (1872).
17. *Id.* at 141 (Bradley, J., concurring).
18. Minor v. Happersett, 88 U.S. 162, 177–78 (1873).
19. Goesaert v. Cleary, 335 U.S. 464, 466 (1948).
20. Reed v. Reed, 404 U.S. 71, 76–77 (1971).
21. Frontiero v. Richardson, 411 U.S. 677, 679–81 (1973).
22. *Id.* at 678–91.
23. *Id.* at 691–92 (Powell, J., dissenting).

24. U.S. Const. amend. I.

25. U.S. Const. amend. IX.

26. Letter from Thomas Jefferson to James Madison, Founders Online (Dec. 20, 1787), https://founders.archives.gov/documents/Madison/01-10-02-0210.

27. Letter from James Madison to Thomas Jefferson, Founders Online (Oct. 17, 1788), https://founders.archives.gov/documents/Madison/01-11-02-0218.

28. Letter from Thomas Jefferson to James Madison, Founders Online (Mar. 15, 1789), https://founders.archives.gov/documents/Jefferson/01-14-02-0410.

29. James Madison, *Amendments to the Constitution*, Founders Online (June 8, 1789), https://founders.archives.gov/documents/Madison/01-12-02-0126.

Chapter 1

1. *See* Griswold v. Connecticut, 381 U.S. 479, 499–502 (1965) (Harlan, J., concurring); Poe v. Ullman, 367 U.S. 497, 539–55 (1961) (Douglas, J., dissenting).

2. This is clear from his dissenting opinion in Griswold v. Connecticut, 381 U.S. at 507–27, discussed later.

3. *See* Ruth Bader Ginsburg, *Some Thoughts on Autonomy and Equality in Relation to* Roe v. Wade, 63 N.C. L. Rev. 375 (1985).

4. John Hart Ely, *The Wages of Crying Wolf: A Comment on* Roe v. Wade, 82 Yale L.J. 920 (1973).

5. For a summary offered by a conservative critic of *Roe*, *see* Timothy P. Carney, *Honest Pro-Choicers Admit* Roe v. Wade *Was a Horrible Decision*, Wash. Exa'r (Jan. 22, 2011), https://www.washingtonexaminer.com/honest-pro-choicers-admit-roe-v-wade-was-a-horrible-decision.

6. Dobbs v. Jackson Women's Health Org., 142 S. Ct. 2228 (2022).

7. *See, e.g.,* Mary Ziegler, Dollars for Life: The Anti-Abortion Movement and the Fall of the Republican Establishment (New Haven: Yale Univ. Press, 2022).

8. Ginsburg, *supra* note 3, at 385–86.

9. *See, e.g.,* Linda Greenhouse and Reva B. Siegel, *Before (and After)* Roe v. Wade: *New Questions About Backlash*, 120 Yale L.J. 2028, 2071–87 (2011).

10. Ely, *supra* note 4, 82 Yale L.J. at 935–36.

11. *Id.* at 947.

12. Alexander Bickel, The Least Dangerous Branch 3 (New Haven: Yale Univ. Press, 2d ed. 1986).

13. United States v. Carolene Products Corp., 304 U.S. 144, 152–53 n.4 (1938). The footnote said, in part (citations omitted):

> [L]egislation which restricts those political processes which can ordinarily be expected to bring about repeal of undesirable legislation [may] be subjected to more exacting judicial scrutiny . . . than are most other types of legislation. . . . [S]imilar considerations enter into the review of statutes directed at particular religious or national or racial minorities . . . [and] prejudice against discrete and insular minorities may be a special condition, which tends seriously to curtail

the operation of those political processes ordinarily to be relied upon to protect minorities, and which may call for a correspondingly more searching judicial inquiry.

14. Lochner v. New York, 198 U.S. 45 (1905).

15. West Coast Hotel Co. v. Parrish, 300 U.S. 379, 391 (1937).

16. Bowers v. Hardwick, 478 U.S. 186 (1986).

17. Lawrence v. Texas, 539 U.S. 558 (2003).

18. *Bowers*, 478 U.S. at 194–95.

19. Ginsburg, *supra* note 8, at 382–83.

20. *See* Kenneth Karst, *Foreword: Equal Citizenship under the Fourteenth Amendment*, 91 HARV. L. REV. 1, 53–59 (1977).

21. *See* Ely, *supra* note 4, at 932–35.

22. Hoyt v. Florida, 368 U.S. 57, 62 (1961).

23. Reed v. Reed, 404 U.S. 71 (1971).

24. *See* Craig v. Boren, 429 U.S. 190 (1976).

25. *See* Planned Parenthood v. Casey, 505 U. S. 833, 852, 856 (1992) (plurality opinion).

26. Roe v. Wade, 410 U.S. 113, 164 (1973); *see also id.* at 163 ("[F]or the period of pregnancy prior to [the end of the first trimester,] the attending physician, in consultation with his patient, is free to determine, without regulation by the State, that, in his medical judgment, the patient's pregnancy should be terminated.").

27. Dobbs v. Jackson Women's Health Org., 142 S. Ct. 2228, 2246–47 (2022) (citing Geduldig v. Aiello, 417 U.S. 484 (1974)).

28. Geduldig, 417 U.S. at 496 n.20.

29. *Geduldig* was, perhaps, not a case on which the *Dobbs* Court should have relied so heavily. Congress abrogated the Court's parallel interpretation of the sex discrimination provision of Title VII of the Civil Rights Act of 1964, the principal federal employment discrimination statute. *Compare* General Elec. Co. v. Gilbert, 429 U.S. 125 (1976), *with* The Pregnancy Discrimination Act of 1978, 2000e(k). Four justices have called for *Geduldig* to be overruled. *See* Coleman v. Maryland Court of Appeals, 566 U.S. 30, 54–57 (2012) (Ginsburg, J., dissenting, joined by Breyer, Sotomayor, and Kagan, JJ.). And, of course, a central theme of the *Dobbs* opinion is that precedents are not sacrosanct, especially when, like *Geduldig* and *Roe* (according to *Dobbs's* portrayal of it), they are not well reasoned and have been repeatedly and credibly criticized.

30. *See, e.g.*, United States v. Virginia, 518 U.S. 515 (1996), *and* Califano v. Goldfarb, 430 U.S. 199 (1977).

31. For an argument to this effect, *see* David A. Strauss, *Abortion, Toleration, and Moral Uncertainty*, 1992 SUP. CT. REV. 1 (1992).

32. For example, *compare* South Carolina v. Katzenbach, 383 U.S. 301 (1966), *with* Shelby County v. Holder, 570 U.S. 2 (2013); *compare* Heart of Atlanta Motel v. United States, 379 U.S. 241 (1964), and Katzenbach v. McClung, 379 U.S. 294 (1964), *with* United States v. Morrison, 529 U.S. 598 (2000), *and* Lopez v. United States, 514 U.S. 549 (1995); *compare* Katzenbach v. Morgan 384 U.S. 641 (1966), *with* City of Boerne v. Flores, 521 U.S. 507 (1997).

33. Obergefell v. Hodges, 135 S. Ct. 2584, 2611, 2615 (2015) (Roberts, C.J., dissenting).

34. *Id.* at 2625.
35. *See Constitutional Amendments and Major Civil Rights Acts of Congress Referenced in Black Americans in Congress*, U.S. HOUSE OF REPRESENTATIVES HISTORY, ART & ARCHIVES, https://history.house.gov/Exhibitions-and-Publications/BAIC/Historical-Data/Constitutional-Amendments-and-Legislation/ (last visited Dec. 21, 2022).
36. *See* Nat'l Fed'n of Indep. Bus. v. Sebelius, 567 U.S. 519 (2012).
37. Griswold v. Connecticut, 381 U.S. 479, 514–15 (1965) (Black, J., dissenting).
38. Roe v. Wade, 410 U.S. 113, 128, 152 (1973).
39. *Id.* at 500 (quoting Palko v. Connecticut, 302 U.S. 319, 325 (1937)).
40. *See, e.g.,* Obergefell v. Hodges, 135 S. Ct. at 2597–98, *and* Washington v. Glucksberg, 521 U.S. 702, 720 (1997).
41. Dobbs v. Jackson Women's Health Org., 142 S. Ct. 2228, 2300–04 (2022) (Thomas, J., concurring).
42. *Id.* at 2242 (quoting Washington v. Glucksberg, 521 U.S. 702, 721 (1997)).
43. *Id.* at 2301 (Thomas, J., concurring).
44. *Id.* at 2258.
45. *See, e.g., id.* at 2277–78 ("[T]o ensure that our decision is not misunderstood or mischaracterized, we emphasize that our decision concerns the constitutional right to abortion and no other right. Nothing in this opinion should be understood to cast doubt on precedents that do not concern abortion.").
46. *Id.* at 2257–58 (citations omitted).
47. Griswold v. Connecticut, 381 U.S. 479, 501 (1965) (Harlan, J., concurring) (citations omitted).
48. Lawrence v. Texas, 539 U.S. 558, 578 (2003).
49. *Dobbs,* 142 S. Ct. at 2317 (Breyer, J., Sotomayor, J., and Kagan, J., dissenting) (citations omitted).

Chapter 2

1. Dobbs v. Jackson Women's Health Org., 142 S. Ct. 2228 (2022).
2. Roe v. Wade, 410 U.S. 113 (1973).
3. *See* Melissa Murray, *Race-ing* Roe: *Reproductive Justice, Racial Justice, and the Battle for* Roe v. Wade, 134 HARV. L. REV. 2025, 2042–49 (2021); Douglas NeJaime & Reva Siegel, *Answering the* Lochner *Objection: Substantive Due Process and the Role of Courts in a Democracy,* 96 N.Y.U. L. REV. 1902, 1922–29 (2021).
4. *See* LINDA GREENHOUSE & REVA B. SIEGEL, BEFORE ROE V. WADE: VOICES THAT SHAPED THE ABORTION DEBATE BEFORE THE SUPREME COURT'S RULING 207–10 (New Haven: Yale Law School, 2d ed. 2012), https://documents.law.yale.edu/sites/default/files/beforeroe2nded_1.pdf (discussing 1972 Gallup poll showing 57% of respondents supported the idea that "abortion should be a decision made by a woman and her physician"). Polling conducted in the immediate aftermath of *Roe* showed continuing popular support for abortion rights. William Ray Arney & William H. Trescher, *Trends in Attitudes Toward Abortion, 1972–1975,* 8 FAM. PLAN. PERSPS. 117,

117–18 (1976). In June 2022, after the draft opinion leaked, 58% of Americans told Gallup they opposed overturning *Roe*, and 63% told Gallup that overturning *Roe* and allowing each state to establish its own abortion policies would be a "bad thing." Megan Brenan, *Steady 58% of Americans Do Not Want* Roe v. Wade *Overturned*, GALLUP (June 2, 2022), https://news.gallup.com/poll/393275/steady-americans-not-roe-wade-overturned.aspx. After the Court handed down *Dobbs*, 57% of those polled told Pew they disapproved of the ruling, including 43% who strongly disapproved. *Majority of Public Disapproves of Supreme Court's Decision to Overturn Roe v. Wade*, PEW RSCH. CTR. (July 6, 2022), https://www.pewresearch.org/politics/2022/07/06/majority-of-public-disapproves-of-supreme-courts-decision-to-overturn-roe-v-wade. Sixty-two percent said abortion should be legal in all or most cases. *Id.*

5. *Roe* was engulfed in politics the decision itself did not cause. Republicans used *Roe* to realign conservative Catholics who had long voted with the Democratic Party. *See* GREENHOUSE & SIEGEL, *supra* note 4, 263–318.

6. Planned Parenthood v. Casey, 505 U.S. 833 (1992).

7. *See* Reva B. Siegel, *Memory Games: Dobbs's Originalism as Anti-Democratic Living Constitutionalism—and Some Pathways for Resistance*, 101 TEX. L. REV. 1176 (2023).

8. Dobbs v. Jackson Women's Health Org., 142 S. Ct. 2228, 2245 (2022) (citing two amicus briefs focused on recent developments in sex-based equal protection law). In *Dobbs*, Justice Alito asserted that equal protection was not an independent ground for abortion rights even though he knew there was no equal protection claim in the case. (Judge Carlton Reeves pointed out that the plaintiffs had amended their complaint to drop their equal protection challenge to Mississippi's statute. Jackson Women's Health Org. v. Currier, 349 F. Supp. 3d 536, 539 (S.D. Miss. 2018)).

9. *Casey*'s account of a woman's constitutionally protected liberty to make decisions about bearing children is deeply informed by the Court's sex-equality jurisprudence, in its restatement of the liberty interest, its discussion of reliance and stare decisis, and its applications of undue burden to strike a spousal notice requirement. Planned Parenthood v. Casey, 505 U.S. 833, 852, 856, 895–98 (1992). Justice Blackmun made a direct appeal to the Equal Protection Clause. *See id.* at 928 & n.4 (Blackmun, J., concurring in part) (quoted *infra* text at note 77).

10. Justice Blackmun and Justice Ginsburg have each addressed this question. *See Casey*, 505 U.S. at 928 & n.4 (Blackmun, J., concurring in part); Gonzales v. Carhart, 550 U.S. 124, 171, 185 (2007) (Ginsburg, J., dissenting).

11. *See, e.g.*, Kate Zernike, *Medical Impact of* Roe *Reversal Goes Well Beyond Abortion Clinics, Doctors Say*, N.Y. TIMES (Sept. 10, 2022), https://www.nytimes.com/2022/09/10/us/abortion-bans-medical-care-women-html; *see also infra* notes 49–54 and accompanying text.

12. *See supra* note 9.

13. Frontiero v. Richardson, 411 U.S. 677, 685 (1973) (plurality opinion) (quoting Bradwell v. State, 16 Wall. 130, 83 U. S. 141 (1873) (Bradley, J., concurring)).

14. Griswold v. Connecticut, 381 U.S. 479 (1965).

15. *See* Cary Franklin, *The New Class Blindness*, 128 YALE L.J. 2, 23–24 (2018).

16. *See* Reva B. Siegel, Roe's *Roots: The Women's Rights Claims That Engendered* Roe, 90 B.U. L. Rev. 1875, 1897 (2010) (quoting Roe v. Wade, 410 U.S. 113, 162–66 (1973)).

17. *See* NeJaime & Siegel, *supra* note 3, at 1924 ("In 1968, only six women were federal judges and only twelve women served in Congress.") (citation omitted); Catherine J. Lanctot, *Women Law Professors: The First Century (1896–1996)*, 65 Vill. L. Rev. 933, 957 (2020) ("As of 1965, only about thirty women had ever served as full-time tenure-track law professors.") (citation omitted).

18. *See* Siegel, *supra* note 16, at 1889–92; NeJaime & Siegel, *supra* note 3, at 1928–29.

19. *See* Linda Greenhouse, Becoming Justice Blackmun: Harry Blackmun's Supreme Court Journey 98–99 (New York: Times Books, 2005); Nancy Stearns, *Commentary,* Roe v. Wade: *Our Struggle Continues,* 4 Berkeley Women's L.J. 2–5 (1988–90).

20. *See* Greenhouse, *supra* note 19, at 96–101.

21. Frontiero v. Richardson, 411 U.S. 677, 684 (1973).

22. Reva Siegel, *Reasoning from the Body: A Historical Perspective on Abortion Regulation and Questions of Equal Protection*, 44 Stan. L. Rev. 261, 267 (1992) [hereinafter Siegel, *Reasoning from the Body*]; *see also* Reva B. Siegel, *The Pregnant Citizen, from Suffrage to the Present*, Geo. L.J. 19th Amend. Special Ed. 167, 189 (2020) [hereinafter Siegel, *The Pregnant Citizen*]; *id.* at 189 n.127 ("According to the logic of physiological naturalism, because reproductive differences are objective, real, and categorically distinguish the sexes, (1) judgments about pregnancy are free of stereotypes and constitutionally suspect assumptions about social roles and (2) laws imposing unique burdens on one sex are reasonable.").

23. Siegel, *The Pregnant Citizen*, *supra* note 22, at 189 n.127.

24. Siegel, *Reasoning from the Body*, *supra* note 22, at 333.

25. Siegel, *The Pregnant Citizen*, *supra* note 22, at 191–99 (discussing understandings of the feminist litigators and the justices of the Burger Court in pregnancy cases of the 1970s).

26. Pregnancy Discrimination Act of 1978, 42 U.S.C. § 2000e(k).

27. United States v. Virginia, 518 U.S. 515 (1996).

28. *Id.* at 533; *see also* Cary Franklin, *Biological Warfare: Constitutional Conflict Over "Inherent Differences" Between the Sexes*, 2017 Sup. Ct. Rev. 169.

29. *Virginia*, 518 U.S. at 533 (citations omitted).

30. *Id.* at 534.

31. California Federal Savings & Loan Association v. Guerra, 479 U.S. 272 (1987).

32. *Virginia*, 518 U.S. at 533.

33. Siegel, *Reasoning from the Body*, *supra* note 22.

34. Geduldig v. Aiello, 417 U.S. 484, 496 n.20 (1974) (citations omitted).

35. Nevada Department of Human Resources v. Hibbs, 538 U.S. 721 (2003).

36. *Id.* at 731.

37. *Id.* at 736 (quoting *The Parental and Medical Leave Act of 1986: Joint Hearing Before the Subcomm. on Labor-Management Relations and the Subcomm. on Labor Standards of the H. Comm. on Education and Labor*, 99th Cong., 2d Sess. 33, 100 (1986)).

38. On Blackmun, see GREENHOUSE, *supra* note 19, at 72–101; on Rehnquist, see Reva B. Siegel, *You've Come a Long Way, Baby: Rehnquist's New Approach to Pregnancy Discrimination in* Hibbs, 58 STAN. L. REV. 1871, 1882–83 (2006).

39. *See* Cal. Fed. Savings & Loan Ass'n v. Guerra, 479 U.S. 272 (1987); United Auto. Workers v. Johnson Controls, Inc., 499 U.S. 187 (1991).

40. Dobbs v. Jackson Women's Health Org., 142 S. Ct. 2228, 2245 (2022) (citing Brief for the United States as Amicus Curiae Supporting Respondents, *Dobbs*, 142 S. Ct. 2228 (2022) (No. 19-1392), 2021 WL 4341731, and Brief of Equal Protection Constitutional Law Scholars Serena Mayeri, Melissa Murray, and Reva Siegel as Amici Curiae in Support of Respondents, *Dobbs*, 142 S. Ct. 2228 (2022) (No. 19-1392), 2021 WL 4340072); *see also* Reva B. Siegel, Serena Mayeri, & Melissa Murray, *Equal Protection in* Dobbs *and Beyond: How States Protect Life Inside and Outside of the Abortion Context*, 43 COLUM. J. GENDER & L. 68–69 (2022), https://papers.ssrn.com/sol3/pap ers.cfm?abstract_id=4115569.

41. Justice Alito also attempted to bolster his claim that the Equal Protection Clause supplies no grounds for challenging abortion bans by citing a case about the applicability of a civil rights statute to Operation Rescue protests at an abortion clinic. *See Dobbs*, 142 S. Ct. at 2246 (citing Bray v. Alexandria Women's Health Clinic, 506 U.S. 263, 273–74 (1993)). In *Bray*, Justice Antonin Scalia held that the protesters did not express "invidiously discriminatory animus" against women as a class under 42 U.S.C. § 1985(3), the Ku Klux Klan Act. *Bray*, 506 U.S. at 274. In construing the *mens rea* requirement of § 1985(3), Justice Scalia held that persons who oppose abortion do not (or do not necessarily?) reason from views, beliefs or assumptions about women. He asserted that "opposition to voluntary abortion cannot possibly be considered such an irrational surrogate for opposition to (or paternalism towards) women," and went on to observe, "Whatever one thinks of abortion, it cannot be denied that there are common and respectable reasons for opposing it, other than hatred of, or condescension toward (or indeed any view at all concerning), women as a class." *Id.* at 270.

Justice Alito cited *Bray* to bolster his assertion in *Dobbs* that abortion regulations do not constitute sex-based state action under the Equal Protection Clause. But *Bray* is not an equal protection case. *Bray* was a statutory case about the purposes of private actors protesting at an abortion clinic. The case is concerned about whether "some racial, or perhaps otherwise class-based, invidiously discriminatory animus [lay] behind the" protestors' actions, sufficient to trigger liability under § 1985(3). *Id.* at 268 (alteration in original). *Bray* has nothing to do with state action or the question of whether a law classifies.

42. *Dobbs*, 142 S. Ct. at 2245 (citing Brief for the United States as Amicus Curiae Supporting Respondents, *supra* note 40, and Brief of Equal Protection Constitutional Law Scholars Serena Mayeri, Melissa Murray, and Reva Siegel as Amici Curiae in Support of Respondents, *supra* note 40).

43. *See infra* notes 79–80 and accompanying text.

44. *See State Bans on Abortion Throughout Pregnancy*, GUTTMACHER INST. (Dec. 1, 2022), https://www.guttmacher.org/state-policy/explore/state-policies-later-abortions.

45. *See State Legislation Tracker*, GUTTMACHER INST. (Nov. 15, 2022), https://www.gut tmacher.org/state-policy.

46. *See* Oliver O'Connell, *South Carolina Lawmaker Chokes Up Describing How Teen Almost Lost Uterus Due to Abortion Law He Voted For*, INDEP. (Aug. 17, 2022, 4:50 PM), https://www.independent.co.uk/news/world/ississi/abortion-law-ban-south-carolina-b2146982.html; Caitlin Cruz, *Republicans Are Surprised to See the Abortion Bans They Fought for in Effect*, JEZEBEL (Aug. 10, 2022), https://jezebel.com/republic ans-are-surprised-to-see-the-abortion-bans-they-1849396750; Oriana Gonzalez, *How States Enforce Anti-Abortion Laws*, AXIOS (June 24, 2022), https://www.axios. com/2022/06/08/abortion-bans-penalty-fines-prison-us-states.

47. For example, Wisconsin's 1849 ban, as amended in 1858, was revived by *Dobbs*. This threat became even more pressing after the Sheboygan County district attorney announced he would prosecute abortion cases under the 1849 ban. *Sheboygan County D.A. Advises Law Enforcement He'll Prosecute Abortion Cases*, WBAY (July 1, 2022, 12:33 PM EDT), https://www.wbay.com/2022/07/01/sheboygan-county-da-advises-law-enforcement-hell-prosecute-abortion-cases/.

48. Nadine El-Bawab, *Texas Abortion 'Trigger' Law Allowing Criminal Civil Penalties Set to Go into Effect in August*, ABC NEWS (July 27, 2022), https://abcnews.go.com/ US/ississi-abortion-trigger-law-allowing-criminal-civil-penalties/story?id=87485720; *see also* Blake Ellis & Melanie Hicken, *These Male Politicians Are Pushing for Women Who Receive Abortions to Be Punished with Prison Time*, CNN (Sept. 21, 2022), https://www.cnn.com/2022/09/20/politics/abortion-bans-murder-charges-invs/ index.html; Sabrina Tavernise, *The Effort to Punish Women for Having Abortions; An Extreme Wing of the Anti-Abortion Movement Wants to Criminalize the Procedure as Homicide*, THE DAILY, Aug. 23, 2022, https://www.nytimes.com/2022/08/23/podca sts/the-daily/abortion-abolition-roe-v-wade.html?showTranscript=1.

49. *See* Mark Kelly, *Lawyer Explains What Tennessee's Abortion Ban Means for Doctors*, WKRN (Nov. 3, 2022), https://www.wkrn.com/special-reports/lawyer-explains-what-tennessees-abortion-ban-means-for-doctors; Kavitha Surana, *"We Need to Defend This Law": Inside an Anti-Abortion Meeting with Tennessee's GOP Lawmakers*, PROPUBLICA (Nov. 15, 2022), https://www.propublica.org/article/inside-anti-abort ion-meeting-with-tennessee-republican-lawmakers.

50. *See* Elizabeth Nash, *Focusing on Exceptions Misses the True Harm of Abortion Bans*, GUTTMACHER INST. (Dec. 2022), https://www.guttmacher.org/article/2022/12/focus ing-exceptions-misses-true-harm-abortion-bans? ("Anti-abortion policymakers see exceptions as loopholes and designed them to be difficult if not outright impossible to use even for the few who qualify under their narrow limits.").

51. *See* Dov Fox, *Medical Disobedience*, 136 HARV. L. REV. 1100–1101 (2023), https://ssrn. com/abstract=4152472; Kate Zernike, *What Does "Abortion" Mean? Even the Word Itself Is Up for Debate*, N.Y. TIMES (Oct. 18, 2022), https://www.nytimes.com/2022/10/ 18/us/abortion-roe-debate.html.

52. *See* Pam Belluck, *They Had Miscarriages, and New Abortion Laws Obstructed Treatment*, N.Y. TIMES (July 17, 2022), https://www.nytimes.com/2022/07/17/health/ abortion-miscarriage-treatment.html; Leah Torres, *Doctors in Alabama Already Turn*

Away Miscarrying Patients; This Will Be America's New Normal, SLATE (May 17, 2022, 3:12 PM), https://slate.com/news-and-politics/2022/05/roe-dobbs-abortion-ban-reproductive-medicine-alabama.html.

53. *See* Zernike, *supra* note 11; Carrie Feibel, *Because of Texas Abortion Law, Her Wanted Pregnancy Became a Medical Nightmare*, NPR (July 26, 2022), https://www.npr.org/sections/health-shots/2022/07/26/1111280165/because-of-texas-abortion-law-her-wanted-pregnancy-became-a-medical-nightmare.

54. Roe v. Wade, 410 U.S. 113, 173 (1973).

55. *See* sources cited *supra* notes 52–53.

56. *See* Zernike, *supra* note 51 (reporting on efforts by anti-abortion lawmakers and advocates to redefine "abortion" so that it excludes pregnancy terminations in situations where even they believe terminations are warranted, including cases involving ectopic pregnancies, miscarriages, fetal abnormalities, and pregnant ten-year-olds).

57. Under the intermediate scrutiny standard set forth in *Virginia*, a state must show that its decision to regulate health and life by sex-discriminatory means is substantially related to the achievement of an important governmental end. *Virginia* requires the state to offer an "exceedingly persuasive justification" for its use of any sex-based classification; that is, *Virginia* requires the government to justify its use of sex-based (and coercive) means without relying on "overbroad generalizations about the different talents, capacities, or preferences of males and females." Sex classifications may be used to promote equal opportunity, but sex "classifications may not be used, as they once were . . . to create or perpetuate the legal, social, and economic inferiority of women." United States v. Virginia, 518 U.S. 515, 533–34 (1996).

58. Mississippi's abortion ban explicitly classifies by sex, prohibiting physicians from performing an abortion on "a maternal patient" after fifteen weeks. Gestational Age Act, H.B. 1510 § 1(4), MISS. CODE ANN. § 41-41-191 (West 2018). Kentucky's fifteen-week ban refers to the "maternal patient" and "pregnant woman" throughout. 2022 Ky. H.B. 3 (2022). Oklahoma's ban repeatedly refers to the "pregnant woman." 2022 Okla. Sess. Law Serv. Ch. 11 (S.B. 612) (West 2022).

59. *See* L. B. Finer & M. R. Zolna, *Declines in Unintended Pregnancy in the United States, 2008–11*, 374 NEW ENG. J. MED. 843 (2016); Joerg Dreweke, *New Clarity for the U.S. Abortion Debate: A Steep Drop in Unintended Pregnancy Is Driving Recent Abortion Declines*, GUTTMACHER POL'Y REV. (Mar. 18, 2016), https://www.guttmacher.org/gpr/2016/03/new-clarity-us-abortion-debate-steep-drop-unintended-pregnancy-drivingrecent-abortion.

60. For an illustration of this analysis, *see* Siegel, Mayeri & Murray, *supra* note 40.

61. Isabelle Taft, *Mississippi Remains Deadliest State for Babies, CDC Data Shows*, MISS. TODAY (Sept. 29, 2022), https://mississippitoday.org/2022/09/29/mississippi-remains-deadliest-state-for-babies.

62. *Id.*

63. Asha DuMonthier, Chandra Childers, & Jessica Milli, *The Status of Black Women in the United States*, INST. FOR WOMEN'S POL'Y RSCH. 66 (June 26, 2017), https://iwpr.org/wp-content/uploads/2020/08/The-Status-of-Black-Women-6.26.17.pdf.

64. *See* Angela Grayson, *Op-Ed: Extending Postpartum Medicaid Coverage Is Important to Addressing the Black Maternal Health Crisis*, G93 WPMZ (Oct. 1, 2022), https://g93w mpz.com/2022/10/01/op-ed-extending-postpartum-medicaid-coverage-is-import ant-to-addressing-the-black-maternal-health-crisis.

65. *See* Emily Wagster Pettus, *Mississippi House Leaders Kill Postpartum Medicaid Extension*, AP NEWS (Mar. 9, 2022), https://apnews.com/article/health-mississi ppi-medicaid-c49dcbdc7b356f593485853aee5458c1; Sarah Fowler, *Mississippi Banned Most Abortions to Be the "Safest State" for the Unborn; Meanwhile, One in Three Mississippi Kids Lives in Poverty*, BUS. INSIDER (Nov. 26, 2021), https://www. businessinsider.com/mississippi-defends-abortion-ban-one-in-three-kids-in-pove rty-2021-11.

66. AMERICA'S HEALTH RANKINGS, 2019 HEALTH OF WOMEN AND CHILDREN REPORT 4–7 (2019), https://www.americashealthrankings.org/learn/reports/2019-health-of-women-and-children-report; *see also* UNITED HEALTH FOUND., HEALTH OF WOMEN AND CHILDREN REPORT 8 (2019), https://assets.americashealthrankings.org/app/uploads/executive-highlights-ahr-health-of-women-and-children.pdf   (ranking Mississippi fiftieth in women's and children's health).

67. The Gestational Age Act at issue in *Dobbs* prohibited the performance of abortion past fifteen weeks, "[e]xcept in a medical emergency or in the case of a severe fetal abnormality." MISS. CODE ANN. § 41-41-191 (2018). *Dobbs* sent Mississippi's trigger ban into effect; the state now bans all abortions, except "where necessary for the preservation of the mother's life or where the pregnancy was caused by rape." MISS. CODE ANN. § 41-41-45(2) (2022).

68. For an illustration of this dynamic in Texas, *see* Cary Franklin, Whole Woman's Health v. Hellerstedt *and What It Means to Protect Women*, in REPRODUCTIVE RIGHTS AND JUSTICE STORIES 223 (St. Paul: Foundation Press, Melissa Murray, Kate Shaw, & Reva B. Siegel eds., 2019); for Louisiana, *see* Reva B. Siegel, *Why Restrict Abortion? Expanding the Frame on* June Medical, 2020 SUP. CT. REV. 277, 321–27. *See generally* sources cited *supra* note 70 (sources demonstrating that states with the most restrictive abortion laws tend to rank lowest in social provision and safety-net policies). Some studies suggest that the provision of contraception may be the most effective of these policies. *See, e.g.*, Oberman, *infra* note 71, at 6 ("The single most effective way to help people avoid unwanted pregnancies, thereby deterring abortion, is by increasing contraception rates.").

69. *See* AMERICA'S HEALTH RANKINGS, *supra* note 66, at 5.

70. For sources examining the safety-net policies of so-called pro-life jurisdictions in comparison to other states, *see* Emily Badger, Margot Sanger-Katz, & Claire Cain Miller, *States with Abortion Bans Are Among Least Supportive for Mothers and Children*, N.Y. TIMES (July 28, 2022), https://www.nytimes.com/2022/07/28/upshot/abortion-bans-states-social-services.html; Dylan Scott, *The End of* Roe *Will Mean More Children Living in Poverty*, VOX (June 24, 2022), https://www.vox.com/pol icy-and-politics/23057032/supreme-court-abortion-rights-roe-v-wade-state-aid; Chris J. Stein, *After* Roe, *Are Republicans Willing to Expand the Social Safety Net?*, GUARDIAN (July 5, 2022, 2:00 PM EDT), https://www.theguardian.com/us-news/

2022/jul/05/roe-v-wade-abortion-republicans-social-safety-net;   Lauren   Camera, *States Where Abortion Is Illegal Also Have the Worst Support Systems for Mothers*, U.S. NEWS & WORLD REP. (Aug. 8, 2022), https://www.usnews.com/news/national-news/ articles/2022-08-08/states-where-abortion-is-illegal-also-have-the-worst-support-systems-for-mothers; *and* Rachel Treisman, *States With the Toughest Abortion Laws Have the Weakest Maternal Supports, Data Shows*, NPR (Aug. 18, 2022), https:// www.npr.org/2022/08/18/1111344810/abortion-ban-states-social-safety-net-hea lth-outcomes. *See also* Dobbs v. Jackson Women's Health Org., 142 S. Ct. 2228, 2340 (2022) (Breyer, Sotomayor, & Kagan, JJ., dissenting) ("[A] state-by-state analysis by public health professionals shows that States with the most restrictive abortion policies also continue to invest the least in women's and children's health."). For a re-port on a study of lives saved and lost through policy choices made by red and blue states, *see* Akilah Johnson, *Can Politics Kill You? Research Says the Answer Increasingly Is Yes.*, WASH. POST (Dec. 16, 2022, 6:00 AM EST), https://www.washingtonpost.com/ health/2022/12/16/politics-health-relationship, which observed that "[w]ith abor-tion services no longer legal nationwide, university researchers have estimated that maternal deaths could increase by up to 25 to 30 percent, worsening the nation's ma-ternal mortality and morbidity crisis. [America] . . . is the worst place among high-income countries to give birth." For a wide-ranging policy study demonstrating that "[o]n nearly every measure, people in banned and restrictive states have worse outcomes than their counterparts in supportive states," and that restrictive states "are less likely to enact policies, like paid parental leave, which have been shown to im-prove outcomes for new parents and babies," *see* GENDER EQUITY POLICY INST., THE STATE OF REPRODUCTIVE HEALTH IN THE UNITED STATES 3 (2023), https://thegepi. org/wp-content/uploads/2023/01/GEPI-State-Repro-Health-Report.pdf.

71. Michelle Oberman notes that abortion rates are lower in Europe than in Latin America despite much higher prevalence of criminalization in Latin America and observes that the "single biggest predictor of abortion rates is not the legal status of abortion, but rather, the percentage of pregnancies that occur among those who were not looking to have a baby." Michelle Oberman, *What Will and Won't Happen When Abortion Is Banned*, 9 J.L. & BIOSCIENCES 11 (2022), https://academic.oup.com/jlb/ article/9/1/lsac011/6575467.

72. Caroline Kitchener, *Conservatives Complain Abortion Bans Not Enforced, Want Jail Time for Pill "Trafficking,"* WASH. POST (Dec. 14, 2022), https://www.washingtonpost. com/politics/2022/12/14/abortion-pills-bans-dobbs-roe.

73. *See Prenatal Care*, DEP'T HEALTH & HUM. SERVS. OFF. ON WOMEN'S HEALTH (APR. 1, 2019), https://www.womenshealth.gov/a-z-topics/prenatal-care.

74. Brief of Amici Curiae Economists in Support of Respondents at 23, *Dobbs*, 142 S. Ct. 2228 (2022) (No. 19–1392), 2021 WL 4341729, at *24; *see also* Richard V. Reeves & Joanna Venator, *Sex, Contraception, or Abortion? Explaining Class Gaps in Unintended Childbearing*, BROOKINGS INST. (Feb. 26, 2015), https://www.brookings.edu/resea rch/sex-contraception-or-abortion-explaining-class-gaps-in-unintended-child bearing (finding that access to abortion reduces the disparity between affluent and

low-income women by one-third and access to contraception reduces the same disparity by one-half).

75. *See supra* notes 63–64 and accompanying text.

76. *See* United States v. Virginia, 518 U.S. 515, 533–34 (1996); *see supra* note 57.

77. Planned Parenthood of Se. Pa. v. Casey, 505 U.S. 833, 928 (1992) (Blackmun, J., concurring in part); *see id.* at 928 & n.4 (Blackmun, J., concurring in part).

78. *See* Brief of Equal Protection Constitutional Law Scholars Serena Mayeri, Melissa Murray, & Reva Siegel as Amici Curiae in Support of Respondents, *supra* note 40 (expanding on these arguments).

79. Dobbs v. Jackson Women's Health Org., 142 S. Ct. 2228, 2284 (2022).

80. *Id.* at 2279 ("26 States expressly ask us to overrule *Roe* and *Casey* and to return the issue of abortion to the people and their elected representatives.").

81. *Id.* at 2255 (discussing arguments of brief arguing that abortion bans "were enacted for illegitimate reasons").

82. *Id.* at 2256.

83. Minor v. Happersett, 88 U.S. 162 (1874); *see also* Siegel, *supra* note 7, at 58–59.

84. Bradwell v. Illinois, 83 U.S. 130 (1872). For an account of this portion of the *Dobbs* opinion, see Siegel, *supra* note 7, at 58–59.

85. *See supra* text accompanying notes 21–25.

86. James C. Mohr, Abortion in America: The Origins and Evolution of National Policy, 1800–1900, at 147–170 (New York: Oxford Univ. Press, 1978); *see also Before* Roe: *The Physicians' Crusade*, NPR Throughline (May 19, 2022), https://www.npr.org/2022/05/18/1099795225/before-roe-the-physicians-crusade.

87. *See* Mohr, *supra* note 83, at 33–37 (1978); Leslie J. Reagan, When Abortion Was a Crime: Women, Medicine, and Law in the United States, 1867–1973, at 10–11 (Berkeley: Univ. of California Press, 1997).

88. For examples, *see* Siegel, *Reasoning from the Body, supra* note 22, at 287–92.

89. *See* Siegel, *supra* note 7, at 59–63 (discussing primary and secondary sources).

90. Horatio Robinson Storer, Why Not? A Book for Every Woman 75–76 (Boston: Lee and Shepard, 1866).

91. *Id.* at 36–37.

92. Horatio R. Storer, On Criminal Abortion in America 101 (Philadelphia: J. B. Lippincott & Co., 1860) ("If . . . the community were made to understand and to feel that marriage, where the parties shrink from its highest responsibilities, is nothing less than legalized prostitution, many would shrink from their present public confession of cowardly, selfish and sinful lust."). For more on physicians' use of this term, *see* Siegel, *Reasoning from the Body, supra* note 22, at 308–11.

93. *See* Siegel, *Reasoning from the Body, supra* note 22, at 311–14. At common law, a wife was presumed to consent to sex with her husband when she consented to marriage. For a history of that presumption and nineteenth-century challenges to it, *see* Jill Hasday, *Contest and Consent: A Legal History of Marital Rape*, 88 Calif. L. Rev. 1373 (2000).

94. *See* Siegel, *Reasoning from the Body, supra* note 22, at 307–8; *see also* Tracy A. Thomas, *Misappropriating Women's History in the Law and Politics of Abortion*, 36 SEATTLE U. L. REV. 1, 27–30, 60–63 (2012). Of course, women in other freedom movements of the era sought and advocated for reproductive justice employing different frameworks of appeal. For examples drawn from the antislavery movement and Reconstruction, *see* PEGGY COOPER DAVIS, NEGLECTED STORIES: THE CONSTITUTION AND FAMILY VALUES (New York: Hill and Wang, 1997).

95. D. A. O'Donnell & W. L. Atlee, *Report on Criminal Abortion*, 22 TRANSACTIONS AM. MED. ASS'N 239, 241 (1871).

96. MOHR, *supra* note 86, at 104 (quoting Montrose A. Pallen, *Foeticide, or Criminal Abortion*, 3 MED. ARCHIVES 193, 205 (1869)). For more on the antifeminism of the physicians' campaign, *see* Siegel, *Reasoning from the Body, supra* note 22, at 280–314.

97. *See* Comstock Act ch. 258, 17 Stat. 598, 599 (1873) (repealed 1909) (prohibiting any person from selling or distributing in U.S. mail articles used "for the prevention of conception, or for causing unlawful abortion" or sending information concerning these practices as "obscene"); Siegel, *Reasoning from the Body, supra* note 22, at 314–15 (discussing passage of Comstock Act and state analogues that banned abortifacients and contraceptives, which enabled nonnatalist sex, as obscene); MOHR, *supra* note 86, at 219–21 (describing the passage of such laws in, *inter alia*, Nevada, Michigan, Kansas, Connecticut, and Massachusetts); Carol Flora Brooks, *The Early History of the Anti-Contraceptive Laws in Massachusetts and Connecticut*, 18 AM. Q. 3, 4 (1966); *cf.* JANET FARRELL BRODIE, CONTRACEPTION AND ABORTION IN NINETEENTH-CENTURY AMERICA 253 (Ithaca: Cornell Univ. Press, 1994) ("[T]he campaigns against abortion and contraception . . . shared important similarities in the opponents' motivations, in the imagery and symbolism of their public campaigns, and in the consequences.").

98. HORATIO R. STORER & FRANKLIN FISKE HEARD, CRIMINAL ABORTION: ITS NATURE, ITS EVIDENCE, AND ITS LAW 97 (Boston: Little, Brown, 1868).

99. *Id.* at 98.

100. *Id.* ("[I]f said offender be a married woman, the punishment may be increased at the discretion of the court."); *see generally* MOHR, *supra* note 86, at 225 (describing legislators in the 1870s as revoking the common law immunities of women who sought abortions); REAGAN, *supra* note 87, at 13 (noting that some mid-nineteenth-century abortion bans "included punishment for the women who had abortions"); *id.* at 60 (describing the AMA's shift from "urg[ing] the prosecution of abortionists . . . to recommending prosecution of women").

101. MOHR, *supra* note 86, at 200; *see also id.* at 139 (observing that "so many . . . anti-abortion code revisions" in this period were "directly attributable to the influence of a regular physician with access to the lawmaking process"); *id.* at 200–245 (recounting the achievements of the physicians' campaign with respect to legislation enacted and the alteration of reproductive medicine more generally).

102. *Id.* at 200; *see also* Aaron Tang, *After* Dobbs: *History, Tradition, and the Uncertain Future of a Nationwide Abortion Ban*, 75 STAN. L. REV. 1091 (2023), https://ssrn.com/

abstract=4205139 (showing significant errors in the ways that *Dobbs* characterized and counted nineteenth-century abortion laws).

103. Mary Ziegler, *Some Form of Punishment: Penalizing Women for Abortion*, 26 WM. & MARY BILL OF RTS. J. 735, 740–46 (2018); Clarke Forsythe, *Why States Did Not Prosecute Women for Abortion Before* Roe v. Wade, AMS. UNITED FOR LIFE (Apr. 23, 2010), https://aul.org/2010/04/23/why-the-states-did-not-prosecute-women-for-abortion-before-roe-v-wade (observing that regardless of statutory text, legal actors in this period almost uniformly "determined that states could *not* prosecute women under *any* theory of criminal liability"); Ashley Gorski, Note, *The Author of Her Trouble: Abortion in Nineteenth- and Early Twentieth-Century Judicial Discourses*, 32 HARV. J.L. & GENDER 431, 434 (2009).

104. State v. Carey, 56 A. 632, 636 (Conn. 1904).

105. State v. Pearce, 56 Minn. 226, 230 (1894).

106. Jonathan M. Purver, Annotation, *Woman Upon Whom Abortion Is Committed or Attempted as Accomplice for Purposes of Rule Requiring Corroboration of Accomplice Testimony*, 34 A.L.R. 3d 858 (1970).

107. *See* Siegel, *The Pregnant Citizen*, *supra* note 22, at 170 ("At the founding, the law gave male heads of household authority over women and the ability to represent them in voting and the market; this understanding of women as dependent citizens, defined through family relations to men, continued to shape the law even after women's enfranchisement, despite women's efforts to democratize family structure in order to secure equal citizenship.") (citation omitted).

108. For an illustration of how these different forms of judgment coalesced, *see, e.g.*, 1867 OHIO SENATE J. APP. 233. This Ohio report is often discussed by anti-abortion advocates as monist, as illustrating fetal-protective concern only, when it is plainly dualist, combining arguments about protecting unborn life with arguments for enforcing wives' roles and preserving the ethnic character of the nation. *Compare* John Finnis, *Abortion Is Unconstitutional*, FIRST THINGS (Apr. 2021), https://www.firstthings.com/article/2021/04/abortion-is-unconstitutional *with* Siegel, *supra* note 7, at 60–63 (discussing text of report and the selective ways it is discussed by anti-abortion advocates).

109. Siegel, *Reasoning from the Body*, *supra* note 22, at 321.

110. *Id.*

111. *Id.* at 331 ("[T]oday, as in the past, physiological modes of reasoning about women are invoked to limit principles recognizing woman's commonality with man and equality to him. Indeed, this mode of reasoning about women seems to acquire cultural force as women's claims to equality acquire cultural force.").

112. A Massachusetts court recognized in 1984, "Since at least the fourteenth century, the common law has been that the destruction of a fetus in utero is not a homicide. . . . The rule has been accepted as the established common law in every American jurisdiction that has considered the question." Commonwealth v. Cass, 467 N.E.2d 1324, 1328 (Mass. 1984). *See also* Keeler v. Superior Ct., 2 Cal. 3d 619, 627 (1970) ("By the year 1850 [the common law rule that homicide required live birth] had long been accepted in the United States."); *see generally* Marka B. Fleming, *Feticide*

Laws: Contemporary Legal Applications and Constitutional Inquiries, 29 PACE L. REV. 43, 47 (2008) ("By 1850, the 'born alive' rule was widely adopted in the United States' legal system. Moreover, '[e]very American jurisdiction to consider the issue [of fetal homicide] on the basis of common law, rather than a specific feticide statute, followed some form of the born alive rule until 1984, when the Supreme Judicial Court of Massachusetts extended its vehicular homicide statute to a viable fetus.' ").

113. DAVID DUDLEY FIELD, NEW YORK FIELD CODES 1850–1865, at 112 (Union: The Lawbook Exchange, Ltd., 1998). Field's New York Penal Code was submitted to the legislature in 1865 and enacted in 1881, remaining in effect until its replacement by the New York Penal Law of 1967. *See* Paul H. Robinson & Markus D. Dubber, *The American Model Penal Code: A Brief Overview*, 10 NEW CRIM. L. REV. 319, 322 (2007). Field's approach proved highly influential, directly and derivatively. Field's New York Penal Code was adopted by Dakota in 1865 and California in 1872, which led to its adoption by several western states that followed the California model, including Arizona, Idaho, Montana, Oregon, Utah, and Wyoming. Sanford H. Kadish, *Codifiers of the Criminal Law: Wechsler's Predecessors*, 78 COLUM. L. REV. 1098, 1137–38 (1978). For examples of state codes listing abortion under "Crimes against Public Decency and Good Morals," *see* THE PENAL CODE OF CALIFORNIA: ENACTED IN 1872; AS AMENDED IN 1889, at 124–25 (San Francisco: Bancroft-Whitney Co., Robert Desty, ed., 1889) (classifying abortion with abandonment and neglect of children, bigamy, incest, lotteries, gaming, and indecent exposure); NEV. REV. STAT. ANN. § 201.120 (1911) (classifying abortion with bigamy, incest, obscenity, and open or gross lewdness); *and* Oklahoma, OKLA. STAT. ANN. tit. 21, § 861 (1910) (classifying abortion with adultery, bigamy, incest, and desertion of wife or child).

114. *See* DAVID ALAN SKLANSKY, A PATTERN OF VIOLENCE: HOW THE LAW CLASSIFIES CRIMES AND WHAT IT MEANS FOR JUSTICE 53 (Cambridge: Harvard Univ. Press, 2021).

115. MODEL PENAL CODE § 230.3 (AM. L. INST. 1962).

116. MODEL PENAL CODE § 207.11, Comments (AM. L. INST., Tentative Draft No. 9, 1959).

117. *Id.*

118. MODEL PENAL CODE §§ 230.1–230.5 (AM. L. INST. 1962).

119. *America's Abortion Quandary*, PEW RES. CTR (May 6, 2022), https://www.pewresea rch.org/religion/2022/05/06/americas-abortion-quandary.

120. *See, e.g.*, Brief of Texas Right to Life as Amicus Curiae in Support of the Petitioners at 19, *Dobbs*, 142 S. Ct. 2228 (2022) (No. 19-1392), 2021 WL 4264275, at *20 ("Women can 'control their reproductive lives'; without access to abortion; they can do so by refraining from sexual intercourse.").

121. *See, e.g.*, Opinion No. 22-12, Applicability of the Human Life Protection Act to the Disposal of Human Embryos That Have Not Been Transferred to a Woman's Uterus (Tenn. A.G. 2022), https://www.tn.gov/content/dam/tn/attorneygeneral/docume nts/ops/2022/op22-12.pdf (explaining that "the disposal of a human embryo that has not been transferred to a woman's uterus [is not] punishable as 'criminal abortion' under Tennessee's Human Life Protection Act," which "only applies when a

woman has a living unborn child within her body"); W. Va. Code § 16-2R-4(a)(5) (2022) (providing that "[a]bortion does not include . . . [i]n vitro fertilization"); Ind. Code. § 16-34-1-0.5 (2022) (providing that Article 34, which covers "Abortion," "does not apply to in vitro fertilization"); *cf.* Okla. Stat. tit. 63, § 63-1-730(A)(1) (2022) (defining "abortion" as "the use or prescription of any instrument, medicine, drug, or any other substance or device intentionally to *terminate the pregnancy of a female known to be pregnant* with an intention other than to increase the probability of a live birth" (emphasis added)).

122. *See* Zernike, *supra* note 51 and text accompanying note 56.

123. *See* Siegel, *supra* note 68, at 296–309. For discussion of the woman's health protective laws at issue in *Whole Woman's Health v. Hellerstedt*, 136 S. Ct. 2202 (2016) and *June Medical Services L.L.C. v. Russo*, 140 S.Ct. 2103 (2020), *see* Siegel, *supra* note 68. For the law in *Dobbs*, see Miss. H.B. 1510 § 1(2)(b)(i) (finding that banning abortion protects fetal life); *id.* § 1(2)(b)(ii)–(v) (finding that banning abortion protects women); Brief of Equal Protection Constitutional Law Scholars Serena Mayeri, Melissa Murray, & Reva Siegel as Amici Curiae in Support of Respondents, *supra* note 40, at 12–13. The reasoning Mississippi offers for banning abortion after fifteen weeks—to protect the health of the "maternal patient" (Miss. H.B. 1510 § 1(2)(b) (ii), (iii))—echoes the sex-role assumptions of the nineteenth-century anti-abortion campaign: a pregnant woman's "health" will suffer if she deviates from her natural maternal role.

124. *See* Siegel, *supra* note 68, at 215–16.

125. *See supra* note 123.

126. Justice Kavanaugh uses the word "neutral" no fewer than eight times, and "neutrality" five times, throughout his concurring opinion. *See Dobbs*, 142 S. Ct. at 2304–11 (Kavanaugh, J., concurring).

127. *See* sources cited *supra* note 48.

128. *See supra* notes 123–124 and accompanying text; *see also* Reva B. Siegel, *The Right's Reasons: Constitutional Conflict and the Spread of Woman-Protective Antiabortion Argument*, 57 Duke L. J. 1641 (2008).

129. Sharon Bernstein, *Louisiana Lawmakers Withdraw Bill Declaring Abortion Homicide*, Reuters, May 13, 2022 (5:22 AM EDT), https://www.reuters.com/world/us/louisiana-lawmakers-withdraw-bill-declaring-abortion-homicide-2022-05-13/.

130. Morgan v. State, 256 S.W. 433, 434 (Tenn. 1923) ("It is usually said that the umbilical cord must have been severed, and an independent circulation established."); Keeler v. Superior Ct., 2 Cal. 3d 619, 625–26 (1970) ("[A]n infant could not be the subject of homicide at common law unless it had been born alive."); Mamta K. Shah, Note, *Inconsistencies in the Legal Status of an Unborn Child: Recognition of a Fetus' as Potential Life*, 29 Hofstra L. Rev. 931, 937 (2001); Louis Westerfield, *The Born Alive Doctrine: A Legal Anachronism*, 2 S.U. L. Rev. 149, 149–51 (1975).

131. *See State Homicide Laws That Recognize Unborn Victims*, Nat'l Right to Life (Apr. 2, 2018), https://www.ncsl.org/research/health/fetal-homicide-state-laws.aspx; *State Laws on Fetal Homicide and Penalty-Enhancement for Crimes Against Pregnant*

Women, NAT'L CONF. STATE LEGISLATURES (May 1, 2018), https://www.nrlc.org/
federal/unbornvictims/statehomicidelaws092302.

132. Josh Hammer, *The Case for the Unconstitutionality of Abortion*, NEWSWEEK (July
30, 2021), https://www.newsweek.com/case-unconstitutionality-abortion-opin
ion-1614532; Robert P. George, *Public Reason and Political Conflict: Abortion and
Homosexuality*, 106 YALE L.J. 2475, 2475 (1997) ("From the pro-life point of view,
any regime of law (including one whose pedigree is impeccably democratic) that
deprives unborn human beings of their right to legal protection against homicide is gravely unjust.") (citation omitted); *id.* at 2489 (arguing that "like all other
human beings, [[h]uman beings in the embryonic and fetal stages] are entitled to the
(equal) protection of the laws against homicide") (citations omitted). *See also* Sherif
Girgis, *Update: Why the Equal-Protection Case for Abortion Rights Rises or Falls with
Roe's Rationale*, 17 HARV. J. L. & PUB. POL'Y PER CURIAM 1, 6–7 (2022) (discussing
equality arguments in terms of protection of homicide laws).

133. Brief of Amici Curiae Scholars of Jurisprudence John M. Finnis and Robert
P. George, *Dobbs*, 142 S. Ct. 2228 (2022) (No. 19-1392), 2021 WL 3374325 at 2.

134. *Id.* at 32 (citations omitted).

135. *See* Christine Rousselle, *March for Life Announces 2022 Theme of "Equality,"*
CATHOLIC NEWS AGENCY (Oct. 27, 2021), https://www.catholicnewsagency.com/
news/249416/march-for-life-announces-2022-theme-of-equality (reporting the
president of the March for Life before *Dobbs* as saying, "There's little agreement on
the definition of what 'equality' is and who it applies to. We want to expand this rigorous debate about equality to unborn children.").

136. United States v. Virginia, 518 U.S. at 534.

137. *See supra* notes 51–56 and accompanying text.

138. MICH. CONST. art. I, § 28; VT. CONST. chap. 1, art. 22.

139. 10. S.C.A. 10, 2021 S., Reg. Sess. (Cal. 2021).

140. Mitch Smith & Katie Glueck, *Kansas Votes to Preserve Abortion Rights Protections in
Its Constitution*, N.Y. TIMES (Aug. 2, 2022), https://www.nytimes.com/2022/08/02/
us/kansas-abortion-rights-vote.html; Bruce Schreiner & Beth Campbell, *Kentucky
Voters Reject Constitutional Amendment on Abortion*, PBS NEWSHOUR (Nov. 9,
2022), https://www.pbs.org/newshour/politics/kentucky-voters-reject-constitutio
nal-amendment-on-abortion.

141. *See supra* note 129 and accompanying text.

142. Ashley Kirzinger et al., *How the Supreme Court's* Dobbs *Decision Played in 2022
Midterm Election: KFF/AP VoteCast Analysis*, KFF (Nov. 11, 2022), https://www.kff.
org/other/poll-finding/2022-midterm-election-kff-ap-votecast-analysis.

143. *See supra* text at note 82. Professor Sherif Girgis argues that imposing abortion bans
does not discriminate on the basis of sex. Following Justice Alito, he appeals to physiological naturalism: "The costs of pregnancy . . . cannot be transferred"; "[W]e
would have to find something similarly morally egregious that prolife states would
tolerate to benefit men, if we're to establish a double standard." Girgis, *supra* note
132, at 6. The failure of anti-abortion states to provide support for those whom they
would coerce into carrying pregnancies evinces no sex-role stereotyping, he argues.

To demonstrate sex-role stereotyping in an abortion ban, opponents would have "to identify situations where prolife states not only fail to effectively promote life but do something as callous toward life as withdrawing the protection of homicide laws from a class of innocents." *Id.* at 7 (emphasis omitted); *see also* Girgis, *supra* note 132 at 8 (arguing that "[t]he fact that prolife or antiabortion views are barely more common among men than women, and are quite common among women, is a serious point against suspect-judgment arguments").

144. Elizabeth S. Anderson & Richard H. Pildes, *Expressive Theories of Law: A General Restatement*, 148 U. Pa. L. Rev. 1503, 1525 (2000).

145. *Id.*

146. *Id.*

147. *See supra* note 120.

148. Perry Undem, *Assessing the State of Public Opinion Toward Women, Gender, Equality—and Abortion: Analysis From National PerryUndem Survey* 10 (Nov. 2022), https://perryundem.com/wp-content/uploads/2022/12/PerryUndem-Landscape-of-Views-toward-Women-Gender-and-Abortion-F.pdf. Anti-abortion advocates often cite the fact that substantial numbers of women support abortion bans as evidence that these bans do not enforce gender-based stereotypes or judgments. *See, e.g., supra* note 143. But this polling shows why that's a weak argument: the greatest predictor of anti-abortion sentiment is belief in traditional sex stereotypes, and anti-abortion women hold these beliefs in high numbers. *See id.* at 9, 60.

149. *Id.* at 51. For a recent study analyzing the role of gender attitudes in anti-abortion activism, *see* Eric Swank, *The Gender Conservatism of Pro-life Activists*, 42 J. Women, Pol & Pol'y 124 (2021).

150. For a discussion of this crisis, *see* Khiara M. Bridges, *The Supreme Court, 2021 Term—Foreword: Race in the Roberts Court*, 136 Harv. L. Rev. 23, 46, 48–49 n.127 (2022).

151. *See* Geoff Pender, *"We're 50th by a Mile": Experts Tell Lawmakers Where Mississippi Stands with Health of Mothers, Children*, Miss. Today (Sept. 27, 2022), https://missi ssippitoday.org/2022/09/27/where-mississippi-stands-with-health-of-mothers-children.

152. Charles L. Black, Jr., *The Lawfulness of the Segregation Decisions*, 69 Yale L.J. 421, 424 (1959–60).

Chapter 3

1. *See* John Hart Ely, *The Wages of Crying Wolf: A Comment on Roe v. Wade*, 82 Yale L.J. 920, 949 (1973) ("[T]he Court . . . is under an obligation to trace its premises to the charter from which it derives its authority. A neutral and durable principle may be a thing of beauty and a joy forever. But if it lacks connection with any value the Constitution marks as special, it is not a constitutional principle and the Court has no business imposing it.").

2. *See* Planned Parenthood of Southeastern Pa. v. Casey, 505 U.S. 833, 979–81 (1992) (Scalia, J., concurring in the judgment in part and dissenting in part).

3. *See* Dobbs v. Jackson Women's Health Organization, 142 S. Ct. 2228, 2241 (2022) ("*Roe* was 'not constitutional law' at all and gave 'almost no sense of an obligation to try to be.'") (quoting Ely, *supra* note 1, at 947).

4. Griswold v. Connecticut, 381 U.S. 479 (1965).

5. Loving v. Virginia, 388 U.S. 1 (1967).

6. Brown v. Board of Education, 347 U.S. 483 (1954).

7. *See* Ely, *supra* note 1, at 929–30.

8. *See* Ely, *supra* note 1, at 927–28.

9. *See* JOHN HART ELY, DEMOCRACY AND DISTRUST (Cambridge: Harvard Univ. Press, 1980).

10. *See* Planned Parenthood of Southeastern Pa. v. Casey, 505 U.S. 833, 980 (1992) (Scalia, J., concurring in the judgment in part and dissenting in part).

11. Dobbs v. Jackson Women's Health Organization, 142 S. Ct. 2228, 2242 (2022) (quoting Washington v. Glucksberg, 521 U.S. 702, 721 (1997) (internal quotation marks omitted)).

12. *See, e.g.*, Moore v. City of East Cleveland, 431 U.S. 494, 503 (1977); Washington v. Glucksberg, 521 U.S. 702, 720–21 (1997).

13. *See* David A. Strauss, *Common Law Constitutional Interpretation*, 63 U. CHI. L. REV. 877 (1996).

14. *See* 18 U.S.C. §§ 1461–62 (1964); *see also* Pub. L. 91-662, § 3(1) (1971) (repealing the contraceptive-related provisions of the laws).

15. PEGGY PASCOE, WHAT COMES NATURALLY: MISCEGENATION LAW AND THE MAKING OF RACE IN AMERICA 2, 6 (New York: Oxford Univ. Press, 2009); RANDALL KENNEDY, INTERRACIAL INTIMACIES: SEX, MARRIAGE, IDENTITY, AND ADOPTION 219 (New York: Pantheon, 2003) ("*Every* state whose black population reached or exceeded 5 percent of the total eventually drafted and enacted antimiscegenation laws."); NANCY F. COTT, PUBLIC VOWS: A HISTORY OF MARRIAGE AND THE NATION 43 (Cambridge: Harvard Univ. Press, 2000) ("Community sentiment against whites marrying African Americans was not limited to the south in the antebellum decades. Intermarriage bans and penalties echoed each other from state to state, north and south, east and west, together composing an American system.").

16. *See Dobbs*, 142 S. Ct. 2228, 2280–81; *but see id.* at 2301 (Thomas, J., concurring) (calling for the reconsideration of *Griswold* while remaining silent on *Loving*).

17. *See* Richard A. Epstein, *In Defense of the Contract at Will*, 51 U. CHI. L. REV. 947 (1984).

18. *See* Cass R. Sunstein, Lochner's *Legacy*, 87 COLUM. L. REV. 873 (1987).

19. *See* ADRIAN VERMEULE, LAW AND THE LIMITS OF REASON 75–77 (New York: Oxford Univ. Press, 2009) (explaining the "Burkean paradox").

20. *See* John Harrison, *Substantive Due Process and Constitutional Text*, 83 VA. L. REV. 493 (1997).

21. *See* Ely, *supra* note 9, at 43–72.

22. Dobbs v. Jackson Women's Health Organization, 142 S. Ct. 2228, 2242 (2022) (quoting Washington v. Glucksberg, 521 U.S. 702, 721 (1997) (internal quotation marks omitted)).

23. Roe v. Wade, 410 U.S. 113, 125 (1973).

24. *Id.* at 156–59.

25. *See* Akhil Reed Amar, *Intratextualism*, 112 HARV. L. REV. 747, 773–75 (1999).

26. For an excellent discussion of the justiciability problems in *Roe*, *see* Richard A. Epstein, *Substantive Due Process by Any Other Name: The Abortion Cases*, 1973 SUP. CT. REV. 159, 160–67 (1973). *See also* DAVID P. CURRIE, THE CONSTITUTION IN THE SUPREME COURT 1888–1986 465–66 (Chicago: Univ. of Chicago Press, 1990) (criticizing the mootness analysis in the *Roe* opinion).

27. *See, e.g.*, Sosna v. Iowa, 419 U.S. 393, 401–2 (1975) (holding that a certified class may have a live controversy with the defendants even if the class representative's claims have become moot).

28. *Roe*, 410 U.S. at 125.

29. *See* Sosna, 419 U.S. at 401–2; U.S. Parole Commission v. Geraghty, 445 U.S. 388, 397 (1980) ("[M]ootness of the named plaintiff's individual claim *after* a class has been duly certified does not render the action moot.").

30. *See* Epstein, *supra* note 26 at 164 ("[T]he Court was mistaken when it held that the mootness requirement must be relaxed in the abortion cases because they present questions which will constantly arise yet be incapable of review. The criminal trial of the doctor would provide him with every opportunity to challenge the abortion statute on its face.").

31. *See* Singleton v. Wulff, 428 U.S. 106, 118 (1976) (plurality opinion) ("[I]t generally is appropriate to allow a physician to assert the rights of women patients as against governmental interference with the abortion decision, and we decline to restrict our holding to that effect in *Doe* to its purely criminal context."); DeFunis v. Odegaard, 416 U.S. 312, 318–19 (1974) (a claim does not "evade review" when someone else remains capable of litigating the claim to its conclusion).

32. *See Roe*, 410 U.S. at 125 ("If that termination makes a case moot, pregnancy litigation seldom will survive much beyond the trial stage, and appellate review will be effectively denied.").

33. *See Roe*, 410 U.S. at 164–65.

34. *See* Ely, *supra* note 1.

35. Loving v. Virginia, 388 U.S. 1, 12 (1967).

36. Planned Parenthood of Southeastern Pa. v. Casey, 505 U.S. 833, 847–48 (1992) (plurality opinion).

37. *Casey*, 505 U.S. at 847–49; *id.* at 858.

38. *See* Dobbs v. Jackson Women's Health Organization, 142 S. Ct. 2228, 2326 (2022) (Breyer, Sotomayor, and Kagan, JJ., dissenting) ("The Fourteenth Amendment's ratifiers did not think it gave black and white people a right to marry each other. To the contrary, contemporaneous practice deemed that act quite as unprotected as abortion.").

39. *See Casey*, 505 U.S. at 980 (Scalia, J., concurring in the judgment in part and dissenting in part) ("The Court's suggestion that adherence to tradition would require us to uphold laws against interracial marriage is entirely wrong. Any tradition in that case was contradicted *by a text*—an Equal Protection Clause that explicitly establishes racial equality as a constitutional value.") (citations omitted).

40. *Id.*

41. *See* Jonathan F. Mitchell, *Textualism and the Fourteenth Amendment*, 69 STAN. L. REV. 1237, 1275–90 (2017).

42. *See, e.g.*, John Harrison, *Reconstructing the Privileges or Immunities Clause*, 101 YALE L.J. 1385, 1390 (1992) ("[T]he Equal Protection Clause's function . . . rests on a piece of textual sleight of hand familiar from *Yick Wo v. Hopkins*, which asserts that 'the equal protection of the laws' means 'the protection of equal laws.' If that seems obvious to us, it is because custom has run a groove in our minds. By shifting the focus from 'protection' to 'laws,' the *Yick Wo* maneuver draws our attention away from the embarrassing fact that the subject of the Equal Protection Clause is protection. That word suggests either the administration of the laws or, if it is about their content, laws that protect as opposed to laws that do other things. In order for the clause to be a requirement of equality in everything the states do, [the] word 'protection' must simply drop out, so that the text would read 'equal laws' rather than 'the equal protection of the laws.'").

43. *See Dobbs*, 142 S. Ct. at 2258 ("What sharply distinguishes the abortion right from the rights recognized in the cases on which *Roe* and *Casey* rely is something that both those decisions acknowledged: Abortion destroys what those decisions call 'potential life' and what the law at issue in this case regards as the life of an 'unborn human being.' None of the other decisions cited by *Roe* and *Casey* involved the critical moral question posed by abortion. They are therefore inapposite. They do not support the right to obtain an abortion, and by the same token, our conclusion that the Constitution does not confer such a right does not undermine them in any way.") (citations omitted); *id.* at 2268 ("[N]one of these decisions [including *Loving*] involved what is distinctive about abortion: its effect on what *Roe* termed 'potential life.'").

44. *Dobbs*, 142 S. Ct. at 2242 (quoting *Glucksberg*, 521 U.S. at 721 (internal quotation marks omitted)); *see also id.* at 2246–47; *id.* at 2253.

45. Griswold v. Connecticut, 381 U.S. 479 (1965).

46. Eisenstadt v. Baird, 405 U.S. 438 (1972).

47. *See* Robert H. Bork, *Neutral Principles and Some First Amendment Problems*, 47 IND. L.J. 1, 7–16 (1971).

48. *See supra* note 14, and accompanying text.

49. *See Dobbs*, 142 S. Ct. at 2258; *id.* at 2268.

50. *See* notes 17–18 and accompanying text.

51. *See, e.g.*, Snyder v. Massachusetts, 291 U.S. 97, 105 (1934) ("The commonwealth of Massachusetts is free to regulate the procedure of its courts in accordance with its own conception of policy and fairness, unless in so doing it offends some principle of justice so rooted in the traditions and conscience of our people as to be ranked as fundamental.").

52. Civil Rights Act of 1866, ch. 31, § 1, 14 Stat. 27, 27.

53. *See, e.g.*, William Blackstone, Commentaries *421 ("Our law considers marriage in no other light than as a civil contract.... [T]he law treats it as it does all other contracts."); Meister v. Moore, 96 U.S. 76, 78 (1877) ("Marriage is everywhere regarded as a civil contract."); Elizabeth S. Scott & Robert E. Scott, *Marriage as Relational Contract*, 84 VA. L. REV. 1225, 1230 (1998) (analyzing contemporary marriage as a "long-term relational contract").

54. Civil Rights Act of 1866, ch. 31, § 1, 14 Stat. 27, 27 (emphasis added).

55. *See* 18 U.S.C. §§ 1461-62 (1964).

56. *See* Pub. L. 91-662, § 3(1) (1971).

57. *See* 42 U.S.C. § 300gg-13(a)(4); 45 C.F.R. § 147.130(a)(1)(iv), 29 C.F.R. § 2590.715–2713(a)(1)(iv), *and* 26 C.F.R. § 54.9815–2713(a)(1)(iv).

58. *See* 42 U.S.C. § 2000d.

59. Brown v. Board of Education, 347 U.S. 483 (1954).

60. *See* David A. Strauss, *Originalism, Precedent, and Candor*, 22 CONST. COMMENT. 299, 304–6 (2005) (describing the challenges that confront efforts to defend *Brown's* holding on textualist or originalist grounds).

61. *See, e.g.*, Equal Employment Opportunity Act of 1972, Pub. L. No. 92-261, 86 Stat. 103 (codified as amended in 42 U.S.C. § 2000e (2015)); Fair Labor Standards Amendments of 1974, Pub. L. No. 93-259, 88 Stat. 55 (codified as amended in scattered sections of 29 U.S.C.); Education Amendments of 1972, Pub. L. No. 92-318, § 901, 86 Stat. 235, 373–74 (codified as amended at 20 U.S.C. §§ 1681–88 (2015)); Pregnancy Discrimination Act of 1978, Pub. L. No. 99-555, sec 1 § 701, 92 Stat. 2076, 2076 (1978) (codified at 42 U.S.C. § 2000e(k)).

62. *See, e.g.*, David A. Strauss, *The Common Law Genius of the Warren Court*, 49 WM. & MARY L. REV. 845, 845 (2007) (defending the Warren Court while acknowledging that its "most important decisions cannot be easily justified on the basis of the text of the Constitution or original understandings").

63. *See, e.g.*, Cass R. Sunstein, *Must Formalism Be Defended Empirically?*, 66 U. CHI. L. REV. 636, 642 n.25 (1999) ("Many people can agree that cost-benefit analysis makes sense, but they may disagree, sharply, over what should count as a cost or a benefit, and how much various things that count should be allowed to count.").

64. *See, e.g.*, ADRIAN VERMEULE, JUDGING UNDER UNCERTAINTY 153–82 (Cambridge: Harvard Univ. Press, 2006) (noting that judges suffer from limited information and bounded rationality, which distort their efforts to assess the consequences of their decisions); Antonin Scalia, *Originalism: The Lesser Evil*, 57 U. CIN. L. REV. 849, 854 (1989) (arguing that the legislature is a "more appropriate expositor of social values" than the judiciary).

65. *See* Vermeule, *supra* note 64 (defending formalistic interpretive methodologies on rule-consequentialist grounds).

66. *See, e.g.*, Amar, *supra* note 25 at 793 (acknowledging the possibility of "chameleon words," which "should sensibly mean different things in different clauses").

67. *See* Planned Parenthood of Southeastern Pa. v. Casey, 505 U.S. 833, 867 (1992) (plurality opinion) (purporting to "call[] the contending sides of a national

controversy to end their national division by accepting a common mandate rooted in the Constitution").

68. *See Casey*, 505 U.S. 833.

69. *See* Ely, *supra* note 9, at 44 ("There is absolutely no assurance that the Supreme Court's life-tenured members (or the other federal judges) will be persons who share your values."); Vermeule, *supra* note 64, at 281 ("There is no general mechanism that can produce only happy endings.").

70. *See, e.g.*, District of Columbia v. Heller, 554 U.S. 570, 576–77 (2008) ("In interpreting this text, we are guided by the principle that '[t]he Constitution was written to be understood by the voters; its words and phrases were used in their normal and ordinary as distinguished from technical meaning.'").

71. *See* TransUnion LLC v. Ramirez, 141 S. Ct. 2190 (2021).

72. *See* Allen v. Cooper, 140 S. Ct. 994 (2020).

73. *See* Seila Law LLC v. Consumer Financial Protection Bureau, 140 S. Ct. 2183 (2020); Free Enterprise Fund v. Public Company Accounting Oversight Board, 561 U. S. 477 (2010).

74. *See* Shelby County v. Holder, 570 U.S. 529 (2013).

75. *See* Ruth Bader Ginsburg, *Some Thoughts on Autonomy and Equality in Relation to* Roe v. Wade, 63 N.C. L. REV. 375 (1985).

Chapter 4

1. Roe v. Wade, 410 U.S. 113 (1973).

2. Dobbs v. Jackson Women's Health Org., 142 S. Ct. 2228 (2022).

3. *Id.* at 2265.

4. *Id.* at 2266.

5. *Id.* at 2270.

6. Planned Parenthood v. Casey, 505 U.S. 833 (1992).

7. Throughout this essay, I refer to the abortion issue as affecting pregnant "women." I do not mean in any way to lessen the importance of this issue to transgender men who can become pregnant and seek abortions. Yet it is overwhelmingly women who become pregnant, and I worry that to not acknowledge that is to fail to recognize the disproportionate impact of prohibiting abortion on women's lives. Therefore, though I speak of women in this essay, I very much mean to include transgender men as well.

8. *Dobbs*, 142 S. Ct. at 2242.

9. John Hart Ely, *The Wages of Crying Wolf: A Comment on* Roe v. Wade, 82 YALE L.J. 920, 947 (1973) (emphasis omitted).

10. *See, e.g.*, J. Harvie Wilkinson III, *Of Guns, Abortions, and the Unraveling Rule of Law*, 95 VA. L. REV. 253, 254 (2009) (critiquing *Roe*'s "absence of a commitment to textualism").

11. Griswold v. Connecticut, 381 U.S. 479, 485 (1965).

12. Eisenstadt v. Baird, 405 U.S. 438, 453 (1972) (emphasis omitted).

13. Pierce v. Soc'y of Sisters, 268 U.S. 510, 531–32, 534–35 (1925); Meyer v. Nebraska, 262 U.S. 390, 400, 403 (1923).

14. Skinner v. Oklahoma, 316 U.S. 535, 541, 543 (1942).

15. Loving v. Virginia, 388 U.S. 1, 12 (1967).

16. Obergefell v. Hodges, 135 S. Ct. 2584, 2589–90, 2598, 2603 (2015).

17. *See, e.g.,* Troxel v. Granville, 530 U.S. 57, 65–66 (2000).

18. Moore v. City of E. Cleveland, 431 U.S. 494, 503–4 (1997).

19. Cruzan v. Dir., Mo. Dep't of Health, 497 U.S. 261, 277–78 (1990).

20. Lawrence v. Texas, 539 U.S. 558, 578–79 (2003).

21. *See, e.g.,* Bradley P. Jacob, Griswold *and the Defense of Traditional Marriage*, 83 N.D. L. Rev. 1199, 1214, 1221 (2007) (arguing against nontextual rights in general and "the 'rights' to have sex outside of marriage, to redefine marriage, to engage in homosexuality, and to abort children" in particular).

22. Cass R. Sunstein, Radicals in Robes: Why Extreme Right-Wing Courts Are Wrong for America 81–82 (New York: Basic Books, 2005).

23. Dobbs v. Jackson Women's Health Org., 142 S. Ct. 2228, 2301 (2022) (Thomas, J., concurring).

24. *Id.* at 2332 (Breyer, Sotomayor, Kagan, JJ., dissenting).

25. *Id.* at 2258.

26. *Id.* at 2278–79.

27. *Id.* at 2280.

28. *Id.* at 2309 (Kavanaugh, J., concurring).

29. Eisenstadt v. Baird, 405 U.S. 438, 453 (1972).

30. Roe v. Wade, 410 U.S. 113, 153 (1973).

31. *Id.*

32. *Id.*

33. *Id.*

34. *Id.*

35. Dobbs v. Jackson Women's Health Org., 142 S. Ct. 2228, 2259 (2022).

36. Planned Parenthood v. Casey, 505 U.S. 833, 843–901 (1992) (plurality opinion of Justices O'Connor, Kennedy, and Souter).

37. *See, e.g.,* Stenberg v. Carhart, 530 U.S. 914 (2000).

38. Roe v. Wade, 410 U.S. 113, 163 (1973).

39. *Casey*, 505 U.S. at 870–71.

40. Laurence H. Tribe, *Foreword: Toward a Model of Roles in the Due Process of Life and Law*, 87 Harv. L. Rev. 1, 11 (1973).

41. *Id.*

42. *See* A. Kurjak, *The Beginning of Human Life and Its Modern Scientific Assessment*, 30 Clinics Perinatology 27, 27 (2003) (discussing the "seemingly endless debate" about when human life begins).

43. Tribe, *supra* note 40, at 19.

44. *Id.*

45. Dobbs v. Jackson Women's Health Org., 142 S. Ct. 2228, 2323 (2022) (Breyer, Sotomayor, Kagan, JJ., dissenting).

46. *See People & Events: Anthony Comstock's "Chastity" Laws,* PBS AMERICAN
EXPERIENCE,   http://www.pbs.org/wgbh/amex/pill/peopleevents/e_comstock.html
[https://perma.cc/JYC7-Y62W] (last visited Dec. 24, 2022) ("In 1872 Comstock set
off for Washington with an anti-obscenity bill, including a ban on contraceptives, that
he had drafted himself. . . . The statute defined contraceptives as obscene and illicit,
making it a federal offense to disseminate birth control through the mail or across
state lines. . . . Soon after the federal law was on the books, twenty-four states enacted
their own versions of Comstock laws to restrict the contraceptive trade on a state
level.").

47. Tribe, *supra* note 40, at 21.

48. Stanford Univ. Med. Ctr., *Which Fertilized Eggs Will Become Healthy Human Fetuses?
Researchers Predict with 93% Accuracy,* SCIENCEDAILY (Oct. 4, 2010), https://
www.sciencedaily.com/releases/2010/10/101003205930.htm   [https://perma.cc/
J64B-3YM5].

49. *Id.*

50. ERWIN CHEMERINSKY, THE CONSERVATIVE ASSAULT ON THE CONSTITUTION 174
(New York: Simon & Schuster, 2010) (internal citations omitted).

51. *See* Paul VI, Humanae Vitae 14–15 (1968) (proclaiming that contraceptives that interfere with the procreative aspect of marital intercourse are "unlawful"); *see also*
Catholic Church, Catechism of the Catholic Church § 2370 (documenting the
church's teaching that methods of contraception other than "[p]eriodic continence"
are "intrinsically evil").

Chapter 5

* My thanks to Lee Bollinger, Linda Greenhouse, Mark Graber, Reva Siegel, and Geof
Stone for their comments on previous drafts.

1. Dobbs v. Jackson Women's Health Org., 142 S. Ct. 2228 (2022).

2. Roe v. Wade, 410 U.S. 113 (1973).

3. JACK M. BALKIN, CONSTITUTIONAL REDEMPTION: POLITICAL FAITH IN AN UNJUST
WORLD 179–82 (Cambridge: Harvard Univ. Press, 2011).

4. Jack M. Balkin & Sanford Levinson, *Understanding the Constitutional Revolution,* 87
VA. L. REV. 1045, 1050 (2001); *cf.* Bruce Ackerman, *Revolution on a Human Scale,* 108
YALE L. J. 2279, 2287–88 (1999) (arguing that constitutional moments must occur
within a decade).

5. Wickard v. Filburn, 317 U.S. 111 (1942).

6. Griswold v. Connecticut, 381 U.S. 479 (1965).

7. Jack M. Balkin & Sanford Levinson, *The Processes of Constitutional Change: From
Partisan Entrenchment to the National Surveillance State,* 75 FORDHAM L. REV.
489 (2006); Jack M. Balkin & Sanford Levinson, *Understanding the Constitutional
Revolution,* 87 VA. L. REV. 1045 (2001). *See also* Howard Gillman, *How Political*

Parties Can Use the Courts to Advance Their Agendas: Federal Courts in the United States, 1875–1891, 96 Am. Pol. Sci. Rev. 511 (2002).

8. *See* David Yalof, The Pursuit of Justices: Presidential Politics and the Selection of Supreme Court Nominees 41–46, 55, 60–61 (Chicago: Univ. of Chicago Press, new ed. 2001).

9. *See* Sheldon Goldman, Picking Federal Judges: Lower Court Selection from Roosevelt Through Reagan 116 (New Haven: Yale Univ. Press, 1997).

10. Jack M. Balkin, The Cycles of Constitutional Time 78 (New York: Oxford Univ. Press, 2020).

11. *See* Kevin J. McMahon, Nixon's Court: His Challenge to Judicial Liberalism and Its Political Consequences 6 (Chicago: Univ. of Chicago Press, 2011) (arguing that Nixon only cared about a handful of key issues when making his Supreme Court appointments and "that politics far more than ideology drove all six of his choices for the Court"); *id.* at 172, 177–79 (noting that Nixon did not regard abortion as an important constitutional issue).

12. Reva B. Siegel, *Memory Games: Dobbs's Originalism as Anti-Democratic Living Constitutionalism—and Some Pathways for Resistance*, 101 Texas L. Rev. 1127 (2023).

13. *See* Dobbs v. Jackson Women's Health Org., 142 S. Ct. 2228, 2310–11 (2022) (Roberts, C.J., concurring in the judgment) (arguing for getting rid of the viability standard in *Roe* and *Casey* and upholding a ban on abortions after fifteen weeks).

14. Bruce Ackerman, We the People Volume 1: Foundations (Cambridge: The Belknap Press of Harvard Univ., 1991); Bruce Ackerman, We the People Volume 2: Transformations (Cambridge: The Belknap Press of Harvard Univ., 1998); Bruce Ackerman, We the People, Volume 3: The Civil Rights Revolution (Cambridge: The Belknap Press of Harvard Univ., 2014).

15. Bruce Ackerman, *The Living Constitution*, 120 Harv. L. Rev. 1737 (2007).

16. Balkin & Levinson, *Understanding the Constitutional Revolution, supra* note 7, at 1073–74.

17. *Id.* at 1067; Balkin & Levinson, *The Processes of Constitutional Change, supra* note 7, at 501.

18. Balkin, Cycles of Constitutional Time, *supra* note 10, at 117; Mark A. Graber, *The Coming Constitutional Yo-Yo? Elite Opinion, Polarization, and the Direction of Judicial Decision Making*, 56 How. L.J. 661 (2013).

19. *Id.* at 687–88.

20. *Id.* at 665–66.

21. Balkin, Cycles of Constitutional Time, *supra* note 10, at 118–19.

22. *Id.* at 121–22.

23. *Id.* at 96, 149; Ian Ayres & Kart Kandula, *How Long Is a Republican-Nominated Majority on the Supreme Court Likely to Persist?*, Balkinization (July 3, 2022), https://balkin.blogspot.com/2022/07/how-long-is-republican-nominated.html.

24. Frank Staheli, *Warren Burger, "2nd Amendment Fraud,"—1991 PBS Hews Hour*, YouTube (Aug. 28, 2016), https://www.youtube.com/watch?v=Eya_k4P-iEo.

25. STEVEN M. TELES, THE RISE OF THE CONSERVATIVE LEGAL MOVEMENT: THE BATTLE FOR CONTROL OF THE LAW (Princeton: Princeton Univ. Press, 2008).

26. Siegel, *Memory Games, supra* note 12.

27. *See* ERIC J. SEGALL, ORIGINALISM AS FAITH 4 (Cambridge: Cambridge Univ. Press, 2018).

28. *See* Dobbs v. Jackson Women's Health Org., 142 S. Ct. 2228, 2300–2301 (2022) (Thomas, J., concurring) (opposing substantive due process and calling for revisiting Supreme Court precedents that use it).

29. *See* AMANDA HOLLIS-BRUSKY, IDEAS WITH CONSEQUENCES: THE FEDERALIST SOCIETY AND THE CONSERVATIVE COUNTERREVOLUTION (New York: Oxford Univ. Press, 2015).

30. *Id.*

31. *See* Logan E. Sawyer III, *Principle and Politics in the New History of Originalism*, 57 AM. J. LEGAL HIST. 198 (2017) (listing people serving in the Reagan administration who went on to prominent positions in the conservative legal movement); Steven M. Teles, *Transformative Bureaucracy: Reagan's Lawyers and the Dynamics of Political Investment*, 23 STUD. AM. POL. DEV. 61 (2009) (describing the attempt to build the conservative legal movement within the Reagan administration and its Justice Department).

32. Planned Parenthood of Southeastern Pennsylvania v. Casey, 505 U.S. 833 (1992).

33. YALOF, *supra* note 8, at 192.

34. *Id.* at 192–93.

35. BALKIN, CYCLES OF CONSTITUTIONAL TIME, *supra* note 10, at 120; Ann Southworth, *Lawyers and the Conservative Counterrevolution*, 43 LAW & SOC. INQUIRY 1698, 1705 (2018); HOLLIS-BRUSKY, *supra* note 29, at 20–21, 155–64.

36. *See* NEAL DEVINS & LAWRENCE BAUM, THE COMPANY THEY KEEP: HOW PARTISAN DIVISIONS CAME TO THE SUPREME COURT, 24–25, 40–46 (New York: Oxford Univ. Press, 2019); LAWRENCE BAUM, JUDGES AND THEIR AUDIENCES: A PERSPECTIVE ON JUDICIAL BEHAVIOR 43–49 (Princeton: Princeton Univ. Press, 2006).

37. *See* HOLLIS-BRUSKY, *supra* note 29, at 26, 45–47, 50, 54–55, 78, 84–85, 135–39 (showing how amicus briefs signed by Federalist Society members signaled the views of conservatives and offered legal arguments and materials for judges to use).

38. DEVINS & BAUM, *supra* note 36, at 151, 155–57; HOLLIS-BRUSKY, *supra* note 29, at 20–21, 155–64.

39. BALKIN, CYCLES OF CONSTITUTIONAL TIME, *supra* note 10, at 120–21.

40. Lawrence Baum & Neal Devins, *Federalist Court: How the Federalist Society Became the De Facto Selector of Republican Supreme Court Justices*, SLATE (Jan. 31, 2017), https://scholarship.law.wm.edu/cgi/viewcontent.cgi?article=1406&context=popular_media [https://perma.cc/UUW6-UXLB].

41. *Id.*; Joan Biskupic, *Trump's Supreme Court Nominee List Reflects His Us-versus-Them Approach to Judges*, CNN (Sept. 10, 2020), https://www.cnn.com/2020/09/10/politics/supreme-court-trump-judiciary-rule-of-law/index.html [https://perma.cc/GJ5G-SZT2]; Jeremy Diamond, *Trump Unveils His Potential Supreme Court*

Nominees, CNN (May 18, 2016), https://www.cnn.com/2016/05/18/politics/donald-trump-supreme-court-nominees/index.html [https://perma.cc/YA8B-WSAD].

42. *See* Nicholas Stephanopoulos, *The Anti-Carolene Court*, 2019 SUP. CT. REV. 11 (2019); BALKIN, CYCLES OF CONSTITUTIONAL TIME, *supra* note 10, at 143 (describing effects of constitutional rot).

43. *See* BALKIN, CYCLES OF CONSTITUTIONAL TIME, *supra* note 10, at 144 (offering as an example Department of Commerce, v. New York, 139 S. Ct. 2551 (2019)).

44. Robert A. Dahl, *Decision-Making in a Democracy: The Supreme Court as a National Policy-Maker*, 6 J. PUB. L. 291 (1957); ROBERT G. MCCLOSKEY, THE AMERICAN SUPREME COURT 261 (Chicago: Univ. of Chicago Press, Sanford Levinson ed., 5th ed. 2010).

45. Mark A. Graber, *The Nonmajoritarian Difficulty: Legislative Deference to the Judiciary*, 7 STUD. AM. POL. DEV. 35, 36–37 (1993).

46. *Id.* at 38. *See also* E. E. SCHATTSCHNEIDER, THE SEMI-SOVEREIGN PEOPLE: A REALIST'S VIEW OF DEMOCRACY (New York: Holt, Rinehart, and Winston, 1960).

47. Brown v. Board of Education, 347 U.S. 483 (1954).

48. LINDA GREENHOUSE & REVA B. SIEGEL, BEFORE *ROE V. WADE*: VOICES THAT SHAPED THE ABORTION DEBATE BEFORE THE SUPREME COURT'S RULING 286–303 (New York: Kaplan Publishing, 2d ed. 2012).

49. Jack Balkin, *A Ruling the G.O.P. Loves to Hate*, N.Y. TIMES (Jan. 25, 2003), https://www.nytimes.com/2003/01/25/opinion/a-ruling-the-gop-loves-to-hate.html.

50. *Id.*

51. BALKIN, CYCLES OF CONSTITUTIONAL TIME, *supra* note 10, at 76 ("Perhaps paradoxically, the pro-life Republican Party can form a larger coalition with *Roe* than without it.").

Chapter 6

1. Dobbs v. Jackson Women's Health Org., 142 S. Ct. 2228 (2022).

2. Roe v. Wade, 410 U.S. 113 (1973). *Dred Scott* brought the nation to civil war, but in a decade was reversed by constitutional amendment. I expressed my views on the abortion issue some thirty years ago. Michael W. McConnell, *How Not to Promote Serious Debate on Abortion*, 58 U. CHI. L. REV. 1181 (1991).

3. Most famously John Hart Ely, a supporter of abortion rights, wrote, "[*Roe*] is bad because it is bad constitutional law, or rather because it is not constitutional law and gives almost no sense of an obligation to try to be." John Hart Ely, *The Wages of Crying Wolf: A Comment on* Roe v. Wade, 82 YALE L.J. 920, 947 (1973).

4. *See* WHAT ROE V. WADE SHOULD HAVE SAID (Jack Balkin ed., New York: New York University Press, 2005).

5. On the significance of the full form of the maxim, *see* Clarke Forsythe & Regina Maitlin, *Stare Decisis, Settled Precedent, and* Roe v. Wade: *An Introduction*, 34 REG. U. L. REV. 385, 388–89 (2022).

6. Brief for Respondents, Dobbs v. Jackson Women's Health Org., 142 S. Ct. 2228 (2022) (No. 19-1392), 2021 WL 4197213 (U.S.).

7. *Dobbs*, 142 S. Ct. at 2332 (Breyer, Sotomayor, & Kagan, JJ., dissenting).

8. Payne v. Tennessee, 501 U.S. 808, 828 (1991).

9. Hertz v. Woodman, 218 U.S. 205, 212 (1910).

10. Agostini v. Felton, 521 U.S. 203, 235 (1997).

11. Burnet v. Coronado Oil & Gas Co., 285 U.S. 393, 407–8 (1932) (Brandeis, J., dissenting).

12. Mitchell v. W. T. Grant Co., 416 U.S. 600, 627–28 (1974) (Powell, J., concurring) (emphasis added).

13. Michael J. Gerhardt, *The Role of Precedent in Constitutional Decisionmaking and Theory*, 60 GEO. WASH. L. REV. 68, 76 (1991) (emphasis added).

14. Randy J. Kozel, *Stare Decisis as Judicial Doctrine*, 67 WASH. & LEE L. REV. 411, 414 (2010).

15. Lemon v. Kurtzman, 403 U.S. 602 (1971).

16. Kennedy v. Bremerton School District, 142 S. Ct. 2407, 2434 (2022).

17. *Table of Supreme Court Decisions Overruled by Subsequent Decisions*, CONST. ANNOTATED, https://constitution.congress.gov/resources/decisions-overruled/ (last visited Sept. 30, 2022).

18. Burnet v. Coronado Oil & Gas Co., 285 U.S. 393, 406 (1932) (Brandeis, J., dissenting) (italics omitted).

19. Henry P. Monaghan, *Stare Decisis and Constitutional Adjudication*, 88 COLUM. L. REV. 723, 748 (1988).

20. DAVID STRAUSS, THE LIVING CONSTITUTION 38 (New York: Oxford Univ. Press, 2010).

21. Washington v. Glucksberg, 521 U.S. 702, 703 (1997).

22. Lawrence v. Texas, 539 U.S. 558 (2003).

23. Bivens v. Six Unknown Named Agents of Fed. Bureau of Narcotics, 403 U.S. 388 (1971). *Bivens* created an action for damages against federal officials for some constitutional violations, without statutory basis.

24. *See, e.g.,* Bush v. Lucas, 462. U.S. 367, 374–78 (1983); FDIC v. Meyer, 510 U.S. 471, 484–86 (1994); Minneci v. Pollard, 565 U.S. 118, 129–30 (2012).

25. J. I. Case Co. v. Borak, 377 U.S. 426 (1964). *Borak* was distinguished by Alexander v. Sandoval, 523 U.S. 275 (2001); Stoneridge Inv. Partners v. Scientific-Atlanta, 522 U.S. 148 (2008); Ziglar v. Abbasi, 137 S. Ct. 1843, 1855 (2017) (distinguishing *Borak's* "different approach" as relics of an "*ancien regime*"). *Borak* created an implied cause of action for damages for certain securities law violations.

26. Helms v. Picard, 151 F.3d 347, 350 (5th Cir. 1998).

27. *See* Agostini v. Felton, 521 U.S. 203, 235 (1997) (overruling Aguilar v. Felton, 473 U.S. 402 (1985), & most of School District of Grand Rapids v. Ball, 473 U.S. 373 (1985); Mitchell v. Helms, 500 U.S. 793 (2000) (overruling Meek v. Pittenger, 421 U.S. 349 (1975), & Wolman v. Walter, 433 U.S. 299 (1977)); Kennedy v. Bremerton School District, 142 S. Ct. 2407 (2022) (apparently overruling Lemon v. Kurtzman, 403 U.S. 602 (1971)).

28. Gonzales v. Carhart, 546 U.S. 1169 (2006); Stenberg v. Carhart, 530 U.S. 914 (2000).

29. 1 JAMES KENT, COMMENTARIES ON AMERICAN LAW *442 (1826).

30. Planned Parenthood v. Casey, 505 U.S. 833, 867 (1992) ("[O]nly the most convincing justification under accepted standards of precedent could suffice to demonstrate that a later decision overruling the first was anything but a surrender to political pressure.").

31. Professor (later Utah Supreme Court Justice) Thomas Lee concluded that the special rule for constitutional cases was adopted in the early to mid-twentieth century. Thomas Lee, *Stare Decisis in Historical Perspective*, 52 VAND. L. REV. 647 (1999).

32. Smith v. Allwright, 321 U.S. 649, 665 (1944).

33. Burnet v. Coronado Oil & Gas Co., 285 U.S. 393, 406–7 (1932) (Brandeis, J., dissenting).

34. Ring v. Arizona, 536 U.S. 584 (2002); United States v. Gaudin, 515 U.S. 506 (1995); Hubbard v. United States, 514 U.S. 695 (1995); 44 Liquormart, Inc. v. Rhode Island, 517 U.S. 484 (1996); Fulton Corp. v. Faulkner, 516 U.S. 325 (1996); State Oil Co. v. Khan, 522 U.S. 3 (1997); Hudson v. United States, 522 U.S. 93 (1997); Hohn v. United States, 524 U.S. 236 (1998); Minnesota v. Mille Lacs Band of Chippewa Indians, 526 U.S. 172 (1999); United States v. Hatter, 532 U.S. 557 (2001); United States v. Cotton, 535 U.S. 625 (2002); Lapides v. Bd. of Regents of Univ. Sys. of Georgia, 535 U.S. 613 (2002); Atkins v. Virginia, 536 U.S. 304 (2002); Lawrence v. Texas, 539 U.S. 558 (2003); Crawford v. Washington, 541 U.S. 36 (2004); Roper v. Simmons, 543 U.S. 551 (2005); Cent. Virginia Cmty. Coll. v. Katz, 546 U.S. 356 (2006); Pearson v. Callahan, 555 U.S. 223 (2009); Alleyne v. United States, 570 U.S. 99 (2013); Obergefell v. Hodges, 576 U.S. 644 (2015); Johnson v. United States, 576 U.S. 591 (2015); Hurst v. Florida, 577 U.S. 92 (2016); South Dakota v. Wayfair, Inc., 138 S. Ct. 2080 (2018); Herrera v. Wyoming, 139 S. Ct. 1686 (2019); Ramos v. Louisiana, 140 S. Ct. 1390 (2020); Arizona v. Evans, 514 U.S. 1 (1995) (Ginsburg, J., dissenting); Arkansas v. Sullivan, 532 U.S. 769 (2001) (Ginsburg, J., concurring); Watson v. United States, 552 U.S. 74 (2007) (Ginsburg, J., concurring); John R. Sand & Gravel Co. v. United States, 552 U.S. 130 (2008) (Ginsburg, J., dissenting); AT&T Corp. v. Hulteen, 556 U.S. 701 (2009) (Ginsburg, J., dissenting); Michigan v. Bay Mills Indian Cmty., 572 U.S. 782 (2014) (Ginsburg, J., dissenting); Gamble v. United States, 139 S. Ct. 1960 (2019) (Ginsburg, J., dissenting); United States v. International Business Machines Corp., 517 U.S. 843 (1996) (Kennedy, J. dissenting); Bush v. Vera, 517 U.S. 952 (1996) (Souter, J., dissenting); Kimel v. Fla. Bd. of Regents, 528 U.S. 62 (2000) (Stevens, J., concurring in part); Harris v. United States, 536 U.S. 545 (2002) (Thomas, J., dissenting), (overruled by Alleyne v. United States, 570 U.S. 99 (2013)); McDonald v. City of Chicago, Ill., 561 U.S. 742 (2010) (Breyer, J., dissenting); Trump v. Hawaii, 138 S. Ct. 2392 (2018) (Sotomayor, J., dissenting).

35. William O. Douglas, *Stare Decisis*, 49 COLUM. L. REV. 735, 736 (1949).

36. *See* John O. McGinnis & Michael Rappaport, *Original Methods Originalism: A New Theory of Interpretation and the Case Against Construction*, 103 NW. U. L. REV. 751 (2009).

37. Marbury v. Madison, 5 U.S. 137 (1803); Hylton v. United States, 3 U.S. 171 (1796).

38. The Passenger Cases, 48 U.S. (7 How.) 283, 470 (1849) (Taney, J., dissenting).

39. *See generally* MICHAEL KLARMAN, FROM JIM CROW TO CIVIL RIGHTS: THE SUPREME COURT AND THE STRUGGLE FOR RACIAL EQUALITY (New York: Oxford Univ. Press, 2004).

40. "*Roe v. Wade* sparked public opposition and academic criticism, in part, I believe, because the Court ventured too far in the change it ordered and presented an incomplete justification for its action." Ruth B. Ginsburg, *Some Thoughts on Autonomy and Equality in Relation to* Roe v. Wade, 63 N.C. L. REV. 375 (1985).

41. There have been a handful of cases in which lower courts explicitly defy Supreme Court precedent but are affirmed. *See, e.g.*, Ableman v. Booth, 62 U.S. 506 (1858); West Virginia Bd. of Ed. v. Barnette, 319 U.S. 624 (1943).

42. *See generally* ROBERT AXELROD, THE EVOLUTION OF COOPERATION (New York: Basic Books,1984); SHAUN HEAP & YANIS VAROUFAKIS, GAME THEORY: A CRITICAL TEXT (London: Routledge, 2004).

43. Garcia v. San Antonio Metro. Transit Authority, 469 U.S. 258 (1985) (overruling Nat'l League of Cities v. Usery, 426 U.S. 833 (1976)).

44. Carson v. Makin, 142 S. Ct. 1987, 2012 (2022) (Sotomayor, J., dissenting).

45. Gamble v. United States, 139 S. Ct. 1960, 2006 (2019) (Ginsburg, J., dissenting).

46. Peter Overby, *Presidential Candidates Pledge to Undo "Citizens United." But Can They?*, NATIONAL PUBLIC RADIO (Feb. 14, 2016), https://www.npr.org/2016/02/14/466668949/presidential-candidates-pledge-to-undo-citizens-united-but-can-they.

47. Mark Tushnet, *Abandoning Defensive Crouch Liberal Constitutionalism*, BALKINIZATION (May 16, 2016), https://balkin.blogspot.com/2016/05/abandoning-defensive-crouch-liberal.html.

Chapter 7

1. Dobbs v. Jackson Women's Health Org., 142 S. Ct. 2228 (2022).

2. Griswold v. Connecticut, 381 U.S. 479, 485–86 (1965).

3. Eisenstadt v. Baird, 405 U.S. 438, 453, 562, 577–78 (1972).

4. Lawrence v. Texas, 539 U.S. 558, 564, 578 (2003).

5. Obergefell v. Hodges, 576 U.S. 644, 681 (2015).

6. *Dobbs*, 142 S. Ct. at 2319 (Breyer, J., dissenting).

7. In light of allegations that undocumented persons recently were subjected to coercive sterilizations at an immigrant detention facility in Georgia, it is timely to note that the method of constitutional interpretation that the *Dobbs* majority utilizes also imperils *Skinner v. Oklahoma*, 316 U.S. 535 (1942), which struck down a compulsory sterilization law under the Equal Protection Clause. Nicole Narea, *The Outcry Over ICE and Hysterectomies, Explained*, VOX (Sept. 18, 2020), https://www.vox.com/policy-and-politics/2020/9/15/21437805/whistleblower-hysterectomies-nurse-irwin-ice; Victoria Bekiempis, *More Immigrant Women Say They Were Abused by ICE Gynecologist*, GUARDIAN (Dec. 22, 2020), https://www.theguardian.com/us-news/2020/dec/22/ice-gynecologist-hysterectomies-georgia; Maya Manian, *Immigration*

Detention and Coerced Sterilization: History Tragically Repeats Itself, ACLU (Sept. 29, 2020), https://www.aclu.org/news/immigrants-rights/immigration-detention-and-coerced-sterilization-history-tragically-repeats-itself. State and federal governments did not recognize the right to bear children in 1868. Indeed, when the Court was asked in 1927 whether the Constitution protected such a right, it infamously answered the question in the negative. *See* Buck v. Bell, 274 U.S. 200, 207 (1927) ("It is better for the world if, instead of waiting to execute degenerate offspring for crime or to let them starve for their imbecility, society can prevent those who are manifestly unfit from continuing their kind. . . . Three generations of imbeciles are enough."). Thus, *Dobbs* puts *Skinner*—like *Griswold, Eisenstadt, Lawrence,* and *Obergefell*—on shaky ground.

We might also note that the method of constitutional interpretation embraced by the *Dobbs* majority imperils *Loving v. Virginia* as well. 388 U.S. 1 (1967). Indeed, Justice Breyer points this out in dissent, "According to the majority, no liberty interest is present—because (and only because) the law offered no protection to the woman's choice in the 19th century. But here is the rub. The law also did not then (and would not for ages) protect a wealth of other things. . . . It did not protect the right recognized in *Loving* to marry across racial lines" (*Dobbs,* 142 S. Ct. at 2332 (Breyer, J., dissenting)). Although the Court invoked the Equal Protection Clause in *Loving* to reach the holding that the Constitution proscribes antimiscegenation laws, it relied on the Due Process Clause as well (388 U.S. at 11–12). There should be no doubt that in 1868, precious few people believed that the Due Process Clause protected the right to marry someone of a different race. Indeed, one could point to numerous laws in 1868 that proscribed miscegenation—a fact that, pursuant to the *Dobbs* Court's interpretive method, would be fatal to the claim that the Constitution protects the right to interracial marriage (*U.S. Legal Map,* LOVING DAY, https://lovingday.org/legal-map/ (last visited Sept. 22, 2022) (reporting that thirty-one states had laws effective in 1868 that made interracial marriage illegal. Of the nineteen states that did not, five states—Iowa, Kansas, Massachusetts, Pennsylvania, and Washington—had laws voiding interracial marriages that ended on or before 1868. Five states that would gain statehood after 1868—Montana, North Dakota, Oklahoma, South Dakota, and Wyoming—later passed laws voiding interracial marriages)).

8. *Dobbs,* 142 S. Ct. at 2261. Justice Clarence Thomas's concurring opinion says the quiet part out loud. That is, it explicitly states that which is only implied in the *Dobbs* majority opinion: *Dobbs* puts substantive due process and the Court's decisions in *Griswold, Lawrence,* and *Obergefell* in grave danger. *See id.* at 2301 (Thomas, J., concurring) (arguing that the Court "should reconsider all of [its] substantive due process precedents, including *Griswold, Lawrence,* and *Obergefell,*" as "any substantive due process decision is 'demonstrably erroneous'").

9. *Dobbs,* 142 S. Ct. at 2261.

10. *Id.*

11. *Id.* at 2305–7, 2310 (Kavanaugh, J., concurring).

12. *Id.* at 2305. Of course, Kavanaugh and the other justices who joined the majority opinion ignore that the Court has returned the question of abortion's legality to the people to "resolve through the democratic process in the States or Congress" at a time

when the Court has revealed itself to be unwilling to protect voting rights and many states with Republican majorities in their legislatures have worked fastidiously to disenfranchise people who are likely to support Democratic candidates, that is, people of color, poor people, young people, and people with disabilities. *See* Amy Gardner, Kate Rabinowitz, & Harry Stevens, *How GOP-Backed Voting Measures Could Create Hurdles for Tens of Millions of Voters*, WASH. POST (Mar. 11, 2021), https://www.was hingtonpost.com/politics/interactive/2021/voting-restrictions-republicans-states/ (detailing, among many other disenfranchising laws, a proposal to eliminate automatic registration for absentee voting, forcing voters to reapply each election cycle; restrictions to mail and early voting proposed in thirty-three states; a proposal in Michigan and legislation in Texas that would add identification requirements to absentee voting; and a new Georgia law that tightens absentee ballot identification requirements); *see also The Impact of Voter Suppression on Communities of Color*, BRENNAN CTR. FOR JUST. (Jan. 10, 2022), https://www.brennancenter.org/our-work/ research-reports/impact-voter-suppression-communities-color ("strict voter ID laws disproportionately impact voters of color"); K. A. Dilday, *Voting Rights Aren't Just a Black Issue: They Affect Poor People of All Races*, BLOOMBERG (Nov. 13, 2018), https:// www.bloomberg.com/news/articles/2018-11-13/voter-suppression-targets-blacks-but-affects-all-poor; Charlotte Hill, *It's Harder for Young People to Vote*, DEMOCRACY DOCKET (Sept. 3, 2020), https://www.democracydocket.com/opinion/its-harder-for-young-people-to-vote/ (finding that young people "are less likely to have the voter ID documentation they think they need to vote" and tend to vote at higher rates in states that allow same-day registration and mail ballots in advance to all registered voters); Andrew Pulrang, *7 Ways New Voting Laws Can Affect People with Disabilities*, FORBES (July 25, 2021), https://www.forbes.com/sites/andrewpulrang/2021/07/25/7-ways-new-voting-laws-can-affect-people-with-disabilities/?sh=4025c4ee6289 ("Most of the new anti-voter laws we have seen enacted in a number of states will make voting more difficult for disabled folks."). Thus, the Court leaves the resolution of the question of abortion's legality to the democratic process precisely when the Court has permitted that process to be marginally democratic, at best.

13. *Dobbs*, 142 S. Ct. at 2236 (arguing that "many [common-law] authorities asserted that even a pre-quickening abortion was 'unlawful' and that, as a result, an abortionist was guilty of murder if the woman died from the attempt").

14. *See Planned Parenthood, Media Guide: For Writing Accurately and Objectively About Abortion*, PLANNED PARENTHOOD 6, https://www.plannedparenthoodaction.org/ uploads/filer_public/1e/7f/1e7f4f58-7073-42d6-a32f-0970d9e8fcb0/writing_abou t_abortion_ppaf.pdf (last visited Sept. 22, 2022) (noting that the term "abortionist" "connote[s] suspicion and distrust" and stating that "abortion providers are licensed medical professionals and should be referred to accordingly").

15. *Dobbs*, 142 S. Ct. at 2250, 2254.

16. *Id.* at 2244 (quoting the Mississippi Gestational Age Act, whose ban on abortion after fifteen weeks was justified on the grounds that "most abortions after 15 weeks employ 'dilation and evacuation procedures which involve the use of surgical instruments to crush and tear the unborn child'").

17. Stenberg v. Carhart, 530 U.S. 914, 958–60, 974–76 (2000) (Kennedy, J., dissenting).

18. Gonzales v. Carhart, 550 U.S. 124, 135–41 (2007).

19. *Dobbs*, 142 S. Ct. at 2244 (quoting the Mississippi Gestational Act's description of the dilation and evacuation abortion procedure as "a barbaric practice").

20. *See* Stuart v. Loomis, 992 F. Supp. 2d 585, 599 n.24 (M.D.N.C. 2014) (arguing that "even outside the abortion context, it does not take much imagination to identify serious problems with allowing the government to justify compelled speech on one basis when its primary purpose is otherwise" and noting that "[u]nder the guise of promoting informed consent, for example, the state might require physicians to show gruesome videos of surgery to patients, when the real purpose was to reduce medical costs by discouraging patients from choosing expensive surgery"); Sarah Runels, *Informed Consent Laws and the Constitution: Balancing State Interests with a Physician's First Amendment Rights and a Woman's Due Process Rights*, 26 J. OF CONTEMP. HEALTH L. & POL'Y 185, 193 (2009) ("In reality, a detailed description of any major medical procedure would be gruesome.").

21. *Dobbs*, 142 S. Ct. at 2312.

22. *Id.* at 2241–44, 2249, 2268, 2270, 2281.

23. *Id.* at 2241–44, 2252, 2256, 2258–59, 2261, 2265–67, 2271, 2273, 2284.

24. *Id.* at 2243–44. The majority notes that the Mississippi legislature found that "at 5 or 6 weeks' gestational age an 'unborn human being's heart begins beating'; at 8 weeks the 'unborn human being begins to move about in the womb'; at 9 weeks 'all basic physiological functions are present'; at 10 weeks 'vital organs begin to function,' and '[h]air, fingernails, and toenails . . . begin to form'; at 11 weeks 'an unborn human being's diaphragm is developing,' and he or she may 'move about freely in the womb'; and at 12 weeks the 'unborn human being' has 'taken on "the human form" in all relevant respects.'" *Id.*

25. *See* Khiara M. Bridges, *When Pregnancy Is an Injury: Rape, Law, and Culture*, 65 STAN. L. REV. 457, 471 (2013).

26. *See* Brief for the National Abortion Rights Action League et al. as Amici Curiae in Support of Appellees at *5, Thornburgh v. Am. Coll. of Obstetricians & Gynecologists, 476 U.S. 747 (1986) (Nos. 84-495, 84-1379), 1985 WL 669630, at *5.

27. *Id.* at *29.

28. *Id.* at *21.

29. *Id.* at *28.

30. DIANA GREENE FOSTER, THE TURNAWAY STUDY: TEN YEARS, A THOUSAND WOMEN, AND THE CONSEQUENCES OF HAVING—OR BEING DENIED—AN ABORTION 37 (New York: Scribner, 2020).

31. *Id.* at 177.

32. *Id.* at 230–31.

33. *See* David J. Garrow, *Abortion Before and After* Roe v. Wade: *An Historical Perspective*, 62 ALB. L. REV. 833, 834 (1999) (observing that in the days before *Roe*, "there were hundreds upon hundreds of doctors in this country who secretly performed abortions for women whom they knew and who could pay").

34. It is important to observe that even before the Court's decision in *Dobbs*, abortion care in the United States had been rendered inaccessible to the most marginalized. This is because there has never been a positive right to an abortion, obligating the state to ensure that individuals can access this form of healthcare. The right to an abortion in the United States has always been the right to purchase abortion services in the market—a negative right that is meaningless to those without the means to pay. Moreover, the Hyde Amendment, which prevents the expenditure of federal funds on abortion care except in narrow circumstances, has meant that low-income people cannot rely on their health insurance, Medicaid, to cover the costs of abortion care; it has also meant that indigenous people cannot turn to Indian Health Services, the agency that purports to fulfill the U.S. government's treaty obligation to provide healthcare to members of federally recognized tribes, for abortion care. *See* Deborah Kacanek et al., *Medicaid Funding for Abortion: Providers' Experiences with Cases Involving Rape, Incest and Life Endangerment*, 42 PERSP. ON SEXUAL & REPROD. HEALTH 79, 79–80 (2010) (discussing the difficulties providers have experienced when seeking Medicaid reimbursement for abortions that qualify for funding); Julie Andrews et al., *Indigenous Women's Reproductive Justice: A Survey of Sexual Assault Policies and Protocols Within Indian Health Service Emergency Rooms*, NATIVE AM. WOMEN'S HEALTH EDU. RES. CTR. 3 (2004) (discussing how the Indian Health Service fails to provide abortion access to Native women due to the Hyde Amendment).

35. Self-managing abortion today is less dangerous than it was in the past due to the advent of misoprostol and mifepristone, that is, medication abortion. *See* Aziza Ahmed, *Floating Lungs: Forensic Science in Self-Induced Abortion Prosecutions*, 100 B.U. L. REV. 1111, 1123 (2020) ("A medication abortion is safe and legal—according to advocates and health professionals—when the abortion is done within legal and medical time limits, provided by the legally required health professional, and done with medication received from a pharmacy.") (footnotes omitted). Although medication abortion carries extremely low risks, the medication must be ingested at earlier stages of the pregnancy in order to ensure its safety. The risk of complications increases when the pills are taken after the medical time limits—up to the tenth week of pregnancy. *See* Greer Donley, *Medication Abortion Exceptionalism*, 107 CORNELL L. REV. 627, 655 (2022). Thus, there is the likelihood that the most unprivileged individuals will not be able to discover their pregnancies and gather the money necessary to pay for the medication within the medical time limits. These marginalized individuals will be forced to ingest the medication after the tenth week of pregnancy (when complications are more likely to arise), resort to more dangerous methods of self-managed abortion (i.e., the coat hangers of yesteryear), or carry their pregnancies to term unwillingly.

36. *See* GEOFFREY R. STONE, SEX AND THE CONSTITUTION: SEX, RELIGION, AND LAW FROM AMERICA'S ORIGINS TO THE TWENTY-FIRST CENTURY 373 (New York: Liveright, 2017). It is difficult to overstate the horrors of back-alley and self-managed abortion in the pre-*Roe* era. As Professor Stone describes:

> Women who resorted to self-induced abortion typically relied on such methods as throwing themselves down a flight of stairs or ingesting, douching with, or inserting into themselves a chilling variety of chemicals and toxins ranging from

bleach to potassium permanganate to turpentine to gunpowder to whiskey. Knitting needles, crochet hooks, scissors, and coat hangers were among the tools commonly used by women who attempted to self-abort.... Women who sought abortions from "back-alley" abortionists encountered similar horrors.... The vast majority of these abortions were performed either by persons with only limited medical training, such as physiotherapists, midwives, and chiropractors, or by rank amateurs, including elevator operators, prostitutes, barbers, and unskilled laborers.

Id. at 373. As Stone explains, more than two hundred women died annually from unsafe, illegal abortions, with the mortality rate for Black and Latinx people being twelve times the rate of their white counterparts. *Id.*

37. Roe v. Wade, 410 U.S. 113, 153 (1973).

38. Planned Parenthood of Southeastern Pennsylvania v. Casey, 505 U.S. 833, 860 (1992).

39. *Id.* at 852.

40. *Id.*

41. *Id.* at 853.

42. *Id.*

43. Dobbs v. Jackson Women's Health Org., 597 U.S. 2228, 2305 (2022) (Kavanaugh, J., concurring).

44. Julie Rikelman, who argued on behalf of the abortion clinics in the litigation, made this point during oral arguments after Kavanaugh asked her to engage with the claim that "neutrality requires the Court to interpret the Constitution as silent on abortion rights." Transcript of Oral Argument at 43, Dobbs v. Jackson Women's Health Org., 597 U.S. 2305 (2022) (No. 19-1392). She responded that this would not be a "neutral position. The Constitution provides a guarantee of liberty. The Court has interpreted that liberty to include the ability to make decisions related to childbearing, marriage, and family." *Id.* at 78.

45. Amita Kelly, *McConnell: Blocking Supreme Court Nomination "About a Principle, Not a Person,"* NPR POLITICS (Mar. 16, 2016), https://www.npr.org/2016/03/16/470664561/mcconnell-blocking-supreme-court-nomination-about-a-principle-not-a-person.

46. Dan Mangan, *Trump: I'll Appoint Supreme Court Justices to Overturn* Roe v. Wade *Abortion Case*, CNBC ELECTIONS (Oct. 19, 2016), https://www.cnbc.com/2016/10/19/trump-ill-appoint-supreme-court-justices-to-overturn-roe-v-wade-abortion-case.html.

47. Susan Davis, *Senate Pulls "Nuclear" Trigger to Ease Gorsuch Confirmation*, NPR POLITICS (Apr. 6, 2017), https://www.npr.org/2017/04/06/522847700/senate-pulls-nuclear-trigger-to-ease-gorsuch-confirmation.

48. Seung Min Kim & John Wagner, *Kavanaugh Sworn in as Supreme Court Justice After Divided Senate Votes for Confirmation*, WASH. POST (Oct. 6, 2018), https://www.washingtonpost.com/politics/kavanaugh-vote-divided-senate-poised-to-confirm-trumps-nominee/2018/10/06/64bf69fa-c969-11e8-b2b5-79270f9cce17_story.html.

49. That politics courses through *Dobbs* is demonstrated by the fact that Mississippi even asked the Court to reverse *Roe* in its entirety. In its petition of certiorari, Mississippi only asked the Court to overturn *Roe* and *Casey* to the extent of discarding the

viability line. *See* Reply Brief for Petitioners at 9, Thomas E. Dobbs, M.D., M.P.H., In His Official Capacity as State Health Officer of the Mississippi Department of Health, et al., Petitioners, v. Jackson Women's Health Organization, On Behalf of Itself and Its Patients, et al., Respondent., 142 S. Ct. 2228 (2022) (No. 19-1392), 2020 WL 3317135 (U.S.). However, in its brief on the merits, Mississippi asked for the complete reversal of *Roe*. *See* Brief for Petitioners at 1, Thomas E. Dobbs, M.D., M.P.H., In His Official Capacity as State Health Officer of the Mississippi Department of Health, et al., Petitioners, v. Jackson Women's Health Organization, On Behalf of Itself and Its Patients, et al., Respondent., 142 S. Ct. 2228 (2022) (No. 19-1392). We can explain the evolution of Mississippi's requests in terms of the Court's personnel. Between the filing of the petition for certiorari and the merits brief, Ginsburg had died and Barrett had been hurriedly nominated and confirmed to the Court. Thus, Mississippi knew it did not have to be modest by simply asking for the eradication of the viability line. Mississippi knew that it could go big.

Mississippi modified its request in the *Dobbs* litigation from *Roe*'s evisceration (through discarding the viability line) to *Roe*'s elimination (through its reversal) not because the law had changed, the facts and science around abortion and fetal life had changed, or the essential nature of abortion access for people capable of pregnancy had changed. Instead, the request shifted because the Court's personnel had changed. Mississippi did no more than ask the Court to allow the law around abortion to hew more closely to the shifts in the Court's composition that politics had made possible.

50. *See* Transcript of Oral Argument at 14–15, Dobbs v. Jackson Women's Health Org., 142 S. Ct. 2228 (2022) (No. 19-1392).
51. *Id.* at 15.
52. Glenn Kessler, Salvador Rizzo, & Meg Kelly, *Trump's False or Misleading Claims Total 30,573 Over 4 Years*, WASH. POST (Jan. 24, 2021), https://www.washingtonpost.com/politics/2021/01/24/trumps-false-or-misleading-claims-total-30573-over-four-years.
53. Establishing the Marxist Roots of Critical Race Theory and Detail the Threat This Divisive Ideology Poses to the American Republic, H.R. Res. 1303, 117th Cong. (2022), https://www.congress.gov/bill/117th-congress/house-resolution/1303/text?r=16&s=1.
54. That is, we will likely witness the inverse of the scenario that followed the release of *Roe*, in which supporters of abortion rights decried the decision's reasoning. As the *Dobbs* majority triumphantly writes of the reception of *Roe* in the legal academy:

> [A]cademic commentators, including those who agreed with the decision as a matter of policy, were unsparing in their criticism. John Hart Ely famously wrote that *Roe* was "not constitutional law and g[ave] almost no sense of an obligation to try to be." Archibald Cox, who served as Solicitor General under President Kennedy, commented that *Roe* "read[s] like a set of hospital

rules and regulations" that "[n]either historian, layman, nor lawyer will be persuaded . . . are part of . . . the Constitution." Laurence Tribe wrote that "even if there is a need to divide pregnancy into several segments with lines that clearly identify the limits of governmental power, 'interest-balancing' of the form the Court pursues fails to justify any of the lines actually drawn." Mark Tushnet termed *Roe* a "totally unreasoned judicial opinion."

Dobbs v. Jackson Women's Health Org., 142 S. Ct. 2228, 2270 (2022) (citations omitted).

Chapter 8

*. I am grateful to Lawrence B. Solum, Geoffrey Stone, and Adrian Vermeule, and various others, for valuable comments, discussions, ideas, and suggestions. I am also grateful to Davy Perlman for terrific research assistance.

1. Dobbs v. Jackson Women's Health Org., 142 S. Ct. 2228, 2240–300 (2022).
2. Roe v. Wade, 410 U.S. 113 (1973).
3. *Dobbs*, 142 S. Ct. at 2241.
4. *Id.* at 2246.
5. For an illuminating and in some ways startling discussion, *see generally* Lawrence B. Solum and Max Crema, *The Original Meaning of "Due Process of Law" in the Fifth Amendment*, 108 Va. L. Rev. 447 (2022).
6. *Dobbs*, 142 S. Ct. at 2246.
7. *Id.*
8. *Id.* at 2240.
9. *Id.* at 2247.
10. *See* Cass R. Sunstein, *Due Process Traditionalism*, 106 Mich. L. Rev. 1543 (2008).
11. *Dobbs*, 142 S. Ct. at 2247.
12. *See, e.g.*, Washington v. Glucksberg, 521 U.S. 702, 720–21 (1997); Michael H. v. Gerald D., 491 U.S. 110, 122–24 (1989); Moore v. City of E. Cleveland, 431 U.S. 494, 503 (1977).
13. *Michael H.*, 491 U.S. at 127 n.6.
14. *Id.*
15. *Id.*
16. *Glucksberg*, 521 U.S. at 703.
17. Dobbs v. Jackson Women's Health Org., 142 S. Ct. 2228, 2247 (2022).
18. *Id.*
19. *Id.* at 2248.
20. *Id.*
21. *Id.*
22. *Id.* at 2248–49.
23. *Id.* at 2249–52.
24. *Id.* at 2257.

25. If it is applied to the Fifth Amendment as well as the Fourteenth, due process traditionalism is also hard to square with the "equal protection component of the Due Process Clause." For example, *Califano v. Goldfarb*, 430 U.S. 199 (1977) would be impossible to defend.

26. *Dobbs*, 142 S. Ct. at 2258.

27. *Id.*

28. Here is a sympathetic understanding of what the Court is doing here: Due process traditionalism is meant to set out the appropriate boundaries of substantive due process. But it is not meant to suggest that every decision that departs from due process traditionalism will be *overruled*. The reference to the uniqueness of the abortion question is meant to suggest why *Roe* and *Casey* should be overruled. Decisions like *Griswold* and *Obergefell* might have been wrong when decided (given due process traditionalism), but they need not and perhaps should not be overruled.

29. *Dobbs*, 142 S. Ct. at 2258. I do not deal here with the very lengthy, and implication-filled, discussion of the limits of *stare decisis*. It would be possible, of course, to embrace due process traditionalism without voting to overrule *Roe v. Wade* if one had a particularly strong commitment to *stare decisis*. This is of course the approach urged by Chief Justice John Roberts in his concurrence. *See id* at 2310–17 (Roberts, C.J., concurring in the judgment).

30. *Id.* at 2284.

31. *See supra* notes 29–30.

32. *Dobbs*, 142 S. Ct. at 2245.

33. I am grateful to Lawrence Solum for help with this point.

34. In Burke's famous words:

> We are afraid to put men to live and trade each on his own private stock of reason; because we suspect that this stock in each man is small, and that the individuals would do better to avail themselves of the general bank and capital of nations and of ages. Many of our men of speculation, instead of exploding general prejudices, employ their sagacity to discover the latent wisdom which prevails in them. If they find what they seek, and they seldom fail, they think it more wise to continue the prejudice, with the reason involved, than to cast away the coat of prejudice, and to leave nothing but the naked reason; because prejudice, with its reason, has a motive to give action to that reason, and an affection which will give it permanence.

EDMUND BURKE, REFLECTIONS ON THE REVOLUTION IN FRANCE 129–30 (1790).

35. *See* Sunstein, *supra* note 11.

36. *See id.*

37. I emphasize the word "might"; I am not attempting here to offer a view on interpretation of the Privileges or Immunities Clause, originalist or otherwise, and so not insisting that the right interpretation is (3) or (4). On one view, for example, the category of privileges or immunities is very large, but anything within the category is subject to reasonable regulation.

38. There are also questions about the Ninth Amendment. On a reasonable view, that amendment applies to the national government (whatever it means), and if it applies to the states, it would be because it is incorporated via the Fourteenth Amendment,

most plausibly through the Privileges or Immunities Clause. (As they say: awkward.) It is broadly consistent with the overall approach of the Court to say that if the Ninth Amendment does anything of relevance (a big if), it adds nothing to the Fourteenth Amendment, even if it is incorporated.

39. For a more detailed discussion of due process traditionalism, *see* Sunstein, *supra* note 11.

40. *See* Ronald Dworkin, *The Forum of Principle*, 56 N.Y.U. L. REV. 469, 518 (1981) ("Learned Hand warned us that we should not be ruled by philosopher-judges even if our judges were better philosophers. But that threat is and will continue to be a piece of hyperbole. We have reached a balance in which the Court plays a role in government but not, by any stretch, the major role. Academic lawyers do no service by trying to disguise the political decisions this balance assigns to judges. Rule by academic priests guarding the myth of some canonical original intention is no better than the rule by Platonic guardians in different robes. We do better to work, openly and willingly, so that the national argument of principle that judicial review provides is [a] better argument for our part. We have an institution that calls some issues from the battleground of power politics to the forum of principle. It holds out the promise that the deepest, most fundamental conflicts between individual and society will once, someplace, finally, become questions of justice. I do not call that religion or prophesy. I call it law.")

41. BLAISE PASCAL, THOUGHTS, LETTERS AND MINOR WORKS 449 (New York: P. F. Collier & Son, O. W. Wight trans., Charles W. Eliot ed. 1910) (1648).

42. JEREMY BENTHAM, THE BOOK OF FALLACIES 71 (London: John and H. L. Hunt, 1824).

43. *See* ALEXANDER BICKEL, THE LEAST DANGEROUS BRANCH (New Haven: Yale Univ. Press, 1962), for an argument to this general effect in what might seem to be a surprising place. As of this writing, the view sketched in this paragraph seems to be a historical retrospective, or perhaps also a bit of science fiction, pointing to a history-that-will-never-be. (There aren't five votes for it!) But as we will see in the next section, it is science fact, more or less, with respect to other parts of the Constitution.

44. Dobbs v. Jackson Women's Health Org., 142 S. Ct. 2228, 2240 (2022).

45. The Fifteenth and Twenty-Fourth Amendments are exceptions. U.S. CONST. amend. XV & XXIV.

46. With the exception of the Nineteenth Amendment. U.S. CONST. amend. XIX.

47. Originalists would, of course, have their own ways of answering these questions; whether we should be traditionalists would depend on the original public meaning (suitably defined) and perhaps on "the construction zone."

48. Some people have argued that restrictions on the right to choose abortion violate the Equal Protection Clause. The Court briefly rejects that argument, largely by reference to precedent. I do not explore the issue here.

49. *Dobbs*, 142 S. Ct. at 2247.

50. On that issue, *see* Cass R. Sunstein, *Sexual Orientation and the Constitution: A Note on the Relationship between Due Process and Equal Protection*, 55 U. CHI. L. REV. 1161 (1988).

51. In my view, we should not be. There is of course an originalist alternative to tradition-alism and to the approach that I sketch in this paragraph; there is also common good constitutionalism. *See* ADRIAN VERMEULE, COMMON GOOD CONSTITUTIONALISM (Medford: Polity Press, 2022).

Chapter 9

*. Thanks to Will Baude, Rachel Bayefsky, Naomi Cahn, Olive Eisdorfer, Randy Kozel, Liz Sepper, and Nina Varsava, among others.

1. Dobbs v. Jackson Women's Health Org., 142 S. Ct. 2228 (2022). "Gradualism" here encompasses any means of temporally extending a court's decisional process across multiple steps.

2. Richard M. Re, *The Doctrine of One Last Chance*, 17 GREEN BAG 2D 173 (2014).

3. U.S. CONST. art. III, § 1.

4. On backlash, *see* text accompanying *infra* note 70.

5. For evidence that the doctrine of one last chance has changed outcomes and improved briefing, *see* Richard M. Re, *Second Thoughts on "One Last Chance"?*, 66 UCLA L. REV. 647 (2019).

6. *See* Petition for Writ of Certiorari at i, Dobbs v. Jackson Women's Health Org., 142 S. Ct. 2228 (2022) (No. 19-1392).

7. *See id.* at 5.

8. *See* Brief for Petitioners, Dobbs v. Jackson Women's Health Org., 142 S. Ct. 2228 (2022) (No. 19-1392).

9. *See* Sherif Girgis, *Two Obstacles to (Merely) Chipping Away at* Roe *in* Dobbs, SSRN (Aug. 19, 2021), http://dx.doi.org/10.2139/ssrn.3907787 ("[M]any on both sides . . . assume . . . the Justices would stop short of eliminating *Roe*'s constitutional right to elective abortions.").

10. *See* Transcript of Oral Argument at 50, Dobbs v. Jackson Women's Health Org., 142 S. Ct. 2228 (2022) (No. 19-1392).

11. Dobbs v. Jackson Women's Health Org., 142 S. Ct. 2228, 2273 (2022) (discussing the undue burden standard).

12. *Dobbs* at 2242 (quoting Respondents).

13. Brief for Respondents at 43, Dobbs v. Jackson Women's Health Org., 142 S. Ct. 2228 (2022) (No. 19-1392).

14. *Dobbs* at 2349 (dissent).

15. *See* Planned Parenthood v. Casey, 505 U.S. 833 (1992).

16. *See* Richard M. Re, *Hard-line Advocacy in* Dobbs—*and* Casey, RE'S JUDICATA (Dec. 8, 2021), https://richardresjudicata.wordpress.com/2021/12/08/hard-line-advocacy-in-dobbs-and-casey/.

17. *Id.*

18. *Dobbs* at 2316 (Roberts, C.J., concurring in the judgment).

19. *See* June Medical Services v. Russo, 140 S. Ct. 2103 (2020).

20. *Dobbs* at 2277. For criticism of the Court's narrow view of reliance, *see* Nina Varsava, *Reliance*, 136 HARV. L. REV. 1845 (2023).

21. *See* Lora Kelley, *Major Indiana Employers Criticize State's New Abortion Law*, N.Y. TIMES (Aug 6, 2022), https://www.nytimes.com/2022/08/06/business/indiana-companies-abortion.html.

22. *See* Aaron Blake, *Buyer's Remorse Could Be Creeping in for GOP on Abortion*, WASH. POST (Aug. 25, 2022), https://www.washingtonpost.com/politics/2022/08/25/repu blicans-abortion-politics/.

23. *See* Frances Stead Sellers & Fenit Nirappil, *Confusion Post-*Roe *Spurs Delays, Denials for Some Lifesaving Pregnancy Care*, WASH. POST (July 16, 2022), https://www.was hingtonpost.com/health/2022/07/16/abortion-miscarriage-ectopic-pregnancy-care/.

24. Citing democratic inertia and other political pathologies, Rosalind Dixon and David Landau argue for a delayed remedy that would have afforded time for legislative updating. *See* Rosalind Dixon & David Landau, Dobbs, *Democracy and Dysfunction*, SSRN (Aug. 17, 2022), http://dx.doi.org/10.2139/ssrn.4185324. That approach could be viewed as gradualism as to decisional effects alone, without gradualism as to decision-making.

25. *Cf. Dobbs* at 2305 (Kavanaugh, J., concurring).

26. *Dobbs* at 2277.

27. *See* Whole Women's Health v. Jackson, 141 S. Ct. 2494 (2021).

28. *Id.*

29. *See Dobbs* Oral Argument, *supra* note 10.

30. *See* Josh Gerstein & Alexander Ward, *Supreme Court Has Voted to Overturn Abortion Rights, Draft Opinion Shows*, POLITICO (May 3, 2022), https://www.politico.com/news/2022/05/02/supreme-court-abortion-draft-opinion-00029473.

31. *See* Richard M. Re, *Who's Afraid of Gradualism in* Dobbs, RE'S JUDICATA (Nov. 29, 2021), https://richardresjudicata.wordpress.com/2021/11/29/whos-afraid-of-gra dualism-in-dobbs/.

32. *See* Brief of Scholars of Court Procedure as Amici Curiae in Support of Respondents, Dobbs v. Jackson Women's Health Org., 142 S. Ct. 2228 (2022) (No. 19-1392); *see also* Richard M. Re, *Good Reasons to Go Slow on Abortion Precedents*, WALL ST. J. (Dec. 2, 2021), https://www.wsj.com/articles/supreme-court-go-slow-roe-v-wade-abortion-precedents-gradualism-mississippi-dobbs-11638475763.

33. Petition for Writ of Certiorari at i, Dobbs v. Jackson Women's Health Org., 142 S. Ct. 2228 (2022) (No. 19-1392).

34. Dobbs v. Jackson Women's Health Org., 142 S. Ct. 2228, 2281 (2022).

35. *Id.* at 2281–83.

36. *See* Richard M. Re, *Narrowing Supreme Court Precedent from Below*, 104 GEO. L. J. 921 (2016).

37. *But see* Girgis, *supra* note 9.

38. *Dobbs* at 2315 (Roberts, C.J., concurring in the judgment).

39. *Id.* at 2314 (Roberts, C.J., concurring in the judgment).

40. *See* Planned Parenthood v. Casey, 505 U.S. 833, 870 (1992).

41. *See* Gonzales v. Carhart, 550 U.S. 124, 157–60 (2007).

42. *Dobbs* at 2315 (Roberts, C.J., concurring in the judgment) .

43. *Id.* at 2270 (majority opinion) (collecting sources).

44. *See* CASS R. SUNSTEIN, ONE CASE AT A TIME: JUDICIAL MINIMALISM ON THE SUPREME COURT (Cambridge: Harvard Univ. Press, 2001).

45. *Dobbs* at 2317 (Roberts, C.J., concurring in the judgment).

46. *See* Re, *supra* note 2.

47. *Dobbs* at 2316 (Roberts, C.J., concurring in the judgment).

48. *Id.*

49. *Id.* at 2315 (Hertz v. Woodman, 218 U.S. 205, 212 (1910)).

50. *See* Richard M. Re, *Precedent as Permission*, 99 TEX. L. REV 907 (2021).

51. *Dobbs* at 2301 (Thomas, J., concurring).

52. Citizens United v. FEC, 558 U.S. 310, 384 (2010) (Roberts, C.J., concurring).

53. *Dobbs* at 2281 (quoting *Citizens United*, 558 U.S. at 384 (Roberts, C.J., concurring)).

54. *Id.*

55. *Id.* at 2283 (quoting *Citizens United*, 558 U.S. at 375 (Roberts, C.J., concurring)).

56. Planned Parenthood v. Casey, 505 U.S. 833, 861, 870, 873 (1992).

57. Harris v. Quinn, 573 U.S. 616 (2014); Abood v. Detroit Bd. of Ed., 431 U.S. 209 (1977).

58. Citizens United v. FEC, 558 U.S. 310, 328 (2010).

59. *Dobbs* at 2283.

60. *Id.*

61. *Id.* at 2316 (Roberts, C.J., concurring).

62. *See* Maria Cramer & Jesus Jiménez, *Armed Man Traveled to Justice Kavanaugh's Home to Kill Him, Officials Say*, N.Y. TIMES (June 8, 2022), https://www.nytimes.com/2022/06/08/us/brett-kavanaugh-threat-arrest.html.

63. *See Dobbs* Oral Argument, *supra* note 29.

64. *See* Reynolds v. Sims, 377 U.S. 533 (1964).

65. *Dobbs* at 2315 (Roberts, C.J., concurring).

66. *Dobbs* at 2283.

67. Plessy v. Ferguson, 163 U.S. 537 (1896).

68. *Dobbs* at 2265.

69. Brown v. Board of Education, 347 U.S. 483, 491 (1954).

70. *See* MICHAEL J. KLARMAN, FROM JIM CROW TO CIVIL RIGHTS: THE SUPREME COURT AND THE STRUGGLE FOR RACIAL EQUALITY 204–12, ch. 6 (New York: Oxford Univ. Press, 2004).

71. *See id.*; SUNSTEIN, *supra* note 44, at 38.

72. *See* KLARMAN, *supra* note 70, at 318–20 (discussing the "all deliberate speed" standard); JUSTIN DRIVER, THE SCHOOLHOUSE GATE: PUBLIC EDUCATION, THE SUPREME COURT, AND THE BATTLE FOR THE AMERICAN MIND 262–63 (New York: Pantheon Books, 2018).

73. *Dobbs* at 2278.

74. *Id.* at 2279.

75. *Id.* at 2277. For deep criticism of this point, *see* Varsava, *supra* note 20.

76. *Dobbs* at 2265.

77. *Id.*

78. *Id.*

79. *Id.*

80. *Id.* at 2277–78.

81. *Id.* at 2330 (Breyer, Sotomayor, & Kagan, JJ., dissenting).

82. *Id.* at 2334 (Breyer, Sotomayor, & Kagan, JJ., dissenting).

83. *See, e.g.*, Franchise Tax Bd. v. Hyatt, 139 S. Ct. 1485, 1499 (2019); Payne v. Tennessee, 501 U.S. 808, 827 (1991) ("[W]hen governing decisions are . . . badly reasoned, this Court has never felt constrained to follow precedent.") (internal quotation marks omitted).

84. *Dobbs* at 2334 (Breyer, Sotomayor, & Kagan, JJ., dissenting) (citation omitted).

85. *Id.* at 2342.

86. *See* KLARMAN, *supra* note 70, at 301 ("Once a majority had agreed to invalidate segregation, potential dissenters faced strong pressures to conform.").

87. *See Dobbs* at 2242.

88. *Id.* at 2320 (Breyer, Sotomayor, & Kagan, JJ., dissenting) (quotation omitted).

89. *Id.*; *see also* RANDY R. KOZEL, SETTLED VERSUS RIGHT: A THEORY OF PRECEDENT (Cambridge: Cambridge Univ. Press, 2017).

90. *Dobbs* at 2348 (Breyer, Sotomayor, & Kagan, JJ., dissenting) (citing Payne v. Tennessee, 501 U.S. 808, 844 (1991) (Marshall, J., dissenting)).

91. *Id.* at 2350 (citation omitted). The quote is from Justice Stephen Breyer's bench dissent at 32:53 in *Parents Involved v. Seattle School*, 551 U.S. 701 (2007).

92. South Carolina v. Gathers, 490 U.S. 805, 824 (1982) (Scalia, J., dissenting).

93. *See, e.g.*, Robert Post & Reva Siegel, Roe *Rage: Democratic Constitutionalism and Backlash*, 42 HARV. C.R.-C.L. L. REV. 373, 381 (2007) ("One important avenue for influencing constitutional decision-making is the appointment of Supreme Court Justices.").

94. Planned Parenthood v. Casey, 505 U.S. 833, 960 (1992).

95. *See* Post & Siegel, *supra*; Reva B. Siegel, *Memory Games:* Dobbs's *Originalism as Anti-Democratic Living Constitutionalism—and Some Pathways for Resistance*, 101 TEX. L. REV. 1128 (2023); MARY ZIEGLER, DOLLARS FOR LIFE: THE ANTI-ABORTION MOVEMENT AND THE FALL OF THE REPUBLICAN ESTABLISHMENT (New Haven: Yale Univ. Press, 2022).

96. *See* Aaron Blake, *Trump Makes Clear Roe Is on the Chopping Block*, WASH. POST (July 2, 2018), https://www.washingtonpost.com/news/the-fix/wp/2018/07/02/trump-makes-clear-roe-v-wade-is-on-the-chopping-block/.

97. NAMUDNO v. Holder, 557 U.S. 193 (2009).

Chapter 10

* Our thanks for terrific research assistance to Cardozo Law student Lauren Chamberlin, NYU Law students Ry Walker and Kelsey Brown, and University of Pennsylvania Carey Law student Megan Bird. For insightful comments and critiques,

we thank Serena Mayeri, Reva Siegel, Nelson Tebbe, and participants in the NYC-Area Family Law Scholars Workshop.

1. *See Abortion on the Ballot*, N.Y. TIMES (Dec. 20, 2022), https://www.nytimes.com/interactive/2022/11/08/us/elections/results-abortion.html ("The proposal [to] create a constitutional right to personal reproductive autonomy" in Vermont passed with 76.8% of the vote. The Michigan proposal to "create a state constitutional right to reproductive freedom, including decisions 'about all matters relating to pregnancy,' such as abortion and contraception," passed with 56.7% of the vote. California voters adopted a state constitutional amendment "to protect a person's reproductive freedom" with 66.9% of the vote.).

2. *Id.* ("An amendment [that] would state there is no right to abortion . . . in the State Constitution" failed in Kentucky with 52.3% voting no. A measure that "would enact a law making any infant 'born alive' at any gestational age a legal person" and would "criminalize health care providers who do not make every effort to save the life of the infant" failed in Montana with 52.6% of voters voting no.).

3. *See* Craig Palosky, *Analysis Reveals How Abortion Boosted Democratic Candidates in Tuesday's Midterm Election*, KFF (Nov. 11, 2022), https://www.kff.org/other/press-release/analysis-reveals-how-abortion-boosted-democratic-candidates-in-tuesd ays-midterm-election/ ("About four in ten (38%) voters overall said that the Supreme Court decision ending the constitutional right to an abortion had a major impact on their decision about whether to vote in this year's election."); Alice Miranda Ollstein & Megan Messerly, *A Predicted "Red Wave" Crashed Into Wall of Abortion Rights Support on Tuesday*, POLITICO (Nov. 9, 2022), https://www.politico.com/news/2022/11/09/abortion-votes-2022-election-results-00065983 ("Michigan Democrats, who campaigned on their opposition to the state's 1931 near-total abortion ban and ran on newly drawn maps that made districts more competitive, flipped control of the state Legislature for the first time in decades."); Elaine Kamarck & William A. Galston, *It Wasn't Just "the Economy Stupid"—It Was Abortion*, BROOKINGS (Nov. 10, 2022), https://www.brookings.edu/blog/fixgov/2022/11/10/it-wasnt-just-the-economy-stupid-it-was-abortion/ ("Although the Democrat, John Fetterman gave a halting performance because he was still recovering from a serious stroke, his opponent, Republican Mehmet Oz, managed to make what had to be one of the most damaging comments on abortion ever," and the comment distracted voters.); Ruby Belle Booth et al., *The Abortion Election: How Youth Prioritized and Voted Based on Issues*, TUFTS U. TISCH COLL.– CIRCLE (Nov. 14, 2022), https://circle.tufts.edu/latest-research/abortion-election-how-youth-prioritized-and-voted-based-issues (finding youth prioritized abortion data over all other issues).

4. *See After* Roe *Fell: Abortion Laws by State*, CTR. REPROD. RTS., https://reproductiverig hts.org/maps/abortion-laws-by-state/ (last visited Jan. 30, 2023).

5. Dobbs v. Jackson Women's Health Organization, 142 S. Ct. 2228 (2022).

6. Roe v. Wade, 410 U.S. 113 (1973).

7. Planned Parenthood v. Casey, 505 U.S. 833 (1992).

8. *Dobbs*, 142 S. Ct. at 2243. *See* Editorial Board, *Kansas, Abortion and the Supreme Court*, WALL ST. J. (Aug. 4, 2022), https://www.wsj.com/articles/kansas-and-the-supr

eme-court-samuel-alito-roe-v-wade-john-harris-david-von-drehle-abortion-dobbs-11659650794 ("[T]he vote defeating a constitutional amendment to overturn a state Supreme Court ruling on abortion is a rousing vindication of Justice Alito's majority opinion overturning *Roe v. Wade*.").

9. *Dobbs*, 142 S. Ct. at 2277.

10. *Id.* at 2265.

11. *Id.*

12. *Id.* at 2259.

13. Douglas NeJaime & Reva Siegel, *Answering the* Lochner *Objection: Substantive Due Process and the Role of Courts in a Democracy*, 96 N.Y.U. L. Rev. 1902, 1910 (2021).

14. *Id. See also* Jeremy Waldron, Political Theory 37 (Cambridge: Harvard University Press, 2016).

15. *See* Amy Gutmann & Dennis Thompson, Democracy and Disagreement (Cambridge, MA: Belknap Press, 1996); *see also* Robert C. Post, *Between Democracy and Community: The Legal Constitution of Social Form, in* Democratic Community: Nomos XXXV 163, 172 (New York: New York University Press, John W. Chapman & Ian Shapiro eds., 1993).

16. *Dobbs*, 142 S. Ct. at 2277 (emphasis added).

17. *Id.* (emphasis added).

18. *Id.* at 2283–84 (emphasis added).

19. Miriam Seifter, *Countermajoritarian Legislatures*, 121 Colum. L. Rev. 1733, 1755–76 (2021); Jessica Bulman-Pozen & Miriam Seifter, *The Democracy Principle in State Constitutions*, 1119 Mich. L. Rev. 859, 859 (2020).

20. Hodes & Nauser, MDS, P.A. v. Schmidt, 440 P.3d 461, 502 (Kan. 2019); Planned Parenthood of the Heartland, Inc. v. Iowa Bd. Med., 865 N.W.2d 252 (Iowa 2015), *overruled by* Planned Parenthood of the Heartland, Inc. v. Reynolds, 975 N.W.2d 710 (Iowa 2022).

21. *See* David E. Pozen, *Judicial Elections as Popular Constitutionalism*, 110 Colum. L. Rev. 2047, 2117–18 (2010). A striking example here is Wisconsin, where the gulf between statewide preferences and legislative majorities is especially striking. Members of the state supreme court are typically elected with over 50% of the state-wide support. For example, Jill Karofsky was elected to the Wisconsin Supreme Court in 2020 with 55.2% of the vote (855,573 votes), beating Daniel Kelly, the incumbent, who received 44.7% (693,134 votes). *Jill Karofsky*, Ballotpedia, https://ballotpe dia.org/Jill_Karofsky (last visited Nov. 19, 2022). In 2022, the Democratic governor, Tony Evers, won 51.2% statewide (1,358,664 votes). And yet in the same election that produced Evers's statewide victory, the Republican Party retained control of both chambers of the legislature in the state by a significant margin. *Wisconsin Governor Election Results*, N.Y. Times, https://www.nytimes.com/interactive/2022/11/08/us/elections/results-wisconsin-governor.html (last visited Nov. 19, 2022); *Party Control of Wisconsin State Government*, Ballotpedia, https://ballotpedia.org/party_con-trol_of_Wisconsin_state_government (last visited Nov. 19, 2022); Hope Karnopp, *Did Wisconsin Republicans Achieve a Veto-Proof Supermajority in the Legislature in the 2022 Election?*, Wis. Watch (Nov. 14, 2022), wisconsinwatch.org/2022/11/

did-wisconsin-republicans-achieve-a-veto-proof-supermajority-in-the-legislature-in-the-2022-election/ (reporting that beginning in 2023, Wisconsin Republicans will hold approximately 64% of seats in the state assembly and 67% of seats in the state senate).

22. Pozen, *supra* note 21, at 2048–49.

23. Seifter, *supra* note 19, at 1756. For a discussion of the Supreme Court's role in facilitating the type of gerrymandering necessary to produce these results, see *infra*.

24. *See* Katherine Shaw, *Constitutional Nondefense in the States*, 114 Colum. L. Rev. 213, 231 (2014).

25. *See, e.g.*, Bruce Schreiner, *Kentucky Governor Vetoes Restrictive 15-Week Abortion Ban*, Associated Press (April 8, 2022), https://www.pbs.org/newshour/politics/kentucky-governor-vetoes-proposed-15-week-abortion-ban.

26. *See* Cameron v. EMW Women's Surgical Ctr., 142 S. Ct. 1002 (2022).

27. William P. Marshall, *Break Up the Presidency? Governors, State Attorneys General, and Lessons from the Divided Executive*, 115 Yale L.J. 2446, 2448 (2006).

28. Miriam Seifter, *State Institutions and Democratic Opportunity*, 72 Duke L.J. 275, 280, 299, 325 (2022); *see generally* Katherine Shaw, *State Administrative Constitutionalism*, 69 Ark. L. Rev. 527 (2016).

29. Bulman-Pozen & Seifter, *supra* note 19, at 883–84; John J. Dinan, The American State Constitutional Tradition 94 (Lawrence: University Press of Kansas, 2006).

30. Mitch Smith & Katie Glueck, *Kansas Voters to Preserve Abortion Rights Protections in Its Constitution*, N.Y. Times (Aug. 2, 2022), https://www.nytimes.com/2022/08/02/us/kansas-abortion-rights-vote.html; Aprile Rickert, *Kentucky Voters Reject Amendment That Would Have Affirmed No Right to Abortion*, NPR (Nov. 9, 2022), https://www.npr.org/2022/11/09/1134835022/kentucky-abortion-amendment-midterms-resulting; Olivia Weitz, *Montana Voters Reject So-called "Born Alive" Ballot Measure*, NPR (Nov. 10, 2022), https://www.npr.org/2022/11/10/1134833151/montana-midterms-results-born-alive-abortion; Mitch Smith & Ava Savani, *Michigan, California, and Vermont Affirm Abortion Rights in Ballot Proposals*, N.Y. Times (Nov. 9, 2022), https://www.nytimes.com/2022/11/09/us/abortion-rights-ballot-proposals.html.

31. Partial-Birth Abortion Ban Act of 2003, 18 U.S.C. § 1531.

32. Gonzales v. Carhart, 550 U.S. 124 (2007).

33. Dobbs v. Jackson Women's Health Org., 142 S. Ct. 2228, 2305 (2022) (Kavanaugh, J., concurring) ("The Constitution is neutral and leaves the issue for the people and their elected representatives to resolve through the democratic process in the States *or Congress*—like the numerous other difficult questions of American social and economic policy that the Constitution does not address.") (emphasis added). *See* Aaron Tang, *After* Dobbs: *History, Tradition, and the Uncertain Future of a Nationwide Abortion Ban*, 75 Stan. L. Rev. 1091 (2023).

34. *See, e.g.*, Exec. Order No. 14076, Executive Order on Securing Access to Reproductive and Other Healthcare Services, 87 FR 42053 (2022), https://www.whitehouse.gov/briefing-room/presidential-actions/2022/08/03/executive-order-on-securing-access-to-reproductive-and-other-healthcare-services/.

35. *See, e.g.,* Jane Mayer, *State Legislatures Are Torching Democracy,* THE NEW YORKER (Aug. 6, 2022).

36. Aliza Forman-Rabinovici & Olatunde C. A. Johnson, *Political Equality, Gender, and Democratic Legitimation in* Dobbs, 46 HARV. J. L. & GENDER 81, 103 (2023).

37. *See e.g.,* Matthew A. Baum, Alauna Safarpour, & Kristin Lunz Trujillo, *Kansas Vote for Abortion Rights Highlights Disconnect Between Majority Opinion on Abortion Laws and Restrictive State Laws Being Passed After Supreme Court Decision,* THE CONVERSATION (Aug. 3, 2022), https://theconversation.com/kansas-vote-for-abort ion-rights-highlights-disconnect-between-majority-opinion-on-abortion-laws-and-restrictive-state-laws-being-passed-after-supreme-court-decision-187138; Jeff Diamant & Aleksandra Sandstrom, *Do State Laws on Abortion Reflect Public Opinion?,* PEW RSCH. CTR. (Jan. 21, 2020), https://www.pewresearch.org/fact-tank/2020/01/21/do-state-laws-on-abortion-reflect-public-opinion/.

38. *Dobbs,* 142 S. Ct. at 2284.

39. *Id.* at 2265.

40. *Id.* at 2257 ("In some States, voters may believe that the abortion right should be even more extensive than the right that *Roe* and *Casey* recognized. Voters in other States may wish to impose tight restrictions based on their belief that abortion destroys an "unborn human being.") (quoting Miss. Code Ann. §41–41–191(4)(b)).

41. *Id.* at 2309 (Kavanaugh, J., concurring) ("[M]ay a State bar a resident of that State from traveling to another State to obtain an abortion? In my view, the answer is no based on the constitutional right to interstate travel.").

42. *Id.* at 2305.

43. *Id.*

44. *Id.* at 2277 (noting women's ability "to seek to affect the legislative process by influencing public opinion, lobbying legislators, voting, and running for office," and observing that "women are not without electoral or political power").

45. As support for its claim that "women are not without political power," the majority notes that "the percentage of women who register to vote and cast ballots is consistently higher than the percentage of men who do so"; it specifically points to Mississippi, where, in 2020 "women, who make up around 51.5 percent of the population of Mississippi, constituted 55.5 percent of the voters who cast ballots." *Id.* at 2277 (citing Dep't of Commerce, U.S. Census Bureau, Voting and Registration in the Election of November 2020, Table 4b, Reported Voting and Registration, by Sex, Race, and Hispanic Origin, for States: November 2020, https://www.census.gov/data.html).

46. *Gender Differences in Voter Turnout,* CTR. FOR AM. WOMEN AND POL., https://cawp.rutgers.edu/facts/voters/gender-differences-voter-turnout#NPGR (last visited Nov. 22, 2022).

47. *Women in State Legislatures 2022,* CTR. FOR AM. WOMEN AND POL., https://cawp.rutgers.edu/facts/levels-office/state-legislature/women-state-legislatures-2022#table (last visited Nov. 23, 2022).

48. *Id.*

49. *Women in the U.S. Congress 2022*, CTR. FOR AM. WOMEN AND POL., https://cawp.
rutgers.edu/facts/levels-office/congress/women-us-congress-2022 (last visited Nov.
23, 2022).

50. Timothy M. LaPira, Kathleen Marchetti, & Herschel F. Thomas, *Gender Politics in the*
Lobbying Profession, 16 POL. & GENDER 816, 816 (2019).

51. Kira Sanbonmatsu & Claire Gothreau, *The Money Race for the State Legislature*, CTR.
FOR AM. WOMEN AND POL. 8 (2020), https://cawp.rutgers.edu/sites/default/files/
resources/cawp_money_race.pdf.

52. Jennifer A. Heerwig & Katie M. Gordon, *Buying a Voice: Gendered Contribution*
Careers Among Affluent Political Donors to Federal Elections, 1980–2008, 33 SOCIO.
F. 805, 805, 814 (Sept., 2018) (finding "large and persistent gendered inequalities of
political voice continue to characterize this significant form of political influence").

53. Jacob M. Grumbach, Alexander Sahn, & Sarah Staszak, *Gender, Race, and*
Intersectionality in Campaign Finance, 44 POL. BEHAV. 319, 330 (2022).

54. Forman-Rabinovici & Johnson, *supra* note 36, at 116.

55. *Id.*

56. *See infra.*

57. WIS. CONST. of 1848, art. III, § 1 (amended 1934).

58. Dobbs v. Jackson Women's Health Org., 142 S. Ct. 2228, 2248 (2022).

59. *Id.*

60. Reva B. Siegel, *Memory Games:* Dobbs's *Originalism as Anti-Democratic Living*
Constitutionalism—and Some Pathways for Resistance, 101 TEX. L. REV. 1127, 1185–
87 (2023).

61. *Id.* at 1186–87.

62. *Id.* at 1192.

63. David Landau & Rosalind Dixon, Dobbs, *Democracy, and Dysfunction*, FSU COLL. L.
(Aug. 2022), https://papers.ssrn.com/sol3/papers.cfm?abstract_id=4185324.

64. Siegel, *supra* note 60, at 1196 ("*Dobbs* is antidemocratic because it locates constitutional authority in imagined communities of the past, entrenching norms, traditions,
and modes of life associated with old status hierarchies.").

65. Reva B. Siegel, *She the People: The Nineteenth Amendment, Sex Equality, Federalism,*
and the Family, 115 HARV. L. REV. 947, 1002–3 (2002); Richard L. Hasen & Leah M.
Litman, *Thin and Thick Conceptions of the Nineteenth Amendment Right to Vote and*
Congress's Power to Enforce It, 108 GEO. L.J. 27, 61–62 (2020); Brief of Equal Protection
Const. L. Scholars Serena Mayeri, Melissa Murray, & Reva Siegel as Amici Curiae in
Support of Respondents at 5–7, Dobbs v. Jackson Women's Health Org., 142 S. Ct.
2228 (2022) (No. 18-60868).

66. Brief of Equal Protection Const. L. Scholars Serena Mayeri, Melissa Murray, & Reva
Siegel as Amici Curiae in Support of Respondents at 5–7, Dobbs v. Jackson Women's
Health Org., 142 S. Ct. 2228 (2022) (No. 18-60868).

67. Melissa Murray, *Children of Men: The Roberts Court's Jurisprudence of Masculinity*, 60
HOUSTON L. REV. 799, 859 (2023) ("No actor has done more to distort the landscape

of democratic deliberation—that is, to make it difficult for individuals to register their policy preferences at the ballot box—than the Court itself.").

68. *See* Michael J. Klarman, *Foreword: The Degradation of American Democracy and the Court,* 134 HARV. L. REV. 1, 178–79 (2020) ("The Court is at the peak of its institutional legitimacy when it intervenes to bolster democracy. . . . Unfortunately, today's Republican Justices seem insensitive, or even hostile, to this conception of the Court's constitutional role."); Pamela S. Karlan, *The New Countermajoritarian Difficulty,* 109 CALIF. L. REV. 2323, 2344–45 (2021) ("In sharp contrast to the Warren and Burger Courts, the current Supreme Court has done virtually nothing to make elections more inclusive or more responsive.").

69. *Wisconsin Election Results,* WASH. POST, washingtonpost.com/election-results/2022/wisconsin/ (last visited Nov. 23, 2022).

70. Karnopp, *supra* note 21.

71. Rucho v. Common Cause, 139 S. Ct. 2484, 2506 (2019).

72. *Id.*

73. *Id.* at 2507 ("Our conclusion does not condone excessive partisan gerrymandering. . . . The States . . . are actively addressing the issue on a number of fronts . . . [including] by placing power to draw electoral districts in the hands of independent commissions."); *id.* ("Provisions in state statutes and state constitutions can provide standards and guidance for state courts to apply.").

74. Arizona State Legislature v. Arizona Indep. Redistricting Comm'n, 576 U.S. 787, 825 (2015) (Roberts, C.J., dissenting) ("Art. I, § 4 . . . vests congressional redistricting authority in 'the Legislature' of each State. An Arizona ballot initiative transferred that authority from 'the Legislature' to an 'Independent Redistricting Commission.' The majority approves this deliberate constitutional evasion by . . . revising 'the Legislature' to mean 'the people.' ").

75. Moore v. Harper, 142 S.Ct. 1089 (2023); Leah M. Litman & Katherine Shaw, *Textualism, Judicial Supremacy, and the Independent State Legislature Theory,* 2022 WIS. L. REV. 1235.

76. Brnovich v. Democratic Nat'l Comm., 141 S. Ct. 2321, 2350 (2021) (Kagan, J., dissenting).

77. Shelby County v. Holder, 570 U.S. 529 (2013).

78. *Brnovich,* 141 S. Ct. at 2321.

79. Allen v. Milligan, 143 S.Ct. 1487 (2023).

80. *Id.* at 1519 (Kavanaugh, J., concurring) (describing Justice Clarence Thomas's position that "even if Congress in 1982 could constitutionally authorize race-based redistricting under § 2 for some period of time, the authority to conduct race-based redistricting cannot extend indefinitely into the future," and noting that "Alabama did not raise that temporal argument in this Court, and I therefore would not consider it at this time").

81. Husted v. A. Philip Randolph Inst., 138 S. Ct. 1833, 1835 (2018); Lisa Marshall Manheim & Elizabeth G. Porter, *The Elephant in the Room: Intentional Voter Suppression,* 2018 SUP. CT. REV. 213, 214 (2018).

82. *Husted,* 138 S. Ct. at 1835.

83. *Id.* (permitting Ohio to purge voters where such voters had not voted for two years, had failed to return an official postcard, and had not voted for another four years after failing to submit postcard).

84. Crawford v. Marion County Election Bd., 553 U.S. 181 (2008).

85. *See Voter ID Laws*, NAT'L CONF. OF STATE LEGIS., https://www.ncsl.org/elections-and-campaigns/voter-id#statebystate (last updated Mar. 9, 2023) (listing voter identification requirements in force in thirty-five states).

86. *See, e.g.*, Veasey v. Abbott, 830 F.3d 216 (5th Cir. 2016) (finding that the voter ID law was racially discriminatory under the Voting Rights Act); Holmes v. Moore, 2022-NCSC-122, 881 S.E.2d 486, *reh'g granted*, No. 342PA19-2, 2023 WL 1769462 (N.C. Feb. 3, 2023) (holding that state voter identification legislation was discriminatory in intent and violated the state constitution's equal protection provisions); Applewhite v. Com., No. 330 M.D. 2012, 2014 WL 184988 (Pa. Commw. Ct. Jan. 17, 2014) (holding that the Pennsylvania voter identification law violated state constitution fundamental rights, but not equal protection); Martin v. Kohls, 2014 Ark. 427, 444 S.W.3d 844 (2014) (finding that Arkansas's voter identification law was unconstitutional on its face); Priorities USA v. State, 591 S.W.3d 448 (Mo. 2020) (striking down the affidavit requirement of Missouri's voter identification law).

87. *See Voter ID Laws*, NAT'L CONF. OF STATE LEGIS. (last updated Mar. 9, 2023), https://www.ncsl.org/elections-and-campaigns/voter-id#statebystate (listing voter identification requirements in force in thirty-five states).

88. Matt A. Barreto, Stephen. A. Nuño, & Gabriel R. Sanchez, *The Disproportionate Impact of Voter-ID Requirements on the Electorate—New Evidence from Indiana*, 42 POLI. SCI 111, 114–15 (2009); Bernard L. Fraga & Michael G. Miller, *Who Does Voter ID Keep from Voting?*, 84 J. POLIT. 1091, 1102–3 (2022).

89. Citizens United v. Fed. Election Comm'n, 558 U.S. 310 (2010).

90. *Citizens United* 558 U.S. 310; SpeechNow v. Fed. Election Commission, 599 F.3d 686 (D.C. Cir. 2010); *see also* Jennifer A. Heerwig & Katherine Shaw, *Through a Glass, Darkly: The Rhetoric and Reality of Campaign Finance Disclosure*, 102 GEO. L.J. 1443, 1445 (2014) (discussing *Citizens United*).

91. *Citizens United*, 558 U.S. 310 (2010).

92. Deborah Hellman, *Defining Corruption and Constitutionalizing Democracy*, 111 MICH. L. REV. 1385, 1408–14 (2013); *see* Samuel Issacharoff, *On Political Corruption*, 124 HARV. L. REV. 118 (2010).

93. Nicholas O. Stephanopoulos, *The Anti-Carolene Court*, 2019 SUP. CT. REV. 111, 116 (2019) ("[T]he franchise is a freedom, too, yet the Roberts Court has never found a violation of it.").

94. *Citizens United* 558 U.S. 310; McCutcheon v. Fed. Election Comm'n, 572 U.S. 185 (2014).

95. Shelby County v. Holder, 570 U.S. 529, 556 (2013).

Chapter 11

1. DOROTHY ROBERTS, KILLING THE BLACK BODY: RACE, REPRODUCTION, AND THE MEANING OF LIBERTY (New York: Vintage Books, 1997); BRIANNA THEOBALD, REPRODUCTION ON THE RESERVATION: PREGNANCY, CHILDBIRTH, AND COLONIALISM IN THE LONG TWENTIETH CENTURY (Chapel Hill: University of North Carolina Press, 2019); ELENA R. GUTIÉRREZ, FERTILE MATTERS: THE POLITICS OF MEXICAN-ORIGIN WOMEN'S REPRODUCTION (Austin: University of Texas Press, 2008); JAEL SILLIMAN ET AL., UNDIVIDED RIGHTS: WOMEN OF COLOR ORGANIZE FOR REPRODUCTIVE FREEDOM (Chicago: Haymarket Books, 2016).

2. *Pregnant and Scared? How Fake Clinics Prey on Women*, NAT'L WOMEN'S HEALTH NETWORK (July 9, 2022), https://nwhn.org/expect-need-pregnancy-abortion-help/. Some anti-abortion Christian Evangelicals promote adoption of children from developing countries, including migrant children who were separated from their families at the U.S. border, as an expression of their "pro-life" politics. KATHRYN JOYCE, THE CHILD CATCHERS: RESCUE, TRAFFICKING, AND THE NEW GOSPEL OF ADOPTION (New York: Public Affairs, 2013); Chrissy Stroop, *Are Evangelical Adoption Agencies Stealing Children?*, DAME, (Oct. 1, 2018), https://www.damemagazine.com/2018/10/01/are-evangelical-adoption-agencies-stealing-children/; Jill Filipovic, *Adoption of Separated Migrant Kids Shows "Prolife" Groups' Disrespect for Maternity*, GUARDIAN (Oct. 30, 2019), https://www.theguardian.com/commentisfree/2019/oct/30/adoption-separated-migrant-children-pro-lifers-deep-disrespect-for-maternity.

3. Laura Briggs, *Making Abortion Illegal Does Not Lead to More Adoptions*, 10 ADOPTION & CULTURE (2022).

4. *See* Gretchen Sisson, *The Good Plaintiff*, 10 ADOPTION & CULTURE (2022), https://muse.jhu.edu/pub/30/article/871268/pdf; Mical Raz, *Our Adoption Policies Have Harmed Families and Children*, WASH. POST (Nov. 18, 2022), https://www.washingtonpost.com/made-by-history/2022/11/18/adoption-parental-rights/?utm_campaign=wp_main&utm_medium=social&utm_source=twitter.

5. Susan Matthews, *While Hearing the Case That Could Overturn* Roe, *Amy Coney Barrett Suggests Adoption Could Obviate the Need for Abortion Anyway*, SLATE (Dec. 1, 2021), https://slate.com/news-and-politics/2021/12/amy-coney-barrett-abortion-adoption-comments.html.

6. Dobbs v. Jackson Women's Health Org., 142. S. Ct. 2228, 2259 (2022).

7. *Id.* at note 46.

8. Michele Merritt, *My Adoption, My Abortion: Getting Clear About What Counts as a Reproductive Choice*, 10 ADOPTION & CULTURE (2022), https://muse.jhu.edu/pub/30/article/871266/pdf; Mary Cardaras, *Adoption: Not a Default Setting*, 10 ADOPTION & CULTURE (2022), https://muse.jhu.edu/pub/30/article/871014/pdf. *See also* Erica C. Walker, *Adoption, Abortion, and Nonpersons*, 10 ADOPTION & CULTURE (2022), https://muse.jhu.edu/pub/30/article/871013/pdf ("[I]n the body of common law that Alito cites to cinch his project to criminalize abortion, adoption does not exist.").

9. ANN FESSLER, THE GIRLS WHO WENT AWAY: THE HIDDEN HISTORY OF WOMEN WHO SURRENDERED CHILDREN FOR ADOPTION IN THE DECADES BEFORE *ROE*

v. WADE (New York: Penguin Press, 2006); KAREN WILSON-BUTERBAUGH, THE BABY SCOOP ERA: UNWED MOTHERS, INFANT ADOPTION, AND FORCED SURRENDER (New York: Penguin Press, 2017); GABRIELLE GLASER, AMERICAN BABY: A MOTHER, A CHILD, AND THE SHADOW HISTORY OF ADOPTION (New York: Viking, 2021).

10. DIANA GREENE FOSTER, THE TURNAWAY STUDY: TEN YEARS, A THOUSAND WOMEN, AND THE CONSEQUENCES OF HAVING—AND BEING DENIED—AN ABORTION (New York: Scribner, 2020); Laura Briggs, *Making Abortion Illegal Does Not Lead to More Adoptions*, 10 ADOPTION & CULTURE (2022); Gretchen Sisson, *Who Are the Women Who Relinquish Infants for Adoption? Domestic Adoption and Contemporary Birth Motherhood in the United States*, 54 PERSPECTIVES ON SEXUAL & REPRO. HEALTH 46 (2022); Sydney Trent, *Women Denied Abortion Rarely Choose Adoption. That's Unlikely to Change*, WASH. POST (July 18, 2022), https://www.washingtonpost.com/dc-md-va/2022/07/18/adoption-abortion-roe-dobbs/.

11. FOSTER, *supra* note 10.

12. DOROTHY ROBERTS, TORN APART: HOW THE CHILD WELFARE SYSTEM DESTROYS BLACK FAMILIES—AND HOW ABOLITION CAN BUILD A SAFER WORLD (New York: Basic Books, 2022).

13. *Child Welfare: Purposes, Federal Programs, and Funding*, CONG. RSCH. SERV. (2022), https://sgp.fas.org/crs/misc/IF10590.pdf.

14. Dorothy E. Roberts, *The Racial Geography of Child Welfare: Toward a New Research Paradigm*, 87 CHILD WELFARE 125 (2011); Kelley Fong, *Neighborhood Inequality in the Prevalence of Reported and Substantiated Child Maltreatment*, 90 CHILD ABUSE & NECLECT 13 (2019).

15. Hyunil Kim, Christopher Wildeman, Melissa Jonson-Reid, & Brett Drake, *Lifetime Prevalence of Investigating Child Maltreatment Among US Children*, 107 AM. J. PUB. HEALTH (2017), https://ajph.aphapublications.org/doi/abs/10.2105/AJPH.2016.303 545; Frank Edwards, Sara Wakefield, Kieran Healy, & Christopher Wildeman, *Contact with Child Protective Services Is Pervasive but Unequally Distributed by Race and Ethnicity in Large US Counties*, 118 PNAS (2021), https://www.pnas.org/doi/10.1073/pnas.2106272118.

16. TINA LEE, CATCHING A CASE: INEQUALITY AND FEAR IN NEW YORK CITY'S CHILD WELFARE SYSTEM (New Brunswick: Rutgers University Press, 2016); Kelley Fong, *Getting Eyes in the Home: Child Protective Services Investigations and State Surveillance of Family Life*, 84 AM. SOCIOLOGICAL REV. 610 (2020); Tarek Ismail, *Family Policing and the Fourth Amendment*, 111 CA. L. REV. 1485 (2023).

17. *Child Welfare: Purposes, Federal Programs, and Funding*, CONG. RSCH. SERV. (2022), https://sgp.fas.org/crs/misc/IF10590.pdf.

18. DIANE L. REDLEAF, THEY TOOK THE KIDS LAST NIGHT: HOW THE CHILD PROTECTION SYSTEM PUTS FAMILIES AT RISK (Santa Barbara: Praeger, 2018); Josh Gupta-Kagan, *America's Hidden Foster Care System*, 72 STAN. L. REV. 841, 849–52 (2020).

19. LAURA BRIGGS, TAKING CHILDREN: A HISTORY OF AMERICAN TERROR (Oakland: University of California Press, 2021).

20. *Child Maltreatment 2019*, ADMIN. FOR CHILDREN AND FAMILIES, U.S. DEPT. OF HEALTH & HUMAN SERVS. (2021), https://www.acf.hhs.gov/sites/default/files/documents/cb/cm2019.pdf.

21. Diane L. Redleaf, *Narrowing Neglect Laws Means Ending State-Mandated Helicopter Parenting*, AM. BAR ASS'N. (Sept. 11, 2020), https://www.americanbar.org/groups/litigation/committees/childrens-rights/articles/2020/fall2020-narrowing-neglect-laws-means-ending-state-mandated-helicopter-parenting/.

22. Elizabeth Brico, *"The Civil Death Penalty"—My Motherhood Is Legally Terminated*, FILTER (July 13, 2020), https://filtermag.org/motherhood-legally-terminated/.

23. Christopher Wildeman, Frank R. Edwards, & Sara Wakefield, *The Cumulative Prevalence of Termination of Parental Rights for U.S. Children, 2000–2016*, 25 CHILD MALTREATMENT 32 (2020).

24. Barbara White Stack, *Law to Increase Adoptions Results in More Orphans*, PITT. POST GAZETTE (Jan. 2, 2005), https://www.seattlepi.com/national/article/Law-to-increase-adoptions-results-in-more-orphans-1163211.php.

25. *Young Adults Formerly in Foster Care: Challenges and Solutions*, YOUTH.GOV, https://youth.gov/youth-briefs/foster-care-youth-brief; *Foster Youth and Homelessness*, HOMELESSNESS POL'Y RSCH. INST., https://socialinnovation.usc.edu/wp-content/uploads/2021/05/Foster-Youth-and-Homelessness-final-1.pdf.

26. ROBERTS, *supra* note 1 JACQUELINE JONES, LABOR OF LOVE, LABOR OF SORROW: BLACK WOMEN, WORK, AND THE FAMILY FROM SLAVERY TO THE PRESENT 14, 35 (New York: Basic Books, 1985); ANGELA Y. DAVIS, WOMEN, RACE & CLASS (New York: Vintage Books, 1983); DEBORAH GRAY WHITE, AR'N'T I A WOMAN? FEMALE SLAVES IN THE PLANTATION SOUTH (New York: W. W. Norton, rev. ed. 1999).

27. Dorothy Roberts, *Race*, in THE 1619 PROJECT: A NEW ORIGIN STORY 45 (New York: One World, Nikole Hannah-Jones, Caitlin Roper, Ilena Silverman & Jake Silverstein eds., 2021); RACHEL A. FEINSTEIN, WHEN RAPE WAS LEGAL: THE UNTOLD HISTORY OF SEXUAL VIOLENCE DURING SLAVERY 16–47 (New York: Routledge/Taylor & Francis Group, 2019).

28. Jennifer L. Morgan, *Reproductive Rights, Slavery, and* Dobbs v. Jackson, BLACK PERSPECTIVES (Aug. 2, 2022), https://www.aaihs.org/reproductive-rights-slavery-and-dobbs-v-jackson [https://perma.cc/3LRY-ESWL]; *see also* Dána-Ain Davis, *Trump, Race, and Reproduction in the Afterlife of Slavery*, 34 CULTURAL ANTHROPOLOGY 26, 27–30 (2019).

29. PEGGY COOPER DAVIS, NEGLECTED STORIES: THE CONSTITUTION AND FAMILY VALUES (New York: Hill and Wang, 1997).

30. HEATHER ANDREA WILLIAMS, HELP ME TO FIND MY PEOPLE: THE AFRICAN AMERICAN SEARCH FOR FAMILY LOST IN SLAVERY (Chapel Hill: University of North Carolina Press, 2012).

31. TONI MORRISON, BELOVED 28 (New York: Columbia University Press, 1998).

32. DAVIS, *supra* note 29.

33. *Id.*

34. ROBERTS, *supra* note 1.

35. *Id.* at 92.

36. *Id.* at 37.

37. DAVIS, *supra* note 29; ROBERTS, *supra* note 1 at 96.

38. CONG. GLOBE, 38th Cong., 1st Sess. 1439 (1864) at 1324. For similar statements, *see* CONG. GLOBE, 38th Cong., 1st Sess. 2990 (1864).

39. While ignoring the abolitionist origins of the Fourteenth Amendment, *Dobbs* applied an antidemocratic originalism that "restricts and threatens rights that enable equal participation of members of historically marginalized groups." Reva Siegel, *Memory Games: Dobbs' Originalism as Anti-Democratic Living Constitutionalism—and Some Pathways for Resistance*, 101 TEX. L. REV. 1128 (2023).

40. ANGE-MARIE HANCOCK, THE POLITICS OF DISGUST: THE PUBLIC IDENTITY OF THE WELFARE QUEEN 57–64 (New York: NYU Press, 2004).

41. *The Negro Family: The Case for Nat'l Action*, OFF. POL'Y PLANNING & RSCH., U.S. DEPT. LAB. (Mar. 1965).

42. ELIZABETH HINTON, FROM THE WAR ON POVERTY TO THE WAR ON CRIME: THE MAKING OF MASS INCARCERATION IN AMERICA 63–179 (Cambridge, MA: Harvard University Press, 2016).

43. ROBERTS, *supra* note 1; MICHELE GOODWIN, POLICING THE WOMB (Cambridge: Cambridge University Press, 2020).

44. Lynn Paltrow & Jeanne Flavin, *Arrests and Prosecutions of Pregnant Women, 1973–2020*, NAT'L ADVOCS. FOR PREGNANT WOMEN (Sept. 18, 2021), https://www.nation aladvocatesforpregnantwomen.org/arrests-and-prosecutions-of-pregnant-women-1973-2020 [https://perma.cc/9ENA-UENS].

45. Kate Zernike, *Is a Fetus a Person? An Anti-Abortion Strategy Says Yes.*, N.Y. TIMES (Aug. 30, 2022), https://www.nytimes.com/2022/08/21/us/abortionanti-fetus-per son.html [https://perma.cc/Z778-NPY4]; Erika Bachiochi, *What Makes a Fetus a Person*, N.Y. TIMES (July 1, 2022), https://www.nytimes.com/2022/07/01/opinion/fetal-personhood-constitution.html [https://perma.cc/7L6Q-5CLP].

46. Robert Baldwin III, *Losing a Pregnancy Could Land You in Jail in post-*Roe *America*, NPR (July 3, 2022), https://www.npr.org/2022/07/03/1109015302/abortion-prosecut ing-pregnancy-loss.

47. *See* Jia Tolentino, *We're Not Going Back to the Time Before* Roe. *We're Going Somewhere Worse*, NEW YORKER (June 24, 2022), https://www.newyorker.com/magazine/2022/07/04/we-arenot-going-back-to-the-time-before-roe-we-are-going-somewhere-worse [https://perma.cc/9XPBNETZ]; Cary Aspinwall et al., *They Lost Pregnancies for Unclear Reasons. Then They Were Prosecuted*, WASH. POST (Sept. 12, 2022), https://www.washingtonpost.com/national-security/2022/09/01/prosecutions-drugs-misca rriages-meth-stillbirths [https://perma.cc/P9WZ-MFLL].

48. Khiara Bridges, *Race, Pregnancy, and the Opioid Epidemic: White Privilege and the Criminalization of Opioid Use during Pregnancy*, 133 HARV. L. REV. 800 (Jan. 2020).

49. MOVEMENT FOR FAMILY POWER, "WHATEVER THEY DO, I'M HER COMFORT, I'M HER PROTECTOR": HOW THE FOSTER CARE SYSTEM HAS BECOME GROUND ZERO FOR THE U.S. DRUG WAR (2020), www.movementforfamilypower.org/ground-zero.

50. Amanda Roy et al., *Toxicology Screening Practices for Perinatal Substance Use Among New York State Birthing Hospitals*, UNIV. OF ALBANY, 2018, www.albany.edu/cphce/nyspqcpublic/ToxicologySurveyPosterAMCHP2018.pdf; Sarah C. M. Roberts & Amani Nuru-Jeter, *Universal Alcohol/Drug Screening in Prenatal Care: A Strategy for Reducing Racial Disparities? Questioning the Assumptions*, 15 MATERNAL & CHILD HEALTH J. 1127–34 (2010), https://doi.org/10.1007/s10995-010-0720-6; Sarah C. M. Roberts et al., *Does Adopting a Prenatal Substance Use Protocol Reduce Racial Disparities in CPS Reporting Related to Maternal Drug Use? A California Case Study*, 35 J. OF PARINATOLOGY 146–50 (2015), https://doi.org/10.1038/jp.2014.168.

51. ROBERTS, *supra* note 1 at 175–76; Ira J. Chasnoff, Harvey J. Landress, & Mark E. Barrett, *The Prevalence of Illicit-Drug or Alcohol Use during Pregnancy and Discrepancies in Mandatory Reporting in Pinellas County, Florida*, 322 N. ENGL. J. MED. (1990), https://doi.org/10.1056/NEJM199004263221706; D. R. Neuspiel et al., *Custody of Cocaine-Exposed Newborns: Determinants of Discharge Decisions*, 83 AM. J. PUB. HEALTH 1726–29 (Dec. 1, 1993), https://doi.org/10.2105/ajph.83.12.1726; Sarah C. M. Roberts & Amani Nuru-Jeter, *Universal Screening for Alcohol and Drug Use and Racial Disparities in Child Protective Services Reporting*, 39 J. BEHAV. HEALTH SERV. & RES. 3–16 (2011), https://doi.org/10.1007/s11414-011-9247-x; Michael Fitzgerald, *New York City to Investigate Hospital Drug Tests of Black and Latino New Mothers, Which Can Prompt Foster Care Removals*, IMPRINT (Nov. 16, 2020), https://imprintnews.org/child-welfare-2/new-york-hospital-drug-tests-mothers-foster49384.

52. Emily Badger, Margot Sanger-Katz, & Claire Cain Miller, *States With Abortion Bans Are Among Least Supportive for Mothers and Children*, N.Y. TIMES (July 28, 2022), https://www.nytimes.com/2022/07/28/upshot/abortion-bans-states-social-services.html.

53. *Id.*; Rolanda L. Lister, Wonder Drake, Baldwin H. Scott, & Cornelia Graves, *Black Maternal Mortality—The Elephant in the Room*, 3 WORLD J. GYNECOL. WOMEN'S HEALTH (2019), https://www.ncbi.nlm.nih.gov/pmc/articles/PMC7384760/; Khiara M. Bridges, *Racial Disparities in Maternal Mortality*, 95 N.Y.U. L. REV. 1229 (2020).

54. CTR. FOR REPROD. RIGHTS, SISTERSONG, & THE NAT'L LATINA INST. FOR REPROD. HEALTH, REPRODUCTIVE INJUSTICE: RACIAL AND GENDER DISCRIMINATION IN U.S. HEALTH CARE 13 (2014).

55. Violent Crime Control and Law Enforcement Act of 1994, Pub. L. No. 103-322, 108 Stat. 1796 (1994), https://www.congress.gov/103/statute/STATUTE-108/STATUTE-108-Pg1796.pdf.

56. Personal Responsibility and Work Opportunity Reconciliation Act, Pub. L. No. 104-193, 110 Stat. 2105 (1996), https://www.congress.gov/104/plaws/publ193/PLAW-104publ193.pdf.

57. GWENDOLYN MINK, WELFARE'S END (Ithaca: Cornell University Press, 2001); ANNA MARIE SMITH, WELFARE REFORM AND SEXUAL REGULATION (Cambridge: Cambridge University Press, 2007).

58. Adoption and Safe Families Act of 1997. Pub. L. No. 105-89, 111 Stat. 2115 (1997), https://www.congress.gov/105/plaws/publ89/PLAW-105publ89.pdf.

59. Alison Mitchell, *President Tells Government to Promote More Adoptions*, N.Y. Times (Dec. 15, 1996), https://www.nytimes.com/1996/12/15/us/president-tells-governm ent-to-promote-more-adoptions.html.

60. Kim Phagan-Hansel, *One Million Adoptions Later: Adoption and Safe Families at 20*, The Imprint, (Nov. 28. 2018), https://imprintnews.org/adoption/one-million-adopti ons-later-adoption-safe-families-act-at-20/32582.

61. Cong. Rsch. Serv., R43025, Child Welfare: The Adoption Incentive Program and Its Reauthorization 1 (Apr. 18, 2013–July 15, 2014), https://www.everycrsrep ort.com/files/20140715_R43025_29e04f3cdd52baff8b319fca5ff9ca384e198251.pdf.

62. U.S. Dept. Health & Human Serv., Admin. for Children & Families, The Afcars Report: Final Estimates for FY 1998 Through FY 2002 at 12 (Oct. 2006), https://www.acf.hhs.gov/sites/default/files/documents/cb/afcarsreport12.pdf.

63. *See, e.g.,* Elizabeth Bartholet, Nobody's Children: Abuse and Neglect, Foster Drift, and the Adoption Alternative (Boston: Beacon Press, 1999).

64. Amanda Spake, *Adoption Gridlock*, 124 U.S. News & World Rep. 30 (June 22, 1998).

65. Natalie Pardo, *Losing Their Children: As State Cracks Down on Parents, Black Families Splinter*, Chicago Rep. (Jan. 1, 1999), at 1; *see also* Sarah Karp, *DCFS Policy Spells Pressure for Black Families*, Chicago Rep. (Oct. 1, 1999), at 1.

66. Dakota Engel, *The Unknown Family Separation Policy: Parental Rights and Child Custody during Incarceration*, Pub. Purpose (Feb. 14, 2022), https://thepublicpurp ose.com/2022/02/14/family-separation-during-incarceration/; *see generally* Sylvia A. Harvey, The Shadow System: Mass Incarceration and the American Family (New York: Bold Type Books, 2020); Dorothy E. Roberts, *Prison, Foster Care, and the Systemic Punishment of Black Mothers*, 59 UCLA L. Rev. 1474 (2012).

67. Jean C. Lawrence, *ASFA in the Age of Mass Incarceration: Go to Prison—Lose Your Child*, 40 Wm. Mitchell L. Rev. 990 (2013–14); Emily K. Nicholson, *Racing against the ASFA Clock: How Incarcerated Parents Lose More Than Freedom*, 45 Duq. L. Rev. 83 (2006).

68. Philip M. Genty, *Damage to Family Relationships as a Collateral Consequence of Parental Incarceration*, 30 Fordham Urb. L.J. 1671 (2003).

69. Raz, *supra* note 4.

70. Briggs, *supra* note 19, at 3 (quoting Hillary Clinton (@HillaryClinton), "There's nothing American about tearing families apart," Twitter (June 20, 2018, 9:34 A.M.), https://twitter.com/hillaryclinton/status/1009434414986747906?lang=en.

71. SisterSong Women of Color Reproductive Justice Collective, *What Is Reproductive Justice?*, SisterSong, https://www.sistersong.net/reproductive-justice; *see generally* Lorreta Ross & Rickie Solinger, Reproductive Justice: An Introduction (Oakland: University of California Press, 2017); Loretta Ross et al., eds., Racial Reproductive Justice: Foundations, Theory, Practice, Critique (New York: The Feminist Press at CUNY, 2017).

Chapter 12

1. Roe v. Wade, 410 U.S. 113 (1973), *overruled by* Dobbs v. Jackson Women's Health, 142 S. Ct. 2228 (2022).
2. Minor v. Happersett, 88 U.S. 162, 178 (1873).
3. *See* Bradwell v. State, 83 U.S. 130, 140–42 (1873).
4. *See Roe* at 153.
5. *See* 2 WILLIAM BLACKSTONE, COMMENTARIES *442–45 (discussing the "chief legal effects of marriage during coverture").
6. *Id.* at *442.
7. *Id.*
8. *Id.*
9. MATTHEW HALE, THE HISTORY OF THE PLEAS OF THE CROWN 629 (London: R. Gosling, E. Nutt, & R. Nutt, 1736).
10. Dobbs v. Jackson Women's Health Org., 142 S. Ct. 2228, 2242 (2022).
11. GERALD J. POSTEMA, LAW'S RULE: THE NATURE, VALUE, AND VIABILITY OF THE RULE OF LAW 116 (New York: Oxford Univ. Press, 2022).
12. *Id.*
13. State v. Oliver, 70 N.C. 60, 62 (1874).
14. Abbott v. Abbott, 67 Me. 304, 305 (1877).
15. *Id.* at 305.
16. Roller v. Roller, 37 Wash. 242 (1905).
17. *Id.*
18. *See* Reva B. Siegel, *"The Rule of Love": Wife Beating as Prerogative and Privacy*, 105 YALE L.J. 2117, 2165 (1996).
19. *Id.*
20. Sally F. Goldfarb, *Violence Against Women and the Persistence of Privacy*, 61 OHIO ST. L.J. 1, 22 n. 92 (2000).
21. *See* DOROTHEA L. DIX, TO THE HONORABLE THE LEGISLATURE OF THE STATE OF NEW YORK IN ON BEHALF OF THE INSANE POOR 1, 46–7 (Forest Grove: University Press of the Pacific, 1844) (1971).
22. Emily Feng, Megan Lim, & Sarah Handel, *For Ben Franklin, Abortion Was Basic Arithmetic*, NPR (May 16, 2022), https://www.npr.org/2022/05/16/1099244635/for-ben-franklin-abortion-was-basic-arithmetic.
23. *See, e.g.*, Sarah Hougen Poggi & Cynthia A. Kiemer, *A 1792 Case Reveals That Key Founders Saw Abortion as a Private Matter*, WASH. POST (July 19, 2022), https://www.washingtonpost.com/made-by-history/2022/07/19/1792-case-reveals-that-key-founders-saw-abortion-private-matter/.
24. HORATIO R. STORER, WHY NOT? A BOOK FOR EVERY WOMAN 85 (Boston: Lee and Shepard, 1868) (also quoted in Leslie Reagan, *When Abortion Was a Crime: Women, Medicine, and Law in the United States, 1867–1973, in* THE REPRODUCTIVE RIGHTS READER 82 (New York: New York University Press, Nancy Ehrenreich ed., 2008).
25. Dobbs v. Jackson Women's Health, 142 S. Ct. 2228, 2242 (2022).
26. Dred Scott v. Sandford, 60 U.S. 393, 407 (1857).

27. Plessy v. Ferguson, 163 U.S. 537, 551–52 (1896).

28. Buck v. Bell, 274 U.S. 200 (1927).

29. Whole Woman's Health v. Hellerstedt, 136 S. Ct. 2292, 2̶

30. *Id.* at 2321 (holding that the state of Texas cannot in̶ tion services that substantially burden women seeking concurring).

31. HARRIET A. JACOBS, INCIDENTS IN THE LIFE OF A SLAVE GI̶ the author, L. Maria Child, ed., 1861).

32. Sojourner Truth, *Ain't I a Woman?* (May 29, 1851).

33. Letter from Thomas Jefferson to John Wayles Epps (June 30, 18̶ tjrs.monticello.org/letter/380#:~:text=Jefferson%20Quotes%2 Letters,-Monticello&text=I%20consider%20a%20woman%20w̶ mas%20Jefferson%20Collection.

34. Elizabeth Wolfe et al., *Man Indicted in Rape of a Child Who Tra̶ Indiana for an Abortion*, CNN (July 22, 2022), https://www.cnn.co̶ gerson-fuentes-child-rape-abortion-indictment/index.html.

35. ALEXIS DE TOCQUEVILLE, DEMOCRACY IN AMERICA (London: Saunders Otley, 1835).

36. Ableman v. Booth, 62 U.S. 506, 522–26 (1858).

37. *Id.*

38. *Id.*

39. United States v. Booth, 59 U.S. 476 (1856).

40. Julius Yanuck, *The Garner Fugitive Slave Case*, 40 J. AM. HISTORY 47, 50 (1953).

41. *See, e.g.,* Michele Goodwin, *A Different Type of Property: White Women and the Human Property They Kept*, 119 MICH. L. REV. 1081 (2021).

42. *See, e.g.,* Prigg v. Pennsylvania, 41 U.S. 539, 543 (1842); *see also* RICHARD BELL, STOLEN: FIVE FREE BOYS KIDNAPPED INTO SLAVERY AND THEIR ASTONISHING ODYSSEY HOME (New York: 37 INK, 2019).

43. *See* Brentin Mock, *The Dark "Fugitive Slave" History of Rikers Island,* BLOOMBERG (July 23, 2015), https://www.bloomberg.com/news/articles/2015-07-23/what-sho uld-be-done-about-rikers-island-s-dark-fugitive-slave-history.

44. In 1662, the Virginia Grand Assembly enacted one of its first "slave laws" to address this issue:

> Whereas some doubts have arrisen whether children got by any Englishman upon a negro woman should be slave or free, Be it therefore enacted and declared by this present grand assembly, that all children borne in this country shalbe held bond or free only according to the condition of the mother, And that if any christian shall committ fornication with a negro man or woman, hee or shee soe offending shall pay double the fines imposed by the former act.

> 2 WILLIAM WALLER HENING, STATUTES AT LARGE; BEING A COLLECTION OF ALL THE LAWS OF VIRGINIA 170, 260, 266, 270 (1823).

45. Yanuck, *supra* note 40 at 58.

46. Dred Scott v. Sandford, 60 U.S. 393, 407 (1857).

Speech on the Fugitive Slave Law, Delivered at Lancaster, SLAVERY: LETTERS AND SPEECHES 511–12 (Boston: B. B. Mussey &

400

GIDDINGS, *Compromise Measures, in* SPEECHES IN CONGRESS 495–96 J. P. Jewett and Co., 1853).

v. Wade, 410 U.S. 113, 153 (1973).

id.

achel Benson Gold, *Lessons from Before* Roe: *Will Past Be Prologue?*, 6 GUTTMACHER POL'Y REV. 8, 8 (2003).

. Symposium, *Law, Morality, and Abortion*, 22 RUTGERS L. REV. 415, 420–21 (1967) (statement of Dr. Alan F. Guttmacher).

55. LESLIE J. REAGAN, WHEN ABORTION WAS A CRIME: WOMEN, MEDICINE, AND LAW IN THE UNITED STATES 1867–1973, at 214 (Berkeley: Univ. of California Press, 1997).

56. *Id.* at 210.

57. *Id.* at 210–11.

58. *See, e.g.*, Frances Stead Sellers & Fenit Nirappil, *Confusion Post-*Roe *Spurs Delays, Denials for Some Lifesaving Pregnancy Care*, WASH. POST (July 16, 2022), https://www.washingtonpost.com/health/2022/07/16/abortion-miscarriage-ectopic-pregnancy-care/.

59. Minyvonne Burke, *Woman Carrying Fetus Without a Skull to Seek Abortion in Another State Following Louisiana Ban*, NBC NEWS (Aug. 26, 2022), https://www.nbcnews.com/news/us-news/louisiana-woman-carrying-fetus-skull-seek-abortion-another-state-rcna45005.

60. Jackson Women's Health Org. v. Currier, 349 F.Supp. 3d 536, 540 n.22 (S.D. Miss. 2018).

61. Lauren Coleman-Lochner et. al, *Doctors Fearing Legal Blowback Are Denying Life-Saving Abortions,* BLOOMBERG L. (July 12, 2022), https://news.bloomberglaw.com/health-law-and-business/doctors-fearing-legal-blowback-are-denying-life-saving-abortions.

Chapter 13

* I am very grateful to Linda Greenhouse and Martha Minow for their valuable comments on a previous draft.

1. Dobbs v. Jackson Women's Health Org., 197 S. Ct. 2228 (2022).

2. *See id.* at 2254 ("[T]hey have found no support for the existence of an abortion right that predates the latter part of the 20th century—no state constitutional provision, no statute, no judicial decision, no learned treatise.").

3. *Id.* at 2252.

4. Roe v. Wade, 410 U.S. 113 (1973).

5. Lawrence v. Texas, 539 U.S. 558, 571–72 (2003) provides a telling contrast: "[W]e think that the laws and traditions of the past half century are of most relevance here."

6. *Dobbs*, 197 S. Ct. at 2248–49; *see id.* at 2249–57, especially 2249 and n. 24.

7. *Id.* at 2235.

8. Lochner v. New York, 198 U.S. 45 (1905). In *Lochner* the Court struck down a maximum-hours law for bakers, claiming that New York State could not abridge the "liberty of contract" (implied in the due process guarantee) that workers and employers both deserved, allowing them to choose a killingly long work day. It was a 5–4 decision, its constitutional rationale soon condemned as a cover for big-business sympathies, since the dissenters saw that public health and safety warranted such laws. The Court's hidebound majority stuck there for years, stymying much of the ambitious legislation of the New Deal. *West Coast Hotel v. Parrish,* 300 U.S. 379 (1937) effectually negated *Lochner* when it overruled *Adkins v. Children's Hospital,* 261 U.S. 525 (1923). The much-criticized *Adkins* decision in 1923 had struck down a state law regulating women's wages on the reasoning that women's "liberty of contract" should mimic men's now that women were voters and presumably equal citizens. There are faint echoes of *Adkins* in *Dobbs,* in the latter's blithe assessment that women's life chances have changed so significantly since *Planned Parenthood of Southeastern Pa. v. Casey,* 505 U.S. 833 (1992) as to warrant no sex-based concern.

9. Griswold v. Connecticut, 381 U.S. 470 (1965).

10. Poe v. Ullman, 367 U.S. 497 (1961).

11. *Id.* at 516. Douglas had tried out his conception of privacy in regard to a different issue years earlier in dissent, in *Public Utilities Commission of District of Columbia v. Pollak,* 343 U.S. 451, 467 (1952). Justice Harlan as well as Douglas dissented in *Poe v. Ullmann,* being willing to invoke privacy reasoning to strike down the Connecticut law then: "The home derives its preeminence as the seat of family life. And the integrity of that life is something so fundamental that it has been found to draw to its protection the principles of more than one explicitly granted Constitutional right. . . . Of this whole 'private realm of family life,' it is difficult to imagine what is more private or more intimate than a husband and wife's marital relations." *Poe,* 367 U.S., at 551–52.

12. Meyer v. Nebraska, 262 U.S. 390 (1923).

13. *Id.* at 399.

14. Griswold v. Connecticut, 381 U.S. 479, 485–86 (1965).

15. *Id.* at 500 (Harlan, J., concurring).

16. The two dissenters, Justices Potter Stewart and Hugo Black, both thought the law was bad but saw no constitutional basis on which to strike it down without treading the path of *Lochner* by inventing "natural law due process," in Justice Black's words. *Id.* at 516 (Black and Stewart, JJ., dissenting).

17. Pierce v. Soc'y of Sisters, 268 U.S. 510 (1925).

18. Prince v. Massachusetts, 321 U.S. 158 (1944).

19. Loving v. Virginia, 388 U. S. 1 (1967).

20. Skinner v. Oklahoma *ex rel.* Williamson, 316 U.S. 535 (1942). *Skinner,* which struck down an Oklahoma statute that prescribed sterilization for certain felons and not others convicted of comparable crimes, was decided on equal protection grounds, but

the majority opinion included relevant dicta, for example, "We are dealing here with legislation which involves one of the basic civil rights of man. Marriage and procreation are fundamental to the very existence and survival of the race. There is no redemption for the individual whom the law touches. Any experiment which the State conducts is to his irreparable injury. He is forever deprived of a basic liberty." Two concurring justices thought the law was "an invasion of personal liberty" and should fail on due process liberty grounds. *Id.* at 541, 545.

21. Eisenstadt v. Baird, 405 U. S. 438 (1972).

22. *Id.,* at 453 (citing Stanley v. Georgia, 394 U.S. 557 (1969) (protecting the private possession of obscene matter at home).

23. *Roe v. Wade* had come to the Court in the fall of 1970, but its consideration was delayed both by jurisdictional questions and by retirements that reduced the Court to seven members. In the interim the Court addressed not only *Eisenstadt v. Baird* but also another abortion case, *United States vs. Vuitch*, which challenged the D.C. criminal abortion law for its vagueness in allowing doctors to perform an abortion to preserve a woman's life or "health." The federal district court had declared the law unconstitutional for vagueness. While the Supreme Court did not agree, its mixed opinion held that the word "health" must be interpreted very broadly. For an effective summary of this foreground as well as the politics of abortion at the time, I am much indebted to LINDA GREENHOUSE, BECOMING JUSTICE BLACKMUN: HARRY BLACKMUN'S SUPREME COURT JOURNEY 72–87 (New York: Henry Holt and Company, LLC, 2005).

24. *Id.* at 72.

25. Quoted in *id.* at 83. LINDA GREENHOUSE & REVA B. SIEGEL, BEFORE ROE V. WADE: VOICES THAT SHAPED THE ABORTION DEBATE BEFORE THE SUPREME COURT'S RULING (New York: Kaplan, 2010) ably lays out the partisan political strategies in play and the extent of public dissension over abortion before the Court ruled in January 1973.

26. Doe v. Bolton, 410 U.S. 179 (1973).

27. I am very much indebted to Greenhouse, *supra* note 23, at 80–99, for my discussion of Blackmun.

28. Greenhouse, *supra* note 23, at 91–93. The "fundamental" phrase is quoted from his notes; the second phrase quoted was in his subsequent draft and appeared in the opinion as filed as "broad enough to encompass a woman's decision whether or not to terminate her pregnancy." Roe v. Wade, 410 U.S. 113, 153 (1973).

29. Greenhouse, *supra* note 23, at 94. In the interim, a federal district court in Connecticut struck down Connecticut's criminal abortion law (which resembled the one in Texas) by citing and quoting *Eisenstadt* on the protected liberty to choose "whether to bear or beget a child" without government intrusion. Though the Second Circuit Court agreed, the Supreme Court stayed enforcement because *Roe* was pending. *Abele v. Markle*, 351 F. Supp. 224. (Conn. 1972), *and see* Fred P. Graham, *Justices to Weigh Pregnancy Issue*, N.Y. TIMES, Oct. 25, 1972, at 8.

30. *See* Greenhouse, *supra* note 23, at 152–53; *cf.* cases cited in *Griswold*, *supra* notes 17– 20. Justice Stewart's concurrence also quoted from *Abele v. Markle*, *supra* note 29, at 227, "Certainly the interests of a woman in giving of her physical and emotional self

during pregnancy and the interests that will be affected throughout her life by the birth and raising of a child are of a far greater degree of significance and personal intimacy than the right to send a child to private school protected in *Pierce v. Society of Sisters*, 268 U. S. 510 (1925), or the right to teach a foreign language protected in *Meyer v. Nebraska*, 262 U. S. 390 (1923)." Roe v. Wade, 410 U.S., at 170 (Stewart, J., concurring).

31. *Id.* at 165–66.

32. *Id.* at 154.

33. The word "arbitrary" appeared in a letter to his colleagues. *See* Greenhouse, *supra* note 23, at 95. Blackmun linked his choice to the medical finding that through the first trimester, abortion was no more dangerous to a woman's health than pregnancy. *Roe,* 410 U.S. at 163.

34. Greenhouse, *supra* note 23, at 95–99.

35. *Roe*, 410 U.S., at 113, 159, 163, 164. In his dissent, Rehnquist said the three-stage scheme "partakes more of judicial legislation than it does of a determination of the intent of the drafters of the Fourteenth Amendment." *Id.* at 174 (Rehnquist, J. dissenting).

36. *Id.*at 129–52.

37. *Id.* at 129.

38. *Id.* at 149–51.

39. *Id.* at 140–41.

40. *Id.* at 138–40. *Cf.* Brief for Amici Curiae American Historical Ass'n and Organization of American Historians in Support of Respondents, Dobbs v. Jackson Women's Health Org., 197 S. Ct. 2228 (2022) (No. 19-1392).

41. Important examples include Robert Byrn, *An American Tragedy: The Supreme Court on Abortion*, 41 FORDHAM L. REV. 807 (1973); Joseph W. Dellapenna, *Nor Piety nor Wit: The Supreme Court on Abortion,* 6 COLUM. HUMAN RIGHTS L. REV. 379 (1974); Joseph W. Dellapenna, *The History of Abortion: Technology, Morality, and Law*, 40 U. PITT. L. REV. 359 (1979); James S. Witherspoon, *Reexamining* Roe: *Nineteenth-Century Abortion Statutes and the Fourteenth Amendment*, 17 ST. MARY'S L.J. 29 (1985); Joseph W. Dellapenna, *Abortion and the Law: Blackmun's Distortion of the Historical Record, in* DENNIS J. HORAN ET AL., ABORTION AND THE CONSTITUTION: REVERSING ROE v. WADE THROUGH THE COURTS 137–58 (Washington, D.C.: Georgetown Univ. Press, 1987); Dennis J. Horan et al., *Two Ships Passing in the Night: An Interpretivist Review of the White-Stevens Colloquy on* Roe v. Wade, 6 St. LOUIS U. PUB. L. REV. 229 (1987); Philip Rafferty, Roe v. Wade: *A Scandal Upon the Court*, 7 RUTGERS J. L. & RELIGION 1 (2005); John Keown, *Back to the Future of Abortion Law:* Roe's *Rejection of America's History and Traditions*, 22 ISSUES IN L. & MED. 3 (2006); JOSEPH DELLAPENNA, DISPELLING THE MYTHS OF ABORTION HISTORY (Durham: Carolina Academic Press, 2006); Joseph Dellapenna, *Recycling the Myths of Abortion History*, 5 FIRST THINGS (2008); Justin Buckley Dyer, *The Politics of Abortion History, in* SLAVERY, ABORTION, AND THE POLITICS OF CONSTITUTIONAL MEANING 105–32 (New York: Cambridge

Univ. Press, 2013); Justin Buckley Dyer, Roe *v. History*, 1 TOUCHSTONE MAGAZINE (2014); Clarke Forsythe, *A Draft Opinion Overruling Roe v. Wade*, 16 GEORGETOWN J. OF L. & PUB. POL'Y 445, 460–64 (2018); Justin Buckley Dyer, *Wrong Then, Wrong Now: The Fake Abortion History of* Roe v. Wade, THE PUB. DISCOURSE (Sept. 29, 2021), https://www.thepublicdiscourse.com/2021/09/78200/; John Finniss & Robert George, *An Enhanced Amicus Brief in* Dobbs, Soc. Sci. RSCH. NETWORK (2022), http://dx.doi.org/10.2139/ssrn.3955231.

42. *See* Brief for Amici Curiae, *supra* note 40, for a more accurate account. Unfortunately, few scholars have confronted the work cited *supra* note 41 directly. One able riposte is Carla Spivack, *To Bring Down the Flowers: The Cultural Context of Abortion Law in Early Modern England*, 14 WM. & MARY J. WOMEN & L. 107 (2007); *and see* WOLFGANG P. MULLER, THE CRIMINALIZATION OF ABORTION IN THE WEST (Ithaca: Cornell Univ. Press, 2012).

43. On Means's involvement with the lawyers behind *Roe*, see DAVID J. GARROW, LIBERTY AND SEXUALITY: THE RIGHT TO PRIVACY AND THE ROAD TO ROE V. WADE 356–57, 500ff. (Berkeley: Univ. of California Press, 1994). The attack literature has kept Means alive as a whipping boy, sustaining his name long after his death in 1992. Without naming Means in the text, *Dobbs* fell into line with typical overstatement, asserting that "*Roe* relied largely on two articles by a pro-abortion advocate who claimed that Coke had intentionally misstated the common law because of his strong anti-abortion views." Dobbs v. Jackson Women's Health Org., 197 S. Ct. 2228, 2254–55 (2022).

44. *See* Brief, *supra* note 40, 11–14.

45. *E.g.*, Forsythe, *supra* note 41. *Cf.* Brief, *supra* note 40, 14–17.

46. *Dobbs*, 197 S. Ct. at 2249–52.

47. Both *Mills v. Commonwealth*, 13 Pa. 631, and F. Wharton's CRIMINAL LAW departed from the consensus, and these are the cases cited by the majority opinion. *See* Brief, *supra* note 40, at 9–10, for explication of both.

48. *Dobbs*, 197 S. Ct. at 2252.

49. *Id.* at 2254–55.

50. *Lochner* supplied the ever-invocable devil to avoid: "[W]hen the Court has ignored the '[a]ppropriate limits' imposed by 'respect for the teachings of history,' *Moore*, 431 U. S., at 503 (plurality opinion), it has fallen into the freewheeling judicial policymaking that characterized discredited decisions such as *Lochner* v. *New York*, 198 U.S. 45 (1905). The Court must not fall prey to such an unprincipled approach." *Id.* at 2248. For evidence of the Court's move over time, *compare* Moore v. East Cleveland, 431 U.S. 494 (1977) *with* Bowers v. Hardwick, 478 U.S. 186 (1986) *and* Michael H. v. Gerald D., 491 U.S. 110 (1989). After *Griswold* (6–1), *Roe* (7–2), and *Eisenstadt* (6–1), due process cases resulted in more severely split outcomes.

51. *Bowers v. Hardwick*, 478 U.S. 186 (1986), and *Michael H. v. Gerald D.*, 491 U.S. 110 (1989), strongly illustrated that "traditions" were backward-looking. Both showed overt discord among the justices on deciding what constitutes "tradition," as well. In *Michael H.*, three justices dissented, and two others concurring in the judgment disagreed with the test given by Justice Antonin Scalia in his opinion for the majority. *See* relevant discussions of what has been called "due process traditionalism" in Brian

Hawkins, *The* Glucksberg *Renaissance: Due Process Traditionalism since* Lawrence v. Texas, 105 MICH. L. REV. 409 (2006); *see also* Ronald Turner, *Marriage Equality and* Obergefell's *Generational (Not* Glucksberg's *Traditional) Due Process Clause*, 23 DUKE J. GENDER L. & POL'Y 145 (2016).

52. Snyder v. Massachusetts, 291 U.S. 97, 105 (1934).

53. Palko v. Connecticut, 302 U.S. 319, 325 (1937).

54. Moore v. East Cleveland, 431 U.S. 494, 503 (1977).

55. Washington v. Glucksberg, 521 U.S. 702 (1997). *But cf.* County of Sacramento v. Lewis, 523 U.S. 823, 857 (1998) (Kennedy, J., concurring) ("[H]istory and tradition are the starting point, but not in all cases the ending point of the substantive due process inquiry."). Kennedy made this point again, quoting himself, in *Lawrence v. Texas*, 539 U.S. 558, 572 (2003).

56. For an incisive critique of the *Dobbs* majority's version of "history and traditions," *see* Reva Siegel, *Memory Games:* Dobbs' *Originalism as Anti-Democratic Living Constitutionalism—and Some Pathways for Resistance*, 101 TEXAS L. REV. 1127 (2023).

57. Minor v. Happersett, 88 U.S. 162, 174–75 (1875).

58. Aaron Tang, who has researched this issue more deeply than any previous scholar, including case law in states where criminal statutes were passed, puts the number of states effectively criminalizing abortion before quickening in 1868 at only sixteen. *See* Aaron Tang, *After* Dobbs: *History, Tradition, and the Uncertain Future of a Nationwide Abortion Ban*, 75 STAN. L. REV. 1091 (2023); Aaron Tang, *The Supreme Court Flunks Abortion History*, L.A. TIMES (May 5, 2022), https://www.latimes.com/opinion/story/2022-05-05/abortion-draft-opinion-14th-amendment-american-history-quickening; Aaron Tang, *What Justice Alito Can Learn from a 114-Year-Old Sex Abuse Scandal*, SLATE (June 2, 2022), https://slate.com/news-and-politics/2022/06/justice-alito-abortion-history-roe-v-wade-constitution.html.

59. Justices Clarence Thomas, Brett Kavanaugh, Neil Gorsuch, and Amy Coney Barrett joined the opinion; Chief Justice John Roberts concurred only in part, rejecting the viability standard in *Roe* and *Casey*, thus crediting Mississippi's fifteen-week ban but not overthrowing the right to choose abortion.

60. Planned Parenthood v. Casey, 505 U.S. 833 (1992).

61. Brief for Petitioners at 16, Dobbs v. Jackson Women's Health Org., 197 S. Ct. 2252 (2022) (No. 19-1392), (quoting Harris v. McRae, 448 US 297, 325 (1980)).

62. This claim is inferential only. No historian has found a shred of evidence to indicate that any state legislator linked the two.

63. *See, e.g.,* Tang, *supra* note 58; Laura Briggs, *Originalists Are Misreading the Constitution's Silence on Abortion*, WASH. POST (May 3, 2022), https://www.washingtonpost.com/outlook/2022/05/03/originalists-misreading-constitution-silence-abortion/; Melissa Murray, *Alito's Aggressive Ruling Would Reach Way Beyond* Roe, WASH. POST (May 4, 2022), https://www.washingtonpost.com/opinions/2022/05/04/justice-alito-leaked-supreme-court-abortion-ruling-way-beyond-roe/; Jill Lepore, *Of Course the Constitution Has Nothing to Say about Women*, NEW YORKER (May 4, 2002), https://www.newyorker.com/news/daily-comment/why-there-are-no-women-in-the-constitution; Timothy Bella et al., *Abortion Protests Continue after Supreme Court*

Ends Roe v. Wade; *Biden Criticizes Court's Terrible Decisions*, WASH. POST (June 25, 2022), https://www.washingtonpost.com/nation/2022/06/25/roe-v-wade-abortion-supreme-court-ruling/; Linda Greenhouse, *Abortion Questions for Justice Alito and His Supreme Court Allies*, N.Y.TIMES (May 24, 2022), https://www.nytimes.com/2022/05/24/opinion/abortion-oklahoma-supreme-court.html; Linda Greenhouse, *Requiem for the Supreme Court*, N.Y.TIMES (June 24, 2022), https://www.nytimes.com/2022/06/24/opinion/roe-v-wade-dobbs-decision.html; Patricia Cline Cohen, *The* Dobbs *Decision Looks to History to Rescind* Roe, WASH. POST (June 24, 2022), https://www.washingtonpost.com/outlook/2022/06/24/dobbs-decision-looks-history-rescind-roe/.

64. Eisenstadt v. Baird, 405 U. S. 438, 454 (1972).

65. Poe v. Ullman, 367 U.S. 497, 542 (1961) (Harlan, J., dissenting).

66. Dobbs v. Jackson Women's Health Org., 142 S. Ct. 2228, 2317 (2022) (Kagan, J., dissenting).

67. *Poe*, 367 U.S. 497, 542 (1961) (Harlan, J., dissenting).

Chapter 14

1. Because the need to reduce fertility could be a matter of life and death, some practiced infanticide as a form of birth control, and this too was stringently regulated: an infanticide would be legal only in specific circumstances and generally needed to be performed immediately after birth.

2. *See* JUDITH WALZER LEAVITT, BROUGHT TO BED: CHILDBEARING IN AMERICA, 1750–1950 (New York: Oxford Univ. Press, 1988); *see also* LESLIE J. REAGAN, WHEN ABORTION WAS A CRIME: WOMEN, MEDICINE, AND LAW IN THE UNITED STATES (Berkeley: Univ. of California Press, 1997).

3. Rachel Benson Gold, *Lessons from Before* Roe: *Will Past Be Prologue?*, GUTTMACHER INST. (Mar. 1, 2003), https://www.guttmacher.org/gpr/2003/03/lessons-roe-will-past-be-prologue.

4. LINDA GORDON, THE MORAL PROPERTY OF WOMEN: A HISTORY OF BIRTH CONTROL POLITICS IN AMERICA 29, 34 (Urbana: Univ. of Illinois Press, 2002).

5. *See* REAGAN, *supra* note 2.

6. GEOFFREY R. STONE, SEX AND THE CONSTITUTION 189 (New York: Liveright Publishing Company, 2017).

7. *See* GORDON, *supra* note 4.

8. *See id.*

9. DANIEL OKRENT, THE GUARDED GATE: BIGOTRY, EUGENICS, AND THE LAW THAT KEPT JEWS, ITALIANS, AND OTHER EUROPEAN IMMIGRANTS OUT OF AMERICA 237 (New York: Scribner, 2019).

10. *See* LAURA KAPLAN, THE STORY OF JANE: THE LEGENDARY UNDERGROUND FEMINIST ABORTION SERVICE (New York: Pantheon Books, 1995).

11. The Tariff Act of 1930 had incorporated the anticontraceptive provisions of the Comstock Act.

12. Griswold v. Connecticut, 381 U.S. 479 (1965).

13. The Court did not extend the right to contraception to unmarried persons until 1972 in *Eisenstadt v. Baird*, 405 U.S. 438 (1972).

14. Gold, *supra* note 3.

15. *CPI Inflation Calculator*, U.S. BUREAU OF LAB. STAT., https://www.bls.gov/data/infla tion_calculator.htm.

16. ANDREA TONE, DEVICES AND DESIRES: CONTRACEPTION IN AMERICAN HISTORY 203–61 (New York: Hill and Wang, 2001).

17. *See, e.g.*, Very Reverend George C. Higgins of the National Conference of Catholic Bishops, quoted in *Two Abortion Views That Will Never Mix*, BOS. SUNDAY GLOBE, Sept. 28, 1980.

18. Randall Balmer, *The Religious Right and the Abortion Myth*, POLITICO (May 10, 2022), https://www.politico.com/news/magazine/2022/05/10/abortion-history-right-white-evangelical-1970s-00031480. For more extensive discussion of these ideas, see RANDALL BALMER, BAD FAITH: RACE AND THE RISE OF THE RELIGIOUS RIGHT (Grand Rapids: Wm. B. Eerdmans Publishing Co., 2021).

19. TIM LAHAYE & BEVERLY LAHAYE, THE ACT OF MARRIAGE: THE BEAUTY OF SEXUAL LOVE (New York: Bantam, 1976), a New Right sex manual, is tolerant of abortion. GARY K. CLABAUGH, THUNDER ON THE RIGHT: THE PROTESTANT FUNDAMENTALISTS (Chicago: Nelson-Hall, 1974) does not mention abortion.

20. Paul Weyrich, *Family Issues*, *in* THE NEW RIGHT AT HARVARD 17–22 (Vienna: Conservative Caucus, Howard Phillips, ed., 1983).

21. Phil Gailey, *Politics; Abortion Knits Religious Right into G.O.P. Fabric*, N.Y. TIMES, June 19, 1986, at B8.

22. Rosalind Pollack Petchesky, *Fetal Images: The Power of Visual Culture in the Politics of Reproduction*, 13 FEMINIST STUD. 263, 263–92 (1987).

Chapter 15

1. *See* Dobbs v. Jackson Women's Health Organization, 142 S. Ct. 2228, 2235 (2022).

2. *See, e.g.*, Caroline Kitchener, *Louisiana Republicans Gut a Bill That Would Have Charged Abortion as Murder*, WASH. POST (May 12, 2022), https://www.washingtonp ost.com/politics/2022/05/12/la-republicans-gut-bill-that-would-have-classified-abortion-homicide/.

3. *See* LESLIE J. REAGAN, WHEN ABORTION WAS A CRIME: WOMEN, MEDICINE, AND LAW IN THE UNITED STATES, 1867–1973 23–47 (Oakland: Univ. of California Press, 1997); JAMES C. MOHR, ABORTION IN AMERICA: THE ORIGINS AND EVOLUTION OF NATIONAL POLICY 19–33 (New York: Oxford Univ. Press,1979).

4. *See* Brief of American Historical Association et al., at 8–11, Dobbs v. Jackson Women's Health Organization, 142 S. Ct. 2228 (2022) (No. 19-1392); PATRICIA CLINE COHEN, TIMOTHY J. GILFOYLE, & HELEN LEFKOWITZ HOROWITZ, THE FLASH

PRESS: SPORTING MALE WEEKLIES IN NEW YORK 185–203 (Chicago: Univ. of Chicago Press, 2008).

5. American Medical Association, *Thirteenth Annual Meeting, First Day's Proceedings*, 5 ATLANTA MED. SURGICAL J. 392, 465–68 (1860); *see also* Horatio Robinson Storer, *The Criminality and Evils of Forced Abortions, Being the Prize Essay Which the American Medical Association Awarded the Gold Medal for MDCCCLXV*, 16 TRANSACTIONS OF THE AM. MED. ASS. 735, 736 (1865).

6. *See* Brief of American Historical Association et al., *supra* note 4 at 24.

7. *See* REAGAN, *supra* note 3 at 23; LINDA GORDON, THE MORAL PROPERTY OF WOMEN: A HISTORY OF BIRTH CONTROL POLITICS IN AMERICA 29–30 (Urbana: Univ. of Illinois Press, 2002).

8. On Finkbine's story, *see* LESLIE REAGAN, DANGEROUS PREGNANCIES: MOTHERS, DISABILITIES, AND PREGNANCIES IN MODERN IN AMERICA (Berkeley: Univ. of California Press, 2010). On the ALI bill and its significance, *see* MARY ZIEGLER, ABORTION AND THE LAW IN AMERICA: *ROE V. WADE* TO THE PRESENT 13–20 (New York: Cambridge Univ. Press, 2020).

9. *Finkbines Deny Crime Charge in Abortion*, CHI. TRIB. (Aug. 20, 1962), at 3A.

10. On the spread of the ALI bill, *see* DAVID J. GARROW, LIBERTY AND SEXUALITY: THE RIGHT TO PRIVACY AND THE MAKING OF *ROE V. WADE* 253–308 (Berkeley: Univ. of California Press, 1998).

11. George Dugan, *Ask Fight on Abortion Bill: Pastoral Letter Read*, N.Y. TIMES (Feb. 13, 1967), at 1.

12. *State's Roman Catholic Bishops Amplify Stand on Abortion*, L.A. TIMES (Dec. 9, 1966), at 3.

13. *Nine-Man Vice Squad Faces Big Responsibility*, HARTFORD COURANT (Nov. 2, 1960), at 28.

14. Lynn Lilliston, *Areas of Concern in Law Change*, L.A. TIMES (Feb. 24, 1967), at D1. On the short 1960 abortion sentence, *see Abortionist Gets Two-Year Sentence*, N.Y. TIMES (July 23, 1964), at 28.

15. Stephen Aug, *Repeal Sex Laws, Panel Urges*, BOSTON GLOBE (May 8, 1967), at 1.

16. Thomas J. Higgins, *Abortion Equated with Assassination*, N.Y. TIMES (Apr. 15, 1965), at 28.

17. *Catholics Begin "Pro-Life" Drive Against Permitting Abortions*, PHIL. INQUIRER (Sept. 20, 1967), at 27.

18. *Buckley Pushes Curb on Abortion*, N.Y. TIMES (June 1, 1973), at 1.

19. Letter from Joseph Witherspoon to Executive Committee, National Right To Life Committee, Inc. (Aug. 14, 1973), *in* The American Citizens Concerned for Life, Box 6, Constitutional Amendment 1973 Folder, GERALD R. FORD PRESIDENTIAL LIBR., https://www.fordlibrarymuseum.gov/library/document/0048/004800066.pdf.

20. Memorandum from Nellie Gray to Members of the Pro-Life Movement (Dec. 1, 1973), *in* The American Citizens Concerned for Life, Box 6, Constitutional Amendment 1973 Folder, GERALD R. FORD PRESIDENTIAL LIBR., https://www.fordlibrarymuseum.gov/library/document/0048/004800066.pdf. For Rice's view, *see* Letter

from Charles Rice to Joseph Witherspoon (Sept. 5, 1973), *in* The American Citizens Concerned for Life, Box 6, Constitutional Amendment 1973 Folder, GERALD R. FORD PRESIDENTIAL LIBR., https://www.fordlibrarymuseum.gov/library/document/0048/004800066.pdf.

21. Letter from Robert Byrn to Joseph Witherspoon (Sept. 4, 1973), *in* The American Citizens Concerned for Life, Box 6, Constitutional Amendment 1973 Folder, GERALD R. FORD PRESIDENTIAL LIBR., https://www.fordlibrarymuseum.gov/library/docum ent/0048/004800066.pdf.

22. John Noonan, Excerpt, Appendix E (n.d., ca. 1973), *in* The American Citizens Concerned for Life, Box 6, Constitutional Amendment 1973 Folder, GERALD R. FORD PRESIDENTIAL LIBR., https://www.fordlibrarymuseum.gov/library/document/0048/004800066.pdf.

23. *See* Mary Ziegler, *Beyond Backlash: Legal History, Polarization, and* Roe v. Wade, 71 WASH. & LEE L. REV. 969, 975–88 (2014).

24. On Ford, *see* Daniel K. Williams, *The GOP's Abortion Strategy: How Pro-Choice Republicans Became Pro-Life in the 1970s*, 34 J. POL'Y HIST. 513, 513–39 (2022). On Carter, *see* Myra McPherson, *Carter's Abortion Aid Stance Assailed*, WASH. POST (July 16, 1977), https://www.washingtonpost.com/archive/politics/1977/07/16/cart ers-abortion-aid-stance-assailed/1b08dd08-eef8-411d-adc2-e38182eeb3ae/. On the increasing abortion rate, *see* Lisa M. Koonin et al., *Abortion Surveillance, 1986–1987*, 39 MMWR SURVEILLANCE SUMMARIES 23, 23–27 (1990). On decreasing morbidity and mortality, *see* H. W. Lawson, *Abortion Mortality, United States, 1972 through 1987*, 171 AM. J. OBST. & GYNEC. 1365, 1365–72 (1992). On problems with contraception, *see* Nancy Hicks, *Birth Control*, N.Y. TIMES (Sept. 23, 1973), at 8; Philip J. Hilts, *U.S. Is Decades Behind Europe in Contraceptives, Expert Report*, N.Y. TIMES (Feb. 15, 1990), at 1.

25. On Reagan's approach to crime, *see* JOHN HAGAN, WHO ARE THE CRIMINALS? THE POLITICS OF CRIME FROM THE AGE OF ROOSEVELT TO THE AGE OF REAGAN 104–40 (Princeton: Princeton University Press, 2012). On the demise of a fetal-protective amendment, *see* ZIEGLER, *supra* note 8 at 54–82. On the spread of anti-abortion arguments for fetal homicide and the fetal victimization in the 1980s, *see* William Schmidt, *Murder Trial Adds Facet to the Abortion Debate*, N.Y. TIMES (June 15, 1990), at B5; Andrew Patner, *Handful of Prosecutors Start Treating Pregnant Drug Users as Child Abusers*, WALL. ST. J. (May 12, 1989), at A1. On the targeting of pregnant people of color, *see* MICHELE GOODWIN, POLICING THE WOMB: INVISIBLE WOMEN AND THE CRIMINALIZATION OF MOTHERHOOD (Cambridge: Cambridge Univ. Press, 2020).

26. *See* MARY ZIEGLER, ROE: THE HISTORY OF A NATIONAL OBSESSION 64, 79 (New Haven: Yale Univ. Press, 2023). On the uptick in anti-abortion violence, *see* JOHANNA SCHOEN, ABORTION AFTER ROE 145–53 (Chapel Hill: Univ. of North Carolina Press, 2015).

27. *Letter to the Westchester Editor: Safety, Legal Abortions Are Not Synonymous*, N.Y. TIMES (Nov. 15, 1981), at WC27. On "The Abortionists" and response to it, *see* SCHOEN, *supra* note 26 at 98–111.

28. Colman McCarthy, *Looking Back on the Backward Abortion Decisions*, L.A. TIMES (Jan. 13, 1983), at D11.

29. Linda Greenhouse, *Court Affirms Abortion Right and Bars Variety of Local Curbs*, N.Y. TIMES (June 16, 1983), at A1. For Nathanson's book, *see* BERNARD NATHANSON, ABORTING AMERICA (Garden City: Doubleday,1979).

30. Richard Glasow, *Planned Parenthood Operates Nation's Largest Abortion Clinic Chain*, NAT. RIGHT TO LIFE NEWS (Dec. 21, 1982), at 7.

31. Richard Glasow, *PP's Abortion Litigation: A Successful Strategy*, NAT. RIGHT TO LIFE NEWS (Dec. 21, 1982), at 7.

32. Jerome Watson, *Ruling Sparks Political Battles*, CHI. SUN-TIMES (July 3, 1989), at 3. On NRLC's model bill, *see States Testing the Limits on Abortion*, N.Y. TIMES (Apr. 2, 1990), https://www.nytimes.com/1990/04/02/us/states-testing-the-limits-on-abort ion.html.

33. On the prosecution of pregnant people of color in the late 1980s and early 1990s, *see* Dorothy Roberts, *Punishing Drug Addicts Who Have Babies: Women of Color, Equality, and the Right of Privacy*, 104 Harv. L. Rev. 1419, 1419 (1991). On the abortion rate in the late 1980s, *see* L. M. Koonin et al., *Abortion Surveillance, United States—1990*, 42 MMWR SURVEILLANCE SUMMARIES 29, 30 (1993). On the health effects of maternal incarceration, *see* Christopher Wildeman, *Imprisonment and Infant Mortality*, 59 SOCIAL PROBLEMS 228 (2012).

34. *See* Planned Parenthood of Southeastern Pennsylvania v. Casey, 505 U.S. 833, 857–82 (1992) (plurality decision).

35. Judith Koehler, *Being Pro-Life Is Good Politics*, CHI. TRIB. (Sept. 17, 1997), at NW26.

36. On the rise and importance of Targeted Regulations on Abortion Providers (TRAP laws), *see* Reva B. Siegel, *Why Restrict Abortion? Expanding the Frame on June Medical*, 2020 SUP. CT. REV. 1, 1–87 (2021).

37. On political party realignment at the federal and state level, *see* JAMES E. CAMPBELL, POLARIZED: MAKING SENSE OF A DIVIDED AMERICA 141–80 (Princeton: Princeton Univ. Press, 2018).

38. *See* ROBERT PERKINSON, TEXAS TOUGH: THE RISE OF AMERICA'S PRISON EMPIRE 6 (New York: Metropolitan Books, 2010); Noah Robertson & Patrik Jonsson, *How Race Shaped the South's Punitive Approach to Justice*, CHRISTIAN SCI. MONITOR (June 28, 2021), https://www.csmonitor.com/USA/Justice/2021/0628/How-race-shaped-the-South-s-punitive-approach-to-justice.

39. James Taranto, *An Echo, Not a "Choice": Trump's Blunder Is No Breath of Fresh Error*, WALL ST. J. (May 31, 2016).

40. Ginger Adams, *Punisher in Chief*, N.Y. DAILY NEWS (Mar. 31, 2016), at 4.

41. *See* Amy Howe, *Decade in Review: Brett Kavanaugh's Confirmation Hearing*, SCOTUS BLOG (Dec. 31, 2019), https://www.scotusblog.com/2019/12/decade-in-review-just ice-brett-kavanaughs-confirmation-hearing/.

42. For the decision of *June Medical, see* June Medical Services v. Russo, 140 S. Ct. 2103 (2020). On the spread of heartbeat bans, *see* ZIEGLER, *supra* note 26 at 131–44.

43. *See* ZIEGLER, *supra* note 26, at 144–48.

44. On Louisiana's abortion bill, *see* Kitchener, *supra* note 2.

45. Charlie Camosy, *Fighting for Life in the Golden State*, PILLAR (June 3, 2022), https://www.pillarcatholic.com/p/fighting-for-life-in-the-golden-state?s=r. On Germany's approach to abortion law, *see* Vanessa McDonald & Jula Hughes, *The German Abortion Decisions and the Protective Function in German and Canadian Constitutional Law*, 50 OSGOODE HALL L.J. 999, 999–1050 (2013).

46. On the decline of abortion rates, *see* Elizabeth Nash et al., *The U.S. Abortion Rate Continues to Drop*, GUTTMACHER INST. (Sept. 18, 2019), https://www.guttmacher.org/gpr/2019/09/us-abortion-rate-continues-drop-once-again-state-abortion-restrictions-are-not-main. On the stability of popular opinion on abortion, *see Abortion*, GALLUP, https://news.gallup.com/poll/1576/abortion.aspx (last visited Oct. 24, 2022).

47. *See* Rachel K. Jones et al., *Long-Term Decline in U.S. Abortions Reverses, Showing Need for Abortion as Supreme Court Is Poised to Overturn* Roe v. Wade, GUTTMACHER INST. POL'Y ANALYSIS (June 2022), https://www.guttmacher.org/article/2022/06/long-term-decline-us-abortions-reverses-showing-rising-need-abortion-supreme-court.

Chapter 16

1. For a recent summary of the evidence, see Michelle Oberman, *What Will and Won't Happen When Abortion Is Banned*, 9 J. LAW & THE BIOSCIENCES 1 (2022).

2. Some policies might ameliorate some quality-of-life concerns. These include social supports for childrearing such as generous programs of paid maternity leave and easily accessible institutions for infant and child care, and policies that make adoption readily available. Quality-of-life concerns survive adoption-related policies because, for example, having gone through an entire pregnancy the new mother might have developed affectional ties to her child that lead her to accept a lower quality of life instead of pursuing adoption. (As far as I am aware, Western European abortion-related policies don't generally incorporate attention to adoption as an alternative to abortion.)

3. The German Constitutional Court sought to enhance this "thinking seriously" by mandating counseling of women seeking abortions that would seek to guide them noncoercively to continue the pregnancy. Directive counseling of this sort exists elsewhere in Western Europe but is not characteristic of the Western European approach.

4. *See, e.g.,* DeShaney v. Winnebago County, 489 U.S. 189 (1989) *and* Town of Castle Rock v. Gonzales, 545 U.S. 748 (2005) for examples of decisions imposing such responsibility at a high level in what would seem to be rather compelling circumstances.

5. Traditional Catholic teaching does describe consensual intercourse not aimed at conception as wrongful. Unlike the Church's teaching on abortion, the teaching on contraception is apparently almost universally ignored by U.S. Catholics (and Catholics elsewhere, though I have less information about that).

6. On some reasonably standard views of Christian theology we are all fallen and "guilty," even women who are raped—though not with respect to *that* event.

7. My daughter, who regularly counsels pregnant women at a crisis-pregnancy center, reports that many of the women she talks to are ambivalent about both their relationship with the man with whom they had intercourse—suggesting that at least sometimes they experience the circumstances as partially voluntary, partially coerced—and about terminating the pregnancy. My sense is that such ambivalence, again about both the circumstances leading to pregnancy and about terminating the pregnancy, is quite widespread (though not of course universal).

8. For a useful expression of this view, *see* Tracy A. Weitz, *Rethinking the Mantra That Abortion Should Be "Safe, Legal, and Rare,"* 22 J. WOMEN'S HIST. 161 (2010).

9. The Church's teachings about abortion are very slightly more authoritative than its teachings about capital punishment, but most of the margin deals with conditions other than those obtaining in the United States and Eastern Europe.

Chapter 17

* Thanks to Mary Kathryn Healy, Natalie Hoge, and Lara Sachdeva for research assistance.

1. Roe v. Wade, 410 US 113 (1973); Dobbs v. Jackson Women's Health Organization, 142 S. Ct. 2228 (2022).

2. *Abortion*, GALLUP (2022), https://news.gallup.com/poll/1576/abortion.aspx.

3. *Dobbs*, 142 S. Ct.

4. Elyssa Spitzer & Nora Ellmann, *State Abortion Legislation in 2021: A Review of Positive and Negative Actions*, CTR. FOR AM. PROGRESS (Sept. 21, 2021), https://www.americanprogress.org/article/state-abortion-legislation-2021/.

5. Bundesverfassungsgericht [Federal Constitutional Court of Germany], Feb. 25, 1975, 39 BVerfGE 1, (Ger.); Gerald L. Neuman, Casey *in the Mirror: Abortion, Abuse and the Right to Protection in the United States and Germany*, 43(2) AM. J. COMPAR. L. 273–314 (1994).

6. *See* AHARON BARAK, PROPORTIONALITY (New York: Cambridge Univ. Press, 2022); *see also* ALEC STONE SWEET & JUD MATHEWS, PROPORTIONALITY BALANCING AND GLOBAL CONSTITUTIONALISM (New York: Oxford Univ. Press, 2019).

7. *See* ROBERT ALEXY, A THEORY OF CONSTITUTIONAL RIGHTS (Oxford: Oxford Univ. Press, Julian Rivers, trans., 2002).

8. Jamal Greene, *Foreword: Rights as Trumps?*, 132 HARV. L. REV. 28 (2018); Vicki Jackson, *Constitutional Law in an Age of Proportionality*, 124(8) YALE L.J. 2680–3203 (June 2015).

9. R. v. Morgenthaler, [1988] 1 S.C.R. 30 (Can.).

10. Tremblay v. Daigle, [1989] 2 S.C.R. 530 (Can.).

11. Puri M. et. al, *Abortion and Unintended Pregnancy in Nepal*, GUTTMACHER INST. (Feb. 2017). https://www.guttmacher.org/fact-sheet/abortion-unintended-pregnancy-in-nepal.

12. *Lakshmi v. Government of Nepal (Supreme Court of Nepal)*, CTR. FOR REPROD. RTS. (Feb. 22, 2007), https://reproductiverights.org/case/lakshmi-dhikta-v-government-of-nepal-amici-supreme-court-of-nepal/.

13. *See Safe Motherhood and Reproductive Rights Act, 2018*, CTR. FOR REPROD. RTS./ F. FOR WOMEN, L. AND DEV. (Sept. 18, 2018), https://reproductiverights.org/sites/defa ult/files/2020-01/Safe%20Motherhood%20and%20Reproductive%20Health%20Rig hts%20Act%20in%20English.pdf.

14. Janet F. Wang, *Attitude Toward and Use of Induced Abortion Among Taiwanese Women*, 3(3) ISSUES IN HEALTH CARE OF WOMEN 179–202 (1981).

15. *Genetic Health Act*, L. AND REGUL. DATABASE OF THE REPUBLIC OF CHINA (TAIWAN), https://law.moj.gov.tw/Eng/LawClass/LawAll.aspx?PCode=L0070001#:~:text= This%20Act%20is%20duly%20enacted,subject%20to%20other%20Act%20co ncerned.

16. *See* Hunbeobjaepanso [Const. Ct.], Aug. 23, 2012, 24-2(A), KCCR 471, 2010Hun— Ba402 (S. Kor.).

17. Hunbeobjaepanso [Const. Ct.], Apr. 11, 2019, 2017Hun-Ba127 (S. Kor); *see also* English-language summary at *Major Decisions: [Rights of Freedom] Case on the Crime of Abortion*, CONST. CT. OF KOR. (Apr. 11, 2019), https://www.law.utoronto.ca/utfl_ file/count/documents/reprohealth/south_korea_2019_constitutional_court_abort ion.pdf.

18. Eighth Amendment of the Constitution Act 1983 (Act No. C8/1983) (Ir.), https:// www.irishstatutebook.ie/eli/1983/ca/8/enacted/en/print#sec2.

19. *What is the Eighth Amendment?*, IRISH COUNCIL FOR C.L., https://www.iccl.ie/her-rig hts/what-is-the-eighth/ (last visited Nov. 7, 2023).

20. *Eighth Amendment Repealed After Bill Is Signed into Law*, BBC NEWS (Sept. 18, 2018), https://www.bbc.com/news/world-europe-45568094.

21. *See* JAMES S. FISHKIN, DEMOCRACY WHEN THE PEOPLE ARE THINKING: REVITALIZING OUR POLITICS THROUGH PUBLIC DELIBERATION (Oxford: Oxford Univ. Press 2018); *see also* HÉLÈNE LANDEMORE, DEMOCRATIC REASON: POLITICS, COLLECTIVE INTELLIGENCE, AND THE RULE OF THE MANY (Princeton: Princeton Univ. Press, 2012); *see also* HÉLÈNE LANDEMORE, OPEN DEMOCRACY: REINVENTING POPULAR RULE FOR THE TWENTY-FIRST CENTURY (Princeton: Princeton Univ. Press, 2020).

22. *American Convention on Human Rights, "Pact of San Jose," Costa Rica* art. 4, Organization of American States (OAS), Nov. 22, 1969.

23. Elena Moore, *Argentina Legalizes Abortion in Historic Senate Vote*, NPR (Dec. 30, 2020), https://www.npr.org/2020/12/30/951001451/argentina-legalizes-abortion-in-historic-senate-vote.

24. ROBERTO GARGARELLA, THE LAW AS A CONVERSATION AMONG EQUALS 260 (New York: Cambridge Univ. Press, 2022).

25. Law No. 27610, Jan. 15, 2021, B.O. 34.562 (Arg.); for English translation, see Tradoctas, trans., *Access to the Voluntary Termination of Pregnancy, Law No. 27,610,*

L

Red de Acceso al Aborto Seguro (REDAAS) Argentina, https://www.redaas. org.ar/archivos-recursos/521-Law%2027,610%20-%20Access%20to%20the%20Vo luntary%20Termination%20of%20Pregnancy.pdf.

26. *Access to the Voluntary Termination of Pregnancy, supra* note 25, at 1.

27. *Id.* at 4.

28. *Colombia's Highest Court Rules to Decriminalize Abortion*, Ctr. for Reprod. Rts. (Feb. 2, 2022), https://reproductiverights.org/colombia-court-decriminalize-abortion/.

29. Constitución Política de Colombia [C.P.] art. 11; for English translation, see Max Planck Inst., trans., *Colombia 1991 (rev. 2015)*, Constitute, https://www. constituteproject.org/constitution/Colombia_2015?lang=en (last visited Nov. 9, 2022).

30. Corte Constitucional [C.C.] [Constitutional Court], May 10, 2006, MP: J. Rentería, C. Hernandez, Sentencia C-355/06 (Colom.), https://www.corteconstitucional.gov. co/relatoria/2006/c-355-06.htm.

31. Constitución Política de Colombia [C.P.] art. 93; for English translation, see Max Planck Inst., trans., *Colombia 1991 (rev. 2015)*, Constitute, https://www. constituteproject.org/constitution/Colombia_2015?lang=en (last visited Nov. 9, 2022).

32. Salvador Rivera, *Abortion Legal in 9 Mexican States, Including Baja California*, Border Rep. (June 24, 2022), https://www.borderreport.com/health/abortion-legal-in-9-mexican-states-including-baja-california/.

33. Constitución Política de law República de Chile [C.P.] art. 19; for English translation, see Rodrigo Delaveau Swett, trans., *Chile 1980 (rev. 2021)*, Constitute, https://www.constituteproject.org/constitution/Chile_2021?lang=en.

34. Michele Oberman, Her Body, Our Laws: On the Frontlines of the Abortion War from El Salvador to Oklahoma 10 (Boston: Beacon Press, 2018).

35. At this writing, France's National Assembly has proposed a constitutional amendment to guarantee access to abortion.

36. Oberman, *supra* note 34, at 43.

37. *Dominican Republic 2015*, Constitute, https://www.constituteproject.org/constitut ion/Dominican_Republic_2015?lang=en (last visited Nov. 9, 2022).

38. Rafael Romo, *Pregnant Teen Dies After Abortion Ban Delays Her Chemo Treatment For Leukemia*, CNN (Aug. 18, 2012), https://edition.cnn.com/2012/08/18/world/ americas/dominican-republic-abortion/index.html?fb_action_ids=1015101529 7108671&fb_action_types=og.recommends&fb_source=aggregation&fb_aggrega tion_id=288381481237582.

39. *Dominican Republic Constitutional Court Repeals Abortion Law*, Ctr. for Reprod. Rts. (Dec. 4, 2015), https://reproductiverights.org/dominican-republic-constitutio nal-court-repeals-abortion-law/.

40. *Poland: A Year on, Abortion Ruling Harms Women*, Hum. Rts. Watch (Oct. 19, 2021), https://www.hrw.org/news/2021/10/19/poland-year-abortion-ruling-harms-women.

41. Erin M. Kwolek, *Alone on an Island: The Impact of COVID-19 Containment Measures on Access to Abortion Care in Malta*, 7 VOICES IN BIOETHICS (Sept. 1, 2021), https://journals.library.columbia.edu/index.php/bioethics/article/view/8663.

42. Sara Monetta, *Fears for US Woman's Life as Abortion Denied in Malta*, BBC NEWS (June 22, 2022), https://www.bbc.com/news/world-61898437.

43. *The World's Abortion Laws*, CTR. FOR REPROD. RTS, https://reproductiverights.org/maps/worlds-abortion-laws/.

44. *Madagascar 2021*, AMNESTY INT'L, https://www.amnesty.org/en/location/africa/southern-africa/madagascar/report-madagascar/.

45. U.S. DEP'T OF STATE, BUREAU OF DEMOCRACY, HUM. RTS., AND LAB., *Madagascar 2019 Human Rights Report*, https://www.state.gov/wp-content/uploads/2020/02/MADAGASCAR-2019-HUMAN-RIGHTS-REPORT.pdf.

46. HARMONIZED DRAFT CONSTITUTION ART. 35 (2009) (Kenya).

47. REVISED HARMONIZED DRAFT CONSTITUTION OF KENYA ART. 25(4) (2010) (Kenya) ("Abortion is not permitted unless in the opinion of a registered medical practitioner, the life of the mother is in danger.").

48. CONSTITUTION ART. 26(4) (Kenya), https://www.constituteproject.org/constitution/Kenya_2010?lang=en.

49. Steven Ertelt, *Kenya Government Starts Campaign for Pro-Abortion Constitution, Attacks Church*, LIFENEWS (Apr. 20, 2010); *Kenya: Abortion Harms Women's Health, U.S. Physicians Say*, CATH. INFO. SERV. FOR AFR. (NAIROBI) (Mar. 31, 2010), https://allafrica.com/stories/201003310624.html.

50. They also opened up an office in Zimbabwe. *See* Kapya Kaoma, *Colonizing African Values: How the Christian Right Is Transforming Sexual Politics in Africa* vii, POL. RSCH. ASSOC. (2012), https://politicalresearch.org/sites/default/files/2018-10/Colonizing-African-Values.pdf.

51. *More U.S. Taxpayer Funds for Pro-Abortion Kenyan Constitution: Rep. Smith*, LIFESITE (May 26, 2010), http://www.lifesitenews.com/ldn/2010/may/10052606.html.

52. Jeffrey Gettleman, *Kenyans Approve New Constitution*, N.Y. TIMES (Aug. 5, 2010), at A7.

53. Kaoma, *supra* note 50, at 12.

54. Jeff Sagnip & Steven Ertelt, *Probe: Obama Admin. Broke Law to Push Abortion in Kenya*, LIFENEWS (Nov. 16, 2011), http://www.lifenews.com/2011/11/16/probe-obama-admin-broke-law-to-push-abortion-in-kenya/.

55. Jordan Sekulow, *The New ACLJ: All About the African Center for Law & Justice Online*, AM. CTR. FOR L. AND JUST. (July 24, 2012), https://aclj.org/aclj/the-new-aclj-all-about-the-african-center-for-law-justice-.

56. Sarah Posner, *Pat Robertson's Women Warriors Leading Spiritual Warfare in Zimbabwe*, RELIGION DISPATCHES (Aug. 2, 2010), https://religiondispatches.org/pat-robertsons-women-warriors-leading-spiritual-warfare-in-zimbabwe/.

57. *Our History*, WOMEN, WEAPONS OF WARFARE, http://www.womenweaponsofwarfare.com/ourhistory.html.

58. Rebecca Gomperts, *Women on Waves: Where Next for the Abortion Boat?*, 10(19) REPROD. HEALTH MATTERS 180–83 (2002).

59. Protocol to the African Charter on Human and Peoples' Rights on the Rights of Women in Africa, art. 14, July 11, 2003.

60. Mildred Mapingure v. Minister of Home Affairs and 2 Others, Civil Appeal No. SC 406/12, Supreme Court (2014) (Zim.).

61. These are protected under the Convention. The relevant aspect of Article 3 reads, "No one shall be subjected to . . . inhuman or degrading treatment." Article 8 states in its relevant section, "1. Everyone has the right to respect for his private . . . life. . . . 2. There shall be no interference by a public authority with the exercise of this right except such as is in accordance with the law and is necessary in a democratic society in the interests of national security, public safety or the economic well-being of the country, for the prevention of disorder or crime, for the protection of health or morals, or for the protection of the rights and freedoms of others." The relevant part of Article 14 is as follows: "The enjoyment of the rights and freedoms set forth in [the] Convention shall be secured without discrimination on any ground such as sex, race, colour, language, religion, political or other opinion, national or social origin, association with a national minority, property, birth or other status." Council of Europe, European Convention on Human Rights, Nov. 4, 1950, C.E.T.S. No. 005.

62. *See* Women on Waves and Others v. Portugal, No. 31276/05 Eur. Ct. H.R. (2009), https://hudoc.echr.coe.int/fre?i=002-1667.

63. Case of A, B and C v. Ireland, No. 25579/05 Eur. Ct. H.R. (2010), https://hudoc.echr.coe.int/fre?i=001-102332.

64. R.R. v. Poland, No. 27617/04 Eur. Ct. H.R. (2011), https://hudoc.echr.coe.int/fre?i=001-104911.

65. *Manuela v. El Salvador (Inter-American Court of Human Rights)*, CTR. FOR REPROD. RTS. (Dec. 2, 2021), https://reproductiverights.org/case/Manuela-v-el-salvador-inter-american-court-of-human-rights/.

66. Jimmy Chia-Hsin Hsu, *The Right to Life, in* OXFORD HANDBOOK OF COMPARATIVE CONSTITUTIONAL LAW IN ASIA (Oxford: Oxford Univ. Press, David Law, Holning Lau, &Alex Schwartz, eds., 2022).

67. CONST., (1987) art. II, § 12 (Phil.); *see* Imbong v. Ochoa, G.R. No. 204819 (Apr. 8, 2014) (Phil.), (confirming that legislature does not enjoy power to legalize abortion).

68. The UN committee responsible for interpreting the Convention on the Elimination of Discrimination Against Women has since 1999 positioned reproductive health as a central element of the convention and called for the decriminalization of abortion. Comm. on the Elimination of Discrimination Against Women, General Recommendation No. 24: Article 12 of the Convention (Women and Health), UN Doc. A/54/38/Rev/1, chap. 1, at para. 31 (1999).

69. OBERMAN, *supra* note 34, at 11.

Chapter 18

* I thank Carli Sley for excellent research assistance pertinent to this chapter. I thank Stephen Sachs, Reva Siegel, Maya Manian, and attendees at the faculty workshop at the American University Washington College of Law and Berkeley Law for helpful comments.

1. Dobbs v. Jackson Women's Health Org., 142 S. Ct. 2228, 2301 (2022) (Thomas, J., concurring) (quoting Ramos v. Louisiana, 140 S. Ct. 1390, 1424, and Gamble v. United States, 139 S. Ct. 1960, 1984–85, (Thomas, J., concurring)).

2. Dobbs v. Jackson Women's Health Org., 142 S. Ct. 2228, 2258 (2022).

3. Dobbs v. Jackson Women's Health Org., 142 S. Ct. 2228, 2332 (2022) (Joint Dissent).

4. *Dobbs*, 142 S. Ct. at 2258.

5. IVF is "a medical procedure in which a woman's eggs are extracted from her ovaries and mixed with sperm in the laboratory. The resulting embryos are grown for three to five days, then transferred back to the woman's uterus through the cervix."

An IVF cycle has four phases:

Phase 1: Ovarian Stimulation and Monitoring. A woman is treated with a sequence of drugs, generally administered through injection, to induce multiple follicles to mature so that several eggs can be retrieved. Drug treatment usually begins midway through a woman's menstrual cycle and continues until the eggs are retrieved.

Phase 2: Egg Collection. Egg retrieval is done in a surgical procedure in which either general anesthesia or a combination of sedation and pain medications are administered to the woman. Physicians insert an ultrasound-guided needle through the vaginal wall and into a developed ovarian follicle. Using suction, the fluid inside the follicle is withdrawn, along with the egg it contains. This removal technique is repeated for each follicle that has developed.

Phase 3: Fertilization and Embryo Culture. Each normal-appearing egg is placed in a separate petri dish containing culture medium. Semen is obtained from the male partner and is processed to obtain a high concentration of motile sperm. The sperm is then introduced into the dish. The contents of the dish are examined under a microscope after one day to determine if the egg is fertilized.

Phase 4: Embryo Transfer. Embryos are generally transferred to the woman's uterus two or three days after egg retrieval, when they are comprised of four to eight cells. Under certain circumstances the embryo will be transferred after five days when it has become a blastocyst. The transfer is accomplished using a sterile tube with a syringe on one end. Droplets of fluid containing one embryo are drawn into the tube, which is inserted through the cervix and then injected into the uterus. Embryo transfer generally requires no anesthesia or sedation.

Following embryo transfer, a woman will wait approximately ten to fourteen days before undergoing a blood test to determine if she is pregnant.

JUDITH DAAR ET AL., REPRODUCTIVE TECHNOLOGIES AND THE LAW 1114–15 (Durham: Carolina Academic Press, 3d ed. 2022).

6. I. Glenn Cohen, Judith Daar, & Eli Y. Adashi, *What Overturning* Roe v Wade *May Mean for Assisted Reproductive Technologies in the U.S.*, 328 JAMA 15, 15 (2022) (citing *2019 Assisted Reproductive Technology: Fertility Clinic and National Summary Report*, US Ctrs. for Disease Control and Prevention (2019), https://www.cdc.gov/art/reports/2019/pdf/2019-report-art-fertility-clinic-national-summary-h.pdf). Cryopreservation is "freezing at a very low temperature, such as in liquid nitrogen (−196°C) to keep embryos, eggs, or sperm viable." *Cryopreservation and Storage*, Am. Soc'y for Reproductive Med., https://www.asrm.org/topics/topics-index/cryopreservation-and-storage/ (last visited Nov. 22, 2022). Once embryos are fertilized in the lab, "there may be more resulting embryos than can be safely transferred back to the woman's uterus," in which case additional embryos can be cryopreserved (frozen) for later use, "which allows a woman to avoid additional injections and surgeries if the initial IVF fails or she chooses to gestate the embryos at a later time." Daar et al., *supra* note 5, at 38.

7. Henry T. Greely, *The Death of* Roe *and the Future of Ex Vivo Embryos*, 9 J.L. & Biosciences 1, 12 (2022) (citing Practice Comm. of the Am. Soc'y for Reprod. Med. & the Prac. Comm. for the Soc'y for Assisted Reprod. Techs., *Guidance on the Limits to the Number of Embryos to Transfer: A Committee Opinion*, 116 Fertility & Sterility 651 (2021)). In theory, couples could implant more than that and engage in what those involved in reproductive medicine call "[s]elective reduction" or "multifetal pregnancy reduction," which involves a "surgical procedure [that is] performed between the late first and early second trimester of pregnancy to 'reduce' the number of fetuses in a multiple pregnancy, typically to enhance the survival and well-being of the remaining fetuses." Judith Daar, *The Outdated Pregnancy: Rethinking Traditional Markers in Reproduction*, 35 J. Legal Med. 505, 512 (2014). But in the post-*Dobbs* world such actions may also be prohibited by some states' restrictions on abortion. Indeed, there continue to be debates *within* reproductive medicine as to whether it would show more solidarity with women fighting for abortion rights to call these "abortions" rather than "selective reduction."

8. *See* Daar et al., *supra* note 5, at 669–775 (discussing cases, statutes, and data).

9. Cohen et al., *supra* note 6, at 15 (citing U.S. Centers for Disease Control and Prevention, *supra* note 6).

10. La. Stat. Ann. § 9:129 (1986). The 1986 enactment date of the statute may be relevant to my discussion below of the political support for such restrictions; in 1986 familiarity, usage, and likely support for IVF was much less widespread than today. I do wonder whether even Louisiana would be able to pass such a law with today's electorate.

11. I return to this issue of transfer out of state after *Dobbs* in the conclusion.

12. Ky. Rev. Stat. Ann. § 311.715 (West 1984). When it comes to the destruction of embryos for research purposes—for example, stem cell derivation—at least eleven states have banned or effectively banned the practice. Kirsten R. W. Matthews & Daniel Morali, *Can We Do That Here? An Analysis of U.S. Federal and State Policies Guiding Human Embryo and Embryoid Research*, 9 J.L. & Biosciences 1, 10 (2022); *see* Greely, *supra* note 7, at 22.

13. DAAR ET AL., *supra* note 5, at 743.

14. *Id.*

15. *Id.* at 749–53. The terminology here is quite fraught, and some rightly chafe at "adoption" presupposing the moral equivalence between embryo and a child that is already born.

16. *See* I. Glenn Cohen, *The Right(s) to Procreate and Assisted Reproductive Technologies in the United States, in* THE OXFORD HANDBOOK OF COMPARATIVE HEALTH LAW 1009, 1011–16 (New York: Oxford Univ. Press, Tamara K. Hervey & David Orentlicher eds., 2021).

17. *See id.*

18. Heather Silber Mohamed, *Embryonic Politics: Attitudes about Abortion, Stem Cell Research, and IVF*, 11 POL. & RELIGION 459, 467 (2018) (quoting Erin Allyson Heidt-Forsythe, Reconceiving the State (May, 2013) (PhD dissertation, Rutgers University) (on file with the Rutgers University Community Repository)).

19. *Id.* at 469–70. Her analysis of views by religious group is also quite interesting in finding less reliable correlations between denomination and attitudes toward IVF:

> [N]o relationship exists between Evangelical Protestants and IVF attitudes. Additionally, while the Catholic Church has been outspoken in opposition to procedures regarding human embryos, in comparison with mainline Protestants, I find that Catholics are no more likely to describe these procedures as morally wrong. Likewise, despite expectations that Jewish respondents would hold the most liberal views about embryonic politics, this variable was significant only for views on abortion.

> *Id.* at 482.

20. One very recent data point in favor of my prediction is West Virginia's new tough abortion law, HB-302, enacted in September 2022, which explicitly excludes IVF from its definition of abortion. HB-302, W. Va. Code §16-2R-4(5) (2022), available at https://www.wvlegislature.gov/Bill_Status/bills_text.cfm?billdoc=HB302%20ENG.htm&yr=2022&sesstype=3X&i=302. The carve-out refers to IVF specifically, not the destruction of frozen embryos created as part of IVF, but other parts of the statute might be plausibly read to exclude them from the prohibition as well. Another good recent example comes from Tennessee, which amended its abortion statute shortly after *Dobbs*. It adopts a very broad definition of "unborn child," which it defines as "an individual living member of the species, homo sapiens, throughout the entire embryonic and fetal stages of the unborn child from fertilization until birth." TENN. CODE ANN. § 39-15-213(a)(4) (2022). This definition would capture fertilized embryos. But then in its definition of abortion it adopts limiting language that excludes embryo destruction from the acts it prohibits in this section. It defines abortion as "the use of any instrument, medicine, drug, or any other substance or device with intent to terminate the pregnancy of a woman known to be pregnant with intent other than to increase the probability of a live birth, to preserve the life or health of the child after live birth, or to remove a dead fetus." *Id.* at (a)(1). Pregnancy is the touchstone for its abortion definition, and it in turn specifies, "'Pregnant' means the human female reproductive condition of having a living unborn child *within her body throughout* the entire

embryonic and fetal stages of the unborn child from fertilization until birth." *Id*. at (a) (3) (emphasis added). Thus it excludes embryo destruction. This reading comports with that of the Tennessee Attorney General Opinion issued on October 20, 2022, which considered the question "Is the disposal of a human embryo that has not been transferred to a woman's uterus punishable as 'criminal abortion' under the Human Life Protection Act?" and answered, "No. The Human Life Protection Act only applies when a woman has a living unborn child within her body." State of Tennessee, Office of the Attorney General, Opinion No. 22-12, Oct. 20, 2022, available at https://www.tn.gov/content/dam/tn/attorneygeneral/documents/ops/2022/op22-12.pdf.

21. One can, from one's armchair, offer some sociological or political explanations as to why the political process might have different attitudes toward restricting abortion versus embryo destruction. One set of explanations might draw on race and class differences among users of IVF abortion. Black and poor individuals face difficulties accessing IVF, in part because of only very limited (if any) insurance coverage, high out-of-pocket cost, referral patterns, and more. *See, e.g.*, Aziza Ahmed, *Race and Assisted Reproduction: Implications for Population Health*, 86 FORDHAM L. REV. 2801, 2807 (2018); Usha Lee McFarling, *For Black Women, the Isolation of Infertility Is Compounded by Barriers to Treatment*, STAT NEWS (Oct. 14, 2020), https://www.statn ews.com/2020/10/14/for-black-women-isolation-of-infertility-compounded-by-barriers-to-treatment/. Some label this a problem of "stratified reproduction, in which medical technology is used to enhance the fertility of married, rich, white women, but not that of poor Black and brown women." *Id*. This population is much more likely to successfully resist state regulation, the argument goes, than does that burdened by abortion. One might also layer on a historical argument that (in the words of one of the historian briefs in *Dobbs*) "States Restricted Abortion More Stringently Following an Elite-Driven Physicians' Campaign Built on Mixed and Discriminatory Motives." Dobbs v. Jackson Women's Health Org., Brief for Amici Curiae American Historical Association and Organization of American Historians in Support of Respondents 18 (2021), available at http://www.supremecourt.gov/DocketPDF/19/19-1392/192957/20210920133840569_19-1392%20bsac%20Historians.pdf. *See also id*. at 21 ("While [key abortion prohibition leader Dr. Horatio] Storer believed that abortion was always morally wrong, two other concerns were inextricable from his condemnation of abortion on that ground: his ethnocentric concerns about rising immigrant birthrates and his blame of married Protestant women for abandoning their primary responsibility of motherhood, thus becoming especially culpable for the falling birth rate.").

A different explanation points to gender. Restrictions on abortion affect women in the first instance, whereas restrictions on embryo destruction directly burden both men and women—though not equally given the much greater maternal costs and risks of egg retrieval and also differences as to when each sex "ages out" of fertility. Such explanations seem plausible to me as an explanation of why the difference in regulation of the two areas might persist, but my focus in this piece is instead on whether the differences are justified, normatively speaking.

22. Like many, I do not like these terms and all the baggage associated with them, the assumptions they make of the other side, the rhetorical traps they invite, but I rely

on them because they are the useful shorthand. One particularly interesting wrinkle in their usage here is that they help illuminate that some who oppose abortion restrictions are *both* pro-life and pro-choice, but in the case of embryo destruction the two unravel. That is, to skip slightly ahead, there are those who oppose abortion who believe in Premise 1 (the personhood of the fetus) and reject Premise 2 (that said personhood trumps women's control of their bodies).

23. Leon R. Kass, *The Wisdom of Repugnance*, in THE ETHICS OF HUMAN CLONING 3, 19, 38–39 (Washington, D.C.: AEI Press, Leon R. Kass & James Q. Wilson eds., 1998). Indeed, if one looks at the history of IVF, in the decade before the world's first IVF birth in 1978, Kass was one of the loudest voices opposing it. *See* MARGARET MARSH & WANDA RONNER, THE PURSUIT OF PARENTHOOD: REPRODUCTIVE TECHNOLOGY FROM TEST-TUBE BABIES TO UTERUS TRANSPLANTS 46–48 (Baltimore: Johns Hopkins Univ. Press, 2019) (discussing Kass's and Princeton theologian Paul Ramsey's very public opposition).

24. *See, e.g.*, Courtney Megan Cahill, *After Sex*, 97 NEB. L. REV. 1, 4 (2018) ("If marital supremacy is what happens when the law makes ideal marriage the measure of non-marital relationships, then sexual supremacy is what happens when the law makes ideal sexual procreation the measure of non-sexual procreation. In both cases, a non-traditional relationship or practice is regulated in the shadow of ideas and ideals about a traditional relationship or practice."). This strand may be especially prominent in opposition to the newest and most disruptive technologies, like mitochondrial replacement techniques and, in the future, in vitro gametogenesis. For more on these technologies, *see, e.g.*, HENRY T. GREELY, THE END OF SEX AND THE FUTURE OF HUMAN REPRODUCTION (Cambridge, MA: Harvard Univ. Press, 2018); NAT'L ACADS. OF SCIS., ENG'G & MED., MITOCHONDRIAL REPLACEMENT TECHNIQUES: ETHICAL, SOCIAL, AND POLICY CONSIDERATIONS (2016); I. Glenn Cohen et al., *The Regulation of Mitochondrial Replacement Techniques Around the World*, 21 ANN. REV. GENOMICS & HUM. GENETICS 565 (2020); I. Glenn Cohen, George Q. Daley, & Eli Y. Adashi, *Disruptive Reproductive Technologies*, 9 SCI. TRANSLATIONAL MED. eaag2959 (2017); Sonia M. Suter, In Vitro *Gametogenesis: Just Another Way to Have a Baby?*, 3 J.L. & BIOSCIENCES 87 (2016).

25. *See, e.g.*, Marsh & Ronner, *supra* note 23, at 54–55, 64–67.

26. I. Glenn Cohen, *Are All Abortions Equal? Should There Be Exceptions to the Criminalization of Abortion for Rape and Incest?*, 43 J. LAW MED. & ETHICS 87, 88 (2015). As I acknowledge there, it may be that there are some arguments against abortion that do not approach it this way, but they are outliers. Indeed, the fact that we call the movement "pro-life" emphasizes just how important that first premise is.

Some might challenge the whole method of this chapter—to suggest it misses the point to take seriously the normative premises underlying opposition to abortion and examining where those premises take us. For them, the sociology of the culture wars is what matters, not philosophical arguments. I guess I agree insofar as there are many people for whom close examination of what they believe and why is beside the point for thinking about what the law should be, but disagree insofar as the suggestion is that this renders the approach I take here not worthwhile. I am not naïve enough to think reasoned argument is the way to win everyone over, but believe it is essential as at least a first step to determine whether it is the game one should be trying to win at all.

27. When I use the term "early embryo" in this chapter, I mean to refer to the embryo in the period of two to seven days of development and culturing after insemination, that is, the period in which embryos are typically either transferred to the uterus as part of IVF or cryopreserved for a future use. *E.g.*, Practice Committee of the American Society for Reproductive Medicine, *Fertility Preservation in Patients Undergoing Gonadotoxic Therapy or Gonadectomy: A Committee Opinion*, 12 FERTILITY & STERILITY 1022 (2019), https://www.asrm.org/globalassets/asrm/asrm-content/news-and-publications/practice-guidelines/for-non-members/fertility_preservation_in_patients_undergoing_gonadotoxic_therapy_or_gonadectomy.pdf. It is conceivable that for some views on personhood the exact timing of the two to seven days might matter, though for most of the views I canvass below it will not.

28. For this typology of procreative rights, *see generally* I. Glenn Cohen, *The Right Not to Be a Genetic Parent?*, 81 S. CAL. L. REV. 1115 (2008).

29. *See generally id.* In some ways this is similar to the claim a person might make in embryo disposition disputes surrounding divorce—if you use an embryo made up of my sperm and your egg over my contemporaneous objection I would argue you are forcing me into genetic parenthood. *See generally id.*

   One might wonder whether a distinction between IVF and abortion can be made on the basis of the principle of double effect, a set of ideas in Catholic bioethics tracing back to Thomas Aquinas, that "sometimes it is permissible to cause a harm as a side effect (or 'double effect') of bringing about a good result even though it would not be permissible to cause such a harm as a means to bringing about the same good end." Alison McIntyre, *Doctrine of Double Effect*, STAN. ENCYCLOPEDIA OF PHIL. (Spring 2019 ed.), https://plato.stanford.edu/archives/spr2019/entries/double-effect/. With IVF the goal is producing a child, and embryo destruction is double effect; not so with abortion, where the goal, not merely the double effect, is the destruction of the fetus. A full discussion of how embryo destruction relates to double effect is beyond the scope of this chapter, but here are some brief reasons why I do not think this will work. First, this argument may prove too much in that is does not distinguish abortion and embryo destruction—that is, if one accepts a double effect argument here, it is not clear why fetal destruction in abortion could not also be labeled a double effect in some instances—the permissible cause being to live a certain kind of life that continuing the pregnancy would make impossible. The case of abortion sought by a rape victim, and the psychological trauma that the woman seeks to avoid, might be the easiest case to characterize this way. Second, it is not clear that embryo destruction as part of IVF satisfies the requirement for double-effect-type arguments, in that they typically require that "[t]he agent may not positively will the bad effect but may permit it. If he could attain the good effect without the bad effect he should do so. The bad effect is sometimes said to be indirectly voluntary." *Id.* (quoting F. J. Connell, *Double Effect, Principle of*, 4 NEW CATHOLIC ENCYCLOPEDIA 1020, 1021 (1967)).

The possibility of fertilizing only the embryos one intends to implant may constitute a violation of this necessity requirement, as might egg freezing (discussed below). Even for embryos whose implantation is ruled out by preimplantation genetic diagnosis (PGD), the alternative of indefinite cryopreservation as opposed to destruction might defeat the necessity claim. All that said, it is certainly plausible that for the general public who may not have delved deeply into the matter, folk intuitions about double effect are in the background causing them to have very different reactions to IVF and abortion.

30. I say "wonder" because to me it depends heavily on the framing. To see this, consider the fact that many states do not cover IVF *at all* or do so with significant limitations. *See, e.g.*, I. Glenn Cohen & Daniel L. Chen, *Trading-Off Reproductive Technology and Adoption: Does Subsidizing IVF Decrease Adoption Rates and Should It Matter?*, 95 MINN. L. REV. 485, 537–39 (2010). It is hard to know how to square this with the rights claim here. On the one hand, it may seem "bougie" to make claims about the cost of engaging in multiple rounds of IVF when many cannot afford any IVF and we have not recognized a general duty on the part of the state to fix that. On the other hand, the need for multiple rounds stems from a negative liberty restriction on how many may be created per cycle rather than a positive liberty claim for financial assistance, and perhaps that is relevant in the analysis?

A different but related point is that we may be experiencing some of the gulf between reproductive rights and reproductive justice types of claims. The fact that many people's ability to pursue their reproductive goals in the way they want in these examples stems not only from the restriction imposed by the state but background facts about lack of resources, racialized and class-based lack of access to IVF, and so forth. One is reminded of the American idiom "Don't bring a knife to a gun fight" (probably derived from a line in the film *The Untouchables*). The potential problem seems to be in bringing claims about reproductive justice to a fight centered around rights claims—that of women's rights to control their bodies and the rights of the fetus to inviolability. This raises the question of whether debates about embryo destruction might permit us to get away from rights talk in terms of reproductive regulation, and whether doing so would be good or would cede too much ground to the camp one opposed.

31. Here the state might retort that egg freezing, discussed at the end of this chapter, is a possible alternative.

32. Judith Jarvis Thomson, *A Defense of Abortion*, 1 PHIL. & PUB. AFFS. 47 (1971).

33. Cohen, *supra* note 26, at 96. It is worth reading her work in its entirety—this is just a sketch of the argument.

34. Thomson, *supra* note 32, at 56.

35. McFall v. Shimp, 10 Pa. D. & C. 3d 90, 92 (Pa. Com. Pl. 1978). *See also* Bertha Alvarez Manninen, *Rethinking* Roe v. Wade: *Defending the Abortion Right in the Face of Contemporary Opposition*, 10 AM. J. BIOETHICS 33 (2010).

36. *See, e.g.*, Andrew Koppelman, *Originalism, Abortion, and the Thirteenth Amendment*, 112 COLUM. L. REV. 1917 (2012); Dov Fox, *Thirteenth Amendment Reflections on Abortion, Surrogacy, and Race Selection*, 104 CORNELL L. REV. ONLINE 114 (2019).

37. *See, e.g.*, Koppelman, *supra* note 36; Fox, *supra* note 36; Cohen, *supra* note 26; Jason T. Eberl, *Fetuses Are Neither Violinists nor Violators*, 10 Am. J. Bioethics 53 (2010).

38. Congregation for the Doctrine of the Faith, *Instruction on Respect for Human Life in Its Origin and on the Dignity of Procreation: Replies to Certain Questions of the Day* (Feb. 22, 1987), https://www.vatican.va/roman_curia/congregations/cfaith/docume nts/rc_con_cfaith_doc_19870222_respect-for-human-life_en.html.

39. Robert P. George & Patrick Lee, *Embryonic Human Persons: Talking Point on Morality and Human Embryo Research*, 10 EMBO Reps. 301, 303 (2009). One might also characterize their view as a potentiality view, discussed below, that starts at the moment of fertilization. I prefer to treat them separately because not all potentiality views will start with fertilization.

   George and Lee very explicitly suggest the question of personhood is a binary: "[T]he answer must be either yes or no—there is no in between." I think that is true for the rights claim (moral or legal) as to inviolability or at least whether the entity is such that it has a particular sets of rights claims of this type. It remains possible, though, that the actual property of personhood is a continuum—it accretes over time, and/or an entity can have more or less of it, but we are forced to place a moral and legal binary on that continuum. Because the choice of the law is always binary in this respect—should fetal/embryo destruction be permitted in this *particular* circumstance, yes or no—I am not sure it matters for this project whether one thinks the actual underlying property of personhood is discrete or continuous.

40. *E.g.*, Thomas Douglas & Julian Savulescu, *Destroying Unwanted Embryos in Research: Talking Point on Morality and Human Embryo Research*, 10 EMBO Reps. 307 (2009) ("However, if embryos are persons, then surely you should save them, as it is morally permissible—if not obligatory—to save thousands of persons in preference to one."); Rob Lovering, *The Substance View: A Critique*, 27 Bioethics 263, 266–67 (2013) ("After all, saving ten intrinsically valuable beings is clearly better than saving only one when all parties are equally intrinsically valuable. But that one ought to save the ten frozen human embryos rather than the five-year-old girl is strongly counterintuitive if not absurd.").

41. Cynthia Cohen, Renewing the Stuff of Life: Stem Cells, Ethics, and Public Policy 66 (Oxford: Oxford Univ. Press, 2007).

42. *Id* (citing B. J. Cummings et al., *Human Neural Stem Cells Differentiate and Promote Locomotor Recovery in Spinal Cord–Injured Mice*, 102 PNAS 14069 (2005)).

43. *Id*. at 67.

44. *Id*. at 68.

45. *E.g., id*. at 69–73.

46. *Id*. at 69–73. Cohen captures some of the strangeness of the "special respect" idea well by discussing Daniel Callahan's position, noting that he "finds the view that the early embryo is owed 'special respect' both sensible and yet puzzling. He confesses to a 'nagging uneasiness' about such respect, as it is 'an odd form of esteem—at once high-minded and lethal.' " *Id*. at 70.

47. *See, e.g.*, Giulia Cavaliere, *A 14-Day Limit for Bioethics: The Debate Over Human Embryo Research*, 18 BMC Med. Ethics 38 (2017); Eli Y. Adashi & I. Glenn Cohen,

Who Will Oversee the Ethical Limits of Human Embryo Research?, 40 NATURE BIOTECH. 463 (2022); Karen Weintraub, *Should Scientists Be Allowed to Grow Human Embryos in a Dish Beyond 14 Days? Is It Scientifically Important or Morally Wrong?*, USA TODAY (May 2, 2021), https://www.usatoday.com/in-depth/news/health/2021/05/02/embryo-research-14-day-rule-under-review-raising-ethical-questions/6916582002/. The current debate concerns whether fourteen days is too limiting and should be extended to a later point, not whether it is too permissive, but in the course of the debate some have suggested the reasoning behind it is arbitrary. *See id.*

48. Davis v. Davis, 842 S.W.2d 588, 597 (Tenn. 1992).

49. *See* John A. Robertson, *Sex Selection for Gender Variety by Preimplantation Genetic Diagnosis*, 78 FERTILITY & STERILITY 463 (2002).

50. A more sympathetic take on the "special respect" approach is that it is not meant to be proscriptive but is instead meant to capture an expressive dimension—to structure the way we think and talk about the early embryo rather than cordon off certain behaviors as prohibited. That may be right, but it is not very clear to me what that should mean for attempts to reconcile views on abortion and embryo destruction, especially in a rights-based discourse.

51. There is a huge amount of literature on this topic; to pick out a few citations of folks discussing the propriety of one or more of these capacities as a definition of personhood, *see, e.g.*, JEFF MCMAHAN, THE ETHICS OF KILLING: PROBLEMS AT THE MARGINS OF LIFE 4 (New York: Oxford Univ. Press, 2002); I. Glenn Cohen & Sadath Sayeed, *Fetal Pain, Abortion, Viability, and the Constitution*, 39 J. L. MED. & ETHICS 235, 240 (2011); Bonnie Steinbock, *The Morality of Killing Human Embryos*, 34 J. L. MED. & ETHICS 26, 26–34 (2006); Mary Anne Warren, *On the Moral and Legal Status of Abortion, in* BIOMEDICAL ETHICS 456, 458 (New York: McGraw-Hill Higher Education, Thomas A. Mappes & David DeGrazia eds., 5th ed. 2001); Norman L. Cantor, *The Real Ethic of Death and Dying*, 94 MICH. L. REV. 1718, 1723 (1996).

52. As Alta Charo put it almost twenty years ago:

> [A criteria of] brain activity later in development, when it is sufficient to support sentience, pain awareness, and sense of self, would be entirely analogous to the condition of many non-human animals that are used for laboratory experimentation. Use of these later developmental criteria to explain the onset of a human's right to life or a right to be free of experimentation requires an explanation as to why. . . . [Conversely], many newborn babies, who are granted the same moral status as older children and adults by most Americans, would fail to demonstrate some of these characteristics.

Alta Charo, *The Hunting of the Snark: The Moral Status of Embryos, Right-to-Lifers, and Third World Women*, 6 STAN. L & POL'Y REV. 11, 16 (1995). It would also exclude from personhood individuals with severe developmental disabilities. *See, e.g.*, Bonnie Steinbock, *Moral Status and Human Embryos, in* THE OXFORD HANDBOOK OF BIOETHICS 416, 427 (Oxford: Oxford Univ. Press, Bonnie Steinbock, ed., 2006).

53. COHEN, *supra* note 41, at 73.

54. *Id.* at 74.

55. Imagining a parallel argument applied to animals or already-born humans demonstrates some of why I think it is a problem. That said, perhaps I am being too harsh here. There is a family resemblance, after all, between this move and the idea of viability as being important to legal status that underlay the pre-*Dobbs* abortion jurisprudence. Viability was just as "external" to the entity, in terms of the medical technology available, as this is. To me, though, that just helps explain why the viability standard was such a strange one on which to hinge abortion jurisprudence, as I have suggested elsewhere. *See* Cohen & Sayeed, *supra* note 51, at 236–37; *cf.* Bruce P. Blackshaw & Daniel Rodger, *Why We Should Not Extend the 14-Day Rule*, 47 J. MED. ETHICS 712 (2021).

56. COHEN, *supra* note 41, at 75.

57. *See id.* at 76.

58. *Id.*

59. *Id.* at 77–78. This problem is related to but also distinct from the argument that twinning is possible before up to fourteen days, an argument discussed as to the time-of-fertilization view which would also apply to any potentiality argument that "activates" before fourteen days. The arguments are distinct because even if, counterfactually, embryonic twinning was *not* possible, the question of continuity between the early embryo and the fetus it becomes would still be a challenge.

60. ProPublica accessed the recording of a webinar held on October 27, 2022, with GOP Tennessee legislators by a Tennessee affiliate of National Right to Life wherein Representative Susan Lynn asked how to respond to questions about IVF. In response Stephen Billy, Susan B. Anthony Pro-Life America's vice president for state affairs, said, "Maybe your caucus gets to a point next year, two years from now, three years from now, where you do want to talk about IVF, and how to regulate it in a more ethical way, or deal with some of those contraceptive issues. . . . But I don't think that that's the conversation that you need to have now." Kavitha Surana, *"We Need to Defend This Law": Inside an Anti-Abortion Meeting with Tennessee's GOP Lawmakers*, PROPUBLICA (Nov. 15, 2022 (https://www.propublica.org/article/inside-anti-abort ion-meeting-with-tennessee-republican-lawmakers?utm_source=sailthru&utm_ medium=email&utm_campaign=majorinvestigations&utm_content=feature#).

61. *See, e.g.*, I. Glenn Cohen, *Travel to Other States for Abortion After* Dobbs, 22 AM. J. BIOETHICS 42 (2022).

62. Dobbs v. Jackson Women's Health Org., 142 S. Ct. 2228, 2309 (2022) (Kavanaugh, J., concurring).

63. For more on this technology, *see, e.g.*, DAAR ET AL., *supra* note 5, at 632–35.

64. *E.g.*, Tamar Lewin, *Industry's Growth Leads to Leftover Embryos, and Painful Choice*s, N.Y. TIMES (June 17, 2015), https://www.nytimes.com/2015/06/18/us/embryos-egg-donors-difficult-issues.html.

Chapter 19

*. This chapter draws on a longer academic work published in the *NYU Law Review*.

1. Roe v. Wade, 410 U.S. 113, 153 (1973).

2. Daniel J. Solove, *A Taxonomy of Privacy*, 154 U. PA. L. REV. 477, 581 (2006).

3. *See, e.g.*, Rory Van Loo, *Privacy Pretexts*, 108 CORNELL L. REV. 1 (2023).

4. Neil M. Richards, *The Information Privacy Law Project*, 94 GEO. L.J. 1087 (2006) (surveying information privacy law scholarship); Julie Cohen, *Examined Lives: Informational Privacy and the Subject as Object*, 52 STAN. L. REV. 1373, 1375 (2000) (using the phrases "informational privacy" and "data privacy" interchangeably).

5. Mariano-Florentino Cuéllar & Aziz Z. Huq, *Privacy's Political Economy and the State of Machine Learning: An Essay in Honor of Stephen J. Schulhofer*, 76 N.Y.U. ANN. SURV. AM. L. 317 (2021).

6. Dobbs v. Jackson Women's Health Organization, 142 S. Ct. 2228 (2022).

7. Oriana Gonzalez, *New Wave of Abortion Clinic Closings after* Roe v. Wade *Overturned*, AXIOS (July 23, 2022), https://www.axios.com/2022/07/28/abortion-clinics-close-dobbs-roe-supreme-court.

8. Mariana Lenharo, *After* Roe v. Wade: *US Researchers Warn of What's to Come*, 607 NATURE 15 (2022).

9. *Id.*

10. Elizabeth Nash and Isabel Guarnieri, *13 States Have Abortion Trigger Bans—Here's What Happens When* Roe *Is Overturned*, GUTTMACHER INSTITUTE (May 2022), https://www.guttmacher.org/state-policy/explore/state-policies-later-abortions.

11. *Arrests and Prosecutions of Pregnant Women, 1973–2020*, NAT'L ADVOC. FOR PREGNANT WOMEN (Sept. 21, 2021), https://www.nationaladvocatesforpregnantwo men.org/arrests-and-prosecutions-of-pregnant-women-1973-2020/.

12. TEX. HEALTH & SAFETY Code ANN. S.B.8 § 171.208(a)(1) & (2) (2021); Aziz Z. Huq, *The Private Suppression of Constitutional Rights*, 101 TEX. L. REV. 1259 (2023), https://papers.ssrn.com/sol3/papers.cfm?abstract_id=4072800.

13. Josh Merchant, *Nearly Half of Abortions in Kansas Are for Missourians. A Vote Next Year Could Change That,* KAN. CITY BEACON (Nov. 20, 2021), https://missouriinde pendent.com/2021/11/22/nearly-half-of-abortions-in-kansas-are-for-missourians-a-vote-next-year-could-change-that/.

14. Kate Robertson, *Facts Were Sparse on an Abortion Case. But That Didn't Stop the Attacks*, N.Y. TIMES (July 14, 2022), https://www.nytimes.com/2022/07/14/business/media/10-year-old-girl-ohio-rape.html.

15. Pam Belluck, *Abortion Pill Providers Experiment With Ways to Broaden Access*, N.Y. TIMES (Sept. 3, 2022), https://www.nytimes.com/2022/09/03/health/abortion-pill-access-roe-v-wade.html?searchResultPosition=1.

16. Joseph Johnson, *Internet Usage in the United States—Statistics & Facts*, STATISTA (Mar. 24, 2022), https://www.statista.com/topics/2237/internet-usage-in-the-united-states/ [https://perma.cc/SQS7-RFSD].

17. SHOSHANA ZUBOFF, THE AGE OF SURVEILLANCE CAPITALISM: THE FIGHT FOR A HUMAN FUTURE AT THE NEW FRONTIER OF POWER 80–81 (New York: Public Affairs, 2018).

18. *Stigler Committee on Digital Platforms: Final Report*, U. CHI. BOOTH SCH. BUS., at 7 (Sept. 16, 2019), https://www.chicagobooth.edu/-/media/research/stigler/pdfs/digital-platforms—committee-report—stigler-center.pdf.

19. Matthew Crain, *The Limits of Transparency: Data Brokers and Commodification*, NEW MEDIA & SOC. 1, 11 (2016).

20. GINA NEFF & DAWN NAFUS, SELF-TRACKING 2 (Cambridge, MA: MIT Press, 2016).

21. Emily A. Vogels, *About One-in-Five Americans Use a Smart Watch or Fitness Tracker*, PEW RSCH. CTR. (Jan. 9, 2020), https://www.pewresearch.org/fact-tank/2020/01/09/about-one-in-five-americans-use-a-smart-watch-or-fitness-tracker/.

22. Donna Rosato, *What Your Period Tracker App Knows About You*, CONSUMER REPS. (Jan. 28, 2020), https://www.consumerreports.org/health-privacy/what-your-period-tracker-app-knows-about-you/.

23. Elizabeth A. Brown, *The Femtech Paradox: How Workplace Monitoring Threatens Women's Equity*, 61 JURIMETRICS J. 289, 306 (2021).

24. Bobbly Allyn, *Privacy Advocates Fear Google Will Be Used to Prosecute Abortion Seekers*, NPR (July 11, 2022), https://www.npr.org/2022/07/11/1110391316/google-data-abortion-prosecutions.

25. Tony Arnold, *How Your Private Illinois Tollway Data Is Shared With Cops and Divorce Lawyers*, WBEZ (Sept. 19, 2019), https://www.wbez.org/stories/how-your-private-illinois-tollway-data-is-shared-with-cops-and-divorce-lawyers/cea68ea0-4b13-481a-80a1-50bf0e9db738.

26. Martin Kaste, *Nebraska Cops Used Facebook Messages to Investigate an Alleged Illegal Abortion*, NPR (Aug. 12, 2022), https://www.npr.org/2022/08/12/1117092169/nebraska-cops-used-facebook-messages-to-investigate-an-alleged-illegal-abortion.

27. *Instagram and Facebook Begin Removing Posts Offering Abortion Pills*, NPR (June 28, 2022), https://www.npr.org/2022/06/28/1108107718/instagram-and-facebook-begin-removing-posts-offering-abortion-pills.

28. Andrea M. Matwyshyn, *Unavailable*, 81 U. PITT. L. REV. 349, 369 (2019).

29. Suzanne van Geuns & Corinne Cath-Speth, *How Hate Speech Reveals the Invisible Politics of Internet Infrastructure*, BROOKINGS TECHSTREAM (Aug. 20, 2020), https://www.brookings.edu/techstream/how-hate-speech-reveals-the-invisible-politics-of-internet-infrastructure.

30. *How Does DNS Filtering Work?*, WEBTITAN (Aug. 30, 2019), https://www.spamtitan.com/web-filtering/how-does-dns-filtering-work.

31. *Global Requests for User Information*, GOOGLE TRANSPARENCY REPORT, https://transparencyreport.google.com/user-data/overview?user_requests_report_period=authority:US (last visited July 14, 2022).

32. Title III of the Omnibus Crime Control and Safe Streets Act of 1968, 18 U.S.C. §§ 2510–22 (1968).

33. Carpenter v. United States, 138 S. Ct. 2206, 2217 (2018).

34. *Geofence Warrants and the Fourth Amendment*, 134 HARV. L. REV. 2508, 2509 (2021).

35. *Cf.* United States v. Chatrie, 2022 WL 628905 (E.D. Va. 2022).

36. Andrew Manuel Crespo, *Probable Cause Pluralism*, 129 YALE L.J. 1276, 1280 (2020).

37. Christopher Slobogin, *Subpoenas and Privacy*, 54 DEPAUL L. REV. 805, 805–7 (2005).

38. United States v. R. Enters., 498 U.S. 292, 299 (1991).

39. *Id.* at 301.

40. United States v. Morton Salt Co., 338 U.S. 632, 652–53 (1950).

41. 18 U.S.C. §§ 2701–11.

42. United States v. Warshak, 631 F. 3d 266 (6th Cir. 2010).

43. 18 U.S.C. § 2702.

44. 18 U.S.C. § 2703(d).

45. 45 C.F.R. § 160 (2000); 45 C.F.R. §§ 164.102–164.106 (2000); 45 C.F.R. §§ 164.400–164.414 (2000).

46. 45 C.F.R. § 164.512(f)(1) (2000).

47. *HIPAA for Professionals: Covered Entities and Business Associations*, DEP'T OF HEALTH AND HUMAN SERVICES (June 16, 2017), https://www.hhs.gov/hipaa/for-profession als/covered-entities/index.html.

48. 15 U.S.C. § 6802(e)(5) (1999).

49. *See, e.g.*, Bennett Cyphers, *How the Federal Government Buys Our Cell Phone Location Data*, EFF (June 13, 2022), https://www.eff.org/deeplinks/2022/06/how-federal-gov ernment-buys-our-cell-phone-location-data.

50. Joseph Cox, *Data Broker Is Selling Location Data of People Who Visit Abortion Clinics*, VICE MOTHERBOARD (May 3, 2022), https://www.vice.com/en/article/m7vzjb/locat ion-data-abortion-clinics-safegraph-planned-parenthood.

51. *See generally* SARAH LAMDAN, DATA CARTELS: THE COMPANIES THAT CONTROL AND MONOPOLIZE OUR INFORMATION (Stanford: Stanford Univ. Press, 2022).

52. Alfred Ng, *Data Brokers Resist Pressure to Stop Collecting Info on Pregnant People*, POLITICO (Aug. 1, 2022), https://www.politico.com/news/2022/08/01/data-informat ion-pregnant-people-00048988.

53. Cox, *supra* note 43.

54. Jonathon W. Penney & Bruce Schneier, *Platforms, Encryption, and the CFAA: The Case of* Whatsapp v. NSO Group, 36 BERKELEY TECH. L.J. 469, 472 (2021).

55. Aziz Z. Huq, *Constitutional Rights in the Machine-Learning State*, 105 CORNELL L. REV. 1875, 1929 (2020).

56. David Freeman Engstrom et. al., *Government by Algorithm: Artificial Intelligence in Federal Administrative Agencies*, REPORT SUBMITTED TO THE ADMINISTRATIVE CONFERENCE OF THE UNITED STATES 10 (Feb. 2020).

57. Jen Fitzpatrick, *Protecting People's Privacy on Health*, GOOGLE BLOG (July 1, 2022), https://blog.google/technology/safety-security/protecting-peoples-privacy-on-hea lth-topics/.

58. Alan Martin, *Period-Tracking Apps Respond to* Roe v. Wade *Ruling*, TOM'S GUIDE (June 25, 2022), https://www.tomsguide.com/news/period-tracking-apps-respond-to-roe-v-wade-ruling.

59. Kashmir Hill, *Imagine Being on Trial With Exonerating Evidence Trapped on Your Phone*, N.Y. TIMES (Nov. 22, 2019), https://www.nytimes.com/2019/11/22/business/law-enforcement-public-defender-technology-gap.html.

60. For a timely comparison, the Just Futures nonprofit has recommended that tech companies take a similar stance of routinely seeking judicial review of ICE administrative subpoenas for user data. *ICE Administrative Subpoenas to Tech Companies for Account Holder Data*, JUST FUTURES LAW 3 (August 2022), https://www.justfutures law.org/s/JFL-ICE-admin-subpoenas-factsheet-final-edits-1-xak2.pdf.

61. My Body, My Data Act of 2022, S. 4434, 117th Cong. (June 16, 2022).

62. Aziz Z. Huq & Rebecca Wexler, *Digital Privacy for Reproductive Choice After Roe*, 98 N.Y.U. L. REV. 555 (2023); Aziz Z. Huq & Rebecca Wexler, *Big Tech Can Help Women in a Post-Roe World: Will It?*, WASH. POST (June 1, 2022), https://www.washingtonp ost.com/outlook/2022/06/01/roe-dobbs-big-tech/?variant=15bc93f5a1ccbb65.

63. Aziz Z. Huq & Rebecca Wexler, *Digital Privacy for Reproductive Choice After Roe*, 98 N.Y.U. L. REV. 555 (2023).

64. EDWARD J. IMWINKELRIED, THE NEW WIGMORE: A TREATISE ON EVIDENCE: EVIDENTIARY PRIVILEGES § 1.1 (Philadelphia: Wolters Kluwer, 2002).

65. FED. R. CIV. P. 45(d)(3)(A)(iii).

66. Bowman Dairy Co. v. United States, 341 U.S. 214, 221 (1951).

67. *See, e.g.,* 18 U.S.C. § 2517(4).

68. 18 U.S.C. § 2517(4).

69. *See generally*, EDWARD J. IMWINKELRIED, *The Recognized Exceptions Common to Most of the Recognized Absolute Communications Privileges*, § 6.13.2, *in* THE NEW WIGMORE: A TREATISE ON EVIDENCE: EVIDENTIARY PRIVILEGES § 1.1 (Philadelphia: Wolters Kluwer, 2002).

Chapter 20

*. Thanks to Nancy Cott, Gene Chang, Gabrielle Crofford, Cynthia Dwork, Arka Gupta, Carolina Rabinowicz, and Joe Singer for invaluable comments and assistance.

1. *The Unraveling—Political Performance Art by Adrienne Sloane*, 13FOREST (Jan. 15, 2020), https://13forest.com/news/the-unraveling. The artist Adrienne Sloane describes the work while unraveling some of it in a video. *See* Adrienne Sloane, *Unraveling* (hand-knit art) *at* Fuller Craft Museum (Jan. 31, 2018) ("[T]he way I designed it, it's the whole piece will come apart ultimately; not the stars, the stars will come up. We're hoping we won't get there.").

2. *The Unraveling—Political Performance Art by Adrienne Sloane*, 13FOREST (Jan. 15, 2020), https://13forest.com/news/the-unraveling.

3. *Id.*

4. Russell Wheeler, *Trump's Judicial Campaign to Upend the 2020 Election: A Failure but Not a Wipe-out*, BROOKINGS (Nov. 30, 2021), https://www.brookings.edu/blog/fixgov/2021/11/30/trumps-judicial-campaign-to-upend-the-2020-election-a-fail

ure-but-not-a-wipe-out/. *See* Ryan Teague Beckwith, *These 14 Republican Candidates Actively Sought to Overturn the 2020 Election*, BLOOMBERG (Sept. 28, 2022), https://www.bloomberg.com/graphics/us-election-risk-index/2022-candidates-challenge-presidential-election-results/?leadSource=uverify%20wall; Jane C. Timm & Henry J. Gomez, *Trump's Stolen Election Lie Is on the Ballot, Thanks to These Candidates*, NBC (Oct. 16, 2021), https://www.nbcnews.com/politics/donald-trump/trump-s-stolen-election-lie-ballot-2022-thanks-these-candidates-n1281680.

5. *See* Marshall Cohen & Avery Cox, *The January 6 Insurrection: Minute by Minute*, CNN (July 29, 2022), https://www.cnn.com/2022/07/10/politics/jan-6-us-capitol-riot-timeline/index.html. The inspector general in Hartford, Connecticut, warned that Trump's disrespect for the rule of law would continue unless halted by impeachment and resignations. Liam Brennan, *Trump's Disrespect for the Rule of Law Continues*, JUST SECURITY (Sept. 10, 2018), https://www.justsecurity.org/60663/trumps-disresp ect-rule-law-spreads/ ("We are only protected by the Constitution to the extent that we adhere to constitutional principles. It is a fragile republic. To keep it, we must re-spect it.").

6. Shira A. Scheindlin, *Trump's Judges Will Call the Shots for Years to Come*, GUARDIAN (Oct. 25, 2021), https://www.theguardian.com/commentisfree/2021/oct/25/trump-judges-supreme-court-justices-judiciary.

7. *See* Dobbs v. Jackson Women's Health Organization, 142 S. Ct. 2228 (2022). Because several states had enacted laws banning or suppressing abortion in case the Court overturned *Roe*, 80 million people lost access to abortion within one hundred days after the *Dobbs* decision, and more will as more states take up the issue. *See 100 Days since Roe Fell*, CTR. FOR REPRODUCTIVE RTS. (Sept. 30, 2022), https://reproductiverig hts.org/100-days-since-roe-fell/.

8. Overturning precedents, while not unheard of, has historically involved a tiny frac-tion of Supreme Court decisions. David Schultz, *The Supreme Court Has Overturned Precedents Dozens of Times, Including Striking Down Legal Segregation and Reversing Roe*, THE CONVERSATION (June 30, 2022), https://theconversation.com/the-supr eme-court-has-overturned-precedent-dozens-of-times-including-striking-down-legal-segregation-and-reversing-roe-185941#:~:text=In%20my%20book%2C%20 %E2%80%9CConstitutional%20Precedent,145%20times%20%E2%80%93%20bar ely%200.5%25 ("[F]rom 1789 to 2020, there were 25,544 Supreme Court opinions and judgments after oral arguments. The court has reversed its own constitutional precedents only 145 times—barely 0.5%."). The number of reversals remains small. "From 1953 until 2020, under the successive leadership of Chief Justices Earl Warren, Warren Burger, William Rehnquist and now John Roberts, the court overturned constitutional precedent 32, 32, 30 and 15 times, respectively. That is well under 1% of decisions handled during each period in the court's history." Whether that rate continues or accelerates, as Justice Thomas seems to promote, *see* text at n. 9. now re-mains to be seen.

9. *Dobbs*, 142 S. Ct. at 2300–2304 (Thomas, J., concurring).

10. Robert Barnes, *Supreme Court, Dogged by Questions of Legitimacy, Is Ready to Resume*, WASH. POST (Sept. 29, 2022), https://www.washingtonpost.com/politics/2022/09/29/

supreme-court-roberts-kagan-legitimacy/; Paul M. Collins Jr. & Artemus Ward, *Why Have So Many Americans Come to Mistrust the Supreme Court?*, WASH. POST (Sept. 30, 2022), https://www.washingtonpost.com/politics/2022/09/30/supreme-court-new-term-public-approval/. Even before the *Dobbs* decision, 62% of Americans surveyed reported that they saw the courts motivated by partisan concerns rather than legal ones. Grinnell College, *62% of Americans Say Politics, Not Law, Drives Supreme Court Decisions*, GRINNELL COLL. NEWS (Oct. 20, 2021), https://www.grinn ell.edu/news/62-americans-say-politics-not-law-drives-supreme-court-decisions. State legislatures, engaged in partisan conflicts, are also seeking to confine the powers of state courts. *See also* Patrick Berry, Alicia Bannon, & Douglas Keith, *Legislative Assaults on State Courts—2022*, BRENNAN CTR. (June 22, 2022), https://www.brenna ncenter.org/our-work/research-reports/legislative-assaults-state-courts-2022. The nonpartisan group Freedom House reported in 2021 growing concerns about partisan distortion of both state and federal courts as well as chronic weaknesses such as perceptions of racial discrimination and prosecutorial misconduct especially in the states. *Freedom in the World 2021: United States*, FREEDOM HOUSE (2021), https:// freedomhouse.org/country/united-states/freedom-world/2021.

11. Journalists have explored the issue already. *See, e.g.,* Olivia Goldhill, *Supreme Court Decision Suggests the Legal Right to Contraception Is Also Under Threat*, STAT (June 24, 2022), https://www.statnews.com/2022/06/24/supreme-court-decision-suggests-the-legal-right-to-contraception-is-also-under-threat; Becky Sullivan & Juliana Kim, *These 3 Supreme Court Precedents Could Be At Risk After* Roe *Was Overturned*, NPR (June 24, 2022), https://www.npr.org/2022/05/05/1096732347/roe-v-wade-implicati ons-beyond-abortion.

12. Griswold v. Connecticut, 381 U.S. 479 (1965).

13. Eisenstadt v. Baird, 405 U.S. 438 (1972).

14. Carey v. Population Services International, 431 U.S. 678 (1977).

15. An empirical study recently showed the reduction of wages for women of child-bearing age in states with increased abortion restrictions even before the reversal of *Roe*. Itay Ravid & Jonathan Zandberg, *The Future of* Roe *and the Gender Pay Gap: An Empirical Assessment*, 98 IND. L. J. 1089, 1115 (2023). Although not all women can become pregnant and some who can become pregnant do not identify as women, this chapter will use "women" as shorthand to refer to those most directly affected by abortion. *See* Julie Compton, *Transgender Dads Tell Doctors: "You Can Be a Man and Have a Baby,"* NBC NEWS (May 19, 2019), https://www.nbcnews.com/feature/nbc-out/trans-dads-tell-doctors-you-can-be-man-have-baby-n1006906.

16. Dobbs v. Jackson Women's Health Organization, 142 S. Ct. 2228, 2258 (2022). Use of the word "inapposite" to refer to the very cases relied upon in *Roe v Wade* is curious as the word means "not apt" or not "pertinent." *Inapposite*, MERRIAM-WEBSTER DICTIONARY, https://www.merriam-webster.com/dictionary/inapposite.

17. *Dobbs*, 142 S. Ct. at 2261 (citing the term used by *Roe* for embryo or fetus).

18. *Id.* at 2280.

19. *Id.* at 2281.

20. *Id.* at 2309 (Kavanaugh, J., concurring).

21. *Id.* at 2305 (Kavanaugh, J., concurring).

22. *Id.* at 2300–2304 (Thomas, J., concurring).

23. *Id.* at 2301 (Thomas, J., concurring) (starred note omitted).

24. *See id.* at 2281–83 (opinion for the Court); *See also id.* at 2349–50 (Breyer, Sotomayor, and Kagan, JJ., dissenting) [hereinafter Dissent] ("We believe that The Chief Justice's opinion is wrong, too, but no one should think that there is not a large difference between upholding a 15-week ban on the grounds he does and allowing States to prohibit abortion from the time of conception.").

25. *Id.* at 2301, 2302, 2304 (Thomas, J., concurring).

26. *Id.* at 2303 (Thomas, J., concurring).

27. *Id.* at 2302 (Thomas, J., concurring).

28. *Id.* at 2303 (Thomas J., concurring).

29. Loving v. Virginia, 388 U.S. 1 (1967).

30. *Id.*

31. *Dobbs*, 142 S. Ct. at 2319 (Dissent). The dissent also exposes the near silence of the majority opinion about women. In contrast, this is the steady focus of the dissent. *See, e.g., id.* at 2319 (Dissent) (quoting *Casey*, 505 U.S. at 852) ("When an unplanned pregnancy is involved—because either contraception or abortion is outlawed—'the liberty of the woman is at stake in a sense unique to the human condition.' ").

32. *Id.* (The issues of pregnancy and abortion affect anyone who can become pregnant, which includes most women of childbearing age and also others who were born with and retain that capacity.)

33. *Id.*

34. *Id.*

35. *Id.* at 2319 (Dissent).

36. *Id.*

37. *Id.* at 2319, 2332 (Dissent).

38. *Id.* at 2319 (Dissent).

39. *Id.* 2332 (Dissent).

40. *Id.* at 2319 (Dissent). Commentators have often described the collection of cases as *Griswold* and its progeny. *See, e.g.,* Joanna L. Grossman, Griswold v. Connecticut: *The Start of the Revolution*, VERDICT (June 8, 2015), https://scholarlycommons.law.hofstra.edu/faculty_scholarship/943; Vivian E. Hamilton, *On Griswold and Women's Equality*, J. GLOB. JUST. & PUB. POL'Y 171 (2016), https://jgjpp.regent.edu/wp-content/uploads/2021/12/ON-GRISWOLD-AND-WOMENS-EQUALITY.pdf; Douglas NeJaime, Griswold's *Progeny: Assisted Reproduction, Procreative Liberty, and Sexual Orientation Equality*, 124 YALE L.J. F. 340 (2015). The Senate's refusal to endorse the nomination of Judge Robert Bork to the Supreme Court turned in no small part on Bork's rejection of that line of cases. *See* Lackland H. Bloom Jr., *The Legacy of* Griswold, 16 OHIO N.U. L. REV. 511, 537–43 (1989).

41. *Id.* at 2330 (Dissent).

42. *Id.* at 2331 (Dissent).

43. *Id.* at 2339 (Dissent).

44. *Id.* at 2339 & n.9 (Dissent).

45. *Id.* at 2333 (Dissent).

46. *Id.* at 2350 (Dissent).

47. Little Sisters of the Poor Saints Peter & Paul Home v. Pennsylvania, 140 S. Ct. 2367 (2020).

48. *Id. See* Martha Minow, *Not in the Room Where It Happens: Adversariness, Politicization, and* Little Sisters of the Poor, 2020 Sup. Ct. Rev. 35 [hereinafter *Not in the Room*].

49. *Dobbs*, 142 S. Ct. at 2337 (Dissent). Medical personnel may be worried or uncertain in the face of the post-*Dobbs* regulatory context and deny timely care for life-threatening medical conditions such as preeclampsia.

50. For definition of ectopic pregnancy, *see Ectopic Pregnancy*, Mayo Clinic, https://www.mayoclinic.org/diseases-conditions/ectopic-pregnancy/symptoms-causes/syc-20372088. On legal and medical treatment after *Dobbs*, *see* Elizabeth R. Kirk & Ingrid Skop, *Why the* Dobbs *Decision Won't Imperil Pregnancy-Related Medical Care*, SCOTUS Blog (July 7, 2022), https://www.scotusblog.com/2022/07/why-the-dobbs-decision-wont-imperil-pregnancy-related-medical-care/.

51. Frances Stead Sellers & Fenit Nirappil, *Confusion Post-*Roe *Spurs Delays, Denials for Some Life-saving Pregnancy Care*, Wash. Post (July 16, 2022), https://www.washingtonpost.com/health/2022/07/16/abortion-miscarriage-ectopic-pregnancy-care/.

52. Joerg Dreweke, *Contraception Is Not Abortion: The Strategic Campaign of Antiabortion Groups to Persuade the Public Otherwise*, 17 Guttmacher Po. Rev. 14, 15 (2014); *Is Antiabortion Movement Undermining Contraception?*, 133 Contraceptive Tech. Update (1991). After the decision in *Dobbs*, some spokespersons for religious groups targeted "emergency contraception" and the right to contraception as their next targets. Molly Olmstead, *"Today Is a Major Victory": How the Christian Right Reacted to the end of* Roe, Slate (June 24, 2022), https://slate.com/news-and-politics/2022/06/dobbs-ruling-christian-right-roe-wade-overturned.html (citing Bill Donahue and Church Militant). Due to political pressures, presidents of both parties have restricted access to the "morning after" pill. *See* Minow, *Not in the Room* (discussing alterations of FDA recommendations under administrations of Presidents George W. Bush and Barack Obama).

53. For an exquisite description of these steps and of the scientific research illuminating them, *see* Magdalena Zernicka-Goetz & Roger Highfield, The Dance of Life: The New Science of How a Single Cell Becomes a Human Being (New York: Basic Books, 2020). Religious views of "potential life" could lead to laws banning the kind of research behind the scientific field reporting on these steps.

54. *Fetal Development: Stages of Growth*, Cleveland Clinic, https://my.clevelandclinic.org/health/articles/7247-fetal-development-stages-of-growth ("Within 24 hours after fertilization, the egg that will become your baby rapidly divides into many cells. By the eighth week of pregnancy, the embryo develops into a fetus. There are about 40 weeks to a typical pregnancy.").

55. *Id.*

56. *See* Damir Sapunar, *Prenatal Development*, ENCYCLOPEDIA BRITANNICA, https://www.britannica.com/science/prenatal-development; *Embryo*, ENCYCLOPEDIA BRITANNICA, https://www.britannica.com/science/embryo-human-and-animal.

57. B. Alberts et al., *Eggs, in* MOLECULAR BIOLOGY OF THE CELLS (New York: Garland Science, 4th ed. 2002), available at https://www.ncbi.nlm.nih.gov/books/NBK26842/. Human sperm can live outside the body for several days. *Facts About Sperm Health and Lifespan*, MED. NEWS TODAY (Oct. 12, 2017), https://www.medicalnewstoday.com/articles/319669.

58. Alex Mira, *Why Is Meiosis Arrested?*, 194 J. OF THEORETICAL BIOLOGY 275–87 (Sept. 1998);

David Diaz, *What Is an Oocyte?*, WEST COAST FERTILITY CTRS. (July 6, 2015), https://www.eggfreezing.com/what-is-an-oocyte/.

59. *What Is Ovulation?*, AM. PREGNANCY ASS'N, https://americanpregnancy.org/getting-pregnant/infertility/understanding-ovulation/. *See* Kailey Remien & Leela Sharath Pillarisetty, *Female Development, in* STATPEARLS [INTERNET] (Treasure Island: StatPearls Publishing, updated May 8, 2022), available at https://www.ncbi.nlm.nih.gov/books/NBK539695/.

60. Kelly Malcom, *New Insights on Sperm Production Lay Groundwork for Solving Male Infertility*, U. OF MICH. HEALTH LAB (Aug. 24, 2018), https://labblog.uofmhealth.org/lab-report/new-insights-on-sperm-production-lay-groundwork-for-solving-male-infertility.

61. "Plan B works like other birth control pills to prevent pregnancy. Plan B acts primarily by stopping the release of an egg from the ovary (ovulation). It may prevent the union of sperm and egg (fertilization). If fertilization does occur, Plan B may prevent a fertilized egg from attaching to the womb (implantation). If a fertilized egg is implanted prior to taking Plan B, Plan B will not work." U.S. Food and Drug Administration, *FDA's Decision Regarding Plan B: Questions and Answers*, U.S. FOOD AND DRUG ADMIN. (Aug. 24, 2006).

62. Medication abortion "drugs stop a pregnancy from growing and then cause the uterus to contract and expel it. Medication abortion is approved by the Food and Drug Administration for use within the first 10 weeks of pregnancy, and people can take the pills at home or in any location." Dani Blum, *What's the Difference Between Plan B and the Abortion Pill?*, N.Y. TIMES (June 27, 2022), https://www.nytimes.com/2022/06/27/us/abortion-pill-plan-b.html.

63. John R. Vile, *Religious Rights of Pharmacists and Morning After Pills*, THE FIRST AMEND. ENCYCLOPEDIA (Aug. 1, 2022), https://www.mtsu.edu/first-amendment/article/2152/religious-rights-of-pharmacists-and-morning-after-pills. In fact, emergency contraception such as Plan B reduces the mobility of sperm through the use of progestins, which are biologically similar to progesterone, the pregnancy hormone, and prevent pregnancy by thickening the cervical mucus. *Levonorgestrel*, ENCYCLOPEDIA BRITANNICA, https://www.britannica.com/science/levonorgestrel. Progestins may also thin the lining of the uterus and prevent implantation. Rather than imitate progesterone, abortion medications interfere with progesterone

and its ability to bind to receptors and also may stimulate the uterus to contract and eject the endometrial lining as well as the embryo. *Medical Abortion*, MAYO CLINIC (July 29, 2022), https://www.mayoclinic.org/tests-procedures/medical-abortion/about/pac-20394687#:~:text=Oral%20mifepristone%20(Mifeprex)%20 and%20oral%20misoprostol%20(Cytotec).&text=These%20medicines%20are%20 usually%20taken,from%20staying%20implanted%20and%20growing; *see also* B. Couzinet et al., *Termination of Early Pregnancy by the Progesterone Antagonist RU 486 (Mifepristone)*. 35 NEW ENGL. J. MED. 187–91 (1986); *see also Mifepristone (Oral Route)*, MAYO CLINIC, https://www.mayoclinic.org/drugs-supplements/mifeprist one-oral-route/side-effects/drg-20067123?p=1#:~:text=Mifepristone%20is%20u sed%20in%20a,of%20the%20uterus%20are%20expelled. *Birth Control Methods*, OFF. ON WOMEN'S HEALTH, https://www.womenshealth.gov/a-z-topics/birth-control-methods#:~:text=Short%2Dacting%20hormonal%20methods%2C%20s uch,from%20getting%20to%20the%20egg. In fact, emergency contraception occurs before fertilization and must occur within a few days of intercourse to be effective. *Birth Control*, MAYO CLINIC, https://www.mayoclinichealthsystem.org/ locations/fairmont/services-and-treatments/obstetrics-and-gynecology/birth-control (last visited Oct. 30, 2022). Abortion occurs following fertilization and can take place medically up to seventy days (ten weeks) following the last menstrual period. *Mifepristone Information*, FOOD AND DRUG ADMINISTRATION (2021), https:// www.fda.gov/drugs/postmarket-drug-safety-information-patients-and-providers/ mifeprex-mifepristone-information.

64. *E.g.*, Dobbs v. Jackson Women's Health Organization, 142 S. Ct. 2228, 2257–58, 2261 (2022).

65. *Id.* at 2241; *see also id.* at 2243, 2259.

66. *Id.* at 2261.

67. Vile, *supra* note 63.

68. Sarah Varney, *When Does Life Begin? As State Laws Define It, Science, Politics and Religion Clash*, NPR (Aug. 27, 2022), https://www.npr.org/sections/health-shots/ 2022/08/27/1119684376/when-does-life-begin-as-state-laws-define-it-science-politics-and-religion-clash.

69. *Dobbs*, 142 S. Ct. at 2280.

70. *Dobbs*, 142 S. Ct. at 2300–2304 (Thomas, J., concurring).

71. *Id.* at 2332 (Dissent).

72. Christine Vestal, *New Research Shows State Restrictions Reduce Contraception Use*, PEW RSCH. CTR. (Sept. 22, 2022), https://www.pewtrusts.org/en/research-and-analysis/blogs/stateline/2022/09/22/new-research-shows-state-restrictions-red uce-contraception-use.

73. Michael Ollove, *Some States Already Are Targeting Birth Control*, PEW CHARITABLE TRS. (May 19, 2022), https://www.pewtrusts.org/en/research-and-analysis/blogs/ stateline/2022/05/19/some-states-already-are-targeting-birth-control. Scholars esti-mate profound impacts from contraception restrictions on women's economic par-ticipation. *See* Sheelah Kohlhatkar, *Restrictions on Contraception Could Set Women*

Back Generations, NEW YORKER (July 1, 2022), https://www.newyorker.com/busin
ess/currency/restrictions-on-contraception-could-set-women-back-generati
ons#:~:text=Access%20to%20contraception%20was%20established,same%20ri
ght%20to%20unmarried%20people (citing work by Claudia Goldin and Lawrence
Katz). *See also The Economic Effects of Contraceptive Access: A Review of the Evidence,*
INST. FOR WOMEN'S POLICY RSCH., (2019), https://iwpr.org/iwpr-issues/reproduct
ive-health/the-economic-effects-of-contraceptive-access-a-review-of-the-evide
nce/ (report by Anna Bernstein and Kelly M. Jones) (reviewing studies of positive
effect of contraception access on women's participation in paid labor force).

74. *See* Geoffrey Skelley & Holly Fuong, *How Americans Feel About Abortion and Contraception*, FIVETHIRTYEIGHT (July 12, 2022), https://fivethirtyeight.com/featu res/abortion-birth-control-poll/. Compare *Abortion*, GALLUP, https://news.gallup. com/poll/1576/abortion.aspx, *with Public Attitudes About Birth Control*, ROPER CTR., https://ropercenter.cornell.edu/public-attitudes-about-birth-control.

75. William Saletan, *Do Pro-Lifers Oppose Birth Control?*, SALON (Jan. 15, 2014), https://slate.com/news-and-politics/2014/01/do-pro-lifers-oppose-birth-control-polls-say-no.html (citing a May 2012 Gallup Poll); *Use a Scalpel, Don't Amputate Obamacare, U.S. Voters Tell Quinnipiac University National Poll; Voters Oppose Fund Cut for Planned Parenthood 7–1*, INS. NEWSNET (Feb. 6, 2017), https://insur ancenewsnet.com/oarticle/use-scalpel-dont-amputate-obamacare-u-s-voters-tell-quinnipiac-university-national-poll-voters-oppose-fund-cut-for-planned-par enthood-7-1. On public attitudes about insurance coverage for contraception, *see generally* Robert P. Jones et al., *The State of Abortion and Contraception Attitudes in All 50 States*, PUB. RELIG. RESRCH. INST. (2019), https://www.prri.org/wp-cont ent/uploads/2019/08/PRRI_Aug_2019_Abortion_Contraception-D.pdf. In the early 1970s, even those opposed to premarital sexual activity showed widespread support for access to contraception. Richard Pomeroy & Lynn C. Landman, *Public Opinion Trends: Elective Abortion and Birth Control Services to Teenagers*, 4 FAMILY PLANNING PERSPECTIVES 44, 45, 52 (1972).

76. Skelley & Fuong, supra note 74.

77. Shirin Ali, *Most Americans Support Free, Widely Available Birth Control If Abortion Is Banned*, THE HILL (May 12, 2022), https://thehill.com/changing-america/resp ect/accessibility/3486584-most-americans-support-free-widely-available-birth-control-if-abortion-is-banned-poll/.

78. Lara Cartwright-Smith & Sara Rosenbaum, *Controversy, Contraception, and Conscience: Insurance Coverage Standards Under the Patient Protection and Affordable Care Act*, 127(5) PUB. HEALTH REPS. 541–45 (2012), https://www.ncbi. nlm.nih.gov/pmc/articles/PMC3407856/.

79. *Contraceptive Use in the US by Demographics*, GUTTMACHER INST. (May 2021), https://www.guttmacher.org/fact-sheet/contraceptive-use-united-states; Rachel K. Jones, *People of All Religions Use Birth Control and Have Abortions*, GUTTMACHER INST. (Oct. 19, 2020), https://www.guttmacher.org/article/2020/10/people-all-religi ons-use-birth-control-and-have-abortions (reporting that 99.0% of Catholics,

99.4% of mainline Protestants, and 99.3% of Evangelical Protestants have used contraception other than natural family planning).

80. Allie Volpe, *What You Need to Know About Birth Control Post-*Roe, Vox (July 20, 2022), https://www.vox.com/even-better/23271306/birth-control-roe-v-wade-america. *See Polycystic Ovarian Syndrome*, MAYO CLINIC, https://www.mayoclinic.org/diseases-conditions/pcos/diagnosis-treatment/drc-20353443.

81. I am grateful to Gene Chang for his analysis as well.

82. *Dobbs*, 142 S. Ct. at 2242.

83. *Washington v. Glucksberg*, 521 U.S. 702 (1997). In *Obergefell v. Hodges*, 576 U.S. 644, 671 (2015), the Court concluded that *Glucksberg's* formula that rights had to be "deeply rooted" in history was "inconsistent" with the approach the Court had used in other cases, such as *Loving v. Virginia*, 388 U.S. 1 (1967) and *Lawrence v. Texas*, 388 U.S. 1 (2003).

84. Dobbs v. Jackson Women's Health Organization, 142 S. Ct. 2228, 2257 (2022).

85. *Id.* at 2254.

86. *Id.* at 2248.

87. *Id.* at 2324–25 (Dissent).

88. *The 19th Amendment*, NAT'L ARCHIVES, https://www.archives.gov/exhibits/featured-documents/amendment-19.

89. *See* MARY WARE DENNETT, BIRTH CONTROL LAWS: SHALL WE KEEP THEM, CHANGE THEM, OR ABOLISH THEM 192 (New York: Frederick H. Hitchcock, 1926), https://archive.org/details/in.ernet.dli.2015.219265.

90. *Dobbs*, 142 S. Ct. at 2319 (Dissent).

91. *See,* e.g., *History, the Supreme Court, and* Dobbs v. Jackson Women's Health Organization: *Joint Statement of the American Historical Association and the Organization of American Historians*, AM. HIST. ASS'N (July 2022), https://www.historians.org/news-and-advocacy/aha-advocacy/history-the-supreme-court-and-dobbs-v-jackson-joint-statement-from-the-aha-and-the-oah-(july-2022) [hereinafter Joint Statement of Historians]; Hanna Struckstroff, *An Historian's Reaction to* Dobbs v. Jackson Women's Health Organization, WOMEN IN THEOLOGY (July 18, 2022), https://womenintheology.org/2022/07/18/an-historians-reaction-to-dobbs-v-jackson-womens-health-organization/. The problems with the method may come whether one sides with the *Dobbs* majority or the dissent. *See* Buckley Dryer, *Selective History in the* Dobbs *Dissent*, LAW AND LIBERTY (July 21, 2022), https://lawliberty.org/selective-history-in-the-dobbs-dissent/ (criticizing selective uses of history in the dissent and the briefs on which it relies; concluding, "[H]istory and tradition cannot be the only guide to constitutional interpretation"). For similar criticisms of the Court's treatment of history in *New York Rifle & Pistol Association v. Bruen, see* Saul Cornell, *Cherry Picked History and Ideology Driven Outcomes*, SCOTUS BLOG (June 27, 2022), https://www.scotusblog.com/2022/06/cherry-picked-history-and-ideology-driven-outcomes-bruens-originalist-distortions/.

92. Joint Statement of Historians. *See also* Nancy Cott, *Where History Fails, in* ROE v. DOBBS (New York: Oxford Univ. Press, Lee C. Bollinger & Geoffrey Stone eds., 2024) (examining uses and misuses of history in Supreme Court abortion decisions).

Criminal laws addressing abortion emerged after 1820 and become more common between the 1860s and 1880s as medicine became professionalized, medical schools grew, and competition increased between orthodox and nonorthodox physicians. Shauna Devine, *Health Care and the American Medical Professor, 1830–1880*, J. OF THE CIVIL WAR ERA (July 2017), https://www.journalofthecivilwarera.org/2017/07/health-care-american-medical-profession-1830-1880/.

93. Phyllis L. Brodsky, *Where Have All the Midwives Gone?*, 17 J. PERINAT. EDUC. 48 (2008), https://www.ncbi.nlm.nih.gov/pmc/articles/PMC2582410/; *Midwives in 19th Century America*, HIST. OF AM. WOMEN, https://www.womenhistoryblog.com/2014/06/19th-century-midwives.html; Jane V. Donegan, *"Safe Delivered," but by Whom? Midwives and Men-Midwives in Early America, in* WOMEN AND HEALTH IN AMERICA 302 (Madison: Univ. of Wisconsin Press, Judith Walzer Leavitt, ed., 1984); Frances E. Kobrin, *The American Midwife Controversy: A Crisis of Professionalism, in* WOMEN AND HEALTH IN AMERICA 318 (Madison: Univ. of Wisconsin Press, Judith Walzer Leavitt, ed., 1984); Nancy Dye Schrom, *History of Childbirth in America*, 6 WOMEN, SEX, AND SEXUALITY 97 (1980); Deborah A. Sullivan, *The Decline of Traditional Midwifery in America, in* LABOR PAINS: MODERN MIDWIVES AND HOME BIRTH 1 (New Haven: Yale Univ. Press, Rose Weitz, ed., 1988); Laurel Thatcher Ulrich, *"The Living Mother of a Living Child": Midwifery and Mortality in Post-Revolutionary New England*, 46 THE WILLIAM AND MARY Q. 27 (Jan. 1989).

94. LESLIE J. REAGAN, WHEN ABORTION WAS A CRIME: WOMEN, MEDICINE, AND LAW IN THE UNITED STATES, 1867–1973 (Oakland: Univ. of California Press, 2022).

95. LINDA GORDON, WOMAN'S BODY, WOMEN'S RIGHT 26–46 (New York: Penguin Books, 1990). *See* Lawrence Stone, *The Family, Sex and Marriage in England 1500–1800* (New York: Harper & Row, 1977). Following ancient and medieval methods to control reproduction, scientific developments in the nineteenth century introduced birth control devices and medicines. JOHN M. RIDDLE, EVE'S HERBS: A HISTORY OF CONTRACEPTION AND ABORTION IN THE WEST (Cambridge, MA: Harvard Univ. Press, 1999); ROBERT JÜTTE, CONTRACEPTION: A HISTORY (Cambridge, UK: Polity, 2008).

96. James Reed, *Doctors, Birth Control, and Social Values, 1830–1970, in* WOMEN AND HEALTH IN AMERICA 124 (Madison: Univ. of Wisconsin Press, Judith Walzer Leavitt, ed., 1984). An 1888 editorial in the *Journal of the American Medical Association* noted, "We do not exaggerate: everyone that knows anything of American society in cities (at least) knows that there are very few married people that do not or have not discussed methods of preventing conception, and the majority of physicians will have no difficulty in remembering instances in which they have been consulted on this subject." *Mother's Friend: Birth Control in Nineteenth-Century America*, NAT'L MUSEUM OF CIVIL WAR MED. (Feb. 5, 2017), https://www.civilwarmed.org/birth-control/ (*quoting The Ethics of Marriage*, THE JOURNAL OF THE AM. MED. ASS'N (Sept 1, 1888)).

97. Reed, *supra* note 96.

98. JOHN HUMPHREY NOYES, MALE CONTINUENCE 10–11 (Oneida: Office of the American Socialist, 1872), *quoted in* Carroll Smith-Rosenberg & Charles Rosenberg, *The Female Animal: Medical and Biological Views of Woman and Her*

Role in Nineteenth-Century America, in WOMEN AND HEALTH IN AMERICA 17–18 (Madison: Univ. of Wisconsin Press, Judith Walzer Leavitt, ed., 1984).

99. Andrea Tone, *Black Market Birth Control: Contraceptive Enterpreneurship and Criminality in the Gilded Age*, 87 THE J. OF AM. HIST. 435, 439 (2000); Gordon, *supra* note 95, at 24, 65. Before the Civil War, preventing conception primarily involved abstinence or timing intercourse to avoid fertile periods, although information circulated as well about contraceptive methods with variable effectiveness, including douches, the ancient vaginal sponge, pessary contraptions, and condoms made of animal skins. Lauren Sharkey, *Birth Control in the 1880s: How Far Have We Come?*, HEALTHLINE (Sept. 27, 2021), https://www.healthline.com/health/birth-control/birth-control-in-the-1800s. Contraceptive devices were available in the United States and became cheaper with the development of the rubber condom in United States. *See, e.g.*, Vern L. Bullogh, *A Brief Note on Rubber Technology and Contraception: The Diaphragm and the Condom*, 22 TECH. AND CULTURE 104 (1981); Hunter Oatman-Stanford, *Getting It On: The Covert History of the American Condom*, COLLECTORS WEEKLY (Aug. 16, 2012), https://www.collectorsweekly.com/articles/getting-it-on-the-covert-history-of-the-american-condom/. Contraception teacher and advocate Margaret Sanger reported how advocacy groups in the late nineteenth and early twentieth centuries in the United States sought to spread to people of all socioeconomic classes information and techniques used by upper-class families. MARGARET SANGER & KATHRYN CULLEN-DUPOINT, MARGARET SANGER: AN AUTOBIOGRAPHY 128–130 (Pleasantville: Reader's Digest Association, 1971, originally published 1938).

100. The law was known as the Comstock Act, U.S. Code 17 Stat. 598 (1873). It directed:

> No obscene, lewd, or lascivious book, pamphlet, picture, paper, print or other publications of an indecent character, or any article or thing designed or intended for the prevention of conception or procuring of abortion, nor any article or thing intended or adapted for indecent or immoral use or nature, nor any written or printed card, circular, book, pamphlet, advertisement or notice of any kind giving information, directly or indirectly, where, or how, or of whom, or by what means either of the things before mentioned may be obtained or made, nor any letter upon the envelope of which, or postal-card upon which indecent or scurrilous epithets may be written or printed, shall be carried in the mail.

> *Quoted in* Jeffrey Escoffier, Whitney Strub, & Jeffrey Patrick Colgan, *The Comstock Apparatus, in* INTIMATE STATES: GENDER, SEXUALITY, AND GOVERNANCE IN MODERN US HISTORY 41 (Chicago: Univ. of Chicago Press, Margot Canaday, Nancy F. Cott, & Robert O. Self, eds., 2021). An 1842 law, enforced by customs officials, prohibited importation of obscene literature. *Id.*

101. *The 19th Amendment*, NAT'L ARCHIVES, https://www.archives.gov/exhibits/featured-documents/amendment-19.

102. Brandon R. Burnette, *The Comstock Act of 1873*, THE FIRST AMEND. ENCYCLOPEDIA, https://www.mtsu.edu/first-amendment/article/1038/comstock-act-of-1873.   *See* CHARLES G. TRUMBULL & SCOTT MATTHEW DIX, OUTLAWED! HOW ANTHONY COMSTOCK FOUGHT AND WON THE PURITY OF A NATION (n. pub., Scott Matthew Dix ed., 1913, reprinted 2013); AMY WERBER, LUST ON TRIAL: CENSORSHIP AND THE RISE OF AMERICAN OBSCENITY IN THE AGE OF ANTHONY COMSTOCK (New York: Columbia Univ. Press, 2018).

103. ELAINE TYLER MAY, AMERICA AND THE PILL: A HISTORY OF PROMISE, PERIL, AND LIBERATION 16, 18 (New York: Basic Books, 2010); Burnette, *supra* note 102; Tone, *supra* note 99.

104. Carol Flora Brooks, *The Early History of the Anti-Contraceptive Laws in Massachusetts and Connecticut*, 18 AM. Q. 2 (1966), https://www.jstor.org/stable/2711107?seq=1#metadata_info_tab_contents; Jeffrey Escoffier, Whitney Strub, & Jeffrey Patrick Colgan, *The Comstock Apparatus, in* INTIMATE STATES: GENDER, SEXUALITY, AND GOVERNANCE IN MODERN US HISTORY 41, 42 (Chicago: Univ. of Chicago Press, Margot Canaday, Nancy F. Cott, & Robert O. Self, eds., 2021). Some in the "social purity" movement, in contrast, supported access to contraceptives for married couples while treating sexual activity outside of marriage as illicit. Support for access to contraceptives also came from the eugenics movement, while opposition grew in the wake of national leaders and scientists sounding an alarm as white middle-class women chose smaller families in what became known as "race suicide." LINDA GORDON, THE MORAL PROPERTY OF WOMEN: A HISTORY OF BIRTH CONTROL POLITICS IN AMERICA 86–100 (Urbana: Univ. of Illinois Press, 2007); MARVIN N. OLASKY, ABORTION RITES: A SOCIAL HISTORY OF ABORTION IN AMERICA 127 (Washington, D.C.: Regnery Publishing, 1992). *See Warren S. Thompson, Race Suicide in the United States*, 5 SCI. MONTHLY 22 (1917), https://www.jstor.org/stable/22426?seq=14#metadata_info_tab_contents.

105. Reed, *supra* note 96, at 126.

106. Connecticut's law lasted into the 1960s until overturned in *Griswold v. Connecticut*.

107. *See* GORDON, *supra* note 104. *See also* Neil S. Siegel & Reva B. Segel, *Contraception as a Sex Equality Right*, YALE L. J. FORUM (Mar. 2, 2015), https://www.yalelawjournal.org/forum/contraception-as-a-sex-equality-right. *See* PETER C. ENGELMAN, A HISTORY OF THE BIRTH CONTROL MOVEMENT IN AMERICA (Santa Barbara: Praeger, 2011); ANDREA TONE, DEVICES AND DESIRES: A HISTORY OF CONTRACEPTIVES IN AMERICA (New York: Hill and Wang, 2002); Ranana Dine, *Scarlet Letters: Getting the History of Abortion and Contraception Right*, CTR. FOR AM. PROGRESS (Aug. 8, 2013), https://www.americanprogress.org/article/scarlet-letters-getting-the-history-of-abortion-and-contraception-right/.

108. *Id.*; *see* Christopher Tietze, *History of Contraceptive Methods*, 1 J. SEX RES. 69 (1965), https://www.jstor.org/stable/3811880?seq=15#metadata_info_tab_contents.

109. Linda Gordon, *Voluntary Motherhood: The Beginnings of Feminist Birth Control Ideas in the United States, in* WOMEN AND HEALTH IN AMERICA 104, 104–5 (Madison: Univ. of Wisconsin Press, Judith Walzer Leavitt, ed., 1984).

110. *See* AMY SOHN, THE MAN WHO HATED WOMEN: SEX, CENSORSHIP, AND CIVIL LIBERTIES IN THE GILDED AGE (New York: Farrar, Straus and Giroux, 2021); Gordon, *supra* note 95, at 183–242.

111. Gordon, *supra* note 95, at 210–13, 217.

112. *Id.* at 218–25, 317–19, 337–85.

113. Amita Kelly, *Fact Check: Was Planned Parenthood Started to "Control" the Black Population?*, NPR (Aug. 14, 2015), https://www.npr.org/sections/itsallpolitics/ 2015/08/14/432080520/fact-check-was-planned-parenthood-started-to-control-the-black-populatio; Reuters Fact Check Team, *Fact Check: Planned Parenthood Founder Margaret Sanger's 1939 Quote on Exterminating Black Population Taken Out of Context*, REUTERS (May 9, 2022), https://www.reuters.com/article/factch eck-pp-exterminating/fact-check-planned-parenthood-founder-margaret-sang ers-1939-quote-on-exterminating-black-population-taken-out-of-context-idUSL2 N2X11YN.

114. *Early Literature*, DITTRICK MED. HIST. CTR., https://artsci.case.edu/dittrick/onl ine-exhibits/history-of-birth-control/contraception-in-america-1800-1900/early-literature/ (discussing *Aristotle's Masterpiece, Displaying the Secrets of Nature in the Generation of Man*). *See id.* (discussing Charles Knowlton, *Fruits of Philosophy, or the Private Companion of Young Married People* (1832)).

115. GORDON, *supra* note 111.

116. JANET FARRELL BRODIE, CONTRACEPTION AND ABORTION IN NINETEENTH-CENTURY AMERICA (Ithaca: Cornell Univ. Press, 1994).

117. DONNA J. DRUCKER, CONTRACEPTION: A CONCISE HISTORY (Cambridge, MA: MIT Press, 2020); *Mother's Friend: Birth Control and Nineteenth Century America*, NAT'L MUSEUM OF CIVIL WAR MED. (Feb. 5, 2017), https://www.civilwarmed.org/birth-control/.

118. Hence even while defending its restrictions on abortion before the Court in *Dobbs*, Mississippi distinguished contraception because "[i]n invalidating a state law regulating the use of contraceptives, *Griswold* vindicated the textually and histori-cally grounded Fourth Amendment protection against government invasion of the home—which would likely have been necessary to prosecute under the statute. *E.g.*, *id.* at 480, 484–85. *Griswold* also vindicated our history and tradition of safeguarding 'the marriage relationship'—which raises privacy interests 'older than the Bill of Rights.' *Id.* at 486." Brief for Petitioners at 15, Dobbs v. Jackson Women's Health Organization, 142 S. Ct. 2228 (2022) (No. 19-1392). The methodology adopted by the *Dobbs* Court, however, would allow a future decision to reject this analysis as too general to be sustained as grounded in "history" and "tradition," and in particular, to reject *Eisenstadt v. Baird*, 405 U.S. 438 (1972) and *Carey v. Population Services Int'l*, 431 U.S. 678 (1977), as lacking historical foundation for contraceptive use by single people, outside marriage or the marital home.

119. J. C. Ruppenthal, *Criminal Statutes on Birth Control*, 10 J. AM. INST. CRIM. L. & CRIMINOLOGY 48 (May 1919–Feb. 1920), https://scholarlycommons.law.northwest ern.edu/cgi/viewcontent.cgi?referer=https://www.google.com/&httpsredir=1&arti cle=1616&context=jclc.

120. *See* Dobbs v. Jackson Women's Health Org., 142 S. Ct. 2228, 2300–2304 (2022) (Thomas, J., concurring).

121. *See Intrauterine Devices*, AM. PREGNANCY ASS'N., https://americanpregnancy.org/ unplanned-pregnancy/birth-control-pills-patches-and-devices/iud-intrauterine- devices/ ("The released progesterone or copper creates changes in the cervical mucus and inside the uterus that kills sperm or makes them immobile. The IUD changes the lining of the uterus, preventing implantation should fertilization occur."); *FDA's Decision Regarding Plan B: Questions and Answers*, U.S. FOOD AND DRUG ADMIN. (Dec. 7, 2015), https://www.fda.gov/drugs/postmarket-drug-safety-informat ion-patients-and-providers/fdas-decision-regarding-plan-b-questions-and-answ ers#:~:text=Plan%20B%20works%20like%20other,to%20the%20womb%20 (im- plantation) ("Plan B acts primarily by stopping the release of an egg from the ovary (ovulation). It may prevent the union of sperm and egg (fertilization). If fertilization does occur, Plan B may prevent a fertilized egg from attaching to the womb (implan- tation)."). *FDA's Decision Regarding Plan B: Questions and Answers*, U.S. FOOD AND DRUG ADMIN. (Dec. 7, 2015), https://www.fda.gov/drugs/postmarket-drug-safety- information-patients-and-providers/fdas-decision-regarding-plan-b-questions- and-answers. *But see Emergency Contraception*, THE AM. COLL. OF OBSTETRICIANS AND GYNECOLOGISTS (Sept. 2015), https://www.acog.org/clinical/clinical-guida nce/practice-bulletin/articles/2015/09/emergency-contraception ("emergency con- traception is unlikely to prevent implantation of a fertilized egg" and instead inhibits ovulation, affects sperm viability and function, and only works "before a pregnancy is established").

122. *See* Sellers & Nirappil, *supra* note 51.

123. *See Contraception*, STUDENTS FOR LIFE OF AM., https://studentsforlife.org/learn/ contraception/.

124. *See* text & *supra* note 83. In *Planned Parenthood v. Casey*, 505 U.S. 833 (1992), the plurality opinion deemed precedent important to uphold even if unpopular, for un- less the ruling had proven intolerable, the law had not developed in such a way that left the rule "no more than a remnant of abandoned doctrine"; the facts had changed significantly, and in the case of preserving *Roe v. Wade*, as "[a]n entire generation has come of age free to assume *Roe*'s concept of liberty in defining the capacity of women to act in society, and to make reproductive decisions." *Id.*, at 860.

125. *Dobbs*, 142 S. Ct. at 2265.

126. *Id.* (citation omitted).

127. Eisenstadt v. Baird, 405 U.S. 438, 453 (1972).

128. *Dobbs*, 142 S. Ct. at 2248 (discussing *Casey*).

129. *Id.* at 2276 (citation omitted).

130. *Id.* (citing *Casey*, 505 U.S. at 856). Law professor Robert Tsai observed, "The *Casey* plurality had concluded that it would affirm *Roe* in part because millions of Americans had since 1973 relied upon that precedent to order their lives. In his draft opinion in *Dobbs*, Alito merely shrugged at that key point and observed, 'that form of reliance depends on an empirical question that is hard for anyone—and in partic- ular, for a court—to assess.' In other words, the fact that ordinary citizens have found

a right to be valuable will not stop an emboldened conservative court in overruling precedent and erasing a constitutional right in the future." Robert Tsai, *What Rights Could Unravel Next*, POLITICO (May 3, 2022), https://www.politico.com/news/magazine/2022/05/03/supreme-court-abortion-draft-other-precedents-00029625.

131. *Dobbs*, 142 S. Ct. at 2345–47 (Dissent).

132. *Id.* at 2334–35, 2337–38, 2341–43, 2349–50 (Dissent). Several current members of the Court show willingness to overturn precedents that they find inadequately reasoned in a way that seems to depart from prior practices. *See* David Schultz, *The Supreme Court Has Overturned Precedents Dozens of Times, Including Striking Down Legal Segregation and Reversing* Roe, THE CONVERSATION (June 30, 2022), https://theconversation.com/the-supreme-court-has-overturned-precedent-doz ens-of-times-including-striking-down-legal-segregation-and-reversing-roe-185 941#:~:text=In%20my%20book%2C%20%E2%80%9CConstitutional%20Preced ent,145%20times%20%E2%80%93%20barely%200.5%25.

133. Erwin Chemerinsky, *Even the Founders Did Not Believe in Originalism*, THE ATLANTIC (Sept. 2022), https://www.theatlantic.com/ideas/archive/2022/09/supr eme-court-originalism-constitution-framers-judicial-review/671334/. For example, Thomas Jefferson wrote, "[L]aws and institutions must go hand in hand with the progress of the human mind." Extract from Thomas Jefferson to "Henry Tompkinson" (Samuel Kercheval) (July 12, 1816), https://tjrs.monticello.org/let ter/1384.

134. Washington v. Glucksberg, 521 U.S. 702 (1997) (rejecting challenges to a statutory ban against assisted suicide).

135. *Id.*

136. While rejecting the claim against the ban on physician-assisted suicide, the Court did affirm that "[i]n a long line of cases, we have held that, in addition to the specific freedoms protected by the Bill of Rights, the 'liberty' specially protected by the Due Process Clause includes the rights to marry; to have children; to direct the education and upbringing of one's children; to marital privacy; to use contraception; to bodily integrity . . . to abortion . . . [and] the traditional right to refuse unwanted lifesaving medical treatment." *Id.*, at 720. Noting that some members of the Court had identified a liberty interest in refusing unwanted treatment prolonging life, the Court's opinion observed "earnest and profound debate about the morality, legality, and practicality of physician-assisted suicide," and the Court concluded, "Our holding permits this debate to continue, as it should in a democratic society." *Id.*, at 48. Such debate did continue and led the state of Washington to adopt by referendum the 2008 Death with Dignity Act, which approved and exempted from legal liability services by physicians to assist individuals in terminating their lives. *Death with Dignity Act*, WASH. DEP'T OF HEALTH, https://doh.wa.gov/you-and-your-fam ily/illness-and-disease-z/death-dignity-act.

137. Washington v. Glucksberg, 521 U.S., at 752, 756–73 (Souter, J., concurring in the judgment). Justice Souter notably warned against "the all-or-nothing analysis that tends to produce legal petrification instead of an evolving boundary between the domains of old principles." *Id.*, at 770.

138. Jacob Neu, *The Short History and Checkered Tradition of "History and Tradition,"* Ius & Iustitium (July 8, 2022), https://iusetiustitium.com/the-short-history-and-checkered-tradition-of-history-and-tradition/.

139. *See* Adrian Vermeule, Common Good Constitutionalism (Cambridge, UK: Polity Press, 2022) (critiquing "originalism" for failing to draw on Justinian, Aquinas, Blackstone, and other antecedents to American law); Neu, *supra.* note 138; *see also* Morton Horwitz, The Transformation of American Law, 1780–1860 (New York: Oxford Univ. Press, 1979) (demonstrating that the actual history of American law in the nineteenth century involved major changes in legal doctrines and procedures in support of economic development).

140. *See* Martha Minow, *We, the Family: Constitutional Rights and American Families,* 74 J. Am. Hist. 959 (1987).

141. Dobbs v. Jackson Women's Health Org., 142 S. Ct. 2228, 2325 (2022) (Breyer, Sotomayor, & Kagan, JJ., dissenting).

142. Bob Smietana, Dobbs *Decision and Fall of* Roe *Met With Rejoicing, Dismay From Faith Groups,* Religion News Service (June 24, 2022), https://religionnews.com/2022/06/24/roe-wade-scotus-dobbs-abortion-rejoicing-dismay-from-faith-gro ups/; Carl R. Trueman, *Christians Should Rejoice Over* Dobbs, First Things (July 2022), https://www.firstthings.com/web-exclusives/2022/07/christians-should-rejo ice-over-dobbs.

143. James L. Gibson, *Losing Legitimacy: The Challenges of the* Dobbs *Ruling to Conventional Legitimacy Theory,* SSRN (Sept. 1, 2022), https://ssrn.com/abstract= 4206986; Robert Barnes, *Supreme Court Dogged by Questions of Legitimacy, Is Ready to Resume,* Wash. Post (Sept. 29, 2022), https://www.washingtonpost.com/politics/2022/09/29/supreme-court-roberts-kagan-legitimacy/; Sara Savat, *WashU Expert: Post-*Dobbs, *Supreme Court's Legitimacy at Risk,* The Source (Wash. U. in St. Louis) (Oct. 12, 2022), https://source.wustl.edu/2022/10/washu-expert-post-dobbs-supreme-courts-legitimacy-at-risk/ (discussing views of James L. Gibson).

144. John Ketcham, *Midnight Orders: Increased Use of the Shadow Docket Could Undermine Trust,* City Journal (Oct. 21, 2021), https://www.city-journal.org/supreme-court-shadow-docket-could-undermine-trust; Collin Mitchell, *The Shadow Docket: What Is Happening and What Should Be Done,* 36 BYU L. Rev. 189 (2022), https://scholarsarchive.byu.edu/byuplr/vol36/iss1/13; Nathan Richardson, *Antideference: COVID, Climate, and the Rise of the Major Questions Canon,* 108 Va. L. Rev. Online 174 (2022), https://www.virginialawreview.org/articles/antide ference-covid-climate-and-the-rise-of-the-major-questions-canon/.   Professor Charles Fried, former solicitor general, described the current Court as "reactionary" and wrote:

> [T]he best description of what they are doing is a program to repeal the twentieth century. And by that I would include the reforms of Theodore Roosevelt and Woodrow Wilson. Think of administrative law and administrative agencies' regulation of business, regulation of elections and campaign finance laws (through *McConnell v. FEC* in 2003), the empowerment and regulation of public- and private-sector labor unions, the secularization of publicly funded

primary and secondary education—in all these areas in the last few years the Court has overturned precedents and doctrines, understandings and practices reaching back at least to 1903.

Charles Fried, *Letters*, THE N.Y. REV. OF BOOKS (Nov. 24, 2022). The Court is altering or questioning precedents dealing with criminal treatment of juveniles, the status of American Indians and tribes and also technical legal subjects, such as personal jurisdiction, federalism, and deference to administrative agencies. *See* Nina Totenberg, *Supreme Court Rejects Restrictions on Life Without Parole for Juveniles*, NPR (Apr. 22, 2021), https://www.npr.org/2021/04/22/989822872/supreme-court-rejects-restrictions-on-life-without-parole-for-juveniles (describing Court's "U-turn"); Rachel Reed, *Supreme Court Preview:* Brakeen v. Haaland, HARV. L. TODAY (Oct. 31, 2022), https://hls.harvard.edu/today/supreme-court-preview-brackeen-v-haaland/ ("Harvard Law Professor Joseph Singer says the Court's decision in *Brackeen v. Haaland* has the potential to upset tribal sovereignty."); Matthew Bush, Alvin Lee, & Shaila Rahman Diwan, *Supreme Court Issues Landmark Personal Jurisdiction Decision*, JD SUPRA (March 29, 2021), https://www.jdsupra.com/legalnews/supreme-court-issues-landmark-personal-9824939/; Celine L. Shirooni & Robert L. Duckels, *The Changing Landscape of Personal Jurisdiction*, ABA (July 17, 2017), https://www.americanbar.org/groups/litigation/committees/products-liability/practice/2017/the-changing-landscape-of-personal-jurisdiction/; Sanford V. Levinson, *Is the Supreme Court Moving Us Backward or Back Toward Federalism?*, DALLAS NEWS (July 31, 2022), https://www.dallasnews.com/opinion/commentary/2022/07/31/is-the-supreme-court-moving-us-backward-or-back-toward-federalism; Andrew T. Blum, Matthew J. Greenberg, & Larry J. Saylor, *Supreme Court Signals Move Away from Judicial Deference to Administrative Agencies*, NAT'L REV. (July 20, 2022), https://www.natlawreview.com/article/supreme-court-signals-move-away-judicial-deference-to-administrative-agencies.

145. Louis Capozzi, *The Past and Future of the Major Questions Doctrine*, 84 OHIO STATE L. J. 192, 226, 241–42 (2023), https://ssrn.com/abstract=4234683 or http://dx.doi.org/10.2139/ssrn.4234683; Jessica Gresko, *Supreme Court Justices Spar Over Court Legitimacy Comments*, AP NEWS (Oct. 26, 2022), https://apnews.com/article/abortion-us-supreme-court-elena-kagan-samuel-alito-government-and-politics-10bf92ae6830573054da5f756a029d1c; Colleen Slevin, *Chief Justice Roberts Defends Legitimacy of Court*, AP NEWS (Sept. 10, 2022), https://apnews.com/article/abortion-us-supreme-court-denver-public-opinion-john-roberts-6921c22df48b105cdff5fabdc6c459bb.

146. *Dobbs*, 142 S. Ct. at 2349 (Dissent) ("Neither law nor facts nor attitudes have provided any new reasons to reach a different result than *Roe* and *Casey* did. All that has changed is this Court.").

147. *Id.*

148. *See* Tara Leigh Grove, *The Supreme Court's Legitimacy Dilemma*, 132 HARV. L. REV. 2240, 2270–72 (2019). Even before the *Dobbs* decision, criticisms of the Supreme Court captured public attention sufficiently to prompt President Biden to establish a commission looking into potential reforms—a commission with members of

diverse views who therefore did not agree upon any large changes. Nina Totenberg, *Biden's Supreme Court Commission Steers Clear of Controversial Issues in Draft Report*, NPR (Dec. 6, 2021), https://www.npr.org/2021/12/06/1061959400/bidens-supreme-court-commission-releases-draft-report.

149. RICHARD FALLON JR., LAW AND LEGITIMACY IN THE SUPREME COURT 21–36 (Cambridge, MA: The Belknap Press of Harvard Univ. Press, 2018).

150. *Supreme Court Public Opinion Project: 2022 Survey Results*, HARV. U. (2022), https://projects.iq.harvard.edu/scotus-poll/2022-survey-results. For historical trends and comparison of views held by political party affiliation, *see Positive Views of Supreme Court Decline Sharply Following Abortion Ruling*, PEW RSCH. CTR. (Sept. 1, 2022), https://www.pewresearch.org/politics/2022/09/01/positive-views-of-supreme-court-decline-sharply-following-abortion-ruling/ ("Just 28% of Democrats and Democratic-leaning independents now view the [C]ourt favorably, down 18 percentage points since January and nearly 40 points since 2020. Positive views of the [C]ourt among Republicans and Republican leaners have increased modestly since the start of the year (73% now, 65% then).").

151. Revealing disagreements within as well as across groups, public opinion, religious, and philosophical views display sharp divisions around abortion. *See* Carrie Blazina, *Key Facts About the Abortion Debate in America*, PEW RSCH. CTR. (July 15, 2022), https://www.pewresearch.org/fact-tank/2022/07/15/key-facts-about-the-abortion-debate-in-america/; *Open Letter to Religious Leaders on Abortion as a Moral Decision*, RELIGIOUS INST. (Jan 18, 2005), http://religiousinstitute.org/open-letters/open-letter-to-religious-leaders-on-abortion-as-a-moral-decision/ (Written by theologians representing Jewish, Protestant, and Catholic traditions, the Open Letter outlines the religious foundations for affirming abortion as a morally justifiable decision.); *The Ethics of Abortion*, THE PLURALISM PROJECT—HARV. U. (Mar. 2020), https://pluralism.org/the-ethics-of-abortion; John Baker, *Philosophy and the Morality of Abortion*, 2 J. APPLIED PHIL. 261 (1985) (reviewing conflicting positions and arguments).

152. ALEXANDER BICKEL, THE LEAST DANGEROUS BRANCH: THE SUPREME COURT AT THE BAR OF POLITICS (New Haven: Yale Univ. Press, 2d. ed., 1986); Fallon, *supra* note 149.

153. PAUL KENS, LOCHNER V. NEW YORK: ECONOMIC REGULATION ON TRIAL (Lawrence: Univ. Press of Kansas, 1998).

154. *See* MARK V. TUSHNET, THE HUGHES COURT: FROM PROGRESSIVISM TO PLURALISM, 1930 TO 1941, 296–310 (Cambridge: Cambridge Univ. Press, 2022).

155. *Id.* (reviewing and assessing scholarly debate about the "switch in time").

156. *See* BARRY FRIEDMAN, THE WILL OF THE PEOPLE: HOW PUBLIC OPINION HAS INFLUENCED THE SUPREME COURT AND SHAPED THE MEANING OF THE CONSTITUTION (New York: Farrar, Straus and Giroux, 2010); James F. Smith, *U.S. Supreme Court v. American Public Opinion: The Verdict Is In*, HARV. KENNEDY SCHOOL (July 13, 2020), https://www.hks.harvard.edu/faculty-research/policy-topics/democracy-governance/us-supreme-court-v-american-public-opinion.

157. U.S. Constitution, Art. II, § 2.

158. Rucho v. Common Cause, 139 S. Ct. 2484, 2506 (2019) (deeming partisan gerrymandering "incompatible with democratic principles" but nonetheless beyond the reach of federal court review); Citizens United v. Federal Election Commission, 558 U.S. 310 (2010) (prohibiting restrictions on independent campaign expenditures by corporations and nonprofit organizations). Thanks to Gene Chang for underscoring this point.

159. MARY ZIEGLER, DOLLARS FOR LIFE: THE ANTI-ABORTION MOVEMENT AND THE FALL OF THE REPUBLICAN ESTABLISHMENT (New Haven: Yale Univ. Press, 2022).

160. Jonaki Metha & Courtney Dorning, *One Man's Outsized Role in Shaping the Supreme Court and Overturning* Roe, NPR (June 30, 2022), https://www.npr.org/2022/06/30/1108351562/roe-abortion-supreme-court-scotus-law (tracing role of the Federalist Society and Leonard Leo in judicial selections leading to *Dobbs*). *See* MICHAEL AVERY & DANIELLE MCLAUGHLIN, THE FEDERALIST SOCIETY: HOW CONSERVATIVES TOOK THE LAW BACK FROM LIBERALS (Nashville: Vanderbilt Univ. Press, 2013); AMANDA HOLLIS-BRUSKY, IDEAS WITH CONSEQUENCES: THE FEDERALIST SOCIETY AND THE CONSERVATIVE COUNTERREVOLUTION (Oxford: Oxford Univ. Press, 2015).

161. Sheldon Whitehouse, *The Scheme Speech 5: The Federalist Society* (July 27, 2021), https://www.whitehouse.senate.gov/news/speeches/the-scheme-speech-5-the-federalist-society.

162. *Compare Public Opinion on Abortion*, PEW RSCH. CTR. (May 17, 2022), https://www.pewresearch.org/religion/fact-sheet/public-opinion-on-abortion/ (61% support legal abortion) *with* Geoffrey Skelley & Hooly Fuong, *How Americans Feel About Abortion and Contraception*, FIVETHIRTYEIGHT (July 12, 2022), https://fivethirtyeight.com/features/abortion-birth-control-poll/ ("90 percent of Americans said condoms and birth control pills should be legal in 'all' or 'most' cases, and 81 percent said the same of IUDs (intrauterine devices)"). And there is very little difference in support for the legality of each of these contraceptives across party lines.

163. Gini Ehrlich, *Opinion: Birth Control Gives Women Power to Decide*, NBC (Mar. 8, 2017), https://www.nbcnews.com/news/latino/opinion-birth-control-gives-women-power-decide-n730751 (opinion piece citing research from University of Michigan and *Bloomberg Businessweek*).

164. *Compare Public Opinion on Abortion*, THE CONVERSATION (Feb. 6, 2015), https://theconversation.com/the-contraceptive-pill-was-a-revolution-for-women-and-men-37193#:~:text=They%20enhanced%20women's%20opportunities%20to,labour%20market%20options%20and%20earnings. Sonia Oreffice, *The Contraceptive Pill Was a Revolution for Women and Men*,

165. *Complications of Pregnancy*, JOHN HOPKINS MED., https://www.hopkinsmedicine.org/health/conditions-and-diseases/staying-healthy-during-pregnancy/complications-of-pregnancy.

166. *Contraception and Reproduction: Health Consequences for Women and Children in the Developing World*, NAT'L RSCH. COUNCIL COMM. ON POPULATION, CONTRACEPTION AND REPRODUCTION ch. 4 (1989), https://www.ncbi.nlm.nih.gov/books/NBK235069/.

167. *Id.*; *Birth Control: Benefits Beyond Pregnancy Prevention*, WEBMD, https://www.webmd.com/sex/birth-control/other-benefits-birth-control.

168. *Birth Control: Benefits Beyond Pregnancy Prevention*, WebMD, *supra* note 167.

169. *See, e.g.*, Olivia Goldhill, *Supreme Court Decision Suggests the Legal Right to Contraception Is Also Under Threat*, Stat (June 24, 2022), https://www.statnews.com/2022/06/24/supreme-court-decision-suggests-the-legal-right-to-contraception-is-also-under-threat.

170. *Access to Emergency Contraception*, Am. Coll. of Obstetricians and Gynecologists (July 2017, reaffirmed Dec. 2019), https://www.acog.org/clinical/clinical-guidance/committee-opinion/articles/2017/07/access-to-emergency-contraception.

171. *See The Difference Between the Morning-After Pill and the Abortion Pill*, Planned Parenthood (2003) (citing Horatio B. Croxatto et al., *Mechanisms of Action of Emergency Contraception*, 68 Steroids 1095–98 (2003)).

172. James Trussell & Beth Jordan, *Mechanism of Action of Emergency Contraceptive Pills*, 74 Contraception 87–89 (2006).

173. *FDA's Decision Regarding Plan B: Questions and Answers*, Food and Drug Admin. (Dec. 7, 2015), https://www.fda.gov/drugs/postmarket-drug-safety-information-patients-and-providers/fdas-decision-regarding-plan-b-questions-and-answers.

174. *Emergency Contraception*, Kaiser Family Found. (Aug. 4, 2022), https://www.kff.org/womens-health-policy/fact-sheet/emergency-contraception/.

175. As of October 2022, nine states had already passed bills prohibiting or limiting the sale/provision of emergency contraception. *Emergency Contraception*, Guttmacher Inst. (Nov. 1, 2022), https://www.guttmacher.org/state-policy/explore/emergency-contraception; *Don't Be Fooled: Birth Control Is Already at Risk*, Nat'l Women's L. Ctr. (June 17, 2022), https://nwlc.org/resource/dont-be-fooled-birth-control-is-already-at-risk/. In fact, abortion aims to end a pregnancy *after* fertilization rather than preventing fertilization.

176. Rachel Cohen, *U of I Warns Employees to Stay Neutral on Abortion or Risk Prosecution*, Boise State Public Radio (Sept. 26, 2022), https://www.boisestatepublicradio.org/news/2022-09-26/u-of-i-warns-employees-to-stay-neutral-on-abortion-or-risk-prosecution; Oriana Gonzales, *Post* Dobbs *Birth Control Fight Heads to College Campuses*, Axios (Sept. 30, 2022), https://www.axios.com/2022/09/30/dobbs-roe-abortion-university-birth-control.

177. Thanks to Arka Gupta for this point, analogized to requirements in the context of medical abortions. *Medication Abortion*, Guttmacher Inst. (Oct. 1, 2022), https://www.guttmacher.org/state-policy/explore/medication-abortion.

178. *See* Sara Morrison, *Should I Delete My Period Tracking App? And Other Post-*Roe *Privacy Questions*, Vox (July 6, 2022), https://www.vox.com/recode/2022/7/6/23196809/period-apps-roe-dobbs-data-privacy-abortion; *Rewards Cards: How Much Personal Information Is Collected?*, CBS News (Aug. 26, 2015), https://www.cbsnews.com/dfw/news/rewards-cards-how-much-personal-information-is-collected/. Prosecutors have been using search history to prove that women had the intent of getting an abortion (if a woman searched how/where to get one, that demonstrated intent). Cynthia Conti-Cook, *Surveilling the Digital Abortion Diary*, 50 U. of Baltimore L. Rev. 1 (2020), https://scholarworks.law.ubalt.edu/ublr/vol50/iss1;

https://scholarworks.law.ubalt.edu/cgi/viewcontent.cgi?article=2078&context=ublr; Kevin Collier, *What Digital Information Could Prosecutors Use in Abortion-Related Cases?*, ABC NEWS (June 29, 2022), https://www.nbcnews.com/tech/security/abortion-digital-information-privacy-rcna35543. Similar approaches could affect individuals looking for where to access emergency contraception or IUDs—a woman's search history can show where she went to get emergency contraception/an IUD, and that can be used against the provider of the contraception. Similar and perhaps even more issues arise regarding data collection and abortion as, after *Dobbs* and the new state laws it permitted, many need to travel out of state, leaving a data trail of gas purchases, mapping service information, bus and airline schedule searches, and mobile phone location history. Bobby Allyn, *Privacy Advocates Fear Google Will Be Used to Prosecute Abortion Seekers*, NPR (July 11, 2022), https://www.npr.org/2022/07/11/1110391316/google-data-abortion-prosecutions. Thanks to Carolina Rabinowicz for these details.

179. Edward Helmore, *Tech Companies in Spotlight as US Abortion Ruling Sparks Privacy Threat*, GUARDIAN (July 2, 2022), https://www.theguardian.com/us-news/2022/jul/02/abortion-tech-companies-data-police-privacy.

180. *Fact Sheet: President Biden to Sign Executive Order Protecting Access to Reproductive Health Care Services*, WHITE HOUSE (July 8, 2022), https://www.whitehouse.gov/briefing-room/statements-releases/2022/07/08/fact-sheet-president-biden-to-sign-executive-order-protecting-access-to-reproductive-health-care-services/.

181. Ilya Shapiro, *An Exit Survey of Trump's Constitutional Misdeeds*, CATO INST. (Jan. 24, 2021), https://www.cato.org/commentary/exit-survey-trumps-constitutional-misdeeds. *See* Tsai, *supra* note 130.

182. Ariana Lee, *Fiber Artist Adrienne Sloane Unravels Our Concepts of Democracy*, WBUR (June 20, 2019), https://www.wbur.org/news/2019/06/10/artist-adrienne-sloane-the-unraveling-american-flag. Another artist, Sonya Clark, invites visitors to her art shows to pick apart a Confederate flag, piece by piece. *Id.* That undoing has a generative, hopeful consequence.

Closing Dialogue

1. Dobbs v. Jackson Women's Health Org., 142 S. Ct. 2228 (2022).

2. Roe v. Wade, 410 U.S. 113 (1973).

3. *See Dobbs*, 142 S. Ct. at 2240–85.

4. *See id.*

Index

For the benefit of digital users, indexed terms that span two pages (e.g., 52–53) may, on occasion, appear on only one of those pages.